CHILDREN'S LITERATURE

Critical Concepts in Literary and Cultural Studies

Edited by
Peter Hunt

Volume III
Cultural Contexts

LONDON AND NEW YORK

First published 2006
by Routledge
2 Park Square, Milton Park, Abingdon, Oxon OX14 4RN

Simultaneously published in the USA and Canada
by Routledge
270 Madison Avenue, New York, NY 10016-0602

Routledge is an imprint of the Taylor & Francis Group, an informa business

Typeset in 10/12pt Times by Graphicraft Limited, Hong Kong
Printed and bound in Great Britain by
MPG Books Ltd, Bodmin, Cornwall

British Library Cataloguing in Publication Data
A catalogue record for this book is available from the British Library

Library of Congress Cataloging in Publication Data
A catalog record for this book has been requested

ISBN10: 0–415–37228–3 (Set)
ISBN10: 0–415–37226–7 (Volume III)

ISBN13: 978–0–415–37228–2 (Set)
ISBN13: 978–0–415–37226–8 (Volume III)

Publisher's note

References within each chapter are as they appear in the original complete work

CHILDREN'S LITERATURE

CONTENTS

ACKNOWLEDGEMENTS

The Publishers would like to thank the following for permission to reprint their material:

The Children's Literature Association for permission to reprint Kenneth Kidd, 'Children's Culture, Children's Studies, and the Ethnographic Imaginary', *Children's Literature Association Quarterly* 27(3) (2002): 146–155. Reprinted by permission of the Children's Literature Association.

The Children's Literature Association for permission to reprint Nina Christensen, 'Childhood Revisited: On the Relationship between Childhood Studies and Children's Literature', *Children's Literature Association Quarterly* 28(4) (2003–2004): 230–239. Reprinted by permission of the Children's Literature Association.

Rosemary Ross Johnston, 'Childhood: A narrative chronotope', in Roger D. Sell (ed.), *Children's Literature as Communication*, Amsterdam/Philadelphia: John Benjamins, 2002, pp. 137–157. With kind permission by John Benjamins Publishing Company. www.benjamins.com.

Blackwell Publishing for permission to reprint Valerie Krips, 'Imaginary childhoods: memory and children's literature', *Critical Quarterly* 39(3) (1997): 42–50.

Stephen Thomson, 'Substitute Communities, Authentic Voices: the Organic Writing of the Child', in Karín Lesnik-Oberstein (ed.), *Children in Culture: Approaches to Childhood*, Basingstoke: Macmillan, 1998, pp. 248–273, reproduced with permission of Palgrave Macmillan.

Thimble Press for permission to reprint Peter Hollindale, 'Ideology and the Children's Book', *Signal* 55 (1988): 3–22.

The University of Chicago Press and Anne Scott MacLeod for permission to reprint Anne Scott MacLeod, 'Censorship and children's literature', *Library Quarterly* 53(1) (1983): 26–38. Copyright © 1983 by the University of Chicago. All rights reserved.

The Children's Literature Association for permission to reprint Opal Moore and Donnarae MacCann, 'The Uncle Remus Travesty, Part I', *Children's Literature Association Quarterly* 11(2) (1986): 96–99. Reprinted by permission of the Children's Literature Association.

The Children's Literature Association for permission to reprint Opal Moore and Donnarae MacCann, 'The Uncle Remus Travesty, Part II: Julius Lester and Virginia Hamilton', *Children's Literature Association Quarterly* 11(4) (1986–1987): 205–209. Reprinted by permission of the Children's Literature Association.

Indiana University Press for permission to reprint Jack Zipes, 'Breaking the Disney Spell', in Elizabeth Bell, Lynda Haas and Laura Sells (eds), *From Mouse to Mermaid: The Politics of Film, Gender, and Culture*, Bloomington: Indiana University Press, 1995, pp. 21–42.

The Horn Book, Inc. for permission to reprint Philip Pullman, 'The Republic of Heaven', *The Horn Book Magazine* 57(7) (November/December 2001): 655–667.

Flynn, Elizabeth A. and Patrocinio P. Schweickart. *Gender and Reading: Essays on Readers, Texts and Contexts*, 1986, pp. 165–186. Reprinted with permission of the Johns Hopkins University Press.

Thimble Press for permission to reprint Lissa Paul, 'Enigma Variations: What Feminist Theory Knows about Children's Literature', *Signal* 54 (1987): 186–202.

Ursula K. Le Guin for permission to reprint Ursula K. Le Guin, *Earthsea Revisioned*, Cambridge: Children's Literature New England in association with Green Bay Publications, 1993, pp. 5–26.

The Children's Literature Association for permission to reprint Beverly Lyon Clark, 'Fairy Godmothers or Wicked Stepmothers? The Uneasy Relationship of Feminist Theory and Children's Criticism', *Children's Literature Association Quarterly* 18(4) (1993–1994): 171–176. Reprinted by permission of the Children's Literature Association.

Thacker, Deborah. Feminine Language and the Politics of Children's Literature. *The Lion and the Unicorn* 25 (2001): 3–16. © The Johns Hopkins University Press. Reprinted with permission of the Johns Hopkins University Press.

Springer Science and Business Media and Ann M. Trousdale and Sally McMillan for permission to reprint Ann M. Trousdale and Sally McMillan, '"Cinderella was a Wuss": A Young Girl's Responses to Feminist and Patriarchal Folktales', *Children's Literature in Education* 34(1) (March 2003): 1–28. With permission from Springer Science and Business Media.

Thimble Press for permission to reprint Michael Rosen, 'Raising the Issues', *Signal* 76 (1995): 26–44.

Sage Publications Ltd for permission to reprint Hannah Davies, David Buckingham and Peter Kelley, 'In the worst possible taste: Children, television and cultural value', *European Journal of Cultural Studies* 3(1) (2000): 5–24. Copyright © Sage Publications 2000, by permission of Sage Publications Ltd.

Taylor & Francis for permission to reprint Nicholas Tucker, 'Good Friends, or Just Acquaintances? The Relationship between Child Psychology and Children's Literature', in Peter Hunt (ed.), *Literature for Children: Contemporary Criticism*, London: Routledge, 1992, pp. 156–173.

Kidd, Kenneth. Psychoanalysis and Children's Literature: The Case for Complimentarity. *The Lion and the Unicorn* 28(1) (2004): 109–130. © The Johns Hopkins University Press. Reprinted with permission of the Johns Hopkins University Press.

Papers for permission to reprint Ann Grieve, 'Metafictional Play in Children's Fiction', *Papers: Explorations into Children's Literature* 8(3) (1998): 5–15.

Style for permission to reprint Maria Nikolajeva, 'The Changing Aesthetics of Character in Children's Fiction', *Style* 35(3) (Fall 2001): 430–453.

Wyile, Andrea Schwenke. The Value of Singularity in First- and Restricted Third-Person Engaging Narration. *Children's Literature* 31 (2003): 116–141. © The Hollins University Corporation. Reprinted with permission of the Johns Hopkins University Press.

Disclaimer

INTRODUCTION TO VOLUME III

> Because many of society's concerns are reflected in children's literature more rapidly than in other literary studies . . . critics of children's literature are uniquely able to reach out from their studies and embrace other critical and social concerns. With the potential for, almost necessity of, drawing heavily upon other studies, good criticism of children's literature could in the future become a model for much literary study.
>
> (Pickering 1982, p. 16)

Childhood studies

Children's Literature is essentially interdisciplinary, and so it is appropriate that it should be closely associated with a newly developing interdisciplinary area – Childhood Studies. Kehily sums up the principles:

> A growing body of literature points to the importance of childhood as a conceptual category and as a social position for the study of a previously overlooked or marginalised group – children. Childhood studies as a field of academic endeavour offers the potential for interdisciplinary research that can contribute to an emergent paradigm wherein new ways of looking at children can be researched and theorised.
>
> (Kehily 2004, p. 1)

Characteristic of the field is a series of texts from the UK Open University, introduced thus:

> The growing field of childhood and youth studies provides an integrative framework for interdisciplinary research and teaching, as well as analysis of contemporary policy and practice in, for instance, education, health and social work. Childhood is now a global issue, forcing a reconsideration of conventional approaches to study. Childhood is also a very personal issue for each and every one of us – scholars, policy-makers, parents and children.
>
> (Kehily and Swann 2003, p. ii)

The child as constructed in fiction, and the child-reader as constructed by writers and critics, may or may not have some things in common with children and childhood as they are constructed (or exist) in the real world. However, as Krips (Chapter 60) puts it: 'the literary child may be a construct of writing, but it is one with which both readers and writers must come to terms (p. 73)'. Texts for children show us how the societies that produced the texts see the child, wish the child to be or to be seen; this provides valuable evidence for socio-cultural studies and there can be a symbiotic relationship between the child in the book and the child outside the book. (See also Chapters 18, 27, 31, 82, 84, 89 and 96.)

Ideology, race and politics

> Oh, they say, what a shame, Le Guin has politicised her delightful fantasy world, Earthsea will never be the same. I'll say it won't. The politics were there all along, the hidden politics of the hero-tale, the spell you don't know you're living under until you cast it off.
>
> (Le Guin, Chapter 70, p. 234)

> If children's literature fails to offer young people ways of thinking about themselves and their world that suggest that they can make a difference and help them construct a discourse of their own to empower them as political subjects, it cannot be excluded from the other social forces implicated in the gelding of youth and youth culture.
>
> (Reynolds 2004, p. 147)

Some newcomers to children's literature assume, or hope, that the texts will reflect an innocent childhood. Such an attitude commonly stems from a nostalgic or idealistic yearning for a simpler, more wholesome, less troublesome world than the one that the adult inhabits and can seriously influence critical thinking (see Chapter 49). However, children's literature and childhood do not exist outside ideology, and in any case, as a best-selling novelist, Judy Blume, puts it:

> I don't know what childhood innocence is supposed to mean. Children are inexperienced, but they are not innocent. Childhood can be a terrible time of life. No kid wants to stay a kid. It is only adults who have forgotten who say, 'If only I could be a kid again.' The fantasy of childhood is to *be* an adult.
>
> (West 1988, pp. 11–12)

Even from the point of view of the 'controlling' adult, innocence, in whatever form, is not necessarily a virtue. The British illustrator, Edward Ardizzone has written:

> I think we are possibly inclined, in a child's reading, to shelter him too much from the harder facts of life. Sorrow, failure, poverty, and possibly even death, if handled poetically, can surely all be introduced without hurt. After all, books for children are in a sense an introduction to the life that lies ahead of them. If no hint of the hard world comes into these books, then I am not sure that we are playing fair.
>
> (Egoff, Stubbs and Ashley 1980, p. 293)

In short, ideology is inescapable and, given the power structures inherent in children's literature, a natural consequence is that adults exercise control over books, from conception to delivery. Censorship of children's literature is exercised at all levels, directly or indirectly, according to the surrounding culture. Mark West sums up the situation:

> Throughout the history of children's literature, the people who have tried to censor children's books, for all their ideological differences, share a rather romantic view about the power of books. They believe, or at least profess to believe, that books are such a major influence in the formation of children's values and attitudes that adults need to monitor nearly every word that children read. Because the proponents of censorship invest books with so much power, they reject as too dangerous the idea that children should be exposed to a wide variety of books and be trusted to make their own selections. The people who seek to censor children's books may be practising intolerance, but in their own eyes, they are protecting innocent children and working for the benefit of society.
>
> (West 1994, p. 689)

Censorship is, of course, relative and must be put in the context of the change in, or disappearance of, childhood, especially when the commodification of the child seems to be so extensive (see Chapter 66).

All of this discussion, which implies a direct and perceptible connection between text and response/affect is in rather sharp contrast to the views both of the theorists who question affect of language (Chapters 51, 59 and 61) and the practitioners who question the accessibility of the response (Chapters 27, 29 and 34). It also suggests, as did Mitzi Myers, in a famous analysis of potential directions for children's literature criticism, that a more complex reading of history and ideology, and their relation to young readers, is required:

> A New Historicism of children's literature would integrate text and socio-historic context, demonstrating on the one hand how

extraliterary cultural formations shape literary discourse and on the other how literary practices are actions that make things happen – by shaping the psychic and moral consciousness of young readers but also by performing many more diverse kinds of cultural work, from satisfying authorial fantasies to legitimating or subverting dominant class and gender ideologies, from mediating social inequalities to propagandizing for causes, from popularizing new knowledges and discoveries to addressing live issues like slavery and the condition of the working class. It would want to know how and why a tale or poem came to say what it does, what the environing circumstances were (including the uses a particular sort of children's literature served for its author, its child and adult readers, and its culture), and what kinds of cultural statements and questions the work was responding to. It would pay particular attention to the conceptual and symbolic fault lines denoting a text's time-, place-, gender-, and class-specific ideological mechanisms, being aware that the most seemingly artless and orthodox work may conceal an oppositional or contestatory subtext. It would examine too a book's material production, its publishing history, its audiences and their reading practices, its initial reception, and its critical history, including how it got inscribed in or deleted from the canon. It would need to do all these things and more to elucidate significant links between social and aesthetic forms, the particular cultural meanings codified in particular aesthetic expressions, for formal properties can't be sealed off from their social and historical matrix. Recognizing that human subjectivity itself, much less its literary expression, is culture-bound, it couldn't reify or essentialize The Child and Children's Literature (or even Literature) and What Children Like. If the Romantics . . . dictated the organicist and idealist terms in which subsequent critics have obligingly construed their poems, so too have Wordsworthian notions of child nature and nurture informed subsequent discussion of literature for the young; witness, for example, the Romantics' privileging of fairy tale over more realistic fiction, the context of which is only beginning to be explored critically, though we have long starred fantasy, glorified 'imagination', and relied on Romantic ideologies of childhood to structure our thinking about 'appropriate' literature. What a New Historical orientation could not make central to its program is what much historically-based study of children's literature still does: organize material within preconceived patterns implying an evolutionary view of historical progress. Linearly organized, always toward, most literary histories aren't analytic history, but teleology.

(1998, p. 42)

Gender

Gender has been one of the more visible issues in children's literature. One of the earliest British books for children was published by John Newbery in 1744, with the title:

> A Little Pretty Pocket Book, intended for the Instruction and Amusement of little Master Tommy and Pretty Miss Polly, with an agreeable Letter to read from Jack the Giant Killer, as also a Ball and a Pincushion, the use of which will infallibly make Tommy a good Boy, and Polly a good Girl.

A majority of publishers and editors of children's books have been female (see Goldthwaite's trenchant objection to this (in Chapter 74)), and boys' and girls' educations and responses to texts have been very different (see, for example, Millard 1997 and Chapters 30 and 33). From the male-dominated British imperialist genre (see Chapter 89) to the 'self-help' texts in the USA, and from books across the world emphasising appropriate female conduct to modern feminist texts, writers have been acutely aware of the potential power of the form for social engineering. As Roberta Seelinger Trites put it, with regard to feminism:

> The important thing is that girls – and boys – have choices and that they know they have choices. A major goal of feminism is to support women's choices, but another that is equally important is to foster societal respect for those choices. And since childhood is the time in our lives when our options seem most unlimited, it is a time when respect for choices about self and others can have serious import.
>
> (1997, p. 2)

There has been a tendency for writers on children's literature (also a majority of females) to deal with women's issues, although almost all of the articles collected here have an equal amount to say about the situation of the male, by implication. They also reflect the rapid changes that have taken place in *some parts* of society, and so although Lissa Paul's groundbreaking article (Chapter 69) on feminist theory is less than 20 years old (1987), it should be read in the context of her more recent thoughts on the subject:

> There is a lot of very good feminist-inspired criticism about – and it has changed the landscape of children's literature studies. What's over is the feminist movement that supported the development of feminist criticism in the 1970s and 1980s. Feminism is over in the same way that romanticism is over, and rationalism is over and

existentialism is over and Marxism is over. We've been changed by those critical movements and they all continue to influence our readings of texts. But the movements themselves have been relegated to their particular historical periods. Although feminism as a critical movement is over, its influence is alive and well and exerting itself on what we read, and on how we interpret and value what we read.

(2004, pp. 1, 140–153)

Publishing and television, psychology and special topics

> There are . . . few of us who have not felt unnerved at some time by the fact that when children read stories there is no observable outcome. . . . The story has happened inside the child's head.
>
> (Michael Benton, quoted in Fox 1983, p. 19)

The remaining chapters in this volume demonstrate the inevitable relationship between texts, readers, means of production and the cultural values embedded in them. Andrea Schwenke Wyile regards her analytic approach to narration (Chapter 81) as a method that 'can teach us a lot about the constructedness of texts and reader response' (p. 416); Rosen's satirical account of the contemporary publishing scene (Chapter 75) links commercial pressures to concepts of literary quality (compare Chapters 10, 32 and 74), to the influence of other media (compare Chapter 66) and finally to psychology:

> children's literature enters the discourse of child psychology . . . because it provides a forum in which children's agency is recognised. . . . So children's literature inevitably draws on whatever is the contemporary level of understanding of children's abilities. . . . [I]t is actually part of the discourse about children's thinking and child psychology.
>
> (Chapter 75, p. 315)

Kidd (Chapter 78), similarly, makes links to literary and psychological theory, gender, play and finally folklore (see also Chapters 93–95), Grieve (Chapter 79) makes links to play, and so on. Together these chapters exemplify the complex interweaving of ideas that constitute the discipline of Children's Literature.

References

Egoff, S., Stubbs, G. T., and Ashley, L. F. (1980) *Only Connect: Readings on Children's Literature*, Toronto: Oxford University Press.

Fox, G. (ed.) (1983) *Responses to Children's Literature*, Munich: K. G. Saur.
Kehily, M. J. (2004) *An Introduction to Childhood Studies*, Maidenhead and New York: Open University Press/McGraw Hill Education.
Kehily, M. J. and Swann, J. (2003) *Children's Cultural Worlds*, Milton Keynes: Open University Press/John Wiley.
Millard, E. (1997) *Differently Literate: Boys, Girls and the Schooling of Literacy*, London: Falmer Press.
Myers, M. (1998) 'Missed Opportunities and Critical Malpractice: New Historicism and Children's Literature', *Children's Literature Association Quarterly* 13(1): 41–43.
Paul, L. (2004) 'Feminism Revisited', in Hunt, P. (ed.) *International Companion Encyclopedia of Children's Literature*, 2nd edn, London and New York: Routledge.
Pickering, S. (1982) 'The Function of Criticism in Children's Literature', *Children's Literature in Education* 13(1): 16.
Reynolds, K. (2004) 'Alchemy and Alco Pops: Breaking the Ideology Trap', in Keenan, C. and Thompson, M. S. (eds), *Studies in Children's Literature 1500–2000*, Dublin: Four Courts Press.
Trites, R. S. (1997) *Waking Sleeping Beauty: Feminist Voices in Children's Novels*, Iowa City: University of Iowa Press.
West, M. (1988) *Trust Your Children: Voices Against Censorship in Children's Literature*, New York: Neal-Schuman.
—— (1994) 'Censorship', in Hunt, P. (ed.) *International Companion Encyclopedia of Children's Literature*, London and New York: Routledge.

Part 10

CHILDHOOD STUDIES

57

CHILDREN'S CULTURE, CHILDREN'S STUDIES, AND THE ETHNOGRAPHIC IMAGINARY

Kenneth Kidd

Source: *Children's Literature Association Quarterly* 27(3) (2002): 146–155.

Within the last decade, and particularly in the last several years, scholars of children's literature have seen exciting new work on "children's culture." New York University Press alone has put out three representative anthologies: *The Children's Culture Reader, Generations of Youth: Youth Cultures and History in Twentieth-Century America* (both 1998), and *Childhood in America* (2000). Obviously the term "culture" means many things to many people. Like "discourse" and "ideology," "culture" is at once a problematic and useful term. On the one hand, the culture idea is so generic or universal that it threatens to mean nothing at all, as some scholars have pointed out. Yet that is exactly why we like it. We rely on its vagueness. Its wide range of designation (alongside more specific meanings) allows for the greatest possible expansion of our critical efforts, such that "children's culture," as we are now imagining it, refers to music, film, television, toys, and other material goods, as well as to literature proper. Articles in the above volumes address (among other topics) the history of childhood, child-rearing practices, food and nutrition, interactive technology and cyberspace, sports and athleticism, fan clubs, and beauty pageants. The idea of children's culture allows us to claim greater interdisciplinarity and intellectual freedom.

"Children's studies" is usually articulated along the same lines, appealing directly or indirectly to the conceit of children's culture. The debate about children's studies and its alternate terms—among them "child studies" and "childhood studies"—attests to the very success of an interdisciplinary zeitgeist. We would not be having this conversation were there not already some consensus about the importance of interdisciplinary, or at least extra-literary, scholarship. Of course, both children's culture (as a domain) and children's studies (as a practice) raise interesting questions for literary scholars. How are we to think about our work these days? To what extent are we, as teachers and students of children's literature, already identifying as something else? How will our relationship to a long-devalued, now re-valued form of literature shift in the wake of a more general appreciation of objects and practices long disdained by the defenders of legitimate culture? For so long children's literature wasn't taken seriously, and just as it's being granted greater respect, the academy is turning to cultural and area studies, theory, and "everyday life."[1] Will our emergent interest in children's culture be indulged at the expense of the literary tradition we have worked so hard to champion?

No doubt scholars will continue to explore such questions, and I want to make clear my enthusiasm about the shift away from a narrow vision of literature, criticism, and academic life. This is an exciting period, and children's culture and children's studies make possible new projects and perspectives. Even so, I'd like to suggest that as children's culture and children's studies gain popularity, we are not so much venturing into uncharted territory as we are reshaping the academic field to meet current needs. The nomenclature may be different, but our practices are largely the same, not despite differences in the material we study but indeed *as is evidenced by* those differences. That is, the very shift in focus from literature to culture attests to the staying power and adaptability of analysis as a vocation, and of "culture" as an organizing field. Culture may be a new thematic interest, but it has been there all along in more diffuse form, securing the very place of literature.

I want to sound a cautionary note, not about the decline of literature, but about our current faith in culture, often too utopian and ahistorical. To begin with, the culture idea has been around for a while. And however much we benefit from its fungibility, the culture idea has an intellectual history that we can trace in and around anthropology, cultural studies, and the historiography of English studies. Current formulations of children's studies appeal to the culture idea ideologically and rhetorically but usually without acknowledging that history. At least two dimensions of the culture idea underwrite current critical efforts. The first is the classic anthropological understanding of culture as, in E. B. Tylor's words, "that complex whole which includes knowledge, belief, art, morals, law, custom, and any other capabilities and habits acquired by man as a member of society." That expansive definition opens Tylor's *Primitive Culture* (1871), setting the stage not only for anthropology but also for the humanities and social sciences more generally. Culture was a positive term for Tylor, the so-called father of anthropology; it meant something comprehensive, if not entirely comprehensible. By the 1920s, however, this sense of culture had yielded to the cultural or comparative anthropology of Franz Boas, Ruth Benedict, and Margaret Mead. Central to cultural anthropology is ethnographic fieldwork, the close observation of local cultures, often conducted to debunk claims of universality. To this day, the holistic, more archetypal idea of culture persists alongside a variable, pluralistic, ethnographic sense of culture.[2]

At the risk of gross oversimplification, I would argue that these two anthropological modes of culture-think are residual in children's studies. This essay historicizes the ever-morphing yet weirdly familiar idea of culture to suggest that "children's culture" doesn't automatically mean something new or progressive. A deeper understanding of the culture idea will also help shed light on children's studies and debates about how that field should be formed. Some scholars have been harshly critical of poststructuralist approaches to children's forms, arguing for interdisciplinarity, practicality, and realism in the familiar name of culture. In his introduction to *The Children's Culture Reader*, for instance, Henry Jenkins appeals to an unreconstructed idea of culture in order to indict wild theory. Jenkins appeals repeatedly to "real children" to authorize children's culture against an otherwise empty poststructuralist mode of analysis. (Here I think of Wednesday's query in one of the *Addams Family* films: "[D]o your Girl Scout cookies have real Girl Scouts in them?") In such declarations of new (inter)disciplinarity, culture gets no treatment as an evolving idea or cluster of ideas.[3]

As poststructuralist theory makes clear, appeals to real children and the real world themselves derive from anthropological and sociological methods of observation and research, and from the texts that such work generates: case studies, field reports, statistical analyses, and so forth. Realism is never self-evident: it must be produced. While the holistic idea of culture apparently migrated to literary study in the 1930s, ethnography did not really take root in the field of English until the advent of cultural studies, beginning, perhaps, with the Birmingham Centre for Contemporary Cultural Studies in the 1960s. With varying degrees of emphasis, the ethnographic approach to culture also informs children's studies, for better and for worse. What I am calling the "ethnographic imaginary" is a descriptive rather than a prescriptive term. It refers to field research with children and their materials, as well as the symbolic repertoire of classic ethnography—the familiar language of observer and observed, the practices of ethnographic writing that estrange as much as bring close their subjects. Although allied with comparative anthropology, ethnographic work can also support essentialist or centrist understandings of culture.

I have in mind as a model Michèle Le Doeuff's term "the philosophical imaginary." By this, she means not only philosophy's repertoire of images and conceits, but also its claim to objectivity, its disavowal of literariness or subjectivity. An intellectual discipline's imaginary, she proposes, works to cope with—often to mask or disguise—problems posed by the theoretical enterprise. I'm similarly interested in the ethnographic imaginary of children's studies, as it claims objectivity, generates and recycles images and metaphors, and collaborates as well as conflicts with a more holistic sense of culture.[4] Some of the fiercest critics of poststructuralist excess in children's studies put their faith not only in the idea of culture as "a complex whole" but also in the ethnographic imaginary. Even so, it's unfair to imply that poststructuralist thinkers aren't also inspired by the ethnographic imaginary, particularly since poststructuralism emphasizes the relativity of culture(s). I thus address also the compatibilities of poststructuralism and the ethnographic imaginary.

My goal is to trace the origins and effects of the culture idea in children's studies, not so that we can correct all our biases—that might not be possible or even desirable—but so that we may better understand the current enthusiasm for culture as representing continuity as well as innovation. Although this essay is deconstructive to an extent, I hope that a stronger sense of history and disciplinarity will help alleviate the tension between poststructuralist and more traditionally humanist assessments of culture.

Literature and/as culture

Children's literature, of course, has long been more eclectic and interdisciplinary than other academic specialties, perhaps necessarily so. Children's literature has often meant children's culture, embracing not only a diverse group of written texts but also oral narrative. Scholars in the field have been writing about film and television for quite a while, even if film and media theory is a more recent arrival. Scholars of children's literature already know quite a bit about children's work and children's play, drawing from both representation and direct personal experience. Still, we've not paid much attention to the culture idea's influence on our discipline.

Literature used to mean something similar to culture. It did not signal, as it often does now, a limited body of texts, often traditional ones (a canon), but rather a set of values, ideals, and traditions. There are different explanations for the resemblances between literature and culture, which are really variations on a larger theme of mutual influence. Scholars have persuasively shown that advocates of literature borrowed the anthropological idea of culture in the early twentieth century, recognizing the advantages of linking literature to that "complex whole" of Tylor's vision. At the same time, as other scholars have emphasized, the late nineteenth-century anthropological idea of culture derives from a belletristic vision of literature as holistic and ennobling. Belletristic criticism, a weird mix of aesthetic appreciations and moral analyses of literature, preceded and helped clarify the anthropological project. So familiar was the language of culture to men of letters that Frederic Harrison, Matthew Arnold's frequent antagonist, called the talk of culture "the silliest cant of the day," noting that such talk "sits well on a possessor of belles lettres" (qtd. in Guillory, "Literary Study" 26). John Guillory notes that culture and literature alike were expected to be ambiguous and non-utilitarian, and that literature especially "has been made to play a kind of allegorical role in the development of the disciplines, as the name of the principle antithetical to the very scientificity governing discipline formation in the modern university" ("Literary Study" 37).

English departments were founded in the last quarter of the nineteenth century, although most came into being later on. Previously, professors of oratory or rhetoric or even classics had taught Shakespeare and sometimes the British Romantic poets. The earliest literary scholars were philologists, many of them trained in Germany. As a number of scholars have shown working from different angles, English studies has always been a nationalistic project, inspired by European romanticism and nineteenth-century interest in native language and culture (recall here Perrault, the Brothers Grimm, and the great civilizing project of folklore as traced by Jack Zipes). A comprehensive story of the rise of English has yet to be told, one that brings together domestic histories of the field with Marxist and post-colonial accounts of English abroad. In any case, the study of literature has long been coterminous with the study of culture.

It was the 1930s, claims Susan Hegeman, that witnessed the incorporation of the culture idea into literary studies. Hegeman's book *Patterns for America* documents the rich exchanges between anthropology and literature during this period, alongside problematic assertions of aesthetic superiority and the national psyche. Anthony Easthope confirms that the study of literature, as advocated in the 1930s, demanded a separation of literature from everything else. Culture was at once denigrated in the form of the popular or the mass, and redeemed/rewritten in the idiom of literature's organism, wholeness, and transformative power. F. R. Leavis, for instance, hated popular culture but tried to preserve the culture idea by distinguishing between culture—known best as literature, art, and music—and civilization, the repository of everything trashy. For Leavis, civilization was the enemy, and culture the savior. "This golden time," writes Hegeman, "was the moment of high modernism, when the intellectual was seen to have operated as a critically distanced, but engaged, commentator on society" (170).

Raymond Williams effectively turned the tables on Leavis in his *Culture and Society* (1958). Taking a longer historical view, Williams also argues for culture's wholeness, but a wholeness spanning industry and labor and class formations, the whole sorry underbelly of capitalism. Williams strategically appealed to the classic Anglo-American formulation of culture á la Tylor precisely to challenge the Leavisite assumption that culture means only high culture. *Culture and Society* shows how the fantasy of cultural wholeness was highly selective and served as a defense against modern industrial life.

Accompanying the disenchantment with holistic views of literature and culture, though, was the sense that critical practice itself might be suspect, no matter its methodology or objects. Cultural studies calls into question all forms of symbolic activity, including its own claims to social relevance. As Bruce Robbins points out, Williams' intervention in the scene of culture also showed how

> "criticism" in the narrow disciplinary sense—the study of literary texts—could base its ascent on the grandiose claim to be a kind of self-appointed conscience of modern society. And it explains how this rise in the pretensions of literary criticism could have taken place during a period when literature itself was being relegated to an increasingly marginal role within the cultures of Britain and the U.S. How could literary criticism become the staging ground for social critique when literature itself was losing its social influence? It was precisely because literature was not central to society or representative of its dominant trends that it could serve as a condensation and epitome of culture.
>
> (60–61)

Thus, cultural studies has had to acknowledge its debt to literary study and that strategy of estrangement, and to urge relevance along different lines. Cultural studies has tried to bridge the gap between society and art, to challenge academic elitism. But as critics point out, cultural studies has its own formalist and estranging tendencies. How can it not, as a mode of analysis that demands at least some remove from the everyday?

It is not that literature is only lately losing its relevance, as opposed to cultural studies or children's studies; rather, literature's relevance or cultural power has long (if not always) depended upon its remove from the public sphere. If this is true, then we might think differently about the current "crisis" of the humanities. Literature's estrangement from society is simply becoming more problematic, as competing forms of cultural capital—internet knowledge, for one—promise both cultural and economic legitimacy. If students are now less invested in the humanities, it's probably because they know that the humanities aren't as profitable as business or engineering, and that the cultural (compensatory) capital of literature is on the wane.

In *Cultural Capital* (1993), a brilliant account of literature and its discontents across the centuries, John Guillory proposes that critical theory has become a supplement to literature, a form of cultural and linguistic capital in its own right. He contends further that theory effects a "transference of transference," transforming the student's love for the teacher into the love of the teacher's subject or discourse (181–207). Theory thus becomes both a middle-class form of cultural capital and a mode of cultural transmission. For Guillory, whose debt to French sociologist Pierre Bordieu is clear, theory is less a bold new intellectual adventure than another form of what Bordieu calls "distinction." Guillory does not address the culture idea per se, but clearly culture is a sustaining link between literature and theory (perhaps even a compromise of sorts between them). For Guillory, "cultural" is an adjective rather than a noun, but we could easily reverse the terms: if literature is a form of cultural capital, as he holds, then culture is also a form of literary capital, perhaps now more than ever.

There is nothing especially natural about a career in English. And disciplinary and methodological shifts are the very stuff of intellectual life. Given these realities, it is surprising how many literary critics bemoan the decline of literature at the hands of culture. In his recent book *The Fateful Question of Culture* (1997), for example, Geoffrey H. Hartman argues that the adoption in anthropology of what Clifford Geertz called the "text analogy" has weakened rather than refined our understanding of literature. "After a heady period," Hartman writes, "during which the semiotic theory of culture drew every human activity into its net, students and scholars of literature are no longer sure what they profess" (2). But Hartman's own book quite clearly illustrates how literary criticism profits by the "text analogy." Not being sure of what we profess has its perks. How else could Hartman, an English professor (not an anthropologist), explore the fateful question of culture, and through such loving attention to Wordsworth? Denis Donoghue assures us in a blurb that Hartman is uniquely qualified for that project in part because "he has read everything," establishing a baseline for cultural knowledge that echoes Tylor's faith in totality. Culture, it seems, has gone literary, even if literature has vanished into culture. Hartman is not shy about playing anthropologist and social critic, postulating that the culture idea keeps the hope of embodiment alive, against the ghostliness of daily living. Given such assessments, it is odd that Hartman seeks as he does to recuperate literature, since clearly literature's disciplinary expansion made "fateful" the question(s) of culture.

Again and again, critics concentrate on the failures of culture as a concept rather than appreciating culture's generative power (which depends on that "failure"). While Hartman questions the excesses of cultural studies in order to redeem literature, Terry Eagleton, one of our sharpest and most socially progressive critics, contends in his own recent monograph *The Idea of Culture* (2000) that "we are trapped at the moment between disablingly wide and discomfortingly rigid notions of culture," that we need to move beyond both (32). Is moving beyond either possible or desirable, I wonder? "It is hard," writes Eagleton, "to resist the conclusion that the word 'culture' is both too broad and too narrow to be greatly useful" (32). He is taking his cue in part from anthropologists themselves, who have questioned the viability of the culture idea. Adam Kuper, for instance, concludes that "the more one considers the best modern work on culture by anthropologists, the more advisable it must appear to avoid the hyper-referential word altogether, and to talk more precisely of knowledge, or belief, or art, or technology, or tradition, or even of ideology" (x). In *The Faded Mosaic*, English professor Christopher Clausen likens the culture idea to a cult.[5] But what most scholars downplay is that literary criticism has always authorized itself through/as culture-writing, even if (precisely as) the terms of culture have changed.[6]

Disciplining children's studies

What does all this mean for children's studies? It means, first of all, that we ought to study the dialectical relationship of English and anthropology. We should also pay more attention to the history of English studies These fields show that culture is far from a new idea in our discipline. I am not arguing that we should not aspire to ideals of wholeness or interdisciplinarity; rather, we need to remember that the idea of culture has long enabled the professing of literature.

In his recent essay "The Future of the Profession," Jerry Griswold urges scholars of children's literature to publish and network outside our field, so that we do not wind up "only talking to ourselves and our protégés" (237). He cites Jack Zipes's recent book *Sticks and Stones: The Troublesome Success of Children's Literature from* Slovenly Peter *to* Harry Potter, remarking that Zipes, too, is worried about the profession's narcissism, if from a different angle. At first glance, then, Griswold seems to urge a wider vision, at least within the field of English. Griswold offers five measured recommendations for sustaining the enterprise of children's literature. His final suggestion, which he knows will be controversial, is that we make more careful distinctions between children's literature and "children's reading." Quick to acknowledge how easily such distinctions might seem reactionary, he nonetheless feels that children's literature should not be confused with just any children's texts. He hopes that future generations of scholars will manage to weave "their way between the Scylla of a needed openmindedness and the Charybdis of worries about becoming reactionary" (241). "It seems to me," he remarks further, "that when we are able to talk about Children's Literature as literature, we will be able to address others outside our discipline with genuine confidence and authority" (241).

Put another way, literary expertise is still the key to our success as professionals. Here Griswold sounds much like Hartman. If we write only about comic books or the Teletubbies, he implies, we'll forget *The Odyssey* and lose scholarly face. Too broad or popular a sense of culture might lead to disciplinary disaster, whereas retaining a literary sensibility will safeguard our cultural voice. Griswold's concern about professional insularity, then, actually comes out of a fairly traditional commitment to literature. Griswold does take an unusual approach to the problem of cultural studies. Rather than argue, as many do, that cultural studies is troubling because it diminishes the value of literature (end of story), Griswold worries that cultural studies will prevent us from talking about literature, which will in turn prevent us from participating fully in the academy. It seems to me, however, that children's literature scholars now *benefit* from their knowledge about popular culture, even when it displaces literary knowledge. A firm command of *Toy Story* in tandem with some knowledge of Baudrillard makes better career sense these days than a firm command of Dickens. Why police the border between literature and reading, since that border is mythical anyway, and since culture has again become a dominant term?

Contributors to the recent special issue of *The Lion and the Unicorn* on children's studies (April 2001) also urge a professional vision that is less novel than it seems at first. In her introductory essay, sociologist Gertrud Lenzer pleads for an integrated, multi-disciplinary approach to childhood and children, commenting that "we cannot arrive at a comprehensive understanding of children by simply accumulating, aggregating, or adding up segmented findings from a far-flung variety of inquiries in the various disciplines" (183). That a "comprehensive picture" is even possible and desirable is assumed from the start. Co-founder and Director of the Children's Studies Program and the Children's Studies Center at Brooklyn College, Lenzer aspires to a humanistic, holistic understanding of child and culture alike. She is not invested in literature, or rather, her vision of culture does not privilege literature. Children's studies, she writes, "makes the ontological claim that children must be viewed in their fullness as human beings. The various child-focused disciplinary endeavors must contribute to such a holistic understanding of children rather than reducing them to specialized abstract fragments" (183). Lenzer does a little reducing of her own, dismissing poststructuralism. She wants to cultivate "enlightened knowledge among our students," to be sure that children are viewed "not merely as objects of specialized scholarly research or of social policies and social action" (185). Lenzer hopes to reconstitute at the disciplinary level the wholeness of childhood not realized elsewhere, because it is not otherwise achievable. Such wholeness, in my view, is sheer fantasy; the point is that it is not a new fantasy.

Lenzer's scheme finds a close counterpart in Mary Galbraith's "Hear My Cry: A Manifesto for an Emancipatory Childhood Studies Approach to Children's Literature," the next essay in the special issue. Galbraith, a psychologist, is even more dismissive of poststructuralist theory, although she's quite happy to embrace Habermas' utopian faith in the public sphere. A proponent of "emancipatory" theory, she identifies as useful the work of Alice Miller and Lloyd de Mause (both problematic in my book, especially de Mause). I could not be happier to hear of efforts to empower children and assure their rights, but I doubt that the academy's "postmodern skeptics" are blocking the way, as Galbraith holds. Is emancipatory criticism significantly different—institutionally, rhetorically, disciplinarily—from the skeptical work that Galbraith does not like? Isn't she advocating a different critical canon as much as anything else? Galbraith's passion is admirable, deriving (as she acknowledges) from an Enlightenment faith in humanistic rationality. But to accept uncritically the culture idea seems just as presumptuous as to interrogate dubious assumptions about identity, representation, and power.

The children's culture wars (of which my essay is obviously a part) turn on the issue of what constitutes a good-faith scholarly enterprise, and/or what our real subjects should be (so much so, in fact, that these questions seem foundational to the enterprise). Do we write about books or about real kids? Is writing even worthwhile? Galbraith and others seem to believe that writing does not matter as much as other kinds of care and feeding of children, and they may be right. But aren't we always (already?) writing, and in professional contexts, for each other? Is writing really incompatible with and less important than parenting, teaching, and other kinds of fieldwork?

Richard Flynn makes the same point in his critique of Peter Hunt's distinction between "book people" and "child people." Both Flynn and Karen Coats defend the importance of "books" in children's studies, by which they mean literature and criticism alike. In her essay assessing the shape and fortunes of children's studies, Coats suggests that we keep children's studies plural, meaning that we try to respect as much as bridge disciplinary differences, and strike a balance between the study of representation(s) as informed by critical theory and the study of actual children. Proposing an "alternative manifesto," she points out that even the most emancipatory project presumes that "wholeness is possible" and that lack is de facto traumatic, presumptions that she challenges from a Lacanian perspective (144).

Clearly, theoretical differences underscore these discussions, and I don't mean to sound disrespectful. Still, it is troubling that some advocates of children's studies idealize culture while objecting to poststructuralist insight. In his introduction to *The Children's Culture Reader*, Henry Jenkins at once embraces and criticizes poststructuralism, in order to recuperate the holistic culture idea in a contemporary theoretical vein. Jenkins avers that the displacement of the child from children's culture (studies) was a "necessary first step for critiquing the mythology of childhood innocence" (23). Now, he says, it is time to bring the child back into culture, and here the discussion gets weird. Jenkins suggests that if we do not study real children, the child exists "purely as a figment of pedophilic desire" (23). The implication is that children's studies without actual children amounts not merely to narcissism or insularity, as Griswold worries, but indeed to pedophilia.

In their introduction to *Disciplinarity at the Fin de Siècle*, Amanda Anderson and Joseph Valente point out that we usually associate interdisciplinarity with freedom and disciplinarity with constraint, forgetting that "the dialectic of agency of determinism, currently distributed across the disciplinary/interdisciplinary divide, was at the heart of disciplinary formation itself" (2). It is as if discipline and disciplinarity are dirty words, connoting—like didacticism or sentimentality—narrative and/or moral inflexibility.

The ethnographic imaginary

Like the culture concept, ethnography has come under fire in anthropological circles. Although he affirms ethnography as a practice, Martyn

Hammersley, in his monograph on the subject, remarks, "I no longer believe 'ethnography' to be a useful category with which to think about social research methodology" (203). Ethnography, of course, has long been the heart of anthropology, first as a method of participant observation of and reportage from the field, as codified by Bronislaw Malinowski in *Argonauts of the Western Pacific* (1922), and later as a reconstructed, more self-conscious and experimental practice of writing about cultural others, and about the otherness of self. Thanks largely to the textualization of fieldwork, anthropology often treats culture as a series of texts to be interpreted, so it is not surprising that Margaret Mead and other early practitioners emphasized the hermeneutic and aesthetic powers of the anthropologist.

Given this heritage, what James Clifford calls the post-1950s "dispersion of ethnographic authority" is also/instead a redistribution of that authority along familiar, if now postmodern and poststructuralist, lines that authorize the literary critic to hold forth on culture (24). Clifford's book is titled *The Predicament of Culture* (1988), but we might think also about the culture of predicament and how we sustain it. Analysis of culture and its ills, after all, has been one of culture's centripetal forces. Furthermore, in some of the critical literature the deconstruction of culture seems little more than a plea for the restoration of literature; there is little in either Hartman or Eagleton about anthropology or ethnography, residual in children's culture work.

Near the end of his review of *The Children's Culture Reader*, Richard Flynn asks this question: "After Rose, after Ariès, after Kincaid, what are the cultural and historical effects of the persistence of developmental models of childhood? Where are the descriptive ethnographies of the child at the end of the twentieth century?" (473). It is worth asking (with Flynn) what kind of ethnographies of childhood we want to write and why. What methods of textualization and collection/display are strategic? How might we deal productively with ethnography's rhetoric of realism, its reputation as a mimetic mode of mapping and description? Might not a seemingly innocuous title like *Children's Culture* tend to establish authority, much in the manner of classic texts named "simply" after the people they describe: *The Andaman Islanders, Street Corner Society, The Mountain People*? Until the twentieth century, the ethnographer and the anthropologist were separate creatures, with different tasks; do we now expect the scholar of children's culture to gather data, translate customs, interpret and theorize, all of the above? What happens to the model of participant observation in the field when we observe our own children, or when we remember our own childhoods? Jenkins argues that we should give kids the right "tools" with which they can "realize their own political agendas or to participate in the production of their own culture" (30). I agree, but isn't this language familiar? What are the pros and cons of imagining children as primitive people with a distinct culture, along the lines of early comparative anthropology? Should we cheer on the "dispersion" of ethnographic authority when children talk back?

These are difficult questions, and here I can only emphasize that, for better and for worse, the ethnographic imaginary takes different narrative forms in children's studies, among them pop-journalistic exposés of youth culture as well as more academic and theoretical treatments of childhood. If children's studies is to encompass non-academic as well as academic work, then we might want to pay more attention to discussions of youth in the popular press. We can see ethnographic language and methods most obviously in some recent books about American adolescence. Consider, for instance, *A Tribe Apart: A Journey Into the Heart of American Adolescence* (1998). The synopsis on the dust jacket makes even clearer than the title the book's ethnographic spirit:

> For three fascinating, disturbing years, writer Patricia Hersch journeyed inside a world that is as familiar as our own children and yet as alien as some exotic culture—the world of adolescence. As a silent, attentive partner, she followed eight teenagers in the typically American town of Reston, Virginia, listening to their stories, observing their rituals, watching them fulfill their dreams and enact their tragedies. What she found was that America's teens have fashioned a fully defined culture that adults neither see nor imagine—a culture of unprecedented freedom and baffling complexity, a culture with rules but no structure, values but no clear morality, codes but no consistency.

Here the language of culture is comparativist rather than singular, in keeping with ethnography. The ethnographic imaginary can accommodate both the traditional holistic sense of culture, as codified by Tylor, and the comparative idea of culture as introduced by Boas. Another example would be Elinor Burkett's recent ethnography *Another Planet: A Year in the Life of a Suburban High School* (2001), whose cover looks like a field notebook and/or a diary (as if Margaret Mead and Harriet the Spy were collaborating).

Also invoking adolescence as the undiscovered country is Thomas Hine's *The Rise and Fall of the American Teenager* (1999). In chapter 3, "Coming of Age in Utter Confusion," Hine appeals to Mead's work as a model for defamiliarizing and illuminating the culture of American adolescence, which (like Mead before him) he alternately sees as stable and as vanishing. "Strange stories from exotic locales," he writes, "can provide perspectives on our own culture and its weird and painful practices" (44). His penultimate chapter, "Goths in Tomorrowland," surveys today's "tribes of youth," whom he regards largely as "modern primitives," fond of tattoos, piercing, and other enigmatic practices (277). These books on adolescence resemble most contemporary studies of boyhood, girlhood, and the family, which make frequent appeals to anthropological knowledge and the ethnographic imaginary.

But what about more properly academic writing? How does the ethnographic imaginary work to cope with problems posed by the theoretical enterprise known as children's culture? My impression is that the ethnographic imaginary has not only survived the poststructuralist revolution but has inhabited it rather fully, or, as we might say after Michel Foucault, rather productively. Poststructuralism has changed the terms of the critical conversation, but it has also appropriated ethnography to its own narrative ends, for better and for worse. Foucault's work has been especially influential in children's literature studies as well as in the emergent field of children's studies. We tend now to think of children as docile bodies, as subjects of an institutional and disciplinary surveillance previously affirmed as the positive, necessary experience of schooling and socialization. Foucault's critique of the repressive hypothesis in and around modern subjectivity has done much to undermine what I would call the progressive hypothesis of children's literature and culture, the tale of ever-expanding autonomy and rationality.

At the same time, despite Foucault's emphasis on reverse discourses and so forth, Foucauldian analysis rewrites the story of children's freedom as the story of discipline through discourse and commodification. Simply put, Foucauldian analysis often assumes that children and other populations are subaltern victims of oppressive social norms. Foucauldian analysis is organized around key figures of social specification and regulation—among them the (masturbating) child—and children's culture may likewise depend upon an estranging sense of childhood at the level of rhetoric if not the analysis, per se.

One way to defamiliarize childhood is to suggest a significant divide between child and adult, and their respective cultures, such that the child is always other to the adult (self). But in order for the inquiry to be worthwhile, that otherness must also be manageable: this is the delicate economy of poststructuralist ethnographic writing, which appeals less to the wholeness of culture than to the otherness of subjectivity. Along these lines, consider Christopher Jenks' *Childhood*, one of Routledge's "Key Ideas" books, a sociological analysis of construction(s) of childhood past, present, and future, organized around issues such as child innocence, child abuse, and the alleged "disappearance" of childhood. Early in the first chapter, Jenks proposes that in developmental psychology and socialization theory (he singles out the work of Jean Piaget and Talcott Parsons respectively), the project of accounting for the experiences of childhood "proceed[s] rapidly to an overattentive elaboration of the compulsive processes of integration," or of becoming an adult (4). In his view, we never really examine what a child is, because we are too preoccupied with that child's evolution into adulthood. Jenks suggests, in effect, that we do not sufficiently understand the child as other. "Simply stated," he writes, "the child is familiar to us and yet strange, he or she inhabits our world and yet seems to answer to another, he or she is essentially of ourselves and yet appears to display a systematically different order of being" (3). This chapter, which ruthlessly questions the idea of development, resorts to an ethnographic thematic of otherness. We might see this as standard procedure; don't we often defamiliarize our subject in order to make it our own, especially in writing?

Maybe so, maybe not. In any case, Jenks specifically invokes anthropology and its language of estrangement. Throughout this first chapter, he appeals to the classic child-savage analogy of evolutionary science and anthropology even as—or alternatively, *by*—ostensibly disavowing it. This discussion begins in a section actually titled "The Child as 'Savage,'" in which select quotation marks and rhetorical markers identify the association as troubling. And yet Jenks consistently likens the work of the child culture theorist to that of the anthropologist, such that the section title winds up a faithful description of his assumptions. It is as if the child-savage analogy is so useful that Jenks thinks he can ditch the equivalence but keep the discursive field and protocol.

In fairness, Jenks admits that the child-savage analogy is political and politicized, that the "manner of our assembling and the character of our distancing are significant in the constitution of either savage or child" (5). But as that very sentence shows, the analogy persists, not as an example of a practice to be shunned, but as a narrative of how childhood analysis has worked up to this point, and as a more politically problematic antecedent of a more useful poststructuralist theorization of the child as strange, and of children's culture as distinct, even unknowable. It is not a good idea to keep the child-savage equivalence in circulation, since that equivalence descends from centuries of colonial encounter that gave us much classic children's literature and helped authorize English studies. Several times Jenks invokes "our early anthropologist" as the foil-turned-model for the childhood theorist, who is likewise witnessing a sea change. That theorist, in his view, is "addressing the somewhat more diffuse and volatile boundaries that mark off childhood today, and the fact that we are considering such a transition from within the mores and folkways of a modern secular society, is no guarantee that that ritualism will be any less present" (7). As compelling as his analysis is, we do not have to accept either the assumption that childhood is more vulnerable today than in days past or the description of the childhood scholar as interpreter-theorist of modern mores, folkways, and ritualism.

I dwell on Jenks' work because it illustrates how powerfully the ethnographic imaginary persists in even the most sophisticated poststructuralist analysis. We're light years away from *A Tribe Apart*, and yet much of the rhetoric is the same. The ethnographic imaginary, of course, is not exclusive to literature or anthropology. We can see it in psychoanalysis especially, and we shouldn't forget the significance of Freud's own fieldwork and ethnographic case studies. Freud wrote about a host of exotic creatures, adapted from sexology, and classified in typically bourgeois ways: the neurotic, the homosexual, the fetishist, and so on (not entirely unlike Foucault). It's no surprise that Malinowski sought to debunk the Oedipus Complex in his anthropological work in the early part of the century; he understood psychoanalysis as a rival discipline to anthropology, equally ambitious and resilient, another imaginative refashioning of humanist science that promised to decode culture(s) through contact with real people. Psychoanalysis and the modern social sciences depend upon the ethnographic imaginary, as do cultural studies and children's studies after them.

* * *

The potential of children's studies is exciting. But we need in children's studies and discussions of children's culture a stronger sense of intellectual and disciplinary history. Identifying and challenging the holistic idea of culture as it resurfaces in current debates is fairly easy. Ethnography is trickier to deal with, for while the ethnographic imaginary is often troublesome, fieldwork with children can be responsibly conducted. But so far, children's studies has not demonstrated the kind of critical self-consciousness about ethnography that is now crucial to anthropology and sociology, which makes it harder to distinguish between more and less legitimate forms of child study.

As Le Doeuff shows with respect to philosophy, an intellectual discipline's imaginary is intimately bound up with its critical concepts and rhetorical strategies. Perhaps we cannot divest ourselves of culture or its more troubling metaphors unless we stop thinking of ourselves as academics working in the humanities. I am not sure exactly where to go from here, but why not push for a children's studies informed by self-reflexive field research *and* poststructuralist theory (not just the optimistic stuff) *and* what we might call disciplinary studies—a children's studies that acknowledges to the fullest possible degree its debts to anthropology, cultural studies, and so on?

"Culture is a deeply compromised idea I cannot quite do without," writes James Clifford (qtd. in Buzard 312). We may share Clifford's ambivalent attitude, but we should know by now that ambivalence is fundamental (if not necessary) to academic work. Clifford's very career attests to the critical fortunes of the culture idea and to the generative effects of ambivalence. Clifford is not technically an anthropologist, as one might surmise from his writings, but rather, he is a literary theorist and intellectual historian teaching in the History of Consciousness Program at UC-Santa Cruz. He has played deconstructive anthropologist for some time now, capitalizing on yet another migration of the culture idea to English studies. As James Buzard shows in "Notes on the Defenestration of Culture," just as comparative anthropology began to doubt the culture idea around the middle of the twentieth century, that idea invigorated and authorized cultural studies (in which poststructuralist anthropological theory remains a staple).

For all its progressive impulses and self-conscious posturing, cultural studies has one major blind spot: disciplinarity. Buzard argues persuasively that cultural studies arrogantly positions itself as anthropology's brighter and politically promising sibling without admitting as much, reclaiming culture as its central concern but refusing to see itself as a discipline informed by other disciplines. Whether or not children's culture is a deeply compromised idea we cannot quite do without, children's studies must learn from this tendency of cultural studies to deny its own disciplinary history.

Notes

1 The academic discourse on "everyday life" had its heyday in 1950s and 1960s France, later inspiring British and American cultural studies as well as Marxist criticism. We might identify Henri Lefebvre's *Critique of Everyday Life* (1947) as the inaugural text, though Situationist writing was also influential. Interest in the "everyday" has intensified again in the wake of cultural studies and a renewed interest in sociology; for more information on this body of work and its current purchase, see *The Everyday Life Reader*, edited by Ben Highmore.

2 As anthropology became more sophisticated in the twentieth century, the twin issues of representation and interpretation were hotly contested, such that anthropology now is an incredibly self-conscious discipline, hyper-aware of (even hyper-apologetic about) its own procedures. Even so, the holistic idea persists, most often as a fantasy of critical reconstruction. A field study is still supposed to tell you something important about a culture, as well as legitimate the author.

3 As Richard Flynn notes in his review, *The Children's Culture Reader* is useful as an introductory textbook but has little to offer beyond the standard poststructuralist insight that childhood isn't, well, so natural after all. At the same time, the book appeals to an undertheorized, ahistorical idea of culture, perhaps as compensation for the deconstruction of "childhood." NYU Press' *Generations of Youth*, by contrast, makes an effort to engage more locally with issues such as race and class bias, often against a monolithic culture idea. It is also more successful as an anthology, cohesive while wide-ranging, perhaps because youth culture is already an established topic of cultural studies.

4 Obviously, the ethnographic imaginary, like other such sweeping concepts—Le Doeuff's philosophical imaginary, or the "political unconscious" of Frederic Jameson—threatens to be nearly as totalizing as the culture idea. Even so, I think it will be useful in this context, as a rhetorical and theoretical counterpart to other discursive conceits, among them the culture idea.

5 Thanks to J. D. Stahl for directing me to this text.

6 "A literary education has many values," Eagleton wryly observes, "but systematic thought is not one of them" (239). But as Eagleton also acknowledges, we've benefited from our resistance to systematic thought; literature is in many ways articulated against such.

Works cited

Anderson, Amanda, and Joseph Valente. "Discipline and Freedom." *Disciplinarity at the Fin de Siècle*. Ed. Amanda Anderson and Joseph Valente. Princeton: Princeton UP, 2002. 1–15.

Austin, Joe, and Michael Nevil Willard, eds. *Generations of Youth: Youth Cultures and History in Twentieth-Century America*. New York: New York UP, 1998,

Bourdieu, Pierre. *Distinction: A Social Critique of the Judgment of Taste*. Trans Richard Nice. Cambridge: Harvard UP, 1984.

Burkett, Elinor. *Another Planet: A Year in the Life of a Suburban High School*. New York: Harper, 2001.

Buzard, James. "Notes on the Defenestration of Culture." *Disciplinarity at the Fin de Siècle*. Ed. Amanda Anderson and Joseph Valente. Princeton: Princeton UP, 2002. 312–31.

Clausen, Christopher. *Faded Mosaic: The Emergence of Post-Cultural America*. Chicago: Dee, 2000.

Clifford, James. *The Predicament of Culture: Twentieth-Century Ethnography, Literature, and Art*. Cambridge, MA: Harvard UP, 1988.

Coats, Karen. "Keepin' It Plural: Children's Studies in the Academy." *Children's Literature Association Quarterly* 26 (2001): 140–50.

Eagleton, Terry. *The Idea of Culture*. London: Blackwell, 2000.

Easthope, Antony. *Literary into Cultural Studies*. New York: Routledge, 1991.

Fass, Paula S., and Mary Ann Mason. *Childhood in America*. New York: New York UP, 2000.

Flynn, Richard. "The Intersection of Children's Literature and Childhood Studies." *Children's Literature Association Quarterly* 22 (1997): 143–45.

——. Rev. of *The Children's Culture Reader*, ed. Henry Jenkins. *The Lion and the Unicorn* 24 (2000): 468–73.

Galbraith, Mary. "Hear My Cry: A Manifesto for an Emancipatory Childhood Studies Approach to Children's Literature." *The Lion and the Unicorn* 25 (2001): 187–205.

Griswold, Jerry. "The Future of the Profession." *The Lion and the Unicorn* 26 (2002): 236–42.

Guillory, John. *Cultural Capital: The Problem of Literary Canon Formation*. Chicago: U of Chicago P, 1993.

——. "Literary Study and the Modern System of the Disciplines." *Disciplinarity at the Fin de Siècle*. Ed. Amanda Anderson and Joseph Valente. Princeton: Princeton UP, 2002. 19–43.

Hammersley, Martyn. *What's Wrong with Ethnography? Methodological Explorations*. New York: Routledge, 1992.

Hartman, Geoffrey H. *The Fateful Question of Culture*. New York: Columbia UP, 1997.

Hegeman, Susan. *Patterns of Culture: Modernism and the Concept of Culture*. Princeton: Princeton UP, 1999.

Hersch, Patricia. *A Tribe Apart: A Journey into the Heart of American Adolescence*. New York: Ballantine, 1998.

Highmore, Ben, ed. *The Everyday Life Reader*. New York: Routledge, 2002.

Hine, Thomas. *The Rise and Fall of the American Teenager: A New History of the American Adolescent Experience*. New York: Harper, 1999.

Jenkins, Henry, ed. *The Children's Culture Reader*. New York: New York UP, 1998.

Jenks, Chris. *Childhood*. New York: Routledge, 1996.

Kuper, Adam. *Culture: The Anthropologists' Account*. Cambridge: Harvard UP, 1999.

Le Doeuff, Michèle. *The Philosophical Imaginary*. Trans. Colin Gordon. Stanford: Stanford UP, 1989.

Lenzer, Getrud. "Children's Studies: Beginnings and Purposes." *The Lion and the Unicorn* 25 (2001): 181–86.

Robbins, Bruce. *Secular Vocations: Intellectuals, Professionalism, Culture*. London: Verso, 1993.

Travisano, Thomas. "Of Dialectic and Divided Consciousness: Intersections between Children's Literature and Childhood Studies." *Children's Literature* 28 (2000): 22–29.

Tylor, E. B. *Primitive Culture: Researches into the Development of Mythology, Philosophy, Religion, Language, Art, and Custom*. 2 vols. New York: Putnam, 1920.

Williams, Raymond. *Culture and Society, 1780–1950*. 2nd ed. New York: Columbia UP, 1983.

58

CHILDHOOD REVISITED

On the relationship between childhood studies and children's literature

Nina Christensen

Source: *Children's Literature Association Quarterly* 28(4) (2003–2004): 230–239.

The different positions of scholars working with children's literature creates rich opportunities for critical analysis. In this article, the focus is on the interaction between children's literature both as literature and as a representation of childhood, on scholars' awareness of the relationship of such representations to ideas of childhood in a certain historical period, and finally on the self-conception of scholars in relation to the object of study.

This discussion is designed to help scholars think about keeping a balance between different forms of awareness. First, they must be aware of the fact that children's literature is literature, that it is, among other things, fiction, which needs no legitimization outside itself. Second, scholars must have an awareness that children's literature, like literature in general, is created and shaped under certain conditions and exists within a certain reality influencing the final product. Although children's literature can be discussed in its own right without focus on factors external to the text, "real" children read the books, and discussions concerning children in society, for instance, influence the portrayal of the characters. Discussions of "real" and "ideal" children are required of us, which points to the necessity of metacritical awareness in the researcher or scholar of children's literature.

Different countries, different research traditions

Recent theories within a number of fields reflect a turn from a focus on the interpretation of specific texts to an interest in the construction of texts in the broadest sense of the word. One consequence of this is that words such as history, identity, and reality are put in the plural or in quotation marks in order to reflect the writer's awareness of the impossibility of stable meaning. This turn has been both rejected and welcomed in children's literature criticism: it is rejected by critics who primarily see children's literature as a useful and unproblematic tool in making the child connect subject and object through representation in language and images, while other critics see it as a most welcome opportunity for discussing such fundamental concepts as reality, child, and identity. In children's literature criticism, this turn has led to a growing interest in the implications of integrating childhood studies into children's literature criticism, and the subject has been widely discussed, especially among English-speaking academics.

Only to a very limited extent has this been the case in Denmark, where the theoretical foundations for the study of children's literature are still under construction and where children's literature is rarely taught or acknowledged as a serious object of study at universities. This is probably due to the fact that children's literature was accepted at universities for a brief period in the seventies as part of ideological criticism, where its pertinence to the integration of literatures had been previously neglected in literary departments. In the beginning of the 1980s, when academics were quick to turn their backs on ideological criticism, the study of children's literature was abandoned. When the Centre for Children's Literature was inaugurated in 1998, it was established as an independent unit at the Danish University of Education. This independent status can, of course, be seen as a strength, but it can also be read as a sign of the marginalization of the field. Either way, the small size of the research community in Denmark adds to the necessity of dialogue with the international research community in the field. Here the researcher will have to engage in theoretical discussions concerning the relationship between childhood studies and children's literature in a foreign language, and the debate will be based on different historical developments, different academic traditions, and different primary source material and canons. The possibility of asking questions that arise on the basis of another perspective can be regarded as a challenge.

My interest in these subjects is based on reflections arising from my Ph.D. thesis, *Den danske billedbog 1950–1999. Teori, analyse, historie* (*The Danish Picture Book 1950–1999. Theory, Analysis, History*). In a central argument of my thesis, I argue that the development of Danish picture books is the result of various interests on many different levels. The production of picture books in Denmark is closely linked to the development of the welfare state, since most picture books are sold to public libraries and school libraries. Therefore, laws, reports, and other official documents concerning this development provide important source material. Since librarians and teachers decide which books are to be bought for these public collections, their critical standards are of utmost importance and must therefore be investigated. Articles, reviews, and debates concerning, for instance, the defining characteristics of "good" children's literature also provide valuable sources. Naturally, the books actually produced are the center of focus, but here my study demonstrates that different interests blend: since the market is part of the educational system—the education of the citizen through libraries and the education of the child through schools and kindergartens—picture books offer representations of role models for child and adult. Different images of child and adult are to be seen in the books, both through the depiction of the characters in texts and illustrations and through the implicit and explicit address of an audience of children and adults.

Picture books are interesting starting points for the study of representations of childhood for at least two reasons. First, they are traditionally aimed at smaller children and have a strong socializing function (Stephens 152). Children in picture books are supposed to function as role models for identification, but picture books are evidently also an interesting object of study because the representation takes place through two different code systems: the visual and the verbal code. Thus, we have the opportunity to study the simultaneous fictionalization of the child in text and image.

Herein, I wish to present analyses of how children are represented and addressed in six Danish picture books from 1950 until today. Although the sources are related to a specific national (literary) history, the general conclusions are not. I have chosen the examples I include because they point to some characteristic conceptions of children's literature and of children in different periods. The underlying question motivating this historical and analytic endeavour is my investigation of why it is important to combine studies of children's literature with childhood studies. This leads to a general discussion of positions the researcher can assume when working in this field.

A self-reliant child from the 1950s

Within children's literature criticism it is often assumed that children will identify with the main character. Although this point of view could and should be questioned, as it has been by Karín Lesnik-Oberstein in *Children's Literature* and "Defining Children's Literature and Childhood," an investigation of such fictive characters as "signs of childhood" is relevant. This can be done, for instance, by analyzing descriptions of the appearance and inner qualities of the children depicted, of their social relations, of their physical surroundings, and of the rules of behavior described. In picture books produced in a certain period one can, of course, also detect different and sometimes contradicting images of the child. However, some general traits reveal themselves. One example of a typical child represented in picture books from the 1950s is [the child shown in Thea Bank Jensen and Lis Lund-Hansen's *Trine kan . . .* (*Trine can . . .*) (Copenhagen: Høst and Søn, 1955)].

As the title [. . .] implies, the book is a description of all the abilities of a girl of approximately five years of age. The black-and-white photographs are taken at close range and show how the girl performs activities using her body and her senses: what she can do with her hands, her mouth, her ears, her eyes, her nose, and her feet. The first-person narrator uses short, simple sentences with repetitive patterns, and the verbal text is a confirmation of what is in the photos. The child appears very absorbed in her activities, which she performs on her own. She is not portrayed either in the company of other adults or other children. All the photos show her with attitudes and expressions of absorption and concentration on her activities, and none of them show any negative emotions, such as sorrow or anger.

Although the narrative takes place within one day, her physical appearance changes: she wears different outfits—dresses, trousers, blouses, etc., all of them presenting her as a child dressed in clothes that allow her to move and to play. A casual, short hairstyle adds to the staging of the child not as a neat, restrained little girl, but as a child curiously and actively experiencing the world. The surroundings within which she does this are a home where she has her own child-sized furniture and her own children's books and toys. Outside the house she plays with water on a terrace and plays football in a meadow near some houses. All in all, the child represented is living in a protected environment where the physical surroundings are adjusted to her needs. Accordingly, the child is independent, secure, and apparently satisfied with her situation.

This image is reflected in the author's postscript addressed to parents stating that, since children enjoy recognizing familiar situations, the scenes in the book from the everyday life of a child will bring pleasure to the reading child. Because the written text is very simple, the postscript also states, child readers will quickly be able to "read" the text on their own. Thus, the expected reader of the book is supposedly a child who identifies with the child represented and finds pleasure in recognition and a simple story told in simple language. Simultaneously, the book instructs parents in ideal, progressive, contemporary child life.

Discussions concerning children's books in Denmark of the 1950s

A picture book of this kind reflects certain trends concerning the raising of children and the role the book was thought to play in that connection. In the 1930s, Danish educators began to see the picture book as a means of disseminating a "modern" view of the child, where children were the center of their own existence, and the books had contemporary children and their needs in mind. In "Keepin it plural," Karen Coats describes three different images of the child: romantic, modern, or post-modern (140–50). A representation of the child in a book like *Trine kan . . .* could certainly be said to conform to her description of a modernist child in that parents are supposed to secure and facilitate the natural "capacity for growth and development" in the child (Coats 146).

The Swedish researcher Kristin Hallberg describes how these ideas resulted in what she calls a "pedagogical poetics" in books for small children. She describes how such a poetics is characterized by, among other things, taking the everyday life of children as a starting point, by adopting the point of view of a child, by using "the language of the child"—simple and straightforward language—and by an often repetitive narrative structure (Hallberg 83). All these traits are characteristic of *Trine kan . . .*, so it is a very clear example of how a certain image of the child, based on certain ideas of childhood, is represented in picture books. In this case the image did not have national limits: in an edition with drawings the book was translated into, for instance, Spanish, Swedish, German, Finnish, and French until the 1980s.

Another, and very different, variation on the picture book used for educational purposes are the books by Egon Mathiesen. His books are not primarily meant to support the linguistic development of the child or to show children—and adults—the ideal conditions of a well-stimulated child. The primary goal for Mathiesen, who was associated with progressive educational groups in the 1930s, was to introduce the child to aesthetic expressions and a view of human beings based on democratic ideals—what he called "modern humanism" (96).

The general characteristics of Mathiesen's texts are that they are in very rhythmical verse, use playful expressions, and address the listening child in a humorous and direct manner. The child is often addressed explicitly through rhetorical questions throughout the text, which helps to connect pictures and text. Often his illustrations are quasi-naive depictions of objects on a white background. He uses bright colors, which sometimes fill the whole page, sometimes only a very small part of the page. These visual characteristics are used in order to draw the attention of the child to aspects of visual grammar, such as dimension, form, and color. To Mathiesen, picture books are a means of introducing the child to the visual arts. In his writing on picture books, he argues that the child has an instinct for art, a natural sense of color and form, which is to be seen, for instance, in the drawings of children. By extension, picture books can contribute to developing a sense of art, of form, color, lines, and proportions in the child.

But this aesthetic education is linked to the view that picture books could and should educate children to become responsible citizens in a democratic society. Contrary to the dominant realistic tendency of the era, Mathiesen often uses a nonrealistic setting and small animals to represent children. He demonstrates how this can be done in a sensible way in *Oswald the Monkey* [(*Aben Osvald*) (Copenhagen: Gyldendal, 1947)] which tells the story of a flock of small monkeys living under the oppressive rule of a big monkey tyrant, until the small monkey Oswald rebels. This is told in the following way:

> But suddenly Oswald says NO!
> he even scares himself
> and here he sits
> and looks around
> with eyes so big and dark.
>
> And all the monkeys they get nappy
> oh, no, I mean they get so happy
> they all do just like Oswald,
> and ev'ry monkey
> now shouts "no
> and no and no and no!"[1]

[T]he word "no" is emphasized in the verbal text: it appears underneath the first picture of the little monkey in red letters followed by a blue exclamation mark.

In the following illustration, the word is repeated underneath each of the small monkey faces with colored letters. The written letters thus find a visual expression that the preliterate child must perceive as "the image of the word no." This knowledge can then be used on the following double spread, where the image of the monkey and the image of the word are repeated several times. In this way the child is introduced to decoding, to the interaction of verbal, auditory, and visual codes, as well as to the importance of taking a moral stand. Perhaps the combination of an explicit awareness of the child as audience and of the importance of aesthetic quality is not the only reason why Mathiesen's books are still so popular. What he calls the "ethical quality" also plays a part, an influential librarian on the jury noted when he received the first Children's Literature Prize awarded by the Ministry of Cultural Affairs in 1954:

> In 1944, the year when the people of this country were weighed down by thoughts of the fate of the deported Jews, a picture book was published which in the most enchanting and obvious way expressed everything we wanted to explain to our children . . . With these books . . . Egon Mathiesen has created a series of picture books which you could call today's moral picture books . . . Egon Mathiesen has built his books on one of the most important and positive thoughts in modern pedagogy: that admonitions, advice and threats are of no use when you want to reach children. But if you give them an experience, set an example, so to speak, in a way

> that captures their minds and imaginations, and especially their feelings, you can make them listen and understand.
>
> (Bredsdorff 29–30)

One can conclude that the two books by Egon Mathiesen and Thea Bank Jensen represent an image of the child as someone who needs the guidance and support of adults. This perception of the child is explicitly stated in contemporary discussions concerning the role of picture books in the upbringing of children. The persons involved in these discussions are primarily librarians, who choose and evaluate books for the increasing number of public libraries, and educators, who provide guidance to children (and parents) concerning the leisure reading of children.

Generally speaking, discussions about children's literature in the 1950s focuses on two matters: the moral of the book and its realism. Children's books were supposed to present children with acceptable modes of behavior, and this tendency was reinforced by a fierce critique of comic books. The fear that children would uncritically accept and internalize the violent attitudes and explicit sexuality in comic books led to the appointment of a committee known as "Det kulørte udvalg" (The Pulp Committee). The committee discussed what could be done to encourage children to read books of literary quality, and censorship was proposed. But the less authoritarian point of view that "good writing is the enemy of poor writing" won strong support and led to various initiatives to further what was considered quality literature.

Concerning the issue of realism in literature, the debate was based on the fear that the reading of fantastic literature would harm the development of what was called a "secure and positive relationship to reality" in the consciousness of the child (Kragh-Müller 12). In such debates educators also discussed whether the originality of Mathiesen's books was acceptable. In the only contribution to reflections on picture book criticism in the 1950s, "On judging Picture Books," the influential Danish critic Torben Gregersen praised Mathiesen's books, but also used them to discuss whether imaginative picture books were harmful to the psychological development of the child. In his opinion, picture books should be recognizably related to the world the child knows: "I think one can say that, generally, it is an advantage if a picture book in its choice of topic has a relation to lived reality" (Gregersen 52). In the 1950s, one could detect a similar adult attitude toward children's literature as toward children's reading habits: the role of the adult is to protect children, provide them with secure living conditions, and guide them—especially when it comes to reading.

Which reality and whose reality? Criticism in the 1970s

Throughout the 1960s, 1950s attitudes toward children were challenged. A new library act issued in 1964 explicitly stated that small children, too, had a right to access books from public collections, and thus the production of picture books increased. This led to debates on the quality of the books, not least of which were discussions of the critical standards of librarians in relation to children's books. In the beginning of the 1970s, these improved market conditions contributed to the publication of a wide range of revolutionary—in all senses of the word—picture books.

The interest in children's culture increased in Denmark in this period. Changing critical standards occasioned by, among other things, academics at Danish universities with an interest in ideological criticism beginning to analyze and evaluate children's literature were also of importance to the development of a new kind of picture book in Denmark. From the point of view of ideological criticism, children's literature was an important means of questioning well-established stereotypes concerning, for instance, gender, society, politics, and history, and could thus profitably form a part of the desired consciousness-raising of children and adults. As a result, a large number of Danish picture books from the 1970s are like textbooks in that they are not "free" aesthetic, fictitious expressions. In such books, the aim was primarily to inform, for instance, about different jobs, environmental problems, and living conditions in less developed countries. This development can also be viewed as a natural extension of the demand for realism in children's books. Needless to say, it was a demand for a certain conception of realism in which too-fanciful solutions to problems were criticized.

The discussion of one specific book, *Røgen* (*Smoke*), [(Copenhagen: Gyldendal, 1970)] reflects this situation. In *Røgen*, Ib Spang Olsen tells the story of a family who wants to go to the countryside and breathe some fresh air. But they are prevented from doing so because of the smoke coming from factory chimneys, from polluting oil burners, and from their own car's exhaust pipe. In one case, the family helps a factory owner by covering the chimneys with objects at hand, in another by helping him to pay for a depolluting system, the oil burner is fixed by the father of the family, and their car's exhaust system is improved. Finally, they can go to the woods and enjoy the fresh air.

The following year another book on environmental problems was published: the translation of a Swedish picture book by Annika Almquist, *Sprätten satt på toaletten* (*Sprätten Sat on the Toilet*). In this case the solution was explicitly socialist: the pollution of the factory was stopped when the workers took over the factory. Both books were reviewed in a new progressive magazine on children's culture, *Bixen. Sprätten satt på toaletten* was praised, while *Røgen* was criticized in the following way: "What on earth is the point of letting the family in *Røgen* give the owner of the factory their savings, because he can't afford to install a depolluting system? This is simply a neglect of responsibility. The book reveals a political naivety, which unfortunately corresponds to the superficial measures adopted by the responsible authorities" (Egebak and Olsen 78). The review focuses exclusively on the content of the book and the solution presented. In reply, the author states that he wrote the book the way he did because it was aimed at smaller children, and that he considered other criteria than the strictly political to be of relevance ("Om" 85–87).

When a researcher compares the two books thirty years later, the point of view is, of course, different. It is particularly striking that the illustrations in *Sprätten satt på toaletten* seem primitive and unprofessional, the storyline uninteresting and simplified, and there is an apparent lack of awareness of the implied reader being a child. By contrast, *Røgen* appears to be an aesthetically beautiful book by an experienced and professional illustrator with a strong awareness of the demands of a child audience. However, the main concern of contemporary reviewers was whether the child was exposed to a reality that conformed to an adult ideal.

Children and parents as equal human beings

In the 1970s some of the stereotypes most frequently challenged in Danish picture books were the roles of women and men, and of children and parents. This is clearly evidenced in *Der hvor Linda bor* (*The Place Where Linda Lives*) written by Bodil Bredsdorff and illustrated by Lilian Brøgger [(Copenhagen: Fremad, 1975)]. The most obvious change in the description of the life of the child is in its physical surroundings: Linda lives in the city with her single mother and younger brother in a flat in an old building without bathing facilities, and she spends most of her day in a kindergarten. As in *Trine kan . . .*, the daily life of children is thematized, but in a very different way. In *Der hvor Linda bor*, the child is described as a social being interacting with several different persons: she relates to her kindergarten teacher, to her friend Bo, and to her little brother, and the center of the action is the relationship to her mother. The narrative starts late in the afternoon when Linda is picked up from kindergarten, and she and her mother go home, where the mother immediately starts cooking. Linda provokes her mother's anger when she plays with water and when she "can't eat properly." As a result, she is sent to bed in tears. The mother regrets her anger and authoritarian behavior and says to Linda, "I am sorry that I got so angry . . . but I was so tired" (n.p.). She thoroughly explains her reasons —how she had to get up, make breakfast, take the children to kindergarten, go to work as a cleaner in a hospital, go shopping, back to pick up the children and home to cook dinner. The mother addresses the child as a rational, equal human being and expects to gain her sympathy. The child does not explicitly exhibit such an understanding attitude, but the explanation ends the conflict. In contrast to Danish picture books from the 1950s and 1960s, adults, too, could be at the center of the action in picture books, and the parent-child relationship is described as being based on an ideal of mutual respect and understanding.

Other traits in the depiction of children in *Der hvor Linda bor* reveal new tendencies. In the illustration showing a fight between Linda's friend Bo and his sister (from an incorporated sequence recounting an evening in that family), children are depicted in extreme close-up, with an explicit focus on their emotions. The fear and sorrow and aggression expressed in the faces of the children demonstrate how the accepted norms of "childlike" behavior have changed by this point. Another significant change is to be seen in the cause of conflict between the children: the girl, Lis, wants her brother to play the part of a traditional husband and leave the den to go to work, but the boy insists on his right to stay home. This conflict concerning gender roles is later repeated by the children's parents, when the mother tries to make her husband help in the kitchen. It leads to a quarrel where the mother says, "I am just sick and tired of doing everything myself, can't you understand that?" (n.p.). As the implicit narrator states, the father "knows very well that Kirsten [the mother] is right," and so the father finally does the dishes with the help of his son (n.p.).

The changing images of children and adults are not only apparent in the fictive characters, but also in the implicit reader of the text. The characters in focus are the children, but to a great extent so are the two women in the story. This and the discussions of gender roles suggest that the audience of the book is supposed to be both children and adults—especially women. Although a book like *Trine kan . . .* also must be seen as being implicitly addressed to parents, the dual audience of children and adults is much more obvious in *Der hvor Linda bor.*

The 1990s: childhood for adults

Der hvor Linda bor anticipates a general turn in Danish picture books from the 1980s onward: instead of expecting the child to engage in conflicts on a larger scale, portraits of children focus on conflicts in the family and the emotional life of children. One of the author-illustrators who first described the changing conditions of life for children in the 1980s is Dorte Karrebæk. In the 1990s, her work *Pigen der var go' til mange ting* (*The Girl who was Good at Many Things*, [Copenhagen: Forum] 1996) was very much debated and also criticized—a criticism that I think can be traced back to adults' rejection of the image of the child conveyed in the book.

A short summary may serve to partly explain these changes. The story is about a girl whose parents are very good at partying but not very interested in their daughter. The parents fight a lot, and she wonders whether she is raising them the right way or if it would be better to be more authoritarian. She decides to try to change them by having a fancy dress party, and they turn up dressed like a cat and a dog. But afterwards they are unable to take off their masks and her conclusion, which is the [. . .] the following: "Then the girl knew that everything was too late and that you can't change a dog and a cat. So she forgot about her childhood and started growing as fast as she could. And then she left home" (n.p.).

The text and illustrations emphasize childhood as being a function of the child's will: the moment she decides to abandon childhood, her physical appearance changes in three stages. The reader is confronted with a sad, frightened, powerless, and bleary-eyed girl in the two smallest images, and an insistent, almost aggressively direct look at the reader from the tallest girl. Size equals power.

The child has all the practical duties that are normally attributed to adults and is so busy ironing, cleaning the house, and doing the dishes that she does not have time to go to school. She is the responsible person in the family, the one who thinks about upbringing and about how to make the family work better and has none of the advantages of childhood as they are depicted in, for instance, *Trine kan. . . .* The preconditions for an ideal child life in the book from the 1950s were that adults provided the child with safe and stimulating surroundings, but the statement in *Pigen der var go' til mange ting* shows that it is not naturally given that adults accept this role. And if a child takes over these tasks, the only thing separating child from adult is size. In relation to fictitious characters, this small difference is easily overcome, as the illustration shows.

The difference between child and adult readers of the text seems to be less easily overcome. Karrebæk's text is written in simple, straightforward language, in a matter-of-fact tone, with an undercurrent of irony. The illustrations focus on the child's point of view through repeated frontal depictions of the child in the foreground of the illustrations, thus showing her emotional reactions to the actions of the parents in the background. Her look addresses the reader/spectator directly and thus demands identification and contact, and both adults and children are in the first instance supposed to relate to the child. As the first sentence shows, the story is told by an omniscient and apparently objective narrator: "Once upon a time there was a girl. She was good at many things, and she had to be: there was so much she had to do" (n.p.). There is not an explicit narrator in the story until the end where he/she addresses the audience: "And I can tell you that the girl who was good at many things was also good at finding herself a good place to stay" (n.p.). This sentence reveals a narrator who, contrary to the adults in the story, is reassuring and assumes some measure of responsibility in relation to the (child) reader: after the unfolding of a tough story, where the audience is confronted with parents unable to take care of their child, the narrator explicitly and directly tells a child reader that the girl will be fine—without her parents.

I think it obvious that a child reader is addressed through the staging of point of view in the illustrations and through the voice of the narrator in the text. However, the book has been discussed as an example of the increasing "adulteration" of children's books, and some libraries even place the book on a separate shelf in order not to expose small children to it. This might be done with the best of intentions, but it can also be read as a deliberate exclusion in order to protect readers—adults as well as children—from an unacceptable view of adults and childhood.

This indeed seems to be the case when one considers other contemporary picture books thematizing the relationship between adults and children. Generally speaking, Danish picture books from the 1990s introduced several examples of the child depicted as a rational, mature, and powerful being. Accordingly, the parent emerged as the imperfect, uncontrolled, and immature figure. A strikingly frequent theme in contemporary Danish picture books is that of children who run away from their parents. This is for instance the case in *Mor* (*Mum*) written by Kim Fupz Aakeson and illustrated by Mette-Kirstine Bak [(Copenhagen: Gyldendal, 1998)]. The first-person narrator of the story is a young boy who lives alone with his mother, who is incredibly fat. He tries to make her eat less and eat more vegetables, but, as she says, "I'm not a rabbit." He tells the reader about how embarrassed he feels on various occasions, and since she does not listen to his complaints he decides to leave her for the skinny woman next door. The only problem is that this woman insists on him calling her "mother," and he is unable to do so. Strange words pop out of his mouth instead, words like "mackerel" and "mussels" and "mattress," instead of the real m-word. He gives up and goes home to his real mother, who, as is to be seen in the last illustration, embraces him in a "Madonna with child"-like image. The child tries one last time to suggest that she could eat more carrots; she repeats that she is not a rabbit, and the story ends with the words: "'No,' I said. 'You are a mother. You are my mother'" (n.p.).

Aside from the fact that this is an interesting book from an aesthetic point of view, one that has many qualities for both child and adult reader (not least of which is its humor), the book is a striking example of how picture books also represent certain role models for adults and for adult behavior. Through the illustrations, the importance of the mother is foregrounded; she takes up most of the space and the child is placed in the corners and margins of the illustrations. The mother is a grand figure in many senses of the words: she is depicted as a loving, erotic, and all-embracing figure, wearing eccentric, tight, and brightly colored costumes and fancy hairdos. Her opposite is the slim lady: blond, pale, inhibited, and unattractive in her controlled position. The ideal is free expression and satisfaction of desire; the adult's control of desire is evil. The child has to accept this in order to have a loving mother.

It is noteworthy that none of the skepticism that met *Pigen der var go' til mange ting* met this book. The story, which was reviewed in all of the major Danish newspapers, was praised for being humorous and well-written; and the depiction of the mother received comments such as "Mum is great"

(Larsen). To me, this is an indication that one of the rarely explicitly stated critical standards of children's literature is whether the books convey an acceptable image of the adult, which would be reasonable, if only it were stated explicitly and reflected upon.

Images of adulthood: the author and the critic

In the above, I have attempted to provide a broad overview of the ways in which children and adults are positioned through text and illustrations and how these images are discussed—more or less explicitly—in the reception of the books. My study of Danish picture books from 1950–1999 shows that, to a very high extent, the books are expressions and confirmations of certain culturally-valued images.

An analysis of the depiction of child and adult in a historical perspective goes some way toward answering the question of why it is important to combine studies of children's literature with childhood studies. The depiction of children and adults in certain periods does not arise from purely artistic considerations. The use of other sources than picture books leads to an awareness of how much the sign of the child can change over a relatively short period of time, while the referent is thought of as being the same, be it child or adult (Flynn 143–45; Myers 41–43). The fact that both sign and referent change only becomes apparent through an exploration of both representations of children and statements concerning conceptions of children drawn from contemporary sources.

At the turn of the millennium, many scholars think of identity as something that can be negotiated. Within children's literature criticism, Karín Lesnik-Oberstein has stated that childhood should be seen as "a narrative of identity which changes from time to time, from culture to culture, and from one political ideology to another" (*Childhood and Textuality* 8). But I think it is of utmost importance that we include an awareness of the changing identities of adults and, not least, critics and researchers.

In a crucial article, "*Kinderliteratur als Medium der Entdeckung von Kindheit*" ("Childhood Explored through Children's Literature"), German critic Hans-Heino Ewers discusses how and if children's literature can provide the source material for investigations into childhood (47–62). He describes four different types of authors writing on childhood throughout the history of German children's literature in particular. The first type he calls the "literary educator" ("*die literarische Erzieher*"), since children's literature before the nineteenth century was primarily seen as a means to teach children right and wrong. Authors wrote about children and childhood seen from a distance, and childhood was seen as a stage to be passed. With Romanticism and its different conception of childhood, two new types emerged: the naive and the sentimental poet of childhood ("*Naive*" and "*sentimentalische Kindheitsdichter*"). Ewers describes how the naive poet writing about childhood in the period of late Romanticism in Germany still perceives him/herself as a child and has preserved the "naivety, the spontaneity and the innocence" of a child" (57), qualities which were supposed to live on in this type of sensitive poet. From a Danish perspective, H. C. Andersen is an example of this kind of poet who can describe childhood in poor and less than ideal conditions, and at the same time idealize it and praise his own preserved childlike self. Such a naive poet of childhood would not see childhood as a finite period of time, while the sentimental type would have a permanent longing for a childhood lost. Ewers cites Milne and Barrie as obvious examples of sentimental poets of childhood. Finally, Ewers discusses the most recent type: the critical poet of childhood as the child's literary advocate ("kritischen Kindheitsdichter als literarischem Anwalt des Kindes"). This type of author focuses on the child as a reader and wants to generate reflection and consciousness in the child. The author feels a responsibility toward a social reality, and can through his/her writings influence the child, and thus the world, by taking a moral or political stand. As Ewers rightly states, this type bears resemblances to the first type, the literary educator.

This short and, indeed, reductive summary does not reflect the many interesting aspects of Ewers' article. However, I was struck by how these different types can also occur in different positions assumed by researchers in the field of children's literature criticism, both on a diachronic and a synchronic level. The following positions of researchers, or critics of children's literature in general, could thus be outlined as follows:

1. **The researcher as educator.** From this point of view, reading of children's literature should lead to greater wisdom. The reading child will and should identify with the main character, and through the actions of the fictional character learn about right and wrong. Critics and researchers should be concerned with books that aim at achieving this and investigate how children's literature does it best.
2. **The naive researcher.** Seen from this perspective, reading of children's literature is also a way for the adult to communicate with his/her "inner child." A double viewpoint is supposed to exist: the child's and the adult's. From this point of view the good critic or researcher is someone who somehow has managed to preserve the child's perspective. Peter Hunt's plea for "childist" criticism, for instance, seems to bear traits of such a view of the critic.
3. **The sentimental researcher.** The sentimental critic or researcher knows that childhood is different from adulthood, but tends to advocate that children be protected from adult life as long as possible. Neil Postman provides an example of this position in the 1980s: "it is clear that if we turn over to children a vast store of powerful adult material, childhood cannot survive. By definition adulthood means mysteries solved and

secrets uncovered. If from the start the children know the mysteries and the secrets, how shall we tell them apart from anyone else?" (88).

4. **The critical researcher as the child's advocate.** Assuming the position of the critical adult acting as the child's advocate, some critics and adults claim to speak on behalf of children. The critical adult would often take an explicit stand and claim, as Coats has, that "many of us love children and most of us care deeply about the future of our society" or "Most people will come to Children's Studies out of a genuine love for children and a desire to ease their suffering and make their lives better" (141).

These four positions are, of course, caricatures, and most of us would find a hint of all of them in our reflections on our own work, on children's literature and on reading. This is precisely why I would add a fifth position:

5. **The meta-critical researcher.** A meta-critical adult reader of children's literature would be aware of the fact that children's literature, aside from being a fictitious artifact, is an expression of images of children and adults on various levels. Thus, it is crucial that the adult is conscious of the difference between representations of childhood/adulthood and actual childhoods. On this point I must agree with Coats, who states that researchers have to establish their childhood selves as "a kind of Other." A meta-critical adult reader would never use personal childhood memories or experiences with actual children in the present as an argument. This would amount to taking the child, or even the apparent memory of a child, hostage.

Conclusion

My study of Danish picture books from 1950–1999 shows that picture books must be seen as an expression of a certain image of the child at the same time as they indeed play a significant role in perpetuating this sign. Thus, analyses of this image, through text and pictures, including an analysis of the intended audience, are both necessary and valuable. Instead of criticizing the apparent "adulteration" of picture books, one might also view this shift as an explication of what has been implicit for many years, namely that picture books are most often read aloud by adults, and that communication between book and child does not, in the first place, occur without a mediator.

Moreover, if one is to understand such changing images, I am convinced that the researcher has to combine an analysis of actual works of fiction with other source material. In my thesis, examples of such sources included, for instance, official reports and laws concerning children, libraries and book production, curricula, and debates in newspapers and magazines devoted to children and their reading habits. My thesis shows that picture books are produced under specific historical and ideological conditions; not acknowledging this fact will lead to a reductionist reading.

Additionally, a disregard of the fact that the transmission of images of childhood is one aim of picture books could lead to naive criticism and the deliberate exclusion of books with non-acceptable images of children or adults. In criticism of children's literature, there has been an apparent "aesthetic turn" in Denmark, where focus is on the artistic qualities of text and pictures and often on the actual reading experience: was the reader entertained, bored, or indifferent while reading? These considerations can, of course, form parts of criticism, but they should not be used as a means of avoiding critical reflection on the image of the child conveyed. Lack of reflection too often results in a sentimental or naive reading from an adult position or in a modern kind of moral criticism wherein books are rejected because they challenge dominant ideas of childhood. What is protected here is not a possible child audience but the adult critic.

Finally, I think the integration of childhood studies into children's literature criticism would strengthen the researcher's ability to reflect on his/her own practice. If children's literature criticism does not wish to be thought of as a field inhabited by naive and/or sentimental individuals longing in some way to preserve a romantic idea of childhood, language, and identity, continuous reflection on the relationship between ideal and real childhoods—without quotation marks—are necessary.

Notes

A version of this article appeared in *Fundevogel* 149 (2003): 5–27.

1 All translations of Danish texts are the author's.

Works cited

Aakeson, Kim Fupz. Illus. Mette-Kirstine Bak. *Mor* (*Mother*). Copenhagen: Gyldendal, 1998.

Bank Jensen, Thea. Photos. Lis Lund-Hansen. *Trine kan . . .* (*Trine can . . .*). Copenhagen: Høst & Son, 1955.

Bredsdorff, Aase. "Egon Mathiesen." *Børn og Bøger* 3–4 (1954): 29–30.

Bredsdorff, Bodil. Illus. Lilian Brøgger. *Der hvor Linda bor*. (*The Place Where Linda Lives*). Copenhagen: Fremad, 1975.

Christensen, Nina. *Den danske billedbog 1950–1999. Teori, analyse, historie* (*The Danish Picture Book 1950–1999. Theory, Analysis, History*). Copenhagen: Roskilde Universitetsforlag, 2003.

Coats, Karen. "Keepin' it Plural: Children's Studies in the Academy." *Children's Literature Association Quarterly* 26 (2001): 140–50.

Egebak, Birte, and Hanne Olsen. "Den bevidst politiske børnebog" ("The Consciously Political Children's Book"). *Bixen* 1 (1971): 77–79.

Ewers, Hans-Heino. "Kinderliteratur als Medium der Entdeckung von Kindheit." (Childhood Explored through Children's Literature"). *Kinder. Kindheit. Lebensgeschichte*. Ed. Imbke Behnken and Jürgen Zinnecker. Seeelsze-Velber: Kallmeyer, 2001. 47–62.

Flynn, Richard. "The Intersection of Children's Literature and Childhood Studies." *Children's Literature Association Quarterly* 22 (1997):143–45.

Gregersen, Torben. "Lidt om bedømmelse af billedbøger." (*On Judging Picture Books*). *Børn og Bøger* 5 (1950): 49–54 and *Børn og Bøger* 6 (1950): 63–70.

Hallberg, Kristin. "Pedagogik som poetik. Den moderna småbarnslitteraturens berättande." ("Pedagogics as Poetics. The Narration of Modern Literature for Small Children"). *Konsten att berätta för barn*. Ed. Anne Banér. Stockholm: Centrum för barnkulturforskning, 1996. 83–101.

Hunt, Peter. "Passing on the Past: The Problem of Books that are for Children and that were for Children." *Children's Literature Association Quarterly* 21 (1997): 200–02.

Karrebæk, Dorte. *Pigen der var go' til mange ting*. (*The Girl who was Good at Many Things*). Copenhagen: Forum, 1996.

Kragh-Müller, C. C. "Børnelitteraturen som opdragelsesfaktor." ("The Role of Children's Literature in Education"). *Unge Pædagoger*, Special issue D (1952): 9–12.

Larsen, Steffen. "Mum is great." Rev. *Aktuelt*. 3. Dec. 1998.

Lesnik-Oberstein, Karín. *Children's Literature. Criticism and the Fictional Child.* Oxford: Clarendon, 1994.

——. "Defining Children's Literature and Childhood." *International Companion Encyclopaedia of Children's Literature*. Ed. Peter Hunt. London: Routledge, 1996. 17–31.

——. "Childhood and Textuality: Culture, History, Literature." *Children in Culture: Approaches to Childhood.* Ed. Karín Lesnik-Oberstein. Basingstoke: Macmillan, 1998. 1–28.

Mathiesen, Egon. *Aben Osvald.* (*Oswald the Monkey*). Copenhagen: Gyldendal, 1947.

——. "The Artist and the Picture Book." *The Horn Book Magazine* 1 (1966): 93–98.

Myers, Mitzi. "Missed Opportunities and Critical Malpractice: New Historicism and Children's Literature." *Children's Literature Association Quarterly* 22 (1988): 41–43.

Postman, Neil. *The Disappearance of Childhood.* New York: Delacorte, 1982.

Spang Olsen, Ib. "Om politisk bevidsthed i billedbøger." (About Political Consciousness in Picture Books.) *Bixen* 2 (1972): 85–87.

——. *Røgen*. (*Smoke*). Copenhagen: Gyldendal, 1970.

Stephens, John. *Language and Ideology in Children's Fiction*. London: Longman, 1992.

Travisano, Thomas. "Of Dialectic and Divided Consciousness: Intersections Between Children's Literature and Childhood Studies." *Children's Literature* 28 (2000): 22–29.

59

CHILDHOOD

A narrative chronotope

Rosemary Ross Johnston

Source: Roger D. Sell (ed.), *Children's Literature as Communication*, Amsterdam/Philadelphia: John Benjamins, 2002, pp. 137–157.

1. Chronotope as a term

The word *chronotope* (*xronotop*) was not Bakhtin's own coinage, but his use of it has certainly led to new ways of considering relationships in narrative between people and events on the one hand and time and space on the other. The term itself (from *chronos*, time, and *topos*, space) was originally a mathematical one connected with Einstein's theory of relativity, which re-described time not as the objective absolute of Newtonian physics, but as a subjective variable, dependent on the position of the observer. Bakhtin noted that he was using *chronotope* metaphorically, then added in a parenthesis, "almost, but not entirely" (Bakhtin, 1981, p. 84). Be that as it may, as a literary concept chronotope is an important critical tool. In Michael Holquist's words, it is "an optic for reading texts as x-rays of the forces at work in the culture system from which they spring" (in Bakhtin, 1981, pp. 423–4). It can help us to read beyond the mechanics of "setting", and to re-think depictions of narrative time-spaces in ideological terms, as subjective, changeable, and interwoven with the observer's positionality.

In seeing things this way, we need to relate chronotope to certain other aspects of Bakhtin's thought. As Michael Holquist and Caryl Emerson write, what emerges from the "thickening" of time as it "takes on flesh" and fuses with space to create the artistic chronotope is a "living impulse" (in Bakhtin, 1986, p. 84). In Bakhtin's work, this living impulse is soaked in his ideas about "outsideness" and the "superaddressee", and about language. For Bakhtin, language is dialogical; is heteroglossic and polyphonic; is heterogeneous; is intonated with the richness and complexity of the ordinary and the everyday, which often pass unnoticed; is potentially marked by both "great time" (the perspectives of centuries (Bakhtin, 1986, pp. 1–9)) and the "presentness" of each moment; is ultimately characterized by unfinalizability (*nezavershennost*); and most important of all, is inherently and immanently creative. In various ways all these ideas affect the concept of the artistic chronotope, and offer an analytical language for its discussion. They also highlight the fact that the organization of time-spaces in narrative is complex and multifarious, reflecting attitudes and beliefs which, whether explicit or implicit, are deeply rooted in historical phases of society.

In what follows here, I shall not be linking the notion of chronotope to particular genres of children's literature; I shall not be speaking of an "adventure" or "fantasy" chronotope, for instance (cf. Nikolajeva, 1996, p. 134). Nor shall I use Bakhtin's term as a way of examining some particular aspect of narrative — say, subjectivity (cf. McCallum, 1999). Altogether more broadly, my concern is with a major chronotope type: a chronotope of childhood in narrative. I shall be trying to suggest what is distinctive about such a chronotope, and why.

2. Outsideness

Children's literature can be thought of as an artistically mediated form of the communication which a society has with its young (Johnston, 2001, p. 303). As such it involves an intersection of real and narrative time-spaces: at its simplest, the time-spaces of the fiction, of the writer, and of the reader. This obviously applies to any other kind of book as well. But children's literature is different in that it is almost always written *by* adults, but *for* children. This means that its chronotopes — its organization of people and events in relation to time and space — will tend to reflect some kind of negotiation — a dialogic interchange — between generations. In one sense, this will be inherently one-sided. It will favour the adult writers who write, and the adult publishers who choose what to publish. But in another sense, the imbalance will be counteracted, since the adult writer has no choice but to envisage the main addressees as children. Both the writer and the publisher will be hoping for children's response.

Given such dialogism between the two different cultural groups of adults and children, the use of the chronotope as a research optic may reveal, not only how a society feels about its children, but also how it feels about itself. In fact the chronotope can sharpen our focus in an area where criticism has perhaps been rather fuzzy. In the lives of grown-ups, childhood is a palimpsistic presence whose remembered time-space blurs comfortably into myth. Bakhtin's ideas about outsideness warn us that as adults we cannot enter into the cultural time-space of childhood, and that we should not want to. Rather, we can create a more fruitful dialogue by remembering that, as members of an adult culture, we are now outsiders to childhood. In this way we can paradoxically learn more about ourselves. In Bakhtin's words (1986, p. xiii),

> [a] pure projection of myself into the other, a move involving the loss of my own unique place outside the other, is, on the whole, hardly possible; in any event it is quite fruitless . . . Aesthetic activity proper actually begins at the point when we return into ourselves and to our place outside the other person.

Here there are two related points with clear implications for children's literature, both of them pertaining to the chronotope's element of space. First, we can never really see from the other's point of view anyway. Although we may be in exactly the same surroundings (*okruzheniia*), our field of vision (*krugozor*) will inevitably be different. You can see me in a way that I cannot possibly see myself. It is this very difference, however, which provides the potential for creative understanding. As Morson and Emerson (1990, p. 185) outline Bakhtin's ideas:

> The essential aesthetic act of creating such an image of another is most valuable when we seek not to merge or duplicate with each other, but rather to supplement each other, to take full advantage of our field of vision.

In other words, our fullest participation in the aesthetic act of creating images of childhood will be along the borders of our difference, precisely because we are not children but a creative other. This is where the second point comes in as a direct consequence. Our fullest view of ourselves becomes possible only when we see ourselves in relation to others; we need an other as a reference point. This is true for both adults and children. So what is particularly significant for a narrative chronotope of childhood is that, thanks to the creative other of the adult, and thanks to the images of the adult's aesthetic act itself, children may come to see themselves, just as they are taken to see themselves as modelled in commercial advertizing.

Another paradox concerns the chronotope's time element. On the one hand, narrative time-space is a series of moments of presentness, each with its own meanings. They are meanings which are peculiar to precisely that conjunction of time and space, which are cultural, social, and historical, and which depend on who is speaking and listening, how they feel towards each other, what has just happened, the time of day, the weather, and so on. On the other hand, a story's time-space also involves a dialogized heteroglossia: an accumulation of meanings that go far beyond specific presentness. Heteroglossia (*raznorečie*) refers to the way actual usages (the "talks" or languages of the everyday) play on established meanings of words, taking away their semblance of neutrality, and surrounding them with the great host of other utterances heretofore.

Such heteroglossia is dialogized, because it can only emerge as part of communicative exchanges; it is inherent in the many dialogues of the everyday. This is a phenomenon of which writers take full advantage, by inserting into it their own voices and intentions. So here we can speak of the "double voice" of discourse: both the voice of a fictional character who speaks, and — behind and around and through that voice — the "refracted" voice of the author, working to achieve his or her narrative purposes. Bakhtin (1981, p. 324) writes:

> Heteroglossia, once incorporated into the novel (whatever the forms of its incorporation) is another's speech in another's language, serving to express authorial intentions but in a refracted way. Such speech constitutes a special type of double-voiced discourse. It serves two speakers at the same time and expresses simultaneously two different intentions: the direct intention of the character who is speaking, and the refracted intention of the author.

As a result words become multi-voiced, polyphonic and polysemic.

Take the word "space" itself. When we think about its contemporary usage in the expressions *cyberspace* and *I need my own space*, the openings for polysemy become rather obvious. Traditional notions of a novel's "setting" generally referred to "place" rather than "space". Bakhtin's concept of "space", by contrast, includes not just descriptions of place as a geographical location, but the *perception* of place. This overtly attributes a temporal frame, and means that a single objective place can be thought of as multiple subjective spaces, inner as well as outer. To adapt a suggestion made by John Shotter (1993, pp. 21, 35), such perceptions tend to function as "extensions of ourselves" — Shotter stresses the "complex relation between people's identities and their 'hook-up' to their surroundings". This is a familiar tradition in the history of children's literature, as even many titles tend to hint. There is *Anne of Green Gables* (Montgomery, 1908), for instance, or *Hannah and the Tomorrow Room* (Gleeson, 1999), a short chaptered novel about a child looking forward to moving into her own bedroom. The Australian text *Do not go around the edges* (Utemorrah and Torres, 1990) is in one sense about objective places of Daisy Utemmorah's life, but is much more accurately described as being about space — her *perceptions* of place, of spaces where she belonged and did not belong, her yearning for spaces which do not include her, and her infilling of current space with dreaming. Many of the spaces in children's books are imaginative spaces in much the same way — spaces of the mind. We think of Burningham's *Come away from the water, Shirley* (1977) and Baillie and Tanner's *Drac and the Gremlin* (1988). Gleeson and Greder's *The Great Bear* (1999) is about metaphors of space. In generic terms its chronotope is that of a folk tale, "the fullness of time in it" (Bakhtin, 1986, p. 52), though it plays on ideas of cosmic space as well.

3. Ideologies and assumptions

Decisions about what to depict as part of the relationship between time-space and people and events reflect artistic and ideological assessments of worth. G. S. Morson and Caryl Emerson (1990, p. 369) note that "because for Bakhtin all meaning involves evaluation, chronotopes also define parameters of value." In Bakhtin's own words (1981, p. 250):

> chronotopes are the organizing centres for the fundamental narrative events of a novel. The chronotope is the place where the knots of narrative are tied and untied. It can be said without qualification that to them belongs the meaning that shapes narrative.

So in Peter Pohl's *Johnny, my Friend* ([1985] 1991), the organizing centre of narrative events is an authentically geographical location in the Stockholm of the 1950s. And Pohl links maps of place with a mapping of that period's youth culture, in this way providing a realism which works, from the opening lines, as an aesthetic validation of the characters as portrayed:

> Now then, lads, do you recognize this? says the cop, lifting out Johnny's bicycle.
>
> We flash the whites of our eyes to each other, but nobody feels the urge to volunteer. The cop's mate is still sitting there in the cop car, wittering into his mike. The corner of Swedenborgsgatan and Maria Prästgårdsgata. About ten young lads. I'll get back to you.
>
> (Pohl, [1985] 1991, p. 9)

Tove Jansson organizes her Moomin stories around the time-spaces of a valley which is removed from most specifics of time and place, where "the clocks stopped ticking" in winter, where fairytale isolation is clearly marked as beauty and space for adventure, and where any fear of such isolation is softened by favourite symbols of care and security:

> When they reached the top [of the hill] the March wind gambolled around them, and the blue distance lay at their feet. To the west was the sea, to the east the river looped around the Lonely Mountains; to the north the great forest spread its green carpet, and to the south the smoke rose from Moomintroll's chimney, for Moominmamma was cooking the breakfast.
>
> (Jansson, [1948] 1961, p. 18)

J. K. Rowling has chosen to organize her Harry Potter books around a centre in which the space element — the suburbs, attitudes and language of an ironically stereotypical English social class — is clearly defined from the first few lines but in which the time element is vague:

> Mr and Mrs Dursley, of number four, Privet Drive, were proud to say that they were perfectly normal, thank you very much. They were the last people you'd expect to be involved in anything strange and mysterious, because they just didn't hold with such nonsense.
>
> (Rowling, 1997, p. 7)

The first page of *Dance on my Grave*, by Aidan Chambers, overlays his description with ironic metaphor and clearly indicates the time-space of his teenage narrator:

> The beach, that first day, was a morgue of sweating bodies laid out on slabs of towels. Sea and sand at sunny Southend.
>
> We had lived in this Londoners' playground at the mouth of the Thames for seventeen months, my father, my mother and me, and I was still not used to a town whose trade was trippers.
>
> There was talent about, bared to the imagination.
>
> (Chambers, 1982, p. 9)

Consciously or unconsciously, all these writers have made decisions about what is valuable and significant in the organization of their narratives, and what will be most effective in communicating their chosen time-spaces to their readers. In each, we can perceive the double voice. In the excerpt from *Johnny, my Friend*, for example, the voice of the young narrator reporting the voice of the policeman clearly establishes the importance of peer solidarity in adolescence, and its "othering" of authority; this is part of Pohl's narrative intent. In a further refraction, we first "see" the boys in a time-space described by the adult other, but reported by one of themselves.

The chronotope, writes Bakhtin (1981, p. 250), "provides the ground essential for the showing-forth, for the representability of events." Note how quickly a few lines describing narrative time-space establish this ground in the examples quoted above. Or as an example of a different type of text, consider the first few lines of Bunyan's *The Pilgrim's Progress* (1678):

> As I walk'd through the wilderness of this world, I lighted on a certain place, where there was a Denn; And laid me down in that place to sleep: And as I slept I dreamed a Dream.
>
> (Bunyan, [1678] 1960, p. 8)

What are the impulses which lie behind that which society "shows forth" to its young in children's literature? Applying the idea of the chronotope in this way will not give all the answers, but it does gives us a point of departure. Three main considerations arise: one that is sociocultural, relating to theoretical understandings of the young; one that is pedagogical, relating to perceptions of teaching the young; and one that is literary, relating to the significance of story as pleasure.

First, that a society seeks to show forth anything at all reflects a confidence in young people's receptiveness. In a discussion of the adolescent novel, Julia Kristeva (1990, p. 8), who in her early years was very much influenced by Bakhtin, says she understands the term "adolescent" less as an age category and more as "an open psychic structure." She discusses adolescence in psychoanalytical terms, noting that it "opens itself to the repressed at the same time that it initiates a psychic reorganization of the individual". This provides an obvious and immediate insight into many books for somewhat older children, including *Johnny, my Friend*, in which the protagonists are clearly involved in an organization-reorganization of identity initiated by the conflicts, paradoxes and tensions between new-found freedoms and pre-existing social and moral realities and constraints. It also suggests interesting possibilities for discussing adolescence in Bakhtinian terms of creative boundaries. Kristeva's analogy of the "open systems" of living organisms, which "maintain a renewable identity through interaction with another" (Kristeva, 1990, p. 8), is not only a particularly fruitful way to consider the culture of adolescence as represented in fiction; it also provides a metaphor for the chronotope in action.

This clearly leads to the second consideration. Part of the organizing impulse of the chronotope of childhood in narrative is pedagogical. Historians of children's literature have traditionally noted that children are taken to be, if not "open psychic structures" or *tabulae rasae*, then certainly receptive to influence and guidance, and acutely sensitive to interaction with each other. Books for children have been organized around conventions designed to "teach" and "socialize" and "acculturate", in earlier times with respect to religious and moral concerns, in later times as a more general education, and most recently in connection with specific social issues. This organizing principle shaped both story and discourse. Thus the book usually described as "beginning" Australian children's literature (Saxby, 1998, p. 12), Charlotte Barton's *A Mother's Offering to her Children: by a Lady long resident in New South Wales* (1841), not only transparently teaches the child characters about such things as the botany and flora of the new colony. The highly contrived format within which Mamma (Mrs Saville) and her children interact also expresses a chronotope which is organized around ideas about the value of such information:

> Julius. — Mamma we ought not to overlook the Fig Tree.
> Mrs. S. — Indeed, we ought not, Julius. It is not only splendid, but a very remarkable tree. The stem or trunk of the tree appears to be enveloped in drapery. The Red Cedar is also a handsome tree, and

> so is the Sassafras. I think the smell of the bark very agreeable; and you know it is used medicinally.
>
> (Barton, 1841, p. 17)

Children, such narratives imply, need to be taught, and books should teach. It is important to note, however, that from the beginning the very notion of teaching through a book supposedly being read for pleasure involved a particular type of teaching strategy, and a particular view of children. This leads to the third main consideration: the attraction of story. Apparently assuming that children may not want to sit and be taught, many authors have chosen to coat the pill with sugar. Their books seek to announce very publicly that they are neither formal school books, nor textbooks. Hence the use of illustrations and decorative prints and cover pictures, and most important of all, the pretence (or if that is too harsh a term, the layering) of *story*. It is just such a pretence of story that is the organizing centre of the otherwise bald explanations in books such as *A Mother's Offering to her Children*. "Story", then, is conceived as pleasure. This is part of a long multicultural tradition of societies communicating their histories and beliefs to themselves and to their children through story.

The assumption that children can and should learn from the pleasure of story is still with us. Even a cursory survey of the last twenty years of at least Australian children's literature reveals that the impulse to teach remains alive and well. While there is certainly a great variety of beautiful books, the ideological impulse of many of them is the advocacy of particular stances on social issues. Especially during the final years of the old millennium, these issues included the environment, indigenous cultures, multiculturalism, the changing shape of families, and gender and gender roles. To use Bakhtinian language (1981, pp. 243, 253), the matrix of people and events, and time and space in these books is "shot through with chronotopic values of varying degree and scope" which reflect the concerns of "the world that creates the text".

4. Paratexts and the addressee

This world that creates the text is a provocative concept. At the very least, it clearly refers to an author and a publisher, and to the children, parents and teachers who represent market forces. In pragmatic terms, the author is doubtless mainly concerned to be published and successfully marketed. So although the author is the text's creator and is writing for children, we can already glimpse the shadow of adult readers, whose presence is by convention not generally acknowledged. How much do children's writers write for these other adults, and how much does this influence a chronotope of childhood in narrative? According to Shavit (1995), authors write in varying degrees for adult and/or child. Yet such a view is too simplistic.

When we shift the focus from the reader to the created text, this is seen to be the product, not only of author and illustrator, but of forces at work in the sociocultural context.

The significance of this context-world can be seen in what Genette (1987) calls paratexts, i.e. the material which is liminal to the text, in the zone between off-text and on-text — the "public" part of the book that includes blurbs, dedications, excerpts from reviews, afterwords and so on. This paratextual material is designed to communicate, but not always to the implied reader of the actual text, and it is not always written (or seen to be written) by the author of the actual text. For example, the Australian picturebook-maker, Jeannie Baker, includes at the end of her books, after the story and her beautifully-wrought pictures have come to an end, a serious message and explanation. That of her most recent publication, *The Hidden Forest*, gives information about kelp forests, and describes how she actually constructed the artwork. It reads in part:

> Jeannie Baker made a number of visits to Tasmania's Tasman Peninsula where she went snorkelling and scuba-diving to explore at first hand the magic of its kelp forests. Jeannie constructed the artwork using a multitude of collected natural materials including seaweed, sponges and sands. The kelp was modelled with a translucent artist's clay and the wet seawater with resin.
>
> (Baker, 2000)

Compare the languages of text and afterword in an earlier book by Baker, *Where the Forest meets the Sea.* The first and second pages read:

> My father knows a place
> we can only reach by boat.
>
> Not many people go there,
> and you have to know the way through the reef.
>
> (Baker, 1987)

The text of the afterword reads:

> The place, the people, and the predicament are real. This forest is part of the wilderness between the Daintree River and Bloomfield in North Queensland, Australia. There remain at the making of this book only 296,000 acres of wet tropical rain forest wilderness that meet the ocean waters of the Great Barrier Reef. Small as it is, this is the largest pristine area of rain forest left in Australia.
>
> The artist made two extensive field trips to the Daintree Wilderness to research and collect materials.

> These relief collages are constructed from a multitude of materials, including modeling clay, papers, textured materials, preserved natural materials, and paints.
>
> The collages are mostly the same size as the reproductions.
>
> (Baker, 1987)

Such an afterword is clearly included so as to give authenticity to the text's advocacy. But it also reflects a great deal about the world that creates the text, ideas of story as pleasure, and the desires of a culture to "show forth." When an important issue is at stake, someone — perhaps the author, perhaps not — decides that story has to be explained, contextualized, authenticated, in some cases so that teachers and parents will be armed with more facts, in some cases to justify the stand being taken, and perhaps even to persuade these adult readers themselves.

In Barbara Wall's opinion, the marker of writing *for* children is actually writing *to* them. In developing this idea, she further suggests that the distinctive feature of a children's book is less the relationship between the implied reader and the implied author than that between a narrator and a narratee.

> While the presence of the implied author pervades the text and colours and controls the reader's response, at any and every given moment it is the narrator who "speaks." And although the idea of the implied reader is being shaped by the gradual unfolding of the text as a whole, at any and every given moment it is the narratee to whom the narrator speaks.
>
> (Wall, 1991, pp. 7–8)

Wall describes this relationship as one of single address, with the writer addressing children without consciousness of the possible presence of adults, or of double address, with the writer consciously addressing both audiences in a variety of ways, or of dual address, which is "a fusion of the two". She argues that children's literature has broken away from some of the condescending practices of earlier times, such as talking to adults above the heads of children, and has developed a mode of address that is more genuinely and specifically a form of single address directed to children.

There is certainly less condescension, but Wall's claim does perhaps call for qualification. As we have seen, not only are there other implied readers of contemporary children's books who exert a powerful influence on the organization of the text, but there are strong social forces that also have a great deal to do with its popular advocacies. Indeed, it is the growth of interest in children's literature, both as an academic field and as an area of enhanced community awareness, which has in some quarters led to an exaggerated kind of political and literary correctness. I would not include Baker in this condemnation; she is a committed and gifted artist with a genuine passion for the environment. And in some ways the phenomenon has also had its positive sides. Writers and illustrators have become increasingly aware of postmodernist theory, and they deliberately experiment with multiple focalizations, metafictional devices, gaps, intertextuality and multiple time-spaces. Yet even so, all this does still involve the presence of multiple addressees who influence the telling of the tale.

On the other hand, the children's books now highlighting fashionable social themes and seeking the approval of academics and literary judges can also be considered in a gentler way, which is demeaning neither to the implied child reader nor to the writer. Bakhtin (1986, p. 126) noted that as part of the organizing structure of any text there is a "higher" superaddressee who is "a constitutive aspect of the whole utterance", and whose "absolutely just reponsive understanding" is simply taken for granted. It can of course be argued that this superaddressee ought to be the child, but sometimes is not, or perhaps ought to be "wise" adults, well equipped to re-iterate the text's messages. In many children's books, however, I think the superaddressee — the person who, deeply and inherently, is a constitutive part of the whole utterance — may be neither the child nor the adult as such, but rather *the adult the child will become.* For it seems to me that, if there is one particular distinctive characteristic of the chronotope of childhood in narrative, it is the creation of a present that has a forward thrust.

This is not to deny the obvious: that the implied reader is the present child. But it is that child conceptualized as both present and potential, as unfinalizable and creatively alive, within a sense of "great time" — within a much larger perspective. Note that I am also implying here an idea of reading that reaches beyond an enclosed and finished meeting event of text and reader. As a physical and cognitive process, reading may end when the book is closed, but reading as a dialogue which draws in the reader's own experience and worldview (past, present and yet to come), reading which, in Bakhtin's words, involves the reader in "renewing the work" of art, may continue for a lifetime. Reading, as well as writing, can be seen as a creative process:

> The work and the world represented in it enter the real world and enrich it, and the real world enters the work and its world as part of the process of its creation, as well as part of its subsequent life, in a continual renewing of the work through the creative perception of listeners and readers.
>
> (Bakhtin, 1981, p. 254)

In fact the whole *raison d'être* of teaching is to prepare children for adulthood; the equipping for "now" is part of this process. Here, then, over and above the present child there hovers another presence, a sort of incipient otherness, in the forthcoming future of the child, who is caught up in a process of continual "recreation" (Johnston, 1998). This shadowy presence is the adult who will actually have the agency to care for the environment, to respect indigenous rights, to take a responsible social role. Again, this is not to play down the agency of children, who by caring for their own space — their home, their school, their community — can certainly do their bit. But their period of greatest agency will be as adults.

This is why the chronotope is such a helpful term in the discussion of children's literature. The time element in children's books — represented as it is in multiple ways — takes on a different type of flesh, a thickening that is specific to itself, a thickening that is fluid and temporary and likely to change. Its present is sometimes unending, but even an unending present, and even a moment of presentness that is terrifying, is underwritten with future, and the possibility of change and transformation. If we consider "the process of the reading" to extend, as I have argued, beyond the immediate physical and cognitive act, this gives an interesting perspective to Eco's words (1994, p. 24):

> . . . [T]he model author and the model reader are entities that become clear to each other only in the process of reading, so that each one creates the other.

The forward thrust of children's narratives implies possibilities and options. This potential to create circumstantial differences is not only the essence of the fairy tale, but is present in a text such as *Dance on my Grave*, which, among other things, is about coming to terms with death. Consider these lines which occur a page or so before the end:

> There's something ahead for me; I can't see what it is yet, but I know it is there, waiting.
>
> (Chambers, 1982, p. 250)

Perhaps we could say that the chronotope of childhood in narrative is a chronotope which inherently, and sometimes obviously, sometimes less obviously, focusses on change, growth and becoming. So when there are afterwords and other paratextual materials, they are written for the child to grow into, perhaps to be helped into, achronologically, sometimes in hindsight, sometimes very quickly. This represents part of the potential of childhood, part of the notion of children as open psychic structures, as well as clearly being another expression of pedagogical activity, which is similarly concerned with deliberate interventions in the processes of change and growth. Children's books, then, imply a notion of what Bakhtin (1981) called "open wholeness" — the child reader who is wholly child at this moment, but who is open to change, for whom change is inevitable, and who will ultimately become wholly "other."

5. An ethics of hope

This insight may help to clarify the vexed discussion of what counts, and what does not count, as a children's book. The texts most likely to be rejected as books for children are the ones which lack this forward thrust, texts enclosed and closed in time, and proposing no possibility of change. This rejection emphasizes the way that the social forces of the community outside the text, which is essentially looking *back*, wants to conceive of the future it projects in the time-spaces of children's narrative. I believe that this forward thrust and this momentum towards another wholeness of present indicate that, while children's books should be realistic as well as fantastic, should be diverse as well as particular, should present different versions of what it is to be, was to be, and can be, they should also be characterized, immanently, by the idea of an ethics of hope.

The potential for this hope emerges from the fact that childhood, despite its inevitable relationship with some particular present, and perhaps because of it, is an unfinished state. Childhood has the space for time, and the time for space. As we have seen, we can link this to Bakhtin's idea about *unfinalizability*, which accepts the world's general chaos, mess and incompleteness, but perceives this as an open potential for freedom and creativity:

> Nothing conclusive has yet taken place in the world, the ultimate word of the world and about the world has not yet been spoken, the world is open and free, everything is still in the future and will always be in the future.
>
> (Bakhtin, 1984, p. 166)

If, as suggested above, children do indeed see themselves through the aesthetic images that are created for them, then an ethics of hope is more than a philosophical nicety. It is surely a social imperative. In part it entails the presentation of many different images and possibilities of being, something which many picture books are already doing extremely well. Especially at a time when a globalized commerce is bombarding young people with images of similarity and conformity, urging them to admire just a certain narrow range of body shapes, clothing brands, food, and toys, and to speak certain languages, to act out only certain behaviours, we do need to consider the implications of the texts children read very seriously. Do their images of childhood and adolescence have an appropriately hopeful orientation, and is it towards a future that is appropriately varied?

So with some notable exceptions, one of the features of a narrative chronotope of childhood is a present infused with a future, whereas what many books for adults offer is a present infused with a past. The orientation towards the future can even be seen in books where the time that is being constructed is a sentimental version of pastoral perfection — what Bakhtin (1981, p. 103) called a "bucolic-pastoral-idyllic chronotope". This time-space is like a cameo, or a Victorian miniature, tiny and perfect, framed and separated from the incursions of the real-time world. It is the "dream-time" or "idyllic time" of fairy tales, or of books such as *The Wind in the Willows, Winnie-the-Pooh,* and the Moomin stories. It has been constructed as a retrospect by adults who would like it to remain sacrosanct, even though they know this is impossible. It, too, is time with a forward thrust, but the thrust does not come from an excitement and growth within, but is an inevitable, sorrowful propulsion by immutable forces without.

6. Future-in-the-present

Any such future-in-the-present can bring to mind the principle of simultaneity applied in mediaeval art, when a number of events which must obviously have occupied different pockets of *time* are expressed in the same *space.* Maria Nikolajeva (1996, p. 134) relates this to the depictions of story in the visual art of picturebooks. It can also be applied to considerations of the time-spaces of verbal narrative, helping us to clarify the distinctive chronotopical feature of a forward thrust in the midst of present concerns. A brief comparison of two books, one a book for older children and one a book for adults, may help to demonstrate this idea. Both these books have won honours, which signifies cultural endorsement for what they "show forth." Brian Caswell and David Phu An Chiem's *Only the Heart* was named as the Children's Book Council of Australia Notable Book in 1998 and has also been set as a school text in at least one Australian state. *Beloved* is a Pulitzer Prize winner and its author, Toni Morrison, received the Nobel Prize for Literature in 1993.

My point has nothing to do with whether the one book is more realistic than the other, nor with their relative merits as literature. As in earlier studies (e.g. Johnston, 2001), I am assuming that children's literature *is* literature, and is part of a literature continuum. Its texts deal with kinds of issue which concern the entire continuum, and in different ways address similarly complex and abstract themes and ideas. In so doing, it trains a receptiveness to later encounters with more complex texts, extending young people's conceptual horizons. The themes which attract older readers' attention are viewed against the horizons of what they have read in earlier life.

So *Only the Heart* and *Beloved* are different in scale, but do have a number of similarities: both are based on historical fact and overtly seek to confront the horrors of the past; both deal with the aftermath of war; both focus on displaced families which are isolated by time-events into spaces allowing little or no agency — the plight of Vietnamese boat people in *Only the Heart* and, in *Beloved*, the condition of Afro-Americans before and after the Civil War. Both books are chronotopically organized around legacies of wars and operate on a type of simultaneity principle, the composition circling in and out of time spaces that span a number of years and places. Both have child and adult characters who are sometimes assigned a narrative voice. In both, people die in terrible circumstances, and children grow into adults.

The differences in the time-space organization of these two books begin with the paratexts. The dedication of *Only the Heart* begins "*For all those who lived the Nightmare, in search of the Dream*" and follows this up with expressions of personal thanks which suggest an element of collaboration and authenticity. Morrison's dedication is cryptic and succinct: "*Sixty Million and more.*" Here is a glimpse of two different time inscriptions. Morrison's is horrifying and complete, circumscribed and enclosed. Caswell and Chiem's acknowledges the horror, but focusses on the possibility of escape.

Equally revealing are the following passages from the texts proper:

> Paul D had only begun, what he was telling her was only the beginning when her fingers on his knee, soft and reassuring, stopped him. Just as well. Saying more might push them both to a place they couldn't get back from. He would keep the rest where it belonged: in that tobacco tin buried in his chest where a red heart used to be. Its lid rusted shut. He would not pry it loose now in front of this sweet sturdy woman, for if she got a whiff of its contents it would shame him. And it would hurt her to know that there was no red heart bright as Mister's [a rooster] comb beating in him.
>
> Sethe rubbed and rubbed, pressing the work cloth and the stony curves that made up his knee. She hoped it calmed him as it did her. Like kneading bread in the half-light of the restaurant kitchen. Before the cook arrived she stood in a space no wider than a bench is long, back behind and to the left of the milk cans. Working dough. Working, working dough. Nothing better than to start the days serious work of beating back the past.
>
> (Morrison, 1997, pp. 72–3)

> Daily life took as much as she had. The future was sunset; the past something to leave behind. And if it didn't stay behind, well, you might have to stomp it out. Slave life; freed life — every day was a test and trial.
>
> (Morrison, 1997, p. 256)

> But you grow out of everything, even despair. Sure, there's a certain satisfaction to be got out of feeling bitter, but it hurts

people, especially the people you love, and you can't keep doing it. Either you let it destroy you, or you start doing drugs or booze, which is about the same thing. Or you shake the crap out and get on with what's left of your life.

(Caswell and Chiem, 1997, p. 201)

I don't know why the gangs have to be part of a community which is almost obsessively law-abiding. It just doesn't seem to make any sense.

My grandmother would probably see it in terms of balance. Good and evil light and dark, the yin and the yang.

Me, I don't think the universe is organized quite so neatly.

(Caswell and Chiem, 1997, p. 205)

Then we make our way outside and the tin-can sound of a scooter rises above the noise of the crowd. It moves like a memory across my path and for a moment the years drop away [the protagonist is now an adult, a father himself]. But only for a moment. I am tired from the trip and I can feet the sweat on my hands. I grip the urn more lightly.

Not long now.

Soon she will lie next to my grandfather, and I will say the words to give her spirit rest. Though a medium of Quan Yin should have no need of words to give her peace.

Thanh has written a poem of farewell, and he asks that I read it to her when she is at her final resting place. He's printed it out for me; I've got it folded up in the pocket of my shirt.

But it isn't really necessary. I know it by heart.

To Vo Kim Tuyet 1919–1996

Our years, like leaves,
Drift and fall away;
Piling up, memory upon memory,
Joy upon sadness,
Until the smile and the tear
Become One.

And the One becomes All.

Our dreams, like children
Grow from a song of the heart;
We know the melody;
But we cannot tie it down
To sounds the ear can taste.
And yet it lives within us

Through our dreams,
Through our children.

And the words are like years,
Drifting like leaves;
And the rhythm is a pulse,
The beat of life and death.

For the song is a journey
And the journey is a song

That only the heart can sing . . .
(Caswell and Chiem, 1997, pp. 209–212)

It is of course impossible to generalize from only two texts, and there will be many exceptions to any rule. Nonetheless, I suspect that subsequent research may lead to more agreement than disagreement with the argument I am supporting through this comparison. Discourse lives, writes Bakhtin (1981, p. 292), in a living impulse (*napravlennost*) toward the object; if we detach ourselves completely from this impulse all we have left is the naked corpse of the word, from which we can learn nothing about the social situation or the fate of a given word in life (cf. Johnston, 1997).

7. Conceptualizing the visual chronotope

As the reference above makes clear, Bakhtin was referring to a chronotope expressed in the language of words — in the verbal text of the novel. However, the literary concept of the chronotope, and the idea of a chronotope of childhood in narrative, becomes even more interesting when we contemplate the idea of a *visual* chronotope, and consider its application to the text of picturebooks.

A visual chronotope is the representation of time-space in picturebook art and illustration. Just as Bakhtin's original concept of the chronotope recognizes ideological loadings, so will its extension into the idea of a visual chronotope. Whatever is selected to illustrate time-space will reflect personal and social values and attitudes. For example, a clock on the space of a wall is a clear time marker, but its repeated presence with different times (particularly short intervals), and as a central presence, may also reflect pressures and stress (Johnston, 2001).

But the visual chronotope not only helps us discuss the way meaning emerges from picturebooks' interplay of words pictures. It can also enlarge our sense of the chronotopical images themselves. A picturebook's verbal and visual chronotopes may actually differ from each other, and this difference may account for meanings which as readers we perceive yet find difficult to pin down. In Bakhtin's words (1981, p. 252):

> Chronotopes are mutually inclusive, they co-exist, they may be interwoven with, replace or oppose one another, contradict one another or find themselves in ever more complex relationships.

It is in this spirit that Bakhtin speaks of an *intervalic chronotope*, where as part of the narrative two different constellations of time and space play out against each other, the action being perceived from two quite different chronotopical perspectives. One of these may be "hidden". But the interaction between them means that "both of them take on metaphoric significance" (Bakhtin, 1981, p. 165). Here is one way to describe, say, Burningham's *Come away from the water, Shirley* (1977), or Baillie and Tanner's *Drac and the Gremlin* (1997), or *Jag såg, jag ser*, by Håkan Jaensson and Gunna Grähs (1997). It describes particularly well the wonderful book by Thomas and Anna-Clara Tidholm, *Resan till Ugri-La-Brek* (1995), where the child protagonists go searching for their dead grandfather, across the football field, through the snowy forest, through the desert, across a beach, right to the other side of the world into an icy land, where they find and talk with him, and then return home. The hidden intervalic chronotope hints that all this has happened during play in their yard. Their parents on the balcony were glimpsed as the children made their campfire in the snowy forest, and are dearly seen having afternoon coffee on the children's "return." The link with my main point about the forward thrust of children's literature is surely dear. A picturebook's deliberate organization of two different time-spaces typifies the unboundedness of the narrative chronotope of childhood. It represents a setting free from adult perceptions by the adults themselves who are the creators of the text.

Resan till Ugri-La-Brek could also be considered in terms of another type of chronotope identified by Bakhtin (1981, p. 111): the *adventure novel of everyday life*, where time-space is organized as "a new type of adventure time" which is a "special sort of everyday time." Here the emphasis is not on two perspectives of time and space being quite different, but on a perspective of time-space — and of life itself — as being simultaneously, within the single chronotope, both critically personal or individual and, *just as critically*, something which reaches beyond individual experience, so endowing individual experience with further significance. This is a notion of time which draws past and future into the experience of the present moment, but with an inclination towards change. The adventure novel of everyday life is a temporal sequence of "metamorphosis" or "transformation" which is linked with "identity" as part of an "idea of development"; it presents moments of "crisis" — that is, critical points of a development which "unfolds not so much in a straight line as spasmodically, a line with 'knots' in it" (Bakhtin 1981, p. 113). In the early Christian "crisis hagiographies" which Bakhtin notes as belonging to this type, "there are as a rule only two images of an individual" — a sort of "before" and "after" that are both "separated and reunited through crisis and rebirth" (Bakhtin, 1981, p. 115). He goes on to expand this idea:

> [A] novel of this type does not, strictly speaking, unfold in biographical time. It depicts only the exceptional, utterly unusual moments of a man's life, moments that are very short compared to the whole length of a human life.

The novel used as a model for the discussion of this chronotope is Apuleius' *The Golden Ass*, and Bakhtin describes in great detail concomitant features that relate directly to this text, for example themes such as individual initiative, chance, guilt, and redemption. In themselves these are not relevant to my present argument. But once again, the overall type of chronotope Bakhtin distinguishes is certainly relevant to an ethics of hope. A chronotope of the "adventure novel of everyday life", with its representation of critical incidents as "knots" of becoming can clearly express childhood with a sense of forward thrust. It can catch the paradox of childhood both as an intense presentness, acutely and vitally realized, and as a larger moment of "great time".

To take another example of visual chronotope, Jenni Overend and Julie Vivas's *Hello Baby* (1999) tells the story of a home birth, which is focalized through the eyes of Jack, the third child and youngest sibling. The verbal text is clearly organized by the chronological time-space of the labour; time is part of the structure of events, which take place near a "town" more rural than urban — a neighbour drops off "a load of wood" as "a present for the baby" — and which are more or less contemporary: the midwife brings "oxygen" and "a special microphone for listening to the baby's heart", there is a "phone", and the family has "sleeping bags". The illustrations of the visual text depict clothes of an indeterminately modern period, and a similarly indeterminate house; the pictures of preparations for the birth imply rather than detail window, chair and table. The first of the two illustrations of the scene outside the house shows a water tank and a wind-blurred forest of tall trees, so reinforcing the rural impression; the second depicts part of a house and a woodheap, with Jack (the narrator) and his father collecting wood. All this is clearly a critical incident, "a knot", in the life of the mother, the family, and the child about to be born, concentrated around the moment of birth, which becomes the threshold of the "before" and "after." Nothing will be the same again for any of them — and cutting (and knotting) the cord is both end and beginning. However, it is also an everyday moment — babies are born, many of them at home, all the time.

This example quintessentializes my argument: that the chronotope of childhood in narrative is forward-looking, is characterized by an ethics of hope, and most of all constructs childhood within a sense of time-space which, rather than dislocating the personal moment of the child or discounting the significance of the child's present, extends personal moment and present into the spaces and perspectives of "the fullness of time".

True, unassisted by the research optic of the chronotope, traditional critics would still be able to say a great deal here. They could note that the wildness outside stands in a similar relation to the house within which the birth takes place as the macrocosm to the microcosm in Shakespeare; that the illustration of the forest, and of the tall (even phallic) trees which dwarf the figure of the pregnant woman walking into the pressure of the wind, connotes the forests of folk and fairytale — enchanted woods which keep out or keep in; and to pinpoint an Australian context, they could also catch a hint of the bush (or desert or other wild place) as a space of healing and redemption, of finding oneself, of gathering together physical and emotional resources.

The visual chronotope — and the particular chronotope of the adventure time of everyday life — gives us a another way of discussing the richness of this book. The text begins *in medias res*: "We've been waiting a long time for this day, Mum, Dad, Bea, Janie and me." Preparations have started. Although this sense of a long period of waiting refers both back and forward, the verbal text is telling a predictable story of a special but far from unusual occurrence. Yet right from the start the visual chronotope challenges any idea that the present can contain the entire story; it pushes time beyond the everyday into the realm of adventure time, and even of a folkloric "great time." On the title page Jack, the previous baby, holds up the jumpsuit, inviting the reader-viewer to engage not only with the comparative smallness of the coming baby, and the transformational process of his own growing, but also with the sure knowledge that the new baby will similarly transform and outgrow the space of this moment. The swirl of preparations for birth becomes increasingly focussed on the human figures and their relationships, which are made visual in the representation of touch, overlap and interconnection. Most of the time, the space surrounding them is little more than a pinkish-red glow. After the baby's birth this space becomes darker, and the family sleep in front of the golden light of the fire, in a visual image that is almost tribal.

The paucity of space markers reaches its most extreme in the picture of the newly-born baby on just a white page, thrust into present, with the cord as its only connection to the moment before. In a sense, this baby has become Every Baby, just as the illustration immediately following is another version of the iconic Madonna and Child. The next double page spread places the baby in the world, within an aerial perspective which allows his face to become the central focus, and to gaze beyond the page. It also allows the reader-viewer to see the "beautiful" placenta, the life-giving sustenance that as life begins is no longer necessary.

The visual chronotope of *Hello Baby*, and its organization of time-space as reaching beyond the sequential units of verbal text and thrusting towards future, is an example of what a chronotope of childhood in narrative looks like. In different ways, to different degrees, and with sometimes different outcomes, the same kind of chronotope is to be found in a huge range of books, including the Ahlbergs' *Each Peach Pear Plum* (1989), Gleeson's *Eleanor Elizabeth* and *Where's Mum?* (1984, 1992), Paterson's *Bridge to Terabitha* (1978), Marsden's *Tomorrow* series (1994–1999), Hill and Barrett's *Beware, Beware* (1993), Ottley's *Mrs Millie's Painting* (1998), Baum's *The Wonderful Wizard of Oz* (1900), Montgomery's *Anne of Green Gables* (1908), Isadora's *At the Crossroads* (1991), Hutchins' *Rosie's Walk* (1968), Browne's *Piggybook* (1986), Nodelman's *Alice falls apart* (1996), and many others. There are also notable exceptions, where space- and timescape has what Bakhtin (1981, p. 103) calls the "specific insular idyllic landscape" of a pastoral chronotope, and is structured more in terms of "a time saturated with its own strictly limited, sealed-off segment of nature's space". The accompanying sense of wistful nostalgia that characterizes many of these texts in its own way indicates that the future is always a consideration, and that the time they celebrate is already lost.

By exploring children's literature through the optic of the chronotope, we can better understand the impulses underlying this communication which society chooses to have with its young. Such impulses are likely to be characterized by the forward thrust and, generally speaking, the responsible carriage of an ethics of hope: a depiction of a future which may in fact be difficult and imperfect, but which nevertheless is open and has potential. The notion of a chronotope of childhood in narrative draws together literary and pedagogical ideas that emerge out of the common insight that childhood is not stasis, but growth and change. Kristeva (1989, p. 8) notes that "each speaking subject is both the addresser and the addressee of his own message . . ." Is this a message, then, which we would also hope to give ourselves?

References

Ahlberg, J., & A. (1978). *Each Peach Pear Plum.* London: Puffin.

Baillie, A., & Tanner, J. (1988). *Drac and the Gremlin.* Melbourne: Penguin Books.

Baker, J. (1987). *Where the Forest meets the Sea.* London: Walker Books.

Bakhtin, M. M. (1981). *The dialogic imagination.* Austin: University of Texas Press.

Bakhtin, M. M. (1984). *Problems of Dostoevsky's poetics.* Minneapolis: University of Minnesota Press.

Bakhtin, M. M. (1986). *Speech genres and other late essays.* Austin: University of Texas Press.

[Barton, C.] (1841). *A Mother's Offering to her Children: by a Lady long resident in New South Wales.* Sydney: The Gazette.

Baum, F. ([1900] 1956). *The Wonderful Wizard of Oz.* New York: Airmont Publishing Caswell.

Paterson, K. (1982). *Bridge to Terabithia.* Harmondsworth: Penguin.

Browne, A. (1986). *Piggybook.* London: Julia MacRae Books.
Burningham, J. (1977). *Come away from the water, Shirley.* London: Red Fox.
Bunyan, J. ([1678] 1960). *The Pilgrim's Progress from this World to that which is to come.* Oxford: Clarendon Press.
Caswell, B., & Phu An Chiem, D. (1997). *Only the Heart.* St Lucia: University of Queensland Press.
Chambers, A. (1982). *Dance on my Grave.* London: The Bodley Head.
Eco, U. (1994). *Six walks in the fictional woods.* Cambridge, MA: Harvard University Press.
Genette, G. (1987). *Paratexts: Thresholds of interpretation.* Cambridge: Cambridge University Press.
Gleeson, L. (1999). *Hannah and the Tomorrow Room.* Ringwood: Penguin Australia.
Gleeson, L., & Greder A. (1999). *The Great Bear.* Gosford, NSW: Scholastic Australia.
Gleeson, L. (1984). *Eleanor Elizabeth.* Sydney. Angus & Robertson.
Hill, A., & Barrett, J. (1993). *Beware beware.* London: Walker Books.
Hutchins, P. (1968). *Rosie's Walk.* London: The Bodley Head.
Isadora, R. (1991). *At the Crossroads.* London: Red Fox.
Jaensson, H., & Grähs, G. (1997). *Jag såg, jag ser.* Stockholm: Alfabeta.
Jansson, T. (1961) [1948]. *The Finn Family Moomintroll.* London: Penguin.
Johnston, R. R. (1997). Reaching beyond the word: Religious themes as "deep structure" in the *Anne* books of L. M. Montgomery. *Canadian Children's Literature,* 88, 25–35.
Johnston, R. R. (1998). Thisness and everydayness in children's literature: The "being-in-the-world" proposed by the text. *Papers: Explorations into children's literature,* 8, 25–35.
Johnston, R. R. (2001). Children's literature. In G. Winch, R. R. Johnston, M. Holliday, L. Ljungdahl & P. March (Eds.). *Literacy: Reading, writing and children's literature* (pp. 287–437). Melbourne: Oxford University Press.
Kristeva, J. (1990). The Adolescent Novel. In her *Abjection, melancholia and love* (pp. 8–23). London: Routledge.
Kristeva, J. (1989). *Language the unknown: An initiation into linguistics.* Trans. by Anne M. Menke. Hertfordshire: Harvester Wheatsheaf.
Marsden, J. (1994). *Tomorrow when the War began.* Sydney: PanMacmillan.
McCallum, R. (1999). *Ideologies of identity in adolescent fiction: The dialogic construction of subjectivity.* New York: Garland.
Montgomery, L. M. (1972) [1908]. *Anne of Green Gables.* London: Peacock Books.
Morrison, T (1987). *Beloved.* London: Random House.
Morson, G. S., & Emerson, C. (1990). *Mikhail Bakhtin: Creation of a prosaics.* Standford: Stanford University Press.
Nikolajeva, M. (1996). *Children's literature comes* of *age: Towards a new aesthetic.* New York: Garland.
Nodelman, P. (1996). *Alice falls apart.* Winnipeg: Bain & Cox.
Ottley, M. (1998). *Mrs Millie's Painting.* Sydney: Hodder Headline.
Overend, J., & Vivas, J. (1999). *Hello Baby.* Sydney: ABC Books.
Paterson, K. ([1978] 1982). *Bridge to Terabitha.* Harmondsworth: Penguin.
Pohl, P. ([1985] 1991). *Johnny, my Friend.* Woochester Stroud: Turton & Chambers.
Rowling, J. K. (1997). *Harry Potter and the Philosopher's Stone.* London: Bloomsbury.
Saxby, 1998. *Offered to children.* Gosford, NSW: Scholastic.

Shotter, J. (1993). *The cultural politics of everyday life*. Buckingham: Open University Press.

Shavit, Z. (1995). The historical model of the development of children's literature. In M. Nikolajeva (Ed.), *Aspects and issues in the history of children's literature* (pp. 27–37). Westport, CT.: Greenwood Press.

Tidholm, T., & Tidholm, A.-C. (1995). *Resan till Ugri-La-Brek*. Stockholm: Alfabeta.

Utemorrah, D., & Torres, P. (1990). *Do not go around the edges*. Broome: Magabala Books Aboriginal Corporation.

Wall, B. (1991). *The narrator's voice: The dilemma of children's fiction*. London: Macmillan.

60

IMAGINARY CHILDHOODS

Memory and children's literature

Valerie Krips

Source: *Critical Quarterly* 39(3) (1997): 42–50.

Is childhood ending? Rumours of its demise have come thick and fast in the years since Neil Postman wrote *The Disappearance of Childhood* (1982) and blamed it on television's role in blurring the boundaries between childhood and adulthood. According to Postman, our culture is based upon the notion that adults know more than children. One of the constitutive tasks of adulthood is to make knowledge available in an appropriate and timely way so that the child, the adult and society in general benefit. Television's virtually uncontrolled release of information has undone the traditions of slow and careful revelation of knowledge within which so much cultural training and adaptation was accomplished. Further, since watching the television requires little in the way of sophisticated and institutionalised education when compared to the attainment of literacy, the opportunities for disciplining and producing the child in ways particular to formal education are also threatened. One of the consequences is that the interests of adults and children have slowly merged as the differences which marked the state of each have faded. In 1980, Postman notes, the Nielsen Report on television in the USA indicated that adults over 18 and children aged from 2 to 11 listed roughly the same TV shows as their favourites. Further, the entertainment and information provided by television was itself structured to meet the demands of the merging audience. Nor are films immune. Those which twenty years earlier would have been thought fit entertainment only for children (he includes *Raiders of the Lost Ark* in his list) are now fully accepted as adult fare.

The resulting loss of distinction between the states of adulthood and childhood affects both groups. What we have to lose is both the child we knew and the adults we have become, since adulthood is formed in the light of and in response to childhood, and vice versa. What is at stake is literally, in Postman's view, civilisation as we know it.

The childhood that Postman thinks is disappearing was the result of roughly 600 years of development in the West, if we take Philippe Ariès's pioneering study of the family and childhood as a guide.[1] The concept of childhood we have inherited was forged by a wide variety of factors, but there is little doubt in Ariès's mind that the vital conjunction in its development was the rise of formal education in schools and colleges and the reorganisation of the family unit around the child. The resulting focus on childhood was spurred on in the eighteenth and nineteenth centuries by developments in science and medicine that provided ways of thinking about growth, generation and continuity which, when attached to childhood, began to consolidate its imaginary form into something very like the construct with which we are familiar today.

An important but little discussed determinant of that consolidation was children's literature. A literature for children could scarcely be imagined, of course, until it was understood that children had their own needs and desires. Once set in train in the mid-eighteenth century, however, writing and publishing for the young began to add its concepts of childhood to those already in circulation. Early children's books took up new ideas about education, instruction and child-rearing with alacrity. Responding to John Locke's and Jean-Jacques Rousseau's meditations on education, the early books were overtly instructional and eschewed fantasy and fable even as they attempted to find ways of persuading children into their letters by entertaining them, as Locke suggested.[2]

From its inception it was well understood that children's literature was a mechanism for socialising the child. Jack Zipes has recently written extensively on this aspect of children's books, and particularly of the fairytale's part in conceptualising the child in ways which not only reproduced society's understandings of childhood but helped to refine and define them. First written down in France by aristocratic women as diversions, fairytales were recast and appropriated by Charles Perrault as illustrations of the code of *civilité*. Zipes remarks that Perrault informed 'his plots with normative patterns of behaviour to describe an exemplary social constellation'.[3] While Perrault's tales were originally addressed to adults, the first English translation of them, appearing in 1719, was advertised as being 'very entertaining and instructive to children'[4].

However, the early English writers for children shunned the fabulous and fantastic, concerning themselves primarily with the serious business of moral instruction. The stories they wrote were almost without exception earnest and adamantly down-to-earth, not to say literal-minded; Locke's remarks concerning the persuasive effects of linking instruction to entertainment had, it seemed, been forgotten. By the mid-nineteenth century this overlooked idea was revived, abetted by an increasingly sentimentalised view of childhood. The translation of Grimm's fairytales in 1823–6 and of Hans Christian Andersen's in 1846 were thus greeted with enthusiasm rather than suspicion. Indeed, John Ruskin, the first Slade Professor of Fine Art at Oxford declared in the introduction to John Campden Hotten's edition of *German Popular Stories* of 1858 that the child

> should not need to choose between right and wrong. It should not be capable of wrong: it should not conceive of wrong. Obedient, as bark to helm, not by sudden strain or effort, but in the freedom of its bright course of constant life; true, with an undistinguished, painless, unboastful truth, in a crystalline household world of truth; gentle, through daily entreatings of gentleness, and honourable trusts, and pretty prides of child-fellowship in offices of good; strong, not in bitter and doubtful contest with temptation, but in peace of heart, and armour of habitual right, from which temptation falls like thawing hail; self-commanding, not in sick restraint of mean appetites and covetous thoughts, but in vital joy of unluxurious life, and contentment in narrow possession, wisely esteemed.
>
> Children so trained have no need of moral fairytales . . .[5]

The fairy stories then available to English children may not have been overtly moralistic, but it does not follow that they were free from normative effect. The stories of both the Grimm brothers and Andersen acted as adjuncts to the cultural and educational formations which instilled in children the roles which would fall to them in a bourgeois and moralistic society.[6] By the time of the first Education Acts of 1870 and 1880, then, children's literature was a well-established genre in England. Indeed one of the 'classic' English children's books had been published five years earlier: Lewis Carroll's *Alice in Wonderland* appeared in 1865. Before compulsory education was much more than thirty years old, most of the best-known children's novels of the Victorian and Edwardian period were in print: books such as R. L. Stevenson's *Treasure Island* (1883); Rudyard Kipling's *The Jungle Book* (1894); Beatrix Potter's *The Tale of Peter Rabbit* (1902); Kenneth Grahame's *Wind in the Willows* (1908) and Frances Hodgson Burnett's *The Secret Garden* (1910). The scene was set for a consolidation of the imaginary child that children's literature had helped to construct.

In his recent *Theatres of Memory* (1994) Raphael Samuel attends to a collection of trends, responses, events, artefacts and approaches to the past. Retrofitting in pubs and shopping malls, living history events and old photographs, the heritage industry and the works of Charles Dickens on stage and screen are all species of memory work in Samuel's analysis, ways of relating the past to the present in contemporary Britain. His collection, the first volume in a projected series is, as he says, 'object centred', and 'about ways in which history is being rewritten and reconceptualized'.[7] That reconceptualisation, fruit in part of a 'democratizations in the production and dissemination of knowledge' provides a way of thinking about cultural constructions which brings pressure to bear on Postman's powerful polemic with which I began.[8] Importantly, it helps to turn attention to a lacuna in Postman's argument caused by his failure to attend to children's literature. Postman is centrally concerned to understand and elucidate the result of changes to the historically developed relationship between adult and child. That is a relationship which has had an outcome across a range of cultural forms, but crucially has produced an object peculiar to it: children's literature. This is an artefact which bears witness to the distinction between adult and child which Postman thinks is fading, if not almost gone. Thinking about that artefact along the lines that Samuel suggests allows us to bring its existence to bear on Postman's argument. We are reminded that children's literature is not merely an abstract cultural form but consists too of objects which may be some of the child's earliest possessions, cherished life-long.[9] In order to deal critically with Postman's claims, then, we need to focus on the children's book in two distinct ways. First, we need to think of the relationship between adult and child enacted in the genre; secondly, we must try to understand the children's book as an object of and for, the child.

In his *Outside Literature* (1990), Tony Bennett writes of literary genres as 'spheres of sociality of which their textual components are but a part'.[10] Children's literature bears the unmistakable traces of the social relations that construct it. Written, published and generally bought by adults for children, the genre adjusts to the dimensions and particularities of its market as it fashions itself for an ever-renewed audience, an audience which comprises not just the child but the adult too. One of the most important but least remarked aspects of children's books is that they must sustain an appeal to both adult and child. The clearest signs of this necessity can be found in books for the very young, those which are read aloud by adult to child. A. A. Milne's *Winnie-the-Pooh* (1926) is a prime example of narrative full of adult jokes, sometimes at the child's expense, which continues to find devoted audiences of both adults and children. However, all children's books, including the most egregious novels, must first find adult approval – must, in that sense, 'appeal' to the adult. Adults commission, edit, write, publish, promote and, in the main, buy children's books. And adults are called to account for the books they produce and promote by teachers, parents, librarians and, last link in a long chain, children.

A less readily recognised aspect of the sphere of sociality of the genre is its commemorative function. Children's literature is a *lieu de mémoire*, to use the term from Pierre Nora's *Realms of Memory* (1996).[11] History has accelerated in Nora's analysis: things 'tumble with increasing rapidity into an irretrievable past'.[12] Modernity's response is to create archives and records, to replace or even erase memory, the faculty upon which, until a few centuries ago, we mostly relied for our knowledge of the past. In erasing memory we dispose of a precious resource. Memory is 'life, always embodied in living societies and as such in permanent evolution . . . History, on the other hand, is the reconstruction, always problematic and incomplete, of what is no longer'.[13] *Lieux de mémoire* are complex things. Functional, material and symbolic, they are embodied memory. They represent a will to remember, but importantly thrive because they also retain a capacity to change, to generate new meanings and to resurrect old ones. They are sites which, through their representations, offer the promise of re-connection to the past. Instigated when our erstwhile fund of memory disappeared, their purpose is to 'stop time, to block the work of forgetting, to establish the state of things . . . to materialize the immaterial'.[14]

The immaterial that children's literature materialises is both the idea of the child and the adult's memory of a personal childhood. The idea of the child created in children's literature does not exist simply within the pages of books. As Bennett's framework helps us to see, the relationships developed within its sphere of sociality are permeable: the literary child may be a construct of writing, but it is one with which both readers and writers must come to terms. And that coming to terms is itself a process, part of the individual's memorialisation of a personal past. Revisions to the set of concepts which constitute 'the child' are, then, likely to arouse fierce dismay: cathexes to personal and collective memories are at issue.

A visceral response to revisions in a classic children's text found expression in 1987 in a broadsheet newspaper of the left, the *Guardian*. The question as the *Guardian* framed it was one of literary standards. But the terms in which the criticism was couched, the associations evoked, explicit and implicit, suggest that the areas of concern exceeded those of purely literary merit.

Ladybird books had recently published a version of Beatrix Potter's *The Tale of Peter Rabbit*. Inexpensive but well produced, the book both abridged and added to Potter's text, and replaced her watercolour illustrations with photographs of stuffed toys in tableaux that repeated some of the famous Potter iconography. Peter stands on his hind-legs by a garden gate, anxiously looking for a way out; Peter is caught by the buttons of his coat in a gooseberry net; he is dosed with camomile tea by his mother at the end of his adventures.

Ladybird were well known at the time as the publishers of a reading series widely used in English schools, and of fairytales; and other short fiction. Their books, uniform in size and generally so in length, were carefully graded for the beginning reader and, at the time when their version of *Peter Rabbit* appeared, were to be found nationally in bookshops, newsagents, and some supermarkets. With a solid reputation in education and recreational reading, but with no claim to be producing works of abiding literary merit, Ladybird might well have supposed that their foray into the world of Potter's little animals would go as unremarked by the national press as had their other and numerous efforts to entertain and educate the English child.[15]

Potter's books, also uniform in design, were an institution of a different kind. Still produced by Potter's original publisher Warne, they were, according to Potter's wishes, small enough to fit comfortably into a child's hand.[16] Hard-covered and undated, printed on high-quality paper with a page of text and a full-page illustration at every opening, they repeat the original 1902 edition in every particular. Sold primarily in bookshops, and expensive in comparison to Ladybird's offerings, the continuing success of these books in a well-defined market was doubtless an important factor in persuading Ladybird that their own version, tapping a different market, would be successful. Were they not, after all, doing what they had already done so successfully with stories such as *Cinderella*, or the *Three Little Pigs*?

In September 1987 the *Guardian* devoted several column inches to Ladybird's venture, declaring that the new version was 'cloth-eared' and the result of 'levelling-down'.[17] The revisions of Potter's work were thought to be like those perpetrated upon the Book of Common Prayer, which was 'purged', in the columnist's language, 'of its richness and mystery in the name of popular accessibility'. 'Ladybird's true intentions', the newspaper thundered, 'are betrayed by its illustrations. Where Beatrix Potter's Peter is pure rabbit, and her Nutkin pure squirrel, Ladybird's equivalents are cuddly toys. And the language of the stories has been altered to match'.

The literary grounds from which the attack is launched are surprisingly Leavisite: 'levelling-down' brings in its train notions of an élitist literary criticism about which many critics on the left have had severe misgivings. Further, its pleading for the retention of 'richness and mystery' seems to play a tune very like that advanced by conservative, not to say reactionary, advocates of England's 'glorious heritage' many of whom, as Patrick Wright argues in *On Living in an Old Country* (1985), deploy similar concepts to promote their visions of Britain.[18] Since the political left in England has in general been suspicious of the turn to heritage, seeing in it a debilitating and politically regressive nostalgia, the *Guardian*'s response represents a puzzle.

Anyone living in the last ninety years could have owned a copy of Beatrix Potter's *The Tale of Peter Rabbit* just like those available today in bookshops. It symbolises the past and, moreover, has become an article of 'heritage', sold alongside porcelain cottages and reproduction horse-brasses in giftshops, as a souvenir. It is also an embodiment of the past, repeating in its material form the book we owned as children, or the one we could have owned. And importantly, *The Tale of Peter Rabbit* is a small book, an object made to fit the tiny hands of children.

The miniature book, according to Susan Stewart's account in *On Longing* (1993) 'always calls attention to the book as total object.'[19] Tiny as it may be, it retains the capacity to display within its compass whole worlds, including those not known through lived experience or the senses. The social space of the miniature book is, she says, the social space in miniature of all books, of 'the book as talisman to the body and emblem of the self'.[20] But we must also consider, she reminds us, the depiction and description of miniatures in the text. The miniatures most obviously present in books for children are of course the children themselves when understood in terms of the adult's construction of childhood. In children's literature childhood is pictured 'as if it were at the other end of a tunnel – distanced, diminutive, clearly framed'

> not simply because the child is in some physical sense a miniature of the adult, but also because the world of childhood, limited in scope yet fantastic in its content, presents in some ways a miniature and fictive chapter in each life history; it is a world that is part of history, at least the history of the individual subject, but remote from the presentness of adult life.[21]

Childhood is thus seen through the wrong end of a spy-glass: distinct but far away, recognisable but infinitely small and infinitely desirable. This is, of course, the childhood of the ideal, an ideal uncovered now as existing not only within the social space created by the genre of children's literature, but in the social space of the objects themselves, the little books we provide for children.[22] It is to such nostalgic conceptualisation that the *Guardian* responds, seizing 'hold of a memory as it flashes up in a moment of danger', to quote Benjamin.[23]

Both Postman and the *Guardian* respond to the threat of a lost childhood. The antecedent assumptions of the *Guardian*'s visceral response are clear enough, and sufficiently powerful to thrust aside questions which might, in fairness, be put. Is Potter's version of *The Tale of Peter Rabbit* to be judged as a work of art, in which any alteration is necessarily a dimunition? Or is it to be understood as a cultural icon, depending for its survival upon a capacity to change? If it is such an icon, ought we not to rejoice in its dissemination to children otherwise locked out by expense, by availability and, indeed, by language, from what it represents? That the *Guardian* does not take this line of enquiry is evidence not so much of a failure of critical acumen as it is of the complexities the critic of children's literature faces.

Postman's account of the growing similarity of adults and children helps to focus these questions. His is, doubtless, also a response to danger, but one conceived in more general terms than is the *Guardian*'s. The *Guardian* implicitly answers the question of whether childhood is ending in the affirmative as it springs to its defence in a moment of perceived threat. That there is a widespread perception that childhood is endangered is scarcely to be doubted. However, the fact that we have constructed a *lieu de mémoire* associated with it indicates that we have a will to remember childhood, and a desire to keep it alive. Perhaps what we face is a transformation of childhood, rather than its ending.

Notes

1 Philippe Ariès, *Centuries of Childhood*, trans. Robert Baldick (New York: Vintage Books, 1962).
2 These suggestions are set out in detail in John Locke, *Some Thoughts Concerning Education*, ed. J. W. and Jean S. Yolton (Oxford: Clarendon, 1989).
3 Jack Zipes, *Fairytales and the Art of Subversion* (Routledge: New York, 1991), 26–7.
4 Iona and Peter Opie (eds), *The Classic Fairy Tales* (New York: Oxford University Press, 1980), 30. Their introduction to the collection provides a very interesting account of the conditions under which fairytales were introduced to Britain.
5 Quoted in Harvey Darton, *Children's Books in England*, 3rd edn, revised by Brian Alderson (Cambridge: Cambridge University Press, 1982), 241–2.
6 See Zipes's argument, op. cit., 46.
7 Raphael Samuel, *Theatres of Memory* (London: Verso, 1994), p. x.
8 Ibid, p. xi.
9 It is worth noting that, given the vast numbers of children's books which have been published, second-hand copies are a relative rarity. In part this may be due to the child's destructive tendencies, but that would scarcely account for the absolute scarcity of first editions of novels for older children published in the twentieth century. It is reasonable to assume that people often hang on to their childhood books, and perhaps even pass them on to their children.
10 Tony Bennett, *Outside Literature* (London: Routledge, 1990), 105.
11 Pierre Nora, *Realms of Memory*, vol. 1, *Conflicts* and *Divisions*, ed. with foreword by Lawrence D. Kritzman (New York. Columbia University Press, 1996).
12 Ibid., 1.
13 Ibid., 3.
14 Ibid., 15.
15 One of the matters at issue here is the highly charged distinction between books for children understood as 'literature' and books which it is difficult or undesirable to group under that description. Discussion of this vexed topic goes well beyond the scope of the present essay, but it is worth noting that Ladybird books' association with pedagogy and particularly with learning to read marks them as belonging to the 'sphere of sociality' differently from Potter's version. My point would be that the concept of the genre as represented in the term 'literature for children' is not only unhelpful but actually misrepresents what is a very complex and sociologically fascinating genre. But for the present argument the term is retained to mark the difference between books whose primary purpose is to entertain children, as distinct from books which aim to teach.
16 See the discussion of this point in Margaret Lane, *The Tale of Beatrix Potter* (Harmondsworth: Penguin, 1986), ch. 5, p. 62.
17 Unascribed article, *Guardian*, 27 September 1987.
18 Patrick Wright, *On Living in an Old Country* (London: Verso, 1995).
19 Susan Stewart, *On Longing: Narratives of the Miniature, the Gigantic, the Souvenir, the Collection* (Durham, NC: Duke University Press, 1993), 44.
20 Ibid., 41.
21 Ibid., 44.
22 The point can be made differently for the very large books we also produce for children, and further for the restricted narratives and representations of the world found in children's books.
23 Walter Benjamin, *Illuminations*, ed. Hannah Arendt (New York: Schocken Books, 1969), 255.

61

SUBSTITUTE COMMUNITIES, AUTHENTIC VOICES

The organic writing of the child

Stephen Thomson

Source: Karín Lesnik-Oberstein (ed.), *Children in Culture: Approaches to Childhood*, Basingstoke: Macmillan, 1998, pp. 248–273.

> And if a text always gives itself a certain representation of its own roots, those roots live only by that representation, by never touching the soil, so to speak. Which undoubtedly destroys their *radical essence*, but not the necessity of their *racinating function*.[1]

> On the side of experience, a recourse to literature as reappropriation of presence [. . .] of Nature; on the side of theory, an indictment against the negativity of the letter, in which must be read the degeneracy of culture and the disruption of the community.[2]

In Alan Garner's short novel *The Stone Book*,[3] Mary, the central child-character, wants a book. Tired of being a lad, that is of having to help her mason father at work, she craves, at one stroke, and perhaps as part of the same package, a lettered schooling and a big house full of shiny things. With the pawky, tight-lipped wisdom of Garner's own private Cheshire, father warns of the dangers of book-learning and materialism alike, but at length relents so far as to offer Mary a deal. She is to go deep into a certain cave, see what she sees, and if she still wants a book after that, then she can have one. Duly finding the mark of her ancestors, stoneworkers time out of mind, feeling the presence of the past all around her and so on, Mary returns with an apprehension more ancient and wise than any book. Father has won, as he knew he would. Nevertheless, he *does* give Mary a book – a book of fossil-bearing stone, which is 'better than a book you can open'.[4] For it has in it 'all the stories of the world and the flowers of the flood',[5] on which note, this first part of the *Quartet* ends.

In drawing this – inevitably partial – synopsis of Garner's novel, I want to ask what is happening when literature seems to call into question the value of reading? This question could, of course, be qualified and complicated with more detailed reference to the text: the fossil motif, for instance, places father's mistrust of letters in the context of a questioning of established religious dogma, and the text is perhaps not entirely monologic. Still, the fable leans heavily towards, and furthermore ends on, a note of distrust for print. At the very least, it can be confidently stated that it mobilizes a theme that might be called the vanity of reading – a feeling that experience is what matters, and that mere words on a page may prove empty or even harmful. In the context of postwar children's literature, *The Stone Book* is not alone in this. In Jane Gardam's *The Hollow Land*[6] we see canny swains mocking city-born children for reading geology books when the living rock lies underneath them; a whole episode is devoted to the impossibility of describing a cluster of icicles, of the need to be there; for the journalist father immersed in an article he has just written, the children are like shadows, momentarily eclipsed by textual chimeras. Similar strong instances could be cited from William Mayne. It might be argued that Garner, Mayne and Gardam show a particularly marked tendency in this direction. Even so, related attitudes appear throughout much canonic fiction for eight-to-twelve-year-olds of the past 50 years, albeit in a variety of more or less attenuated forms. School-learning – allegedly book-bound, dry, removed from experience – is routinely denigrated in favour of a sort of pastoral truancy that brings the child into the spontaneously educative embrace of Nature, there to learn by doing rather than, or at least *before*, reading. Indeed, a text as decisive in the development of the canon of twentieth-century children's literature as *The Secret Garden*[7] can be made to support the view that where reading precedes experience, a distorted or hystericized relation to one's surroundings sets in. Colin is healed when, instead of looking at animals in picture books in a gloomy interior, he comes out into the garden and watches things growing.

In any case, far from being seen as an aberration, the *Quartet* is widely hailed as a masterpiece, perhaps *the* masterpiece, of modern children's literature. It is this critical response which interests me here for what it has to tell us about the constitution of children's literature, about the construction of a certain idea of literariness thought of as appropriate to the child. The first point, then, is that the *Quartet* is canonized, not in spite of, but precisely by virtue of, its qualms over literature and education. Unsurprisingly, no-one concludes that Garner is telling us that reading is utterly bad. The literary quality of his text is, nevertheless, consistently located not – emphatically not – in literariness *per se*, but in an ethic of peasant simplicity that runs counter to literacy. For one critic, at least, Garner's very career is a sort of process of de-schooling, that culminates in the stripped-to-the-bones peasant lore of the *Quartet*.

> Garner's formal education removed him from his natural background of rural Cheshire craftsmen, with their ancient skills, their language, traditions, stories. In his *Stone Book* quartet – perhaps his masterpiece – he has attempted to resolve his own tensions, re-establishing himself, in his own way, as a writer/craftsman, in his own local culture, and establishing his own identity and place in his long family history.[8]

Education has led the author away from his community, and the final triumph of his art is, by some obscure synthesis, to divest himself of the stigma of letters, and so re-integrate himself as an organic part of a pre-print, oral culture. While this account does not directly describe the text in question, it *does* outline a version of the author's life in terms borrowed from the text. The critic concurs with Mary's father – education *is* a threat to community – but envisages a final redemption which is not so much stated in the text as implied by its very existence. The figure of the 'writer/craftsman' hovers above the text, both inside and outside, identified with it as a whole, but not a character in it. This solution can only work on a level in which life and work are confounded – that of the œuvre. In effect, Garner's stories are read as a diary of his own progress through a sort of adolescent confusion to a mature wholeness. His two previous novels – *Red Shift* and *The Owl Service* – had dealt sympathetically with educated youngsters struggling to find their place in their environment and in their family history. In *The Owl Service*, Gwyn's mother is against his speaking the Welsh of his ancestors but equally, having sent him to Grammar School to improve himself, resents what seems to her a tone of superiority. Meanwhile, Gwyn's mastery of Standard English is not enough to gain acceptance with snobbish English incomers. Though the plot resolution suggests a recognition of his Celtic roots, nowhere in the text is Gwyn entirely at one with his interlocutors. In short, this text *enacts* the 'tensions' that the *Quartet* is supposed to have resolved; it is riddled with the marks of discontinuity. In the later work, the text maintains a single plain-speaking artisan voice throughout, which the narrative shares with all the characters. Here, we are to believe, the author and his art have come home, found peace, all linguistic squabbles smoothed over.

This resolution, on the other hand, still leaves the critic to deal with 'tensions' of his own. The text is necessarily written, and expects a literate readership, but must, in some way, be shown to reincorporate what has preceded, and been lost in, the process of education. Criticism of the *Quartet* is indeed anxious to find in it the traces of something before the printed word, chunks of the real that have lodged in the text, but retain an independent existence. Again the appeal goes out to the oral, craft tradition that, common sense tells us, flourished quite happily in rural communities for long ages before the diffusion of print. 'By exhuming what is embedded in the texts, Neil Philip relocates Garner's work in a kind of traditional innocence of utterance associated with the folk tale'.[9]

Once more, we are to see Garner reaching back to an older, more innocent linguistic moment. Interestingly, however, here it is not just Garner's writing that is cast in this light. One critic is describing the work of another as a sort of archaeology, a retrieval of the very substance of the past rather than an artificial reconstruction. It is as if there were ancient matter living and growing in these texts which is only there provisionally, and can be detached and 'relocated'. This in turn gives a subtle inflection to the work of textual criticism. The critic himself, it would seem, is rolling up his sleeves and raking about in the ancient, honest humus – an activity in keeping with the rural craft-based world which is at stake. The whole text-critic encounter can be read as the work of artisans.

The role of the critic in decoding an original, transparent simplicity might otherwise be problematic. For if Garner's text *does* all that is claimed for it, it shouldn't need critics to tell us. Surely a text ought to partake of 'innocence of utterance' already, manifestly, or not at all. If it is to communicate this to children, it certainly shouldn't need an adult critic to 'relocate' it for other adult critics. Of course, all criticism risks the charge of parasitism. If it sticks too close to the text, it might appear tautologous, hence redundant. If on the other hand it departs too far, it could be seen as an irrelevant imposition. Criticism of the *Quartet* generally constrains itself to the modesty of paraphrase – the simple admiring recognition of what is there. It is a modesty, however, that exceeds itself. For even a seemingly spare inventory such as 'the transmission of skills, the wisdom that resides in work, and continuity of life in an intimately known landscape'[10] implies a whole narrative. We already sense that these elements belong together, are representative parts of a coherent world, whose value is implicitly wholesome and educative. I refer to this as excessive not because it says something the text cannot be made to say, but because it calls on some *common sense* to make the connections. It requires us to draw on something that precedes the text, a previous knowledge of the whole tableau from which these details are drawn. This *sense*, what is more, asks to be thought of not as the effect of a textual game, but of a truth directly apprehended from reality, or from folk memory. Seemingly, this business of a lost community, and the teasing possibility of its recovery, is truly immanent. It is not here or there, the property of the author, text or critic, nor even discourse; it is just *there*, and this, arguably, is the most palpable community that this writing forges for itself: modifications of form aside, critic and author alike share a deep feeling of writing from and with the same stuff.

To put this another way, if the *Quartet* breaks down with suspicious ease into a series of critical commonplaces, we are not to believe that this is because either the critic or Garner himself is writing with these commonplaces in mind. Counter to this, I want to suggest, there is a sense in which

Garner's text is providing critics with the materials to sing one of their favourite songs – if the *Quartet* did not exist, criticism would have to invent it. With reservations, one might say that the *Quartet* is the masterpiece of recent children's literature *because* it is seen to be an adequate vehicle, the perfect occasion, for certain critical narratives and tropes. In outlining other texts that share in this community, I want to suggest how this stuff comes to be the particular property of the child.

We have before us, then, a complex theme that links the disruption of an organic community that existed at some point in the past with an equivocal suspicion of written language. If I propose looking at a variety of other texts that employ similar themes, it is not to suggest a tradition proper. That is to say, I do not mean to claim that similarities are necessarily the sign of the direct influence of, or self-conscious adherence to, a given text. Indeed, the way of thinking which is at stake is so broad and so fundamental as to defy such a description. For the same reasons, the term 'theme' itself is perhaps not entirely just – the role of this motif, if you will, of the loss of nature, is anything but anecdotal. It plays a profound role in structuring thought in a number of domains across a broad stretch of time. My intention nevertheless is to sketch a rough tradition of decisive instances that will help to suggest how the child is, and continues to be, implicated in this whole affair. To begin with, I want to turn to Rousseau, as a writer who assumes the anti-writing position with a rare violence, claiming variously that he hates books,[11] that his literary career is a freakish detour,[12] and that he writes to prevent his readers from copying him.[13] Yet, even in the last instance cited there is still the more or less explicit admission that writing is necessary, even as a means of avoiding further writing. Jacques Derrida has illuminated discussion of this ambivalence enormously in pointing out the prominence of ideas of supplementation and substitution in Rousseau's texts. Briefly, Rousseau is exercised by the simultaneous necessity and danger of making one thing stand in the place of another, or of adding things on to what is already there. To put it very crudely, his text, with its jaundiced view of civilization, is troubled by the recurring question – why can't we just *be*, why all this other nonsense? The question recurs because the recovery of the state of nature – of being, pure and simple – constantly calls for some further artifice which must, in its turn, be given some sort of naturalizing justification. So, as Derrida points out, language and representation are particularly problematic in this current of thought. The word either adds nothing, and so is a pointless distraction, or it threatens to usurp the thing represented.

> As a general rule never substitute the symbol for the thing signified, unless it is impossible to show the thing itself; for the child's attention is so taken up with the symbol that he will forget what it signifies.[14]

Becoming a thing in itself, a fetish, the word risks leading us away from life, from nature. Rousseau's pedagogy constantly warns us that the child must learn by seeing and doing, and not by reading. Reading, on the other hand, has a vexatious habit of reasserting itself. So, for instance, in the *Lettres sur la botanique* he counsels the tutor to avoid the mere naming of plants. The child must learn first to *see*, and names offered too readily will give a false sense of knowledge that can only get in the way of a true apprehension of Nature. For this very reason, however, the tutor will have to learn the names of *parts* of plants so as to be able to direct the child's gaze, to encourage it to see the plant for what it is, to pick out the details that make the whole. Only then, when the object itself has been grasped, will she proceed to name. Rousseau is very insistent that the tutor should not read books, and seems to exclude his own course of letters from that category. At the same time, he occasionally ends a letter with an apology for suffocating the tutor with prose, and an invitation to draw breath. There is, then, some equivocation over the status of the letters as text. The overall impression is that reading, in measured doses, may be a necessary evil – the eventual aim is to breathe freely in the fresh air, in the unmediated pursuit of nature, and reading is only a minimal preparative which will eventually be subsumed in practice.[15]

Derrida suggests that the pedagogical setting of this sort of dilemma, and so also the presence of the figure of the child, is by no means incidental. The child's helplessness at birth, its need of guidance is, in Rousseau's thought, 'the first manifestation of the deficiency which, in Nature, calls for substitution [*suppléance*]'.[16] Indeed, 'without childhood, no supplement would ever appear in Nature'.[17] So the child, as yet unpolluted by the evils of Society, is at once the very type of Nature and the thing that reveals its insufficiency. Education, then, must be described 'as a system of substitution [*suppléance*] destined to reconstitute Nature's edifice in the most natural way.'[18] The child-tutor-nature triangle serves as a paradigm of all communication of knowledge, or at least as a critical instance. For the child is the subject who categorically – rather than merely incidentally or partially – is supposed not to know. In Rousseau's terms, the tutor should as far as possible avoid merely supplying words, and strive to put the child in a situation where s/he will experience, apprehend, work out things for him/herself, from nature as it were. So the role of writing is to be minimized, or at least subordinate to experience. By the same stroke, the tutor ceases to be a communicator, and becomes a facilitator. Taken together, the elision of writing and of the tutor's pedagogical authority are two sides of the same desire to cut Society out of the picture, to interrupt its steady reproduction of itself, so allowing Nature to elaborate itself out of the nature of the child.

It is commonplace to see Rousseau's pedagogical writing as one strand in the broader weave of his social/political thought. This might suggest nothing more than that a certain method of teaching is produced in response to some already worked-out thesis of society; a local technique designed to deal with one aspect of the problem of society. One could, however, go further to claim that education, in the Rousseau tradition, is the central thesis of society; that there is a sense in which, for this tradition, education *is* society. Educational thought in what is usually known as the progressive or child-centred tradition – including the likes of Pestalozzi and Froebel – tends to set up its own spontaneously educative community against a prevailing decadence or insufficiency of Society. The writing need not be explicitly or self-consciously political: the emphasis on learning a whole way of living, of living as learning, posits a future life of altered relations in society, and a present institution (not necessarily the school) that already embodies them. At the limit of this tendency, education becomes the stake in a bid to pre-empt all other sciences or theories of society, or indeed to replace society itself.

To take a relatively modern and lucid example, John Dewey's *Democracy and Education* begins by imagining back to a time when life and learning were co-extensive, when one lived and learned by practising one's craft in a close community.[19] Dewey argues that in Modernity, with the progressive expansion and specialization of knowledge, the demise of this community was inevitable. As the social group becomes more complex, and 'playful imitation is less and less adequate',[20] the content of social life has increasingly to be formulated, taught as a separate subject, in a separate institution. As in Rousseau, writing marks an epoch in this process.

> The invention of writing and of printing gives the operation an immense impetus. Finally the bonds which connect the subject matter of school study with the habits and ideals of the social group are disguised and covered up.[21]

After this divorce, neither life nor learning is ever quite the same again. As the accumulated knowledge of a society is increasingly *written*, and necessarily removed from everyday transmission through speech and practice, so it loses its *vitality*. Formal instruction 'easily becomes remote and dead – abstract and bookish'.[22] Though the latter two adjectives are to some degree qualified as the 'ordinary words of depreciation', Dewey's exposition here is enmeshed in the structural opposition of writing to experience, death to life. Knowledge 'stored in symbols' is at a remove from 'familiar acts and objects', and so 'relatively technical and superficial', lacking the 'depth of meaning' that comes from contact with daily interests. It 'exists in a world by itself, unassimilated to ordinary customs of thought and expression', it is 'isolated' from life-experience, and so on.[23] The litany hammers home Rousseau's motif of writing as a flattening, alienating force that draws knowledge into a dead zone, apart from life and speech. Here lies the danger of the 'ordinary notion of education' as 'the conveying of learning through verbal signs: the acquisition of literacy'.[24] Writing risks becoming an end in itself, the final resting place of dead information, rather than a convenient vehicle. By way of contrast, any shared, practical pursuit is '*at least* personal and vital'.[25] For Dewey, then, activity-based learning would always have as a bare minimum the virtue of remaining within the current of life, of offering a semblance of the old way where one learned on the job.

This, at any rate, is one moment in the argument. Unfortunately, with the loss of community, it is not as simple as that. For in any social group, 'there are many relations that are not yet social'; the simple fact of being drawn into the same space, of associating, is seemingly *not* enough; relations rooted in power and utility alone may remain machine-like.[26] Here, in addition to the complexity of society, 'industrial life' is responsible.[27] In the post-organic society, it is as if life itself has become written. That is to say, the everyday interaction that educated spontaneously and healthily in the old days, may not even be 'personal and vital', once infected by the deadness and the remoteness elsewhere symbolically associated with writing. We reach the perverse position where life as it is lived – which at another moment in the argument must nevertheless be presented as the ideal educative force – may well be positively harmful.

Dewey nevertheless remains adamant that we should not try to 'educate apart from the environment'. This, he suggests, is Rousseau's big mistake when he removes Emile from his family and whisks him off to rural Montmorency. Perversely then, even this reintroduction to Nature could be seen as artificial. Implicitly 'the environment' must be taken to mean the world the child will continue to inhabit, such as it is. If we separate the child from these surroundings, what hope can there be of community? Rather, Dewey proposes, we are 'to provide an environment in which native powers will be put to better uses'.[28] So Dewey attempts to mark out his distance from Rousseau, but in so doing comes up against the limits of his discourse, by choosing with unerring accuracy to differ on precisely the point which cannot be escaped without giving up this particular game altogether. Granted, Dewey has in mind a complementary space *within* current society, whereas Rousseau suggests a wholesale substitution. In either case, however, there is a broad agreement that the naturally-occurring (if you will) environment is deficient, and that a corrective, artificial (yet more natural) version must be supplied. In effect, Dewey does not escape the toils of supplementarity. In response to a malaise seen to spring from the separation of learning from living, he can do no other than offer a separate space for learning. His solution is, nevertheless, a characteristically modern one. For in this century, in the age of democracy and universal suffrage, it is society as a whole that must be educated. The impossibility of admitting everyone into some ideal retreat has never been more apparent. Yet, the challenge remains – a supplementary space must be found in education.

This leads me to what is arguably one of the strongest modern expressions of this motif of disrupted community. Literary studies might, at first glance, seem an unlikely destination for a current of thought which holds that writing threatens to sequester experience. Yet, it is arguably in this field that this discourse has, in this century, in Britain at least, found its surest footing. The narrative of lost community is, indeed, central to F. R. Leavis's project for literary education, and the argument follows lines similar to those taken by Dewey. Where, once, the citizen could be left 'to be formed unconsciously by his environment',[29] modern society is so diseased that education must now work '*against* the environment'.[30] For in place of life, we have what Leavis calls 'substitute-living'. Rather than plugging into each other's lives, we are hooked on newspapers (along with the other media of the culture of mass communication) which are 'designed to dissipate the attention',[31] rather than to spark off fresh energy and intercourse. Leavis faces a problem similar to that faced by Dewey – how to present an artificial substitute for life, when substitution is the problem in the first place, and life is what is ultimately required. In this version, literature will perform the equivocal role of pseudo-environment. Leavis, then, first of all locates the deadening effects of writing firmly in the mass market, in language that can be seen as debased and formulaic, written in bad faith. He could quite easily stop here and relegate all the ill effects of writing to an area of print defined as generically bad and leave literature's excellence to be understood. Interestingly, however, he does not do so. For he himself recognizes that literary education is itself 'to a great extent a *substitute*. What we have lost is the organic community with the living culture it embodied.'[32] Once this supplementary status has been admitted, it remains to be explained how *any* written word can supply the role of community.

In line with the organic tradition, Leavis does not accept without reservation that going to school offers a better education than the unlettered mastery of a craft;[33] what must be learned, by whatever means, is 'the art of living'.[34] On what terms, then, does literature enhance, rather than counter, living? Firstly, we have to see literature as something that has a life outside the school. The living community is that in which 'speech is still an art',[35] and if literature is to be truly alive, it must be part of such a community. Then, rather than dusty arcana, a study apart from life, it is a work of 'collaborative creation',[36] part of an unending conversation. Dickens was perhaps one of the last writers who could count on a public for whom 'speech was still a popular art, belonging to a living culture';[37] his works plugged into this, and so breathed.[38]

It is speech, then, that must animate writing, but today's speech is in a sort of zombie state, a death-in-life – it is only a 'quasiliving language'.[39] Leavis must then argue that literature, in some way, retains the traces of bygone speech, marks of the community that brought it to life, which can themselves be reanimated. It is the unquestioned bedrock of Leavis's thought that literature is the repository, the thesaurus of the riches of the language, 'where its finest and subtlest use is preserved'.[40] Yet, for all that, he does not proceed to declare it simply and unproblematically alive. Rather, it exists in a sort of limbo, 'waiting to be proved living'.[41] Literature offers a resource, a potential for speech and life. That is to say, something is still needed to bring it to life – for even literature could just remain another load of words, dead on the page. Vexingly, this something turns out to be the very tradition, the very community that, we are told, we have lost: 'But if words are our chief link with the past they depend for their life, vigour and potency on being used in association with such traditions as the wheelwright's.'[42] So we come full circle. We need literary education because this tradition/community is dead and gone; yet literature needs that tradition/community if it is to live. The question remains – how *can* we associate with these traditions? In what form are they to be re-presented? Mere words are not enough, and the thing itself is unavailable, so what does this leave? Leavis rather leaves the point hanging, but his constant implication is that some words, at the point of writing, were closer to the world they described, to the language of that world, and retain *in potentia* the glamour of this association. The world depicted in novels valued by Leavis needn't necessarily be rural and artisanal in character. Nonetheless, the author to whom Leavis has most frequent recourse in the more pointedly organicist passages of his writing is D. H. Lawrence, whose novels describe and putatively embody the desired community, or at least its threatened remnants. Implicitly, the direct experience of the author, his/her proximity to Nature, matters. Doubtless any such novel is a representation of a life that is broadly defunct, but at least it is not the representation of a representation.

Leavis himself, it has to be said, is a good deal less facile than many of his contemporaries in this matter. At the back of all this, however, there lies a version of a favourite organicist motif: great writers are close to the soil, to the speech of their forefathers, to the life of a community. In the late nineteenth and early twentieth century, there is a widespread tendency whereby literature is, so to speak, 'greened', assimilated to the natural world. So, for example, we may read that Sir Walter Scott's 'genius is as fresh, and spontaneous, and inexhaustible, as the spring which draws its waters from the depths of the earth'[43] and his writing is 'like the pure air of the mountain [. . .] like the great gifts of nature herself, which seem to come of themselves and to have no ulterior motive'.[44] Literature as a whole is seen as a river meandering through the English landscape, or as a garden. In short, a repertoire of rhetorical turns is elaborated that grants literature honorary vegetable status. Where the rural theme is often prominent in a given text, this sort of rhetoric might at least be granted an illusory self-evidence. To extend similar privileges to texts for which the old life and the countryside are of supreme inconsequence, on the other hand, presents criticism with a challenge which, indeed, it rarely meets head on.

One response might be to demand that all future literature conform to some sort of organic model. According to John Buchan, writing in 1931

– seemingly in response to the verbal experimentation of Modernism – the novel only succeeds 'in so far as it is a development of and akin to the folk and fairy tale'.[45] For these belong to the 'common stock of humanity and are closer to mankind than any written word.'[46] Once upon a time, the storytellers' aim was 'to say clearly what they had to say and to have done with it'; today's literary men, on the other hand, would regard this 'as a sort of black-legging'.[47] In effect, Buchan is saying, we have gone over to the side of words for their own sake; writing has grown too big for its boots and forgotten that its job is to tell stories. The writing that Buchan admires is close to the source, to 'the soil and the traditions of the soil',[48] to a society and realities that exist before and apart from writing. In short, writing must constantly remember that its roots lie outside writing and cultivate an appropriate modesty and simplicity. Hence the folk tale, the narrative harvest of agrarian communities, is to be our guide. The writers offered as models are those, like Hardy, who write both from and about such communities. In short, Buchan synthesizes the various elements of organicism to provide an alternative heritage – and so an alternative future – for the novel. In the present day, I would suggest, it is the canon of children's literature that has claimed this sort of alternative folk heritage as its very own. Though the twin themes of the oral and the soil are often very closely bound up with one another, I propose to examine them separately, starting with the oral.

The influential author and critic John Rowe Townsend argues that the adult novel has gone astray; it has become over-sophisticated and lost its vitality.

> But children's literature has wild blood in it: its ancestry lies partly in the long ages of storytelling which preceded the novel. Myth, legend, fairy-tale are alive in their own right, endlessly reprinted, endlessly fertile in their influence.[49]

Like Buchan, Townsend leans heavily on genetic metaphor (stock, blood, kin, ancestry) without pausing to explain how it works; for it is by no means evident in what sense any text can pass on its blood to another. Certainly, something more than, or indeed quite other than, formal imitation of the fairy-tale is implied; children's literature has, if you like, kept the soul of the old community, and not just the body of its story-forms. The communal, oral 'storytelling' is 'alive', and can pass on its vitality ('fertile'), even *in print*. Like Buchan, Townsend wants to credit his chosen literature with a blood-line that reaches back unbroken to a more ancient, more wholesome time, marking it out from the overbred norm of the modern novel. In making this idea stick, however, the critic of children's literature has at his disposal an additional resource, one that Buchan lacks – quite simply, the child and its proximity to nature and the ancient innocence of mankind.

George Boas[50] locates the child's importance for modern primitivism in the law of recapitulation, the idea that the development of the human individual mirrors the historical development of mankind, from primitive to civilized.[51] The child, then, can be seen as a sort of constantly reproduced primitive, ready-made material for investigation into, and reproduction of, all that is most original and fundamental in man. For primitivists, civilization is 'but an accumulation of superfluities';[52] what they seek in man's origins are clues to a simpler, truer life. In the present century, Boas argues, the child has become, thanks to the (spurious) law of recapitulation, the supreme focus for this sort of investigation. Where other models, such as the noble savage, the canny swain, and even woman, have lost ground, the child has stepped into the breach, subsuming them all.

I would suggest that the passage quoted from Townsend above ultimately rests on this idea. The 'law' is not positively stated or even acknowledged, and Townsend would doubtless be surprised to hear himself referred to as a 'primitivist'. In effect, the assumption that the primitive is the property of the child *by right* is second nature in much current child-discourse. It can be confidently understood, it can be counted on – for is it not evident that the new-born child stands untainted before civilization, and will only gradually be absorbed into its machinery? The child effectively provides the possibility of continued life to an oral tradition: the passage of voice into print is not so hard to conceive if one once accepts that children can '*hear* a story [. . .]; an oral and a print culture are not so separate in their world'.[53] Though the ideas of a separate world, a state before written knowledge and so on are ultimately derived from anthropology, no explicit reference to primitive peoples or far-off places need be made. The daily fact of the birth of fresh children, subjects not yet enmeshed in society and its superfluities, makes possible the constant, naturally-occurring going-back-to-source demanded by someone like Buchan.

So writing for children easily becomes the pretext for recovery of a lost simplicity in writing. The texts that will facilitate this will be shorn of the excess and clutter associated with adult civilization; they will speak to the child with a voice that is simple and direct. Thus praise of simple language in childist criticism strenuously rejects any idea that this reflects a shortcoming on the part of the child – rather, it is an acknowledgement of a moral superiority. The following comes from Candia McWilliam's review of Alison Lurie's *Don't Tell the Grown Ups*.

> The urbane and reserved style – no side-orders of nutty theories, no cherries on the metaphors – is in keeping with the subject of children and what they read, a tone often possessed by those who are genuinely good with children, bespeaking fairness of mind, unembarrassed intimacy and the exact apprehension of what children are [. . .].[54]

I choose this example in particular, firstly because it does not deal with a book *for* children. Seemingly, even a critical text that deals with children's books, but which surely cannot expect a large child-readership, should nevertheless be written in a style 'in keeping with the subject of children'. What is more, this 'style' turns out to be a mode of address, a voice, modelled on an imagined one-to-one encounter between writer and reader. This moment of perfect intimacy, usually denied to reading, has no explicitly anthropological inflection. The child is not likened to, say, savages or peasants, but the idea of an honesty that precedes civilization is implicit. What looks at first like a purely formal, practical comment of a properly literary kind, on literature, arguably rests on an informal anthropology. In effect, the figure of the child reader is used to scorn adult pretension and linguistic over-elaboration from a position of relative purity. As the noble savage could once be held up as the walking critique of civilized man, so the simplicity and intimacy appropriate to the child acts as a lesson for all of us, as a salutary call back to nature, to something simpler and more honest.

Using this theme, with the added support of the oral tradition, childist criticism converts a potential weakness – the childishness of its subject – into a strength. In a sort of inverted rank-pulling, the very youth of the child makes it more ancient, more primordial than anything adult. This can be seen in some detail in a passage of criticism by Margaret Meek.[55] Meek gently chides adult criticism for basing narratology on the novelistic great tradition.[56] It is Garner's *Quartet* that is drafted in to give the lesson. In these texts, 'as lucid as the dawn' – and yet nuanced, layered like an onion – which derive from the 'primary oral tradition', Garner 'shows that the secrets of narrative, in all cultures and subcultures, lie with children making sense of their world'.[57] In this instance, the anthropological theme is discreet, casual, but apparent. The child takes us back to the beginning of beginnings, to a primordial moment where meaning is just about to be made. Indeed, Meek is not shy of the primitivist logic that underpins her argument. So, she tells us, children 'inherit the verbal memory of their *tribe* in a way that contact with more complex narrations will never wholly erase'.[58] The word 'tribe' here is something more than mere metaphor. The child offers up the promise of an ineradicable core; the good, simple, true voice, that will resist the clutter of society, neutralize its more harmful effects. To this way of thinking, the historical beginnings of mankind, and the developmental beginnings of the individual are indeed confounded, under the general rubric of the primary. Why, Meek asks, do we treat children's stories as merely simpler versions of adult literature, when in fact they are the groundwork for them, their '*primary* kinds and structures'?[59] From being dependent or secondary, children's literature is thus granted a novel priority.

The recovery of this primary voice nevertheless calls for a supplement: it will only be effected through children who are properly read to, and this entails the adult production of suitable reading matter. Meek's basic solution to this problem is dominant in recent criticism. Adult writers are seen as getting progressively closer to the authentic, pre-literate voice of childhood, and criticism is constantly looking forward to a time when we will have 'a whole poetics of literature that no one disputes is undoubtedly children's'.[60] So while it looks forward to literacy, children's literature also becomes a sort of bridge *back* to pre-linguistic thought and feeling. Child-readers are on the cusp: they are '*new* readers' whose expectations are based 'not on literary experience'.[61] There is a notional first encounter with story where we can see how the 'surface' of text is 'linked to the *natural* narratives of childhood culture', where we can examine the 'links between the *deep* feelings of childhood and their encoding in texts'.[62] This moment of interface between our deep selves and the world of surfaces lasts as long as the child's relationship with language is oral. It offers a chance of reconnection, of community, but only if we look to 'the voice of the narrator' rather than 'the cult of the author'.[63] So it is down to writers to find the voice that will make the reader 'both the teller and the told',[64] allowing safe passage for the authenticity of the oral into writing. It is as if, thanks to the child, all the classic oppositions – text/world, author/reader, nature/society – could be abolished. Children's literature appears in this light as a sort of on-going experiment, a process of checking the child's response, refining the product based on our findings and so on. So, it is implied, we can get closer and closer to the truth, and produce a supplement that is truly nature-identical.

To set this process rolling, the adult writer already has an imaginary foothold in the child's psyche. For, although we are now adults, we have all been children, and with the will and an appropriate attitude, we may retain our own child. Writers tracing the origins of their own art will thus look for them in the origin of their selves, and critics will take up the relay. So we hear of an author who, as a child, was privileged to listen to one of the last of the travelling storytellers: 'The old woman's technique, her lilting vernacular, her easy relations with her listeners, her compelling formulas, all sank into the child's mind and returned to her when she began to write herself.'[65] This fortunate writer has been exposed to nothing less than the oral tradition itself, in the raw; but it is also important to know that this happened to her as a child. It is the child's receptivity, its capacity to absorb voice, before literacy has had the chance to mould once and for all the patterns of storying, that is supposed to give later writing something of the quality of speech. Looking back over her own childhood writing, another author finds two distinct strains. The origin of the first lies in her childhood reading – from this source come derivative tales. The second strain, however, she can trace to no textual source. Its origin is somehow deeper, more mysterious, lost in a barely-remembered world – yet, at the same time, this origin can be confidently declared 'oral'. This, 'the most primary and spontaneous form of language that we have at our disposal',[66] produces (allegedly) more 'subversive' tales, and it is from the memory of these that the adult author claims to write an authentic children's literature. Only very rarely is any sustained attempt made to explain just what this oral writing might consist of, formally.[67] For that matter, what is to be gained by subtilizing what is, necessarily, a myth of origin? Generally, retrospection into one's own childhood is felt to suffice to claim access to a universal childhood and its voice, clean, unsullied and authentic.

Closeness to the soil is a separate, but closely related theme. It too involves travelling back to a moment of greater purity and connection with nature, from which other authentic voices speak. Unspoiled nature, as well as acting as an analogy for the child's putatively pre-social state, also represents the youth of the planet, the landscape in which the most ancient peoples would have lived. The association of child with nature in some such way is, of course, an old and ingrained one. In the Rousseau tradition, it is commonplace to recommend that the child read the 'book of nature'. It has been of central importance to modern children's literature to convince us that, attentively read, this natural text can be faithfully transliterated.

Modern criticism of children's literature effectively dates from the publication of F. J. Harvey Darton's *Children's Books in England* in 1932. Darton is very much a critic of the organicist epoch, recommending to the child nature, and a writing born of nature, one that shares in nature's enduring presence. For him, true childwriting comes from writers who have 'had a young mind and seen English country sights'.[68] When writing for children leaves behind arid scholasticism – 'Let us leave the schoolroom', says Darton – it steps directly into the open fields.[69] The land, in effect, is the favoured primer of children's literature – the text from which one ought first to learn.

Ideally, reading and rambling are interlocking parts of a single activity. Returning to a place is 'like reading an old book which is still alive'; one enters into 'a dialogue with the past that heighten[s] one's sense of the present'; and it is this continuous, reciprocal acquaintance with the English countryside which, according to his most recent editor, Brian Alderson, particularly qualifies Darton for the job.[70] So even where Darton's undoubtedly vast textual scholarship is being discussed, the reading-as-rambling ethic prevails, and we see him 'pioneering his way through many a bibliographical thicket'.[71] In short, text produced in collusion with the land appears to be, at least in some instances, *symbolically identical* with the land itself – the two practices of reading and observing nature can share and exchange metaphors. Writing for children comes of age when this identity is attained. So Darton says of Stevenson's *A Child's Garden of Verses*, 'It *is* a garden, full of natural flowers growing fom wind-borne seeds'.[72] In an instant, the arbitrariness of metaphor is abolished. It is as if nature, for those attentive enough to hear its voice, had indeed passed into writing. It is as if this were no metaphor at all, but a literal truth.

Not all writing for children aspires to the condition of the garden, but there is a dominant tendency that does. Those texts of the last fifty years held to possess the highest literary value will tend to have a rural setting. Even stories ostensibly set in the city will take flight into a garden, a park, a secondary world, the past. This is not thought of as a mere matter of scene-setting or decorative nature-writing. The sense of place is credited with grounding the text, and the Nature with which it is infused is deeply woven into the text, transmitting a whole world of a piece.

> Rosemary Sutcliff's feeling for 'place' is strong and, as we read, we feel the misty rain of the Lake District, taste the salty tang of the wind over the marshes and see the wide expanse of the Downs.[73]

The element of actual landscape-description involved in proportion to the body of the text need not even be very great – the important point is that a whole place emerges out of every pore of the text. Indeed, if the wind and the rain are revealed to us, it is not necessarily because we have been instructed to see them in so many words. We are to believe in the authentic force of place because we believe the author's experience of Nature to be deep, direct and abiding. The revelation may occur *through* reading but the 'feeling' that guarantees it precedes writing, and could not be reduced to a matter of mere textual analysis.

Some description of natural things is doubtless indispensable to this idea of place, but the Nature evoked in writing has a value that goes beyond the merely picturesque, scenic or external, and involves its adherents in more than mere vicarious pleasure. Ruralist children's literature is ultimately gesturing towards 'the sense of order and continuity which is part of the countryside charm'.[74] The order in question is that of man's earliest and least disruptive relation to the natural world; this may include certain minimal technologies which are seen as quasi-natural in that they do not interrupt the original equilibrium. Continuity is the subsistence through time, be it only as an underlying residue, of this fundamental, primordial way of being. Modern children's literature's move to the country and communion with place is, then, doubly a journey into the past. The true country life already offers, in the present, an essentially unchanged remnant of the innocence of man's encounter with Nature, but in addition, in children's fiction, the past, the essence, of this encounter is eternally present in place. The child, with its affinity for the primitive and natural, has access to this past, and so to a spiritual community in time as well as in space.

This theme has been endlessly rehearsed in modern kiddie-lit. The child protagonist who 'instead of attending school [. . .] reads the landscape',[75] is a familiar figure, a truant from civilization who forgoes letters to receive, from Nature herself, an essential grounding in all that is most human. Such children 'see nature and human relations uncontaminated by received ideas, and speak a language that is both simple and original'.[76] More often than not, the journey into the past implicit in 'uncontaminated', 'simple' and 'original' will be dramatized as a quasi-archaeological quest. The child who declares, 'The history of the countryside is exposed in these layers of earth, if only I could read them. One day I will',[77] is advocating a sort of natural history, if you will, that is seen as an extension, or homologue, of the child's own nature. In the embrace of Nature proper, the child is able to empathize with the true spirit of the past, and realize that 'history in books is a lie' because it is 'printed on nice clean shiny new paper'.[78]

This narrative *works* for kiddie-lit operatives in reassuring them that their own texts are not 'a lie' in so far as it is not, for them, just a convenient or cute rendering of their chosen themes, but indeed deeply informs the image they give themselves as living, interpreting beings. When we are told that writing for kids 'draws heavily on a *feeling* for the primitive and fundamental things of life'[79] we are being asked to subscribe not just to the natural affinities of the child, but also to the existence of adult authors who are themselves prone to '*feeling* history through [their] nerves and seeking it through the soil'.[80] It is a commonplace of About-the-Author blurbs that writers for children live in cottages in whichever part of the countryside inspires their work. Like the heroine of any number of children's novels, a writer may even relocate to her native soil and, once installed, wait for the ancestral voices that will tell her what to write. Then, 'one truly feels the past is speaking to her'.[81] Another will protest that any resemblance her text bears to Virginia Woolf's *To the Lighthouse* is entirely the doing of St Ives.[82] Place, the past, and their voice come together to form a powerful imagined substitute for textuality. That is to say, they offer the possibility of imagining text rooted in something other than itself. Such texts are not just drawn from the life, they spring from it fully formed. Indeed, as a consequence, they are not written, but 'have grown';[83] the writer is 'found by'[84] the story, rather than vice versa; her task is primarily to find 'something alive, something that [will] grow'.[85]

Once more, it is Garner who has, in the *Quartet*, most fully realized the potentials of this narrative: for, according to Margaret Meek, he 'concentrates on time as place, especially the place where his family has lived over centuries. He loops his narrative time to include layers of mythology, traditional tales, legends'.[86] In the *Quartet*, successive generations of a family discover the traces – mason's marks, tools and places on which they have left their mark – of their antecedents, and experience a sense of continuity, belonging and fitness that a documentary genealogy could not provide. In a sense, when time is treated as place, history – written history, chronology – disappears. What is left in its place is the promise of an eternally present core humanity, the child. Time only exists to open a fissure between our double and ourselves, which sensitivity to place instantly heals over.

This last-cited essay by Margaret Meek, 'Speaking of Shifters', will also help to orient us in tracking a movement which has perhaps already been visible, though not avowed, in my exposition of these discourses. For

I have, in an important sense, suppressed time myself in offering no account of the evolution of the motifs in question. Of course Meek's language is in certain important respects quite remote from that of earlier, more effusive or even jingoistic paeans to the joys of the countryside. Granted, the counter-argument might proceed, a certain quasi-mystic rhetoric of nature may have lasted unembarrassed in children's literature criticism longer than in most other places. Now, however, we have attained a new theoretical sophistication, and left all that behind. In short, there is a general feeling that, with the advent of a new formal rigour and self-awareness, an older thematics of childhood has been overcome. And yet, it is strange to witness with what hallucinating precision the old themes re-emerge, like ghosts. So, in the present instance, Meek heralds the linguistic theory of 'shifters' as a new resource; yet, when these shifters have finished with Garner, they have produced nothing but the same peasant community that readings of the *Quartet* have always produced.

Indeed, as long as a formal or language-based approach does its business in collating classic modern texts diligently enough, certain themes will produce themselves, as if naturally. So, for instance, Murray Knowles and Kirsten Malinkjaer, in *Language and Control in Children's Literature*, chart incidence of words, constructions, collocations and so forth, to build up a picture of how texts structure and place the information they convey. A terminology is elaborated according to which, for instance, Carrie, heroine of Nina Bawden's *Carrie's War*, is a 'Senser': her point of view predominates through variants on the tag 'she thought/said'. Thus far, the method displays undivided obedience to itself. When it is applied to a passage in which Carrie describes her strange new acquaintances, it delivers a cargo of imagery. The image applied to each person is drawn up in a list – 'a red squirrel; a worm; claw-like, ringed fingers; a friendly, silly strong bear'. At this point, any method must now declare why this list can function as such. Knowles and Malinkjaer do so as follows: 'This is exactly the sort of language a perceptive and sensitive child might use to record her impressions of the people who have replaced her family and thus her familiar world.'[87]

This moment of bathos – where theoretical elaboration is succeeded by the tendentious reaffirmation of some pre-theoretical commonplace – is not uncommon in the more recent, reportedly theoretical, criticism. There is nothing in the method, or in any other for that matter, that could possibly legitimate this appeal to the real child. Indeed, quite the contrary, it is the – largely unacknowledged – postulate of the real child that underpins the method. In its presence, it goes without saying that this imagery is felt to be apt because it replaces a familiar world with one that is even more familiar – that of nature, the child's special property. Nor is it any surprise to find, a little further on in relation to another passage, that a certain 'parallelism of structure' setting universals like hot and cold against each other 'allows the reader to *hear* the paragraph to be read in the imagination'.[88] Similarly, in *The Narrator's Voice*, Barbara Wall's ultimate appeal is to a real, knowable child, which demands a certain voice that we could all be brought to recognize. Those who have 'the strong tradition of the anonymous oral teller [. . .] behind them'[89] have a head start; they are not plagued by the usual adult 'self-consciousness'.[90] First-person narration may even allow 'one child mind to speak to another'.[91] This most perfect of communities is the particular preserve of the child, and by extension might appear to be a discovery of children's literature. As I hope I have shown, while this figure of the child receives at present a privileged articulation in that literature and its criticism, it by no means originates there. The child – the real child – will, however, continue to produce its effects out of all manner of new methodologies for as long as these do not recognize its immanence in the adult claim to know how to write for children.

Notes

1 Jacques Derrida, *Of Grammatology*, trans. Gayatri Chakravorty Spivak (Baltimore & London: John Hopkins, 1976), p. 101.

2 Derrida, p. 144.

3 This is the first of the four novellas collected in Alan Garner, *The Stone Book Quartet* (London: HarperCollins, 1992). I will refer to the volume as a whole as the *Quartet*.

4 *Quartet*, p. 49.

5 *Quartet*, p. 51.

6 Jane Gardam, *The Hollow Land* (Harmondsworth: Penguin, 1983).

7 Frances Hodgson Burnett, *The Secret Garden* (Harmondsworth: Puffin, 1951).

8 Walter McVitty, 'Alan Garner', in Tracy Chevalier (ed.), *Twentieth-Century Children's Writers* (Chicago and London: St James Press, 1989), p. 377.

9 Margaret Meek, 'Symbolic Outlining: The Academic Study of Children's Literature', *Signal*, 53 (1987), pp. 97–113, p. 104.

10 John Rowe Townsend, *Written for Children: An Outline of English-Language Children's Literature*, 5th edn (London: Bodley Head, 1990), p. 259.

11 'I hate books; they only teach us to talk about things we know nothing about'; Jean-Jacques Rousseau, *Emile* trans. Barbara Foxley (London: Dent, 1911; repr. 1989), p. 147.

12 According to the 'Septième promenade', he was 'jeté dans la carrière littéraire par des impulsions étrangères': Jean-Jacques Rousseau, *Les Rêveries du promeneur solitaire* (Paris: Garnier Flammarion, 1964), p. 125.

13 'You are an author yourself, you will reply. Yes, for my sins; and my ill deeds, which I think I have fully expiated, are no reason why others should be like me. I do not write to excuse my faults, but to prevent my readers from copying me' (*Emile*, p. 160, n.1).

14 *Emile*, p. 133.

15 See 'Lettres sur la botanique', in *Œuvres Complètes*, IV (Paris: Gallimard, 1969). Jean Starobinski discusses with great lucidity Rousseau's use of botany as a system of self-identical signs, a sort of minimal mediation – see 'Friendship among the plants' in *Jean-Jacques Rousseau: Transparency and Obstruction* (Chicago and London: University of Chicago Press, 1988), pp. 234–8.

16 Derrida, p. 146.
17 Derrida, p. 147.
18 Derrida, p. 145.
19 John Dewey, *Democracy and Education: An Introduction to the Philosophy of Education* (New York: Macmillan, 1916).
20 Dewey, p. 9.
21 Dewey, p. 213.
22 Dewey, p. 9.
23 Dewey, p. 10.
24 Dewey, p. 10.
25 Dewey, p. 9; emphasis mine.
26 Dewey, p. 6.
27 Dewey, p. 8.
28 Dewey, p. 138.
29 F. R. Leavis and Denys Thompson, *Culture and the Environment; the Training of Critical Awareness* (London: Chatto & Windus, 1934), p. 5.
30 *Culture*, p. 106.
31 *Culture*, p. 102.
32 *Culture*, p. 1; emphasis mine.
33 *Culture*, pp. 104–5.
34 *Culture*, p. 107.
35 *Culture*, p. 2.
36 F. R. Leavis, *The Living Principle: 'English' as a Discipline of Thought* (London: Chatto & Windus, 1975), passim.
37 *Living Principle*, p. 52.
38 Cf. Leavis's discussion of Bunyan and Blake in 'Literature and Society', in *The Common Pursuit* (London: Hogarth Press, 1984), pp. 182–94.
39 *Living Principle*, p. 52.
40 *Culture*, p. 82.
41 *Living Principle*, p. 52.
42 *Culture*, p. 81.
43 Sir Henry Jones, *Essays on Literature and Education*, ed. H. J. W. Hetherington (London: Hodder & Stoughton, 1924), p. 28.
44 Jones, pp. 43–4.
45 John Buchan, *The Novel and the Fairy Tale*, English Association Pamphlet no. 79, July 1931 (London: Oxford University Press, 1931), p. 7.
46 Buchan, p. 16.
47 Buchan, p. 3.
48 Buchan, p. 9.
49 John Rowe Townsend, *A Sense of Story* (London: Longman, 1971), p. 12.
50 George Boas, *The Cult of Childhood* (London: Warburg Institute, University of London, 1966).
51 The idea finds its classic form in the biogenetic law of Ernst Haeckel, that ontogeny recapitulates phylogeny. For an informative account of the late-nineteenth-century scientific context for this and related ideas, see Laura Otis, *Organic Memory: History and the Body in the Late Nineteenth and Early Twentieth Centuries* (Lincoln and London: University of Nebraska Press, 1994).
52 Boas, p. 8.
53 Fred Inglis, *The Promise of Happiness: Value and Meaning in Children's Fiction* (Cambridge: Cambridge University Press, 1981), p. 56; emphasis mine.
54 Candia McWilliam, 'Trust Hansel and Gretel more than Janet and John', *Independent on Sunday Review*, 27 May 1990, p. 17.

55 Margaret Meek, 'What Counts as Evidence in Theories of Children's Literature?', *Theory into Practice*, vol. 21, no. 4 (Autumn 1982), pp. 284–92; repr. in Peter Hunt (ed.), *Children's Literature: The Development of Criticism* (London: Routledge, 1990), pp. 166–82.
56 'Evidence', pp. 173–4.
57 'Evidence', p. 174.
58 'Evidence', p. 174; emphasis mine.
59 'Evidence', p. 176; emphasis mine.
60 'Evidence', p. 174.
61 'Evidence', p. 176.
62 'Evidence', p. 179; emphasis mine.
63 'Evidence', p. 177.
64 'Evidence', p. 177.
65 Margery Fisher, *Intent upon Reading: A Critical Appraisal of Modern Fiction for Children* (Leicester: Brockhampton Press, 1961), pp. 14–15.
66 Margaret Mahy, 'Joining the Network', *Signal*, 54 (1987), pp. 151–69, p. 155.
67 Cf. Peter Hunt, *Criticism, Theory, and Children's Literature* (Oxford: Basil Blackwell, 1991), pp. 90–6.
68 F. J. Harvey Darton, *Children's Books in England: Five Centuries of Social Life*, 3rd edn, rev. by Brian Alderson (Cambridge: Cambridge University Press, 1982), p. 11.
69 Darton, p. 11.
70 Darton, p. xi.
71 Darton, p. xiii.
72 Darton, p. 314; his emphasis.
73 Eileen Colwell, 'Rosemary Sutcliff – Lantern Bearer', in Elinor Whitney Field (ed.), *Horn Book Reflections* (Boston: The Horn Book, 1969), pp. 122–7 (p. 126).
74 Patricia Craig, *Times Literary Supplement* (1981), p. 1065.
75 Alison Lurie, 'William Mayne', in Gillian Avery and Julia Briggs (eds), *Children and their Books* (Oxford: Clarendon Press, 1990), pp. 369–79 (p. 374).
76 Lurie, p. 371.
77 Scott, *The Haunted Sand* (London: Walker, 1991), p. 54.
78 Robert Westall, *The Watch House* (Harmondsworth: Puffin, 1980), p. 133.
79 Rosemary Sutcliff, 'History is People', in Virginia Haviland (ed.), *Children and Literature: Views and Reviews* (London: Bodley Head, 1974), pp. 306–12, p. 311.
80 Marcus Crouch, *Treasure Seekers and Borrowers: Children's Books in Britain 1900–1960* (London: Library Association, 1962), p. 125.
81 Elaine Moss, 'Barbara Willard: "The Springs of Mantlemass"', in *Part of the Pattern: A Personal Journey Through the World of Children's Books, 1960–1985* (London: Bodley Head, 1986), pp. 64–9. Willard's ancestor was a blacksmith, a practitioner of one of those primitive technologies which, like Garner's stonemasonry, are seen as quasi-natural.
82 Jill Paton Walsh, *Goldengrove* (London: Bodley Head, 1985).
83 Jane Curry, 'On the Elvish Craft', in Nancy Chambers (ed.), *The Signal Approach to Children's Books* (Harmondsworth: Kestrel, 1980), p. 87.
84 Sutcliff, p. 312.
85 Cynthia Harnett, 'From the Ground Upwards', in *Horn Book Reflections*, pp. 97–101, p. 98.
86 Margaret Meek, 'Speaking of Shifters', *Signal*, 45 (1984), pp. 152–67, p. 160.
87 Murray Knowles and Kirsten Malinkjaer, *Language and Control in Children's Literature* (London and New York: Routledge, 1996), p. 118.
88 Knowles and Malinkjaer, p. 119; emphasis mine.

89 Barbara Wall, *The Narrator's Voice: The Dilemma of Children's Fiction* (London: Macmillan, 1991), p. 49. The voice motif, with its air of technical sophistication, seems to be gaining ground. See e.g. Jill Paton Walsh, 'The Masks of the Narrator', in Morag Styles *et al.* (eds), *Voices Off: Texts, Contexts and Readers* (London and New York: Cassell, 1996), pp. 281–90.
90 Wall, pp. 48–9.
91 Wall, p. 68.

Part 11

IDEOLOGY, RACE AND POLITICS

62

IDEOLOGY AND THE CHILDREN'S BOOK

Peter Hollindale

Source: *Signal* 55 (January 1988): 3–22.

> IDEOLOGY 4. A systematic scheme of ideas, usu. relating to politics or society, or to the conduct of a class or group, and regarded as justifying actions, esp. one that is held implicitly or adopted as a whole and maintained regardless of the course of events.
>
> –*Oxford English Dictionary*

I will start with an assortment of disconnected statements.

It is a good thing for children to read fiction.

Children's own tastes are important.

Some novels for children are better than others.

It is a good thing to help children to enjoy better books than they did before.

A good children's book is not necessarily more difficult or less enjoyable than a bad children's book.

Children are individuals, and have different tastes.

Children of different ages tend to like different sorts of books.

Children of different ethnic and social backgrounds may differ in their tastes and needs.

Some books written for children are liked by adults.

Some books written for adults are liked by children.

Adults and children may like (or dislike) the same book for different reasons.

Children are influenced by what they read.

Adults are influenced by what they read.

A novel written for children may be a good novel even if children in general do not enjoy it.

A novel written for children may be a bad novel even if children in general do enjoy it.

Every story is potentially influential for all its readers.

A novel may be influential in ways that its author did not anticipate or intend.

All novels embody a set of values, whether intentionally or not.

A book may be well written yet embody values that in a particular society are widely deplored.

A book may be badly written yet embody values that in a particular society are widely approved.

A book may be undesirable for children because of the values it embodies.

The same book may mean different things to different children.

It is sensible to pay attention to children's judgement of books, whether or not most adults share them.

It is sensible to pay attention to adults' judgements of children's books, whether or not most children share them.

Some of these statements are clearly paired or linked, but they can be read separately in isolation. All of them seem to me to be truisms. It would surprise me if any serious commentator on children's reading were to quarrel seriously with any of them. He or she might wish to qualify them, to respond as to Dr F. R. Leavis's famous 'This is so, isn't it?' with his permitted answer, 'Yes, but . . .'. Even so, I would expect a very wide consensus.

However, if this series of statements is brought to bear on the controversy in recent years between so-called book people and so-called child people, it will be found I think that most of them drift naturally towards either one side or the other. In particular, there is likely to be a somewhat one-sided emphasis on remarks about adult judgements and their importance (book people); about children's judgements and their importance (child people); about differences of literary merit (book people) and about the influence on readers of a book's social and political values (child people).

If these two little exercises do indeed produce the results that I expect them to, much of the division between literary and social priorities which has arisen over the last fifteen years or so may come to seem exaggerated and sterile. We have differences of emphasis disguised as differences of principle. (This may have happened because the extremes of each alternative reflect a much larger public controversy about the chief purpose of education. People slip without realizing it from talking about children's books to talking about educational philosophy.) One result is particularly odd. By my own idiosyncratic but convinced reckoning, the statements which are left over, which seem not to bend towards the critical priorities of either side, are those which concern the individuality of children, and differences of taste or need between children and adults or between one child or group of children and another. It is a curious fact that these, the most obvious truisms of all, are also the most contentious statements. They are contentious because on the one hand they cast doubt on the supremacy of adult literary judgement, and on the other they suggest that we cannot generalize about children's interests.

It is very easy and tempting to simplify a debate until its nature becomes conveniently binary, and matters which are not associated by any kind of logical necessity, or even loosely connected, become coalesced in the same ideological system. Something of this sort has happened in the schism between child people and book people. In the evolution of debate, the child people have become associated not only with a prime concern with the child reader rather than the literary artefact but with the propagation through children's books of a 'progressive' ideology expressed through social values. The book people, on the other hand, have become linked with a broadly conservative and 'reactionary' ideological position. The result is a crude but damaging conjunction of attitudes on each side, not as it necessarily is but as it is perceived by the other. A concern for the literary quality of children's books as works of imagination has become linked in a caricatured manifesto with indifference to the child reader and with tolerance or approval of obsolete, or traditional, or 'reactionary' political values. A concern with the child reader has become linked with indifference to high standards of literary achievement and with populist ardour on behalf of the three political missions which are seen as most urgent in contemporary society: anti-racism, anti-sexism, and anti-classism.

If this is the general divide between book people and child people amongst the critics, a matching divide is said to exist between writers. The book people amongst authors – those who are said by hostile commentators to have produced the prize-winning, dust-collecting, adult-praised, child-neglected masterpieces of the illusory 'golden age' – are those who write 'to please themselves', or 'for the child I once was', or, in C. S. Lewis's famous remark, 'because a children's story is the best art-form for something you have to say.'[1] The child people amongst authors, on the other hand, would accept Robert Leeson's analogy between the modern author and the oral storyteller of days before the printed book:

> . . . is the public, the consumer, obliged to accept such a take-it-or-leave-it attitude, being grateful if the artistic arrows shot in the air find their target? What happened in the old story-telling days? If the audience did not appreciate the genius of the storyteller, did that individual stalk off, supperless, into the night? Actual experience of story-telling suggests something different. You match story to audience, as far as you can.[2]

The trouble with this packaging of attitudes is that it over-simplifies, trivializes and restricts the boundaries of debate. Admittedly most writers on both sides of the notional divide have at times unwisely offered hostages to fortune. One may take for instance Fred Inglis's remark:

> Irrespective of what the child makes of an experience, the adult wants to judge it for himself, and so doing means judging it for *it*self. This judgement comes first, and it is at least logically separable from doing the reckoning for children. *Tom's Midnight Garden* and *Puck of Pook's Hill* are wonderful books, whether or not your child can make head or tail of them.[3]

This carefully formulated and entirely sensible statement offers an important distinction between equally valid but separate ways of reviewing literary experience. Yet I have seen the last sentence removed from its context and made to seem like a wanton dismissal of the child, a typical instance of the book person's negligent aesthetics.

On the other side of the chasm is Bob Dixon, who follows an assault on ancient symbolic and metaphorical uses of the word 'black' by a paragraph which seems ready on ideological grounds to consign Shakespeare and Dickens to the incinerator:

> Adult literature, as might be expected, is full of such figurative and symbolic usages – when it isn't openly racist. Shylock and Fagin, Othello and Caliban all deserve a second look, for there's no need for anyone to accept racism in literature, not even if expressed in deathless blank verse.[4]

This is quite true. Any individual is free to elevate political judgement above literary judgement, and to be contemptuous of all literature which offends a political criterion. The converse is also true. Any individual is free to like and admire a great work of literature, even if its ideology is repellent. These are the private freedoms of a democratic society, and I hope that any commentator would defend both with equal enthusiasm. I make the second choice myself in the case of D. H. Lawrence, whom I admire as a great writer and whose ideology I detest. Neither principle is much use when we confront the problem of introducing children to great works of the past which do not entirely accord with current moral priorities. But if anyone says, 'We should not introduce them; we should ban them,' I begin to hear the boots of Nazis faintly treading, no matter what colour their uniforms.

My particular concern in this article is to argue that, in the very period when developments in literary theory have made us newly aware of the omnipresence of ideology in all literature, and the impossibility of confining its occurrence to visible surface features of a text, the study of ideology in children's literature has been increasingly restricted to such surface features by the polarities of critical debate. A desire on the part of the child people for a particular set of social outcomes has led to pressure for a literature to fit them, and a simplistic view of the manner in which a book's ideology is carried. In turn, this inevitably leads to a situation where too much stress is placed on *what* children read and too little on *how* they read it. At the very point in history when education seemed ready to accept the reading of fiction as a complex, important, but teachable skill, the extremities of critical opinion have devalued the element of skill in favour of the mere external substance.

Diversity and individuality

Things can be made to sound very easy, as they do in Robert Leeson's reassuring comments:

> This *is* a special literature. Its writers have special status in home and school, free to influence without direct responsibility for upbringing and care. This should not engender irresponsibility – on the contrary. It is very much a matter of respect, on the one hand for the fears and concerns of those who bring up and educate children, and on the other for the creative freedom of those whose lives are spent writing for them. I have generally found in discussion with parents or teachers, including those critical of or hostile to my work, that these respects are mutual.[5]

I should like to think that this was true and generally accepted. But it cannot, no matter how true, be so simple. In a socially and culturally, politically and racially divided country such as Britain (and most Western countries to some extent or other) there is not a uniform pattern of 'fears and concerns' on the part of 'those who bring up and educate children'. The 'fears and concerns' of a teacher in a preparatory school in Hampshire are likely to be substantially different from those of a primary school teacher in Liverpool; those of an Irish Catholic parent in Belfast will differ from those of an Asian parent in Bradford. I wish to make only the obvious but neglected point, that the same book, read by four children in the care of these four adults, will not in practice be the same book. It will be four different books. Each of these children needs and deserves a literature, but the literature which meets their needs is unlikely to be a homogeneous one.

It is of course important too for the writer's creative freedom to be respected. But in order to be respected it must be understood, and on that score also I do not share Robert Leeson's optimism. There is too much evidence of pressure on writers (from all points of the politicomoral spectrum) to conform to a predetermined ideology issuing in visible surface features of the text. Here, for example, is Nina Bawden, a writer widely admired by critics of very different approaches (see Fred Inglis, *The Promise of Happiness*, pages 267–70, and Robert Leeson, *Reading and Righting*, page 122):

> Speaking to people who care, often deeply, for children, I have begun to feel that the *child* I write for is mysteriously absent . . . 'Are you concerned, when you write, to see that girls are not forced into feminine role-playing?' 'What about the sexuality of children?' 'All writers are middle class, at least by the time they have become successful as writers, so what use are their books to working class/deprived/emotionally or educationally backward children?' 'Writers should write about modern (*sic*) problems, like drugs, schoolgirl pregnancies. Aren't the books you write rather escapist?' 'What do you know about the problems of the child in the high-rise flat since you have not lived in one?' To take this last question. The reply, that you project your imagination, is seldom taken as adequate; but what other one is there?[6]

Leeson's dictum, 'You match story to audience, as far as you can', is less straightforward than it seems. A diversity of authors exercising their 'creative freedom' – as they must, if they are to write anything worthwhile at all – will *only* match story to audience '*as far as they can*'. If there were indeed a single, uniform audience, a theoretical 'child' who stood for all children, there would be few problems. Either a writer would be able to match her story to this 'child', in which case her credentials as a children's writer would be proved, or she would not be able to, in which case she might have to settle for being a writer of those other children's books supposedly beloved of the book people, the ones admired by literary adults but unread by actual children.

However, one point I hoped to make with my opening anthology of truisms is that the most conspicuous truisms of all are ones which many adult commentators are in practice loth to accept. When Leeson says 'you match story to audience', he must surely be postulating many possible audiences, whether individual (parent reading to child) or socially grouped (teacher or visiting author reading to school class). It is clear that these audiences will differ greatly from each other, whether in age, or sex, or race, or social class, and that these different audiences will perceive the same story in different ways. Otherwise there would be no need for Robert Leeson to do any 'matching'. He is not suggesting that a writer who adjusts and improvises in order to make his story work with one group of children can then sit back, assured of its success with every other group thereafter. And yet at their own self-caricaturing extremes this is precisely the assumption on which both book people and child people seem to act.

For the caricatured book person (a *rara avis*, perhaps) the distinguished children's book has a quality of verbal imagination which can be shown to exist by adult interpretative analysis, and this is a transferable objective merit which the 'ideal' child reader (though unable of course to verbalize his experience) is capable of appreciating and enjoying. The good literary text has an external existence which transcends the difference between reader and reader, even between child and adult. Consequently there is an implicit definition of children's literature which has little *necessarily* to do with children: it is not the title of a readership but of a genre, collateral perhaps with fable or fantasy. Ideology will be admitted to have a place in it, but since the child audience and hence the teaching function are subordinate to literary and aesthetic considerations, it is a small part of the critic's responsibility to evaluate it.

For the caricatured child person the book exists chiefly in terms of audience response. The distinguished children's book is one which the 'kids' will like and which will aid their social growth. Historical periods will differ in the forms of social growth they cherish, but it is an article of faith that the current period will be wiser than its predecessors. The child audience, by some ideological sleight of hand, will be virtually identical or at the very least highly compatible with the preferred social objectives. In an age which desires to propagate imperialist sentiments, children will be an army of incipient colonizing pioneers. In an age which wishes to abolish differences between sexes, races and classes, the readership is a composite 'child' which is willing to be anti-sexist, anti-racist and anti-classist, and does not itself belong to any sex, or race, or class other than those which the equalizing literature is seeking to promote. The 'kids' are a Kid, who is sexless but female, colourless but black, classless but proletarian. Children's literature is implicitly defined as being for this Kid: it is not the tide of a genre but of a readership. Ideology is all-important to it. Literary merit will be admitted to have a place, but it is a minor part of the critic's responsibility to evaluate it.

Both these caricatures exist. Both are extremely intolerant of anything which lies outside their preferred agenda. The first kind is the one which says 'I am almost inclined to set it up as a canon that a children's story which is enjoyed only by children is a bad children's story.'[7] The second is the kind which says, as someone did of Robert Westall's brilliant anti-totalitarian story *Futuretrack 5*, 'The book will appeal greatly to teenage boys, which is the best reason for not buying it.' Both (though naturally for very different reasons) will abominate Enid Blyton, and perhaps it is true to say that both understand the effective working of ideology less well than she did, in practice if not in theory.

My purpose here is emphatically not to argue for or against any single ideological structure in children's books (and certainly not to vindicate Miss Blyton's), but to contend that ideology is an inevitable, untameable and largely uncontrollable factor in the transaction between books and children, and that it is so because of the multiplicity and diversity of both 'book' and 'child' and of the social world in which each of these seductive abstractions takes a plenitude of individual forms. Our priority in the world of children's books should not be to promote ideology but to understand it, and find ways of helping others to understand it, including the children themselves.

Three levels of ideology

Ideology, then, is present in a children's book in three main ways. The first and most tractable is made up of the explicit social, political or moral beliefs of the individual writer, and his wish to recommend them to children through the story. An attractive example is this, offered by the late Henry Treece:

> I feel that children will come to no harm if, in their stories, an ultimate justice is shown to prevail, if, in spite of hard times, the characters come through to receive what they deserve. This, after all, is a hope which most of us share – that all may yet be well provided that we press on with courage and faith. So in my stories I try to tell the children that life may be difficult and unpredictable, and that even the most commendable characters may suffer injustice and misery for a while, but that the joy is in the doing, the effort, and that self-pity has no place. And at the end and the gods willing, the good man who holds to the permanent virtues of truthfulness, loyalty and a certain sort of stoic acceptance both of life's pains and pleasures, will be the fulfilled man. If that is not true, then, for me, nothing is true: and this is what I try to tell the children.[8]

This is the most conspicuous element in the ideology of children's books, and the easiest to detect. Its presence is conscious, deliberate and in some measure 'pointed', even when as with Treece there is nothing unusual or unfamiliar in the message the writer is hoping to convey.

It is at this level of intended surface ideology that fiction carries new ideas, non-conformist or revolutionary attitudes, and efforts to change imaginative awareness in line with contemporary social criticism. This causes difficulties both for writers and critics, which can be exemplified from present-day concern with the depiction of sexual roles. There are hundreds of books which passively borrow and reproduce the sexual stereotyping which they inherit from earlier fiction. No one notices, except radical adult readers (and perhaps some children) who are alert to it and offended by it. On the other hand, any novel which questions the stereotypes and sets out to reflect anti-sexist attitudes will almost inevitably do so conspicuously because it depicts surprising rather than customary behaviour. Ironically, the astonishing effect of *The Turbulent Term of Tyke Tiler* as an anti-sexist story is largely due to its ingenious self-disguise. Much the same is true of anti-racist or anti-classist fiction. In so far as it diverges from stock assumptions about race or class, it may seem crudely didactic. If on the other hand the author seeks to present as natural a society without racial prejudice or class division and to leave out tutelary scenes of conflict, she risks blunting the ideological content and presenting happenings which readers simply do not believe. The writer faces a dilemma: it is very difficult in contemporary Britain to write an anti-sexist, anti-racist or anti-classist novel without revealing that these are still objectives, principles and ideals rather than the realities of predictable everyday behaviour. If you present as natural and commonplace the behaviour you would *like* to be natural and commonplace, you risk muting the social effectiveness of your story. If you dramatize the social tensions, you risk a superficial ideological stridency.

The writer may opt for more circuitous methods. The more gifted the writer, the more likely to do so. If the fictional world is fully imagined and realized, it may carry its ideological burden more covertly, showing things as they are but trusting to literary organization rather than explicitly didactic guidelines to achieve a moral effect. Misunderstandings may follow if you are unlucky or too trusting. The hand of anti-racist censorship has begun to fall occasionally on the greatest anti-racist text in all literature, *Huckleberry Finn*. Twain's ideological error is to be always supremely the novelist rather than the preacher, to present his felt truth uncompromisingly rather than opt for educative adjustments to it, and to trust the intelligence of his readers. Perhaps the most luminous moment in anti-racist storytelling comes when Huck, arriving at the Phelpses' farm and being mistaken for Tom Sawyer, has to fabricate an excuse for late arrival by inventing a river-boat mishap:

> 'It warn't the grounding – that didn't keep us back but a little. We blowed out a cylinder-head.'
>
> 'Good gracious! anybody hurt?'
>
> 'No'm. Killed a nigger.'
>
> 'Well, it's lucky; because sometimes people do get hurt . . .'[9]

This snatch of dialogue is a devastating sign of what comes naturally to Huck's mind as soon as he begins to role-play Tom, but its full effect depends on its late placing in the novel, in the wake of all we have seen already of Huck's 'sound heart and deformed conscience'. It is a crucial point: you cannot experience the book as an anti-racist text unless you know *how to read a novel*. In modern children's writing the consciously didactic text rarely displays such confidence in its readers, with the unhappy result that reformist ideological explicitness is often achieved at the cost of imaginative depth.

The inference is clear: in literature as in life the undeserved advantage lies with *passive* ideology. The second category of ideological content which we must thus take into account is the individual writer's unexamined assumptions. As soon as these are admitted to be relevant, it becomes impossible to confine ideology to a writer's conscious intentions or articulated messages, and necessary to accept that all children's literature is inescapably didactic:

> Since children's literature is didactic it must by definition be a repository, in a literate society almost the quintessential source, of the values that parents and others hope to teach to the next generation.[10]

This is merely to accept what is surely obvious: writers for children (like writers for adults) cannot hide what their values are. Even if beliefs are passive and unexamined, and no part of any conscious proselytising, the texture of language and story will reveal them and communicate them. The working of ideology at this level is not incidental or unimportant. It might seem that values whose presence can only be convincingly demonstrated by an adult with some training in critical skills are unlikely to carry much potency with children. More probably the reverse is true: the values at stake are usually those which are taken for granted by the writer, and reflect the writer's integration in a society which unthinkingly accepts them. In turn this means that children, unless they are helped to notice what is there, will take them for granted too. Unexamined, passive values are widely *shared* values, and we should not underestimate the powers of reinforcement vested in quiescent and unconscious ideology.

Again I will take a pleasant example. It occurs in Richmal Crompton's *William the Bad*. Henry is summing up the salient features of British party politics before the gang hold their elections:

> 'There's four sorts of people tryin' to get to be rulers. They all want to make things better, but they want to make 'em better in different ways. There's Conservatives, an' they want to make things better by keepin' 'em jus' like what they are now. An' there's Liberals, an' they want to make things better by alterin' them jus' a bit, but not so's anyone'd notice, an' there's Socialists, an' they want to make things better by takin' everyone's money off 'em an'

> there's Communists an' they want to make things better by killin' everyone but themselves.'[11]

This is fun, and not to be taken solemnly, but it is not exactly even-handed fun. I do not think Miss Crompton is deliberately making propaganda, but there is not much doubt where her own sympathies lie or where she tacitly assumes that the reader's will follow. The joke about Conservatives and Liberals is a joke about *our sort*, and the joke about Socialists and Communists is a joke about a *different sort*. The interest of the example lies in the gentle, unconsidered bias of the humour. Behind it lies an assumption of uncontroversial familiarity. It can be an instructive exercise to recast the joke, so that its bias dips in the opposite direction – suppose, for example, that it began its list with 'There's Conservatives, an' they want to make things better by makin' rich people richer an' poor people poorer.' It might still be funny, but it would at once acquire a shading of aggressive propagandist intention. As a character remarks in another, more recent and more radical children's book, Susan Price's *From Where I Stand*:

> 'Ah. It'll be something left-wing, then, if *he* calls them "political" in that voice-of-doom. The Tories aren't political, you know. They just are.'[12]

This is a very small instance, introduced simply for illustration's sake, of something which is present to some degree in all fiction and intrinsic to its nature. There is no act of self-censorship by which a writer can exclude or disguise the essential self. Sometimes, moreover, the conscious surface ideology and the passive ideology of a novel are at odds with each other, and 'official' ideas contradicted by unconscious assumptions. Since this is by no means true of fiction only, the skills of analysis applied to different levels of a text should form part of teacher training in any society which hopes for adequate literacy. By teaching children how to develop in alert enjoyment of stories, we are also equipping them to meet linguistic malpractices of more consequential kinds.

To associate the ideology of children's books with ideology in its broader definitions, we need to consider the third dimension of its presence. This is the one to which developments in literary theory, by now familiar and widely accepted, have introduced us, and the one from which domestic skirmishing between book people and child people has tended to distract our attention. In order to affirm its general nature, I take a convenient summary of its position from a study not of children's literature but of sixteenth-century poetry:

> How does ideology affect literary texts? The impact of ideology upon the writings of a particular society – or, for that matter, on

> the conventions and strategies by which *we* read those writings – is no different from the way it influences any other cultural practice. In no case, in Macherey's words, does the writer, as the producer of the text, manufacture the materials with which he works. The power of ideology is inscribed within the words, the rule-systems, and codes which constitute the text. Imagine ideology as a powerful force hovering over us as we read a text; as we read it reminds us of what is correct, commonsensical, or 'natural'. It tries, as it were, to guide both the writing and our subsequent readings of a text into coherence. When a text is written, ideology works to make some things more natural to write; when a text is read, it works to conceal struggles and repressions, to force language into conveying only those meanings reinforced by the dominant forces of our society.[13]

If this is true, as I believe it is, we must think in terms which include but also transcend the idea of individual authorship, and reappraise the relationship between the author and the reader. In the case of children's literature, our thinking may be affected by an over-simplified stereotype of possible authority and influence. The individual writer is likely, as we have seen, to make conscious choices about the explicit ideology of his work, while the uniqueness of imaginative achievements rests on the private, unrepeatable configurations which writers make at subconscious level from the common stock of their experience. Our habit is so much to cherish individualism, however, that we often overlook the huge commonalities of an age, and the captivity of mind we undergo by living in our own time and place and no other. A large part of any book is written not by its author but by the world its author lives in. To accept the point one has only to recognize the rarity of occasions when a writer manages to recolour the meaning of a single word: almost all the time we are the acquiescent prisoners of other people's meanings. As a rule, writers for children are transmitters not of themselves uniquely, but of the worlds they share.

For modern children's writing this has many implications, but I would pick out two. First, the writer's ability to reshape his world is strictly limited. It is in his power (and may be his duty) to recommend an improved world, reflecting not what it is but what he hopes it might be. But this undertaking is bound by the same constraint as the literature of warning, which depicts a corrupted world as the author *fears* it truly is or might be. The starting point for each must be a shared understanding of the present, and an actuality which the young reader believes in.

The second point is that we may live in a period when our common ideology has many local fractures, so that children in different parts of the same national society are caught between bonding and difference. If children who are citizens of one country live in worlds within a world, discrete subcultures within a culture, they will need different storytelling voices to speak to them – voices which can speak within an ideology which for them is coherent and complete. As I hope this discussion has indicated, ideology is inseparable from language, and divergences of language within a national culture point to divisions and fragmentations in its shared ideology. In Britain as in other countries there is indeed a common language, but when that is said it must be qualified. Britain is also a country of many languages, many Englishes, and the children who speak them ideally need both a common national literature and local literatures which speak to and for themselves. Robert Leeson makes this point in his case for 'alternative' publishing for children. He begins by referring specifically to the spoken language and to dialect.

> The very richness of non-standard English is in itself a challenge to the whole system of education and literature, but a challenge that must be met. London schools at the moment are grappling (or not grappling) with new streams of language like Creole.[14]

He goes on to argue that 'alternative' publications need not be subject to the orthodox scrutiny of critics 'provided [they] can meet the critical response of [their] readers'. Interestingly he then goes on to make two significant conflations of ideas: first, he associates linguistic and literary subcultures with the literature of 'progressive' values, and second, he associates alternative publishing of books *for* children with publishing of books *by* children.

> So far the alternative publishers have not made great inroads into the field of fiction for the young. There have been some feminist stories for small children, some teenage writings, original and re-told folk stories from ethnic minorities. These are modest beginnings.[15]

The point which is half made here can be fully understood in its general implications if we define 'ideology' largely and precisely enough. The two points are crucial: subcultures of language are inseparable from the climate of ideas and values which are at work in them, and children inhabiting a subculture need to create a literature of their own, not merely be supplied with one. Leeson's ideas on this point are important and helpful but unnecessarily restricted in their scope. Like many other commentators, he is in practice most concerned with the London community of ethnic minorities and progressive groups. Such critics tend to write as if other places, other social groupings, other sites of active dialects, other schemes of ethical values did not exist, or had no comparable needs. If our thinking about ideology is clear enough, it is apparent that the same considerations apply to *all* children in any part of society (and in practice this probably means all parts of society) where there is tension between a common ideology and local circumstances. To appreciate the implications for children's literature demands acceptance that we do indeed inhabit a fragmented society, where each of the fragments needs and deserves to feel a confident sense of its value. As Leeson argues – but with a wider inference than he draws from it – we need a national children's literature (not to mention an international one) but also local literatures for particular racial or regional or social or (why not?) sexual groups, and also a literature made by the children themselves. Only when we have a coherent definition of ideology does this become adequately clear.

The reader as ideologist

Above all, it emerges from this argument that ideology is not something which is transferred to children as if they were empty receptacles. It is something which they already possess, having drawn it from a mass of experiences far more powerful than literature.

In literature, as in life, we have to start from where the children are, and with their own (often inarticulate) ideology. This offends some commentators, who prefer the literature to begin where they wish the children were, or assume that easy transformations can be made by humanely open-minded critical inquiry, whether based in classrooms or elsewhere. Rob Grunsell, describing his experiences in running an alternative school for chronic truants in London, reports the discomfiting consequences of moving too rationally and openly beyond a pre-existent teenage ideology:

> At lunch they had opinions in plenty, particularly about the blacks and the Pakis. It seemed to me such an obvious place to start, so I planned out a lesson on racial attitudes – a straight survey of what they thought, with no judgements and no 'right' answers. They designed the questionnaire with me, enjoying filling in their answers. From that point on it was a disaster. The answers weren't the same. 'Was Jimmy right?', why were they wrong? I couldn't convince them, because they couldn't listen, that there were no right answers. Here, in a lesson, hating Pakis because they're 'dim' and 'chicken' was obviously wrong. They sensed what I thought, even though I hadn't said it. They had lost, as usual, and more hopelessly than usual since they could do nothing about it. My prize-winning lesson in open-ended exploratory learning produced five miserable, depressed people.[16]

A similar result is produced by much over-confident surface didacticism in modern children's books, as it is by much persuasive rationality in classroom discussion. Where the ideology is explicit, it does not matter how morally unanswerable the substance is if it speaks persuasively only to those who are persuaded already, leaving others with their own divergent ideology intensified by resentful bemusement. Susan Price's *From Where I Stand*, which I referred to earlier, is a passionately anti-racist story which operates very much at the level of conscious authorial intention. At one point a highly intelligent Bangladeshi teenager, Kamla, is interviewed by the headmistress of her comprehensive school about an anti-racist pamphlet she has helped to compose. The headmistress tries to reason with her:

> 'You are going to tell me that Asian and black children are often teased and bullied by white children in this school. This isn't news to me, you know. I am quite aware of it. Whenever I can, I intervene, I punish children who are caught bullying or robbing others – but I punish them for bullying, for blackmail, for theft, not for racism. You see, it isn't always wise to tackle these things head on, my dear; I wonder if you can understand that? These attitudes are entrenched. Unfortunately, many of the children here have parents who are racist in their views. In that case, if you attack the opinion, then you attack the parents, and you are telling the children that their parents are bad people – now, that doesn't help. It only antagonizes them, reinforces their beliefs . . . And they are only *children*, Kamla.'[17]

Susan Price's storytelling is very skilfully organized to discredit the headmistress by presenting her as one who is at best evasive and negligent in her efforts to subdue racist behaviour, and at worst has racist sympathies herself. The speech quoted above is thus placed in a context designed to undermine it. Readers are intended to conclude that the reasons for inaction given in the last sentences – reasons which are put forward often by real teachers in the real world – are merely disreputable rationalizations of unprincipled tolerance, if not something worse, with the implication that such reasons usually are. Susan Price is using literary skills to checkmate her opponents in an ideological chess game. But in the imperfect world these are genuine problems for teachers who try to educate children in anti-racist morality. It is unfortunately true that well-disposed ideological enthusiasm can be counter-productive in school classrooms; and it can be likewise in stories. So the likely effect of Susan Price's storytelling is to deepen children's entrenched attitudes, good and bad alike. If it were not so, the stresses on our social fabric would be a great deal easier to deal with.

Locating the ideology of individual books

I have argued, therefore, that we should accept both the omnipresence of ideology and the realities of fragmentation, divergence, passivity, inertia, conservatism, invisibility, unreasoningness, in much of its expression and reception by the author and the child. Although it is easiest to illustrate the ideological process from the repertoire of *active* ideology in progressive modern fiction, that is only because didactic content is more obtrusive there, not because it is present on a larger scale than it is in traditional fiction. On all sides, in numerous commentaries on children's fiction (not to mention many novels themselves) a customary error is to make the wrong implicit analogy, by treating ideology as if it were a political policy, when in fact it is a climate of belief. The first can be changed, and itemized, and imposed, and legislated into reality and (though not always!) vindicated by pure reason. The second is vague, and holistic, and pliant, and stable, and can only evolve.

The first priority is to understand how the ideology of any given book can be located. Above all, such an understanding is important for teachers, especially primary school teachers and English specialists. Their task is to teach children how to read, so that to the limits of each child's capacity that child will not be at the mercy of *what* she reads. I shall conclude, then, with some examples of the kind of question which teachers in training might usefully be taught to ask about children's books, in order to clarify the ideology which is working in them. They are mostly questions which adults generally might find interesting in order to test their own recreational fiction, and which can easily be modified for use in classrooms. The purpose, as I have tried to indicate throughout, is a modest one: not to evaluate, discredit or applaud a writer's ideology, but simply to see what it is.

The questions are only examples, and teachers and others will readily be able to augment them.

1. What happens if the components of a text are transposed or reversed (as I suggested might be done with Richmal Crompton's political joke in *William the Bad*)? Does examination of the negative, so to speak, show unsuspected blights in the published picture? In particular, do we observe that a book which seems to be asserting a principle is only attacking a symptom? Is this 'anti-sexist novel' in fact sexist itself, and merely anti-male? Does this war story attack the Germans for atrocities which are approved when the British inflict them?

2. Consider the dénouements of some books, and the happy (or unhappy) ending. Does the happy ending of a novel amount to a 'contract of reaffirmation' of questionable values which have earlier seemed to be on trial? Is the conclusion imaginatively coherent, or does it depend on implicit

assumptions which are at odds with the surface ideology? Are there any loose ends (not so much of plot but of thought and feeling)? (Although it is not a children's book, students may find a particularly interesting example in the closing paragraphs of Richard Hughes's *A High Wind in Jamaica*.) If some 'happy endings' reconverge on the dominant ideology, is it also true that an unhappy ending is a device for denying such reconvergence, and hence for reinforcing a blend of ideological and emotional protest? (Students might consider the brilliantly effective unhappy endings of Susan Price's *Twopence a Tub* and Jan Mark's *Divide and Rule*.)

3. Are the values of a novel shown as a 'package' in which separate items appear to interlock? For example, does one story condemn racial prejudice and social class prejudice as if they were automatically interdependent, and does another in the same way celebrate a seemingly inseparable threesome made up of patriotism, courage and personal loyalty? (*Biggles* books are a good source of study on 'packaging' of various kinds.) Are these groups of virtues or vices necessarily or logically connected with each other? Are they being grouped together in order to articulate some larger, aggregated virtue or vice, such as 'white Britishness'? Students may find it interesting to bring this exercise to bear comparatively on the work of W. E. Johns and some current socially progressive fiction. Is it in fact a mark of quality in a book that it differentiates its values rather than fusing them in composite and (perhaps frauduently) homogeneous groups?

4. Is it a noticeable feature of some major 'classic' children's books that they test and undermine some of the values which they superficially appear to be celebrating? (I think it is. Students may find it interesting to perform this experimental inquiry on *Treasure Island, The Wind in the Willows*, and *Stalky and Co*, as well as *Tom Sawyer* and *Huckleberry Finn*.) Are there any modern children's books which seem to work in similar ways? Readers may find, for example, that the novels of John Christopher (notably *Fireball*) and Peter Dickinson (notably *Healer*) are more complex than they seem.

There is an important general point here. As recent studies based in modern critical theory have convincingly shown, many major works will sustain more radical and subversive readings than we are accustomed to. Critiques of children's literature which concentrate on surface ideology tend to ignore such possibilities. They observe only the external conservative values detectable in some major children's books, and overlook the radical questioning to which the text exposes them. The fallacy (as I have earlier suggested in the case of *Huckleberry Finn*) often lies in treating the novel as if it were some other kind of writing, and so ignoring narrative procedures which are basic to its meanings. If critics can make such mistakes, so can children: they need our help in learning how to read. But that is no excuse for suppressing or reclassifying the books.

5. Are desirable values associated with niceness of character, and vice versa? Is it really true that a given attractive philosophy or action could not believably be held or performed by someone whose character was in other ways unpleasant? How much allowance is there (and how much should there be in a children's book) for inconsistency, or for dissonance between ideology and temperament? How far is a book's ideology conveyed by 'moral symmetry' in character delineation?

6. Does anyone in a story have to make a difficult *choice* – of behaviour, loyalties, values, etc. – in which there is more than one defensible course of action? Or does the plot hinge merely on a predetermined choice, and interest depend on whether or not it is successfully carried out?

7. Is any character shown as performing a mixture of roles, especially roles with sharply differentiated contexts of friendship, safety or prestige? Does any character belong as an accepted member in more than one subculture or group, and move without stress between them? If any character does so, is one such group presented by the author as deserving higher value than another? The groups may be as simple as school (both staff and peer group) and family. They may, on the other hand, extend to differences of race, culture, religion, political affiliation and social custom, as they do for example in *Kim*. *Kim* is an excellent text for students to consider, because it exposes the need for caution in using the vocabulary of political judgement, in this case 'racist', as a generalizing critical terminology.

8. Last and most important in this selection is the question of omission and invisibility. Who are the people who 'do not exist' in a given story? This may mean people who are present but humanly downgraded, as if inscribed above the writer's desk were the words 'All human beings are human, but some are more human than others.' Downgraded groups include servants, but may also in a given case include teachers, or even parents. More seriously, they may include criminals and policemen. More seriously still, they may include foreigners, soldiers, girls, women and blacks. These last groups are more serious invisibilities because they do not plausibly represent mere story conventions, but curtailments of humanity embedded in an ideology. Omission takes many forms: for example, the performance of important life-supporting tasks for children without any reference to the workers (such as mothers) who carry them out. Invisibility may take many forms, for example, the denial of names, the identification of people by what they do rather than what they are, and the absorption of individuals into social and racial groups. It can be helpful again to take an 'adult' text before considering children's books with students, and the most rewarding one I know to introduce this inquiry is Conrad's *Heart of Darkness*.

Taken together, questions such as these may serve effectively to lift ideology 'off the page' and bring it from obscure and unexpected places into the light, but it need not and should not suppress the uniqueness of individual stories, or convert them into cadavers for pedagogic dissection or for classroom autopsy. What we call 'ideology', as I have tried to argue, is a living thing, and something we need to know as we need to know ourselves. Very much like that, because it is a part of us.

References

1. C. S. Lewis, 'On Three Ways of Writing for Children', reprinted in *Only Connect* edited by Sheila Egoff *et al.*, Oxford University Press, Canada, 1980, page 208.
2. Robert Leeson, *Reading and Righting*, Collins, 1985, page 161.
3. Fred Inglis, *The Promise of Happiness*, Cambridge University Press, 1981, page 7.
4. Bob Dixon, *Catching Them Young 1, Sex, Race and Class in Children's Fiction*, Pluto Press, 1977, page 95.
5. Leeson, pages 169–170.
6. Nina Bawden, 'The Imprisoned Child', in *The Thorny Paradise* edited by Edward Blishen, Kestrel, 1975, pages 63–4.
7. Lewis, page 120.
8. Henry Treece, 'Writing for Children', in Owens and Marland (eds.). *The Practice of English Teaching*, Blackie, 1970, page 176.
9. Mark Twain, *Huckleberry Finn*, chapter 32.
10. P. W. Musgrave, *From Brown to Bunter: The Life and Death of the School Story*, Routledge & Kegan Paul, 1985, page 17.
11. Richmal Crompton, *William the Bad*, Newnes, 1930, Chapter 3.
12. Susan Price, *From Where I Stand*, Faber & Faber, 1984, page 60.
13. Gary Waller, *English Poetry of the Sixteenth Century*, Longman, 1986, page 10.
14. Leeson, page 179.
15. Leeson, page 180.
16. Rob Grunsell, *Born to be Invisible*, Macmillan Education, 1978, page 50.
17. Price, page 119.

63

CENSORSHIP AND CHILDREN'S LITERATURE

Anne Scott MacLeod

Source: *Library Quarterly* 53(1) (1983): 26–38.

The major arguments against censorship of books for adults have been familiar for a long time. Most of them were well expressed in John Milton's *Areopagitica*, published more than 300 years ago. Milton's notion of a free marketplace of ideas where intellectual wares are available for comparison, his insistence on the right of free adults to choose for themselves their moral and intellectual fare, his argument on the impossibility of suppressing ideas successfully in a free society and on the dangerous weapon that censorship can become in the hands of authority—all these are still basic to the case for uncensored access by adults to printed material. To them must be added another argument, very common in modern (though not in Milton's) discussion: that in any case, it does not much matter, that the written word is but one of many influences on an individual and by no means the most decisive. This attitude was perhaps most succinctly stated by a former mayor of New York, Jimmy Wagner, in a long-ago legal fight over the restriction of pornographic literature, "Well," the Mayor is said to have remarked in laconic defense of liberty, "no girl was ever ruined by a book."

At a time of serious controversy over whether children's reading should or should not be subjected to some kind of restriction, the question arises whether these same arguments are applicable to children and to children's books. Do children have the same intellectual rights that adults have? Or, to put it more basically, are children free citizens of a free society in the same sense that adults are? Should children be encouraged to make comparisons among intellectual and moral concepts freely available to them? Can children be assumed to be as capable as adults of making reasoned choices among ideas? Is the "harmlessness" argument appropriate—that is, should children's books be free of censorship, if for no other reason then because they are a relatively unimportant influence in children's lives? Do the dangers of restricting children's access to the full range of moral, social, and political attitudes outweigh the dangers of exposing the young to pernicious ideas—or is it the other way around? In short, is the concept of intellectual freedom applicable to children? Is that concept, in fact, even compatible with the concept of childhood?

Even to raise the issue suggests that we are in the midst of a historical shift in our thinking about children and childhood. For a long time, certainly for well over 200 years, most adults in Western society would have given an unhesitating no to any and all of these questions. Until quite recently, there existed in our society a very general agreement that the rules on moral and intellectual matters applicable to children belonged to a category altogether separate from those applied to adults. Adults considered that children were beings different from adults intellectually, emotionally, and socially as well as physically, whose proper development required that they be insulated from certain kinds of knowledge and influences, shielded for their own good, from too direct contact with the full range of adult activity.[1]

The idea of childhood as a distinct and, ideally at least, protected period of life has become so familiar as to seem "natural," perhaps even inherent in the human outlook. It is worth remembering, however, that such a view of childhood is neither eternal nor universal. It has a historical beginning and development and, like any other cultural attitude, it is subject to change.

Historians of childhood differentiate between modern concepts of childhood and those that preceded them. Philippe Ariès, whose *Centuries of Childhood* was a seminal work in the field, locates the beginning of modern childhood in the early seventeenth century [2]. According to Ariès, medieval culture separated children from adult life only through the period of infancy, which ended at about the age of seven. After that, children moved into the adult world, living and working alongside adults, hearing, saying, and seeing what adults heard, said, and saw. Ancient and medieval culture made few efforts to protect children from contact with violence, sex, coarse humor, vulgarity, and brutality of various kinds. All those elements of adult life which later generations excluded from the category of knowledge suitable for children were an accepted part of a child's experience once he had left the primary care of mother or nurse.

The rise of the middle class, dating, roughly, from the end of the sixteenth century, brought about fundamental changes in attitudes toward family life in general and toward childhood in particular. Ariès describes a steady in-drawing of the family from that time, a separation of family from the larger world beyond; he sees the extended relationships of medieval society narrowing, and the old, rather careless, attitude toward children giving way to a more anxious and demanding view. Increasingly, middle-class people came to regard childhood as a period of preparation for adult life, and, increasingly, preparation became identified with education. As their concern for the education of their children grew, the middle classes steadily lengthened the period they called childhood. School became the central task of a child's life. In school, children were at a remove from adult life for longer than they had ever been in the medieval society—"quarantined" is Ariès's term.

Whether or not they follow Ariès in all respects, most historians of childhood agree that attitudes toward children began to change in important ways around the turn of the seventeenth century. They generally agree, too, that the change was closely connected with the expansion of the middle classes, and with all the economic and social changes that that expansion implied. Because they were not dependent upon the labor of their children for survival, middle-class families could assign their children to the unproductive (in the immediate economic sense) pursuit of formal education for ever-lengthening periods of time—a process which has continued into the present. Because they increasingly tended to regard children as incomplete or unformed until their education was finished, middle-class parents also tended to emphasize the differences between child and adult, to see childhood as a distinct phase of human life and children as distinctly different from adults.

This is not to say that a single view toward children has prevailed since the seventeenth century. On the contrary: while all "modern" views insist on the differences between childhood and adulthood, there have been important shifts in how adults characterize the nature of children themselves. Over the past several centuries a number of ideas, each quite different from the other, have at various times seemed inseparable from the idea of childhood. In some periods, adults have viewed children as depraved from birth, marked by original sin, in need of the most stringent spiritual training to prepare them for salvation; at other times, they have seen children as innocent creatures, better than adults, whose innocence must be protected as long as possible from the inroads of sordid reality. Adults have sometimes looked on children as a mixture of good and bad, whose goodness must be nurtured and badness suppressed, whose character must be formed and firmed before it was exposed to a corrupt world. At other times, they have thought of children as blank slates, whose characters were written by adults during the childhood years. More recently, adults have tended to see children primarily in psychological terms, to judge influences on children by their psychological rather than their moral effects, and to be concerned for children's mental health more than for their character.

These examples by no means exhaust the list; the adult view of children has changed, sometimes drastically, sometimes subtly, many times over the past 300 or so years. Whatever their differences, however, there are two assumptions common to all modern views of childhood. The first is that children need to be separated to some degree from adult life until they have been educated or ripened in some important way. The second is that adults have something of value to teach children, so that the very concept of childhood in modern history is closely associated with that of the nurture, training, and conscious education of the child by responsible adults.

What these assumptions have meant in practical terms is that modern middle-class childhood is managed, directed, organized, and defined by adults, for the good of the child and for the good of society, as adults see both. And management of childhood implies restriction of children, usually by separating them from some aspects of society and by curtailing their access to some kinds of knowledge, experience, and resources—including books.

A managing approach to childhood reached a high point in the nineteenth century and is closely allied with the whole genesis of a separate literature for children. Ideally, if not always actually, nineteenth-century parents regulated their children's lives fully, certainly including their reading. It is scarcely coincidental that the concept of children's books as a special genre found a congenial home in the nineteenth century and flourished accordingly. Nor is it surprising that adults of the period were at least as concerned with the moral content of children's books as with their literary quality. Nearly all books for children before midcentury were more or less frankly moral tracts, and even when authors set about to write what they were pleased to call "entertaining" stories for children, they often had in view obliterating the folk and fairy tales of which they heartily disapproved. Samuel Goodrich, the "Peter Parley" of early nineteenth-century fame, based a long and busy career on his fervent opposition to fairy tales. Even in the second half of the century, when entertainment and literary merit found a place in children's books, adult concern with the moral content of the literature remained high. The movement that created special collections of children's books, housed in separate children's rooms in public libraries and supervised by specially trained librarians, was very much part of the effort to meet the dangerous challenge of trash literature to provide an attractive alternative to the lurid nickle and dime juveniles so popular in the latter nineteenth century [3, chap. 4]. The idea of selecting children's books for their suitability as moral influences on children was built into library service to children from the beginning.

There is, then, an enormous lot of historical baggage to be sorted through when the question of censorship of children's reading is raised today —as it is with great frequency. Attitudes toward children and childhood have undoubtedly changed in the second half of the twentieth century, as have attitudes toward books and morals. Yet the intensity of current arguments over restriction of children's reading, ringing through journals, meetings, and associations, is ample evidence that the changes have not followed a single direction, nor proceeded at the same pace. The discussion that follows attempts to describe today's situation, together with its background in the first half of the twentieth century, in broadest outline. It cannot detail, though it does try to suggest, the immense intricacies that lie behind today's passionate debates over censorship in children's books. Adult attitudes toward children's books, as toward childhood are, in any period, an amalgam of personal, social, and sometimes political convictions. The mix has rarely been so complex or so explosive as it is today.

The first half of the present century was a burgeoning season for children's books. Publishers built on the successes of the late nineteenth century, adding luster to an already golden period in children's book production. As the market for children's books expanded, more and more publishing houses created separate children's book divisions, presided over by editors who specialized in the genre. By 1900, children's rooms were an established part of many public libraries; later, and more slowly, libraries began to be added to public schools as well. By 1915, most library schools and teachers' colleges offered courses in children's literature; children's librarians became specialists in their field. The specializing trend also affected writers of children's books. Unlike authors of the nineteenth century, who frequently turned their hands to both adult and children's books, those of the twentieth century usually chose between the two audiences, both reflecting and reinforcing the increasingly firm line drawn between the adult and the juvenile fields.[2]

Throughout this time, and indeed until the fateful decade of the 1960s, the issue of censorship within the mainstream of the children's book field was virtually quiescent. While there were sporadic assaults on the evils of comic books and other "trashy" material read by children, the major products of the children's book business, the trade books published by standard, respectable publishing houses and bought by libraries, were pretty much exempt from criticism, or even scrutiny. Libraries generally refused to buy cheap series books—Nancy Drew and Hardy Boys books and such—but the decision was rarely challenged as an act of censorship. If children were disappointed not to find these perennial potboilers in their local public library, few adults chose to raise the banner of intellectual freedom on their behalf.

In fact, the concept of intellectual freedom had little place in most discussions of children's reading in this period. The peace that prevailed was grounded in the common set of values shared by the adults who dealt, whether personally or professionally, with children's books. Those values had evolved since the nineteenth century, but not so far as to make intellectual freedom an issue where children were concerned. Childhood was still considered a stage of life in need of adult protection, a time in which restriction of children, and of the influences on them, was considered a natural duty of adults toward children. The moral preoccupation of the nineteenth century lingered, too, though in far less insistent and preachy form. While authors, publishers, and reviewers of children's books all rejected the openly moral lessons that had dominated books of the past, they had by no means lost interest in what they now called "values" in children's literature—by which they meant moral and social values. Children's books were written, published, reviewed, and purchased in accordance with a remarkably consistent point of view about what was suitable reading for children. The community of adults engaged in bringing children and literature together endorsed, apparently without much real dissension, an implicit code of values which was observed virtually unbroken in thousands of children's books published between 1900 and 1965.

The code is most easily described in the negative, by its taboos. The list is long and often has more to do with how a subject was treated in a book for children than with what the subject was. Violence, for example, was not—as many have assumed—entirely absent from children's books before 1965. Given the plethora of pioneer and frontier stories in children's literature, that would hardly have been possible. What was taboo was a lingering on the details of violence and, even more, the depiction of a child, or even someone near and dear to a child, as the object of serious violence. Neither was death the absolute taboo that many present-day commentators insist it was. But the sentimental death scenes of the nineteenth century were certainly out of favor in the twentieth century, and it is clear that children's book people were concerned that the subject might be harrowing to children unless carefully handled. For this reason, children rarely died in children's books, and the death of parents, if it occurred at all, took place off-stage or in the past: death and grief were rarely central issues in children's stories. That, in fact, was the general approach to such painful topics as were given space in children's books: they were peripheral, rather than central, to the narrative; acknowledged, but not dwelt upon.

A more absolute blackout applied to problems classed as purely adult. Divorce, mental breakdown, alcoholism, rape, drug dependence, suicide, prostitution, sexual deviance—it would never have occurred to most writers of children's books, let alone their editors, that these were suitable topics for the young. Even crime, except for an occasional and relatively innocuous theft, was rare.[3] Racial conflict was touched upon gently and gingerly in a few—very few—books for children before the middle 1960s. Florence Cranall Means, Jerrold Beim, and Frank Bonham were among the early writers on the subject. They wrote honestly but with constraint in a field where most publishers feared to tread.

Most obvious to today's observer was the taboo on the subject of sexuality in books for the young. Not only was prepubescent sexuality unacknowledged in children's books—it was hardly widely acknowledged elsewhere in the culture, either—but even the sexual awareness of teenagers found only restrained, oblique recognition. "Romance" was handled nearly as gingerly as race where the young were concerned. One has but to read Maureen Daly's famous *Seventeenth Summer* (published in 1942) to catch a glimpse. The book was written for older teenagers and, at the time, its portrayal of first love was considered reasonably frank. Today, when it is read at all, it is by eleven- or twelve-year-olds, and to any reader its narrow morality, acute anxieties, and personal naïveté must make it seem a period piece easily as remote from modern experience as *Little Women*.

While these (and other) taboos did not altogether preclude literary realism in children's books, they did ensure that a protective attitude dominated. Reality was tempered and selective for young audiences. Pain and fear were kept at some distance from child protagonists, wrongs were righted, injustice redressed; things generally turned out well at the end. The same protective optimism applied to the child characters the books portrayed. The extreme idealization of the latter nineteenth century had largely disappeared. In twentieth-century stories, children had faults, made mistakes, and strayed (mildly) from the paths of righteousness. But the books insisted that children lived universally within a firm and supportive social and familial system. Parents or other wise adults were always on hand in children's books to correct the wayward child, gently but effectively, and to assert the claims of the community. The message of the books was that American society operated according to a single moral code; that adults were reliable sources of wisdom, justice, and caring; that childhood and children were sheltered under the protection of responsible adults in a responsible society.

It should be emphasized again that the code I have described was not explicit, for the most part, was not an iron set of rules to which writers pledged obedience, was not the result of a conspiracy between book editors and librarians or anyone else. Nor was it imposed, in most instances, by conscious censorship, or against any very fervent opposition. In the first sixty years of the twentieth century, the issue of censorship in children's books simply did not arise very often, for two reasons. First, the community of adults involved in the production and purchase of books for children was both relatively small and relatively homogeneous. Broadly speaking, librarians, teachers, authors, and editors of children's books were the same kind of people, members of a community which shared the general point of view that the code expressed. The rule was one of consensus, rather than coercion.

Second, the children's book field was something of an island in the larger culture. Few adults not professionally involved in children's literature read much or widely in it. Whether the reason was indifference, confidence in the selection processes of public and school libraries, lack of information or misinformation, or the conviction that what children read was unimportant so long as they read—whether it was some of these or all of them, the fact is that until quite recently, most adults, including parents, paid little attention to the content of children's books. Children's literature was sheltered by neglect.

Both consensus and complacency began to break up about the middle of the 1960s. Social upheaval in such manifestations as the Civil Rights movement, the women's movement, the bitter dissensions of the Vietnam era, and the changing mores and altered family structures of a new era raised questions about the world traditionally pictured in children's books. Belatedly, but inexorably, the winds of change sweeping through American society reached children's books, scattering indifference and consensus once and for all. Every group working for social and political change suddenly discovered what the nineteenth century had so often proclaimed; that children's reading is a potentially powerful influence on society. The closed world of children's book production was opened to newcomers who held no brief for the agreed-upon code of the near past. Peace shattered as hundreds of new voices demanded to be heard; unity gave way to a passionate diversity of views. By the 1970s, children's books had become a battleground for the personal, social, and political forces of a changing society.

Again, looked at broadly, the struggle can be seen to have proceeded along two quite contradictory lines. On the one hand, there was a strong movement to loosen the strictures on subject matter in children's books. Slowly at first, then with ever-increasing speed, children's books began to reflect the liberalized moral code and the changing family structures of contemporary society. The old insistence that every American family was intact unless broken by death gave way to facts; divorce was soon nearly as common in children's books as it was in reality. By 1972, Norma Klein could even write of a one-parent family in which the mother had simply chosen not to marry the man who had fathered her child [4]. Teenage sexuality, including homosexuality, became a commonplace topic, discussed with varying degrees of explicitness by such writers as Paul Zindel, John Donovan, Isabelle Holland, and Sandra Scoppettone. Judy Blume casually broke dozens of traditional barriers with her flat-footed but frank stories admitting the interest that even fairly young children had in their own bodies [5, 6]. The so-called "problem novel," dealing with such matters as alcoholism, drug dependence, and a staggering variety of other personal and family troubles, became the major staple of the teen reading market.

There was, to be sure, some shock and some resistance to these books as they came to the hands of traditional selectors of books for the young. But the trend was unstoppable. Times had changed, social attitudes had altered, writers and publishers responded eagerly to new demands for "realism"—and the books were, moreover, an undoubted success with their intended audience. Judy Blume's books sold by the thousands in paperback; libraries that refused to buy her novels lost patrons to drugstores. Besides, there was strong, if not unanimous, sentiment within libraries and schools for greater frankness with children. Most teachers recognized that their students lives were not so sheltered; most librarians were uncomfortable with the role of censor. Those who wanted to maintain protective barriers found themselves at odds with a highly visible, highly vocal liberal-radical coalition which argued forcefully for applying the same standards of intellectual freedom to children's literature as to any other.

Ironically, the concomitant movement ran directly counter to the concept of intellectual freedom. An aroused social consciousness had brought about, at last, an examination of the underlying messages in children's books, and many adults were startled to see what these books did and did not say about race, social responsibility, and the social conditioning of girls or the children of minorities. In the name of social justice long delayed, critics in many quarters began to demand that libraries remove from the shelves books that they, the critics, characterized as racist or sexist. The Council on Interracial Books for Children, founded in 1966, became a powerful voice pronouncing judgment on books for their racial or sexual biases.

Thus, by the later 1960s, the children's book profession found itself confronting two quite contradictory sets of demands. On the one hand, there was enormous pressure to liberalize children's books, to open them and the collections that housed them to every aspect of reality, so that they might better reflect the pluralism of contemporary American society. At the same time, from the other side of a curious equation came an equally strong pressure on writers, publishers, reviewers, and selectors of children's books to rid the literature of racism and sexism. While a raised social consciousness might accomplish this task for present and future books, the only answer to those already written, according to many social critics, was to remove the offending volumes from children's access. Libraries were pressed to review their children's collections for racist or sexist literature and to discard what they found. (The critics, of course, identified many books they wanted removed from the shelves.) It is one of the many ironies of the time that more than a few liberals and radicals found themselves with a foot in each camp, demanding freedom in one cause, censorship in another. Just as remarkable was the fact that many libraries managed to comply with both of these apparently contradictory demands, defending Blume, Klein, and Zindel in their children's collections while retiring *Little Black Sambo*, *Mary Poppins*, and *Dr. Doolittle*.

Whatever the differences of direction, change there surely was: the distance traversed in just over fifteen years is nothing short of astonishing. Its measure may be taken from the books themselves: from Betty Cavanna's prom-centered teen romances of the 1950s and early 1960s to Judy Blume's *Forever*, that 1975 how-to manual of teen-age sex; from Frank Bonham's *Durango Street*, which managed to depict (with commendable realism for its 1965 date) slum gangs without mentioning drugs, lethal weapons, or death, to *Headman* (1975) in which the main character dies with a corkscrew in his stomach. Or it may be taken by adult reactions to the books: from the furor over *Harriet the Spy* (1964) because an adult told a child that it was sometimes necessary to lie, to the silent acceptance of such novels as *Steffie Can't Come Out to Play* [7] (teen-age prostitution). *Are You in the House Alone?* [8] (rape), or any of Lois Duncan's sour tales of high school "life" [9].

However one measures, it is clear that adult attitudes toward children's reading have undergone some major changes during the turbulent years just past. The wide (though not universal) acceptance of a greatly broadened content in children's books seems to stem from the conviction that children should learn as soon as possible the realities of the world they live in—even the hardest and most unsavory realities. The rationale behind the conviction varies: some books are accepted as awful warnings (*Steffie*, surely); some because adults reason that if children's lives are not protected, it is pointless to restrict their reading. And of course, some adults are morally neutral toward the content of children's books, simply endorsing the concept of intellectual freedom for children, as for adults.

At the same time, the arguments for restriction of literature for children have moved to new ground. Barriers of the past were meant to protect the innocence of childhood. Today, it is the good of society that is invoked in favor of censorship more often than children's innocence, and this is true whether the call for censorship comes from the right or from the left.

Liberal censors arguing for the reform of what they call a racist society see no possibility for neutrality if social change is to be effected: "In the end, a failure to work for change actually supports the status quo. . . . At this point in history, directly or indirectly, one serves either the racist past or a humanistic future" [10, p. 11]. Essentially the same argument is made about sexism in children's books: if society is to change, the books cannot be neutral. If they are not liberating, they are by definition damaging. Those who see the issues this way are willing to call for censorship, by libraries, by schools, by authors, editors, and publishers, to bring about social change.

Conservative censors have also cast their argument primarily in social terms. They too want to reform society by eliminating harmful influences in children's books: their target those books they consider "biased toward increasing the centralized power of a secular humanistic state. [books that] will ultimately destroy the family, decent social standards, and basic principles of decentralized government that safeguard every American's individual freedom" [11, p. 9]. In both camps, the ascendant value is social morality.

At the beginning of the 1980s, censorship of children's books continues to be a lively issue. The prospects for peace restored soon to the field of children's reading are, to say the least, dim. Only if all parties to the arguments of the past decade and a half should suddenly agree to agree or, as suddenly, lose all interest in the questions now vigorously debated, could the quiet of earlier years be restored. Neither seems likely.

Nor is it likely that anyone can predict with confidence what the arguments or even who the antagonists will be. We are seeing now a conservative reaction against the liberalism of the 1960s and 1970s. The *Newsletter on Intellectual Freedom* anticipates that the trend will continue, encouraging "would-be censors" to "step up efforts to impose their own moral and social values on library patrons." More than a year ago, Judith Krug, Director of the Office for Intellectual Freedom, American Library Association, saw the conservative movement well underway: "All of the pressures that were just below the surface are now coming out, pressures to remove those materials that people object to on moral grounds or because they believe the materials do not reflect 'traditional American values'" [12, p. 1]. The apparent ascendance of such groups as the Moral Majority lends weight to liberal fears of increased pressure to restrict the content of children's books and to roll back some of the changes of recent years, as do the growing number of attempts to restrict both text and trade books in schools across the country.

But the changes in the literature over the past decade and a half are far-reaching, and many of them grew out of fundamental movements within the society. Reaction may modify how these social transformations are reflected in children's books, but it is unlikely that it can return the literature to the codes of the past. Children's books have been opened to a wider range of influences, as well as to a wider scrutiny since the mid-1960s. Inevitably, they reflect, directly and indirectly, the changing society that produced them. The present situation is neither static nor predictable. The only certainty is that children's books themselves and the debate about children's reading will continue to reflect the shifts and seasons of the American view of childhood, society, and truth.

Notes

1 This is an ideal more often achieved, of course, by the middle and upper-middle classes than by those below. Nevertheless, if lower-class families rarely had the means or the space to make the ideal practicable, they often embraced the concept and deplored their inability to protect their children from too much knowledge too soon: see [1. p. 499].

2 This separation was due to more liberalized adult literature in the twentieth century than to greater restrictions on the content of juvenile books. It also reflected the growing tendency of children's books to revolve around child characters, making the books of limited interest to adults.

3 Even Nancy Drew, whose repetitive adventures usually involved some crime, encountered only the most ludicrously harmless and klutzy thieves. She was often knocked on the head, but never beaten, raped, or murdered.

References

1. Lewis, Oscar. *The Children of Sanchez*. New York: Penguin Books, 1964.
2. Ariès, Philippe. *Centuries of Childhood*. New York: Random House, 1965.
3. Garrison, Dee. *Apostles of Culture*. New York: Macmillan Information, 1979.

4. Klein, Norma. *Mom, the Wolfman, and Me*. New York: Pantheon Books, 1972.
5. Blume, Judy. *Are You There, God? It's Me. Margaret*. Englewood Cliffs, N.J.: Bradbury Press, 1970.
6. Blume, Judy. *Then Again, Maybe I Won't*. Scarsdale, N.Y.: Bradbury Press, 1971.
7. Arrick, Fran. *Steffie Can't Come Out to Play*. Scarsdale, N.Y.: Bradbury Press, 1978.
8. Peck, Richard. *Are You in the House Alone?* New York: Viking Press, 1976.
9. Duncan, Lois. *Killing Mr. Griffin*. New York: Dell Publishing Co., 1978.
10. Council on Interracial Books for Children. *Human (and Anti-Human) Values in Children's Books*. New York: Racism and Sexism Center for Educators, 1976.
11. Jenkinson, Edward B. *Censors in the Classroom*. Carbondale: Southern Illinois University Press, 1979.
12. American Library Association. *Newsletter on Intellectual Freedom* 30 (January 1981): 1, 5, 23–26.

64

THE UNCLE REMUS TRAVESTY

Part I

Opal Moore and Donnarae MacCann

Source: *Children's Literature Association Quarterly* 11(2) (1986): 96–99.

It is a perpetual tug-of-war to decide who will "own" and interpret the art and artifacts of the Black American—determine the use to which historical and cultural materials will be put. This subtle war of wills ensues as a natural result of scholarly Black resistance to further intellectual colonization. The resisters confront the reluctance of white America to relinquish its illegitimate and unnatural proprietorship of valuable and persuasive materials. The nature of this ongoing struggle is encapsulated in the steadily increasing efforts to restore Joel Chandler Harris's Uncle Remus to the "canon" of children's literature.

This misdirected energy in behalf of the Harris version of classic Black folktales has kept pace with the efforts of Black scholars and writers to offer more creditable versions and presentations of the same (as well as other) Black folk material. For instance, Uncle Remus reappears in Macmillan's textbook for children's literature courses, *Classics of Children's Literature* edited by John W. Griffith and Charles H. Frey (1981). In an article in the *Children's Literature Association Quarterly*, Nina Mikkelsen argues for Harris's version of the Black folktale because "it is invariably Harris's version that we remember" (5). And in a two-part article appearing in *Signal*, John Goldthwaite goes even further, crediting Harris with inspiring the major advances in imaginative children's literature over the seventy year period from 1880 to 1950.

It is not for absence of reputable alternative materials that Harris's Remus is being revived. There are texts that offer the Black folktale in a balanced presentation, emphasizing the weight and substance of the story (as contrasted with Harris's depiction of Remus as the prototype of the national "darky" character). The reasons for the Remus revival probably have less to do with the merits of alternative materials than with Mikkelsen's observation: that Harris's Remus-creation is the image already seared in the mature American psyche. The larger-than-life, shuffling, sho-nuffing, grinning image is the sugartit appeasement from which America has refused to be weaned. The contradictions and interpretive difficulties presented by the Remus figure as mouthpiece for the Black folktale are anxiously overlooked, or dismissed with a sympathetic nod in the manner of Goldthwaite, who says: "Talking in dialect and the image of a slave as a man contented with his lot (more or less) did an injury, Blacks knew, to their children, and whites, with the rise of the civil rights movement of the 1960s, quickly abandoned the work as an embarrassment" (91). Goldthwaite then goes on to assert that "An Uncle Remus may have been the right, the necessary, choice of character for the telling of these tales, but he was, everyone agreed, the wrong one for the preserving of them." Finally, however, Goldthwaite devalues these (and presumably all other) objections to the work as "extraliterary."

But the variety of objections leveled against Harris's vision of the folktales turns on the conviction that Remus is *not*, and never was, the right presenter of the tales (that is, if importance is to be given to preserving their context, complexity, and texture). Such objections are decidely textual—raising substantive questions of authenticity and intent—and cannot be brushed aside as nervous-Nelly liberalism, or the over-sensitive nail-biting of a finicky modern Black aesthetic.

Challenges to the authenticity of Harris's work take issue with the "packaging" of the tales more often than with the tales themselves, allowing for the numerous variations and omissions that are possible in an orally preserved story. The charges leveled against Harris are that *he*, rather than the tales, is "inauthentic"; that Remus is a mouthpiece crafted out of stereotype to camouflage, efface, misdirect, or mute the pungency and irreverence of the tales; and that the appropriation of the tales is a bald misuse of the material. Attempts to determine whether it is use or misuse must begin with Harris himself—a man seemingly as contradictory and problematic as his stumbling creation.

In explaining their use of the Harris texts, Griffith and Frey maintain that Harris "grew up on intimate terms with black storytellers" (487). It is an assertion that suggests something more than the four years, from age thirteen, that Harris worked as printer's assistant for *The Countryman*, a newspaper owned by a Georgia planter. R. Bruce Bickley, Jr., a biographer of Harris, says that Harris gained access to the tales during hundreds of hours spent in the "quarters" when he had time on his hands between printings (23). No doubt Harris did have some contact with Black workers and overheard some number of exchanges, but the texture of Harris's adolescent (and later) encounters with Black storytellers is mostly speculation. It cannot be assumed, for example, that four years of employment with a southern planter afforded him an "intimate" relationship with the plantation's slaves. Nor can it be assumed that his collecting of Black folktales reflects on his politics or indicates some unusual affinity for, or understanding of, the Blacks themselves.

In his *Signal* article John Goldthwaite repeats the assumption of Griffith and Frey—that Harris' interest in the tales stemmed from an early contact with the stories. He writes: "Harris retold [the tales] according to the best tellings he had heard, from men he had troubled himself to know since boyhood" (91). These kinds of statements, which claim an unusual intimacy and camaraderie between Harris and his Black sources, are perhaps designed to establish Harris's authority over the material (by suggesting his love of it) as much as to assert the authenticity of his material. However, any clear evidence of his interest in Black folklore stems from the period when a number of columnists were inventing fictional Black informants.

Emphasis on Harris's "intimacy" and "long time familiarity since boyhood" seem designed to soften the obvious fact that the social commentary and worldview of the Black folktale is in direct opposition to that of a press corpsman of the post-Reconstruction "New South." Harris would rapidly achieve notoriety writing for the reactionary *Atlanta Constitution*—the newspaper that spearheaded the 'New South's program to nullify the brief promise of Reconstruction and reconstitute the Black population as a cheap, exploitable labor force.

Prior to Harris's use of a Black stand-in, the *Constitution* had employed another columnist, Sam W. Small, who also created a fictional Black narrator. His "Old Si" mouthed the views of the "New South" in the exaggerated "Negro dialect" made popular through minstrelsy. Southern writers used this as a method of condemning the reforms that would have fully enfranchised the Black population; thus, "Old Si" is supposedly speaking for the Black community when he makes statements like: "Dey [the Northern radicals] gibs de nigger nuffin but de pick'd bone, an' don't gib him dat ef dere's a bonedus fackry any whars handy!" (Hall 89). When Small quit, Harris was offered the opportunity to try his hand at a similar type of column. Harris adopted the familiar format and device—white political commentary delivered through a "new" Negro mouthpiece:

> Hit's agin de mor'l law for niggers fer ter eat w'en dey don't wuk, an w'en you see um 'pariently fattenin' on a'r, you k'n des bet dat ruinashuns gwine on some'rs.
>
> (*Uncle Remus: His Songs and Sayings* 224)

or:

> You slap de law onter a nigger a time or two, an' larn 'im dat he's got fer to look atter his own rashuns an' keep out'n udder

> foke's chick'n coops, an' sorter coax 'im ter feed is own chilluns, an' I be blessed ef you ain't got 'm on risin' ground!
>
> (*Uncle Remus* 232)

It would appear that "Old Si" and propagandist convention were the more immediate inspiration for Harris' later works, rather than the trailing idyllic reminiscences of a youth spent in intimate exchanges with a multitude of Black Remus prototypes.

R. Bruce Bickley's claim that "Harris became one of the most sensitive interpreters of the Southern Negro" is too generous (36). Such an assertion would not seem possible given the vigor with which Harris applied his trade, ridiculing the strivings of Blacks for a symbol of freedom: "The colored people of Macon celebrated the birthday of Lincoln again on Wednesday. This is the third time since last October" (Hall 94). Or, as Wolfe has pointed out, making light of the harsh reality of lynch "law" that necessitated specific civil rights legislation:

> There will have to be another amendment to the civil rights bill. A Negro boy in Covington was attacked by a sow lately and narrowly escaped with his life. We will hear next that the sheep have banded together to mangle the downtrodden race (83).

Undoubtedly Bickley is attempting to draw a distinction between one Joel Chandler Harris and another. It is doubtful, however, that any such clear distinction can be made. "Harris' manipulative political mouthpiece and its direct evolution into the story-telling Remus is too proximitous. It would be naive to expect that the latter could depart radically from his politically inspired progenitor.

At best, Uncle Remus is an ambivalent creation—suggesting a corresponding ambivalence in Harris. At times he is drawn sympathetically, as when he "dis'member'd" his own name or got "some er de facks mix up 'mong deyse'f," reminding the reader of his advanced age, his vulnerability, and possibly, an encroaching senility. At other times, he is the head-scratching "stage darky" as when he remarks to the child, in *Told by Uncle Remus*, "De fus' thing when I get ter de house I'm gwinter be weighed fer ter see how ol' I is. Now, whar wuz I at?" (50–51) And, as Louis J. Budd asks in his essay on Harris, "Did any black actually say 'surgeon er de armies' for 'sergeant at arms?" (203).

It is a difficult task to find the fine line between the exaggerated clowning of the minstrel entertainer and the exaggerated dialect usage employed by Harris. Griffith and Frey state that "Harris took great pains to represent phonetically the dialect of the Southern blacks . . ." (487). But is it a representation or a misrepresentation of Black speech when Uncle Remus calls Atlanta "'Lantmatantarum?" And what is the real purpose of the extensive "eye" dialect—misspellings that nevertheless represent correct pronunciation such as prommus, minnit, frum, wimmen, rashuns, masheen, cubberd? What does it do but create as wide a gulf as possible between the speech (which represents the intelligence) of the Black character and that of the white. The speech of the little boy and the anonymous narrator in the Remus stories is the flattest standard English. Not even a trace of the quite distinctive Southern "tongue" betrays itself in the speech of either.

Goldthwaite claims that "the real satire in these tales lies in the language itself. It is the master's English, but inflected in such a way as to make it, like Brer Rabbit, as big as life and twice as natural" (90). Is "familious wild wunner nudder" an inflection?

Harris himself disavowed any link between his use of dialect and "stage Negro" dialect, stating that the latter was an "intolerable misrepresentation." But while he rejects some features of minstrelsy, he embraces others. For example, the unabashed vulgarity that characterized minstrel shows by the second half of the nineteenth century is not to be found in these works. However, his aim in emphasizing and enlarging the language was, he says, "to wed the (legends) permanently to the quaint dialect . . . and to give the whole a genuine flavor of the old plantation" (Brookes 28–29). This "quaint dialect" was the style employed by Irwin Russell, a Mississippian whose poems were published in the 1870s. Harris wrote an introduction to the collected verses, *Christmas Night in the Quarters and Other Poems* (1888), praising the poems and Russell for capturing in his dialect "the old-fashioned unadulterated negro, who is still dear to the Southern heart" (xi). This "unadulterated negro" resembles the "newly industrious" Black character that Harris and the *Constitution* praised in propagandistic sketches. Russell simply put the theme into unintentionally hilarious doggerel:

> Dis worl' dat we's a-libbin in is like a cotton-row, Whar ebery cullud gentleman has got his line to hoe;
> And ebery time a lazy nigger stops to take a nap, De grass keeps on a-growin' fur to smudder up his crap (74).

While Harris was, as he said, inspired by this dialect, he in turn inspired others. Finally, in 1898, the editor of the *Journal of American Folklore*, called for a halt of so-called Negro dialects. He wrote:

> It is obviously impossible by means of the regular alphabet to reproduce negro dialect with any accuracy. A phonetic alphabet is essential for such purpose. . . . The attempt to indicate the manner of enunciation by the usual English signs results in confusions and contradictions innumerable. . . . An equally serious fault is that the meaning and real interest of the tale is disguised; a dialectic

> story is apt to be a mere piece of jargon, in which the lack of deep human interest is atoned for by a spelling which is usually mere affection.
>
> (Newell 291–292)

There is some indication that such dialect "affectations" thwarted the preservation of Afro-American folktales. Alice Bacon, the leader of the folklore society at Hampton Institute, described in 1898 how difficult it was to procure new examples of folk traditions in the schools. It was "almost impossible for (teachers) to gather from their pupils any folk-lore at all, so certain are they, if they have any, that it is something only to be laughed at . . ." (17). Contrary to the claim that without Harris the tales would have been lost, it can be argued that his minstrel-evoking dialect made them objects of mockery and hence more difficult to collect after 1880.

But, even though dialect versions were embarrassing to Black children, the tales themselves had durability. Goldthwaite asserts that, had Harris not intervened, "all but a few like 'The Tar Baby' would surely have been lost as the Civil War disrupted the flow of story from one generation to the next . . ." (91). This is an extremely dubious speculation. For more than a century the "flow of story" had not been interrupted; the original conditions that generated and fostered storytelling were still in evidence in post-Civil War America: isolating racial oppression, multi-generational family structures, the historical verbal emphasis. These conditions did not alter significantly even with the mass migration to the North. The stories were the tools that "travelled light," entertaining, socializing, teaching, protecting, comforting. In 1880, violence against Blacks was on the increase. The cunning schemes and victories of Brer Rabbit were as pertinent as ever. In fact, storytelling did not seriously falter until modern gadgetry—radio, movies, T.V.—began to usurp the functions of the story ritual.

If the tales are viewed as a kind of psychological weapon against tyranny, there is an ultimate irony in Harris's propagandistic editorials (through Remus) about the work ethic, and, on the other hand, Remus's narration of stories celebrating Brer Rabbit, a work-saboteur *par excellence*. Yet there seems to be little doubt that Harris perceived the tales as allegories when he writes: "The parallel between the case of the 'weakest' of all animals, who must perforce, triumph through his shrewdness, and the humble condition of the slave raconteur, is not without its pathos" (Wolfe 77). However, Harris deleted this sentence from his introduction to later editions of *Uncle Remus: His Songs and His Sayings*, again suggesting his ambivalence, or discomfort with certain aspects of the tales. Or perhaps it was the active conflict of warring selves: the professional journalist and aspiring novelist wishing to perserve the tales intact vs. the Old/New South journalist needing to subvert their message with the myth of the contented slave.

The critic, Bernard Wolfe, has suggested just such an inner conflict as an explanation for the wide disparities and contradictions in Harris's work. Whatever the answer, Wolfe sums it up in a few words: "Harris's inner split—and the South's, and white America's—is mirrored in the fantastic disparity between Remus's beaming face and Brer Rabbit's acts" (84).

Those who are now arguing to re-establish Harris within the children's literature canon are amazingly uncommitted to the stories themselves. Clearly, it was content as well as lively presentation styles that enabled the tales to endure, unwritten, until the last century. But, with Remus, comes a return to obsolete attitudes and historical perspectives as offered in Mark Twain's assessment of the Harris works:

> Uncle Remus is most deftly drawn, & is a lovable and delightful creation; he, & the little boy, & their relations with each other, are bright, fine literature, & worthy to live, for their own sakes." [The stories themselves] are only alligator pears [avocados]—one merely eats them for the sake of the salad-dressing.
>
> (Bickley 41)

Writing in 1974, Louis D. Rubin, Jr., University Distinguished Professor at the University of North Carolina, expressed his agreement with Twain:

> Clearly it is not the folktale subject matter as such that provides the chief appeal of the Uncle Remus stories. . . . The appeal lies in the way that they are told and in the dynamics of the relationship between Uncle Remus, the successive little white boys who listen, and the animal protagonists of the tales themselves, notably Brer Rabbit. . . . Mark Twain was quite right when he told Harris that "in reality the stories are only alligator pears—one merely eats them for the sake of the salad dressing" (165–166).

In his *Signal* articles, Goldthwaite seems to be thinking along similar lines when he writes that "never before had the image of the storyteller or the occasion of the telling been made so real to life or so appealing as with this old Negro and this compliant white child" (90).

How can this distortion be perceived as "real to life?" And what of Black children? What is their importance in this wave of white nostalgia? If the tales are perceived as "alligator pears," bland except for the "dressing" and presented in this manner, then there is nothing positive or useful for Black children to receive.

Harris may be perceived by his proponents as "the most sensitive interpreter" of the Southern Negro" in his time. Fortunately, the tales no longer require the interpretation of the "outsider" narrator. *Black Folktales*, retold by Julius Lester, presents fifteen stories in a lively, assertive voice.

A more recent publication is Virginia Hamilton's *The People Could Fly*, which presents the stories clearly enough for children to read on their own, and includes brief explanatory materials which discuss the dialect and the origins of the works.

Unlike Harris's retellings, these are not likely to make Black children believe that their culture is "something only to be laughed at" as the children of Harris's era feared.

Our next column will look at twentieth century retellings of Black folktales as candidates for the canon of children's literature.

References

Beacon, A. M. "Work and Methods of the Hampton Folk-Lore Society." *Journal of American Folk-Lore* 11(1898): 17–21.

Bickley, R. Bruce, Jr. *Joel Chandler Harris*. Boston: G. K. Hall, 1978.

Brookes, Stella Brewer. *Joel Chandler Harris-Folklorist*. Athens: University of Georgia Press, 1950.

Budd, Louis J. "Joel Chandler Harris and the Genteeling of Native American Humor." *Critical Essays on Joel Chandler Harris*. Ed. R. Bruce Bickley, Jr. Boston: G. K. Hall, 1981.

Goldthwaite, John. "The Black Rabbit: Part One." *Signal* 47(May 1985): 86–111.

Griffith, John W. and **Charles H. Frey, eds.** *Classics of Children's Literature*. New York: Macmillan, 1981.

Hall, Wade. *The Smiling Phoenix: Southern Humor from 1865 to 1914*. Gainesville: University of Florida Press, 1965.

Harris, Joel Chandler. *Told by Uncle Remus: New Stories of the Old Plantation*. New York: Grosset & Dunlop, 1905.

——. *Uncle Remus: His Songs and His Sayings*. New York: D. Appleton and Co., 1895.

Mikkelsen, Nina. "When the Animals Talked—A Hundred Years of Uncle Remus." *Children's Literature Association Quarterly* 8(Spring 1983): 3–5; 31.

Newell, William Wells. "Editor's Note." *Journal of American Folk-Lore* 11(1898): 291–292.

Rubin, Louis D., Jr. "Uncle Remus and the Ubiquitous Rabbit." *Critical Essays on Joel Chandler Harris*. Ed. R. Bruce Bickley, Jr. Boston: G. K. Hall, 1981.

Russell, Irwin. *Christmas Night in the Quarters and Other Poems*. New York: The Century Co., 1888.

Wolfe, Bernard. "Uncle Remus and the Malevolent Rabbit: 'Takes a Limber-Toe Gemmun fer ter Jump Jim Crow." *Critical Essays on Joel Chandler Harris*. Ed. R. Bruce Bickley, Jr. Boston: G. K. Hall, 1981.

65

THE UNCLE REMUS TRAVESTY

Part II: Julius Lester and Virginia Hamilton

Opal Moore and Donnarae MacCann

Source: *Children's Literature Association Quarterly* 11(4) (1986–1987): 205–209.

Part I of this article provided a study of Joel Chandler Harris and the development of his fictional character, Uncle Remus. Our intention was to establish a basis for understanding the original impetus for the creation of Remus, and the ways in which his origins and uses continue to corrupt the tradition of black storytelling. As Zora Neale Hurston's biographer, Robert Hemenway, states: "Joel Chandler Harris had fictionalized animal tales in his Uncle Remus stories . . . but the plantation context for the tale-telling made the folklore seem a childish pastime" (91). Harris' reductionism fettered the tales, disallowing them their complexity, historical weight, and the cultural interaction that promotes a meaningful, rather than a token, survival.

> Negroness is being rubbed off by close contact with white culture.
>
> —Zora Neale Hurston (Hemenway, 87)

In his admiration of the work of Joel Chandler Harris, Mark Twain elevated the figures of Remus and the little boy, referring to them as "bright, fine literature worthy to live for their own sakes." He dismissed the black folk material as "only alligator pears . . . one merely eats them for the sake of the salad dressing" (Bickley, 41). Twain's assessment epitomizes the persisting controversy over the Remus tales. That Remus is a false arbiter for the stories and damaging to their cultural importance is a fact acknowledged even by some Harris advocates, but often shrugged off as a minor loss compared to what is considered the "charm" in the figure of Remus and in the precocity of the little boy.

The question then remains as to the relative importance of Uncle Remus, a literary artifact, and the folktale as a legitimate cultural expression.

The answer is suggested in the observations of Roger D. Abrahams in his extensive introductory material in *African Folktales*, a collection of the folklore of modern Africa. He states that

> The very act of collecting and codifying . . . invariably distorts the "meaning" of a story. . . . Too often we forget that as Westerners, we learn these stories through books that underscore their imaginative and imaginary qualities. Equal emphasis should be placed on their effect on and importance to human interaction (18).

Abrahams' emphasis upon preserving within the folktales the "wisdom of the [African] ancestors", while difficult to accomplish for the African tale, is more difficult still for the African-American stories which have fallen out of active use in the community. Also, the context of the African tales, ancient or modern, is not likely to impinge upon or threaten the self-concept of an American reader. Although Abrahams expresses a degree of concern for "accuracy" in the tales of black America, the stress on authenticity is qualified because of a persistent reticence towards that subject of American slavery. For example, in his introduction to *Afro-American Folktales*, Abrahams bemoans the loss to black American lore of "grand recitations of genealogies . . . the chants accompanying the casting of cowry shells . . . the epic accounts of great heroes and and leaders of the people . . . ," vaguely concluding that "most of the political and philosophical dimensions of African story were lost to us in the Middle Passage" (18). Despite his concern for "equal emphasis" of the folktale to the black American —slave or free—Abrahams suffers from editorial blind spots. Such blind spots are shared by many other editors; one of them it the determination to present Joel Chandler Harris, the man, "more sympathetically."

Sympathy aside, if the Harris tellings are restored as the superlative mode for the black folktale, there are consequences: the tales themselves become subordinate to the entertainment quotient of Remus, "the quaint darky of the South's affections" (to use Twain's phrase). The "political and philosophical" possibilities are supplanted by the fiction of Remus; the stories become static antiques relevant only to the plantation setting; the value-teaching aspect of the tales is negated, both by the setting and by the passive voice of Remus as narrator; and the little white boy becomes, not in fiction, but in fact, the ideal or target audience in place of the black American for whom the tales were created. The Remus factor, so precious to a white audience, has been the alienation factor for blacks. The popularization of the folktale rendered it inaccessible to the "folks".

These effects have been the spur for the re-creation of the black folktale by black writers since Zora Neale Hurston collected material for *Mules & Men* and set out to reclaim a co-opted culture. In the spirit of Hurston, two contemporary writers, Julius Lester and Virginia Hamilton, have contributed to a body of literature aimed at reviving and preserving the integrity of traditional black tales for the benefit of the modern *black* child and, ultimately, all who care to hear. In 1969, Virginia Hamilton published the first of her *Jahdu* tales, folk-like stories for young readers, while Julius Lester stirred controversy with his collection, *Black Folktales*.

Lester defines folktales as "stories that give people a way of communicating with each other about each other . . . it is in stories like these that a child learns who his parents are and who he will become" (viii). Dedicating his volume to the memory of Zora Neale Hurston, "who made me glad I am me" and H. Rap Brown, '60's militant activist, Lester makes it clear that he regards the tales, not as quaint relics, but as an opportunity for a powerful dialogue binding the past to the present and future.

Black Folktales does not accommodate a white audience. Through strategies of voice and context, Lester 'performs' these tales for a private audience of black children. It is this pointed exclusivity of purpose that, according to Lester, earned the volume an overall lukewarm reception, despite occasional enthusiasm for the spiritual verity of the revisions from comrades. John A. Williams was among those who defended the effort:

> Since the essence of the folktale is to relate the life and times of a people, Lester has quite properly updated what was in the tales originally, and made them stories for today (10).

However, *Black Folktales* generated strong rebuke. According to Evelyn Geller in "Aesthetics, Morality and The Two Cultures," *Black Folktales*, though well received, has been criticized for "reverse racism" by some black librarians among others and excluded from several children's collections" (36). Most held a middle ground. The *Kirkus Review* critic suggested that the revisions might be "right and wrongheaded? but to thrash out the problems posed by the book would take many pages . . ." (1118). Undoubtedly so, since "the problems posed by the book" were no less than the problem of the 1960s, the contradictions of the black American presence.

It is the narrative voice of *Black Folktales*, with its bravado, braggadocio, "signifying and lying," innuendo, and at times unyielding bitterness, that is responsible for both the book's liveliness and its censure. It is a shifting narration that is sometimes gentle, as in the "love stories; but most often, it draws from the stringent tones of the 1960s and the strutting verbal play familiar to gatherings of black people. It is a voice selected and crafted for its capacity to deliver a revolutionary entertainment to feed the momentum of black selfhood and community. The stories, as told by Lester, insist upon their privacy and the legitimacy of black linguistic expression and attitudes.

In his zeal to recapture the original African and African-American use of oral art as social bonding agent and catalyst, Lester sacrifices subtlety for broad humor, as in this characterization of the white planters in "High John The Conqueror":

> John lived on one of them bad plantations . . . the white folks was so mean, that the rattlesnakes wouldn't even bite 'em. Fraid they'd poison themselves . . . White folks was so mean up there, they'd shoot a nigger just to bet on whether the body would fall frontwards or backwards. And they'd go whup the dead nigger's moma if the body fell the wrong way. (94)

Or he sacrifices nuance for instructional clarity as in his lesson on non-revolutionary black folks:

> Them was the kind of niggers that would sell their grandmama if it meant they'd get a word of praise from the white folks. . . . Them kind of niggers loved ol' massa so much that if massa's house caught on fire, the house nigger would say, "Massa, our house is on fire." . . . If massa was sick, house nigger would come round and say, "Massa, we sick, ain't we? (98)

Lester goes on to define house niggers as not simply foolish, but dangerous saboteurs of black liberation, observing that "we got some house niggers with us today. . . ," and "living with a house nigger is worse than picking up a hungry rattlesnake and putting it inside your shirt" (a subtle reference to another well-known tale of instruction, "The Nature of the Beast," not included in this collection). The point is that "High John" neutralizes his enemies by recognizing them (not being fooled by "protective coloring"), knowing their nature, taking outrageous but calculated risks, and surviving.

The texture and concerns of *Black Folktales* are so radically different from those of Harris' Remus tales that one might falsely suspect they had evolved from different folk traditions. However, the subversive and political aspects of the black folktale have been extensively explored. Nina Mikkelsen, an advocate of Joel Chandler Harris' work, refers to the obscuring of social and political references in "Brer Rabbit's Laughing Place." According to Mikkelsen, "It is unclear whether Harris understood, as did the black man, that 'laughin place' meant a particular place, The Underground Railroad. In the framework of the tale, he seems to be interpreting the term in a very different way . . ." (4). Later, Mikkelsen admits that "If the story makes sense only within the context of racial implications, it is difficult to imagine that by 1905 Harris did not notice these subtleties, and perhaps he did. But that did not mean . . . the boy should be burdened [with this information]" (5). She seems to suggest that given Harris' audience, the misdirection is acceptable. Using Remus to guide the reader away from the intended message of black liberation, Harris does not delete the reference, but instead, reduces the story's symbol to a literal interpretation that serves his own philosophical purposes. The distortion, which had natural appeal for those readers who liked to think of blacks as humorous, childlike figures or quaint curiosities, is also very persuasive to youngsters—a group that tends to view the world with simple matter-of-factness.

Some of Mikkelsen's observations are consistent with the comments of Robert Hemenway, in his introduction to *Uncle Remus: His Songs and His Sayings*, on the unsettling political potential of the tales:

> The Uncle Remus tales showcase a revolutionary black figure, Brer Rabbit, who must be sanitized for acceptance by the predominantly white American reading public of the nineteenth century. For slaves listening to the Brer Rabbit tales, the rabbit provided an acceptable outlet for an overwhelming hostility, which could lead to self-destruction if openly expressed. Black Brer Rabbit could only be assimilated into the culture of a postslavery America through the mouth of a quasi-Negro whom white readers desperately needed to defuse the stories' revolutionary hostility (29).

As long as blacks were securely restrained within a legal form of bondage, the tales were primarily cathartic. But for the disgruntled not-quite-free ex-slave, or a 1960s radical teacher, the exploits of the rabbit might suggest a new range of possibilities. Remus, therefore, is a fictional shackle.

The prickling narrative voice of *Black Folktales* is Remus' deliberate antithesis, as well as a rejection of the slave's self-protective devices. Lester does not deflect or mask his meaning, but cuts to the bitterness at the core of stories like "Keep On Steppin." He avoids the Brer Rabbit tales, preferring in "High John The Conqueror," the rabbit's less abstract human counterpart. And rather than narrate two separate "trickster John" tales, he joins them, allowing the character's actions to gather momentum, a momentum which climaxes with Massa volunteering for his own death.

In 1970, in an exchange with George Woods, children's book editor for *The New York Times*, Lester commented that "too much of black writing has been blacks writing to whites . . ." (67). Mr. Woods responded to this with a plea for color blindness in society stating, "I try not to look at kids as white or black . . . I want kids in general to have good books" (68). But as the political and social scientist Manning Marable has recently observed, "the phrase 'color blind' has two distinctly different meanings.

For [Martin Luther] King, 'color blind' meant transcending the barriers of legal and de facto segregation . . . [today it] means a public policy invisibility for Afro-Americans" (5).

A congenial invisibility in literature is not the answer. But the pressure for an ahistorical distillation of this material is great. In 1972, with the publication of *The Knee-High Man*, Lester bows to the pressure for non-contextual presentation of the literature. In his "Note About The Stories" he claims that the origins of the tales "are now of importance only to scholars" (31). *The Knee-High Man* is narrated routinely. The illustrations are uninteresting—the rabbit is a bunnyrabbit, the bear is a playfully rotund bear, and the farmer (in "The Rabbit and Mr. Bear") is no longer a symbol of oppression in contest with the subversive rabbit; he is a mild-looking black man, an inaccuracy of visual interpretation that confounds the second level meaning of the tale and destroys the significance of its preservation.

Only three years earlier, in his interview with George Woods, Julius Lester insisted that white Americans "make an effort . . . to meet me on my ground (68). The aggressive voice of *Black Folktales* directly refuted the modulation and flat portrayal of Uncle Remus and attempted to suggest some of the range and complexity both in the tale and the teller. Some of the stories have not since enjoyed as entertaining and un-selfconscious a presentation.

In "Jack and The Devil's Daughter," Lester gives us Jack, who, upon accepting his $1000 inheritance "put the $1000 in one pocket, a deck of cards in the other and took off down the road. . . . It was a very good thing Jack was talented at gambling, because . . . Jack treated work like he treated his mama, and he wouldn't hit his mama a lick . . ." (76). Lester is capable of creating sympathy for Death, overworked, harrassed, and hampered by an antiquated system, as he tries to collect on the anti-hero in "Stagolee."

> Stagolee was sitting on the porch, picking the blues on the guitar and drinking. All of a sudden, he looked up and saw this pale-looking white cat in this white sheet come riding up to his house on a white horse. . . . Death got off his horse, pulled out his address book, and said, "I'm looking for Stagolee Booker T. Washington Nicodemus Shadrack Nat Turner Jones. . . . I'm Death. Come with me. . . . Stagolee started laughing. "You who? . . . Be serious" (124, 125).

The most broodingly memorable tale is "People Who Could Fly," delivering in a straightforward, unembellished language the memory of a deep wish.

> Some of those who tried to go back to Africa would walk until they came to the ocean, and then they would walk into the water, and no

> one knows if they did walk to Africa through the water or if they drowned. It didn't matter (148).
>
> One day, one hot day when the sun singed the hair on the head . . . [a young witch doctor whispered a secret word, and the people] dropped their hoes, stretched out their arms and flew away, back to their home, back to Africa (154).

It is a tale whose theme of lost origins and lost magic has profoundly influenced the imaginations of contemporary black writers. Not by coincidence, it has reappeared as the title story in a collection by Virginia Hamilton. Hamilton's work is by no means an outgrowth of Julius Lester; instead, their work has some parallels. But where Lester left off, perhaps in frustration, Hamilton's efforts to re-establish a folk consciousness and the tradition of storytelling have continued, beginning in 1969 with the publication of *The Time-Ago Tales of Jahdu*, the first in a series of Jahdu stories designed for a young audience.

These stories center around Mama Luka and her afterschool charge, Lee Edward. Like Lester's narrative voice in *Black Folktales*, Mama Luka is a direct challenge to the image of Remus as storyteller. As important as the stories Mama Luka tells, is Hamilton's treatment of the relationship between the old woman and a little boy. Lee Edward is bright and respectful and thrives on the magic and presence of Mama Luka. Her stories fill the air in this "tight little room" in Harlem. Lee Edward need only "point" to the story he desires to hear, "an empty space just above Mama Luka's head," and Mama Luka "reached above her head. She cupped her hands around the place. . . . It has a strong taste to it [she said] for it tells how Jahdu found out he had magic power."

The stories tell of the supernatural power of Jahdu—how he acquires it, how he uses it for creative purposes, and how he misuses it for mischief. The Jahdu tales are not folk stories, but borrow from the conventions of traditional folk tales. Jahdu is a modern trickster; he is full of mischief and learns to shape-shift from the chameleon. He is not nearly as cunning, destructive, or deadly as the African trickster, Anansi, or his American counterpart, Brer Rabbit. Perhaps it is because Jahdu is not as ancient as they; he is "two feet tall. . . . And he had been in the world one year" (11). He is an offspring of the "grandfather" tales and must acquaint himself with the world and its entanglements.

Like the traditional trickster tales, the point of the Jahdu stories is not obvious. Their resemblance to traditional modes might not be apparent or meaningful to a child reader, but offer the opportunity for interpretation by adults reading the tales to children. The symbolism is also very gingerly handled. For example, in the "heavy" story that Mama Luka tells to Lee Edward, Jahdu encounters a family of tumbleweeds hurrying northward.

They advise him to follow their example, "for southward lies trouble" (25). Reminiscent of the traditional tale of the trickster meeting Trouble, Jahdu is curious "who Trouble is" and continues southward. In this case, Trouble is a giant who has a number of captives. Jahdu uses his magic to free them but, as the giant explains to Jahdu, "I don't need to go looking for them [the escapees] for it is the truth that everybody comes looking for Trouble and they always will." The possibilities for symbolic interpretation of the North and South and the Giant are kept open. The only hard fact is that Jahdu, with all of his magic, cannot overcome the Giant. He can only set him back a pace or two.

The direction of Jahdu's travels, in the first volume, is not clear until the final story. Jahdu, using the lesson of the chameleon, changes himself into a variety of things and is not satisfied until he changes into a little Black boy, a boy very much like Lee Edward. Lee Edward is bewildered why Jahdu would want to become a Black boy who has no power. He finally concludes that, "Once he's grown up he'll be a black Jahdu with all his power" (62).

In 1973, Hamilton published the second volume of Jahdu, *Time-Ago Lost: More Tales of Jahdu*. Like Julius Lester's *Knee-High Man* published the year before, *Time-Ago Lost* seems to suffer from over-generalization. Although the writing is still strong and lively, the stories themselves seem to have very little connection to Mama Luka and Lee Edward. Jahdu travels east to replenish his supply of magic Jahdu dust, to be reborn. He emerges from the "oven" full of dust and "glad to be a boy of yellow skin and black, black hair" (46). Clearly, the emphasis is on broadening the audience association of Jahdu. He is a more emphatically "universal" boy, a boy from everywhere and no particular place. While the idea of a universal spirit should not be considered a negative achievement, in *Time-Ago Lost* it seems to be achieved through an agonizing journey, through uncertain symbols and separate cultural references—a journey toward a noncontroversial, apolitical stance.

Still, *Time-Ago Lost* concludes with a powerful dream encounter between Lee Edward and Jahdu. Though Lee Edward cannot see Jahdu's face (no one ever has), he carries a "black lunchbox tucked under his arm" just like Lee Edward's father. And, although the final tale does not seem to evolve from the preceding three, the relationship between Mama Luka and Lee Edward provides a separate storyline, apart from the tales, that is touching and satisfying.

The third volume, *Jahdu* (published in 1980 in Greenwillow's "Read—Alone" series) is a single tale of how Jahdu loses and regains his power. The warmth of the previous books, and Mama Luka, are gone. The reference to Lee Edward is just in passing. But, the treatment of the power theme is strong. Jahdu does not really lose his power, he simply does not recognize it when he sees it. The altered appearances of familiar things, and the difficulty of keeping our personal "magic" in control reveals Hamilton's continued attention to the subtle changes in questions of power since the 1960s. As an allegory of the 1980s, it is quite apt.

Criticism of the Jahdu tales, especially the second volume, has pointed to the fact that the books seem aimed not so much at children as adults. The *Horn Book* critic complains of *Time-Ago Lost* that the "existential weariness pervading the book makes the reader feel that perhaps these stories were not really meant for children" (278). Perhaps they were not, but neither were the traditional folktales. Hamilton is attempting a very delicate balancing act—creating fiction that can be read to children, that will not offend white readers, but that continues to entertain the more serious concerns of a very precarious adult world. Hamilton, unlike Lester, does not choose to announce her troubling themes. She buries them in the light slender dialogue of an impish character, Jahdu, to be rediscovered in time and examined with closer scrutiny. This balancing act continues in the collection, *The People Could Fly: American Black Folktales*. With a simple graceful inversion, the emphasis is placed on "American" rather than "black."

The People Could Fly is a cross-section of folkstories. Some are familiar—Jack and John tales, and tales of Brer Rabbit and Brer Bear—but there are some pleasant surprises. The first is the treatment of the dialect. Rather than completely abandon the difficulties of the verbal patterns, Hamilton offers the tales in modified dialects of various groups of people. This offers the reader in a single volume an idea of the variety (based on geographic location) in spoken English. It ceases to be a common non-language shared by the ignorant.

A second feature of interest is the brief notation provided at the end of every story. Since the tales are phrased in a simplified manner for children, much of the pungency of the familiar tellings is missing. The "endnotes" offer brief historical information on the origins of tales, specific pertinent facts, and keys to the particular dialect in use. For example, the Tar Baby tale is broadened with information about the widespread presence of similar stories in other cultures, and its use as myth, (e.g., "in certain localities of Georgia, the tar baby was considered an actual, living, monstrous creature" (19). One reference is to the social significance of tales like "The Lion, Bruh Bear, and Bruh Rabbit"—a tale that describes the animals' first encounter with the destructive power of men. Hamilton states simply that ". . . the tales satisfied the slaves' need to explain symbolically and secretly the ruling behavior of slaveowners in relation to themselves" (12). Certainly much more could be said in behalf of the social and political implications of the stories, but Hamilton clearly does not care to allow such an emphasis. Her interest here is in the cultural and, to a degree, historical aspects of the folktales.

A third feature of this collection is the inclusion of a section devoted to tales that refer to the ongoing movement towards freedom. The story,

"Carrying the Running-Aways," is an actual slave narrative of a Kentucky slave named Arnold Gragston. The story, given in first person narration, describes how one man became a channel to freedom for others until, one day, he makes his own escape. The story is convincing in its description of a slave's apprehension, his fear based on a total ignorance of what lay on the "other side of the river":

> Now, I had heard about the other side of the river from the other slaves. But I thought it was just like the side where we lived on the plantation. I thought there were slaves and masters over there, too, and overseers and rawhide whips they used on us.

Hamilton lends even more weight to the tale with her personal testimony about the fugitive slave, Levi Perry: "This tale was told to me recently by my mother, Etta Belle Perry Hamilton, who is 92 years old and Levi Perry's oldest daughter" (146).

"Carrying the Running-Aways," and the title story, "The People Could Fly," are the most masterful tales in this collection. In both, the language is sure and powerful poetry:

> They say the people could fly. Say that long ago in Africa, some of the people knew magic. And they would walk up on the air like climbin up on a gate. And they flew like blackbirds over the fields. Black, shiny wings flappin against the blue up there (166).

The narrative voice has obtained the certainty that comes with a tale told many times over. The language is mellow, with sing-song repetition, almost a trance:

> The slaves labored in the fields from sunup to sundown. The owner of the slaves callin himself their Master. Say he was a hard lump of clay. A hard, glinty coal. A hard rock pile wouldn't be moved (167).

The People Could Fly is at home with itself in a way that Hamilton's previous "folk" works were not. They struggled, at times, too self-consciously for a multicultural format, whereas *The People Could Fly* is a work of optimism that presumes the best for the future, while attempting to reconcile the past with the present. The revolutionary black rabbit will always disturb, but here he has been tamed. Hamilton does not explore the dissent of the trickster tales; instead she has rendered the history in the art—the story—with a complexity seldom available to the very young.

The political features of the black rabbit that made him so durable have been consigned to the skeleton closet, but not, let's hope, the graveyard, because the struggle is far from over. Political, social and economic reversals will probably mark the entire decade of the 1980s, a period that has been compared to the Post-Reconstruction of the 1880s when Uncle Remus was created. The tentative, often rhetorical human rights concessions of the 1960s are now being challenged, abandoned, even denounced. Terrorist intimidation abroad has made many white Americans feel disrespected, unwanted, and insecure, and they, as a result, have rallied round the flag and Lady Liberty, and are on the lookout for other comforting memorabilia. A resurging interest in and apologia for Harris and his Uncle Remus should come as no surprise.

The struggle is not over, and young Americans need more than tricks and games. Still, if they know and understand their history—including Remus and the circumstances of his birth, his life and death—they can write their own stories of revolution or love.

References

Abrahams, Roger D. African *Folktales*. New York: Pantheon, 1983.

——. *Afro-American Folktales*. New York: Pantheon, 1985.

Bickley, R. Bruce. *Joel Chandler Harris*. Boston: G. K. Hall, 1978. Rev. of *Black Folktales*, by Julius Lester. *Kirkus Review* 15 Oct. 1969: 1117–1118.

Geller, Evelyn. "Aesthetic, Morality, and Two Cultures." *School Library Journal* (1970).

Hamilton, Virginia, ed. *The People Could Fly*. New York: Knopf, 1985.

——. *Time-Ago Lost: More Tales of Jahdu*. Ray Prather. New York: Macmillan, 1973.

——. *The Time-Ago Tales of Jahdu*. Illus. Nonny Hogrogian. New York: Macmillan, 1969.

Harris, Joel Chandler. *Uncle Remus: His Songs and His Sayings*. 1881. New York: Penguin, 1982.

Hemenway, Robert E. *Zora Neale Hurston: A Literary Biography*. Urbana: U of Illinois P, 1977.

Lester, Julius. *Black Folktales*. Illus. Tom Feelings. New York: Grove, 1969.

——. *The Knee-High Man*. Illus. Ralph Pinto. New York: Dial, 1972.

Lester, Julius, and **George Woods.** "Black and White: An Exchange." *The New York Times Book Review* 24 May 1970: 2; 34; 36–38. Rpt. in *The Black American in Books for Children*. Ed. Donnarae MacCann and Gloria Woodward. Metuchen: Scarecrow, 1985.

Manning, Marable. "America's 'Color Blind' Society." *The Hilltop* (1986).

Mikkelsen, Nina. "When the Animals Talked—A Hundred Years of Uncle Remus." *Children's Literature Association Quarterly* 8.1 (1983): 3–5; 31. Rev. of *Time-Ago Lost: More Tales of Jahdu*, by Virginia Hamilton. *The Horn Book Magazine* 59 (1973): 278.

Williams, John A. Rev. of *Black Folktales*, by Julius Lester. *The New York Times Book Review* 9 Nov. 1969: 10; 12.

66

BREAKING THE DISNEY SPELL

Jack Zipes

Source: Elizabeth Bell, Lynda Haas and Laura Sells (eds), *From Mouse to Mermaid: The Politics of Film, Gender, and Culture*, Bloomington, Indiana University Press, 1995, pp. 21–42.

It was not once upon a time, but at a certain time in history, before anyone knew what was happening, that Walt Disney cast a spell on the fairy tale, and he has held it captive ever since. He did not use a magic wand or demonic powers. On the contrary, Disney employed the most up-to-date technological means and used his own "American" grit and ingenuity to appropriate European fairy tales. His technical skills and ideological proclivities were so consummate that his signature has [obscured] the names of Charles Perrault, the Brothers Grimm, Hans Christian Andersen, and Carlo Collodi. If children or adults think of the great classical fairy tales today, be it *Snow White*, *Sleeping Beauty*, or *Cinderella*, they will think Walt Disney. Their first and perhaps lasting impressions of these tales and others will have emanated from a Disney film, book, or artifact. Though other filmmakers and animators produced remarkable fairy-tale films, Disney managed to gain a cultural stranglehold on the fairy tale, and this stranglehold has even tightened with the recent productions of *Beauty and the Beast* (1991) and *Aladdin* (1992). The man's spell over the fairy tale seems to live on even after his death.

But what does the Disney spell mean? Did Disney achieve a complete monopoly on the fairy tale during his lifetime? Did he imprint a particular *American* vision on the fairy tale through his animated films that dominates our perspective today? And, if he did manage to cast his mass-mediated spell on the fairy tale so that we see and read the classical tales through his lens, is that so terrible? Was Disney a nefarious wizard of some kind whose domination of the fairy tale should be lamented? Wasn't he just more inventive, more skillful, more in touch with the American spirit of the times than his competitors, who also sought to animate the classical fairy tale for the screen?

Of course, it would be a great exaggeration to maintain that Disney's spell totally divested the classical fairy tales of their meaning and invested them with his own. But it would not be an exaggeration to assert that Disney was a radical filmmaker who changed our way of viewing fairy tales, and that his revolutionary technical means capitalized on American innocence and utopianism to reinforce the social and political status quo. His radicalism was of the right and the righteous. The great "magic" of the Disney spell is that he animated the fairy tale only to transfix audiences and divert their potential utopian dreams and hopes through the false promises of the images he cast upon the screen. But before we come to a full understanding of this magical spell, we must try to understand what he did to the fairy tale that was so revolutionary and why he did it.

The oral and literary fairy tales

The evolution of the fairy tale as a literary genre is marked by dialectical appropriation that set the cultural conditions for its institutionalization and its expansion as a mass-mediated form through radio, film, and television. Fairy tales were first *told* by gifted tellers and were based on rituals intended to endow with meaning the daily lives of members of a tribe. As *oral folk tales*, they were intended to explain natural occurrences such as the change of the seasons and shifts in the weather or to celebrate the rites of harvesting, hunting, marriage, and conquest. The emphasis in most folk tales was on communal harmony. A narrator or narrators told tales to bring members of a group or tribe closer together and to provide them with a sense of mission, a *telos*. The tales themselves assumed a generic quality based on the function that they were to fulfill for the community or the incidents that they were to report, describe, and explain. Consequently, there were tales of initiation, worship, warning, and indoctrination. Whatever the type may have been, the voice of the narrator was known. The tales came directly from common experiences and beliefs. Told in person, directly, face-to-face, they were altered as the beliefs and behaviors of the members of a particular group changed.

With the rise of literacy and the invention of the printing press in the fifteenth century, the oral tradition of storytelling underwent an immense revolution. The oral tales were taken over by a different social class, and the form, themes, production, and reception of the tales were transformed. This change did not happen overnight, but it did foster discrimination among writers and their audiences almost immediately so that distinct genres were recognized and approved for certain occasions and functions within polite society or cultivated circles of readers. In the case of folk tales, they were gradually categorized as legends, myths, fables, comical anecdotes, and, of course, fairy tales. What we today consider fairy tales were actually just one type of the folk-tale tradition, namely the *Zaubermärchen* or the magic tale, which has many sub-genres. The French writers of the late seventeenth century called these tales *contes de fées* (fairy tales) to distinguish them from other kinds of *contes populaires* (popular tales), and what really distinguished a *conte de fée*, based on the oral *Zaubermärchen*, was its transformation into a literary tale that addressed the concerns, tastes, and functions of court society. The fairy tale had to fit into the French salons, parlors, and courts of the aristocracy and bourgeoisie if it was to establish itself as a genre. The writers, Mme D'Aulnoy, Charles Perrault, Mlle L'Héritier, Mlle de La Force, etc., knew and expanded upon oral and literary tales. They were not the initiators of the literary fairy-tale tradition in Europe (cf. Zipes 1989). Two Italian writers, Giovanni Francesco Straparola and Giambattista Basile, had already set an example for what the French were accomplishing.[1] But the French writers created an institution, that is, the genre of the literary fairy tale was institutionalized as an aesthetic and social means through which questions and issues of *civilité*, proper behavior and demeanor in all types of situations, were mapped out as narrative strategies for literary socialization, and in many cases, as symbolic gestures of subversion to question the ruling standards of taste and behavior.

While the literary fairy tale was being institutionalized at the end of the seventeenth and beginning of the eighteenth century in France, the oral tradition did not disappear, nor was it subsumed by the new literary genre. Rather, the oral tradition continued to feed the writers with material and was now also influenced by the literary tradition itself. The early chapbooks (cheap books), known as the *Bibliothèque Bleue*, that were carried by peddlers or *colporteurs* to the villages throughout France contained numerous abbreviated and truncated versions of the literary tales, and these were in turn told once again in these communities. In some cases, the literary tales presented new material that was transformed through the oral tradition and returned later to literature by a writer who remembered hearing a particular story.

By the beginning of the nineteenth century when the Brothers Grimm set about to celebrate German culture through their country's folk tales, the literary fairy tale had long since been institutionalized, and they, along with Hans Christian Andersen, Carlo Collodi, Ludwig Bechstein, and a host of Victorian writers from George MacDonald to Oscar Wilde, assumed different ideological and aesthetic positions within this institutionalization. These writers put the finishing touches on the fairy-tale genre at a time when nation-states were assuming their modern form and cultivating particular types of literature as commensurate expressions of national cultures.

What were the major prescriptions, expectations, and standards of the literary fairy tale by the end of the nineteenth century? Here it is important first to make some general remarks about the "violent" shift from the oral to the literary tradition and not just talk about the appropriation of the magic folk tale as a dialectical process. Appropriation does not occur without violence to the rhetorical text created in the oral tales. * * * Such violation of oral storytelling was crucial and necessary for the establishment of the bourgeoisie because it concerned the control of desire and imagination within the symbolic order of western culture.

Unlike the oral tradition, the literary tale was written down to be read in private, although, in some cases, the fairy tales were read aloud in parlors. However, the book form enabled the reader to withdraw from his or her society and to be alone with a tale. This privatization violated the communal aspects of the folk tale, but the very printing of a fairy tale was already a violation since it was based on separation of social classes. Extremely few people could read, and the fairy tale in form and content furthered notions of elitism and separation. In fact, the French fairy tales heightened the aspect of the chosen aristocratic elite who were always placed at the center of the seventeenth- and eighteenth-century narratives. They were part and parcel of the class struggles in the discourses of that period. To a certain extent, the fairy tales were the outcome of violent "civilized" struggles, material representations, which represented struggles for hegemony. As Nancy Armstrong and Leonard Tennenhouse have suggested,

> a class of people cannot produce themselves as a ruling class without setting themselves off against certain Others. Their hegemony entails possession of the key cultural terms determining what are the right and wrong ways to be a human being.[2]

No matter where the literary tale took root and established itself—France, Germany, England—it was written in a standard "high" language that the folk could not read, and it was written as a form of entertainment and education for members of the ruling classes. Indeed, only the well-to-do could purchase the books and read them. In short, by institutionalizing the literary fairy tale, writers and publishers violated the forms and concerns of non-literate, essentially peasant communities and set new standards of taste, production, and reception through the discourse of the fairy tale.

The literary fairy tales tended to exclude the majority of people who could not read, while the folk tales were open to everyone. Indeed, the literary narratives were individualistic and unique in form and exalted the power of those chosen to rule. In contrast, the oral tales had themes and characters that were readily recognizable and reflected common wish-fulfillments. Of course, one had to know the dialect in which they were told. From a philological standpoint, the literary fairy tale elevated the oral tale through the standard practice of printing and setting grammatical rules in "high French" or "high German." The process of violation is *not* one of total negation and should not be studied as one-dimensional, for the print culture enabled the tales to be preserved and cultivated, and the texts created a new realm of pleasurable reading that allowed for greater reflection on the part of the reader than could an oral performance of a tale. At the beginning, the literary fairy tales were written and published for adults, and though they were intended to reinforce the mores and values of French *civilité*, they were so symbolic and could be read on so many different levels that they were considered somewhat dangerous: social behavior could not be totally dictated, prescribed, and controlled through the fairy tale, and there were subversive features in language and theme. This is one of the reasons that fairy tales were not particularly approved for children. In most European countries it was not until the end of the eighteenth and early part of the nineteenth century that fairy tales were published for children, and even then begrudgingly, because their "vulgar" origins in the lower classes were suspect. Of course, the fairy tales for children were sanitized and expurgated versions of the fairy tales for adults, or they were new moralistic tales that were aimed at the domestication of the imagination, as Rüdiger Steinlein has demonstrated in his significant study.[3] The form and structure of the fairy tale for children were carefully regulated in the nineteenth century so that improper thoughts and ideas would not be stimulated in the minds of the young. If one looks carefully at the major writers of fairy tales for children who became classical and popular in the nineteenth century,[4] it is clear that they themselves exercised self-censorship and restraint in conceiving and writing down tales for children.

This is not to argue that the literary fairy tale as institution became one in which the imagination was totally domesticated. On the contrary, by the end of the nineteenth century the genre served different functions. As a whole, it formed a multi-vocal network of discourses through which writers used familiar motifs, topoi, protagonists, and plots symbolically to comment on the civilizing process and socialization in their respective countries. These tales did not represent communal values but rather the values of a particular writer. Therefore, if the writer subscribed to the hegemonic value system of his or her society and respected the canonical ideology of Perrault, the Grimms, and Andersen, he/she would write a conventional tale with conservative values, whether for adults or children. On the other hand, many writers would parody, mock, question, and undermine the classical literary tradition and produce original and subversive tales that were part and parcel of the institution itself.

The so-called original and subversive tales have kept the dynamic quality of the dialectical appropriation alive, for there has always been a danger that the written word, in contrast to the spoken word, will fix a structure, image, metaphor, plot, and value as sacrosanct. For instance, for some people the Grimms' fairy tales are holy, or fairy tales are considered holy and not to be touched. How did this notion emanate?

To a certain extent it was engendered by the Grimms and other folklorists who believed that the fairy tales arose from the spirit of the folk. Yet, worship of the fairy tale as holy scripture is a petrification of the fairy tale that is connected to the establishment of correct speech, values, and power more than anything else. This establishment through the violation of the oral practices was the great revolution and transformation of the fairy tale.

By the end of the nineteenth century the literary fairy tale had the following crucial functions as institution in middle-class society:

(1) It introduced notions of elitism and separatism through a select canon of tales geared to children who knew how to read.

(2) Though it was also told, the fact that the fairy tale was printed and in a book with pictures gave it more legitimacy and enduring value than an oral tale that disappeared soon after it was told.

(3) It was often read by a parent in a nursery, school, or bedroom to soothe a child's anxieties, for the fairy tales for children were optimistic and were constructed with the closure of the happy end.

(4) Although the plots varied and the themes and characters were altered, the classical fairy tale for children and adults reinforced the patriarchal symbolic order based on rigid notions of sexuality and gender.

(5) In printed form the fairy tale was property and could be taken by its owner and read by its owner at his or her leisure for escape, consolation, or inspiration.

(6) Along with its closure and reinforcement of patriarchy, the fairy tale also served to encourage notions of rags to riches, pulling yourself up by your bootstraps, dreaming, miracles, etc.

(7) There was always tension between the literary and oral traditions. The oral tales have continued to threaten the more conventional and classical tales because they can question, dislodge, and deconstruct the written tales. Moreover, within the literary tradition itself, there were numerous writers such as Charles Dickens, George MacDonald, Lewis Carroll, Oscar Wilde, and Edith Nesbit who questioned the standardized model of what a fairy tale should be.

(8) It was through script by the end of the nineteenth century that there was a full-scale debate about what oral folk tales and literary fairy tales were and what their respective functions should be. By this time the fairy tale had expanded as a high art form (operas, ballets, dramas) and low art form (folk plays, vaudevilles, and parodies) as well as a form developed classically and experimentally for children and adults. The oral tales continued to be disseminated through communal gatherings of different kinds, but they were also broadcast by radio and gathered in books by folklorists. Most important in the late nineteenth century was the rise of

folklore as an institution and of various schools of literary criticism that dealt with fairy tales and folk tales.

(9) Though many fairy-tale books and collections were illustrated (some lavishly) in the nineteenth century, the images were very much in conformity with the text. The illustrators were frequently anonymous and did not seem to count. Though the illustrations often enriched and deepened a tale, they were generally subservient to the text.

However, the domination of the word in the development of the fairy tale as genre was about to change. The next great revolution in the institutionalization of the genre was the film, for the images now imposed themselves on the text and formed their own text in violation of print but also with the help of the print culture. And here is where Walt Disney and other animators enter the scene.

Disney's magical rise

By the turn of the twentieth century there had already been a number of talented illustrators, such as Gustave Doré, George Cruikshank, Walter Crane, Charles Folkard, and Arthur Rackham, who had demonstrated great ingenuity in their interpretations of fairy tales though their images. In addition, the broadside, broadsheet, or *image d'Epinal* had spread in Europe and America during the latter part of the nineteenth century as a forerunner of the comic book, and these sheets with printed images and texts anticipated the first animated cartoons that were produced at the beginning of the twentieth century. Actually, the French filmmaker Georges Méliès began experimenting as early as 1896 with types of fantasy and fairy-tale motifs in his *féeries* or trick films.[5] He produced versions of *Cinderella*, *Bluebeard*, and *Little Red Riding Hood* among others. However, since the cinema industry itself was still in its early phase of development, it was difficult for Méliès to bring about a major change in the technological and cinematic institutionalization of the genre. As Lewis Jacobs has remarked,

> this effort of Méliès illustrated rather than re-created the fairy tale. Yet, primitive though it was, the order of the scenes did form a coherent, logical, and progressive continuity. A new way of making moving pictures had been invented. Scenes could now be staged and selected specially for the camera, and the movie maker could control both the material and its arrangement.[6]

During the early part of the twentieth century Walter Booth, Anson Dyer, Lotte Reiniger, Walter Lantz and others all used fairy tale plots in different ways in trick films and cartoons, but none of the early animators ever matched the intensity with which Disney occupied himself with the fairy tale. In fact, it is noteworthy that Disney's very first endeavors in animation (not considering the advertising commercials he made) were the fairy-tale adaptations that he produced with Ub Iwerks in Kansas City in 1922–23: *The Four Musicians of Bremen, Little Red Riding Hood, Puss in Boots, Jack and the Beanstalk, Goldie Locks and the Three Bears*, and *Cinderella*.[7] To a certain degree, Disney identified so closely with the fairy tales he appropriated that it is no wonder his name virtually became synonymous with the genre of the fairy tale itself.

However, before discussing Disney's particular relationship to the fairy-tale tradition, it is important to consider the conditions of early animation in America and role of the animator in general, for all this has a bearing on Disney's productive relationship with the fairy tale. In his important study, *Before Mickey: The Animated Film 1898–1928*, Donald Crafton remarks that

> the early animated film was the location of a process found elsewhere in cinema but nowhere else in such intense concentration: self-figuration, the tendency of the filmmaker to interject himself into his film. This can take several forms, it can be direct or indirect, and more or less camouflaged. . . . At first it was obvious and literal; at the end it was subtle and cloaked in metaphors and symbolic imagery designed to facilitate the process and yet to keep the idea gratifying for the artist and the audience. Part of the animation game consisted of developing mythologies that gave the animator some sort of special status. Usually these were very flattering, for he was pictured as (or implied to be) a demigod, a purveyor of life itself.[8]

As Crafton convincingly shows, the early animators before Disney literally drew themselves into the pictures and often appeared as characters in the films. One of the more interesting aspects of the early animated films is a psychically loaded tension between the artist and the characters he draws, one that is ripe for a Freudian or Lacanian reading, for the artist is always threatening to take away their "lives," while they, in turn, seek to deprive him of his pen (phallus) or creative inspiration so that they can control their own lives. (Almost all the early animators were men, and their pens and camera work assume a distinctive phallic function in early animation.) The hand with pen or pencil is featured in many animated films in the process of creation, and it is then transformed in many films into the tail of a cat or dog. This tail then acts as the productive force or artist's instrument throughout the film. For instance, Disney in his Alice films often employed a cat named Julius, who would take off his tail and use it as stick, weapon, rope, hook, question mark, etc. It was the phallic means to induce action and conceive a way out of a predicament.

The celebration of the pen/phallus as ruler of the symbolic order of the film was in keeping with the way that animated films were actually produced in the studios during the 1920s. That is, most of the studios, largely located in New York, had begun to be run on the Taylor system by men who joined together under the supervision of the head of the studio to produce the cartoons. After making his first fairy-tale films in close cooperation with Ub Iwerks in Kansas City, Disney moved to Hollywood, where he developed the taylorized studio to the point of perfection. Under his direction, the films were carefully scripted to project his story or vision of how a story should be related. The story-line was carried by hundreds of repetitious images created by the artists in his studios. Their contribution was in many respects like that of the dwarfs in *Snow White and the Seven Dwarfs:* they were to do the spadework, while the glorified prince was to come along and carry away the prize.

It might be considered somewhat one-dimensional to examine all of Disney's films as self-figurations, or embodiments of the chief designer's[9] wishes and beliefs. However, to understand Disney's importance as designer and director of fairy-tale films that set a particular pattern and model as the film industry developed, it does make sense to elaborate on Crafton's notion of self-figuration, for it provides an important clue for grasping the further development of the fairy tale as animated film or film in general.

We have already seen that one of the results stemming from the shift from the oral to the literary in the institutionalization of the fairy tale was a loss of live contact with the storyteller and a sense of community or commonality. This loss was a result of the social-industrial transformations at the end of the nineteenth century with the *Gemeinschaft* (community-based society) giving way to the *Gesellschaft* (contract-based society). However, it was not a total loss, for industrialization brought about greater comfort, sophistication, and literacy in addition to new kinds of communication in public institutions. Therefore, as I have demonstrated, the literary fairy tale's ascent corresponded to violent and progressive shifts in society and celebrated individualism, subjectivity, and reflection. It featured the narrative voice of the educated author and publisher over communal voices and set new guidelines for freedom of speech and expression. In addition, proprietary rights to a particular tale were established, and the literary tale became a commodity that paradoxically spoke out in the name of the unbridled imagination. Indeed, because it was born out of alienation, the literary fairy tale fostered a search for new "magical" means to overcome the instrumentalization of the imagination.

By 1900 literature began to be superseded by the mechanical means of reproduction that, Walter Benjamin declared, were revolutionary:

> the technique of reproduction detaches the reproduced object from the domain of tradition. By making many reproductions it

> substitutes a plurality of copies of a unique existence. And in permitting the reproduction to meet the beholder or listener in his own particular situation, it reactivates the object reproduced. These two processes lead to a tremendous shattering of tradition which is the obverse of the contemporary crisis and renewal of mankind. Both processes are intimately connected with the contemporary mass movements. Their most powerful agent is the film. Its social significance, particularly in its most positive form, is inconceivable without its destructive, cathartic aspect, that is, the liquidation of the traditional value of the cultural heritage.[10]

Benjamin analyzed how the revolutionary technological nature of the film could either bring about an aestheticization of politics leading to the violation of the masses through fascism, or a politicization of aesthetics that provides the necessary critical detachment for the masses to take charge of their own destiny.

In the case of the fairy-tale film at the beginning of the twentieth century, there are "revolutionary" aspects that we can note, and they prepared the way for progressive innovation that expanded the horizons of viewers and led to greater understanding of social conditions and culture. But there were also regressive uses of mechanical reproduction that brought about the cult of the personality and commodification of film narratives. For instance, the voice in fairy-tale films is at first effaced so that the image totally dominates the screen, and the words or narrative voice can only speak through the designs of the animator who, in the case of Walt Disney, has signed his name prominently on the screen. In fact, for a long time, Disney did not give credit to the artists and technicians who worked on his films. These images were intended both to smash the aura of heritage and to celebrate the ingenuity, inventiveness, and genius of the animator. In most of the early animated films, there were few original plots, and the story-lines did not count. Most important were the gags, or the technical inventions of the animators ranging from the introduction of live actors to interact with cartoon characters, to improving the movement of the characters so that they did not shimmer, to devising ludicrous and preposterous scenes for the sake of spectacle. It did not matter what story was projected just as long as the images astounded the audience, captured its imagination for a short period of time, and left the people laughing or staring in wonderment. The purpose of the early animated films was to make audiences awestruck and to celebrate the magical talents of the animator as demigod. As a result, the fairy tale as story was a vehicle for animators to express their artistic talents and develop their technology. The animators sought to impress audiences with their abilities to use pictures in such a way that they would forget the earlier fairy tales and remember the images that they, the new artists, were creating for them. Through these moving pictures, the animators appropriated literary and oral fairy tales to subsume the word, to have the final word, often through image and book, for Disney began publishing books during the 1930s to complement his films.

Of all the early animators, Disney was the one who truly revolutionalized the fairy tale as institution through the cinema. One could almost say that he was obsessed by the fairy-tale genre, or, put another way, Disney felt drawn to fairy tales because they reflected his own struggles in life. After all, Disney came from a relatively poor family, suffered from the exploitative and stern treatment of an unaffectionate father, was spurned by his early sweetheart, and became a success due to his tenacity, cunning, courage, and his ability to gather around him talented artists and managers like his brother Roy.

One of his early films, *Puss in Boots* (1922), is crucial for grasping his approach to the literary fairy tale and understanding how he used it as self-figuration that would mark the genre for years to come. Disney did not especially care whether one knew the original Perrault text of *Puss in Boots* or some other popular version. It is also unclear which text he actually knew. However, what is clear is that Disney sought to replace all versions with his animated version and that his cartoon is astonishingly autobiographical.

If we recall, Perrault wrote his tale in 1697 to reflect upon a cunning cat whose life is threatened and who manages to survive by using his brains to trick a king and an ogre. On a symbolic level, the cat represented Perrault's conception of the role of the *haute bourgeoisie* (his own class), who comprised the administrative class of Louis XIV's court and who were often the mediators between the peasantry and aristocracy. Of course, there are numerous ways to read Perrault's tale, but whatever approach one chooses, it is apparent that the major protagonist is the cat.

This is not the case in Disney's film. The hero is a young man, a commoner, who is in love with the king's daughter, and she fondly returns his affection. At the same time, the hero's black cat, a female, is having a romance with the royal white cat, who is the king's chauffeur. When the gigantic king discovers that the young man is wooing his daughter, he kicks him out of the palace, followed by Puss. At first, the hero does not want Puss's help, nor will he buy her the boots that she sees in a shop window. Then they go to the movies together and see a film with Rudolph Vaselino as a bullfighter, a reference to the famous Rudolph Valentino. This spurs the imagination of Puss. Consequently, she tells the hero that she now has an idea that will help him win the king's daughter, provided that he will buy her the boots. Of course, the hero will do anything to obtain the king's daughter, and he must disguise himself as a masked bullfighter. In the meantime Puss explains to him that she will use a hypnotic machine behind the scenes so he can defeat the bull and win the approval of the king. When the day of the bullfight arrives, the masked hero struggles but eventually manages to defeat the bull. The king is so overwhelmed by his performance that he offers his daughter's hand in marriage, but first he wants to know who the masked champion is. When the hero reveals himself, the king is enraged, but the hero grabs the princess and leads her to the king's chauffeur. The white cat jumps in front with Puss, and they speed off with the king vainly chasing after them.

Although Puss as cunning cat is crucial in this film, Disney focuses most of his attention on the young man who wants to succeed at all costs. In contrast to the traditional fairy tale, the hero is not a peasant, nor is he dumb. Read as a "parable" of Disney's life at that moment, the hero can be seen as young Disney wanting to break into the industry of animated films (the king) with the help of Ub Iwerks (Puss). The hero upsets the king and runs off with his prize possession, the virginal princess. Thus, the king is dispossessed, and the young man outraces him with the help of his friends.

But Disney's film is also an attack on the literary tradition of the fairy tale. He robs the literary tale of its voice and changes its form and meaning. Since the cinematic medium is a popular form of expression and accessible to the public at large, Disney actually returns the fairy tale to the majority of people. The images (scenes, frames, characters, gestures, jokes) are readily comprehensible by young and old alike from different social classes. In fact, the fairy tale is practically infantilized, just as the jokes are infantile. The plot records the deepest oedipal desire of every young boy: the son humiliates and undermines the father and runs off with his most valued object of love, the daughter/wife. By simplifying this oedipal complex semiotically in black-and-white drawings and making fun of it so that it had a common appeal, Disney also touched on other themes:

(1) Democracy—the film is very *American* in its attitude toward royalty. The monarchy is debunked, and a commoner causes a kind of revolution.

(2) Technology—it is through the new technological medium of the movies that Puss's mind is stimulated. Then she uses a hypnotic machine to defeat the bull and another fairly new invention, the automobile, to escape the king.

(3) Modernity—the setting is obviously the twentieth century, and the modern minds are replacing the ancient. The revolution takes place as the king is outpaced and will be replaced by a commoner who knows how to use the latest inventions.

But who is this commoner? Was Disney making a statement on behalf of the masses? Was Disney celebrating "everyone" or "every man"? Did Disney believe in revolution and socialism? The answer to all these questions is simple: no.

Casting the commodity spell with *Snow White*

Disney's hero is the enterprising young man, the entrepreneur, who uses technology to his advantage. He does nothing to help the people or the community. In fact, he deceives the masses and the king by creating the illusion that he is stronger than the bull. He has learned, with the help of Puss, that one can achieve glory through deception. It is through the artful use of images that one can sway audiences and gain their favor. Animation is trickery—trick films—for still images are made to seem as if they move through automatization. As long as one controls the images (and machines) one can reign supreme, just as the hero is safe as long as he is disguised. The pictures conceal the controls and machinery. They deprive the audience of viewing the production and manipulation, and in the end, audiences can no longer envision a fairy tale for themselves as they can when they read it. The pictures now deprive the audience of visualizing their own characters, roles, and desires. At the same time, Disney offsets the deprivation with the pleasure of scopophilia and inundates the viewer with delightful images, humorous figures, and erotic signs. In general, the animator, Disney, projects the enjoyable fairy tale of his life through his own images, and he realizes through animated stills his basic oedipal dream that he was to play out time and again in most of his fairy-tale films. It is the repetition of Disney's infantile quest—the core of American mythology—that enabled him to strike a chord in American viewers from the 1920s to the present.

However, it was not through *Puss in Boots* and his other early animated fairy tales that he was to captivate audiences and set the "classical" modern model for animated fairy-tale films. They were just the beginning. Rather, it was in *Snow White and the Seven Dwarfs* (1937) that Disney fully appropriated the literary fairy tale and made his signature into a trademark for the most acceptable type of fairy tale in the twentieth century. But before the making of *Snow White*, there were developments in his life and in the film industry that are important to mention in order to grasp why and how *Snow White* became the first definitive animated fairy-tale film—definitive in the sense that it was to define the way other animated films in the genre of the fairy tale were to be made.

After Disney had made several Laugh-O-Gram fairy-tale films, all ironic and modern interpretations of the classical versions, he moved to Hollywood in 1923 and was successful in producing fifty-six *Alice* films, which involved a young girl in different adventures with cartoon characters. By 1927 these films were no longer popular, so Disney and Iwerks soon developed Oswald the Lucky Rabbit cartoons that also found favor with audiences. However, in February of 1928, while Disney was in New York trying to renegotiate a contract with his distributor Charles Mintz, he learned that Mintz, who owned the copyright to Oswald, had lured some of Disney's best animators to work for another studio. Disney faced bankruptcy because he refused to capitulate to the exploitative conditions that Mintz set for the distribution and production of Disney's films.[11] This experience sobered Disney in his attitude to the cutthroat competition in the film industry, and when he returned to Hollywood, he vowed to maintain complete control over all his productions—a vow that he never broke.

In the meantime, Disney and Iwerks had to devise another character for their company if they were to survive, and they conceived the idea for films featuring a pert mouse named Mickey. By September of 1928, after making two Mickey Mouse shorts, Disney, similar to his masked champion in *Puss in Boots*, had devised a way to gain revenge on Mintz and other animation studios by producing the first animated cartoon with sound, *Steamboat Willie*, starring Mickey Mouse. From this point on, Disney became known for introducing new inventions and improving animation so that animated films became almost as realistic as films with live actors and natural settings. His next step after sound was color, and in 1932 he signed an exclusive contract with Technicolor and began producing his *Silly Symphony* cartoons in color. More important, Disney released *The Three Little Pigs* in 1933 and followed it with *The Big Bad Wolf* (1934) and *The Three Little Wolves* (1936), all of which involved fairy-tale characters and stories that touched on the lives of people during the Depression. As Bob Thomas has remarked, "*The Three Little Pigs* was acclaimed by the Nation. The wolf was on many American doorsteps, and 'Who's Afraid of the Big Bad Wolf?' became a rallying cry."[12] Not only were wolves on the doorsteps of Americans but also witches, and to a certain extent, Disney, with the help of his brother Roy and Iwerks, had been keeping "evil" connivers and competitors from the entrance to the Disney Studios throughout the 1920s. Therefore, it is not by chance that Disney's next major experiment would involve a banished princess, loved by a charming prince, who would triumph over deceit and regain the rights to her castle. *Snow White and the Seven Dwarfs* was to bring together all the personal strands of Disney's own story with the destinies of desperate Americans who sought hope and solidarity in their fight for survival during the Depression of the 1930s.

Of course, by 1934 Disney was, comparatively speaking, wealthy. He hired Don Graham, a professional artist, to train studio animators at the Disney Art School, founded in November 1932. He then embarked on ventures to stun moviegoers with his ingenuity and talents as organizer, storyteller, and filmmaker. Conceived some time in 1934, *Snow White* was to take three years to complete, and Disney did not leave one stone unturned in his preparations for the first full-length animated fairy-tale film ever made. Disney knew he was making history even before history had been made.

During the course of the next three years, Disney worked closely with all the animators and technicians assigned to the production of *Snow White*. By now, Disney had divided his studio into numerous departments, such as animation, layout, sound, music, storytelling, etc., and had placed certain animators in charge of developing the individual characters of Snow White, the prince, the dwarfs, and the queen/crone. Disney spent thousands of dollars on a multiplane camera to capture the live-action depictions that he desired, the depth of the scenes, and close-ups. In addition, he had his researchers experiment with colored gels, blurred focus, and filming through frosted glass, while he employed the latest inventions in sound and music to improve the synchronization with the characters on the screen. Throughout the entire production of this film, Disney had to be consulted and give his approval for each stage of development. After all, *Snow White* was his story that he had taken from the Grimm Brothers and changed completely to suit his tastes and beliefs. He cast a spell over this German tale and transformed it into something peculiarly American. Just what were the changes he induced?

(1) Snow White is an orphan. Neither her father nor her mother are alive, and she is at first depicted as a kind of "Cinderella," cleaning the castle as a maid in a patched dress. In the Grimms' version there is the sentimental death of her mother. Her father remains alive, and she is never forced to do the work of commoners such as wash the steps of the castle.

(2) The prince appears at the very beginning of the film on a white horse and sings a song of love and devotion to Snow White. He plays a negligible role in the Grimms' version.

(3) The queen is not only jealous that Snow White is more beautiful than she is, but she also sees the prince singing to Snow White and is envious because her stepdaughter has such a handsome suitor.

(4) Though the forest and the animals do not speak, they are anthropomorphized. In particular the animals befriend Snow White and become her protectors.

(5) The dwarfs are hardworking and rich miners. They all have names —Doc, Sleepy, Bashful, Happy, Sneezy, Grumpy, Dopey—representative of certain human characteristics and are fleshed out so that they become the star attractions of the film. Their actions are what counts in defeating evil. In the Grimms' tale, the dwarfs are anonymous and play a humble role.

(6) The queen only comes one time instead of three as in the Grimms' version, and she is killed while trying to destroy the dwarfs by rolling a huge stone down a mountain to crush them. The punishment in the Grimms' tale is more horrifying because she must dance in red-hot iron shoes at Snow White's wedding.

(7) Snow White does not return to life when a dwarf stumbles while carrying the glass coffin as in the Grimms' tale. She returns to life when the prince, who has searched far and wide for her, arrives and bestows a kiss on her lips. His kiss of love is the only antidote to the queen's poison.

At first glance, it would seem that the changes that Disney made were not momentous. If we recall Sandra Gilbert and Susan Gubar's stimulating analysis in their book, *The Madwoman in the Attic* (1979), the film follows the classic "sexist" narrative about the framing of women's lives through a male discourse. Such male framing drives women to frustration and some women to the point of madness. It also pits women against women in competition for male approval (the mirror) of their beauty that is short-lived. No matter what they may do, women cannot chart their own lives without male manipulation and intervention, and in the Disney film, the prince plays even more of a framing role since he is introduced at the beginning while Snow White is singing, "I'm Wishing for the One I Love To Find Me Today." He will also appear at the end as the fulfillment of her dreams.

There is no doubt that Disney retained key ideological features of the Grimms' fairy tale that reinforce nineteenth-century patriarchal notions that Disney shared with the Grimms. In some way, they can even be considered his ancestor, for he preserves and carries on many of their benevolent attitudes toward women. For instance, in the Grimms' tale, when Snow White arrives at the cabin, she pleads with the dwarfs to allow her to remain and promises that she will wash the dishes, mend their clothes, and clean the house. In Disney's film, she arrives and notices that the house is dirty. So, she convinces the animals to help her make the cottage tidy so that the dwarfs will perhaps let her stay there. Of course, the house for the Grimms and Disney was the place where good girls remained, and one shared aspect of the fairy tale and the film is about the domestication of women.

However, Disney went much further than the Grimms to make his film more memorable than the tale, for he does not celebrate the domestication of women so much as the triumph of the banished and the underdogs. That is, he celebrates his destiny, and insofar as he had shared marginal status with many Americans, he also celebrates an American myth of Horatio Alger: it is a male myth about perseverance, hard work, dedication, loyalty, and justice.

It may seem strange to argue that Disney perpetuated a male myth through his fairy-tale films when, with the exception of *Pinocchio* (1940), they all featured young women as "heroines": *Sleeping Beauty* (1959), *Cinderella* (1950), and *The Little Mermaid* (1989). However, despite their beauty and charm, these figures are pale and pathetic compared to the more active and demonic characters in the film. The witches are not only agents of evil but represent erotic and subversive forces that are more appealing both for the artists who drew them and the audiences.[13] The young women are helpless ornaments in need of protection, and when it comes to the action of the film, they are omitted. In *Snow White and the Seven Dwarfs*, the film does not really become lively until the dwarfs enter the narrative. They are the mysterious characters who inhabit a cottage, and it is through their hard work and solidarity that they are able to maintain a world of justice and restore harmony to the world. The dwarfs can be interpreted as the humble American workers, who pull together during a depression. They keep their spirits up by singing a song "Hi ho, it's home from work we go," or "Hi ho, it's off to work we go," and their determination is the determination of every worker, who will succeed just as long as he does his share while women stay at home and keep the house clean. Of course, it is also possible to see the workers as Disney's own employees, on whom he depended for the glorious outcome of his films. In this regard, the prince can be interpreted as Disney, who directed the love story from the beginning. If we recall, it is the prince who frames the narrative. He announces his great love at the beginning of the film, and Snow White cannot be fulfilled until he arrives to kiss her. During the major action of the film, he, like Disney, is lurking in the background and waiting for the proper time to make himself known. When he does arrive, he takes all the credit as champion of the disenfranchised, and he takes Snow White to his castle while the dwarfs are left as keepers of the forest.

But what has the prince actually done to deserve all the credit? What did Disney actually do to have his name flash on top of the title as "Walt Disney's Snow White and the Seven Dwarfs" in big letters and later credit his coworkers in small letters? As we know, Disney never liked to give credit to the animators who worked with him, and they had to fight for acknowledgment.[14] Disney always made it clear that he was the boss and owned total rights to his products. He had struggled for his independence against his greedy and unjust father and against fierce and ruthless competitors in the film industry. As producer of the fairy-tale films and major owner of the Disney studios, he wanted to figure in the films and sought, as Crafton has noted, to create a more indelible means of self-figuration. In *Snow White*, he accomplished this by stamping his signature as owner on the title frame of the film and then by having himself embodied in the figure of the prince. It is the prince Disney who made inanimate figures come to life through his animated films, and it is the prince who is to be glorified in *Snow White and the Seven Dwarfs* when he resuscitates Snow White with a magic kiss. Afterward he holds Snow White in his arms, and in the final frame, he leads her off on a white horse to his golden castle on a hill. His golden castle—every woman's dream—supersedes the dark, sinister castle of the queen. The prince becomes Snow White's reward, and his power and wealth are glorified in the end.

There are obviously mixed messages or multiple messages in *Snow White and the Seven Dwarfs*, but the overriding sign, in my estimation, is the signature of Disney's self-glorification in the name of justice. Disney wants the world *cleaned up*, and the pastel colors with their sharply drawn ink lines create images of cleanliness, just as each sequence reflects a clearly conceived and preordained destiny for all the characters in the film. For Disney, the Grimms' tale is not a vehicle to explore the deeper implications of the narrative and its history.[15] Rather, it is a vehicle to display what he can do as an animator with the latest technological and artistic developments in the industry. The story is secondary, and if there is a major change in the plot, it centers on the power of the prince, the only one who can save Snow White, and he becomes the focal point by the end of the story.

In Disney's early work with fairy tales in Kansas City, he had a wry and irreverent attitude toward the classical narratives. There was a strong suggestion, given the manner in which he and Iwerks rewrote and filmed the tales, that they were "revolutionaries," the new boys on the block, who were about to introduce innovative methods of animation into the film industry and speak for the outcasts. However, in 1934, Disney was already the kingpin of animation, and he used all that he had learned to reinforce his power and command of fairy-tale animation. The manner in which he copied the musical plays and films of his time, and his close adaptation of fairy tales with patriarchal codes, indicate that all the technical experiments would not be used to foster social change in America but to keep power in the hands of individuals like himself, who felt empowered to design and create new worlds. As Richard Schickel has perceptively remarked, Disney

> could make something his own, all right, but that process nearly always robbed the work at hand of its uniqueness, of its soul, if you will. In its place he put jokes and songs and fright effects, but he always seemed to diminish what he touched. He came always as a conqueror, never as a servant. It is a trait, as many have observed, that many Americans share when they venture into foreign lands hoping to do good but equipped only with knowhow instead of sympathy and respect for alien traditions.[16]

Disney always wanted to do something new and unique just as long as he had absolute control. He also knew that novelty would depend on the collective skills of his employees, whom he had to keep happy or indebted to him in some way. Therefore, from 1934 onward, about the time that he conceived his first feature-length fairy-tale film, Disney became the orchestrator of a corporate network that changed the function of the fairy-tale genre in America. The power of Disney's fairy-tale films does not reside in the uniqueness or novelty of the productions, but in Disney's great talent for holding antiquated views of society *still* through animation and his use of the latest technological developments in cinema to his advantage. His adaptation of the literary fairy tale for the screen led to the following changes in the institution of the genre:

(1) Technique takes precedence over the story, and the story is used to celebrate the technician and his means.

(2) The carefully arranged images narrate through seduction and imposition of the animator's hand and the camera.

(3) The images and sequences engender a sense of wholeness, seamless totality, and harmony that is orchestrated by a savior/technician on and off the screen.

(4) Though the characters are fleshed out to become more realistic, they are also one-dimensional and are to serve functions in the film.

There is no character development because the characters are stereotypes, arranged according to a credo of domestication of the imagination.

(5) The domestication is related to colonization insofar as the ideas and types are portrayed as models of behavior to be emulated. Exported through the screen as models, the "American" fairy tale colonizes other national audiences. What is good for Disney is good for the world, and what is good in a Disney fairy tale is good in the rest of the world.

(6) The thematic emphasis on cleanliness, control, and organized industry reinforces the technics of the film itself: the clean frames with attention paid to every detail; the precise drawing and manipulation of the characters as real people; the careful plotting of the events that focus on salvation through the male hero.

(7) Private reading pleasure is replaced by pleasurable viewing in an impersonal cinema. Here one is brought together with other viewers not for the development of community but to be diverted in the French sense of *divertissement* and American sense of diversion.

(8) The diversion of the Disney fairy tale is geared toward nonreflective viewing. Everything is on the surface, one-dimensional, and we are to delight in one-dimensional portrayal and thinking, for it is adorable, easy, and comforting in its simplicity.

Once Disney realized how successful he was with his formula for feature-length fairy tales, he never abandoned it, and in fact, if one regards the two most recent Disney Studio productions of *Beauty and the Beast* (1991) and *Aladdin (1992)*, Disney's contemporary animators have continued in his footsteps. There is nothing but the "eternal return of the same" in *Beauty and the Beast* and *Aladdin* that makes for enjoyable viewing and delight in techniques of these films as commodities, but nothing new in the exploration of narration, animation, and signification.

There is something sad in the manner in which Disney "violated" the literary genre of the fairy tale and packaged his versions in his name through the merchandising of books, toys, clothing, and records. Instead of using technology to enhance the communal aspects of narrative and bring about major changes in viewing stories to stir and animate viewers, he employed animators and technology to stop thinking about change, to return to his films, and to long nostalgically for neatly ordered patriarchal realms. Fortunately, the animation of the literary fairy tale did not stop with Disney, but that is another tale to tell, a tale about breaking Disney's magic spell.

Notes

1 See Straparola's *Le piacevoli notti* (1550–53), translated as *The Facetious Nights* or *The Delectable Nights*, and Basile's *Lo Cunto de li Cunti* (*The Story of Stories*, 1634–36), better known as *The Pentamerone*. The reason that the Italians did not "institutionalize" the genre is that the literary culture in Italy was

not prepared to introduce the tales as part of the civilizing process, nor were there groups of writers who made the fairy-tale genre part of their discourse.

2 Nancy Armstrong and Leonard Tennenhouse, eds., *The Violence of Representation: Literature and the History of Violence* (New York: Routledge, 1989), 24.

3 Cf. *Die Domestizierte Phantasie: Studien zur Kinderliteratur, Kinderlektüre und Literaturpädagogik des 18. und frühen 19. Jahrhunderts* (Heidelberg: Carl Winter, 1987).

4 This list would include the Grimms, Wilhelm Hauff, Ludwig Bechstein, Hans Christian Andersen, and Madame De Ségur. In addition, numerous collections of expurgated folk tales from different countries became popular in primers by the end of the nineteenth century. Here one would have to mention the series of color fairy books edited by Andrew Lang in Great Britain.

5 Lewis Jacobs. "George Méliès: Scenes," in *The Emergence of Film Art: The Evolution and Development of the Motion Picture as an Art, from 1900 to the Present*, 2d ed., ed. Lewis Jacob (New York: Norton, 1979).

6 Jacobs, "George Méliès," 13.

7 Cf. Russell Merrit and J. B. Kaufman, *Walt in Wonderland: The Silent Films of Walt Disney*, for the most complete coverage of Disney's early development.

8 Donald Crafton, *Before Mickey: The Animated Film 1898–1928* (Cambridge: MIT Press, 1982), 11.

9 I am purposely using the word designer instead of animator because Disney was always designing things, made designs, and had designs. A designer is someone who indicates with a distinctive mark, and Disney put his mark on everything in his studios. A designing person is often a crafty person who manages to put his schemes into effect by hook or by crook. Once Disney stopped animating, he became a designer.

10 Walter Benjamin, "The Work of Art in the Age of Mechanical Reproduction," in *Illuminations*, trans. Harry Zohn (New York: Harcourt, Brace, and World, 1968), 223.

11 Leonard Mosley, *Disney's World* (New York: Stein and Day, 1985), 85–140.

12 Bob Thomas, *Disney's Art of Animation: From Mickey Mouse to Beauty and the Beast* (New York: Hyperion, 1991), 49.

13 Solomon cites the famous quotation by Woody Allen in *Annie Hall*: "You know, even as a kid I always went for the wrong women. When my mother took me to see 'Snow White,' everyone fell in love with Snow White; I immediately fell for the Wicked Queen" [Charles Solomon, "Bad Girls Finish First in Memory of Disney Fans," *Milwaukee Journal* 17 August 1980, 28].

14 Bill Peet, for example, an "in-betweener" in the early Disney studio, worked for a year and a half on *Pinocchio* (1940). Peet relates that, after watching the film in his neighborhood theatre, "I was dumbfounded when the long list of screen credits didn't include my name" (*Bill Peet: An Autobiography* [Boston: Houghton Mifflin, 1989] 108).

15 Karen Merritt makes the interesting point that "Disney's *Snow White* is an adaptation of a 1912 children's play (Disney saw it as a silent movie during his adolescence) still much performed today, written by a male Broadway producer under a female pseudonym; this play was an adaptation of a play for immigrant children from the tenements of lower East Side New York; and that play, in turn, was a translation and adaptation of a German play for children by a prolific writer of children's comedies and fairy-tale drama. Behind these plays was the popularity of nineteenth- and early twentieth-century fairy-tale pantomimes at Christmas in England and fairy-tale plays in Germany and America. The imposition of childish behavior on the dwarfs, Snow White's resulting

mothering, the age ambiguities in both Snow White and the dwarfs, the 'Cinderella' elements, and the suppression of any form of sexuality were transmitted by that theatrical tradition, which embodied a thoroughly developed philosophy of moral education in representations for children. . . . By reading Disney's *Snow White* by the light of overt didacticism of his sources, he no longer appears the moral reactionary disdained by contemporary critics. Rather, he is the entertainer who elevates the subtext of play found in his sources and dares once again to frighten children" [Karen Merritt, "The Little Girl/Little Mother Transformation: The American Evolution of 'Snow White and the Seven Dwarfs,'" in *Storytelling in Animation: The Art of the Animated Image*, ed. John Canemaker (Los Angeles: American Film Institute, 1994), 106]. Though it may be true that Disney was more influenced by an American theatrical and film tradition, the source of all these productions, one acknowledged by Disney, was the Grimms' tale. And, as I have argued, Disney was not particularly interested in experimenting with the narrative to shock children or provide a new perspective on the traditional story. For all intents and purposes his film reinforces the didactic messages of the Grimms' tale, and it is only in the technical innovations and designs that he did something startlingly new. It is not the object of critique to "disdain" or "condemn" Disney for reappropriating the Grimms' tradition to glorify the great designer, but to understand those cultural and psychological forces that led him to map out his narrative strategies in fairy-tale animation.

16 Richard Schickel, *The Disney Version* (New York: Simon and Schuster, 1968), 227.

67

THE REPUBLIC OF HEAVEN

Philip Pullman

Source: *Horn Book Magazine* 57(7) (November/December 2001): 655–667.

What happens to the Kingdom of Heaven when the King dies? And what has this to do with children's literature?

Children's books [. . .] are capable of expressing just about any idea, and illuminating just about any subject. Well, I certainly haven't read all the children's books there are; I haven't even read very many. What's more, my reading has been unsystematic, butterfly-like, and anything but rigorous. Nevertheless it seems to me that the children's books I love are saying something important about the most important subject I know, which is the death of God and its consequences.

The idea that God is dead has been familiar, and has felt true, to many of us for a long time now. Those who believe that he's still alive will of course disagree with some of what I say, though I hope they'll stay with me till I come to the end. Anyway, I take it that there really is no God anymore; the old assumptions have all withered away. That's my starting point: that the idea of God with which I was brought up is now perfectly incredible.

But not believing in God is not quite like not believing in the tooth fairy. There are bigger consequences. G. K. Chesterton, a stout defender of orthodoxy in religion, said that when people stop believing in God, they don't believe in nothing, they believe in anything. This was a warning against the occult, and astrology, and fashionable religions, especially those from that sinister place, the East. Chesterton was easily excited. He once wrote about seeing "evil shapes" in the pattern of a Turkish carpet—an odd idea that turns up in C. S. Lewis's Narnia too, where the Witch kills Aslan with a knife of "a strange and evil shape." What is an *evil shape*, I wonder? Could a triangle be evil, for example? Are some kinds of triangles decent and God-fearing, whereas others are treacherous and inclined to furtive sodomy? And could you tell that from the *shape*?

Much more grown-up than this penny-dreadful stuff is the famous comment of George Eliot, talking about God, Immortality, and Duty:

"How inconceivable was the first, how unbelievable the second, and yet how peremptory and absolute the third." I like that earnestness. I admire it a great deal. But it points to one of the most important consequences of the death of God, because something's lacking: if Duty is peremptory and absolute, so (given our nature) is the necessity for something else, which one might call joy. George Eliot's universe of duty is a bleak place, and human beings need more than that.

Now it's not legitimate, I know, to argue from the *want* of something to the necessity that it must exist. It's very poor logic. But so much the worse for logic. The heroine of this essay—and why shouldn't an essay have heroes and heroines?—is the young Jane Eyre, and I'm with her on this: "You think I have no feelings," she says to her cold-hearted guardian Mrs. Reed, "and that I can do without one bit of love or kindness; but I cannot live so." She demands love, because of her passionate need of it, and in due course love appears, though not before Jane Eyre the girl has grown and suffered. If we need something, says *Jane Eyre* the book, we must search for it, or create it. I think that the book is right, and I think we need this thing which I've called joy. I might also have called it Heaven.

What I'm referring to is a sense that things are right and good, and we are part of everything that's right and good. It's a sense that we're connected to the universe. This connectedness is where meaning lies; the meaning of our lives is their connection with something other than ourselves. The religion that's now dead did give us that, in full measure: we were part of a huge cosmic drama, involving a Creation and a Fall and a Redemption, and Heaven and Hell. What we did *mattered*, because God saw everything, even the fall of a sparrow. And one of the most deadly and oppressive consequences of the death of God is this sense of meaningless or alienation that so many of us have felt in the past century or so.

However, there is one religion whose peculiar and intense flavor seems to speak very directly to precisely this psychological (or spiritual) condition. I'm talking about Gnosticism. The Gnostic religion, like the Christian one, tells us a story that involves ourselves. To sum it up briefly and crudely, the Gnostic myth says that this world, the material universe we live in, was created not by a good God but by an evil Demiurge, who made it as a kind of prison for the sparks of divinity that had fallen, or been stolen, from the inconceivably distant true God who was their real source. These little sparks of god-ness are known as the *pneuma*, or soul, and each of us has a spark inside us. It's the duty of the Gnostics, the knowing ones, to try and escape from this world, out of the clutches of the Demiurge and his angelic archons, and find a way back to that original and unknown and far-off God.

Now whatever else this is, it's a very good story, and what's more it has an immense explanatory power: it offers to explain why we feel, as so many of us do, *exiled* in this world, *alienated* from joy and meaningfulness and the true connection we feel we must have with the universe, as Jane Eyre feels that she must have love and kindness.

In short, Gnosticism fits the temper of the times. It lends itself to all kinds of contemporary variations: feminism, for example, partly because of the important role the Gnostic story assigns to the figure of the Sophia, or Wisdom, the youngest and paradoxically the rashest of the emanations of the divine being. Somehow we're not surprised to learn that it was all her fault that the material universe came about in the first place.

And Gnosticism appeals powerfully, too, to the sense of being *in the know*, of having access to a truth not available to most people. And, not least, it appeals because the story it tells is all about a massive conspiracy, and we love massive conspiracies. The *X-Files*, for example, is pure Gnosticism. "The truth is out there," says Mulder: not *in here*, because *in here* is permeated by evil conspiracies whose influence reaches the very centers of worldly authority, corrupting politics, the law, the military-industrial complex, and every other center of power in the world. The Demiurge is in charge, *in here*. But *out there* somewhere is the source of all truth, and we belong with that, not with the corrupt and dishonest and evil empire that rules this world.

So it's a powerfully dramatic myth, and it has the great advantage of putting us human beings and our predicament right at the heart of it. No wonder it appeals. The trouble is, it's not true. If we can't believe the story about the shepherds and the angels and the wise men and the star and the manger and so on, then it's even harder to believe in Demiurges and archons and emanations and what have you. It certainly explains, and it certainly makes us feel important, but it isn't true.

And it has the terrible defect of libeling—one might almost say blaspheming against, if the notion had any republican meaning—the physical universe; of saying that this world is just a clumsy copy of a perfect original we can't see because it's somewhere else. In the eyes of some Christian writers, of course, this sort of Platonism is a great merit. C. S. Lewis, at the end of the last book in the Narnia series, has his character the wise old Professor explaining: "Our own world, England and all, is only a shadow or copy of something in Aslan's real world." In fact, the two things are "as different as a real thing is from a shadow or as waking life is from a dream." And then he goes on to add under his breath "It's all in Plato, all in Plato: bless me, what *do* they teach them at these schools!"

Now this is a state of mind which, unless we're careful, can lead to a thoroughgoing hatred of the physical world. It encourages us to see a toad lurking beneath every flower, and if we can't see one, it's because the toads now are extra cunning and have learned to become invisible. The Gnostic would say that the beauty and solace and delight that can be found in the physical world are exactly why we should avoid it: they are the very things with which the Demiurge traps our souls. The Puritanism that so poisoned the human mind later on said just the same sort of thing. I'd say that that position is an unhealthy and distorted one which can only be maintained at the cost of common sense, and of that love and kindness that Jane Eyre demanded, and finally of sanity itself. The Gnostic situation is a *dramatic* one to be in; it's intensely *exciting*; but it's the sort of paranoid excitement felt by those militia groups who collect guns and hide in the hills and watch out for the black helicopters of the evil New World Order as they prepare for Armageddon. It's nuts, basically.

So Gnosticism, intoxicating though it is, won't lead us to the republic of Heaven. We have to realize that our human nature demands meaning and joy just as Jane Eyre demanded love and kindness ("You think we can live without them, but we cannot live so"); to accept that this meaning and joy will involve a passionate love of the physical world, *this* world, of food and drink and sex and music and laughter, and not a suspicion and hatred of it; to understand that it will both grow out of and add to the achievements of the human mind such as science and art. Finally, we must find a way of believing that we are not subservient creatures dependent on the whim of some celestial monarch, but free citizens of the republic of Heaven.

And I think I can see glimpses of such a republic in books that children read, among other places. I think it's possible to point out in children's literature some moments or some qualities that are characteristic of a republican attitude to the great questions of religion, which are the great questions of life.

And these great questions often fix themselves in the tiniest of details: in stockings, for example.

Here is a nonrepublican view of stockings from C. S. Lewis. Near the end of *The Last Battle*, the final book in the Narnia series, Susan is refused entry to the stable, which represents salvation, because, as Peter says, "My sister . . . is no longer a friend of Narnia." "Oh Susan!" says Jill. "She's interested in nothing nowadays except nylons and lipstick and invitations. She always was a jolly sight too keen on being grown-up." In other words, normal human development, which includes a growing awareness of your body and its effect on the opposite sex, is something from which Lewis's narrative, and what he would like us to think is the Kingdom of Heaven, turns with horror.

But I'm interested in those nylons. I think Susan had a point. Here's a passage from William Mayne's recent novel *Midnight Fair* (Hodder, 1997). Paul, a boy of twelve or so, has found his attention increasingly absorbed by Victoria, a strange and solitary girl. He's just summoned up the courage to write a Christmas card for her. They've been in church, and he watches as she leaves with her mother.

> The service ended for the rest of the congregation. For Paul it had not begun, and he would have liked an instant replay, but that was not in prayer books old or new.
>
> He stood up. The girl come along the aisle, nearing him. He would follow her out, catch up in the porch, and present the card. . . . The girl came past. Paul wanted to jump out and give her a hundred cards.
>
> She did not see him. Why should she? She walked with her mother. In a brown skirt, stockings with a small white hole beside one ankle, brown leather shoes with a frilled flap on the instep, a green sweater, and a bronze coat. She was quite plain, but unearthly beautiful; there was nothing else like her, and her uniqueness was the reason for all creation.

Lewis's nylons were not real stockings; they were Platonic stockings, if you like, and their function was simply to carry a symbolic charge. What they mean is that if you give them too much of your attention, you're shut out from the Kingdom of Heaven. In the republic, stockings work differently. They're real stockings; they sometimes have holes in them. That little white hole beside her ankle is one of the things that make Victoria "quite plain, but unearthly beautiful"; and of course Paul *can't* give too much attention to her stockings, and her shoes, and her coat, and everything about her. She is real, and he is in love.

As a matter of fact, Lewis's position as a whole wasn't at all consistent. Whereas the Narnia books illustrate the very antithesis of the republic of Heaven, his critical writing often shows a more generous and sensible spirit. For example, talking about this very business of growing up in his essay "On Three Ways of Writing for Children," he says "surely arrested development consists not in refusing to lose old things but in failing to add new things? I now like hock, which I am sure I should not have liked as a child. But I still like lemon-squash. I call this growth or development because I have been enriched: where I formerly had only one pleasure, I now have two."

There's nothing there which a republican would quarrel with; but the sensible Lewis who wrote it was thrust aside in Narnia by the paranoid bigot who proclaimed that an interest in lipstick and nylons was not an addition to the pleasures of life, but an absolute disqualification for the joys of Heaven.

The ending of *The Last Battle* makes this position even clearer. "The term is over: the holidays have begun," says Aslan to the children, having just let them know that "there *was* a real railway accident. . . . Your father and mother and all of you are—as you used to call it in the Shadowlands—dead."

Using Narnia as our moral compass, we can take it as axiomatic that in the republic of Heaven, people do not regard life in this world as so worthless and contemptible that they leave it with pleasure and relief, and a railway accident is not an end-of-term treat.

Jane Eyre, as so often, got it right and gave the true republican answer when the pious Mr. Brocklehurst asks what she thinks she must do to avoid going to hell: "I must keep in good health, and not die," she says. *This* world is where the things are that matter. If the Narnia stories had been composed in that spirit, the children who have passed through all these adventures and presumably learned great truths from them would be free to live and grow up in the world, even at the price of engaging with the lipstick and the nylons, and *use* what they'd learned for the benefit of others. That would be the republican thing to do. That's why Lewis doesn't let his characters do it, and why the Narnia books are such an invaluable guide to what is wrong and cruel and selfish.

No, if the republic of Heaven exists at all, it exists nowhere but on this earth, in the physical universe we know, not in some gaseous realm far away. Nor can it be truly depicted in most fantasy of the Tolkien sort: closed fantasy, as John Goldthwaite calls it in his brilliant and invaluable study, *The Natural History of Make-Believe* (OUP, 1996). As Goldthwaite points out, such fantasy is both escapist and solipsistic: seeking to flee the complexities and compromises of the real world for somewhere nobler altogether, lit by a light that never was on sea or land, it inevitably finds itself enclosed in a mental space that is smaller, barer, and poorer than reality, because it's sustained by an imagination that strains against the world instead of working with it, refusing and not accepting. The result is a hollowness, a falsity. Tolkien's Shire, his idealized modest English landscape full of comfortable hobbits who know their social places, is no more real than the plastic oak paneling and the reproduction horse-brasses in an Olde English theme-pub. It's a great pity that with the passing of time it's become less easy to see the difference between the artificiality of the Shire and the truthfulness of the great republican fairy tales such as "Jack and the Beanstalk": both the real and the fake now look equally quaint to the uninformed eye.

The difference lies in the connection, or lack of it, with the everyday. Am I saying that there is no fantasy in the republic of Heaven? That everything must be sober and drab, with a sort of earnest sociological realism? Not at all. If the republic doesn't include fantasy, it won't be worth living in. It won't be Heaven of any sort. But *inclusiveness* is the whole point: the fantasy and the realism must connect. "Jack and the Beanstalk" is a republican story because the magic grows out of the most common and everyday thing, a handful of beans, and the beanstalk grows right outside the kitchen window, and at the end of the story, Jack comes home.

Part of the connection which a republican story has to have with our lives—a very important part—is psychological. That's why Wagner's *Ring* is a republican work of art, and Tolkien's isn't. Wagner's gods and heroes are exactly like human beings, on a grand scale: every human virtue and every human temptation is there. Tolkien leaves a good half of them out. No one in Middle-earth has any sexual relations at all; how children arrive must be a complete mystery to them.

So the republic of Heaven is a place where the people behave like us, with the full range of human feelings, even when they don't look like us, even when they look like beings that have never existed, like Tove Jansson's Moomins, or Sylvia Waugh's Mennyms, or Mary Norton's Borrowers. The people in the republic are people like us—even when they're dead. The republic is thronged with ghosts, and they have full democratic rights. A marvelous creepy little tale, Jan Mark's "Who's a Pretty Boy, Then?" exemplifies what I mean: on the patch in the garden where nothing will grow, Dad builds an aviary. But the budgerigars don't thrive, and mysteriously they begin to speak:

> "Oh, I'm so cold," said one.
> "I shall always be very cold," said another, "cold as clay."
> "I shall always be here," said a third.
> "I shall never go away," said the white bird.
> "Pity me."
> "Pity me."

Ghosts that come only to scare us, ghosts that are only special effects, ghosts that might as well be aliens or prehistoric monsters, have nothing to tell us about the republic of Heaven. But ghosts that remind us of our own mortality are citizens like ourselves. In the republic, we honor the dead and maintain a conversation with them, in order to learn more about how to live.

The next essential quality of the republic of Heaven is that what happens there *matters*, and what the characters do *makes a difference*. The republic is a place where, as H. G. Wells's Mr. Polly discovers, "If the world does not please you *you can change it*."

A good example is the two books that Erich Kästner wrote in the thirties about Emil Tischbein: *Emil and the Detectives* and its sequel *Emil and the Three Twins*. In the first book, young Emil goes from the little country town of Neustadt to visit his relatives in the great city of Berlin. On the train he falls asleep, and a thief steals the money Emil's widowed mother has given him to take to his grandmother. Not much money, because they are far from rich, but that's the point: they can't afford to lose it, and Emil feels terribly responsible.

But once he arrives in the city, he finds that he's not alone. Some other boys, strangers at first, quickly join forces to track down and denounce the thief, and the story ends happily, with the money restored. The republican point here is that the children find the solution themselves, out of the everyday qualities they share: resourcefulness, quick wits, determination, and, not least, access to a telephone.

In the sequel, Emil is trying to come to terms with the fact that his widowed mother wants to marry again. He likes his potential stepfather, but that isn't the point, as every stepchild knows. Emil would much rather she didn't marry, but he hasn't told her that. He and his grandmother talk through all the consequences of this, and he learns from her that his mother feels just the same as he does—she would really rather remain alone with Emil; but she's afraid of the future, because Emil will grow up one day, and marry, and leave home; and after all, Herr Jeschke is a good man. Emil says:

> "What am I to do, Granny?"
>
> "One of two things, Emil. When you get home you can ask her not to marry. Then you'll kiss and the thing will be settled."
>
> "Or?"
>
> "Or you can keep silence, but the silence must last till the end of your days, and you must be cheerful in your silence and not go round with a face like a mourner at a funeral. You alone can decide which course to pursue."

He chooses the right way, for Emil is a hero of the republic, which is a place where children learn to grow up, and where cheerfulness and courage do make a difference. Putting your own feelings first and insisting on expressing them, no matter what the cost, is not a republican virtue.

Another work I admire for similar reasons is Edward Ardizzone's *Little Tim and the Brave Sea Captain*. Tim has run away to sea, and has a fine time till a great storm comes up and the ship begins to sink. He and the captain are standing on the bridge.

> "Come," [says the captain,] "stop crying and be a brave boy. We are bound for Davey Jones's locker and tears won't help us now."
>
> So Tim dried his eyes and tried not to be too frightened. He felt he would not mind going anywhere with the captain, even to Davey Jones's locker.
>
> They stood hand in hand and waited for the end.

Little Tim is a picture book for young children, and sure enough, on the next page arrives the lifeboat; but Tim and the captain don't know that when they stand hand in hand waiting for the end. You're never too young to become a citizen of the republic of Heaven.

So part of this *meaning* that I've suggested we need, the sense that we belong and we matter, comes from the moral and social relations that the republic of Heaven must embody. In the republic, we're connected in a moral way to one another, to other human beings. We have responsibilities to them, and they to us. We're not isolated units of self-interest in a world where there is no such thing as society; we cannot live so.

But part of the sense of wider meaningfulness that we need comes from seeing that we have a connection with nature and the universe around us, with everything that is *not* human as well. So the republic of Heaven is also characterized by another quality: it enables us to see this real world, our world, as a place of infinite delight, so intensely beautiful and intoxicating that if we saw it clearly then we would want nothing more, ever. We would know that this earth is our true home, and nowhere else is. In the words of William Blake, one of the founding fathers of the republic of Heaven,

> How do you know but ev'ry Bird that cuts the airy way,
> Is an immense world of delight, clos'd by your senses five?

Lesser writers than Blake have also caught the true tone of this immense world of delight, and made their contribution to the republic. For example, D. J. Watkins-Pitchford, who wrote under the name of "B.B.": his books about the Little Grey Men may be familiar to some older readers. In his novel *Brendon Chase* (first published in 1945, and recently republished in Britain by Jane Nissen Books) he does evoke the kind of delight that Blake speaks of. The three brothers Robin, John, and Harold run away to the forest and live wild for most of a year.

Here is the fifteen-year-old Robin alone in the forest:

> He would sometimes come upon some specially lovely tree, an oak, or a birch, and he would sit down and feast his eyes upon it, just as he would go to the Blind Pool to watch the water and the floating leaves. There was something about the birches which was extremely attractive—their white bark was the colour and texture of kid—sometimes there was a beautiful golden flush on the smooth trunks which felt so soft to the touch. . . . Or perhaps it was another oak which took his fancy, bare and gaunt with each little twig and branch naked to the winds. . . . He would listen to the low hiss of the winter wind among the intricate network, which sang like wires in every passing gust . . . He would put his ear to the kindly grey trunk and hear that wild song much magnified, the whole tree would be pulsing, almost as though a heart beat there inside its rough body.

All in Plato, all in Plato? What utter nonsense.

At the furthest extent, this sense of delight in the physical world can blend into a sort of ecstatic identification with it. "You never enjoy the world aright," said Thomas Traherne, "till the sea itself floweth in your veins, till you are clothed with the heavens, and crowned with the stars: and perceive yourself to be the sole heir of the whole world."

So far I've been talking about various aspects of the republic of Heaven, and not in any particular order; glimpses, little windows opening into it here and there. What we need, if we're going to take it seriously, is something more coherent and solid. We need a story, a myth that does what the traditional religious stories did: it must *explain*. It must satisfy our hunger for a *why*. Why does the world exist? Why are we here?

Of course, there are two kinds of *why*, and our story must deal with both. There's the one that asks *What brought us here?* and the other that asks *What are we here for?* One looks back, and the other looks forward, perhaps.

And in offering an answer to the first *why*, a republican myth must accept the overwhelmingly powerful evidence for evolution by natural selection. The neo-Darwinians tell us that the processes of life are blind and automatic; there has been no purpose in our coming here.

Well, I think a republican response to that would be: *there is now*. We are conscious, and conscious of our own consciousness. We might have arrived at this point by a series of accidents, but from now on we have to take charge of our fate. Now we are here, now we are conscious, we make a difference. Our presence changes everything.

So a myth of the republic of Heaven would explain what our true purpose is. Our purpose is to understand and to help others to understand, to explore, to speculate, to imagine. And that purpose has a moral force.

Which brings in the next task for our republican myth: it must provide a sort of framework for understanding why some things are good and others are bad. It's no good to say, "X is good and Y is evil because God says they are"; the King is dead, and that argument won't do for free citizens of the republic. Of course, the myth must deal with human beings as they are, which includes recognizing that there is a depth of human meanness and wickedness which not even the imagination can fully plumb. But it's no good putting the responsibility for that on a pantomime demon, and calling him Satan; he's dead, too. If we're so undermined by despair at the sight of evil that we have to ascribe it to some extrahuman force, some dark power from somewhere else, then we have to give up the republic, too, and go back to the Kingdom. There's no one responsible but us. Goodness and evil have always had a human origin. The myth must account for that.

But as well as the traditional good things and evil things (and there has never been much disagreement about those in all human history: dishonesty is bad and truthfulness is good, selfishness is wrong and generosity is right—we can all agree about those), I think we need to reinforce another element of a republican morality. We must make it clear that trying to restrict understanding and put knowledge in chains is bad, too. We haven't always understood that; it's a relatively new development in human history, and it's thanks to the great republicans, to Galileo and Milton and those like them, that it's been added to our understanding. We must keep it there, and keep it watered and fed so that it grows ever more strongly: what shuts out knowledge and nourishes stupidity is wrong; what increases understanding and deepens wisdom is right.

The Christian Heaven used to be where we went when we died, if we did what we were told. If the republic of Heaven is here, on this earth, in our lives, then what happens when we die? Is that all? Is that the end of everything for us? That's hard to accept; for some people it's the hardest thing of all. Well, our myth must talk about death in terms that are as true as they can be to what we know of the facts, and it must do what the Christian myth did, and provide some sort of hope or consolation. The myth must give us a way of accepting death, when it comes, of seeing what it means and accepting it; not shrinking from it with terror, or pretending that it'll be like the school holidays. We cannot live so: we cannot die so.

We need a myth, we need a story, because it's no good persuading people to commit themselves to an idea on the grounds that it's *reasonable*. How much effect would the Bible have had for generations and generations if it had just been a collection of laws and genealogies? What seized the mind and captured the heart were the *stories* it contains.

So if we are to see what a republic of Heaven might look like, we must look for evidence of it, as I've been suggesting, in the realm of stories. And one of the few places we can be certain of finding stories, these days, is in books that are read by children.

But I'll end with a nursery rhyme. If the republic of Heaven were to have an anthem, I can't think of a better one than this:

> Boys and girls come out to play,
> The moon doth shine as bright as day;

This is a republic where we live by the imagination. Night can be like day; things can be upside down and back to front and inside out, and still all right.

> Leave your supper and leave your sleep,
> And join your playfellows in the street—

Not in a private playground with security guards where some of us are let in and others are kept out, not in the park that closes its gates before the moon comes out, but in the street, the common place that belongs to everyone.

Come with a whoop, and come with a call,
Come with a good will or not at all.

Like Emil, we must be cheerful and not go round with a face like a mourner at a funeral. It's difficult sometimes, but good will is not a luxury: it's an absolute necessity. It's a moral imperative.

Up the ladder and down the wall,
A tuppenny loaf will serve us all.
You bring milk, and I'll bring flour,
And we'll have a pudding in half an hour.

We can do it. That's the way it happens in the republic of Heaven; we provide for ourselves. We'll have a pudding, and a good nourishing one it'll be, too; milk and flour are full of goodness. And then we can play together in the bright moonlight till we all fall asleep.

Part 12

GENDER

68

"AS THE TWIG IS BENT . . ."

Gender and childhood reading

Elizabeth Segel

Source: Elizabeth A. Flynn and Patrocinio P. Schweickart (eds), *Gender and Reading: Essays on Readers, Texts and Contexts*, Baltimore: Johns Hopkins University Press, 1986, pp. 165–186.

One of the most obvious ways gender influences our experience as readers is when it determines what books are made available to us or are designated as appropriate or inappropriate for our reading. Nowhere is this fact so apparent or its implications so disturbing as in childhood reading. This is partly because the child does not have direct access to books, by and large, but receives them from adult hands. Adults decide what books are written, published, offered for sale, and, for the most part, purchased for children. And over the last century and a half, most adults have firmly believed that literary sauce for the goose is not at all sauce for the gander. The publisher commissioning paperback romances for girls and marketing science fiction for boys, as well as Aunt Lou selecting a fairy tale collection for Susie and a dinosaur book for Sam, are part of a powerful system that operates to channel books to or away from children according to their gender. Furthermore, because the individual's attitudes concerning appropriate gender-role behaviors are formed during the early years, the reader's choice of reading material may be governed by these early experiences long after she or he has theoretically gained direct access to books of all kinds.

To understand how gender operates on this level to condition the reading process, it is useful, first, to look at reading in childhood, ask how the reading lives of girls and of boys have typically differed, and seek out the origins of those differences.

Geoffrey Trease, distinguished British author of children's novels, tells us that in the early 1930s, when he began writing for children, "Books were labelled, as strictly as school lavatories, 'Books for Boys' or 'Books for Girls'."[1] This was also the situation in America, and it prevailed in the same rigid form at least until the 1960s, when the boundaries began to loosen a bit. 'Twas not ever thus, however.

In the few books intended for children's use that were published before the eighteenth century, no distinction seems to have been made between boy readers and girl readers. Manuals of conduct—the various volumes of "a father's counsel" or "a mother's legacy"—were apparently addressed in roughly equal numbers to sons or daughters, depending on the gender of the writer's own offspring. The Puritan tracts depicting godly children on their deathbeds which dominated seventeenth-century juvenile publishing seem to have dwelt with equal fervor on the uplifting spectacle of godly girls and godly boys going meekly to their reward.

The 1740s are generally viewed as marking the coming of age of children's books in England. In that decade, three London publisher-booksellers, Thomas Boreman, Mary Cooper, and John Newbery, began to provide children with books designed to delight as well as instruct them. Increasing middle-class literacy and prosperity set the stage for this development, along with the gradual popular dissemination of John Locke's educational philosophy, which advocated teaching children through play.

One of Newbery's most appealing early publications appears at first glance to herald the publishers' practice of dividing children's books into boys' books and girls' books. *A Little Pretty Pocket-Book* (1744), a miscellany of rhymes and fables in an elegant gilt and flowered binding, opens with two whimsical letters from Jack the Giant Killer to the child reader.[2] One is addressed to Master Tommy, and the other to Pretty Miss Polly. Furthermore, Newbery—canny merchandiser that he was—offered with the book for two pence additional a pincushion (for Pretty Miss Polly, of course) or a ball (for Master Tommy). On closer inspection, however, we see that the wording is exactly the same in each of the two letters, except that one speaks of being a good boy, the other a good girl; where one addresses "my dear Tommy," and the other speaks to "my dear Polly." Both letters praise the child for his or her "Nurse's report": you are, the letters say, "loving and kind to your Play-fellows, and obliging to every body; . . . you rise early in the Morning, keep yourself clean, and learn your Book; . . . when you have done a Fault you confess it, and are sorry for it." Including two letters instead of one was not, it would seem, a way of prescribing different conduct for girls and boys, but a way of personalizing the letter and the book itself in an engaging way.

The two letters also specify the use to which the ball and the pincushion are to be put, and our initial supposition—that Tommy will be gaily playing ball with his fellows while poor Polly sits laboring over her sampler—proves false. No, the objects are to serve the very same function, according to the Giant Killer. Both are red on one side and black on the other, and both come with ten pins. "For every good Action you do, a Pin shall be stuck on the Red Side, and for every bad Action a Pin shall be stuck on the Black Side." Jack rashly promises to send a penny when all the pins arrive on the red side, and a whipping should they all be found on the black. The virtues Newbery and his contemporaries were aiming to develop—obedience, industry, good temper—were evidently the same for both sexes. The reward for such virtues was the same, too, if we can judge from two of Newbery's most popular children's stories: both Goody Two-Shoes and Giles Gingerbread achieve by their goodness and application to studies "the love of all who know them" and the epitome of material success, a fine coach to ride in.

Neither the Puritan aim of saving the child's soul nor the characteristic Georgian aim of developing good character seemed to require a distinction between girl-child and boy-child. The domestic tales of the late eighteenth and early nineteenth centuries, such as Mrs. Trimmer's *The History of the Robins* (1786), the Edgeworths' *Harry and Lucy* stories (1801, 1825), and Mrs. Sherwood's *The Fairchild Family* (1818–1847), all featured children of both sexes as characters and were intended for readers of both sexes. All of these books clearly taught obedience, submission to authority, and selflessness as the cardinal virtues of both girls and boys. The few volumes produced solely for the child's entertainment in the early years of the nineteenth century, such as *The Comic Adventures of Old Mother Hubbard and Her Dog* (1805?) and *The Butterfly's Ball* (1807), also took no account of gender. The latter begins, "Come take up your Hats, and away let us haste / To the Butterfly's Ball, and the Grasshopper's feast," and the illustration shows both girls and boys among the fortunate children who are invited to the unusual party.

Early school stories were an exception. Because boarding schools were for boys or girls, not both, thinly disguised moral tracts with school settings were aimed at one sex or the other. Sarah Fielding's *The Governess; Or, Little Female Academy* specifies on the title page that it is "calculated for the entertainment and instruction of young ladies in their education."[3] Elizabeth Sandham wrote *The Boys' School; Or, Traits of Character in Early Life* (1800). Another of her productions was "an equally purposeful work about girls at school."[4] Mrs. Pilkington's two volumes, *Biography for Boys* (1805) and *Biography for Girls* (1806), suggest that then, as now, it was assumed that the child reader's emulation of the lives of the great would be more likely if girls read about famous women, boys about famous men.

While certain of the school stories and biographies for older children were targeted for boys or for girls, Samuel Pickering's study of eighteenth-century children's books bears out my conclusion that the first "significant differentiation made between books for little girls and for little boys" came with Mary Ann Kilner's *The Adventures of a Pin cushion* (1783?) and *Memoirs of a Peg-Top* (1783).[5] These stories were among the best of the purported biographies of inanimate objects which were popular at the time. The pincushion and the peg-top both travel to boarding school and from one owner to another, in varying stations of life, all the while making improving comments on the scenes they observe. *The Adventures of a Pincushion* was "designed chiefly for the use of young ladies,"[6] *Memoirs of a Peg-Top* for boys. This distinction was apparently based on supposed different interests of girls and boys, rather than on different socializing aims for the two books—a specialization of vehicle rather than message. Indeed, Kilner asserted in her preface to *Memoirs of a Peg-Top* that "the laws of justice, probity, and truth" are "of *general* obligation." Her purpose in addressing the books to the "*different amusements* . . . in which each sex [was] more particularly concerned" was to make her books more interesting to children. It is worth noting that the chief difference between the companion volumes, besides the gender of the child characters, is that the peg-top book departs from the usual standard of gentility in approved children's fiction of the day. The top recounts an incident, for example, in which a blindfolded boy is fed a concoction of custard and cow dung.

Kilner's experiment seems to have had no imitators, and when Victoria came to the throne in 1837, the wholesale fencing off of children's books into books for boys and books for girls had not yet been effected. Elizabeth Rigby's very long article on children's books in the *Quarterly Review* (1844) makes no mention of boys' books or girls' books, either in her critical essay or in the annotations of recommended books which follow.[7] Even in discussing Marryat's *Masterman Ready* (1841), a book invariably referred to today as a boys' book, Rigby noted the danger that parents may "dispute with *their children*"—not with *their sons*—"the possession of it" (my italics).

Within a few years, however, the adventure fiction of Marryat, Ballantyne, Henty, and Kingston would be universally thought of as "boys' books," and domestic chronicles like Susan Warner's *The Wide, Wide World* (1850) and Charlotte Yonge's *The Daisy Chain* (1856) would set a transatlantic pattern for the "girls' book." By the last quarter of the century, articles like William Graham Sumner's "What Our Boys Are Reading"[8] and Edward G. Salmon's "What Girls Read"[9] had become commonplace on both sides of the Atlantic.

How to account for this extensive staking out of boys' and girls' claims on the previously common territory of children's books is the interesting question. Certainly a favorable economic climate was an important precondition. The market had to grow large before publishers would consider restricting sales by excluding potential readers. In 1808 Charles Lamb received a letter from his publisher, William Godwin, suggesting changes in his adaptation of Chapman's *Odyssey* for children, *The Adventures of Ulysses*. Godwin wrote:

> We live in squeamish days. Amid the beauties of your manuscript, of which no man can think more highly than I do, what will the squeamish say to . . . the giant's vomit, page 14, or to the minute & shocking description of the extinguishing the giant's eye, in the page following. You I dare say have no formed plan of excluding the female sex from among your readers, & I, as a bookseller, must consider that if you have, you exclude one half of the human species.[10]

Appropriate subject matter for boys might be judged too "strong" for girls, but for economic reasons publishers at this time preferred to dilute the material rather than limit the book's readers to one sex.

F. J. Harvey Darton, still the ultimate authority on the social history of English children's books, acknowledged the role of economics in making it possible to publish different types of books for boys and for girls by the mid-nineteenth century: "Mere numbers now made sub-division inevitable." Yet he went further, and suggested that this development was a positive step in the evolution of a true children's literature, one that hinged on "the discovery that *The* Child was *a* child, and, on top of that, that he was male and female, and was also different at five years of age and fourteen. . . . Hitherto the young readers had never been clearly defined. They were just 'children', and that meant anything from a baby lisping the alphabet to a young Miss or Master growing like the elder generation."[11]

"The young Miss . . . growing like the elder generation" presented a ticklish problem to her Victorian elders which provided further impetus to develop a distinctive literature for girls. "Girls' literature performs one very useful function," according to Salmon's important 1886 essay. "It enables girls to read something above mere baby tales, and yet keeps them from the influence of novels of a sort which should be read only by persons capable of forming a discreet judgment. It is a long jump from Aesop to 'Ouida', and to place Miss Sarah Doudney or Miss Anne Beale between Aesop and 'Ouida' may at least prevent a disastrous moral fall."[12] Mary Louisa Molesworth, also writing in 1886, cited *Mrs. Overtheway's Remembrances* (1866), by Mrs. Ewing, as a book "more particularly written for girls, and well adapted for that indefinite age, the despair of mothers and governesses, when maidens begin to look down upon 'regular children's stories', and novels are as yet forbidden."[13]

While this literature for older girls, clearly the forerunner of today's "junior novels" or young adult fiction, can legitimately be viewed as being responsive to children's needs (after all, children do need books that fall between Marguerite Henry and Margaret Drabble), Salmon's tone indicates that girls' literature "for that indefinite age" was part of a concerted effort to keep females pure and their imaginations unsullied by restricting their world, even within the home. "The chief end served by 'girls' literature' is that, whilst it advances beyond the nursery, it stops short of the full blaze of the drawing-room," Salmon concluded.[14] It was, by and large, a stopgap, watered down fare, a part of the Victorians' Podsnappian attempt, so well described by Dickens, to proscribe whatever "would . . . bring a blush to the cheek of the young person."[15]

The evidence suggests that more than economic feasibility and increasing dominance of the middle-class made the middle class's definilishment to develop distinctive girls' and boys' books. It was, above all, the sharp differentiation of male and female roles, well underway by the mid-nineteenth century, which mandated separate books for girls and boys.

The polarization of gender roles which accompanied the advance of industrialization and colonization has been well described elsewhere;[16] only the most salient features need be cited here. As work moved out of the home and female leisure became a sign of material success, middleclass women less and less were productive workers, becoming instead consumers confined to the domestic world. At the same time, the increasing dominance of the middle class made the middle class's definition of the role of women society's ideal of womanhood. Man's duties, in contrast, took him into the sordid and fiercely competitive world of industry and commerce and to the four corners of the world—to earn, to fight, and to rule the benighted subjects of empire. The home, under the aegis of the wife as "the angel in the house" was to be the refuge of moral and spiritual values. In place of her former active role of helpmate, the wife was offered the noble mission of influencing husband and children toward the good. This delegation to women of the responsibility for inculcating moral and religious values in men and children, and the generally enthusiastic acceptance of this function (even by women like Louisa May Alcott and George Eliot, who chafed at the restrictions this definition of women's role placed on them), had a profound impact on child-rearing practices and on the relations between the sexes.[17]

Its impact on children's books is unmistakable. For one thing, the women who dominated the ranks of juvenile authors viewed writing for children as the exercise of feminine moral "influence." The content of children's books naturally reflected the doctrine. As Salmon declared:

> Boys' literature of a sound kind ought to help to build up men. Girls' literature ought to help to build up women. If in choosing the books that boys shall read it is necessary to remember that we are choosing mental food for the future chiefs of a great race, it is equally important not to forget in choosing books for girls that we are choosing mental food for the future wives and mothers of that race. When Mr. Ruskin says that man's work is public and woman's private, he seems for the moment insensible to the public work of women as exercised through their influence on their

> husbands, brothers, and fathers. Woman's work in the ordering, beautifying, and elevating of the commonweal is hardly second to man's; and it is this which ought to be borne in mind in rearing girls.[18]

Before the boys' book appeared on the scene, fiction for children typically had been domestic in setting, heavily didactic, and morally or spiritually uplifting, and this kind of earnest family story remained the staple of younger children's fiction. The boys' book was, above all, an escape from domesticity and from the female domination of the domestic world. The adventures of Tom and Huck, of Jim Hawkins and many lesser heroes of boys' books are the epitomy of freedom in part because they are an escape from women, the chief agents of socialization in the culture. Though most boys' books entailed a simple code of honor, earnest introspection and difficult moral choices were taboo; these were books of action and adventure. As Gillian Avery puts it, "Long before girls were allowed amusing books, boys had their Marryat and Ballantyne—books of high adventure with the occasional pious sentiment slipped in as an afterthought, but with no continuous moral message."[19]

The authors of *these* books were not pious female pedagogues, but men of action! Of the British boys' book authors, Frederick Marryat had entered the Royal Navy at fourteen and had taken part in fifty naval engagements before he settled down to write books twenty-four years later. R. M. Ballantyne emigrated to Canada, where he worked for the Hudson Bay Company, often at remote outposts in the Far North. Thomas Mayne Reid, born in Ireland, came to America as a young man and became a trader on the western frontier, living among the native Americans. He fought in the thick of the Mexican War before returning to England to write boys' fiction. And G. A. Henty, chronicler of military history and celebrator of empire, was a war correspondent who had witnessed famous battles all over Europe and Africa for thirty years.

The liberation of nineteenth-century boys into the book worlds of sailors and pirates, forests and battles, left their sisters behind in the world of childhood—that is, the world of home and family. When publishers and writers saw the commercial possibilities of books for girls, it is interesting that they did not provide comparable escape reading for them (that came later, with the pulp series books), but instead developed books designed to persuade the young reader to accept the confinement and self-sacrifice inherent in the doctrine of feminine influence. This was accomplished by depicting the rewards of submission and the sacred joys of serving as "the angel in the house." Whereas in many boys' books, the happy ending is the adolescent "bad boy" successfully escaping socialization, holding out against the Widow Douglasses of the world, and thereby earning the admiration of all, in the girls' book, the protagonist who resists the dictates of genteel feminity must be "tamed," her will broken to accept a submissive and sedentary role. The so-called happy ending of such books is that she herself stops rebelling and chooses the approved role in order to gain or to retain the love and approval of those around her.[20]

The classic example of a girl who is "broken" to the conventional woman's role in a girls' book is the heroine of *What Katy Did*, by Susan Coolidge, which was published in 1872 and widely read in America and Britain for nearly a century.[21] It is a book that repays close attention for the illumination it sheds on the nature of the girls' book.

Katy Carr is the eldest of six motherless children in a well-to-do New England family. A lanky, impulsive, awkward, and passionate twelve year old, she darts from one scrape to another. As crabby Aunt Izzy rails about Katy's missing bonnet-string, torn dresses, and tardiness, the reader responds to Katy's generosity, creativity, and affectionate nature. Moved by the pleadings of her father and of the saintly invalid, Aunt Helen, Katy resolves to conquer her faults, but her resolutions are in vain. One particularly tempestuous day, she vents her frustrations by vigorously swinging, though Aunt Izzy has forbidden it. What Katy doesn't know is that the rope is not secure. Her punishment for this disobedience is a terrible fall and an injury to her back which keeps her in bed and in pain for four years.

In the first months she experiences a deep depression. Then Aunt Helen, beautiful and beloved by all (and an invalid herself, remember), talks to Katy about "God's school," the School of Pain, where the lessons are Patience, Hopefulness, and—believe it or not—Neatness.

The rest of the book chronicles how Katy grows in virtue and gains the love and approval of all. She learns to think of others, not herself, and to fill the place of the dead mother to the younger children. And, of course, being unable to walk for four years effectively cures her coltish exuberance.

The disturbing message that the ideal woman is an invalid is scarcely veiled. Aunt Helen tells Katy that after her own crippling accident she took pains to keep herself and her room looking attractive. It wasn't easy but, she says, "The pleasure it gave my dear father repaid for all. He had been proud of his active, healthy girl, but I think she was never such a comfort to him as his sick one, lying there in her bed" (p. 110). Katy is moved by this chilling vision to wish to "be nice and sweet and patient, and a comfort to people" (p. 111). She succeeds so well that the "happy ending" of the book is not so much the few tottering steps she manages in the last chapter as a compliment from Aunt Helen which ends the book: "You have won the place, which, you recollect, I once told you an invalid should try to gain, of being to everybody 'The Heart of the House'" (p. 166). Since this was the place to which all women were urged to aspire, we may well wonder what the book's effect was on young readers. The book's popularity with previous generations of girls may well be owing to the vivid embodiment in crippled, chastened Katy of the painful limitations that the all too familiar feminine role imposed on active, carefree children.

If one contrasts *What Katy Did* with a comparably popular and respected boys' book of the period—say, *Treasure Island*[22]—one is first struck by the difference in setting: the domestic confinement of one book as against the extended voyage to exotic lands in the other. Also notable is the solemn introspection and moral earnestness that the girls' book expects of its heroine and readers, in contrast to the carefree suspension of moral judgment allowed Jim Hawkins. Good and evil exist in *Treasure Island*, to be sure, but Jim never has to make difficult moral choices (he kills mutineer Israel Hands involuntarily; Long John Silver's escape means Jim doesn't have to turn him over to be executed, etc.). Another revealing contrast is the premium placed on obedience in *What Katy Did*—but not in *Treasure Island*.

Children's books until the mid-nineteenth century had without exception depicted obedience as the most important childhood virtue. Anne S. MacLeod's study of antebellum American juvenile fiction concluded that "no child character was seen to defy authority successfully."[23] There were fictional children who disobeyed, of course, but they were not approved of by their creators. Disobedient children reaping their just deserts abound in early children's fiction: consigned to hellfire, chased by bulls, run over by wagons, or merely left at home when others go on coveted excursions, they are a chastened lot.

The advent of the "good bad boy" in the evolving boys' book marked a radical change in what adults expected of children, or, put another way, in what adults defined as the ideal child—ideal boy-child, that is. Jim Hawkins, Tom Sawyer, and many other rascals disobey adults and get away with it. In fact, their defiance of adult authority constitutes a major part of their charm. Tom's resistance to Aunt Polly's civilizing efforts and his enjoyment of forbidden pleasures are what give him the edge in Aunt Polly's affections over the good boy, Sid. Jim Hawkins's defiance of actual or understood orders of the treasure expedition's adult leaders—going ashore with the mutineers, leaving the stockage, and so on—is what saves all their necks and brings the voyage to a triumphant end.

The reason for this cultural redefinition of the ideal boy is not difficult to deduce. When the man's role will take him into the great world to engage in fierce battles of commerce and empire, pluck and enterprise are the virtues to cultivate in male children, and those are precisely the qualities the boys' book heroes sport in abundance. Obedience was required of the child, but the young man was encouraged to leave that virtue behind him. Thus, we see that the boys' book was every bit as much a tool of socialization as the girls' book—albeit one with more child appeal.

The docile obedience required of adolescent girls in the girls' book stands in marked contrast to the autonomy of the boys' book protagonist. The warning figures of Pandora and Eve seem to shadow many of these stories. To be sure, the appeal of many favorite girls' book heroines rested on their resistance to the confines of the feminine role, but nearly all of them capitulate in the end.[24] In many of these girls' books, the interest derives from the tension between the heroine's drive to activity and autonomy, and the pressure exerted by society to thwart these drives and clip her wings, so to speak. The obedience, self-sacrifice, and docility expected of the young woman in this fiction are the virtues of a dependent. Since until late in the century nearly all women, married or single, were dependent on men, we can see that these books were in fact fulfilling their mission of preparing girls for womanhood (though we can hardly call it adulthood).

We have at bottom, then, not just a divergence of subject matter between boys' books and girls' books, but two forms of literature that were as polar as the ideal man and the ideal woman of the day were. The boys' book, even when entertaining and escapist, was essentially a Bildungsroman, a chronicle of growth to manhood. The approved girls' book depicted a curbing of autonomy in adolescence; while in form purporting to be a Bildungsroman, it is, in Annis Pratt's words, "a genre that pursues the opposite of its generic intent—it provides models for 'growing down' rather than for 'growing up'."[25]

The mass-marketed, syndicate-produced girls' series books that flourished in the late nineteenth and early twentieth centuries—from Elizabeth Champney Williams's Vassar Girls series (1883–1892), which emulated the popular travel adventure books for boys, to that perennial survivor, Nancy Drew—finally provided girls with an escape from domesticity and with active role models. Series titles like The Motor Girls, The Outdoor Girls, The Ranch Girls, The Moving Picture Girls, and The Khaki Girls indicate how far girls series books had roamed by 1920 from Susan Coolidge's bailiwick. But they were shallow, formulaic stories, for the most part, and Mary Thwaite is right when she judges that "the careful separation of stories into series, which publishers and librarians could complacently label 'Boys' or 'Girls', had in fact become a minor oppression of young readers in the later nineteenth century."[26]

This careful separation of books by gender did not affect children's reading as simply as the discussion thus far might suggest, however, for children's actual reading behavior could not be controlled as easily as the content of the books themselves.

For one thing, though girls when they reached "that certain age" could be prevented from joining boys' games and lively exploits, it was harder to keep them from accompanying their brothers on vicarious adventures through the reading of boys' books. And girls were avid readers of boys' books from the start. Amy Cruse, in her survey of reading in the Victorian era, mentioned numerous women, notable and unknown, who were brought up on Scott, the forerunner of the boys' book novelists (Mary Ann Evans began reading him at the age of seven!), Marryat and his cohorts.[27] Salmon quoted a female correspondent who confessed a childhood preference for Jules Verne and Ballantyne—along with *Little Women*.[28] Alice Jordan, writing on American children's reading, asserted that "girls read boys' books then [in the 1870s] as they do today [1947], and it was well that they did, for even when such books were poor they were more vigorous as a whole than stories for girls."[29] Laura Richards, accomplished and prolific writer of children's verse and girls' books, claimed that "all she knew of natural history she learned from Mayne Reid, whose dazzling heroes were her delight."[30] G. A. Henty reported that he received numerous letters from girl readers and that he valued them highly, "for where there is a girl in the same family the brothers' books are generally common stock, and are carefully read, appreciated, and judged. The author declares that girls write more intelligently and evince greater judgment in their criticism."[31]

Cruse suggested that the girl reading her brother's books "risked incurring a painful rebuke for her unladylike tastes,"[32] but Salmon's influential article on girls' reading was sympathetic:

> There are few girls who boast brothers who do not insist on reading every work of Ballantyne's or Kingston's or Henty's which may be brought into the house. . . . The explanation is that they can get in boys' books what they cannot get in the majority of their own—a stirring plot and lively movement. . . . Nor is this liking for heroes rather than heroines to be deprecated. It ought to impart a vigour and breadth to a girl's nature, and to give sisters a sympathetic knowledge of the scenes wherein their brothers live and work.[33]

While it was assumed from the beginning of gender-typed children's books that girls regularly raided their brothers' libraries, the universal opinion was that boys did not and would not read girls' books. This was certainly true of the tamer girls' stories, which were long on submission and short on action—Charlotte Yonge's domestic novels, for instance. As Edith Sichel wrote in 1901: "It is impossible to imagine many men reading Miss Yonge. There is an intemperate tameness about her—at once her charm and her defect—which forbids our associating mankind with her. It would be as if we dreamed of them taking high tea *in perpetuo*."[34] We must suppose that younger male readers would find Yonge even less appealing.

Yet, a few published reminiscences indicate that an occasional boy did cross the gulf from the male side to read a girls' book, and that he enjoyed it. (The confessions are made from the safe distance of adulthood and success.) Alexander Woollcott read *Little Women* and reported it one of the handful of books which retained their appeal in later life.[35] William

Lyon Phelps, distinguished professor and critic, read *Little Women* as a boy and confided to his journal that, like many girls, "he thought the book spoiled by not having Jo marry Laurie."[36]

That boys ventured into the territory of girls' reading only with considerable trepidation is clear from their accounts of the particular circumstances. One boy who grew up in the 1870s described his acquaintance with the quintessential "girls' books" of Sophie May:

> It was a shameful thing for one who had recently enacted Deerslayer and the Young Engineer even to look at such books and I averted my eyes [from sets of Sophie May books at a neighbor's house]; but in the evening with home lessons done and time heavy I bribed my sister to go across the street and borrow *Little Prudy's Captain Horace*—the military title taking off something of the curse. And once drawn in I read the whole lot . . . and I fell for them all, the heroines I mean—sedate Susie and patient Prudy and dashing Dotty Dimple—my first love.[37]

In our own day a similar confession was made by the novelist and broadcaster Melvyn Bragg. He became "hooked" on Alcott after having picked up at a seaside bookshop *Jo's Boys* (the title of which might well have caught a young boy off guard). "I read it countless times," he remembered,

> and the pleasure I found in it must have been powerful, for it enabled me to hurdle the terrible barrier presented by *Little Women*, which I sought out at the library on the hunt for anything else by Louisa May Alcott. . . . For *Little Women*, Miss Alcott announced, firmly, on the title page was *A Story for Girls*. Yet I read it. And I think that this is a rare case of Miss Alcott being mistaken. As years went on I discovered that quite a few men had read it as boys—although most of them would qualify the admission by muttering on about sisters or cousins leaving it lying around . . . or the teacher "forcing" them to read it at school.[38]

Well, then, if most girls were devouring boys' books and a few brave boys were reading girls' books, the categorizing of books by gender in an attempt to enforce restrictive gender roles must have been a failure, right? Not necessarily. The crossing of the well-marked lines by child readers, unfortunately, did not render ineffective the messages of the books regarding the cult of manliness, the counsel of feminine subservience.

For one thing, the restrictiveness of the woman's role as prescribed by girls' books was also embodied in the female characters (when there were any) of boys' books. The docility and dependent fearfulness of Becky

Thatcher or the selflessness of Tom Sawyer's Cousin Mary communicated cultural expectations as effectively as Katy Carr's reformation (maybe more effectively, since minor characters need not be as complex as successful protagonists). Furthermore, the restrictive fate of females which was spelled out in girls' books must have been sharpened and clarified by contrast with the plucky, cocky heroes of boys' wide-ranging fictional adventures.

The girl reader, no doubt, identified with these enviable heroes as she read, and, theoretically, she could have used them as role models in the dearth of fictional female alternatives to tamed tomboys and saintly sisters. Yet it seems likely that this would have entailed such a strong consciousness of inappropriateness that it would render boys' books little more than escapist fantasy for most girls, not much use in expanding the possibilities of their own lives.

Another ramification of the boys' books–girls' books division is that the phenomenon itself constituted a denigration of the female. The very fact that little onus was attached to girls reading boys' books, while boys reading girls' books was surreptitious and was experienced as somehow shameful, revealed to every child the existence of a hierarchy of value favoring the male. Every trespass onto masculine fictional terrain by girls must have reinforced the awareness of their own inferiority in society's view. As students of the still prevalent practice note, "Girls probably feel some internal pressure to adopt the male-typed choices on which society places such high value. One must assume that girls know the difference between first and second place, and have the same inherent desire for status boys have."[39]

Finally, the numbers of boys reading girls' books most likely has always been small. Salmon rejoiced that reading boys' books might "give sisters a sympathetic knowledge of the scenes wherein their brothers live and work." It appears that few boys over the years have gained a similar sympathetic knowledge of the scenes wherein their *sisters* live and work —a knowledge that fiction could have given them.

In recent years, publishers and librarians have been less likely to segregate books and label them "for boys" and "for girls" than the Victorians were, but the old assumptions about what constitutes appropriate reading for boys and for girls are still with us in the guise of attention paid to children's own reading interests. This would seem to be a step forward, since the many twentieth-century studies of children's reading interests appear to have as their goal ascertaining children's own preferences in reading material rather than using books as instruments to mold children to rigid gender-typed ideals.

And, indeed, an increase in sensitivity to children's reading experiences seems to have sparked the initial studies of children's reading interests in the 1920s. The most substantial study was conducted by George Norvell, an educator who collected data on the subject for over forty years, beginning in the early 1920s. His worthy objective was to promote voluntary reading by young people. To achieve this goal, he reasonably suggested that one needs to consider "(1) the reader's ability and interests and (2) the difficulty and attractiveness of the reading materials."[40]

In his attempt to discover what books students actually do enjoy, Norvell queried some fifty thousand subjects in grades seven through twelve concerning 4,993 selected titles. Students were asked to rate each selection they had read on a three-point scale: very interesting, fairly interesting, or uninteresting. Norvell's study admitted at the outset the questionable reliability of its design: "The plan chosen was to examine the reactions of boys and of girls toward a list of selections, each of which was dominated by a single factor, and to depend upon the minimizing of the potency of other factors through cancellation. Undoubtedly the method has pitfalls, since cancellation may not function as expected" (p. 48). In other words, the researcher may categorize a literary work by one characteristic, assuming that the reader's like or dislike of the work stems from that characteristic, when, in fact, the reader is responding to something quite different. For instance, a student may have rated *The Red Badge of Courage* as very interesting, not because its subject is war (as the researcher might assume) but because he was intrigued by Crane's use of symbol. Another student may have found it interesting only in comparison to other titles on the list and may have indicated a preference for it because it is a short novel.

Norvell's recognition of the method's pitfalls did not restrain him from using his accumulated data to draw sweeping conclusions about the dominance of sex as a determinant of young people's reading choices. "The data of this study indicate that sex is so dominant and ever-present a force in determining young people's reading choices that it must be carefully considered in planning any reading program for the schools" (p. 47). "If adolescents are to be provided with satisfactory materials, the reading interests of boys and of girls must receive separate consideration," and "for reading in common, only materials well liked by both boys and girls should be used" (p. 7). Since Norvell asserted elsewhere that "while boys will not tolerate books primarily about women, girls generally read books about men with satisfaction" (p. 51), this means that his recommendation was that no books about females be assigned or read aloud to mixed classes of girls and boys. It is not surprising that, when they were interviewed by a student of mine, a number of boys said that they had never read a book about a girl in their classes. And neither, of course, had their female classmates.

Yet this study, with all its faults, is one of the more sophisticated ones. Others have relied on forced-choice questionnaires, with questions like "Would you rather read a story about spacemen or one about elves?" One of the problems with this method is that the child has to select one, but might well never choose a book on either subject to read. Or the question might be "Which book do you like better, *Black Beauty* or *Alice in*

Wonderland?" The researcher may assume that the child who picks the first prefers animal stories to fantasy, when the child actually enjoys books that make her cry.

Some researchers have described categories of books and asked children which of two types of books they prefer to read. But often the categories are arbitrarily defined. One study concluded that fantasy ranked significantly higher with fourth-grade girls than with their male classmates. Yet fantasy was described on the questionnaire as "a book that is a story of fairies, knights, or imaginary people."[41] This suggests the fairy tale and romance-oriented fantasy, but leaves out many other sorts of literary fantasy. The conclusion is, therefore, misleading.

Samuel Weintraub, whose critique of reading interest studies provides more detail than is possible here, noted that because categories change with each study or are used with different definitions, it has been impossible to synthesize the results of different studies.[42] He concluded:

> In general, the research into children's reading interests has suffered from, among other things, lack of clear definitions and lack of rigor in design, as well as from questionable data-gathering instruments. The instruments appear, for the most part, not to have been scrutinized for reliability or validity, except in the most superficial manner. Through the years the techniques that have been developed seem to have become established by repetition rather than by any careful consideration of their merits or shortcomings.[43]

Weak as the foundation they rest on is, the conclusions of these studies have had a powerful influence on the books boys and girls actually read today. Since it is not possible within the compass of this article to explore all the ways in which this influence has operated, I will focus on the striking effect of the "boys won't read about girls" conclusion of reading-interests researchers.

The following passages are taken from teacher education textbooks published in the last ten years:

> If forced to choose between a book appealing primarily to boys and one to girls, choose the boys' book. Girls might identify with and enjoy *Durango Street, Tuned Out*, or *Swiftwater*, but equally good books appealing chiefly to girls just won't fare equally well with boys.[44]

> The other major factor in reading interest [after age] is sex. Although children may be content to read the same books or have them read aloud, somewhere around the fourth grade, it is made clear to boys that they need special materials appealing to

> them. Unfair or not, after that time boys are not likely to enjoy girls' books, but girls will usually read and enjoy boys' books. Practically, that means the English teacher must choose common reading that will appeal to boys, ignoring *Jane Eyre, Rebecca, Mrs. Mike*, or *Pride and Prejudice*. . . . Getting boys to relate to literature is often a major problem but it can become insoluble if the literature presented is incorrectly oriented.[45]

> It has been found that boys will not read "girl books," whereas girls win read "boy books." . . . Therefore, the ratio of "boy books" should be about two to one in the classroom library collection.[46]

The assumption has become a truism, one to which most teachers and librarians active today subscribe.

One effect of the resulting male domination of the literary curriculum in the schools was, of course, to assert the second-class status of the females as clearly as the boys' book phenomenon had ever done. The message to publishers of studies like Norvell's was to look for even more stories with male protagonists; they sold better. Scott O'Dell has related how his publisher asked him to change the sex of his protagonist in *Island of the Blue Dolphins*, a children's book based on an actual event, the survival for many years of a young Indian girl abandoned on a small Pacific island.[47] (Fortunately, O'Dell stood firm, and the story of Karana has become perhaps the most popular of all the books ever awarded the American Library Association's Newbery Medal.) Textbooks and early-reader trade books were particularly male dominated in the 1960s, since it had been noted with alarm that Johnny rather than Janey was likely to have trouble learning to read, and thus it seemed particularly important to offer at this level stories that appealed to boys.

The consciousness-raising that was at the heart of the women's movement began to awaken sociologists, educators, and literary critics to the staggering imbalance in the male-female ratio in picture books, textbooks, and others.[48] They objected to this practice as restricting the reading options of both boys and girls and negatively influencing the self-esteem of girls. Their protest fell on sympathetic ears, and because it was backed by the willingness of librarians and parents to purchase more balanced books as they became available, change was rapid. In the past ten years many fine books have been published with female characters who are much more varied in temperament and role. As early as 1976 a study of current trade books for children counted approximately equal numbers of male and female protagonists and equal distribution of positive attributes between the two sexes.[49]

Girls now have numerous and varied feminine role models in the books published for children. Real progress has been made, as we can see when we compare the range of books about girls available today as compared to the books of even twenty-five years ago. In historical novels, contemporary fiction, biography, and fantasy, engaging, active heroines abound. Fairy tales featuring spry old ladies, female Paul Bunyans, and capable young girls of perilous quests have been resurrected and published to balance the passive princesses and wicked old witches of the most familiar tales.[50]

Yet what good is this wealth if in 1980 a textbook was telling prospective elementary school teachers that "boys will not read 'girl books'"? And however much we rejoice at the expansion of our daughters' literary horizons, we must recognize that the progress does not benefit our sons if most of them are as reluctant to read girls' books (defined as any book with a female protagonist) as boys were a century ago.

Granted, the appeal of certain books about girls has been strong enough to motivate boys to defy the taboo. Examples include O'Dell's *Island of the Blue Dolphins* (1960), mentioned above; Louise Fitzhugh's *Harriet the Spy* (1964), a revolutionary book in its intrepid, eccentric heroine and its funny yet telling satire of adult mores; and *A Wrinkle in Time*, by Madeleine L'Engle (1962), a rare science-fiction novel for preadolescents in which the heroine's problem of being the homely, awkward daughter of a gorgeous, competent mother is entwined with her quest-mission through a hostile universe to rescue her father and save the world from the powers of darkness.

But the phenomenon of large numbers of boys reading these books is an exceptional event, much remarked on in library and publishing circles. It doesn't happen often, and most adults would never think of giving a boy a book about a girl. Parents often ask me to recommend books for family reading aloud. One of my suggestions, Laura Ingalls Wilder's *Little House* series, is greeted with surprise and skepticism by the parents of boys, though I assure them that my son and all his classmates, male and female, were enthralled by the adventures of Laura and Mary when a creative teacher defied expert opinion and chose it to read to her second-grade class. People who work with children can testify to the sad fact that reading a book about a girl is still cause for embarrassment for many young male readers. The student I mentioned earlier, who interviewed boys about their reading, asked one sixth grader: "Can you remember any books about girls that you enjoyed?" He replied, "No [pause], . . . except *A Wrinkle in Time*." Then he quickly added, "But she wasn't really the main character." But Meg *is* the main character, of course; furthermore, the same boy had earlier named *A Wrinkle in Time* as his favorite book.

This makes clear what has been true all along—that the boys' book–girls' book division, while it depreciated the female experience and so extracted a heavy cost in feminine self-esteem, was at the same time more restrictive of boys' options, of their freedom to read (all the exotic voyages and bold explorations notwithstanding), than of girls'. The fact that girls could roam over the entire territory of children's books while most boys felt confined to boys' books didn't matter much when girls' books were for the most part tame, socializing tools geared to perfecting and indoctrinating young ladies, and virtually all the "good books" from a child's point of view were accessible to boys. But now that many girls' books (whether girls' books are defined as family stories and fairy tales or as all books featuring female characters) are enthralling and enriching stories, boys are the losers. The greater pressure on boys to confine themselves to male-typed reading and behavior, though stemming from the higher status of males, is revealed to be at heart a limitation—one obviously related to all the constraints that preserving the traditional male role impose. We can only speculate about the ramifications of this fact. In a society where many men and women are alienated from members of the other sex, one wonders whether males might be more comfortable with and understanding of women's needs and perspectives if they had imaginatively shared female experience through books, beginning in childhood. At the least, we must deplore the fact that many boys are missing out on one of fiction's greatest gifts, the chance to experience life from a perspective other than the one we were born to—in this case, from the female vantage point.

Patrick Lee and Nancy Gropper, in their article "Sex-Role Culture and Educational Practice," note that because girls experience less pressure than boys to assume same-sex-typed preferences, they tend to be more *bicultural* than boys.[51] (They are referring here to sex-role culture; the term more commonly used is *androgynous*.) They conclude that this biculturalism or androgyny is desirable, and that "boys and girls should be free to approach resources which are currently demarcated along sex-role lines, entirely in accord with individual differences in interests and aptitudes."[52]

If we agree, then an understanding of the subtle influence that restrictive nineteenth-century views on appropriate reading for girls and for boys still exerts on children's reading can help us to identify and challenge its hold.[53] Otherwise, unexamined adult assumptions about divergent reading interests of girls and boys will continue to perpetuate gender-role constraints we thought we had left behind.

Notes

1 Geoffrey Trease, "The Revolution in Children's Literature," in *The Thorny Paradise: Writers on Writing for Children*, ed. Edward Blishen (Harmondsworth, Middlesex: Kestrel, 1975), p. 14.

2 *A Little Pretty Pocket-Book* (London: John Newbery, 1744; 1767 ed. reprinted, London: Oxford University Press, 1966).

3 Sarah Fielding, *The Governess; Or, Little Female Academy*, 2d ed. (London: A. Millar, 1758).

4 Mary Thwaite, *From Primer to Pleasure in Reading*, 2d ed. (London: Library Association, 1972), p. 152.
5 Samuel F. Pickering, Jr., *John Locke and Children's Books in Eighteenth-Century England* (Knoxville: University of Tennessee Press, 1981), p. 244.
6 Mary Ann Kilner, *Memoirs of a Peg-Top* (London: John Marshall, 1783; reprinted, New York: Garland, 1976), p. vi.
7 [Elizabeth Rigby], *Quarterly Review* 74 (1844): 21. Excerpted in *Children and Literature*, ed. Virginia Haviland (Glenview, Ill.: Scott, Foresman, 1973), p. 15.
8 William Graham Sumner, "What Our Boys Are Reading," *Scribner's Monthly* 15 (1878): 681–85.
9 Edward G. Salmon, "What Girls Read," *Nineteenth Century* 20 (1886): 515–29.
10 Charles and Mary Anne Lamb, *The Letters of Charles and Mary Anne Lamb*, 3 vols., ed. Edwin W. Marrs, Jr. (Ithaca: Cornell University Press, 1976), 2: 278–79. Lamb responded: "Dear Godwin,—The Giant's vomit was perfectly nauseous, and I am glad that you pointed it out. I have removed the objection." But he declined to make other suggested changes (p. 279).
11 F. J. Harvey Darton, *Children's Books in England: Five Centuries of Social Life*, 3d ed., rev. Brian Alderson (Cambridge: Cambridge University Press, 1958), p. 217.
12 Salmon, "What Girls Read," p. 522. Sarah Doudney and Anne Beale wrote novels for girls which were noted for their piety and pathos. When Lucy Lyttelton's grandmother began reading aloud *Adam Bede*, "the new novel about which the world raves," it was "duly bowdlerized for our young minds," Lucy reported in her diary. She was eighteen at the time. "In most families George Eliot's works were absolutely forbidden to the young," according to Amy Cruse; those of Charlotte Yonge, on the other hand, were "always open to them" (*The Victorians and Their Reading* [Boston: Houghton Mifflin, 1936], p. 63).
13 Mrs. [Mary Louisa] Molesworth, "Juliana Horatia Ewing," *Contemporary Review* 49 (1886): 675–86; reprinted in *A Peculiar Gift: Nineteenth-Century Writings on Books for Children*, ed. Lance Salway (Harmondsworth, Middlesex: Kestrel, 1976), p. 506.
14 Salmon, "What Girls Read," p. 523.
15 Charles Dickens, *Our Mutual Friend* (Oxford: Oxford University Press, 1952), p. 129.
16 See Walter E. Houghton, *The Victorian Frame of Mind* (New Haven: Yale University Press, 1957), chap. 13; Anne S. MacLeod, *A Moral Tale: Children's Fiction and American Culture, 1820–1860* (Hamden, Conn.: Archon Books, 1975), chap. 1; and Ann Douglas, *The Feminization of American Culture* (New York: Alfred A. Knopf, 1977), chaps. 2 and 3.
17 The doctrine of feminine influence was articulated and embraced in both Britain and the United States, though the social and legal conditions of a frontier society made for interesting complications in America. See Helen Waite Papashvily, *All the Happy Endings* (New York: Harper, 1956), chap. 2; and Elizabeth Segel, "Laura Ingalls Wilder's America: An Unflinching Assessment," *Children's Literature in Education* 8 (1977): 63–70.
18 Salmon, "What Girls Read," p. 526.
19 Gillian Avery, *Childhood's Pattern: A Study of the Heroes and Heroines of Children's Fiction, 1770–1950* (London: Hodder and Stoughton, 1975), p. 166.
20 Papashvily argues persuasively that in popular romances written by women at this time the happy ending is a kind of wish-fulfilling fantasy wherein the woman is recognized as a heroic and noble survivor and her tyrannical or unfaithful husband is reduced to penitent beggary (*All the Happy Endings*, chap. 8). Though

adolescent girls no doubt read some of these books, I do not find this compensating fantasy worked out in the books written by women specifically for girls.

21 Susan Coolidge [Sarah Chauncey Woolsey, pseud.], *What Katy Did* (London: J. M. Dent, 1968). Subsequent references are cited parenthetically in the text.

22 Robert Louis Stevenson, *Treasure Island* (London: Cassell, 1883).

23 MacLeod, *Moral Tale*, p. 10.

24 Whether Jo March, in marrying Professor Bhaer and becoming a sort of Earth-mother, has capitulated is still being debated. My own opinion is that because the final image of Jo is of a strong and successful woman (and because readers, aware of the autobiographical element, consider that she grew up to be a famous writer), Alcott transcended the formula to a great extent, and it is for this reason that the book retained its popularity longer than other girls' books.

25 Annis Pratt, *Archetypal Patterns in Women's Fiction* (Bloomington: Indiana University Press, 1981), p. 14. Pratt notes that in the women's novels about adolescence, "at the same time that the authors . . . suggest psychic dwarfing as the inevitable destiny of young women in British and American society, they manage to introduce a considerable degree of protest into the genre through a vivid depiction of the feelings of its victims" (p. 35). Most girls' books of the nineteenth century, as we might expect, contain few traces of this protest. Women might hint at rebellious feelings to adult women readers, but the sacred duty of preparing girls to accept their assigned role apparently led them to suppress their reservations when writing for girls. The passage describes very well, however, several twentieth-century chronicles of girls' coming of age: Ruth Sawyer's *Roller Skates*, Carol Ryrie Brink's *Caddie Woodlawn*, and Laura Ingalls Wilder's *Little House* books.

26 Thwaite, *From Primer to Pleasure in Reading*, p. 171.

27 Cruse, *Victorians and Their Reading*, pp. 294–97.

28 Salmon, "What Girls Read," p. 524.

29 Alice M. Jordan, *From Rollo to Tom Sawyer and Other Papers* (Boston: Horn Book, 1948), p. 35.

30 Ibid., pp. 48–49.

31 G. Manville Fenn, *George Alfred Henty: The Story of an Active Life* (London: Blackie, 1907); reprinted in Salway, *Peculiar Gift*, p. 430.

32 Cruse, *Victorians and Their Reading*, p. 297.

33 Salmon, "What Girls Read," p. 524.

34 Edith Sichel, "Charlotte Yonge as a Chronicler," *Monthly Review* 3 (1901): 88–97; reprinted in Salway, *Peculiar Gift*, p. 488.

35 Ruth Hill Viguers, "Laura E. Richards, Joyous Companion," in *The Hewins Lectures 1947–1962*, ed. Siri Andrews (Boston: Horn Book, 1963), p. 188.

36 Jordan, *From Rollo to Tom Sawyer*, p. 38.

37 Ibid., p. 37.

38 Melvyn Bragg, "Little Women," *Children's Literature in Education* 9 (1978): 95.

39 Patrick C. Lee and Nancy B. Gropper, "Sex-Role Culture and Educational Practice," *Harvard Educational Review* 44 (1974): 398.

40 George Norvell, *The Reading Interests of Young People*, rev. ed. (Lansing: Michigan State University Press, 1973), p. 3. Subsequent references are cited parenthetically in the text.

41 Lian-Hwang Chiu, "Reading Preferences of Fourth-Grade Children Related to Sex and Reading Ability," *Journal of Educational Research* 66 (1973): 371.

42 Samuel Weintraub, "Two Significant Trends in Reading Research," in *Reading and Writing Instruction in the United States: Historical Trends*, ed. H. Alan Robinson (Urbana: IRA-ERIC, 1977), p. 61.

43 Ibid., p. 63.
44 Steven Dunning and Alan B. Howes, *Literature for Adolescents* (Glenview, Ill.: Scott, Foresman, 1975), p. 198.
45 Dwight L. Burton, *et al.*, *Teaching English Today* (Boston: Houghton Mifflin, 1975), p. 173.
46 Dorothy Rubin, *Teaching Elementary Language Arts*, rev. ed. (New York: Holt, Rinehart, and Winston, 1980), p. 183.
47 Alleen Pace Nilsen, "Women in Children's Literature," *College English* 32 (1971), p. 918.
48 Elizabeth Fisher, "The Second Sex, Junior Division," *New York Times Book Review* (May 21, 1970), pp. 6–7; Nilsen, "Women in Children's Literature," pp. 918–26; Feminists on Children's Literature, "A Feminist Look at Children's Books," *School Library Journal* 17 (1971), pp. 19–24; and Lenore J. Weitzman *et al.*, "Sex-Role Socialization in Picture Books for Preschool Children," *American Journal of Sociology* 77 (1972), pp. 1125–50.
49 Ruth M. Noyce, "Equality of the Sexes in New Children's Fiction," Report prepared at the University of Kansas, 1976. Educational Resources Information Center, ED no. 137/802.
50 Rosemary Minard, *Womenfolk and Fairy Tales* (Boston: Houghton Mifflin, 1975); Ethel Johnston Phelps, *Tatterhood and Other Tales* (Old Westbury, N. Y.: Feminist Press, 1978) and *The Maid of the North: Feminist Folk Tales from around the World* (New York: Holt, Rinehart and Winston, 1981); and Alison Lurie, *Clever Gretchen and Other Forgotten Folktales* (New York: Crowell, 1980).
51 Lee and Gropper, "Sex-Role Culture and Educational Practice," p. 398.
52 Ibid., p. 404.
53 See my article "Choices for Girls, for Boys: Keeping Options Open," *School Library Journal* 28 (1982), pp. 105–7, for practical suggestions for breaking down the gender-determined patterns of children's reading.

69

ENIGMA VARIATIONS

What feminist theory knows about children's literature

Lissa Paul

Source: *Signal* 54 (1987): 186–202.

One thing is certain. The fault lies with *Foreign Affairs* by Alison Lurie. And with a friend who gave me the book. I read it immediately, and in my habitually academic way said that I really liked it because it was a book about masquerade. Then, casting about for a suitable example to support my thesis, I went on: 'especially the raincoat'. 'Yes,' said Nick, 'his [Chuck, the hero's] green plastic-bag packaged raincoat – the one that looks like a dead fish.' That stopped me. I had meant her [Vinnie, the heroine's] raincoat, not his – her new silvery-blue, shimmering silk, extravagantly expensive designer raincoat that makes her feel taller and look like a Druid.

If you haven't read *Foreign Affairs*, don't worry – though it is a terrific book and, as Vinnie is a specialist in children's literature, probably insider's reading for people who read *Signal*. This article is not about *Foreign Affairs* or raincoats or masquerades. At least not exactly. It is about what I saw in that raincoat exchange of words: how very different Nick's reading was from mine – how the words 'masquerade' and 'raincoat' precipitated quite separate constellations of meaning for each of us.[1]

For one, brightly lit moment I caught a glimpse of the doubleness in words and things: raincoats keeping the rain out, but also disguising spies, movie stars, flashers, and other people with something to hide. I saw raincoats concealing and revealing identity and meaning – very like words. And in that initial net of double meanings, I caught something else: something with powerful implications about the content and language of children's literature and children's literature criticism; something to do with 'inside' stories; something of our own fractured sense of the distinctions between self and other; something in tune with our particular moment in Western culture – something articulated in feminist theory.

Bad luck, I thought. It's all very well to have an epiphany, but telling someone else about it is another matter entirely. Though I had understood the need for people – male and female, adult and child – to speak each other's languages and wear each other's clothes, I knew that it would take a long time even to begin to describe, word by word, what had been visible in that moment of illumination. And critics, as Frank Kermode observes in *The Genesis of Secrecy*, prefer enigmas to muddles.

Maybe that is why the idea of masquerade caught me so strongly. I write fiction masquerading as criticism: a mode of discourse that hides and reveals my personal pleasure in a text inside a raincoat of scholarly language. Hence, my 'Enigma Variations'. Both the title and the structure are borrowed (or stolen) from Edward Elgar. He composed thirteen variations, fourteen if you count his own self-portrait. To communicate my epiphany as an enigma rather than a muddle, I have written only two variations, 'The Plot' (pages 195 to 201) and 'Dumb Bunnies' (for a subsequent article) – though three variations might be closer to the truth, if you count my self-portrait that runs like Elgar's 'dark saying' through the whole. And the theme I've composed is the common ground between women's literature and children's literature: a theme that lies in a shared content (the enclosed, interior scenes of the action); and in a shared language (of otherness).

There is good reason for appropriating feminist theory to children's literature. Both women's literature and children's literature are devalued and regarded as marginal or peripheral by the literary and educational communities. Feminist critics are beginning to change that. By tracing the history of women's writing, especially in the nineteenth century, feminist critics are giving definition and value to women in literature and literature by women. As it happens, the forms of physical, economic and linguistic entrapment that feminist critics have been revealing in women's literature match the images of entrapment in children's literature.

The similarity is not surprising. After all, the nineteenth century, give or take a few decades either side, corresponds to 'The Golden Age of Children's Literature', to the age of Lewis Carroll, and Kenneth Grahame, and George MacDonald, and to the age when traditional folktales and fairy tales were gathered up into the children's literature canon.

Inside stories

Children, like women, are lumped together as helpless and dependent; creatures to be kept away from the scene of the action, and who otherwise ought not to be seen or heard. But women make up more than half of the population of the world – and all of us once were children. It is almost inconceivable that women and children have been invisible and voiceless for so long.

There. Now I've named the twin problems feminist critics have: how do you know something is invisible if you can't see it? And how do you know something is inaudible if you can't hear it?

Adrienne Rich, American poet and critic, says in 'When We Dead Awaken: Writing as Re-vision', that feminist critics are engaged in an act of re-vision, that they are waking up, seeing, as if for the first time, all the repressed anger and pain that they have been keeping silent about for so long. Along with other feminist critics Rich is attempting to renegotiate the status quo: to 'review, reimagine, rethink, rewrite, revise and reinterpret' the physical, economic and linguistic entrapment experienced as normal by women and children for roughly, as feminist critic Sandra Gilbert says, 'a thousand years of Western culture'.[2] A frightening prospect, but not a hopeless one. Children's literature, in fact, provides some helpful hints on transcending traps.

Women in literature are disproportionately shown as physically trapped in rooms, attics, in their father's houses, or in their husband's. In those enclosed spaces women go mad or silent, or they die. *Jane Eyre* is the prototypical story of this 'madwoman in the attic'. But the protagonists in children's literature transcend, and, for the most part win, even when the endings of stories are not conventionally happy. Though they have to deal with the same (often overlapping) forms of physical, economic and linguistic entrapment that women do, they are not yet closed in by the rules of adulthood. To illustrate I'm going to draw a few miniatures, naming the hidden stories feminist criticism has been revealing about the contents of traps and the preferred (deceitful) means of escape, but I'll draw the examples from traditional folk and fairy tales and from children's literature. Forgive the thumbnail-sketchiness of the examples, they are not intended as trompe-l'oeil portraits.

Unlike men, women and children can't stray very far from the bounds of home and gardens (at least, not unaccompanied) for Technicolor epic adventures on the scale of, say, *The Odyssey*. So physical entrapment (often connected with economic dependence) is just a fact of life. In 'Rumpelstiltskin' or 'The Three Spinners', for instance, the protagonists are locked in rooms with mountains of spinning to do. To seek their fortunes in the outside world is simply not an option. Though they cry (a perfectly normal response) about their fates at first, they manage to free themselves from both their rooms and their spinning, with a little help from their friends, and with a little trickery and subversion.

Child protagonists from authored texts tend to be equally inventive when it comes to subverting traps and punishment: Max transforms his room (the scene of his punishment) into the land of the wild things (the scene of his power); Colin and Mary transform the dead garden of

Misselthwaite Manor into a blooming, secret one; and Anne (of Green Gables) turns each of the scenes of her early childhood abuse into places of beauty and pleasure. These child protagonists create options that are simply unthinkable to grown-ups whose conditioned responses have already closed in on them. That is one of the reasons why these stories are of value to us as adults. The reader, or listener, looks at life from a very cramped vantage – rooms without views all right, but not without adventures, and not without options. Even a boy who is only as thickasathumb can live an exciting life, and outwit the world from inside a horse's ear, a mouse hole, a snail shell, a cow's belly and a wolf's belly.

Because women and children generally have to stay at home without the affairs of state to worry about, their stories tend to focus on the contents of their traps, the minute and mundane features of everyday life around which their lives revolve: household effects, food, clothes, sewing, interior decorating, and nuances of social relationships. These homely details have been redeemed by feminist critics (see Annette Kolodny, 'A Map for Rereading', *New Feminist Criticism*) as having interest; as being as worthy of critical attention as descriptions of battles or card games or beer drinking.

Harriet (the spy) understands very well that adventure stories are as available inside as they are outside. Although she goes out to follow her spy route, she peeks into the enclosed private spaces of lives of the people on it. She knows how to read the signs. The barrenness of the Robinsons' lives is revealed in their silence and in their monstrous sculpture of a nameless baby. And the tenderness of Harrison Withers is revealed when he addresses each of his twenty-six cats, by name.

The stories Harriet tells are secret stories, founded on voyeurism and gossip. Her adventures are more suited to *Family Circle* than James Bond; more like sociological studies of the family in contemporary urban life than adventures involving the secrets of state. They are private stories, not public, and so subject to the third kind of repression I've named as characteristic of women's stories – linguistic repression.

Harriet's secret writing is typical of the kinds of writing women and children do: small-scale stories, often in the forms of journals, diaries, letters, little poems, or romance novels. These forms are often simply regarded as insignificant, minor, in the face of the epic, grand-scale writings of Dostoyevsky or Dickens or Hemingway, stories that engage the full sweep of human endeavour – war, politics, science, philosophy, areas in which women and children have little experience. Even female writers who have secure places in the canon (Jane Austen, the Brontës, Emily Dickinson, George Eliot, and Virginia Woolf) spent most of their lives feeling not quite a part of the literary establishment (Jane Austen hid her writing if anyone walked into the room, Emily Dickinson published only a few poems in her lifetime).

In children's literature the most famous repressed writer is, I think, the little woman Jo March, Louisa Alcott's alter ego. Jo is, in fact, the perfect nineteenth-century embodiment of physical, economic and linguistic entrapment. She is shut up in her attic, secretly writing romance fiction (to support the family) while her pretentious father holds court in the main-floor study. She is made to feel ashamed of her writing by her husband/father, Professor Bhaer, and to give it up in favour of a really useful profession – raising boys. Dependence is treated as the preferred occupation.

Work and money are the keys to freedom, and women and children don't have much access to either. Unlike adventure stories, or fairy tales where men go out to seek their fortunes, women just have to hope that fortune smiles upon them. In *The Dialectic of Sex* Shulamith Firestone says that women and children live in a condition of 'privileged slavery' under a demoralizing system of patronage:

> . . . the individual eventually appears to be a different kind of human animal with its own peculiar set of laws and behaviour ('I'll never understand women!' [. . .] 'You don't know a thing about child psychology!')
>
> Contemporary slang reflects this animal state: children are 'mice', 'rabbits', 'kittens', women are called 'chicks', (in England) 'birds', 'hens', 'dumb clucks', 'silly geese', 'old mares', 'bitches' . . .
>
> Because the class oppression of women and children is couched in the phraseology of 'cute' it is much harder to fight than open oppression. What child can answer back when some inane aunt falls all over him or some stranger decides to pat his behind and gurgle baby talk? . . . Because it makes them uncomfortable to know that the woman or the child or the black or the workman is grumbling, the oppressed groups must also appear to *like* their oppression – smiling and simpering though they may feel like hell inside. The smile is the child/woman equivalent of the shuffle; it indicates acquiescence of the victim to his own oppression.
>
> (pages 100–1)

The repression about which Firestone writes is easily carried out because women and children are, generally, smaller and weaker than men, regarded as 'other' and so open to abuse. It is not surprising, then, that difficulty being seen and heard is experienced by small protagonists – from Treehorn (who is accused of shirking, when his real problem is that he is shrinking, and no one seems to notice) to Jacob Two-Two (who has to say everything twice to be heard). What makes these characters so engaging is that, despite being small and weak, they win over powers that be. The story is familiar. It is Jack-the-Giant-Killer and David and Goliath. It is the trickster's story. It is also the heroine's story, and the child's.

The quickening of academic interest in women's and children's literature testifies that something in their stories is in touch with the temper of our time. Trickster stories express a contemporary reality; powerlessness is no longer a condition experienced primarily by women, children and other oppressed people. It is a condition we all recognize. And with the new consciousness of the value of the small, weak and powerless protagonist, there is a renewed interest in a survival tactic that has long been out of favour. Deceit.

Deceit, fraud, guile and other forms of trickery have been out of favour for the last thousand (or more) years of Western culture. That wasn't always the case. Tricksters – from mythic Raven and Anansi, to the folk heroes Brer Rabbit and Tolkien's Bilbo Baggins – have all been revered as culture heroes, valued for their craftiness. As deceit isn't a manly virtue, it has been relegated to a lower-order survival tactic, somewhere well below the dignity accorded to a man who fights for his honour, or for 'truth, justice and the American way'.

Academic interest in the tactics of the heroine has generated interest in deceit. In 'Our Lady of Pain: Heroes and Heroines of Romance' (from *The Secular Scripture*) Northrop Frye, taking his terms from Dante, says that heroes fight through the use of 'forza', violence. They usually end up dead, and their stories are tragic more often than not. But heroines who use 'froda', fraud, survive, and their stories resolve happily.

Although 'froda' is a traditional female survival tactic, it is not successfully deployed in times and places in which women are supposed to like being trapped. In the nineteenth century, for instance, girls might start out using guile, but growing up was regarded as a process of civilizing guile out. So Anne in *Anne of Green Gables* is an engaging child, whose imagination allows her to escape from the banality of everyday existence, but in growing up, she actively chooses to stay at home (at Green Gables, on Prince Edward Island) rather than go off to university. She chooses to be trapped. Jo, in *Little Women*, undergoes much the same repressing process. She is also an engaging, even naughty, girl, but as she grows up and learns how to stifle her anger, she becomes much less interesting. For both Anne and Jo, this process is seen (overtly anyway) as a positive one. But I would be willing to bet that one of the reasons that *Anne of Green Gables* and *Little Women* remain such favourites is that readers intuitively understand the tension between the vital girl and the repressed woman. Even if guile gets civilized out, its traces remain.

Still, the point is that though deceit is the traditional tactic of the heroine, it is most visible in the tactics of defenceless child protagonists in children's literature – from Jack, when he meets the Giant Killer, to Jacob Two-Two, when he meets the Hooded Fang. Even *The Secret Garden*, one of the most enduring stories for children of all time, is founded on deceit. Mary and Colin know they have to keep the secret of their growing strength and capacity to survive locked inside the garden wall, until they have managed to undo all the damage done to them by misguided adults. Grown-ups (except for the rustic, childlike sort) are depicted in *The Secret Garden* as destructive and morbid – especially the doctors who prescribe debilitating 'corrective' measures for Colin. Mary and Colin lived in a world where separation between grown-ups and children was possible, and in their case, a positive asset. That separation is no longer possible.

As women and children are increasingly incorporated into the body of the culture, the culture recognizes and incorporates the value of their difference. By naming the physical, economic and linguistic traps in women's and children's literature, and by naming deceit as a survival tactic, I've been naming the previously invisible differences between 'them' (women and children) and 'us' (adults). What follows is an account of the sound of those differences.

And otherness

Feminist critics have been writing about how hard it is to find a voice to talk about women's literature. That is because criticism has traditionally – at least in the now old-school new-critical terms – been deemed objective, and the authority of the text deemed sacrosanct. We now understand that texts don't exist in isolation, and language that pretends to be authoritative and objective is male-order language – not suited to discussions about the inscapes of women's stories.

Male-order criticism is pointed towards the one penetrating strategy that removes even the last G-string of mystery and lays bare the text. But it doesn't quite work; the emperor's magic new clothes degenerate into a low-brow skinflick. Bare texts don't allow for the kind of intellectual play upon which readers (especially critics) thrive. Feminist criticism, on the other hand, is about keeping the voyeur's attention and imagination engaged while the clothes are being taken off. Critical interest centres on the play of meaning, not the sadly naked revelation of meaning.

But as long as the signs and language of women's literature and children's literature are foreign, other, to male-order critics, it is almost impossible to play with meaning. So one of the primary problems feminist critics and children's literature critics have is how to recognize, define, and accord value to otherness.

To make otherness less foreign, feminist critics have been bringing to the body of their critical work all the available power and light from a host of disciplines: semiotic theory to make the signs of otherness visible; linguistic theory to identify the difference between male language and female language; Marxist theory to name the economic entrapment of women and children as comparable to that experienced by the lower classes in class-defined societies; communication theory to focus on the implications of the shift from a print-based, cause-and-effect (essentially male-order) mode of discourse to an audio/visual, storytelling (essentially female) mode of discourse; reader-response theory to give value to the subjective response to texts, and to acknowledge the cultural, social and gender differences between readers; cultural anthropology to explore otherness as a way for us to test the points of likeness and difference between ourselves and others more clearly; psychoanalytic theory to explain the discomfort experienced when we divide 'them' from 'us'. (For reference to specific texts, see 'Useful Books' at the end of this article.)

The capacity to bring together a 'hard body' of critical theory in a 'user friendly', often warm and funny way, is what marks feminist criticism. And I hope it marks my criticism too: the capacity to write with 'hard body' (from a North American predilection for life in the gym) and *jouissance* (Roland Barthes uses the term in *The Pleasure of the Text*; it translates roughly as pleasure – multiple, female orgasmic pleasure). The rewards of writing criticism with this mixture of pain and pleasure make it well worth doing. By bringing scholarship from a variety of disciplines to literary study, and by addressing points of likeness and difference between ourselves and others, feminist critics have breathed life into what was becoming the moribund discipline of literary criticism.

Feminist critics aren't the only ones bringing a range of critical insights into the study of literary texts. The 'impressionistic' criticism (as Nancy Chambers calls it) and 'emotional' criticism (as Eleanor Cameron calls it) that has weakened children's literature criticism for so long is being challenged by something more vigorous and resonant: Aidan Chambers, Hugh Crago and Roger Sale have been bringing various forms of reader-response theory to children's literature, focusing on the points of contact between child-reading and adult-reading; Carolyn Steedman brings Marxist, linguistic and culture theory to writing by children; Jack Zipes draws on Marxist theory to show how fairy tales betray our social values; Peter Hunt is developing what he calls 'childist' (the term sits uncomfortably with me because, I suspect, it maintains them-and-us distinctions) criticism, drawing on the 're-seeing' of the culture; and Eleanor Cameron is bringing a 'wrinkled brow and cool fresh eye' (borrowing her terms from Robert Lowell on Randall Jarrell) to children's literature. I like her approach because she possesses the kind of double-vision that I think is essential in children's literature criticism: the capacity to move freely 'between intuitive thinking and logic' and between adult experience and the freshness of child vision. Cameron says that 'the critic worth reading neither destroys nor chews to shreds; one tries to reveal'. If we are good critics or visionaries, or good sibyls, or good at hermeneutics and semiotics, then we can read the signs and interpret them.

In children's literature, the critical issue no longer involves clarifying distinctions between them (children) and us (grown-ups). It involves looking for the kind of double-vision that Eleanor Cameron advocates and that Aidan Chambers ('All of a Tremble to See His Danger') sees actively operating in *Huckleberry Finn*, when Mark Twain 'stays true to the adolescent self he once openly was and still secretly is' but 'takes with him into his novel the knowledge of life he has acquired since, and transposes it by his craft skill into knowledge that a teenager can discover'. What Aidan reveals is the capacity of the adolescent novel to hold open the signs of the future for the adolescent looking forward, and the signs of the past for the grown-up looking back.

If one of the critical tasks is to look at children's literature as something that keeps childhood and adolescence alive within us, then objective them-and-us conventional approaches to texts look sadly dated. The approach we need is closer to one Richard Shweder, a cultural anthropologist, says is suited to good ethnography: casuistry ('adroit rationalization') to make familiar 'what at first seemed strange, the other' and estranges us 'from what we thought we knew, ourselves'.[3] Simply put, Shweder advocates deceit as a useful tactic for exploring the play of likeness and difference between self and other. It is a language of deceit that tells the truth (reminiscent of raincoats).

As an adult, and as a critic, someone who shares books with children (and with adults who share books with children), I'm responsible. I'm responsible for finding a language that speaks the cultural and aesthetic values of our society in an intelligible way. For me, that is a mode of discourse that incorporates both the *jouissance* of mimetic, storytelling language and the hard body of critical theory: a critical stance that acknowledges both the seriousness and the pleasure of the audience and the text. This only happens if we understand that we explore texts not because the child is the father of the man (or the mother of the woman, one might say, though that seems not to carry the same weight) but because there is something alive in us worth exploring.

The plot – reading the signs in 'The Secret Garden' and 'The Changeover'

I was disappointed by Humphrey Carpenter's *Secret Gardens: The Golden Age of Children's Literature*[4]. When I first encountered it, I eagerly anticipated a book that would give me some keys to *The Secret Garden*, reasons why the story continues to resonate so strongly in me, even though I intensely dislike the way it turns from Mary's story into Colin's (a feeling I know I share with other readers, especially women). Carpenter hits on the right sign: the secret garden itself is the key to the story and to the Golden Age of children's literature. But he doesn't understand the meaning of the sign. He doesn't understand what I now know: the secret garden is a plot.

Plot, says Peter Brooks in *Reading for the Plot: Design and Intention in Narrative*[5], is both the scene of the action and the plan of action, the location and the scheme of a story. The ways that the events of the story are worked out (and the ways the reader reads them) depend on the interpretation of the signs. Humphrey Carpenter's account of secret gardens is disappointing because he depicts the kingpins of the Golden Age of children's literature (especially Kingsley, Carroll, Alcott, and Barrie) as social misfits stuck in some sort of adolescent never-never land. What he doesn't do is explain why their stories remain so compelling. He doesn't explain that they had understood the secret of their secret gardens: the tension between Victorian repression and the archetypal transcendence of a quest romance. They had worked out ways of transforming the repression of their lives into the transcendence of their art. And the traces of their success remain as accessible to readers now as they were then.

In the first part of 'Enigma Variations', I tried to make the signs of feminist poetics (as applicable to children's literature) visible and audible: the physical, economic, and linguistic entrapment of women and children as revealed in the enclosed spaces and small-scale, secret stories of the texts. This part of 'Enigma Variations', 'The Plot', is about what those signs mean. I'm going to use Frances Hodgson Burnett's *The Secret Garden* (1911) and *The Changeover: A Supernatural Romance* by Margaret Mahy (1984)[6] as paradigmatic texts. Both stories tell of the identity quests of their respective protagonists, and both stories locate the scene of the action and the plan of action in enclosed, secret gardens. As in the first part of 'Enigma Variations' I'm going to suggest that there has been a shift in children's literature: from Golden Age entrapment to the transcendence in the young adult fiction of the 1980s.

I've always felt *The Secret Garden* to be as much a monument to the British Empire as are the Crystal Palace and Queen Victoria herself. There is something so compelling about the story that I am prepared to suspend my annoyance with the ending, with the way Burnett puts priggish little Colin front and centre and relegates Mary to the sidelines. My problem is that I have to acknowledge, reluctantly, that Burnett wrote the only possible ending to the story. Like it or not, Burnett got the plot right.

One of the most telling scenes occurs at the end of the book when Colin comes bursting out of the garden, almost knocking his bewildered father off his feet (an obviously Oedipal gesture). Mary comes second. Colin gloats about being able to beat her in a race. Social order is restored. Colin will be king of the castle (of Misselthwaite Manor in this case, displacing the pretender, his uncle Dr Craven). Mary is an also-ran. She fades quietly into the background, the perfect wallflower. The irony implicit in Mary's story is that the secret garden, the place of growth, is the place of her defeat.

Colin is a winner. He is 'Master Colin', who walks 'as strongly and steadily as any boy in Yorkshire' (page 253). I am always dismayed by how far the story drifts from the opening sentence! There we were introduced to the sad image of Mary, who had been 'sent' to Misselthwaite Manor: 'the most disagreeable-looking child ever seen' (page 7). As a reader, I want her to find herself, to complete her quest for selfhood. It is Mary, after all, who divines that the secret of survival is in the garden (the scene of the action) and she is the one who devises a way of acting upon her instinctive knowledge (the plan of action). It is Mary who seeks the garden, finds the key, finds the help she needs to make the garden grow, and finds in herself enough nurturing instinct to help Colin grow. But her story is gradually relinquished to (pretentious, boring) Colin. Though she formulates the plan to save him, she gets little credit. It is Colin, 'the Athlete, the Lecturer, the Scientific Discoverer' (page 251), who stands at the end of the book to tell his story to the adoring assembly of listeners (including Mary) sitting clustered at his feet.

For Colin, growing up in the garden, being nurtured in the garden, means that he has been able to overcome the physical and emotional deprivation of his early childhood – without earning it. For Mary, growing up, outgrowing, her early childhood deprivation means learning to be a follower not a leader, learning that winning selfhood means losing self.

So, there it is, the plot of *The Secret Garden*: the key to the story is the story itself. The signs tell a thwarted story of independence, a thwarted quest romance. Its compelling attraction arises in the tension between the knowledge that the story deteriorates (as Mary's story gives way to Colin's), and the knowledge that Burnett ends the story in accordance with the social and economic truths and values of her particular time and place.

The Changeover, on the other hand, is a success story. Laura, the heroine, completes her quest without losing her story or herself to the male lead. Mahy writes out of a time and place where it is possible for a woman to succeed in a man's world, and where nurturing instincts need not be devalued in relation to science and reason: 'the Scientific Discoverer' doesn't have to suppress the gardener.

The plot traces fourteen-year-old Laura's quest to save her three-year-old brother, Jacko, from succumbing to an incubus, Carmody Braque, who is trying to renew himself (rather more stylishly than a vampire would) by sucking the life out of Jacko. To rescue her brother, Laura must fight Braque's supernatural powers in kind. She must become a witch (through a 'changeover') – aided by sixteen-year-old Sorry (the male lead, who is also a witch and the head prefect at her school) and his witch mother and grandmother.

The plot of Mahy's story, like the plot of Burnett's, is both the scene of the action and the plan of action – and it takes place in a secret garden. But whereas Mary and Colin outgrow their inner secret garden in order to take up life outside, Laura and Sorry learn to take their secret garden with them and incorporate its nurturing powers. In *The Changeover* the everyday, 'outside' world where Laura lives with her mother and brother, is a subdivision called Gardendale. In accordance with the unintentional irony common to such places, it is a perfectly ordinary, raw example of urban blight. The inner secret garden, 'Janua Caeli' (the door of heaven), is where Sorry lives with his mother and grandmother. And it is where Laura recovers her witch nature, and finds the supernatural help she needs to save Jacko.

During the course of her quest Laura finds that her inner and outer gardens are not mutually exclusive: they are, rather, 'like a holograph' in which 'every piece of the world contained the whole of the world' (page 211). In the end, even though she outgrows her immediate need for the secret garden of Janua Caeli, she recognizes its presence all around her:

> Outside in the city, traffic lights changed colours, casting quick spells of prohibition and release. Cars hesitated, then set off again, roaring with urgency through the maze of the Gardendale subdivision, a labyrinth in which one could, after all, find a firebird's feather, or a glass slipper or the footprints of the minotaur quite as readily as in fairy tales, or the infinitely dividing paths of Looking-Glass land.
>
> (page 214)

Throughout *The Changeover* Laura's capacity to fulfil her hero(in)ic quest is tied to an ability to read small-scale signs accurately. When she wanders with Jacko into Carmody Braque's tiny, enticing shop filled with things like 'seven owls made of walnut shells', and 'a peep-show shaped like an egg' – and the smell of stale peppermint (page 19), she recognizes a gingerbread house of a trap. The 'faint used-peppermint smell that made her want to be sick in the gutter' that morning is one of the traces of Carmody Braque that Laura notices. She comments on it every time she is near him, or near Jacko once he is possessed. But it is another of Carmody Braque's small signs that proves almost fatal for Jacko: a rubber stamp, like the Mickey Mouse stamp that the librarian puts on Jacko's hand each week, but this one has Braque's face on it. Jacko begins to wither from the moment his hand receives Braque's image. Laura saves him by tricking Braque into receiving a stamp with her face on it – a magical, powerful stamp won through her changeover.

I like the redemptive ending of *The Changeover*. Laura's quest is personal and domestic, she fights for someone she loves. She uses the tricksterish tactics of the weak and powerless. And she doesn't boast about her success as pretentious Colin does (in a way that makes me cringe) at the end of *The Secret Garden*. The values in Mahy's book are connected with individual humanity rather than public glory. They seem to me to be positive values, especially if we assume that the truth of the story she tells both reflects and is reflected by the truths of our society.

The Secret Garden, on the other hand, has what my colleague Margaret Watson calls a 'blocked ending'.[7] The story can't end with the fairy-tale conclusion in which every protagonist gets what he or she deserves, and gets mated according to his or her personal value. That's why the story (correctly) fades from Mary's quest to Colin's and denies Mary her social integration while allowing Colin his. Archetypal quest romances, or identity quests, or *Bildungsroman* patterns are supposed to be universal. But they are skewed or blurred in the Golden Age of children's literature, as they are in women's literature. The problem with a 'typical' archetypal quest that traces the hero's call to adventure, his descent underground, his battle with the enemy, and his triumphant return (as outlined by the typically male cartographers, Joseph Campbell, or C. G. Jung, or Northrop Frye, for example[8]) is that it is about turning boys into men, not girls into women, or children into people. When the quest ends, the hero gets his rewards, his property, his integrity and, often, a princess thrown in among the other goods and chattels.

A female quest doesn't look quite like that, and a story that simply exchanges a female protagonist for a male one usually ends up making the heroine look like a hero in drag. Annis Pratt, in *Archetypal Patterns in Women's Fiction*, looks at women's stories and illuminates a typical five-phase identity quest that a heroine might travel: a splitting off from family; a green-world guide or token; a green-world lover; confrontation with parental figures; a plunge into the unconscious; and finally an integration with society.[9]

In *The Secret Garden* Mary's female identity quest more or less fizzles out: she goes through all the difficult parts, then Colin gets all the rewards promised in a male quest. The quest romance in *The Changeover* is different. The male and female quest patterns are superimposed, and the story resolves in a much more triumphant way. Margaret Mahy's choice of subtitle, 'A Supernatural Romance', speaks the multiple nature of the quest undertaken by Laura and Sorry. While Laura assumes the role of the male quest hero (she descends into the underworld, and is initiated as a witch in order to do battle with Carmody Braque), Sorry has a supporting female role (as Gatekeeper during her changeover). In accord with Pratt's female quest pattern, Laura: splits off from her (divorced) parents (in contemporary children's literature, parents are often depicted, as they are here, as concerned and interested but largely ineffectual); receives green-world tokens from Sorry's mother and grandmother (they are depicted as women who love the landscape); Sorry is her green-world lover (he wants to be a kind of ranger with the Wild Life Division); she descends to do battle with Carmody Braque; and in coming to terms with her witch nature, Laura finds the maturity to be reconciled with her family.

Besides being a quest romance, *The Changeover* is a romance in the sense that it is a teen-dream love story between Sorry and Laura: good-looking sixteen-year-old male witch disguised as a prefect in love with girl (a latent witch) in fourth form who has never been kissed. That love story has something of the character of the sweet-dreams romances that Sorry – much to Laura's puzzlement – reads. Throughout *The Changeover* these cheap romances counterpoint the serious relationship between Sorry and Laura. In his pursuit of Laura, Sorry refers to them occasionally, only half in clichéd jest: 'If you had read *Wendy's Wayward Heart* . . . you would recognize my expression. I'm trying to look rueful at being caught out in an act of sentimentality' (page 96). Laura is unimpressed. Yet there is a kind of dignity to those romances because Sorry reads them to try to identify the humanity in his witch nature. And readers of *The Changeover* are consciously alerted to the fact that the conventions of sentimental romances are in operation in serious fiction.

By acknowledging that *The Changeover* is both a traditional heroic male quest romance and a sentimental woman's romance, Mahy makes her book reflect the gender-crossing and genre-crossing trends of contemporary young adult fiction – and contemporary society. Mahy 'unvents', to borrow Annis Pratt's term, the conventions of the typical quest romance in her inclusion of the female quest pattern.

Annis Pratt, in her turn, has borrowed the term 'unvention' from a woman who wanted to learn to spin her own wool, but found herself unable to follow the step-by-step male-order instructions. It was not until she actually began to work with the spindle that 'she found that her fingers already seemed to know how to perform motions arcane to her conscious mind. She coined the term "unventing" for the rediscovery of a lost skill through intuition, a bringing of latent knowledge out of oneself in contrast to "invention" from scratch'.

Laura is the kind of heroine I always wanted Mary to be. Laura unvents herself, in a way that Mary never can, in order to bring her story to a redemptive conclusion. Mahy's redemptive, feminist story is only possible in a society which at least accepts the premise that women's stories and natures are of value in and of themselves. In the same way that Laura unvents herself, 'the reading and writing of women's fiction', says Pratt, is a form of 'unvention': 'the tapping of a repository of knowledge lost from Western culture but still available to the author and recognizable to the reader deriving from a world with which she, at some level of her imagination, is already familiar' (page 178).

The capacity (or incapacity) of the heroine to understand her own destiny is mirrored by the reader of *The Secret Garden* or *The Changeover* – or the reader of any book. In order to make meaning out of mystery, in order to understand the plot, one has to be able to read the signs. Just as Laura learns to read the signs of her life (and Mary is inhibited from reading her signs), so readers learn, unconsciously perhaps, to read the signs and plots of feminist poetics.

Story by story, the signs and plots of women's lives begin to find a rightful place, alongside the more familiar male signs, in the mind's eyes of the readers – male and female, adult and child.

Notes

1 It is fitting that this instance of reader-response theory in action should occur in conversation with Nicholas Tucker. In *Signal* 43 Nick argues that Bruno Bettelheim's misguided homogenization of individual readers ignores the idea (put forward by Norman Holland in 5 *Readers Reading*) that 'individuals habitually react towards fiction according to their own imaginative lifestyle, and use each story to re-create their most characteristic psychological processes' (page 35). Nick and I betrayed our individual 'identity themes', as Norman Holland would say.

2 Adrienne Rich, 'When We Dead Awaken: Writing as Re-Vision', *On Lies, Secrets, and Silence: Selected Prose 1966–1978*, Norton, 1979, page 35; Sandra Gilbert, 'What Do Feminist Critics Want?: A Postcard from the Volcano', *The New Feminist Criticism: Essays on Women, Literature and Theory*, edited by Elaine Showalter, Pantheon, 1985, page 32. References to other books of feminist criticism are cited below, under 'Useful Books'.

3 Richard Shweder, 'Storytelling Among the Anthropologists', *New York Times Book Review*, 21 September 1986, page 39.

4 Humphrey Carpenter, *Secret Gardens: The Golden Age of Children's Literature*, Allen & Unwin, 1985.

5 Peter Brooks, *Reading for the Plot: Design and Intention in Narrative*, Knopf, 1984, pages 11–2.

6 Frances Hodgson Burnett, *The Secret Garden*, Puffin, 1951; and Margaret Mahy, *The Changeover: A Supernatural Romance*, Dent, 1984. Future references are to these editions and will be cited in the text.

7 Margaret Watson teaches children's literature at York University in Toronto. She made the remark in the context of Vladimir Nabokov's lecture on *Mansfield Park*. Vladimir Nabokov, *Lectures on Literature*, edited by Fredson Bowers, Harcourt Brace Jovanovich, 1980.

8 I've synthesized a 'typical' male quest from the following sources: Joseph Campbell, *Hero with a Thousand Faces* second edition, Princeton, 1968; C. G. Jung, *Archetypes and the Collective Unconscious*, Princeton, 1969; Northrop Frye, *The Anatomy of Criticism*, Princeton, 1957, and *The Secular Scripture*, Harvard, 1976. Campbell is my main source.

9 Annis Pratt, *Archetypal Patterns in Women's Fiction*, Harvester Press, 1982, pages 139–43. Future references are to this edition and will be cited in the text.

Useful books and articles

On feminist theory

Rachel Brownstein, *Becoming a Heroine: Reading about Women in Novels*, Penguin, 1982

Mary Eagleton, editor, *Feminist Literary Theory*, Basil Blackwell, 1986

Sandra Gilbert and Susan Gubar, *Madwoman in the Attic*, Yale University Press, 1979

Elaine Marks and Isabelle de Courtivron, *New French Feminisms: An Anthology*, Schocken, 1981

Jane Miller, *Women Writing about Men*, Virago, 1986

Elaine Showalter, *A Literature of Their Own: British Women Novelists from Brontë to Lessing*, Princeton University Press, 1977

Elaine Showalter, editor, *The New Feminist Criticism*, Pantheon, 1985 (my favourite)

On contemporary approaches to literature

For semiotic theory, see Julia Kristeva, *Desire in Language: A Semiotic Approach to Literature and Art*, Columbia University Press, 1980

For psychoanalytic/linguistic theory, see Juliet Mitchell and Jacqueline Rose, editors, *Feminine Sexuality: Jacques Lacan and the Ecole Freudienne*, Norton, 1982

For Marxist theory, see Shulamith Firestone, *The Dialectic of Sex*, Morrow, 1970

For communication theory, see Eric Havelock, *The Muse Learns to Write*, Yale University Press, 1986; Walter J. Ong, *Orality and Literacy: The Technologizing of the Word*, Methuen, 1982; Marshall McLuhan, *Understanding Media: The Extensions of Man*, New American Library, 1964

For cultural anthropology, see Clifford Geertz, *The Interpretation of Cultures*, Basic Books, 1973; Richard Shweder and Robert A. LeVine, editors, *Culture Theory: Essays on Mind, Self and Emotion*, Cambridge University Press, 1984

For psychoanalytic theory, see R. D. Laing, *The Politics of Experience*, Penguin, 1967; Jane Gallop, *The Daughter's Seduction: Feminism and Psychoanalysis*, Cornell University Press, 1982

For literary theory, see Roland Barthes, *The Pleasure of the Text*, translated by Richard Miller, Farrar, Straus and Giroux, 1975; Northrop Frye, *The Secular Scripture*, Harvard University Press, 1976; Frank Kermode, *The Genesis of Secrecy: On the Interpretation of Narrative*, Harvard University Press, 1979

On contemporary approaches to children's literature

Eleanor Cameron, 'With Wrinkled Brow and Cool Fresh Eye', *Horn Book* May/June 1985 and July/August 1985

Aidan Chambers, *Booktalk*, Bodley Head 1985; 'All of a Tremble to See His Danger', *Signal* 51, September 1986

Peter Hunt, 'Childist Criticism: The Subculture of the Child, the Book and the Critic', *Signal* 43, January 1984; and 'Questions of Method and Methods of Questioning: Childist Criticism in Action', *Signal* 45, September 1984

Roger Sale, 'Child Reading and Man Reading' in *Fairy Tales and After: From Snow White to E. B. White*, Harvard University Press, 1978

Carolyn Steedman, *The Tidy House: Little Girls Writing*, Virago, 1982

Carolyn Steedman *et al.*, editors, *Language, Gender and Childhood*, Routledge & Keegan Paul, 1985

Jack Zipes, *Fairy Tales and the Art of Subversion: The Classical Genre for Children and the Process of Civilization*, Wildman Press, 1983

70

EARTHSEA REVISIONED

Ursula K. Le Guin

Source: *Earthsea Revisioned*, Cambridge: Children's Literature New England in association with Green Bay Publications, 1993, pp. 5–26.

In our hero-tales of the Western world, heroism has been gendered: The hero is a man.

Women may be good and brave, but with rare exceptions (Spenser, Ariosto, Bunyan?) women are not heroes. They are sidekicks. Never the Lone Ranger, always Tonto. Women are seen in relation to heroes: as mother, wife, seducer, beloved, victim, or rescuable maiden. Women won independence and equality in the novel, but not in the hero-tale. From the *Iliad* to the *Song of Roland* to *The Lord of the Rings*, right up into our lifetime, the hero-tale and its modern form, heroic fantasy, have been a male preserve: a sort of great game-park where Beowulf feasts with Teddy Roosevelt, and Robin Hood goes hunting with Mowgli, and the cowboy rides off into the sunset alone. Truly a world apart.

Since it's about men, the hero-tale has concerned the establishment or validation of manhood. It has been the story of a quest, or a conquest, or a test, or a contest. It has involved conflict and sacrifice. Archetypal configurations of the hero-tale are the hero himself, of course, and often the night sea journey, the wicked witch, the wounded king, the devouring mother, the wise old man, and so on. (These are Jungian archetypes; without devaluing Jung's immensely useful concept of the archetype as an essential mode of thought, we might be aware that the archetypes he identified are mindforms of the Western European psyche as perceived by a man.)

When I began writing heroic fantasy, I knew what to write about. My father had told us stories from Homer before I could read, and all my life I'd read and loved the hero-tales. That was my own tradition, those were my archetypes, that's where I was at home. Or so I thought until – in the enchanting phrase of my youth – sex reared its ugly head.

The late sixties ended a long period, during which artists were supposed to dismiss gender, to ignore it, to be ignorant of what sex they were. For many decades it had been held that to perceive oneself as a woman writer or as a man writer would limit one's scope, one's humanity; that to write as a woman or as a man would politicize the work and so invalidate its universality. Art was to transcend gender. This idea of genderlessness or androgyny is what Virginia Woolf said was the condition of the greatest artists' minds. To me it is a demanding, a valid, a permanent ideal.

But over against the ideal, the fact was that the men in charge of criticism, the colleges, and the society had produced male definitions of both art and gender. And these definitions were set above question. The standards themselves were gendered. Men's writing was seen as transcending gender, women's writing as trapped in it. Why am I using the past tense?

And so the only way to have one's writing perceived as above politics, as universally human, was to gender one's writing male. Writing as a man, to male standards of what is universally human, was centralized, privileged; writing as a woman was marginalized. Masculine judgment of art was definitive; feminine perception and option was secondary, second-rate. Therefore, Virginia Woolf also warned us that a woman's writing will not be adequately judged so long as the standards of judgment are established and defended by men. And this is in the present tense, as it was sixty years ago.

Well, then, if art, if language itself doesn't belong to women, women can only borrow it or steal it. *Le vol*: flighty, women are. Thieves, fly-by-nights. Off on their broomsticks.

And why should men listen to stolen stories unless they concern important things – that is, the doings of men? Children, of course, even manchildren, are supposed to listen to women. Part of women's work is telling stories to children. Unimportant work, but important stories. Stories of the heroes.

From the general to the personal: Since my Earthsea books were published as children's books, I was in an approved female role. So long as I behaved myself, obeyed the rules, I was free to enter the heroic realm. I loved that freedom and never gave a thought to the terms of it. Now that I know that even in Fairyland there is no escape from politics, I look back and see that I was writing partly by the rules, as an artificial man, and partly against the rules, as an inadvertent revolutionary. Let me add that this isn't a confession or a plea for forgiveness. I like my books. Within the limits of my freedom I was free; I wrote well; and subversion need not be self-aware to be effective.

To some extent I pushed against the limits. For example, I followed the intense conservatism of traditional fantasy in giving Earthsea a rigid social hierarchy of kings, lords, merchants, peasants; but I colored all the good guys brown or black. Only the villains were white. I saw myself as luring white readers to identify with the hero, to get inside his skin and only then find it was a dark skin. I meant this as a strike against racial bigotry. I think now that my subversion went further than I knew, for by making my hero dark-skinned I was setting him outside the whole European heroic tradition, in which heroes are not only male but white. I was making him an Outsider, an Other, like a woman, like me.

(You will not see that dark man on most of the covers of the Earthsea books, by the way; publishers insist that jackets showing black people "kill sales," and forbid their artists to color a hero darker than tan. Look at the jackets of Alice Walker's or Paule Marshall's novels to realize how strong this taboo is. I think it has affected many readers' perception of Ged.)

I had a vanilla villainess in the first book, but in the sequel it was my heroine who was white. I'm not sure why. I'd made the Kargish people white in the first book, and had to stick to it; but perhaps also I simply lacked the courage to make my heroine doubly Other.

In *The Tombs of Atuan*, Arha/Tenar is not a hero, she is a heroine. The two English words are enormously different in their implications and value; they are indeed a wonderful exhibition of how gender expectations are reflected/created by linguistic usage.

Tenar, a heroine, is not a free agent. She is trapped in her situation. And when the hero comes, she becomes complementary to him. She cannot get free of the Tombs without him.

But – a fact some critics ignore – neither can Ged get free without her. They are interdependent. I redefined my hero by making him dependent, not autonomous. But heroines are always dependent, not autonomous – even a Fidelio. They act only with and for their man. I had reimagined the man's role, but not the woman's. I had not yet thought what a female hero might be.

No wonder; where are the women in Earthsea? Two of the books of the trilogy have no major female characters, and in all three the protagonist, in the precise sense of the word, is male.

Communities of men in Earthsea are defined as powerful, active, and autonomous; the community of women in Atuan is described as obedient to distant male rulers, a static, closed society. No change can come, nothing can be done, until a man arrives. Hero and heroine depend on each other in getting free of this terrible place, but the man originates the action of the book.

And in all three books the fundamental power, magic, belongs to men; only to men; only to men who have no sexual contact with women.

The women of Earthsea have skills and powers and may be in touch with obscure earth-forces, but they aren't wizards or mages. They know, at most, a few words of the language of power, the Old Speech; they are never methodically taught it by the men who do know it. There are no women at the School of Wizardry on Roke. At best, women are village witches.

But that's at worst, too, for the saying is quoted more than once: "Weak as women's magic, wicked as women's magic."

So, no women in college, no women in power, and that's how things are in Marlboro country. Nobody said anything about it, when the books first came out.

The tradition I was writing in was a great one, a strong one. The beauty of your own tradition is that it carries you. It flies, and you ride it. Indeed, it's hard not to let it carry you, for it's older and bigger and wiser than you are. It frames your thinking and puts winged words in your mouth. If you refuse to ride, you have to stumble along on your own two feet; if you try to speak your own wisdom, you lose that wonderful fluency. You feel like a foreigner in your own country, amazed and troubled by things you see, not sure of the way, not able to speak with authority.

It is difficult for a woman to speak or write with authority unless she remains within a traditional role, since authority is still granted and withheld by the institutions and traditions of men (such as this amazing medieval institution where we are guests this week, on whose august lawns Virginia Woolf was forbidden to walk). A woman, as queen or prime minister, may for a time fill a man's role; that changes nothing. Authority is male. It is a fact. My fantasy dutifully reported the fact.

But is that all a fantasy does – report facts?

* * *

Readers and reviewers of the trilogy did not question Ged's masculinity, as far as I know. He was seen as thoroughly manly. And yet he had no sex life at all. This is of course traditional in the hero-tale: the hero may get a pro-forma bride as final reward, but from Samson and Delilah to Merlin and Nimue to the war stories of our century, sexuality in the hero is shown not as prowess but as weakness. Strength lies in abstinence – the avoidance of women and the replacement of sexuality by non-sexual male bonding.

The establishment of manhood in heroic terms involves the absolute devaluation of women. The woman's touch, in any sense, threatens that heroic masculinity.

By the early seventies, when I finished the third book of Earthsea, traditional definitions and values of masculinity and femininity were all in question. I'd been questioning them myself in other books. Women readers were asking how come all the wise guys on the Isle of the Wise were guys. The artist who was above gender had been exposed as a man hiding in a raincoat. No serious writer could, or can, go on pretending to be genderless. I couldn't continue my hero-tale until I had, as woman and artist, wrestled with the angels of the feminist consciousness. It took me a long time to get their blessing. From 1972 on I knew there should be a fourth book of Earthsea, but it was sixteen years before I could write it.

The fourth book, *Tehanu*, takes up where the trilogy left off, in the same hierarchic, male-dominated society; but now, instead of using the pseudo-genderless male viewpoint of the heroic tradition, the world is seen through a woman's eyes. This time the gendering of the point of view is neither hidden nor denied. In Adrienne Rich's invaluable word, I had "revisioned" Earthsea.

[. . .] Jill Paton Walsh [has] suggested that in *Tehanu* I was "doing penance." Irredeemably secular, I'd call it affirmative action. In my lifetime as a writer, I have lived through a revolution, a great and ongoing revolution. When the world turns over, you can't go on thinking upside down. What was innocence is now irresponsibility. Visions must be revisioned.

In Atuan, Tenar lived in a world apart, a tiny desert community of women and eunuchs; she knew nothing beyond it. This setting was in part a metaphor of the "innocence" long instituted as the value of a girl, her "virtue" (the word deriving from *vir*, man, her worth to men being her only worth). That book and that innocence ended as she entered the "great world" of men and their doings. In *Tehanu*, she has lived in that world for years and knows her part of it well, the part she chose. She chose to leave the mage Ogion, her guardian and guide to masculine knowledge; she chose to be a farmer's wife. Why? Was she seeking a different, an obscurer knowledge? Was she being "womanly," bowing to society's resistance to independently powerful women?

Tenar certainly considers herself independent and responsible; she is ready to decide and to act. She has not abnegated power. But her definition of action, decision, and power is not heroic in the masculine sense. Her acts and choice do not involve ascendance, domination, power over others, and seem not to involve great consequences. They are "private" acts and choices, made in terms of immediate, actual relationships. To those who still believe that the public and the private can be separated, that there is a great world of men and war and politics and business and a little world of women and children and personal relations, and that these are truly worlds apart, one important, the other not – to such readers, Tenar's choice will appear foolish, and her story sadly unheroic.

Certainly, if we discard the axiom *what's important is done by men*, with its corollary *what women do isn't important*, then we've knocked a hole in the hero-tale, and a good deal may leak out. We may have lost quest, contest, and conquest as the plot, sacrifice as the key, victory or destruction as the ending; and the archetypes may change. There may be old men who aren't wise, witches who aren't wicked, mothers who don't devour. There may be no public triumph of good over evil, for in this new world what's good or bad, important or unimportant, hasn't been decided yet, if ever. Judgment is not referred up to the wise men. History is no longer about great men. The important choices and decisions may be obscure ones, not recognized or applauded by society.

Indeed, Ged's first heroic act, in *A Wizard of Earthsea*, was this kind of heroism, a personal choice almost unwitnessed and not sung about in the songs. But it was rewarded, and its reward was immediate: power. His power increased. He was on his way to becoming Archmage. In Tenar's Earthsea, there's neither acclaim nor reward; the outcomes of actions are complex and obscure.

Perhaps it is this lack of applause, of "importance," that has led some reviewers to state that all the men in *Tehanu* are weak or wicked. There are certainly a couple of very nasty villains, but *all* the men? Ogion? I suppose dying is a kind of weakness, but I thought he came through it rather well. As for the young king, he rescues Tenar from a persecutor, just as a hero should, and is clearly going to be an innovative and excellent statesman. Several women readers have objected fiercely that Tenar's son, Spark, is a selfish lout. Are all sons good, then, all wise, all generous? Tenar blames herself for Spark's weakness (just like a woman!), but I blame the society that spoiled the boy by giving him unearned power. After he's managed that farm a while alone, he'll probably shape up. Why do we expect more of the son than of the daughter?

But as for Ged, well, he has indeed lost his job. That's something we punish men for very cruelly. And when your job is being a hero, to lose it means you must indeed be weak and wicked.

In *Tehanu*, Ged's virtues are no longer the traditional male heroic ones: power as domination over others, unassailable strength, and the generosity of the rich. Traditional masculinists don't want heroism revised and unrewarded. They don't want to find it among housewives and elderly goat-herds. And they really don't want their hero fooling around with grown women.

There didn't use to be any sex in Earthsea. My working title for *Tehanu* was *Better Late than Never*.

Tenar always loved Ged, and knew it, but she can't figure out why she now, for the first time, desires him. Her friend the witch Moss explains it to her: Wizards give up one great power, sex, in order to get another, magic. They put themselves under a permanent spell of continence that affects everyone they have to do with. Why didn't I know that? Tenar says, and Moss cackles and explains that the magic of a really good spell is that you don't know it's working. It just "is," the way things "are." But when Ged lost his power as a mage, his spell of chastity went with it, and like it or lump it he's got his manhood back. The witch thinks this is funny.

Moss is a dirty old woman who's led a lively life. It seems that witches don't have to be chaste. They don't make the great sacrifice. Perhaps their powers are even nourished by their sexuality, but that's not clear. In fact curiously little is known about witches in Earthsea, even by witches, even by the author. It looks as if the wizards have generally used their own powers in their own interests to keep their knowledge and skills from women. Women's work, as usual, is the maintenance of order and cleanliness, housekeeping, feeding and clothing people, childbearing, care of babies and children, nursing and healing of animals and people, care of the dying, funeral rites – those unimportant matters of life and death, not part of history, or of story. What women do is invisible. (Since they live without women, the wizards must do a lot of these invisible, "disappeared" things themselves, such as darning and dishwashing: a fact which I, like Moss, find funny. But pleasing, also. I was touched and delighted to discover that Ged was better at mending than I am.)

Old Moss is no revolutionary. She was taught that what men do is what matters. She supports this in her own devious way, saying, "Ours is only a little power, seems like, next to theirs. But it goes down deep. It's all roots. It's like an old blackberry thicket. And a wizard's power is like a fir tree, maybe, great and tall and grand, but it'll blow right down in a storm. Nothing kills a blackberry bramble." I'm afraid Moss is as essentialist as Allen Bloom. But because in this book the witch is allowed to speak, her mere presence subverts the tradition and its rules. If women can have both sex and magic, why can't men?

Continence; abstinence; denial of relationship. In the realm of male power, there is no interdependence of men with women. Manhood, according to Sigmund Freud, Robert Bly, and the hero-tale, is obtained and validated by the man's independence of women. The connection is severed. The heroic man's relation to women is limited to the artificial code of chivalry, which involves the adoration of a woman-shaped object. Women in that world are non-people, dehumanized by a beautiful, worshipful spell – a spell which may be seen, from the other side, as a curse.

A world in which men are seen as independently real and women are seen only as non-men is not a fantasy kingdom. It is every army. It's Washington D. C. and the Tokyo Stock Exchange. It's the corporate boardroom and the executive suite and the board of regents. It's the canon of English Literature. It's our politics. It's the world I lived in when I wrote the first three books of Earthsea. I lived under the spell, the curse. Most of us did, most of do, most of the time. The myth of man alone, or alone with his God, at the center, on the top, is a very old, very powerful myth. It rules us still.

But thanks to the revisioning of gender called feminism, we can see the myth as a myth: a construct, which may be changed; an idea which may be rethought, made more true, more honest.

A rule may be unjust, yet its servants may be just. At the university Virginia Woolf could not enter, Tolkien taught. The mages of Roke were honest and just men, trying to use their power mindfully, keeping Equilibrium according to their lights. When she first came to Gont, Tenar lived as a student with a very wise mage, Ogion. Wouldn't he have taught her the uses of power? Well, we don't know if he would or not, because she refused. She quit grad school. She went off to be a nobody, a wife and mother. And now, as an aging widow not even allowed to own her farm, she's a sub-nobody. Was this a sacrifice? If so, what for?

Ged's bargain seems clearer. In the third book, he sacrifices his power, spending it to defeat a mortal evil. He triumphs, but at the cost of his heroic persona. As Archmage he is dead. And in *Tehanu* we find him weak, ill, depressed, forced to hide from enemies, at best a mere farmhand, good with a pitchfork. Readers who want him to be the Alpha Male are dismayed. They're dubious of a strength that doesn't involve contests and conquests and bossing people around.

Apparently it was the bossing around that Tenar refused, when she stopped studying with Ogion. Maybe Ogion, a maverick mage, would have shared his knowledge with her; but even if the wizardly hierarchy had accepted her, which seems doubtful, she evidently didn't want their kind of power. She wanted freedom.

She doesn't approve of sacrifice. "My soul can't live in that narrow place – this for that, tooth for tooth, death for life . . . There is a freedom beyond that. Beyond payment, retribution, redemption – beyond all the bargains and the balances, there is freedom." And she didn't do any dying to get it. All her former selves are alive in her: the child Tenar, the girl-priestess Arha, who still thinks in Kargish, and Goha the farmwife, mother of two children. Tenar is whole, but not single. She is not pure. The sacrificial image of dying to be reborn is not appropriate to her. Just the opposite. She has borne, she has given birth to, her children and her new selves. She is not reborn, but rebearing. The word seems strange. We think of birth passively, as if we were all babies or all men. It takes an effort to think not of rebirth but of rebearing, actively, in the maternal mode: to think not as the apple but as the apple tree.

But what is Tenar's freedom? A very contingent thing. She lives alone; one night men surround her house, meaning to rape her and take her child from her. Victimized, she panics, she rushes from door to window; at last fear turns to rage, and seizing a knife she flings the door wide open. But it is Ged, playing the man's role to the hilt, who actually stabs one of the assailants. He has been gendered into violence, just as much as they have. And she has been gendered into mere response. Neither acts with genuine freedom, though they do act.

At the end of the book, both Ged and Tenar face the defenders of the old tradition. Having renounced the heroism of that tradition, they appear to be helpless. No magic, nothing they know, nothing they have been, can stand against the pure malevolence of institutionalized power. Their strength and salvation must come from outside the institutions and traditions. It must be a new thing.

* * *

Tenar's last child is one not born of her body, but given to her out of the fire, chosen by her soul. Raped, beaten, pushed into the fire, disfigured, one hand crippled, one eye blinded, this child is innocence in a different sense of the word. This is helplessness personified: disinheritance, a child dehumanized, made Other. And she was the key to this book. Until I saw Therru, until she chose me, there was no book. I couldn't see the story till I could look through her eye. But which eye, the seeing or the blind?

In a story I wrote not long before *Tehanu*, called "Buffalo Gals, Won't You Come Out Tonight?", a child called Myra survives a plane crash in the Oregon desert and is found by a coyote – that is, by Coyote, who created the world, according to the people there, and made quite a mess of it in the process. Myra has lost the sight of one eye in the crash. Some of Coyote's neighbors, Bluejay and Rattler and others, hold a dance and stick an eye made of pine pitch into the socket, and after Coyote licks it, it works fine. And Myra has a kind of double vision. She sees where the animals live not as burrows and dens but as a little village. She sees Coyote as a skinny woman in blue jeans with grayish blonde hair and a lot of nogood boyfriends, and she sees Horse as a beautiful long-haired man, and so on. And though the animals know she's human they see her as one of their own kind – Coyote sees her as a pup, Horse sees her as a filly, and Owl, who isn't paying much attention, sees her as an egg. But when Myra gets near where human beings live, she sees, with one eye, just a town like the one she grew up in, streets and houses and schoolkids. With the other eye, the new one, the wild one, she sees a terrifying hole in the fabric of the world – a noplace where time rushes like a torrent and everything is out of joint – Koyaanisqatsi. In the end she has to go back and live there, with her own people; but she asks Grandmother Spider if she can keep her new eye, and the Grandmother says yes. So maybe she will go on being able to see both worlds.

In *Tehanu*, Tenar is brushing her hair on a windy dry morning, so that it crackles and makes sparks, and the one-eyed child Therru is fascinated, seeing what she calls "The fire flying out all over the sky."

At that moment Tenar first asked herself how Therru saw her – saw the world – and knew she did not know; that she could not know what one saw with an eye that had been burned away. And Ogion's words, *they will fear her*, returned to her; but she felt no fear of the child. Instead, she brushed her hair again, vigorously, so the sparks would fly, and once again she heard the little husky laugh of delight.

Soon after this scene, Tenar herself has a moment of double vision, seeing with two different eyes. An old man in the village has a beautiful painted fan; on one side are figures of lords and ladies of the royal court, but on the other side, usually hidden against the wall:

> Dragons moved as the folds of the fan moved. Painted faint and fine on the yellowed silk, dragons of pale red, blue, green moved and grouped, as the figures on the other side were grouped, among clouds and mountain peaks.
>
> "Hold it up to the light," said old Fan.
>
> She did so, and saw the two sides, the two paintings, made one by the light flowing through the silk, so that the clouds and peaks were the towers of the city, and the men and women were winged, and the dragons looked with human eyes.
>
> "You see?"
>
> "I see," she murmured.

What is this double vision, two things seen as one? What can the blinded eye teach the seeing eye? What is the wilderness? Who are the dragons?

Dragons are archetypes, yes, mindforms, a way of knowing. But these dragons aren't St. George's earthy worm, nor are they the Emperor of China's airy servant. I am not European, I am not Asian, and I am not a man. These are the dragons of a new world, America, and the visionary forms of an old woman's mind. The mythopoeticists err, I think, in using the archetype as a rigid, filled mold. If we see it only as a vital potentiality, it becomes a guide into mystery. Fullness is a fine thing, but emptiness is the secret of it, as Lao Tze said. The dragons of Earthsea remain mysterious to me.

In the first three books, I think the dragons were, above all, wildness. What is *not owned.* A dragonlord wasn't a man who tamed dragons; nobody tamed dragons. He was simply, as Ged said, a man dragons would take notice of. But he couldn't look at them, not eye to eye. The rule was clear: A man must not look into a dragon's eyes.

In the first book we briefly met a young girl who wore a very small dragon on her wrist, like a bracelet; it had consented, temporarily, to be jewelry. Some tiny note was struck here which I remembered when, in the last book, Tenar meets a dragon, a full-scale one. She knows the rule, but then, she's not a man, is she? She and the dragon look at each other, eye to eye, and they know who they are. They recognize each other.

This echoes a legend told early in the book about the time when dragons and human beings were all one people, and how they became separated, and how they might yet be one.

And that legend brings into the European hero-tale tradition the great Native American mythos of the time when animals were people, the time of the making. Myra, the little Buffalo Gal in the Oregon desert, can live for a while in that Dreamtime, that spiritual realm, because she's a child and a child adopted by a coyote, a wolfchild. Tenar doesn't live in it, but she connects with it – she can look the dragon in the eye – because she chose freedom over power. Her insignificance is her wildness. What she is and does is "beneath notice" – invisible to the men who own and control, the men in power. And so she's freer than any of them to connect with a different world, a free world, where things can be changed, remade. And the pledge of that connection is, I think, her adoption of the child who has been destroyed by the irresponsible exercise of power, cast out of common humanity, made Other. Tenar is a wolfmother.

The dragon Kalessin in the last book is wildness seen not only as dangerous beauty but as dangerous anger. The fire of the dragon runs right through the book. It meets the fire of human rage, the cruel anger of the weak, which wreaks itself on the weaker in the endless circle of human violence. It meets that fire and consumes it, for "a wrong that cannot be repaired must be transcended." There's no way to repair or undo what was done to the child, and so there must be *a way to go on from there*. It can't be a plain and easy way. It involves a leap. It involves flying.

So the dragon is subversion, revolution, change – a going beyond the old order in which men were taught to own and dominate and women were taught to collude with them: the order of oppression. It is the wildness of the spirit and of the earth, uprising against misrule.

And it rejects gender.

Therru, the burned child, will grow up to be fully sexed, but she's been ungendered by the rape that destroys her "virtue" and the mutilation that destroys her beauty. She has nothing left of the girl men want girls to be. It's all been burned away. As for Ged and Tenar, they're fully sexed too, but on the edge of old age, when conventional gendering grants him some last flings and grants her nothing but modest grandmotherhood. And the dragon defies gender entirely. There are male and female dragons in the earlier books, but I don't know if Kalessin, the Eldest, is male or female or both or something else. I choose not to know. The deepest foundation of the order of oppression is gendering, which names the male normal, dominant, active, and the female other, subject, passive. To begin to imagine freedom, the myths of gender, like the myths of race, have to be exploded and discarded. My fiction does that by these troubling and ugly embodiments.

Oh, they say, what a shame, Le Guin has politicized her delightful fantasy world, Earthsea will never be the same.

I'll say it won't. The politics were there all along, the hidden politics of the hero-tale, the spell you don't know you're living under till you cast it off. At this conference, Jan Mark made the very simple and profound statement that the "world apart" of a fantasy inevitably refers back to this world. All the moral weight of it is real weight. The politics of Fairyland are ours.

* * *

With her wild eye, Myra sees the wilderness as well as the human realm as her true home. Therru, blinded, sees with the eye of the spirit as well as the eye of the flesh. Where does she see her home?

For a long time we've been seeing with only one eye. We've blinded the woman's eye, said it doesn't see anything worth seeing, said all it can see is kids and cooking, said it's weak, short-sighted, said it's wicked, the evil eye. A woman's gaze is a fearful thing. It looks at a man, and he swells up "twice his natural size," and thinks he did it all himself. But then again the woman's eye looks at a hero and he shrinks. He shrinks right down to human size, man size, a fellow being, a brother, a lover, a father, a husband, a son. The woman looks at a dragon and the dragon looks right back. The free woman and the wild thing look at each other, and neither one wants to tame the other or own the other. Their eyes meet, they say each other's name.

I understand the mythology of *Tehanu* in this way: The child irreparably wronged, whose human inheritance has been taken from her – so many children in our world, all over our world now – that child is our guide.

The dragon is the stranger, the other, the not-human: a wild spirit, dangerous, winged, which escapes and destroys the artificial order of oppression. The dragon is the familiar also, our own imagining, a speaking spirit, wise, winged, which imagines a new order of freedom.

The child who is our care, the child we have betrayed, is our guide. She leads us to the dragon. She is the dragon.

* * *

While I was writing *Tehanu*, I didn't know where the story was going. I held on, held my breath, closed both eyes, sure I was falling. But wings upheld me, and when I dared look I saw a new world, or maybe only gulfs of sunlit air. The book insisted that it be written outdoors, in the sunlight and the open air. When autumn came and it wasn't done, still it would be written out of doors, so I sat in a coat and scarf, and the rain dripped off the verandah roof, and I flew. If some of the wild freedom of that flight is in the book, that's enough; that's how I wanted, as an old woman, to leave my beloved islands of Earthsea. I didn't want to leave Ged and Tenar and their dragon-child safe. I wanted to leave them free.

71

FAIRY GODMOTHERS OR WICKED STEPMOTHERS?

The uneasy relationship of feminist theory and children's criticism

Beverly Lyon Clark

Source: *Children's Literature Association Quarterly* 18(4) (1993–1994): 171–176.

> Now there is no woman, only an overgrown child.
>
> (Margaret Fuller, 1844)

> The cultural myth of cocooning suggests an adult woman who has regressed in her life cycle, returned to a gestational stage. It maps the road back from the feminist journey, which was once aptly defined by a turn-of-the-century writer as "the attempt of women to grow up."
>
> (Susan Faludi, 1991)

> My first mistake was in thinking "children" instead of "child." My second was in seeing The Child as my enemy rather than the racism and sexism of an oppressive capitalist society. My third was in believing none of the benefits of having a child would accrue to my writing.
>
> (Alice Walker, 1979)

Why is it that I still—like Fuller, like Faludi—react so vehemently to being called a girl? Why, if I want to revalue childhood and children and children's literature, do I persist in seeing associations with childhood as negative? The fact is that I, like other feminists, am spoken by a discourse of maturity that devalues children. My feminism and my commitment to children's literature exist in an uneasy relationship—if the relationship is maternal, then there is a constant slippage in the feminism between being a fairy godmother and being a wicked stepmother. The lack of parallelism between the two modifiers in my subtitle—the adjectival "feminist" and the possessive "children's"—is symptomatic of the uneasy relationship between the two fields.[1]

Of course it is true that there are affinities between feminist theory and children's criticism—that, further, if feminist criticism is more "mature," at this point, then it may have more to offer children's criticism. It can be argued, as Perry Nodelman has, that children's literature is a kind of women's writing, writing that responds to repression or, better yet, finds "an alternative way of describing reality," writing that is often nonlinear and contradictory, writing in which "adjustments are made to societal responsibilities" (33, 34). It can be argued, as Lissa Paul has, that the common ground between women's and children's literature "lies in a shared content (the enclosed, interior scenes of the action); and in a shared language (of otherness)" (187)—in entrapment and deceit. Certainly, most of those who write, edit, buy, and critique children's literature—at least in this century—are women. That precedence contrasts strikingly with the situation of women who have written for adults: as of 1992, only 32 percent of the Pulitzer Prizes awarded for fiction had gone to women and only 8 percent of the Nobel Prizes in Literature. Yet women had won some 66 percent of the Newbery Medals. So it should not be surprising if children's literature has addressed some women's concerns.

Not that most feminists have noticed. At the risk of being unsisterly, I want to point to the profound ambivalences that mainstream feminists have about children's literature.[2] If Sandra M. Gilbert and Susan Gubar have argued that women have suffered not so much from a Bloomian "anxiety of influence" as a more primary "anxiety of authorship," a fear that they cannot create, that writing will destroy them (49)—then I would add that women (and other) critics also suffer from an "anxiety of immaturity." They fear that literary creation will be so associated with procreation, and with that which is procreated, that they themselves might be considered childish. And thus they—we—become anxious to dissociate ourselves from immaturity.

Much of the feminist ambivalence about children has been related, I think, to an ambivalence about motherhood. In the early seventies a working-class feminist mother like Tillie Olsen could point out how rare it was for a woman who is a mother also to be a writer (31–32). Other feminists, like Kate Millett, were more specifically resisting male theories and theorists, especially Freud—for whom, with respect to maternity: "It is as if . . . the only self worth worrying about in the mother-child relationship were that of the child" (Suleiman 356). Even now an oppositional stance toward motherhood persists among what can be called liberal feminists, those who favor equal rights, like Susan Faludi, whose recent *Backlash* blames media brainwashing for any resurgent interest in motherhood. By the late seventies a more celebratory stance became possible for cultural feminists (or "difference" feminists), like Nancy Chodorow, who seek commonalities among women, whether biologically or socially induced, and often find one in maternal nurturing. The most clearsighted such theorist—with respect to children—would seem to be Sara Ruddick. In theorizing maternal thinking she acknowledges the complexities of mothers' relationships with children, the need for mothers "to assume, at least temporarily, a child's-eye view, in the interest of acting effectively with and on behalf of their children," and the way in which attentive maternal love "lets difference emerge without searching for comforting commonalities, dwells upon the *other*, and lets otherness be" (37, 122, Ruddick's italics).

Yet feminists who celebrate motherhood continue to be ambivalent about—or to ignore—children. It is indeed important for feminists to claim subjectivity for mothers, especially if, as E. Ann Kaplan claims, "slippage from talking about the mother to talking from the child's perspective seems endemic to research in this area," and especially if "at the very moment when mother-subjects start to gain attention, this subjectivity is displaced into concern with the fetus" (40, 5). Yet "the child's perspective" undergoes a curious slippage in this research too. For critics characteristically mask their ambivalence about children by eliding two meanings of "child"—as defined by age and as defined by family relationship—so that they can continue talking about themselves and hence ignore actual children. Consider the following usage: ". . . I find that while psychoanalytic feminism can add the female child to the male, allowing women to speak as daughters, it has difficulty accounting for the experience and the voice of the adult woman who is a mother" (Hirsch 12). The female child invoked at the beginning of the sentence turns out to be a woman, an adult speaking as a daughter: not a young human. Hence the author of this passage can later make the following claim: "I would submit, then, that to a large degree feminist theorizing itself still argues from the position of the child or, to a lesser extent, that of the childless adult woman and continues to represent the mother in the terms originally outlined by Freud" (169)—as if Marianne Hirsch has in fact been differentiating between the child and the (childless) adult woman. I would submit far otherwise: feminist theorizing has rarely recognized, let alone addressed, the position of the child. We are so adult centered that the only child we adult critics can see is ourselves; we do not recognize what it means to attend to children's perspectives.

Take Julia Kristeva. In the late seventies, even as she deconstructed gender, she was celebrating the possibilities of dissidence and associating it with "the sudden surge of women and children in discourse" ("New Type" 300). But like other feminists she was more concerned with maternity than with juvenility, with the impact not on the child—or fetus—but on the gestating mother of "an identity that splits, turns in on itself and changes without becoming other" ("New Type" 297). This emphasis is largely reiterated in "Stabat Mater," a more concerted theorizing of maternity:

even when she allows some space for her own memory of childhood, she is (like other psychoanalytic theorists) more concerned with the adult whom that child will become than with the child as child. As Jane Flax has remarked of such feminist theory as addresses child rearing, "we still write social theory in which everyone is presumed to be an adult"; we tend to include "almost no discussion of children as human beings or mothering as a relation between persons. The modal 'person' in feminist theory still appears to be a self-sufficient individual adult" (640).

In other words, even those feminists who are not particularly ambivalent about motherhood are more concerned about mothers than about children—and hence continue to devalue children and children's perspectives. Still, maternal theorists are generally less guilty than other theorists of marginalizing children. Whether they smother or other children, mothers are likely at least to acknowledge that children exist.

Another strand of theorizing that could acknowledge children is one that addresses the parameters of marginality. Yet—as if children are still so thoroughly beyond the pale—feminists who theorize marginality have paid virtually no attention to the position of children. Such feminist and cultural critics often address race, gender, class. But not age, not children. The most expansive lists of social cleavage—like Susan Stanford Friedman's adumbration, in addition to gender, of "categories like race, ethnicity, religion, class, national origin, sexual preference, abledness, and historical era" (471)—usually fail to include age. Even those that do include age do so only to acknowledge the elderly, ignoring the young. And that is in spite of the fact that the discursive narrative that leads up to Friedman's list tells of the divergent views of two generations of academic feminists, with their varying allegiances to theory and activism: that is, the experience that grounds her sense of multiple contexts is profoundly influenced by age. Friedman's essay does open some theoretical doors for children's criticism. The "categories like" construction acknowledges that her list is not definitive. Significantly, she provides an accessible account of recent theorizing that attempts to move beyond poststructuralist anti-essentialism to what I am tempted to call a new essentialism, a provisional recognition that the concrete realities of biology, socialization, economics—and, I would add, age—cannot just be deconstructed but do in fact affect who we are.[3] Still, like almost all other feminist theorists, Friedman is blind to children.

Some feminists are, further, not so much blind as downright dismissive of anything they consider juvenile. It is not altogether accidental that in Carol McPhee and Ann FitzGerald's compilation of *Feminist Quotations*—in a context, that is, where "woman as . . ." is likely to be construed as reductive—there are more index entries under "Woman/Women as child" than under any other comparable heading ("as servant," "as redeemer," "as rhododendron"), whether the reference is to Elizabeth Oakes Smith's outrage, in 1853, that wives and mothers are "coerced like unmanageable children," or Vicki Pollard's, in 1969, that doctors force "women into the role of helpless, stupid, ridiculous little girls." I am not the only woman to resent being called a girl.

I have noted elsewhere some of the ways that leading critics Jane Tompkins, Nancy Armstrong, and Barbara Johnson have slighted children and childhood ("Thirteen Ways"). I would like to elaborate one of those examples. Johnson brilliantly addresses the ramifications of abortion and apostrophe, what it means for a poet who is a mother to address what could be considered a dead child, specifically how gender renders problematic the distinction between addressor and addressee: is the fetus part of her body or not? Yet Johnson concludes by assuming that what it means to be a child is unproblematic:

> Whether or not one has ever been a mother, everyone participating in the debate has once been a child. Rhetorical, psychoanalytical, and political structures are profoundly implicated in one another. The difficulty in all three would seem to reside in the attempt to achieve a full elaboration of any discursive position other than that of child. (642)

Social critics would not assume that someone who has left the working class still has an uncomplicated appreciation of what it means to be working class; similarly with a now-male transsexual's appreciation of what it means to be female, or the appreciation of someone who passes for white of what it means to be black. Yet Johnson can still assume that anyone who was once a child requires no "elaboration" of what it means to be in the "discursive position . . . of child"—not recognizing that, as Avi notes, "It is impossible to be a child once one becomes an adult" (45).

Many additional questions arise as well. Why must mainstream feminist critics ignore children's literature when they undertake a broad historical sweep? Why must a study of "the woman writer and the nineteenth-century literary imagination"—to cite the subtitle of Gilbert and Gubar's *Madwoman*—consistently relegate children's literature to subordinate clauses, or at most to a subordinate sentence or two?[4] Gilbert and Gubar write with unconscious irony when they say, "Clearly there is conscious or semiconscious irony in all these choices of the apparently miniature over the assuredly major . . . ," right after describing "Louisa May Alcott's Jo March learning to write moral homilies for children instead of ambitious gothic thrillers" (64). Assuredly, major indeed. Even more strikingly, why must a critic whose avowed topic is the portrayal of children or else "the adolescent idea"—to cite Patricia Meyer Spacks's title—ignore books that consciously address adolescents (Spacks devotes a mere three pages thereto, discussing *The Daisy Chain* and *Tom Brown's Schooldays*). Or to step outside the realm of literary criticism for a moment, to turn to one of the most influential essays in women's studies: why must a feminist squelch another marginalized group in order to assert herself? In "Is Female to Male as Nature Is to Culture?" Sherry B. Ortner challenges the way women have been subordinated through their association with nature. Ortner is then eager, when denying a kind of guilt by association between women and children, to assume a "natural" association between children and nature: "Infants are barely human and utterly unsocialized; like animals they are unable to walk upright, they excrete without control, they do not speak. Even slightly older children are clearly not yet fully under the sway of culture" (77–78). Women should not be degraded by being associated with nature, but it is "natural" for children to be.

Not that feminists are the only ones guilty of literary child abuse; it is just that, nurtured by feminism, I expected more. The real danger here is in using other marginalized groups as stepping stones, as Ortner does. This danger came home to me this semester while teaching a course in American literature before 1865: advocacy of the rights of one group seems to entail metaphorically castigating another. There is Margaret Fuller's put-down of children, cited as an epigraph, as she makes a case for "woman in the nineteenth century." There is Nathaniel Hawthorne, in *The Scarlet Letter*, apparently compensating for creating an uncharacteristically positive portrait of a not-entirely-submissive woman by, in part, reducing her child wholly to a symbol. There is Henry David Thoreau, who allies himself, civilly disobedient, with "the fugitive slave, and the Mexican prisoner on parole, and the Indian come to plead the wrongs of his race," even as he metaphorically disavows boys and women: his fellow townsmen try to punish him by putting him in jail, "just as boys, if they cannot come at some person against whom they have a spite, will abuse his dog. I saw that the State was half-witted, that it was timid as a lone woman with her silver spoons . . ." (Lauter 1974, 1976).

This kind of activity is hardly news to women of color, who have long been aware of the stepping-stone phenomenon. Among the earliest African American women to speak out, in the current wave of feminism, were Barbara Smith in 1977, responding to Elaine Showalter, Ellen Moers, and Spacks; Alice Walker in 1979, responding to Moers and especially Spacks, with whom she had shared an office; and Audre Lorde In 1979, responding to Mary Daly. It is such resistance that led Walker to prefer the term "womanist" to "feminist," the former embracing willfulness, loving other women, sometimes men, and being "Committed to survival and wholeness of entire people, male *and* female" ([Preface], *Search* xi, Walker's italics).[5]

In fact, the stepping-stone phenomenon may be a particular temptation for white members of the middle class, who tend to prize individualism over group effort and hence are willing to image their gain as another's loss. Among other groups this phenomenon seems less common. Because

African Americans, for instance, have "had to work in concert for survival" (Joseph 90), the maternal role may be shared by mothers, sisters, aunts, grandmothers, cousins, not to mention fictive kin, and with so much mutual implication in mothering there has been less temptation to devalue children (see also Collins 119–37). Black women are unlikely to identify motherhood as "a serious obstacle to our freedom as women"; as bell hooks argues: "Historically, black women have identified work in the context of family as humanizing labor, work that affirms their identity as women, as human beings showing love and care, the very gestures of humanity white supremacist ideology claimed black people were incapable of expressing" (133–34). Certainly I have found less evidence of the devaluing of children and childhood in the writings of African-American women critics than in the work of their white counterparts. Walker, for instance, seeks an egalitarian mode with her daughter: "We are together, my child and I. Mother and child, yes, but *sisters* really, against whatever denies us all that we are" ("One Child" 382, Walker's italics).

Does the same respect for children hold among other marginalized groups? A great deal depends on the history and positioning of the group. With lesbians, for instance, the evidence is rather mixed. Eve Kosofsky Sedgwick observes that the epistemology of the closet makes for a complex relationship between lesbians and families, lesbians and motherhood, lesbians and children—not to mention the way stage theories, like Freud's, construct lesbianism as an adolescent stage, giving lesbians an added incentive to claim maturity. Not only do traditional notions of the family exclude lesbians, but the politics of coming out may make for troubled relationships between lesbians and their families of origin or their children from a heterosexual relationship. Lesbian stories may in fact—unlike heterosexual theorizing about maternity—" privilege the moment of separation from the mother rather than the time of unity with her" (Roof 171). And while many lesbians have children, current social mores and social service policies make it difficult for lesbians to adopt a child—when they do not reject motherhood as a patriarchal imposition (Allen).

On the other hand, when a lesbian is herself a mother, she may write of children with considerable sensitivity. Take Adrienne Rich's complex approach to childhood. She may stress the recurring question, "But what was it like for women?", yet she also acknowledges the child's "authentic need" (16, 24). Better still, she acknowledges a common oppression:

> In a tribal or even a feudal culture a child of six would have serious obligations; ours have none. But also, the woman at home with children is not believed to be doing serious work; she is just supposed to be acting out of maternal instinct, doing chores a man would never take on, largely uncritical of the meaning of what she does. So child and mother alike are depreciated, because only

> grown men and women in the paid labor force are supposed to be "productive." (37–38)

Later Rich notes that increasing men's involvement in childcare would change not only gender roles and expectations, for children and adults, but "the entire community's relationship to childhood" (216). In short, she can at times see childhood in its own right.

With few exceptions, though, most feminists do not. Most continue to devalue children, not to mention children's literature. I am still too likely, when reading manuscripts submitted to a mainstream journal or in response to a call for papers on children's literature, to see children's literature belittled—to see perhaps a work of children's literature set up as a straw man so that the critic can go on to discuss how much better a given topic is handled in literature addressed to adults,

Yet perhaps another exception to the tendency that I have been tracing —the tendency of mainstream feminist critics, especially whites, to disavow children as part of their project to claim full adulthood—is the increasing and respectful attention accorded Alcott. Not that feminists have only recently discovered her. But a decade or two ago discussions tended to be tucked away in odd corners of books—Carolyn G. Heilbrun, for instance, writes an appreciation that strains to accommodate itself to a 1982 collection on the twenties. And early critics often invoke Alcott only to disparage her—witness Spacks in 1972. More recently, though, *New Literary History* published an essay by Catharine R. Stimpson, who was able to explore her admiration for *Little Women* in the framework of theorizing about what she calls the paracanon, works that (some) people love: the children's canon becomes the adults' paracanon in a move that simultaneously creates space for children's literature and reinscribes it as subordinate. If, further, prestigious mainstream journals like *New Literary History, Signs*, and *American Literature* publish criticism of children's literature (by, respectively, Stimpson, Ann B. Murphy, and Frances Armstrong), it is almost certain that the criticism addresses Alcott.[6] Alcott now appears in important anthologies like *The Heath Anthology of American Literature*, and Showalter has published an Alcott anthology. Yet Alcott is more often represented in such collections by her works for adults than by those for children, even though the latter are better known and, I would argue, more important. There is still an urge to elevate by discarding what seems juvenile. In my more pessimistic moments I fear that attention to Alcott can take the place of attention to children's literature as a whole—the literary establishment is hardly immune to the lures of tokenism. Given the relative lack of attention, even by children's critics, to the more realistic modes of children's literature, it may be that much easier for adult critics to appropriate domestic fiction like hers for themselves, leaving the children with fantasy and fairy tales. On the other hand, in my more hopeful moments I like to think that Alcott's canonization, even her paracanonization, will make it easier to treat children's literature—hers and others'—with respect. Tokenism may be the first step on the road to genuine dialogue.

So what happens when feminist theory mothers children's literature? I find myself groping for a more adequate metaphor. Perhaps it is time to put aside maternal metaphors and start unearthing, like Walker, the possibilities of sisterhood. Better yet, we can put the two metaphors in dialogue—to invoke sisterhood not so much to replace the maternal as to displace it, to question its underlying assumption of power. At the same time it is important to displace sisterhood as well, at least as it has commonly been used by feminists—to displace the feminist assumption of a sisterhood limited to, certainly governed by, adult females.[7]

Maybe we should turn to a metaphor that acknowledges the social construction of the maternal. Maybe we should place the metaphor and its agent at one remove from biology and likewise underscore the fantasy construction of the maternal: is feminist theory a fairy godmother or a wicked stepmother? True, there are problems with this metaphoric pairing; witness the way it reiterates the dualism stereotypically ascribed to women, here the good woman inhuman, the bad woman not. Yet at least the metaphors are derived from the realm of children's literature, are already grounded in the field. The fairy-tale associations imply a relationship that is constructed, not "natural." They may remind us to question some of the "natural" assumptions that those of us who are no longer children may be tempted to make about children and our relationship to them. The pairing likewise suggests a relationship that is not simple, not simply one or the other. For of course feminist theory is both. Yet, feminist theory can be a fairy godmother. It can offer genuine insights into approaches and politics. Let us use those insights. Let us learn about the images of women (children), about the possibilities of a women's (children's) tradition, about the possibilities for deconstructing binary thinking and giving play to the preoedipal semiotic, about the confluence of race and class and sexuality and imperialism and history (and age) with gender. Let us learn too about the politics of marginalization and appropriation. Sometimes we will use those insights—talk about marginalization and appropriation—against feminist theory itself.

For, too often, feminist theory continues to be a wicked stepmother. Too often, in an effort to establish our own maturity, feminist critics, especially if we are white, want to put away childish things. Maybe it is true that patriarchal society can recuperate an alliance between women and children into enforced domesticity, but that is no reason to continue to ignore children. We continue to be spoken by patriarchy if we simply react against it—or if we assume that an alliance between these two oppressed groups is simply the product of anti-feminist backlash.

It is time for those of us who are feminist critics to realize how much we can learn by attending to children's criticism—radical new perspectives on reader response, as well as what it means to be spoken by a discourse of maturity. It is time to recognize whom we are stepping on, whom we are putting down, and why. It is time, further, for those of us who are children's critics not merely to legitimize our calling by finding connections with feminism but to call feminists to account.

Notes

1 As is the choice of nouns for those adjectives to modify, a choice that admittedly reinforces the hierarchical relationship between the two fields—if, that is, one values theory over criticism.
2 I am not talking about critics like Patricia Pace, Mitzi Myers, or Lynne Vallone—to cite the authors of some recent essays lying on my desk—feminists who have consciously engaged in children's criticism.
3 Other theorists who work this vein include Gayatri Spivak, who speaks in passing of strategic essentializing, and Linda Alcoff, who theorizes positionality; Julia Kristeva's discussion of a "third generation" of feminists, in "Women's Time," can be read as congruent too. Other feminists, like Barabara Christian, have resisted the impulse to deconstruct.
4 With the exception of "Goblin Market"—which, however, they do not treat as a text for or even about children.
5 African-American women writers may portray vexed, even murderous, relationships between mother and child—*Beloved* springs to mind—but there is a sensitivity to the child's perspective, to the possibilities for guilt and renewal.
6 The *Signs* issue, 15.3 (Spring 1990), also addressed Laura Ingalls Wilder and "Snow White."
7 For an illuminating discussion of some of the dangers of the sororal metaphor, how feminists can use it to subsume "Otherness into an increasingly capacious notion of self" (67), see Michie.

Works cited

Alcoff, Linda. "Cultural Feminism versus Post-Structuralism: The Identity Crisis in Feminist Theory." *Signs* 13.3 (Spring 1988): 405–36.

Allen, Jeffner. "Motherhood: The Annihilation of Women." *Mothering: Essays in Feminist Theory*. Ed. Joyce Trebilcot. Ottowa: Rowman, 1983. 315–30.

Armstrong, Frances. "'Here Little, and Hereafter Bliss': *Little Women* and the Deferral of Greatness." *American Literature* 64.3 (Sept. 1992): 453–74.

Avi. "The Child in Children's Literature." *The Horn Book Magazine* Jan./Feb. 1993: 40–50.

Belsey, Catherine, and Jane Moore, eds. *The Feminist Reader: Essays in Gender and the Politics of Literary Criticism*. New York: Blackwell, 1989.

Christian, Barbara. "The Race for Theory." *Cultural Critique* 6 (1987). Rev. and rpt. in *Gender and Theory: Dialogues on Feminist Criticism*. Ed. Linda Kauffman. Oxford: Blackwell, 1989. 225–37.

Clark, Beverly Lyon. "Thirteen Ways of Thumbing Your Nose at Children's Literature." *The Lion and the Unicorn* 16.2 (Dec. 1992): 240–44.

Collins, Patricia Hill. *Black Feminist Thought: Knowledge, Consciousness, and the Politics of Empowerment*. Boston: Unwin Hyman, 1990.

Faludi, Susan. *Backlash. The Undeclared War Against American Women*. New York: Crown, 1991.

Flax, Jane. "Postmodernism and Gender Relations in Feminist Theory." *Signs* 12.4 (Summer 1987): 621–43.

Friedman, Susan Stanford. "Post/Poststructualist Feminist Criticism: The Politics of Recuperation and Negotiation." *New Literary History* 22.2 (Spring 1991): 465–90.

Fuller, Margaret. Excerpt from *Woman in the Nineteenth Century*. 1844. Lauter 1: 1604–26.

Gilbert, Sandra M., and Susan Gubar. *The Madwoman in the Attic: The Woman Writer and the Nineteenth-Century Literary Imagination*. New Haven: Yale UP, 1979.

Heilbrun, Carolyn G. "Louisa May Alcott: The Influence of *Little Women*." *Women, the Arts, and the 1920s in Paris and New York*. Ed. Kenneth W. Wheeler and Virginia Lee Lussier. New Brunswick: Transaction Books, 1982. 20–26.

Hirsch, Marianne. *The Mother/Daughter Plot: Narrative, Psychoanalysts, Feminism*. Bloomington: Indiana UP, 1989.

hooks, bell. *Feminist Theory: From Margin to Center*. Boston: South End P, 1984.

Johnson, Barbara. "Apostrophe, Animation, and Abortion." *Diacritics* 16 (1986). Rpt. in Warhol 630–43.

Joseph, Gloria I. "Black Mothers and Daughters: Their Roles and Functions in American Society." *Common Differences: Conflicts in Black and White Feminist Perspectives*. By Gloria I. Joseph and Jill Lewis. Garden City: Anchor/Doubleday, 1981. 75–126.

Kaplan, E. Ann. *Motherhood and Representation: The Mother in Popular Culture and Melodrama*. London: Routledge, 1992.

Kristeva, Julia. *The Kristeva Reader*. Ed. Toril Moi. New York: Columbia UP, 1986.

——. "A New Type of Intellectual: The Dissident." 1977. Trans. Séan Hand. *The Kristeva Reader* 292–300.

——. "Stabat Mater." 1977. Trans. Léon S. Roudiez. *The Kristeva Reader* 161–86.

——. "Women's Time." Trans. Alice Jardine and Harry Blake. *Signs* 7 (1981). Rev. and rpt. in Belsey 197–217, 240–42.

Lauter, Paul, *et al.*, eds. *The Heath Anthology of American Literature*. 2 vols. Lexington: Heath, 1990.

Lorde, Audre. "An Open Letter to Mary Daly." 1979. *Sister Outsider: Essays and Speeches*. Freedom: Crossing P, 1984. 66–71.

McPhee, Carol, and Ann FitzGerald, eds. *Feminist Quotations: Voices of Rebels, Reformers, and Visionaries*. New York: Crowell, 1979.

Michie, Helena. "Not One of the Family: The Repression of the Other Woman in Feminist Theory." *Discontented Discourses: Feminism/Textual Intervention/Psychoanalysis* (1989). Rpt. in Warhol 58–68.

Millett, Kate. *Sexual Politics*. Garden City: Doubleday, 1970.

Murphy, Ann B. "The Borders of Ethical, Erotic, and Artistic Possibilities in *Little Women*." *Signs* 15.3 (Spring 1990): 562–85.

Myers, Mitzi. "Romancing the Moral Tale: Maria Edgeworth and the Problematics of Pedagogy." *Romanticism and Children's Literature in Nineteenth-Century England*. Ed. James Holt McGavran, Jr. Athens: U of Georgia P, 1991. 96–128.

Nodelman, Perry. "Children's Literature as Women's Writing." *Children's Literature Association Quarterly* 13.1 (Spring 1988): 31–34.

Olsen, Tillie. "One Out of Twelve: Writers Who Are Women in Our Century." 1971. *Silences*. New York: Delta/Seymour Lawrence, 1978. 22–46.

Ortner, Sherry B. "Is Female to Male as Nature Is to Culture?" *Women, Culture, and Society*. Ed. Michelle Zimbalist Rosaldo and Louise Lamphere. Stanford: Stanford UP, 1974. 66–87.

Pace, Patricia. "The Body-in-Writing: Miniatures in Mary Norton's *Borrowers*." *Text and Performance Quarterly* 11.4 (Oct. 1991): 279–90.

Paul, Lissa. "Enigma Variations: What Feminist Theory Knows About Children's Literature." *Signal* 54 (1987): 186–202.

Rich, Adrienne. *Of Woman Born: Motherhood as Experience and Institution*. 1976. 10th Anniversary Ed. New York: Norton, 1986.

Roof, Judith. "'This Is Not For You': The Sexuality of Mothering." *Narrating Mothers: Theorizing Maternal Subjectivities*. Ed. Brenda O. Daly and Maureen T. Reddy. Knoxville: U of Tennessee P, 1991. 157–73.

Ruddick, Sara. *Maternal Thinking: Toward a Politics of Peace*. New York: Ballantine, 1989.

Sedgwick, Eve Kosofsky. *Epistemology of the Closet*. Berkeley: U of California P, 1990.

Showalter, Elaine, ed. *Alternative Alcott*. New Brunswick: Rutgers UP, 1988.

Smith, Barbara. "Toward a Black Feminist Criticism." *Conditions: Two* (1977). Rev. and rpt. in *All the Women Are White, All the Blacks Are Men, But Some of Us Are Brave: Black Women's Studies*. Ed. Gloria T. Hull *et al.* Old Westbury: Feminist P, 1982. 157–75.

Spacks, Patricia Meyer. *The Adolescent Idea: Myths of Youth and the Adult Imagination*. New York: Basic Books, 1981.

——. *The Female Imagination*. 1975. New York: Discus-Avon, 1976.

Spivak, Gayatri Chakravorty. "Three Women's Texts and a Critique of Imperialism." *Critical Inquiry* 12 (1985). Rpt. in Belsey 175–95, 237–40.

Stimpson, Catharine R. "Reading for Love: Canons, Paracanons, and Whistling Jo March." *New Literary History* 21.4 (Autumn 1990): 957–76.

Suleiman, Susan Rubin. "Writing and Motherhood." *The (M)other Tongue: Essays in Feminist Psychoanalytic Interpretation*. Ed. Shirley Nelson Garner *et al.* Ithaca: Cornell UP, 1985. 352–77.

Thoreau, Henry David. "Resistance to Civil Government." 1849. Lauter 1: 1967–81.

Vallone, Lynne. "'A humble Spirit under Correction': Tracts, Hymns, and the Ideology of Evangelical Fiction for Children, 1780–1820." *The Lion and the Unicorn* 15.2 (Dec. 1991): 72–95.

Walker, Alice. *In Search of our Mothers' Gardens*. San Diego: Harcourt, 1983.

——. "One Child of One's Own: A Meaningful Digression Within the Work(s)." 1979. *Search* 361–83.

Warhol, Robyn R., and Diane Price Herndl, eds. *Feminisms: An Anthology of Literary Theory and Criticism*. New Brunswick: Rutgers UP, 1991.

Beverly Lyon Clark teaches English at Wheaton College and has recently completed a study of cross gendered school stories.

72

FEMININE LANGUAGE AND THE POLITICS OF CHILDREN'S LITERATURE

Deborah Thacker

Source: *The Lion and the Unicorn* 25(1) (2001): 3–16.

The academic study of children's literature has undergone a number of transformations over the past twenty years. Once the exclusive concern of educationalists and librarians or, alternatively, a rich source for bibliographers and literary historians, children's literature as a subject of both undergraduate and post-graduate study can now be found frequently placed within departments of literature or cultural studies. In the same way as so much of literary study has been transformed by the challenge of feminist discourses, it is now impossible to think about books for children solely in terms of their effectiveness as educational and socializing tools or as part of the vast popular entertainment industry. Rather, the advent of a feminist perspective has transformed the way that it is possible to think about children's literature (and other non-canonized literatures as well).

The proximity of children's literature to the domestic, nurturing, maternal, and, thus, the feminine sphere can be seen as a contributing factor in the marginalization of the subject in academic discourses.[1] However, it is notion of the silencing of the "Other," whether it be women, children, or those who are racially different, that enriches what it is possible to say about children's texts and that has led to the process of change currently taking place. If the struggle to find a voice within patriarchal, controlling discourse can be considered a prime motivation of feminist theory, "the quest for a kind of 'feminine language' which would articulate pre-oedipal, pre-verbal and pre-symbolic discourses" (Widdowson 88), then children's literature must be seen in terms of its influential role in providing and constructing a variety of reading positions, offering different degrees of autonomy for the reader in the text. Thus, the need to regard children's literature as part of a continuum is encouraged by feminist perspectives that privilege the relationship of power within discourse and seek alternatives to dominant, controlling, "masculine" narratives. More than this, feminist readings also underline the importance of the social contexts within which readings take place, demonstrating how, as part of the State Ideological Apparatus,[2] children's texts reinforce cultural values, either by transparently espousing dominant ideologies or by virtue of the social controls within which adults mediate books for children, and, thus, are silenced by their marginal status. While (a very few) children's authors are able to challenge the controlling, pedagogic aim of most popular and heavily promoted fiction, to provide playful and subversive texts that encourage a lively interaction and favor multiplicity in a disruption of a "masculine" apprehension of the unity of meaning, there are many more factors that seek to control these challenges. From the way in which fiction is taught in schools to the way that children's books are packaged, marketed, and commented upon, the social discourses that surround the texts themselves suppress such provocations, exerting what might be considered to be a repressive political force.

By emphasizing the importance of a broader feminist critique in the study of children's literature and, in turn, the importance of the inclusion of children's literature into a feminist theory of literature, I know that I am neglecting a body of work that arose out of the feminist movement: the challenging of gender stereotyping within children's literature and the recuperation of children's texts by female authors.[3] The latter emphasis challenged male-dominated criticism by reassessing the work of previously ignored female writers, demanding a revised definition of what is considered to be "literary." The inclusion of domestic subject matter, the interweaving of events and possibility, challenges the dominance within the literary tradition of the masculine plots that emphasize the quest, inclusiveness, definition, and unity of meaning. In addition, the emphasis on storytelling and the power of discourse in feminine plots and in the presentation of female characters indicate the awareness, on the part of many of these recuperated female writers, of the power derived from discourse within the oppression of their social circumstances and their cultural invisibility.

> The systematic exclusion of these women from the children's literature canon accords precisely with the ideological reasons for their exclusion from the literary canon—and from positions of power and influence.
>
> (Paul 107)

While the recuperation of women as writers is a prominent and lasting effect of the advent of feminist criticism, children's literature that offers a feminine approach to discourse is not authored exclusively by women, just as female authorship can, and often does, impose a masculinist discourse.

In the same way, feminist challenges to the gendering of children's literature, particularly in the case of fairy tales, have been largely unsuccessful because they retain the oppositional model of gender and refrain from challenging the dominant modes of discourse. The consciousness-raising exercise that arose out of the feminist movement may have led to the rewriting of traditional stories and the acknowledgement of the need for more powerful roles for female characters in new fiction, yet the imposition of unified meanings restrains such efforts from affecting a radical transformation. The passivity of heroines in tales like "Cinderella" and "Sleeping Beauty" has spawned a range of stories that offer reversals of normalized gender roles.[4] However, in most cases, these texts merely switch roles around but retain the stereotyped features of male and female characterization, so that strength, activity, and triumph are still opposed to passivity, beauty, and gentleness. In this way, books that attempt to act as a corrective only impose another way of thinking and reading conventionally, rather than challenging readers with a new way of approaching gender or inviting them to question the imposition of socially constructed modes of behavior.

Invitations to question and to embrace a more flexible view of gender imply a kind of fictional discourse that can be defined in terms of feminist theory. Though rare, the children's book that is able to offer its readers an awareness of their own autonomy is more powerful at combating the restrictions of stereotyping, offering, for instance, the possibility of taking the best of the feminine and the masculine, resulting in an androgynous apprehension of self. A critical perspective of children's texts that investigates the ways in which children, like women, are in a position to be controlled through fictional discourses, particularly the French school of *l'ecriture feminine*, provides the most persuasive parallel between children's literature and feminism.

Children's literature demonstrates much of the theory that circulates around notions of the socially constructed acquisition of subjectivity through language, so it is particularly odd that, while the study of children's literature acknowledges this relationship, there is a silence within feminist theory where children's texts and children-as-readers are concerned.

The absence of children's literature from an understanding of the degree to which power is played out in the socially constructed interactions with language devalues and silences children as readers, divorcing their experience of text from the awareness of the nature of fiction from which notions of literary pleasure derive. Excluding children's literature from the map of a theory of literature constructed in the academic mainstream enforces these silences, by attempting to redefine a literary discourse without acknowledging the relevance of these formative experiences.

However, it is in the area of feminist theory that we come closest to a dialogue, as I have suggested. Feminist reworkings of Lacan's notion of "the fictional direction" identify childhood as the primary site in the development of response to fiction and place storytelling, story-reading, and discursive interactions between parent and child at the heart of the articulation of self.

The ways in which Lacan's theories of identity and language have been re-configured by feminist theorists privilege the social context of the acquisition of subject positions and so suggest perspectives that can include children. Beyond questions of gender, which motivate a revisioning of contemporary psychoanalytic thought and which have provided a way of addressing children's literature as noted above, the notion of the imposition of the *symbolic order* (or the patriarchal law of language) onto the *imaginary* (or a feminine/maternal space) can be extended to include the process by which we are constructed, in a continuous process that begins in childhood, as subjective beings.[5] The *mirror stage*, during which the transformation of the child from the maternal space to the language-bound realm of patriarchy begins, is coterminus with the period of a child's life when narrative, and specifically story, play a crucial role in both language acquisition and identity through subject position.

Those espousing a feminist critique[6] focus on "practices, forms and positions . . . [that] actually help to produce the fixing and channeling of desires by virtue of their production of power-knowledge relations" (Henriques 223). The interactions between parents and children in the negotiation of power are various and contradictory, suggesting that the illusory nature of self-determination and authority are played out in a social context.[7]

Obviously, storytelling and book-based interactions between parent and child are part of social practices during which mutual expectation and negotiation are established through frequency and routine. The *mirror stage* can thus be re-read as the precipitating force by which structural changes in parent/child relationships are engendered, introducing the infant to discourses in which subject positions can be exercised and tested. Book reading is, thus, a social game where the mother plays with the illusion of control. Power is playfully tested, developing the infant's own authority in relation to its mother.[8]

The explicit invitation of modern picture books, for instance, is completely disregarded in this theoretical model, though extremely appropriate. The parent (most often the mother) stands in for the author in these exchanges and, in addition to taking on the voice of the text, may to some degree play within it, adding a personal gloss to the narrative or inviting the child to share in the telling, thus disrupting conventional, controlling modes or storytelling. The child may finish the rhyme, lift the flap, fill in the word, or participate in the narrative to "tell" the pictures, becoming "the teller as well as the told."[9]

In another way, parents often carry the language of the book-reading event into other interactions, disrupting its original meaning(s) and encouraging redefinition and reinterpretation. The use of textual allusion in everyday activities, such as adopting phrases from the text into the language codes of the family (in-jokes, catchphrases, etc.), along with role-play, can offer children powerful positions within fictional discourse and provide an opportunity for playing with illusions of control and self-assertion that contribute to an *active* approach to the invitation of fictional text,[10] and one that accepts the multiplicity and subjectivity of meaning.

The correspondence between the author's voice within the text and the position of the parental reading voice in storytelling exchanges also contributes to an authoritative position for children as participators in the storytelling process. While a shared sense of power within a "writerly" discourse may explain the pleasure children take in repeated rereadings of the same story, the ability to exert authority within discourse encourages a subject position (an "I") that signifies the speaker in this fictionalizing process. In the same way that a child enters into the fictional discourse of book reading, so he/she also enters into the narrative of his/her own life, constructing a self through the "subjunctivizing" force of stories in which the reader can perform the role of author. While a feminist critique emphasizes the gendering of such constructions of self, the extent to which all children are subject to the power relations within language suggests a perspective that implicates the difference between male and female discourse in relation to power relations but also reaches beyond gender.

The process by which the infant enters into the order of language is continually played out in children's literature yet, while Kristeva's consideration of "the moments where language doesn't yet exist such as during a child's apprenticeship to language" (Rice and Waugh 2) and her concern with the socio-cultural context of discourse appear to include a perspective that indicates the universality of such experiences, she does not directly acknowledge either child readers or children's texts.

The disorganized combination of sounds and the associated fluctuations of movement of the body in infancy characterize Kristeva's notion of the *semiotic* and can be found in the babbling, rhythmic, alliterative, melodic play of the young infant and, later, in the playful testing of the limits of language by young children. The imposition of the *symbolic*; the fixing of the sign, gradually overlays this uncontrolled, sensual approach to language, allowing the semiotic material to "bubble up" beneath the pressure of mature socialized language, enabling poetic language to arise.

Although in a minority, linguistic subversion, parody and recognition of a relationship between children and the semiotic force of language is present in some of the most imaginative children's books, the pressure to engage with "correct" usage and conformist language more frequently contests the tendency to "play." But once again, the dimension or process and continuity between child and adult experience of language is ignored in this theoretical map. If the relationship Kristeva sees between the "incandescent" creativity innate in infancy and the controlling, repressive force of the symbolic order exists, then the interaction of children with poetic language must play a significant role in the process she interrogates. The power of the *semiotic*, "this ultimate and primordial leash holding the body close to the mother before it can become a social speaking subject" (Rice and Waugh 30), is implicated in the development of any reader's response.

What is more, the sense in which normative uses of language are disrupted in youthful interactions with story and text can be seen as a parodic gesture that seeks to free the word from its signifying function and defy the law of the symbolic order. This subversion of order at once calls attention to the imposition of order and disturbs its repressive hold. Thus, the disruption of authoritarian discourses with poetic language is a key to radical social change described by a feminist critique, but also characterizes the struggle for authority in the transition from youth to maturity. Authors throughout the history of children's literature have recognized the need for children to be rescued from the dominance of inherited meaning and have provided texts that are, in some senses, radical. By acknowledging the power of children to seek their own interpretations and drawing attention to the making of meaning within narrative, some authors seek to contest dominant and repressive modes of thought by opening out the interaction between author and child-reader, calling attention to the constructedness of language and celebrating a childlike apprehension of the world.

I would like to provide an example of the way that such a feminist perspective illuminates the relevance of children's literature to an understanding of power within discourse by considering the work of two authors, George MacDonald and Maurice Sendak. Though writing at different times, in different countries, and in different genres (if one considers picture books to be a genre), both deliberately address and question notions of power within discourse in their work for children. While both are considered children's writers, they are not exclusively so, and it is often true that those writers who offer a more open relationship with their readers also write for adults or resist the differentiation between audiences. It is therefore important to consider that George MacDonald also embraced similar themes and narrative modes in his adult fantasies, and both writers claimed not to write for children exclusively. MacDonald, in "The Fantastic Imagination," says, "[f]or my part, I do not write for children, but for the childlike, whether of five, or fifty, or seventy-five" (29). Sendak, while seeing himself as a children's writer, similarly refused to accept a restricted view of childhood when characterizing his readership. "Fantasy is the core of all writing for children, as I think it is for the writing of any book—perhaps even for the act of living" (Lanes 65).

Both writers demonstrate an awareness of the implications for self-knowledge and autonomy in children's fantasy literature and in a number of different ways, both challenged the orthodox ideology of their time to suggest that child experience was only part of a continuum. George MacDonald, through the lens of a visionary Christianity, offered a position for his readers that is multiple, fluctuating and dream-like. His belief in the innate goodness of children and their ability to understand higher truths may depend on a romanticism that is long gone, yet such an apprehension of children as readers allows him to provide a relationship with a more "feminine" discourse that calls attention to the autonomy of any individual to pursue his or her own interpretation, rather than, as the author, imposing meaning. In a dialogic exchange in his essay, "The Fantastic Imagination," MacDonald appears to be advocating the "writerly" relation to text suggested by Roland Barthes.

> Everyone . . . who feels the story, will read its meaning after his own nature and development: one man will read one meaning in it, another will read another.
>
> "If so, how am I to assure myself that I am not reading my own meaning in it, but yours out of it?"
>
> Why should you be so assured? It may be better that you should read your meaning into it. That may be a higher operation of your intellect than the mere reading of mine out of it: your meaning may be superior to mine.
>
> "Suppose my child asks me what the fairytale means, what am I to say?"
>
> If you do not know what it means, what is easier than to say so? . . . But indeed your children are not likely to trouble you about the meaning. They find what they are capable of finding, and more would be too much." (29)

Not only does the dialogic form of the argument disrupt the expected polemic of the argument, but it also supports MacDonald's willingness to challenge dominant forms of reading. In a sense, he is espousing a feminine way of reading, and, using the example of a mother's ability to soothe her child's tears without knowing their meaning, he draws a powerful parallel between the dream-like quality of story-language and feminine spaces.

Within his fantasies for children, it is in the company of magical and powerful female figures that the child characters come to their understanding of faith and spiritual truth. The great-great-grandmother in the *The Princess and the Goblin* (1872) and *The Princess and Curdie* (1883), and the North Wind in *At the Back of the North Wind* (1871) demand allegiances that they cannot explain and are always associated with sensuousness and spirit. The existence of these female characters is indeterminate, and, though they embody eternal truths and demand faith, MacDonald uses this lack of definition to provide a gap that the reader must fill.

> The lady and the beautiful room had vanished from her sight, and she seemed utterly alone. But instead of being afraid, she felt more than happy—perfectly blissful. And from somewhere came the voice of the lady, singing a strange sweet song, of which she could distinguish every word; but of the sense she had only a feeling —no understanding. Nor could she remember a single line after it was gone. It vanished, like the poetry in a dream, as fast as it came. In after years, however, she would sometimes fancy that snatches of melody suddenly rising in her brain, must be little phrases and fragments of the air of that song; and the fancy would make her happier, and abler to do her duty.
>
> (*The Princess and the Goblin* 124)

While the implicit meaning must be, in the historical context of the work, of a spiritual kind, a reading that centers on the notion of the *semiotic* must also come into play. Attempts to articulate meanings that are beyond language are central to MacDonald's ability to disrupt assumptions of meaning at the level of the sign and to privilege the feminine. Kristeva's notion of the "sound without sense" or musicality of poetic language is exemplified by MacDonald's frequent use of nonsense rhyme and song. While Curdie is able to combat the hard-headedness of the Goblins by singing nonsense rhymes to them, it is the song that Diamond is able to sing to the baby that characterizes what he has learned while "at the back of the North Wind." This flowing nonsense verse reflects the alliterative, rhythmic play that is associated with presymbolic language, as in the fragment quoted here:

> wake up baby
> sit up perpendicular
> hark to the gushing
> hark to the rushing
> where the sheep are the wooliest
> and the lambs are the unruliest
> and their tails are the whitest
> and their eyes are the brightest
> and baby's the bonniest
> and baby's the funniest
> and baby's the shiniest
> and baby's the tiniest
> and baby's the merriest
> and baby's the worriest (*At the Back of the North Wind* 124)

That children should be at the site of these messages and that the meanings of such language is lost, to be recalled in fragments during adult life, can also be read as the *semiotic* bubbling up beneath the impositions of the *symbolic order* or the repression of a childlike dream-world oppressed beneath the adult world of reality.

Sendak, too, admitting his debt to the inspiration of MacDonald, constructs picture and text that inhabit the world of dream and of mothers, seen and unseen, who exert a powerful, but unspoken, force over the cathartic journeys undertaken by his child characters. The indeterminacy of MacDonald's work, a dependence on the unarticulated, is precisely what appears to attract Sendak to his work.[11]

> Finishing one of his stories is often like waking from a dream—one's own dream. The best of them stimulate long-forgotten images and feelings—the "something profound" that borders frustratingly close to memory without ever reaching it.
>
> (Caldecott 45)

The unreachable quality of remembered feelings and unattainable meanings strikes a chord with MacDonald's own work and with Kristeva's theorizing about poetic language, calling attention to the relevance of feminist discourse to children's literature.

Sendak, like MacDonald, claims the feminine domain as the rightful place for the child. The dream sequence that shows Mickey descending naked into the Night Kitchen,[12] to bring milk to the morning cake, plays out a drama of journey and return to the maternal space of bed.[13] As Mickey utters his "OH!" "HO," "HUM," "YUM," he returns to the nakedness with which he began. His sojourn in the Night Kitchen, with its urban backdrop of skyscrapers made of food packaging, suggests a foray into a masculine world where "making and baking" is insisted upon but concludes with a return, thereby privileging the feminine. *Where the Wild Things Are* also provides a similar return journey: one that takes Max into a dream toward a masculine role as King of all the Wild Things. Here again, Max is called back to the maternal world, where his waiting supper, "still hot," signifies the nurturing mother love that is challenged at the start, when Max's mischief leads him to threaten to eat his mother up. The play of meaning that Sendak offers is never overtly determined, yet each youthful struggle with adult authority results in a return to a presymbolic realm, symbolized by food, comfort, and sound.

In another way, both MacDonald and Sendak may be said to approach a kind of "feminine" discourse in the way that they play with notions of authority over their own narratives, frequently demanding that the child-as-reader contribute to the storytelling process. MacDonald frequently calls attention to what he is unable to say as author and plays with his role as all-knowing author. In *The Princess and the Goblin*, for instance, he describes Princess Irene's rooms:

> You would wonder at that if I had time to describe to you one half of the toys she had. But then you wouldn't have the toys themselves, and that makes all the difference: you can't get tired of a thing before you have it. It was a picture, though, worth seeing—the princess sitting in the nursery with the sky ceiling over her head, at a great table covered with her toys. If the artist would like to draw this, I should advise him not to meddle with the toys. I am afraid of attempting to describe them, and I think he had better not try to draw them. He had better not.
>
> (*The Princess and the Goblin* 8)

The shifting of authority occurs in refusing to provide details, inviting the child, as reader, to share in the description, and to call attention to the wonder of her toys. In *Where the Wild Things Are*, however, Sendak plays with the double narrative of picture and text, as the illustrations gradually encroach upon the white space and written text is pushed to the bottom of the page and finally removed altogether. Not only does this contribute to the potential for the intensification and darkening of the page to draw the reader in, encouraging a participation in the journey to an imaginary space *with* Max, but the absence of written narrative also leaves a gap for the reader to tell the story of the three double-page spreads, in which Max engages in "a wild rumpus" with the Wild Things. The catharsis that the reader is invited to experience, directed at parental suppression of "wildness," during the reading process is enabled by this invitation to enter into the telling: to become the author of fictional events. By thus disrupting the order of authority, Sendak challenges his readers to be autonomous within the storytelling event; to make meaning for themselves, contributing to an illusion of "authority" that is essential for a "creative literary engagement,"[14] but also suggesting a "feminine" approach to text. The narrative, too, celebrates a more feminine discourse, by providing fractures that challenge the directness of meaning in dominant (and dominating) uses of language. For instance, "almost over a day and in and out of weeks"[15] may enhance the dream-like quality of the events, but Sendak also chooses to play with sense-making, so that meaning is de-centered and must be excavated. Here, Sendak demonstrates his affinity with MacDonald most effectively. By making it possible for the reader to interpolate his/her own voice into the text and by portraying the insufficiency of ordered, rule-based language, both of these exceptional authors plead for the child-reader to retain the presymbolic awareness of language.

While some individual authors, like MacDonald and Sendak, attempt to redefine the power relations within fictional language in their children's fiction, the need to test and challenge are finally controlled through social practices and adult mediations. Kristeva calls attention to the fact that the revolutionary sense of resistance to the symbolic order of language is subsumed by the forces of bourgeois ideology, which treat these challenges as a "safety valve for repressed impulses it denies in society" (Selden and Widdowson 142).

Nowhere is this clearer than in the example of children's literature. The encouragement toward openness and testing of adult value systems and the law of language in the most challenging, imaginative, and enlivening children's texts is controlled and contained by those forces that relegate children's literature to the margins of culture. Texts that invite the reader to play with meaning, to question the authority of the author's voice, or to engage with a more feminine discourse, inviting a more "writerly" approach, are threatening to a society that wishes to construct the child as conformist and obedient.[16] The emphasis on marketing the repetitive and conventional fiction for children, such as the *Goosebumps* or *Sweet Valley High* series and the educational need to enforce functional literacy combine to suppress those subversive forces that challenge dominant thinking and create the pleasure of the text. In addition, by denying these texts a place in cultural and academic discourse and by denying them and their readers a place in the continuum of readership, those who define the discourses that surround notions of "literature" are part of that repression and are in danger of subjugating the forces of desire that are at work in our origins.

Feminist discourses have the most to offer children's literature by providing a language that can articulate the power relations within poetic language. However, children will be served better when feminist theory acknowledges the ability of children's books to offer a kind of "feminine" discourse, challenging the dominance of controlling texts and allowing children, regardless of gender, to have a voice.

Notes

1 Peter Hunt suggests this possibility in *Criticism, Theory and Children's Literature* (1991).
2 See Michael Rosen, "Raising the Issues."
3 Lissa Paul, in her entry for the *International Companion Encyclopedia of Children's Literature* entitled "Feminist Criticism: From Sex-Role Stereotyping to Subjectivity," provides an excellent summary of these issues.
4 Munsch's groundbreaking classic, *The Paperbag Princess* (1980), is one of the most influential examples, and the work of Babette Cole (*Princess Smartypants* and *Prince Cinders*) challenge gender stereotyping but retain the conventional binary of passive/active.
5 Other children's literature theorists, such as Lissa Paul and Peter Hunt, have persuasively argued for the close connection between the "feminine" and the

feminist agenda and the current struggles for recognition of children's literature theory. It can certainly be admitted that children and their relationship with story and books is intimately tied to "nurturing practices," as suggested by Michael Rosen.

6 The emphasis that "discursive relations [are] produced by positioning within discursive practices" (Henriques 217) is essential to a feminist position, as it demonstrates the specific positioning that determines psychosexual development and thus a gendered subject.

7 Cathy Urwin invites an inclusion of children's experience of fiction in her discussion of "Power Relations and the Emergence of Language." She argues that "[a] serious consideration of what children contribute to the emergence of language . . . will need both a different view of human subjectivity and a way of articulating its relation to language as it is manifested in particular social practices through which children grow up" (272).

8 There am numerous examples or psychological studies that reveal the ways in which the mother's use of book reading produces the illusion of control. Urwin cites those of Ninio and Bruner, in particular.

9 In Meek. For an explication of these ideas at work in modern picture books, see, in particular, the work of David Lewis in numerous *Signal* articles.

10 For a fascinating account of how role-play initiates negotiation of adult/child power relations, see S. A. Wolf and S. B. Heath (1992).

11 C. S. Lewis, too, claimed to have been inspired by MacDonald in similar terms.

12 See *In the Night Kitchen.*

13 Trites claims that the circular narrative is a common feature of feminist children's novels (11). Both Macdonald and Sendak reject linear narratives in favor of the "nested" narrative (in *At the Back of the North Wind*, we discover late in the book that the narrator is one of the characters and the fairy tale "The Light Princess" is embedded in the narrative).

14 In the sense of Wolfgang Iser's notion of response in *The Act of Reading.*

15 In *Where the Wild Things Are.*

16 See, for instance, Rose.

Works cited

Barthes, Roland. *The Pleasure of the Text*. London: Jonathan Cape, 1975.

Henriques, J., ed. *Changing the Subject: Psychology, Social Regulation and Subjectivity*. London: Methuen, 1984.

Hunt, Peter. *Children's Literature: The Development of Criticism*, London: Routledge, 1990.

——. *Criticism. Theory and Children's Literature*. Oxford: Blackwell. 1991.

Hunt, Peter. ed. *Literature for Children: Contemporary Criticism*. London: Routledge, 1992.

Iser, Wolfgang. *The Act of Reading*. Baltimore: Johns Hopkins University Press, 1974.

Lacan, Jacques. *Écrits*. London: Tavistock Press, 1977.

Lanes, Selma. *The Art of Maurice Sendak*. New York: Abradale Press, 1980.

MacDonald, George. *At the Back of the North Wind*. New York: Signet, 1986.

——. "The Fantastic Imagination." *Signal* 16 (January 1975): 26–32.

——. *The Princess and the Goblin/The Princess and Curdie*. Oxford: Oxford UP, 1990.

Meek, Margaret. *How Texts Teach What Readers Learn*. Stroud: Thimble Press, 1988.

——. "Children Reading—Now." In *After Alice: Exploring Children's Literature*, ed. M. Styles, *et al.* London: Cassell, 1993.

Paul, Lissa. "Feminist Criticism: From Sex-Role Stereotyping to Subjectivity." In *International Companion Encyclopedia of Children's Literature*, ed. Peter Hunt. London: Routledge, 1996.

Rice, P., and P. Waugh, eds. *Modern Literary Theory: A Reader*. London: Edward Arnold, 1992.

Rose, Jacqueline. *The Case of Peter Pan: The Impossibility of Children's Fiction*. London: Macmillan, 1992.

Rosen, Michael. "Raising the Issues." *Signal* 76 (January 1995): 26–44.

Selden, R., and P. Widdowson. *A Reader's Guide to Contemporary Literary Theory*. Hemel Hempstead: Harvester Wheatsheaf, 1993.

Sendak, Maurice. *Caldecott & Co.: Notes on Books and Pictures*. New York: Farrar, Straus and Giroux, 1988.

——. *In the Night Kitchen*. London: Puffin, 1970.

——. *Where the Wild Things Are*. London: Puffin, 1970.

Thacker, Deborah. "Disdain or Ignorance? Literary Theory and the Absence of Children's Literature." *The Lion and the Unicorn* 24.1 (January 2000): 1–17.

——. *An Examination of Children's Inter-action with Fiction, Leading to the Development of Methodologies to Elicit and Communicate Their Responses*. Diss., 1996.

Trites, Roberta S. *Waking Sleeping Beauty Feminist Voices in Children's Novels*. Iowa City: U of Iowa P, 1997.

Urwin, Cathy. "Power Relations and the Emergence of Language." In *Changing the Subject: Psychology, Social Regulation and Subjectivity*, ed. J. Henriques. London: Methuen, 1984.

Widdowson, Peter. *Literature*. London: Routledge, 1999.

Wolf, S. A., and Shirley, B. Heath. *The Braid of Literature: Children's Worlds of Reading*. Cambridge, Mass.: Harvard University Press, 1992.

73

"CINDERELLA WAS A WUSS"

A young girl's responses to feminist and patriarchal folktales

Ann M. Trousdale and Sally McMillan

Source: *Children's Literature in Education* 34(1) (March 2003): 1–28.

In this longitudinal study we examine a young girl's responses to "feminist" and "patriarchal" folktales. Data were collected during five informal interviews with the participant at 8 and at 12 years of age and were analyzed according to grounded theory methodologies. Particularly salient issues raised by tales at both stages had to do with the exercise of personal agency, physical strength on the part of males and females, and the symbolic significance of dress. Findings challenge psychological theories about the appeal of folktales to young children, provide insight into developmental issues in young girls' response to narrative, raise questions about how young girls negotiate cultural scripts in a patriarchal world, and highlight the importance of disrupting the layering of polarized gender norms and ideals through alternative narratives.

A Little Pretty
POCKET-BOOK
Intended for the
Instruction and Amusement
of
Little Master TOMMY
and
Pretty Miss POLLY.
With Two Letters from
JACK the Giant-Killer;

AS ALSO
A Ball and Pincushion;
The Use of which will infallibly make *Tommy*
a good Boy, and *Polly* a good Girl.

From the earliest days of literature produced for children, adults have recognized that stories potentially have a powerful effect on children's self-understanding and behavior. Indeed, from the days when monks copied children's lesson books by hand, through the invention of the printing press in the mid-15th century, and into the early 20th century, didacticism marked children's literature. Published in England in 1744, *A Little Pretty Pocket-Book* represented a new direction in the world of children's books in that it was intended to entertain as well as to instruct. The overall purpose however, is clear: "To make Tommy a good Boy, and Polly a good Girl." The accompanying ball (for little boys) and pincushion (for little girls) reflect the perceived difference in interest between boys and girls; that there were also different perceptions of what exactly it meant for Tommy to become a "good boy" and Polly to become a "good girl" was not an issue that would be raised until much later.

The particular effect that traditional folktales or fairy tales have on children has been a topic of interest and concern at least since the publication of the Grimm Brothers' *Kinder- und Hausmarchen* in the 19th century. According to folklorist Linda Dégh ("Oral folklore: folk narrative", 1965), the Grimms were compelled to consider the suitability of various of their *hausmärchen* for children when the popularity of the tales began to extend from scholars and linguists—their primary intended audience—to children. The Grimms assumed that the tales would give children pleasure and delight; but, along with other adults of the times, the Grimms thought that the frightful elements in the tales would also be useful in disciplining children.

In the 20th century, the influence of fairy tales on children was explored from many perspectives: psychological (Bettelheim, 1977; Estes, 1992; Favat, 1977; Jung, 1959; von Franz, 1980); literary (Auden, 1943; Lewis, 1966; Tolkien, 1965); folkloristic (Dégh, 1965; Stone, 1985); and sociopolitical (Zipes, 1983, 1985, 1986). With the exception of Estes (*Women Who Run with the Wolves*) and Zipes, those who have approached the tales from these perspectives have not interpreted them as conveying particular gendered meaning. Estes' concern is the recovery of the wild woman archetype for women whose free, instinctual, and passionate natures have been "tamed" by a repressive society. Zipes focuses his concern on children. According to Zipes (*Fairy Tales and the Art of Subversion*, 1983), "educated writers [of the 17th through the 19th centuries] purposely appropriated the oral folktale and converted it into a type of literary discourse about mores, values, and manners so that children would become civilized according to the social order of that time" (p. 3). The tales have undergone successive stages of patriarchalization, Zipes says, during which active young heroines were changed to active heroes and matrilineal family ties and relationships became patrilineal. Thus the stories that have come down to children in recent times are stamped by a patriarchal world view.

Others have also expressed concern about the collective weak, silent, and passive females who populate the stories of the Western European canon, females whose chief virtues lie in their physical beauty, their silence, their docility, and their dependence on a stronger male figure to rescue them from a predicament from which they cannot extricate themselves (Bottigheimer, 1986; Davies, 1989; Lieberman, 1972; Phelps, 1978; Stone, 1975, 1981, 1989; Yolen, 1982). In these tales, to use Gilbert's ("And they lived happily ever after: cultural storylines and the construction of gender", 1994) term, a "hierarchical dualism" between masculinity and femininity is reinforced by the juxtaposition of such females with powerful, active, and effective male characters who emerge as the heroes, the rescuers, the saviors of otherwise powerless women (p. 127),

This concern led a number of feminist scholars to search through old folktale anthologies to discover whether among the old tales there were not also stories that featured strong, resourceful, independent, and active females, females whose physical appearance is incidental, females who are quite capable of solving their own (and others') problems in the world. Indeed such tales, neglected or overlooked in a patriarchal culture, were discovered—and recovered. A number of anthologies of these "feminist" tales have been published with the hope that children would find in those tales female role models with whom it is healthier, and more liberating, for little girls to identify (Barchers, 1990; Carter, 1990; Lurie, 1980; Minard, 1975; Phelps, 1978, 1981).

Stories alone do not determine children's perceptions of gender, of course; they are only a part of the complex of societal influences, including television, movies, advertisements, magazines, and popular music, that together send strong messages of gender norms and ideals. Yet, within this complex, stories have a powerful and often subtle effect. As Gilbert (1992) writes:

> By entering into story worlds, and by being inserted into the storylines of their culture, students come to know what counts as being a woman, or being a man, in the culture to which the stories belong. They come to know the range of cultural possibilities available for femininity and masculinity—and the limits to that range. . . . Through constant repetition and layering, story patterns and logic become almost "naturalized" as truths and common sense. (pp. 127–128)

Earlier research in children's responses to traditional tales from the patriarchal tradition indicates that adults are often mistaken when they presume to predict how children respond to traditional folktales; more fruitful than armchair theorizing is asking children themselves what meanings the tales hold for them (Trousdale, "The telling of the tale: children's responses to fairy tales presented orally and through the medium of film", 1987, 1989). What, we wondered, would children's responses be to these more recently recovered "feminist" tales whose protagonists do not conform to patriarchal expectations for females but who counter them, resist them, fly in the face of them? What would their responses to these girls and women reveal about their own constructions of gender, about any tensions or conflicts that they themselves experience in negotiating their roles as females in the world?

Ann conducted the initial research, Sally helping with the later data analysis. Qualitative methodologies guided the overall design of the study, including participant selection and collection and analysis of data.

The stories

Ann read numerous tales from feminist folktale collections and selected three that raised particularly relevant issues. The tales were "Tatterhood," "The Twelve Huntsmen," and "Three Strong Women," all of which came from anthologies edited by Ethel Johnston Phelps (1978, 1981). We also used one "patriarchal" tale, Grimm's "Briar Rose" (*The Complete Fairy Tales*, 1987) for the purpose of contrast and to highlight any differences in response to feminist or patriarchal heroines.

"Tatterhood"

A queen gives birth to twin girls. The first is born with a wooden spoon in her hand, riding a goat, and crying, "Mama!" The second is born fair and sweet. The first twin grows into a little hoyden, always riding about on her goat, dressed in rugged clothes and a ragged hood. This is Tatterhood. Her sister, who is more demure and who dresses cleanly and properly, is much more acceptable to the queen.

One day a pack of trolls invades the castle. Tatterhood tries to drive them away but is successful only after a troll whips off Tatterhood's sister's head, replacing it with a calf's head. Tatterhood resolves to recover her sister's head. She declines the offer of a crew and sets off on a ship with her sister to the land of the trolls. She retrieves her sister's head from the angry trolls, and the two girls decide to travel on a bit to see something of the world. When they reach the shore of another kingdom, a prince rides down to see who has arrived. He immediately falls in love with Tatterhood's sister and wants to marry her, but the sister says she will not marry until Tatterhood marries. The prince rides away wondering who would marry such an odd-looking creature, but he returns with his younger brother to invite the two girls to a feast. Tatterhood, refusing her sister's pleas to clean her face and put on one of her own dresses, rides to the castle alongside the younger prince. The prince asks her why she rides a goat, and she replies, "I can ride on a horse if I choose." Immediately the goat is changed into a fine steed. A similar pattern follows with her ragged cloak, which changes into a circlet of gold and pearls, and her spoon, which changes into a rowan wand. Tatterhood asks the prince if he would like to see her face beneath the streaks of soot and he replies, "That too shall be as you choose." Tatterhood does cause the soot to disappear, and the story ends on the note that the feasting lasted for many days, but that we will never know whether Tatterhood was lovely or plain because it "didn't matter in the least" to Tatterhood or the prince. There is no explicit mention of marriage.

"The Twelve Huntsmen"

Katrine is the only child of a nobleman. She likes to ride out to hunt with her father and has no interest in the many suitors who seek her hand. However, one day a young prince, Wilhelm, comes to the castle, and he and Katrine fall in love. He asks Katrine to marry him and gives her his ring. A messenger arrives from Wilhelm's father, saying that his father is ill and requests Wilhelm to return home. Wilhelm promises to return as soon as he can.

Wilhelm's dying father asks him to marry a princess from a neighboring kingdom. Wilhelm tries to tell his father he is betrothed to another, but in his grief agrees to do as his father wishes. Acting on the advice of a wise lion, Wilhelm delays the marriage. When months pass without Wilhelm's return, Katrine decides to go find out what has caused his delay. She and eleven friends learn the ways of huntsmen, cut their hair, and, dressed as huntsmen, set off to Wilhelm's kingdom. Wilhelm does not recognize Katrine and takes the huntsmen into his service. Katrine learns that Wilhelm is engaged to the princess, but is persuaded to stay until she learns whether Wilhelm really prefers another.

One day Wilhelm, in a state of despair over this proposed marriage, jumps on his horse and gallops recklessly away. Katrine follows and comes upon Wilhelm in the woods, injured in a fall from his horse. She dismounts to help him and Wilhelm, seeing his ring on her finger, recognizes her. They seek the advice of the lion, who tells Wilhelm that his prior betrothal to Katrine releases him from his promise to his father. Their wedding takes place soon after.

"Three Strong Women"

In "Three Strong Women," a Japanese tall tale, the great wrestler Forever-Mountain is on his way to wrestle before the emperor. Strutting along proud of his great strength, he sees a young girl carrying a bucket of water on the road in front of him. Thinking to have some amusement, he comes up behind the girl and tickles her. She brings her arm down and catches Forever-Mountain's hand between her arm and body. To his surprise, he cannot pull his hand away. Over his protests, she drags him along and persuades him to come to her mother's house, where they will make a really strong man of him.

When they arrive, Maru-me's mother returns from the field, carrying a cow on her back. She then picks up a large oak tree and throws it end over end to the next mountainside. Forever-Mountain quietly faints.

The three women put Forever-Mountain through a regimen of hard work. Every evening he wrestles with the grandmother, for Maru-me or her mother might accidentally hurt him if they wrestled with him. He grows stronger, and finally, when Forever-Mountain is able to pin the grandmother for half a minute, they decide he is ready to go to the wrestling match. Before he leaves, Forever-Mountain asks for Maru-me's hand in marriage, promising to return to be a part of the family.

Forever-Mountain, unusually quiet, does not participate in the boasting of the other wrestlers. In the first match, simply by stamping his foot he sends his opponent bouncing into the air and out of the ring like a soap bubble. Forever-Mountain mildly picks up the next challengers and deposits them outside the ring. The emperor proclaims him the winner and gives him all the prize money, but tells him never to wrestle in public again. Forever-Mountain declares that he will become a farmer. He returns to the mountain where Maru-me is waiting for him. The story concludes with the note that up in the mountains when the earth shakes and rumbles, the people say it is Forever-Mountain and Maru-me's grandmother practicing their wrestling.

"Brier Rose"

"Brier Rose" is the Grimm Brothers' variant of "Sleeping Beauty." (*The Complete Fairy Tales of the Brothers Grimm*) In this "patriarchal" tale, a queen gives birth to a long-awaited child who is so beautiful that the king decides to hold a feast. He wants to invite the "wise women" of the kingdom to the feast, but there are 13 wise women and only 12 golden plates from which they can be served, and so one is not invited. At the feast the wise women bestow such gifts as virtue, beauty, and wealth on the young princess. When the thirteenth wise woman enters the hall, angry at not having been invited to the feast, she utters a spell that on her fifteenth birthday the princess will prick herself with a spindle and die. One wise woman who had been invited has not made her wish, and although she cannot undo the spell, she can soften it to a spell of sleep for 100 years.

On her fifteenth birthday the princess comes across an old woman spinning flax. The princess touches the spindle, pricks her finger, and falls into a deep sleep. The spell spreads throughout the entire palace, which is soon covered by a brier hedge. From time to time princes try to break through the hedge, but they are caught and, unable to get loose, die miserable deaths. After many years have gone by, another prince comes to the country and hears the story of the sleeping princess from an old man. Despite the old man's warning, the prince determines to make his way through the hedge. The hundred years have just ended, and the hedge opens before the prince and lets him through. He makes his way to the tower, finds Brier Rose, and kisses her awake. Everyone else in the castle awakens as well. The story ends with the marriage of Brier Rose and the prince.

Nikki, the participant

We interviewed Nikki at two stages of her life, at eight years of age and four years later. She was initially chosen by criterion-based selection (Goetz & LeCompte, *Ethnography and Qualitative Design in Educational Research*, 1984), in accordance with research in children's responses to literature and, particularly, to fairy tales. Favat's (1977) investigations revealed that children's interest in fairy tales peaks between the ages of six and eight. Working from a Piagetian perspective, Favat (*Child and Tale: The Origins of Interest*) notes unique correspondences between characteristics of the young child and characteristics of fairy tales, including animism and a belief in magic, a morality of constraint, an expression of causality by juxtaposition of events, and the egocentrism of the child and the centrality of the fairy tale hero or heroine in the world of the tale. According to Favat, children's interest in fairy tales typically declines after the age of eight, when they begin to seek more realistic reading matter.

Applebee (*A Child's Concept of Story: Ages Two to Seventeen*, 1978) has found that children who have not yet entered concrete operations lack the ability to express responses to narrative beyond a simple retelling of the story, but begin to be able to organize and synthesize responses as they enter concrete operations. We wanted a participant at the upper edge of the six-to-eight age range to maximize her interest in fairy tales as well as to maximize her potential in responding beyond a simple retelling of the story.

Ann met Nikki at church and knew her only slightly when the study began. She comes from a literate, white middle-class background. Her parents divorced when Nikki was three, and the mother had custody of Nikki and her sister, who is three years Nikki's senior. Nikki's mother taught piano at home. Her father was completing an advanced degree in theatre at a local university.

At eight years of age, Nikki freely described herself as a tomboy. She wore her dark curly hair cut short and showed up at the sessions dressed in shorts or pants, high-top tennis shoes, and, often, a baseball cap with its brim turned up at the front or pulled around to the rear. She expressed a strong dislike for ruffles and for the colors pink and purple, saying that she refused to wear them. Nikki was not at all interested in dolls, preferring to play team sports.

Nikki was an avid reader. She had recently finished reading all the Laura Ingalls Wilder books and spoke of a family trip to the Wilder homesite. Nikki's parents had read to her when she was younger, but had not included fairy tales in her early reading. Her knowledge of fairy tales had come primarily from movies, television, and, particularly, seeing fairy tales dramatized in the local amateur children's theatre.

When Ann discussed Nikki's tomboyism with her mother, she confirmed that Nikki would scrutinize clothing, refusing to wear "anything with the hint of a ruffle on it. She could see ruffles we couldn't see." She said that Nikki had been through a period of not wanting to be a girl at all and that she had developed "negative connotations about girls." According to her mother, a neighborhood boy had teased Nikki about being a girl. When her mother saw the effect of this teasing on Nikki she ended the relationship between the children, but she said that from that time, Nikki had refused to wear girlish clothes. She had tried to reassure Nikki that it was okay to be a tomboy, that she herself had been a tomboy, and "that girls can do girl things *and* boy things too," in order to "give her a little bit more permission to return to some of the feminine qualities. She does have a nurturing side."

Nikki's mother said that she and her former husband had not given the children "any messages about being a passive female," but that she had raised her daughters to "be resourceful, to develop their abilities, and to be independent," qualities she saw as neither masculine nor feminine. Living in a single-parent home, the girls shared the household responsibilities with their mother.

In the years between the first and second phases of the study, Nikki and her family moved to another state but returned when Nikki was 12. Ann thought it would be interesting to discover how Nikki, now approaching adolescence, would respond to the same stories at this stage in her development.

At 12, Nikki displayed an interest in acting as a career and in doing television modeling. She had developed a flair for style, now expressing a preference for baggy jeans and overalls worn with a tee shirt and platform tennis shoes. She said that she liked shopping at the Gap, where she could shop for pants without going to a boys department. She volunteered that she had also purchased her first dress, a simple, tailored above-the-knee shift. She explained: "You'll see it in all the magazines. A girl's interest in clothes will change when she begins to notice *boys*!" She was resistant to wearing makeup, however, even though people were "pestering" her about wearing it. "People say, 'You'll become interested in makeup when you begin to notice boys.' I want to say to them, 'I'm almost thirteen years *old*—you don't think I've noticed *boys*?'"

For the most part, Nikki did not clearly remember the feminist stories from four years before, recalling only, several paragraphs into "The Twelve Huntsmen," that Katrine had gone off on a horse somewhere. She did retain a sense of "Brier Rose," a story she had been familiar with from other media and exposure.

The procedures were the same when Nikki was 8 and when she was 12. At both ages Ann met with her five times, in sessions a week apart. The sessions were kept as informal as possible, in Ann's living room where Nikki sat on a sofa and Ann on a chair next to it. The tape recorder was placed on a table between them. At the first session, Ann explained the procedures and assured Nikki that there were no right or wrong answers to any of the questions that she would be asking, that she wanted to find out what she really thought about the stories. She also encouraged Nikki to ask any questions or say anything she might want to say about the stories as they went along.

During the reading of the stories, Ann paused at several places to discuss the story "so far," to tap into ongoing responses. At the end of the reading she asked further open-ended questions. She then asked Nikki to retell the story. The following week, Ann began by asking her to retell the story from the week before, then proceeded with the next story. At the final session, she asked Nikki to retell the last story and then asked summative questions about the stories and story characters.

Ann took field notes, and at the end of the sessions with Nikki she interviewed Nikki's mother. The data were analyzed according to grounded theory methodologies (Glaser & Strauss, 1967). When we analyzed the data from the two sets of interviews, several major themes emerged: issues involving personal agency, physical strength, tensions between autonomy and responsibility, and the symbolic and practical significance of dress. We also noted evidence of developmental difference in Nikki's response.

Findings

Developmental differences

At eight years of age, Nikki seemed to accept the magical elements in the tales without question, in accordance with Favat's (1977) claims about correspondences between young children and fairy tales. By 12 years of age, she had clearly grown beyond belief in magic and took an ironical, almost sarcastic, stance toward the now "unrealistic" elements. For example, Nikki interrupted the reading of "Tatterhood" at the description of Tatterhood's birth. "On a *goat*?" she exclaimed. "She'd have to be big when she was pregnant!" When Ann continued reading, describing the birth of Tatterhood's sister, Nikki laughed. "Was *she* born on a *duck*?"

Similarly, in reading "Brier Rose" when the 100-year-spell was cast, Nikki commented, "She would be, like, 115 years old. 'Thanks to this new aging process, I still look like a 15-year-old.'" Later, when the spell broke, Nikki asked, "Wouldn't you just, while you're sleeping, die of starvation anyway? And I mean everything would just rot. 'All you have is green meat in here!'"

Nikki's responses, however, challenge Favat on one level—his claim for a coincidence of the young child's egocentricity with the centrality of the protagonist in the fairy tale world. Even at eight years of age, Nikki's idea of the story world was not focused exclusively on the protagonist. She demonstrated a notable tendency toward inclusiveness and a concern for secondary characters, an ethic of caring that will be discussed in a later section.

What fairy tales were primarily about changed for Nikki. At eight, she described them as characterized by "fighting or sometimes singing. Women and men mixed together, and there's usually princes and princesses. Sometimes a love story at the end." She identified "Tatterhood," "The Twelve Huntsmen," and "Brier Rose" as fairy tales because they "had princes and princesses in them"; adding that "Tatterhood" also "has a kingdom, a king and queen. I'm used to having fairy tales with kings, queens, prince and princess." She would not call "Three Strong Women" a fairy tale, she said, "because I've never heard a fairy tale with a wrestler in it or strong people." Instead, fairy tales "have people that are dainty, and princesses. People that dress up a lot."

By age 12 her definition of fairy tales had changed. "I think of them as more of the love stories," she said. She identified "Tatterhood," "The Twelve Huntsmen," and "Brier Rose" as fairy tales "because they got married at the end" or "because there's love in it." Now she found Katrine's lack of interest in marrying before Wilhelm arrives "unrealistic."

Again, she would not classify "Three Strong Women" as a fairy tale, but for different reasons. Even though Maru-Me and Forever-Mountain do marry at the end, their romance is not the primary concern of this rather ironic tale that turns ordinary perceptions of men's and women's relative physical strength on end. At age eight, Nikki had found the fact that the women possessed greater physical strength than Forever-Mountain absolutely believable, but her views on this matter had changed significantly by age 12. Now she was also keenly aware of societal constraints on such "unfeminine" physical activities as wrestling. She found another genre for the story: "This would be more of a Japanese fantasy proper," she concluded.

Personal agency

The social and economic dependence of females on males has had a powerful influence in shaping notions of femininity. Over the ages, females have learned to shape their behavior as well as their physical appearance to those expressions that have been likely to gain and retain male approval or desire. Brownmiller (*Femininity*, 1984) has written that the feminine principle historically has been "a grand collection of compromises, large and small, that [a female] must make in order to render herself a successful woman" (p. 16). Femininity, she says, is "a tradition of imposed limitations" (p. 14), "[a] powerful esthetic that is built upon a recognition of powerlessness" (p. 19). According to Brownmiller,

> The masculine principle is better understood as a driving ethos of superiority designed to inspire straightforward, confident success, while the feminine principle is composed of vulnerability, the need for protection, the formalities of compliance and the avoidance of conflict—in short, an appeal of dependence and good will that gives the masculine principle its romantic validity and its admiring applause. . . . Femininity serves to reassure men that women need them and care about them enormously.
>
> (pp. 16–17)

In the late 19th century, George Eliot wrote of girls' susceptibility to adverse judgments by others, which stems from their lack of power and of their consequent inability "to do something for the world" (Gilligan, *In a Different Voice*, 1982, p. 66). Gilligan adds to Eliot's observation the insight, "to the extent that women perceive themselves as having no choice, they correspondingly excuse themselves from the responsibility that decision entails. Childlike in the vulnerability of their dependency and consequent fear of abandonment, they claim to wish only to please, but in return for their goodness they expect to be loved and cared for" (p. 67). Such notions of femininity are the operative principle on which such patriarchal tales as "Cinderella," "Snow White," and "Sleeping Beauty" rely: beautiful, vulnerable, and dependent, these paragons of traditional femininity seem naturally to be unable to extricate themselves from the situations in which they are caught. Their release is dependent on attracting a stronger and more competent male to rescue them, and their future security is assured in their marriage to this strong, protective male, with whom they will "live happily ever after."

In the three "feminist" tales chosen for this study, the female protagonists prove to be capable of taking responsibility for themselves and their situations, of making decisions and acting on them independently of masculine protection or approval. They depend on neither physical beauty nor female wiles to entice a male to act on their behalf. It was in Nikki's responses to "Tatterhood," "The Twelve Huntsmen," and "Brier Rose" that this theme was clearest.

Tatterhood's insistence on self-definition, her independence, and her confidence in her ability to act on the world are evident throughout the story—from her ragged clothing and raucous behavior, her attacking the trolls in the castle, to her decision to set out herself to retrieve her sister's head. She resists any efforts to persuade her to act or dress in a more conventionally feminine way until at the end of the story she transforms her clothing and accoutrements to more conventional ones.

In the first set of interviews (when Nikki was eight), Ann asked Nikki, after reading the story, if there were a character in the story that she would say was her favorite character and, several questions later, if there were a character whom she would like to be like. In both cases Nikki resoundingly chose Tatterhood herself (with one qualification): "because she's like me. I'd like to ride a goat or a horse all day, and wear that kind of stuff except change that hat to a normal hat."

Ann asked Nikki if there were anything in the story that had surprised her. Nikki said that she was surprised that Tatterhood "changed all her stuff." Her retellings of the story reveal her struggle to rationalize the changes. In Nikki's version, when the prince asks Tatterhood why she wears such ragged clothes or carries a spoon, she first replies, "'Cause I want to." The prince asks, "Why don't you ever change it?" Tatterhood responds, "Do you *want* me to change it?" The prince says that that is up to Tatterhood, and she immediately makes the transformation. After finishing the story, Nikki explained, "She was probably thinking, 'Well, I don't think I should be dressed like this. People want me to change, then, well . . . , and nobody's really votin' for me to *stay* like this, guess I'll just have to change!" Seen in the context of Nikki's appreciation of Tatterhood's unconventional ways earlier in the story, one might wonder whether in Nikki's view, Tatterhood was capitulating to the pressure of societal norms or seeking to please a particular male, making the change she assumed he would like. Or it may be that, in the absence of pressure to conform, Nikki's Tatterhood felt free to relax a defensive stance and still retain her integrity. Whatever her understanding of this shift in Tatterhood's resistance to social norms, Nikki seems to interpret her decision in light of what Gilligan (1982) has described as a central concern of young women, that of making decisions that are inclusive of both the self and others.

In Phelps' retelling of "Tatterhood," there is no mention of a marriage at the end of the story. At the end of Nikki's retellings of the story at age eight, Tatterhood remained a free, independent spirit, with no marriage mentioned. At age 12, however, her retelling did end in marriage—of both sisters to the two princes. At this age, her "set" for fairy tales included "marriages, kissing at the end, and a prince and princess." But when Ann asked her if she thought Tatterhood married the prince because she *had* to or because she *wanted* to, Nikki ducked the issue. "I don't know," she countered. "Why don't you ask her?"

In "The Twelve Huntsmen," Katrine's independence and confidence in her ability to solve her problems was manifested in her setting out to discover the truth about why Wilhelm had not returned to marry her. While Nikki said that she would like to do the kinds of things that Katrine did—cutting her hair, dressing as a man, and going to Wilhelm's kingdom—she did not see these actions as the best solution to the problem at hand: "Yeah, why didn't she just say it was the secret police of Nottingham or of Robin Hood . . . and say, 'You tell us the truth.'" Nikki would have solved the problem in a more straightforward and practical way. At another point in the interview, Nikki said that if she were in Katrine's situation she would have sent a "king's messenger" with a "note and get the answer instead of cutting her hair short, learning all that stuff. It's just wasting time." Or, she added, she could have telephoned.

At age eight, Nikki's response to "Brier Rose" was quite different on many levels from her response to the three "feminist" heroines. She was critical of Brier Rose as a person and resistant to the values she represented. Her resistance to Brier Rose seemed to stem from objections to the way Brier Rose dressed and, in Nikki's mind at least, her attitudes and behaviors. When Ann asked Nikki to "tell me about Brier Rose," she replied, "She's okay." Ann prompted, "What was she like?" Nikki responded, "She was a little bit greedy, because—and, you know, seemed like she would brag, just going off and show it because of the magic. Would walk in the house doing this" [tossing her head and shrugging her shoulders proudly].

"You think she would show off like that?" Ann asked.

"Yeah. Because she was so proud of her beauty, and her wealth and her other stuff."

When Ann asked Nikki if she "liked" Brier Rose, she said outright, "No." She went on to explain, "Like, you know, everybody thought she was, you know, so beautiful, and at first she had all these jewels, but if they wouldn't have given her all these gifts, she might just have been a bratty little girl." While Brier Rose is described as physically beautiful in the Grimm Brothers text, the text does not explicitly mention any arrogance or pride in her. This was Nikki's own interpretation. The use to which females put any sense of personal power is clearly important to Nikki; she does not admire a character she sees as proud or self-centered, no matter how "beautiful" she may be.

At eight, the character Nikki was drawn to in "Brier Rose" was the prince—precisely because of his sense of personal agency, along with his impulse to help others. When Ann asked her if there was anyone in the story who she would say was her favorite character, she replied, "The last prince." Why? "He is braver than that guy who was trying to convince him not to go through. And he had a mind, to at least try to save the kingdom. When the other princes just gave up right when they got stuck."

Nikki's insistence on a sense of personal agency was quite clear at age 12. During one interview when she and Ann were discussing such patriarchal heroines as Cinderella, Snow White, Sleeping Beauty, and Rapunzel,

Nikki suddenly exclaimed, "Cinderella was a wuss!" How so? "She could have run away, you know. I mean, like she had the weakest spirit. It's like, 'Do something about your life! You're rotting away here!' She's obviously not stupid, you know. Cinderella." How did Cinderella come to be such a wuss? "Her dad probably was. Weak-willed. She had already resolved to live her whole life as a maid in service. So there's no chance. Now *me, I'd* fight it. I'd run away. Back in those times, you know, you just grab one of the best horses and everything, and they can't track you down." Like Cinderella, Nikki is surrounded by cultural scripts that depict "feminine" passivity as normative. However, unlike Cinderella who accepts the dictates and examples of her environment, Nikki sees herself resisting such constraints.

Her impulse to take an active role in solving problems was also clear in her discussion of "The Twelve Huntsmen." She heartily approved of Katrine's riding off to discover why Wilhelm had not returned. "I think it would be fun," she added, going on to improvise a conversation among the young women, trying out various "masculine" voices.

Physical strength

In these feminist tales, the ability of the heroine to act on the world begins with the self-confidence necessary to make decisions and to act on them; but at issue as well is the actual ability to carry forth those actions, which sometimes involves physical strength or power. According to Bronwyn Davies (*Frogs and Snails and Feminist Tales: Pre-school Children and Gender*, 1989), women are acculturated to view power as "fundamentally contradictory to the *idea* and the idealization of the idea of being female" (p. 71). In her study of preschool children's responses to literary feminist fairy tales, she noted that the female children resisted positioning themselves as powerful except in the domestic sphere and did not even entertain fantasies of themselves as physically powerful. Nikki, older than the children in Davies' study, absolutely did not follow the pattern Davies found.

The story in which physical strength is the most salient issue is "Three Strong Women," the Japanese tale in which the three women are far superior in physical strength to the male wrestler. In responding to this story at age eight, Nikki seemed to be quite comfortable with the idea of females possessing physical strength, and physical strength greater than males'. She did, however, express some qualifications related to age.

Initially Nikki was surprised by Maru-me's physical strength. The initial description of Maru-me is of a "girl," with small dimpled hands, "a round girl with red cheeks and a nose like a friendly button" (pp. 39–40). When Ann paused in the reading of the story at the point when Maru-me has the wrestler firmly in tow and is pulling him along with her, to ask "Is there anything in the story that surprised you so far?" Nikki nodded her head, then said, "Well, a nice, round little girl and she's really strong and stuff. How can a nice little round, dainty girl be, like, a really strong girl?"

At the other end of the scale was the grandmother, whom Nikki described as "stronger than she should be," adding, "and has too much work." When Ann asked her to explain, she replied, "Well, she just lifts trees out the ground when she should be resting." This recommendation seemed to be related to the grandmother's age rather than to her gender. Nikki was very close to her own grandmother and was quite sure that she herself was the stronger of the two. She mentioned the exercise weights that her grandmother owns, which "are green little plastic-covered two-and-a-half-pound [ones], which are pretty light. I could probably use five-pound ones." Other than considerations of age, however, Nikki had absolutely no question in her mind about the relative strength of males and females. When Ann asked, "Do you think women are as strong as men?" she immediately responded, "yes," and went on to describe a race she had had with a boy in her class:

> Okay, you know those blue chairs that you have in preschool? Those blue tin torn-up things? Two of these. Well, we had those outside in the playground and there is a little field space, about like three of these rooms. It started at the beginning of the playground, you know, where you slide and stuff. . . . We started there and we ran all the way across the playground, all the way across the field, and I won. Carrying chairs on our back. And I was also racing against a boy. That just happened so to brag a lot.

Nikki was quite aware, however, that there are perceptions in the world that males are stronger than females, In the story, when Forever-Mountain arrives at the palace grounds to wrestle, all the other wrestlers are comparing weights and telling stories and are surprised that Forever-Mountain does not take part in the boasting. After reading the story, I asked Nikki if she thought Forever-Mountain had changed. She nodded her head and explained, "Well, 'cause I think that he used to see women as, um, sissies. And I thought that, well, I don't guess they really say it in the book, but I bet that those men are boasting, 'Well, if women played against me, I know I'd win.' Forever-Mountain, clearly, had learned his lesson about this matter.

At the end of Nikki's second telling of the story, Forever Mountain is "there and the girl's waiting for him and he's a farmer and uh, the wrestler and wife just live there and he wrestles with the grandma till she dies, every evening. While the women are getting stronger and he's still just the same."

Ann asked, "Do you think that's what happened?" and Nikki responded, very seriously, "Well, the women are stronger than *him*."

Nikki said that her favorite character in the story, and the character she would like to be like, was Maru-me, because she was "strong," adding that then "I could beat out Andrew in my class." At the final session, Nikki chose Maru-me as her favorite of all the characters in all the stories, "because she was strong, and, you know, she could help. It was plain to see she was obviously stronger than this really, really, *really* strong guy."

At 12, Nikki's overall favorite character was not Maru-me but Tatterhood. In contrast with her absolute confidence on the subject of the relative strength of males and females at 8, at 12 she was clearly struggling with conflicting narratives on the subject. In the discussion at the end of "Three Strong Women," Nikki commented, "I liked it a lot, but no woman is allowed to best . . . , to be that strong." Her use of "allowed" implies an understanding of socially constructed boundaries concerning women's manifestation of physical strength. Moments later, however, she reached for another reason, citing another "outside" narrative: "God made it so that women weren't that strong . . . that's like one of the ways he made us different." She seemed to be uncomfortable with this essentialist stance as well, however; later in the interview she qualified this view, saying, "Well, no, I do think that it's realistic that a woman could be a lot stronger than a man, but not that strong."

Not only is it unrealistic for a woman to be that strong, but, at 12, Nikki had come to understand there were other dimensions to the issue. When Ann asked Nikki why she thought the three women did not enter the wrestling match themselves, Nikki explained, "Because they're women and it's unfeminine to wrestle."

"Is it really unfeminine or do people just *think* it's unfeminine?" Ann asked.

"Well, there's a little wrestling move called chest-to-chest," Nikki explained. "Which would kind of hurt. See, one of my old teachers, he was a wrestler; he told us about all this. So it's kinda—it's just really unfeminine."

At the age of 12, Nikki had also expanded her concept of strength to include mental and moral power. Forever-Mountain did not boast in the presence of the other wrestlers, she explained, because "he knew better. Because he had had some good training and everything. You know, he, he had become strong in another way."

An ethic of caring: tensions between autonomy and responsibility

At both ages, Nikki's responses to the characters in the stories revealed a tendency to look beyond the centrality of the protagonist's interests to a concern for other characters. Among the qualities she noted and admired in the characters was their "helpfulness."

Gilligan (1982) writes of females seeing moral actions not in terms of "rights" but in terms of "responsibility," of a female "ethic of nurturance, responsibility, and care" (p. 159). According to Gilligan, girls gain maturity within the context of relationships and an ability to look outside oneself and consider the needs of others. Exerting one's power for solely selfish reasons is seen as uncaring and therefore immoral. Decisions are centered around both the self and the other. This moral sense Gilligan describes as an ethic of caring.

At eight years of age, Nikki was very much drawn to the characters who exhibited physical strength or personal agency. In describing each one, however, she added a layer to their character that went beyond sheer ability to act on the world; in each she also saw an ethic of caring, an ethic of responsibility, or an ability to see beyond one's own needs to consider and act on behalf of the needs of others. When Ann paused during the reading of "Tatterhood" at the point where Tatterhood and her sister start off on the ship to recover the sister's head, Ann asked Nikki what she thought. Nikki responded, "I think the one of the girls that's always riding her goat is more helpful than the one that's always wearing dresses." For Nikki, Tatterhood's independence and resistance to conventionality do not negate an ethic of caring. The passive sister, by implication, is less caring than Tatterhood—or perhaps less able to act on any "caring" she might feel. Her explanation of why Tatterhood "changed all her stuff" at the end of the story is also related to an ethic of caring in its inclusivity of others as well as of herself in making personal decisions.

At eight, Nikki inserted a detail into "The Twelve Huntsmen" that indicated an ethic of caring that extended to living things other than human beings. In the story, Katrine is said simply to like to go hunting with her father. In both her retellings, Nikki emphasized that Katrine went hunting, "but not to kill anything."

Much like Nikki, two of the eight-year-old girls in Anne Dyson's (*Writing Superheroes: Contemporary Childhood, Popular Culture, and Classroom Literacy*, 1997, 1998) research involving folk processes and popular culture also exhibited an ethic of caring when excluded from active roles in their classroom's Author's Theater activity. A popular facet of their second grade language arts curriculum, Author's Theater was a time when students could write and then direct stories that were dramatized by their classmates. However, when classroom scripts based on the cartoon superhero team the *X-men* became pervasive, roles for girls dwindled. As Dyson ("Folk processes and media cultures: reflections on popular for literacy educators", 1998) explains,

> The minimal number of female roles was a source of irritation for many girls, especially for Holly and Tina. These two girls saw their exclusion, not as a matter of individual affront ("you never let me play"), but as a matter of collective exclusion ("you never let girls play").
>
> (p. 55)

Rather than focus on their own experiences of injustice, the outspoken Holly and Tina deemed it appropriate to act as a voice for the other—perhaps less vocal—girls in their class as well. Implicit in both their behavior and outlook was an understanding of personal strength that had little to do with dominance and much more to do with inclusiveness and community protection. Reminiscent of Gilligan's (1990) ethic of care, the two second grade girls appeared to make decisions and exercise power based on the needs of both the self and the other.

Nikki's interpretation of personal strength was similar to that practiced by Holly and Tina (Dyson, 1998). Although Nikki was very much drawn to Maru-Me in "Three Strong Women" because of her physical strength, that was not the only quality she admired in her. At the last interview when Nikki was eight, she chose Maru-Me as her favorite of all the characters in all the stories, "because she was strong, and, you know, she could help. It was plain to see that she was obviously stronger than this really, really, *really* strong guy." Nikki did not interpret Maru-Me's superior strength as enabling her to dominate others but to "help."

At the age of 12, Nikki seemed to have extended this understanding of the use of one's physical strength to the change in Forever-Mountain. As she said, Forever-Mountain "had become strong in another way." From Nikki's point of view, Forever-Mountain had matured beyond the level of his peers in that he no longer deemed boasting—or attempts to demean his rivals—as necessary or appropriate. As Nikki explained, "It just wasn't right to him." Nikki seems to exemplify Gilligan's (1982) observations that, for females, exerting one's power for solely selfish reasons is seen as uncaring and therefore immoral; decisions are centered around both the self and the other.

Nikki's assessment of the prince in "Brier Rose" also linked a sense of personal power with a sense of caring or responsibility. In explaining why the prince was her favorite character in the story, Nikki explained, "He was braver than that guy who was trying to convince him not to go through. And he had a mind, to at least try to save the kingdom. When the other princes just gave up right when they got stuck."

This ethic of caring also seemed to extend to the less powerful or marginalized characters in the stories. At age 12, she was quick to point out that "it's always the prince's brother that's the best," but then realized, "If it was the prince's brother, then he would be a prince too." At this age, in hearing the story "Three Strong Women," she expressed dismay at the mother's excluding Forever-Mountain from household work. "The mother is like, 'No, you watch.' Give the guy a chance, Geez!"

The symbolic and practical significance of dress

Clothing clearly bore both symbolic and practical weight in Nikki's life. Tatterhood's tomboyish and unpretentious clothing and Katrine's donning of masculine attire strongly appealed to Nikki as an eight-year-old. But it was in her discussion of "Brier Rose" and other traditional tales that her understanding of the symbolic, gendered nature of clothing, and the restrictions inherent in feminine dress, were made clear.

Nikki was resistant to Brier Rose as much because of the kind of clothing she wore as for her personal qualities. When Ann asked Nikki if she would "like to be like Brier Rose," she responded, "No."

"No? Why?"

"I'd have to wear dresses."

Even at eight, Nikki had a sense of the political nature of gendered dress. In discussing what it would be like as a girl to live in a castle, Nikki pointed out that it would be "breaking the law to wear pants. 'Cause they didn't, we didn't have our rights yet. Then they could never wear pants. Not in public. They would have to wear those things where you have to pull real tight on their waists, so it looks like your waist is about this big around. But Laura Ingalls, she had to wear dresses a lot, and she got to do her running and playing. In the summer, because they only had to wear thin skirts. But when hoop skirts got in style, ch-ch-ch [gesturing to create a hoop skirt rising up in front of her], because it is always angling up. And she had to go" [pulls imaginary hoop skirt downwards].

The consequences of wearing such limiting clothing seemed to be linked in Nikki's mind to female vulnerability and helplessness. When Ann asked her, "Do you think—if the prince hadn't come—do you think that girls have to get rescued out of their problems by boys?"

"Yeah," Nikki replied. "Those kind of girls."

"Which kind?" I asked.

"Like prissy," she said, "and always have to have those glorying dresses."

"And those girls tend to have to be rescued?"

"Yeah."

"By boys?"

"Yeah."

"And what about you?"

"If I lived in a castle, then I would probably, you know, because how I am, I'd just probably have a dagger nearby."

Nikki clearly resists the trade-off Brownmiller (1984) has noted among females who, recognizing their powerlessness in the world, wish only to please, being loved and cared for in return. Nikki would not succumb to such helplessness. She could imagine herself wielding a dagger, but knew also that wearing pants, symbolic of power permitted only to males, would have been forbidden her. At 8, she was aware of such conflicting expectations and possibilities; at 12 she showed evidence of having had to deal with the subtleties and complexities involved in such a conflict.

As a 12-year-old, Nikki laughed when Ann reminded her of her childhood refusal to wear pink or purple, but when it came to ruffles she was still quite adamant. Her resistance was multilayered: "I still will not wear ruffles. I hate them; they're so gross. They're not elegant! They're just kind of frou-frou. A waste of material." Her initial resistance was expressed at the levels of taste and practicality, yet clothing had retained its symbolic significance. She went on to say, "Why do girls need to wear just a big thing of material around their waist? It doesn't make sense. It's uncomfortable. You can't run in them. I mean, it's just useless."

While still employing her foundational arguments, Nikki also incorporated a strategy of accommodation to strengthen her point. She said that she likes clothing that comes from stores such as the Gap, which are "for girls *and* for boys." Why? "It looks nice." Here Nikki seems to be borrowing from outside narratives (of looking "nice"), while not abandoning her own authentic voice.

At 12 years of age, when retelling the conclusion of "Tatterhood," Nikki refrained from general commentary on the transformation of Tatterhood's clothing, focusing on the transformation of the wooden spoon into a wand. "Why do you need a wand if you're a princess?" Nikki indignantly asked. "You don't need a wand!" Later, in expressing her disappointment at the magic at the end of the story, Nikki said, "Where did those magical powers come from? That was the good thing about her, that she wasn't like, you know, extraterrestrial." Clearly, for Nikki, Tatterhood was enough of a force in the world on her own strength not to need magical trappings, especially such superfluous female trappings as a magic wand. At 12, Nikki still felt a strong identity with Tatterhood. When Ann asked her if there were anybody in the story she would like to be like, she replied, "I'm already like Tatterhood. We're both very outgoing, sort of spunky, and we're not fake." And, she added, she and Tatterhood both dress like "dudes."

Conclusions

This is a study of one child's responses to four fairy tales and, as such, is not intended to be generalized to a larger population. Focusing on one child's responses, however, has allowed us to examine those responses much more closely than would be possible with a larger group of children and to consider particularly salient issues that those responses raise.

Nikki's responses to the stories challenge psychological theories about the appeal of fairy tales to young children, provide insight into developmental issues in response to traditional stories, raise significant questions about how young women negotiate cultural scripts, and underline a need for an expanded literary canon.

While there were consistencies across the ages in such matters as Nikki's strong identification with the character of Tatterhood, the tales themselves were "about" very different things at age 8 and at 12. At eight, Nikki was not struck by the romantic aspects of fairy tales, but saw them as tales of action and adventure. At 12, fairy tales were primarily stories about romance and marriage. Now she found Katrine's lack of interest in marriage before she met Wilhelm "unrealistic" and assumed that, at the end of her independent adventures, Tatterhood married the prince. At eight, Nikki expressed utter confidence and a joyful attitude about the equality—or superiority—of female physical prowess. By the time she was entering adolescence, her ideas of relative female-male strength revealed a struggle with various outside narratives that place physical prowess in the domain of males, not females: societal restrictions on arenas of female activity, notions of what is "feminine," religious teaching about the way God has created males and females to be. Regardless of their physical strength, and not in conflict with her ethic of caring, at both ages Nikki sought characters to identify with who *did* something, were effective, had agency in the world. The "feminist" fairy tales offered Nikki such female protagonists with whom to identify; in the patriarchal tale the only active, effective character was the prince. At 8, Nikki easily identified with him; at 12, perhaps increasingly influenced by gender expectations, she did not. Still resistant to the passivity of Brier Rose, she said she found no one in the story with whom to identify. As Lieberman ("'Some day my prince will come': female acculturation through the fairy tale", 1972) has pointed out, strong women appear in patriarchal tales, but if they are powerful, they are also physically ugly and evil. For a young child, the message becomes a very conflicted one: to identify with a strong female means, implicitly, identifying with someone who is ugly and evil. To identify with an active character who is also "good," one has to identify with a male, something increasingly proscribed as a girl matures.

Nikki's responses challenge dominant psychological theories about children's interest in fairy tales, notably those of Favat (1977) and Bettelheim (*The Uses of Enchantment: The Meaning and Importance of Fairy Tales*, 1977). Her moving beyond a credulous acceptance of the magical elements in the tales at 8 to a more cynical and ironic stance at 12 confirms, in part, Favat's claims, based on Piaget's developmental theory. Yet her responses also contradict his notion that a part of the unique fit between young children and fairy tales has to do with the egocentrism of the young child and the centrality of the protagonist in the fairy tale world. Bettelheim approaches children's interest in the tales from a Freudian perspective. According to Bettelheim, fairy tales are beneficial to children's psyches, regardless of age, in that they provide a central message that "if one . . . steadfastly meets unexpected and often unjust hardships, one masters all obstacles and at the end emerges victorious" (p. 8).

At neither stage did Nikki exhibit interest in the protagonist's dominance or "victory" for its own sake—to the contrary. At age eight she pointed out that the strong and capable characters she admired used their ability to help others, evidencing an expansion in concern beyond the centrality of the protagonist to the needs of other characters. At age 12 she described strength as including inner strength and sufficient self-confidence not to need to lord it over others. Her responses follow much more Gilligan's (1982) observation that girls gain maturity within the context of relationships. For many female adolescents, independence is linked to an ability to look outside oneself and consider the needs of others (p. 79). This was true in Nikki's case even at age eight. Integral to this type of moral and emotional maturity is the idea that exerting one's power for solely selfish reasons is uncaring, and therefore immoral. Decisions are centered around both the self and the other. From Nikki's perspective, in fact, boasting about one's one strength is not a sign of strength, but of weakness. And even at eight, her tomboyism did not extend to an appropriation of such "masculine" power in the world as an impulse toward killing animals. Indeed, an ethic of caring ran through her interviews at both stages of development. Both Favat and Bettelheim were limited in their insights by the patriarchal canon, of course—and, it appears, by a patriarchal mindset.

At age 12, Nikki still identified strongly with Tatterhood and was eager to explain Tatterhood's thoughts and emotions—with one exception. When Ann asked her why Tatterhood married the prince, Nikki ducked the question: "I don't know. Why don't you ask her?" As other comments suggest, Nikki, on the brink of adolescence, seemed to have observed that her culture's dominant scripts demand a great deal of accommodation from women, including the denial of one's own ability effectively to act on the world and a consequent reliance on others'—notably men's—greater power. Marriage has traditionally been one of women's means of achieving such security. Nikki's assumption that Tatterhood married the prince, along with her avoidance of a discussion of Tatterhood's motivation in doing so, suggests an emerging struggle between societal expectations and alternative life scripts that would allow her to face the world with her own independence and integrity intact.

At both ages Nikki was clearly trying to negotiate her way in a world whose prescriptions for gendered behavior conflicted with her own sense of herself and the roles she would choose in life. At 8 she was remarkably forthcoming and sophisticated about gender constraints, but at 12 had obviously noted "where and when women speak and when they are silent," a characteristic that Carol Gilligan ("Teaching Shakespeare's sister: notes from the underground of female adolescence", 1990) observed in 11- and 12-year-old girls "at the edge of adolescence" (p. 25). Moving past the authentic frankness of earlier years, according to Gilbert (1994), many young women become increasingly aware that their lived reality is not easily aligned with the "reality" that is propagated by dominant cultural scripts. Moreover, coming of age in a culture that has long equated maturity with separation from others, North American adolescent girls are put in a double bind since, as Stern ("Conceptions of separation and connection in female adolescents", 1989) and others have explained, they form their identities and even achieve independence within the context of relationships. Unable to achieve supposedly normative psychological maturity (from a Freudian perspective) or to meet accepted feminine social norms, many young women experience a crisis. Confronted by conflicting cultural and self-narratives, girls frequently "go underground" with their thoughts and feelings, which puts them at risk of losing honest relationships with themselves and with others. Brown and Gilligan explain that girls "begin not to know what they once knew, to forget the feelings and thoughts that they once knew, but which they then withdrew to protect" (*Meeting at the Crossroads*, p. 184).

Described as a turning point by Gilligan (1990), this crisis of conflicting life narratives can act in potentially positive ways in girls' lives. Although once forthright girls often become evasive, they also gain keen observational skills, which can equip them to construct their own ways of relating to the world—ways that often enable them to include others without excluding themselves. Authentic voices may then be heard above the din of dominant cultural scripts.

In her study of fifth graders' literature circles, Evans ("A closer look at literature discussion groups: the influence of gender on student response and discourse", 1998) noted girls withdrawing into silence and also suggests that such silence may be a positive thing; it can be interpreted as a form of resistance or as a short-term strategy for maintaining self-worth when girls' experiences do not align with what is culturally pervasive. Yet such silence also has its limits; as Evans says, "[W]e are inclined to agree with those who believe that ultimate silence will not prevent females (or any oppressed group) from being the objects of violence or oppression" (p. 112).

In the case of girls with such strong childhood voices as Nikki's, paying attention to how she negotiates such crises can provide valuable insight and understanding. At age eight, Nikki was remarkably astute about the political dimensions of gender roles and expectations. As a preadolescent more keenly aware of social boundaries, Nikki had learned to hide behind outside narratives, re-emerging with her own lived experiences, moments later altering her voice. Interwoven among all of Nikki's struggles with issues of physical strength, personal agency, the politics of clothing, and relating to others in the world, are an awareness of social boundaries and a struggle to construct a "connected" yet authentic life narrative.

Nikki, like many children, has experienced the "constant repetition and layering" of patterns of female helplessness and passivity to which Gilbert (1994) points. What role might literature play in helping children resist these patterns, in disrupting this layering, in offering alternative views of what makes Polly a "good girl" and Tommy a "good boy"? Certainly it is too much to expect literature alone to bear such a burden, but we can recognize that there are stories, such as the canonized patriarchal fairy tales, that contribute to such layering, reinforcing the notion that polarized gender roles are only natural and logical, ultimately drowning out or silencing the child's inner voice. Should children be "protected" from such stories? Given their ubiquity in the culture, that seems an unlikely—if not impossible—endeavor. But teachers can invite children to take a critical stance to patriarchal stories and the gender roles they prescribe. In the case of adolescent girls, Gilbert (1994) has pointed out that it is important to help them to "locate a space" from which they can critique and rewrite familiar but destructive cultural storylines. Although such critical reflection is not easily accomplished, it is evident that relationships with new and varied texts—both literary and living—can act as key avenues for promoting the spaces girls need to construct their own authentic life stories (Brown & Gilligan, 1992, p. 218; Taylor, *The Healing Power of Stories*, 1996, p. 96). As Gilbert (1994) suggests, it is through a "comparison and juxtaposition" of multiple texts—of conflicting storylines—that young women are offered the possibility of seeing culturally dominant scripts from new perspectives.

Complicating this vital task, however, are the common restrictions of the official school world. Patricia Enciso ("Good/bad girls read together: pre-adolescent girls' co-authorship of feminine subject positions during a shared reading event", 1998) reminds us that in many classrooms students are reluctant "to describe the worlds of reading that matter most to them" due to the fact that "power and social positions often determine who can and cannot speak about reading" (p. 46). For language arts teachers determined to resist and transcend limitations on students' development, it is clear that they must not only expand children's reading experiences beyond the patriarchal canon with its polarized gender roles, but they must also construct learning environments where it is safe for students to vicariously experience alternative ways of being in the world. Both Dyson (1998) and Brown and Gilligan (1992) cite teachers' power to create such an environment by modeling alternative storylines in their daily interactions and classroom instruction. In particular, Dyson (1998) emphasizes that it is teacher encouragement and support that can potentially awaken students to the knowledge that both as individuals and as communities, they have "the right to a different story" (p. 398). Drawing insight from Bakhtin (1981), she also notes that

> the social affiliations and divisions constructed, and revealed, by differentially shared stories can open up dialogic space for teachers and children. Within that space, the emerging official community—the classroom folk—can reflect on "given" stories, imagining other possibilities.
>
> (p. 393)

In such a community, it seems likely that young girls may continue to value their own inner voices rather than feeling that they must "go underground" with their objections and protests, losing their authentic voices, perhaps never to recover them. If the layering of patterns of female helplessness and passivity is to be disrupted through dialogic spaces that emerge from narrative, it would seem that stories such as "Tatterhood," "The Twelve Huntsmen," and "Three Strong Women" are appropriate places to begin.

References

Applebee, A., *A Child's Concept of Story: Ages Two to Seventeen*. Chicago: University of Chicago, 1978.

Auden, W. H., *Forewords and Afterwords*. New York: Random House, 1943.

Barchers, S. I., ed., *Wise Women: Folk and Fairy Tales from Around the World*. Englewood, CO: Libraries Unlimited, 1990.

Bettelheim, B., *The Uses of Enchantment: The Meaning and Importance of Fairy Tales*. New York: Vintage, 1997.

Bottigheimer, R. B., *Fairy Tales and Society: Illusion, Allusion, and Paradigm*. Philadelphia: University of Pennsylvania Press, 1986.

Brown, L. M., and Gilligan, C., *Meeting at the Crossroads*. Cambridge, MA: Harvard University Press, 1992.

Brownmiller, S., *Femininity*. New York: Fawcett Columbine, 1984.

Carter, A., ed., *The Old Wives Fairy Tale Book*. New York: Pantheon, 1990.

Chodorow, N. J., *Feminism and Psychodynamic Theory*. New Haven, CT: Yale University, 1989.

The Complete Fairy Tales of the Brothers Grimm, J. Zipes, trans. New York: Bantam, 1987.

Davies, B., *Frogs and Snails and Feminist Tales: Preschool Children and Gender*. Sydney, Australia: Allen & Unwin, 1989.

Dégh, L., "Oral folklore: folk narrative," in *The Study of Folklore*, A. Dundes, ed. Englewood Cliffs, NJ: Prentice-Hall, 1965.

Dégh, L., "Grimm's *Household Tales* and its place in the household: the social relevance of a controversial classic," *Western Folklore*, 1979, 38.2, 83–103.

Dyson, A. H., *Writing Superheroes: Contemporary Childhood, Popular Culture, and Classroom Literacy*. New York: Columbia University, Teachers College Press, 1997.

Dyson, A. H., "Folk processes and media creatures: reflections on popular culture for literacy educators," *The Reading Teacher*, 1998, 51(5), 392–402.

Enciso, P., "Good/bad girls read together: pre-adolescent girls', co-authorship of feminine subject positions during a shared reading event," *English Education*, February 1998, 30(1), 45–66.

Estes, C. P., *Women Who Run with the Wolves: Myths and Stories of the Wild Woman Archetype*. New York: Ballantine Books, 1192.

Evans, K. S., "A closer look at literature discussion groups: the influence of gender on student response and discourse," *The New Advocate*, 1996, 9(3), 183–196.

Favat, F. A., *Child and Tale: The Origins of Interest*. Urbana, IL: National Council of Teachers of English.

Gilbert, P., "'And they lived happily ever after': cultural storylines and the construction of gender," in *The Need for Story*, A. H. Dyson and C. Genishi, eds. Urbana, IL: National Council of Teachers of English, 1994.

Gilligan, C., *In a Different Voice*. Cambridge, MA: Harvard University Press, 1982.

Gilligan, C., "Teaching Shakespeare's sister: notes from the underground of female adolescence," *Making Connections: The Relational Worlds of Adolescent Girls at Emma Willard School*, C. Gilligan, N. P. Lyons, and T. J. Hammer, eds., pp. 6–29. Cambridge, MA: Harvard University Press, 1990.

Glaser, B. F. and A. L. Strauss, *The Discovery of Grounded Theory: Strategies for Qualitative Research*. New York: Aldine, 1967.

Goetz, J. P. and M. D. LeCompte, *Ethnography and Qualitative Design in Educational Research*. Orlando: Academic Press, 1984.

Jung, C. G., "The phenomenology of the spirit in fairytales," in *The Archetypes and the Collective Unconscious*, Vol. 9, Part 1, pp. 207–254. New York: Pantheon, 1959.

Lewis, C. S., *Of Other Worlds: Essays and Stories*. New York: Harcourt, Brace & World, 1966.

Lieberman, M. K., "'Some day my prince will come': Female acculturation through the fairy tale," *College English*, 1972, 34, 383–395.

A Little Pretty Pocket-Book, London: John Newbery, 1744.

Lurie, A., ed., *Clever Gretchen and Other Forgotten Tales*. New York: Crowell, 1980.

Minard, R., ed., *Womenfolk and Fairy Tales*. Boston: Houghton Mifflin, 1975.

Phelps, E. J., ed., "Tatterhood," in *Tatterhood and Other Tales*. Old Westbury, NY: The Feminist Press, 1978.

Phelps, E. J., ed., "Three strong women," in *Tatterhood and Other Tales*. Old Westbury, NY: The Feminist Press, 1978.

Phelps, E. J., ed., "The twelve huntsmen," in *The Maid of the North: Feminist Folk Tales from Around the World*. New York: Henry Holt, 1981.

Stern, L., "Conceptions of separation and connection in female adolescents," in *Making connections: The Relational Worlds of Adolescent Girls at Emma Willard School*, C. Gilligan, N. Lyons, and T. Hanmer eds., pp. 73–87. Cambridge, MA: Harvard University Press, 1989.

Stone, K., "Things Walt Disney never told us," *Journal of American Folklore*, 1975, 88, 42–49.

Stone, K., "*Marchen* to fairy tale: an unmagical transformation," *Western Folklore*, 1981, 40(3), 232–244.

Stone, K., "The misuses of enchantment: controversies on the significance of fairy tales," in *Women's Folklore, Women's Culture*, R. A. Jordan and S. K. Kalcik, eds., pp. 125–145. Philadelphia: University of Pennsylvania Press, 1985.

Taylor, D., *The Healing Power of Stories*. New York: Bantam Doubleday Dell Publishing Group, 1996.

Tolkien, J. R. R., *Tree and Leaf*. Boston: Houghton Mifflin, 1965.

Trousdale, A. M., "The telling of the tale: children's responses to fairy tales presented orally and through the medium of film." Unpublished doctoral dissertation, The University of Georgia, Athens, GA, 1987.

Trousdale, A. M., "Let the children tell us: the meanings of fairy tales for children," *The New Advocate*, 1989, 2(1), 37–48.

Trousdale, A. M., "I'd rather be normal: a young girl's responses to 'feminist' fairy tales," The New Advocate, 1995, 8(3), 167–181.

von Franz, M. L., *The Psychological Meaning of Redemption Motifs in Fairy Tales.* Toronto: Inner City, 1980.

Yolen, J., "America's Cinderella," in *Cinderella: A Folklore Casebook*, Alan Dundes, ed. New York: Wildman, 1982.

Zipes, J., *Fairy Tales and the Art of Subversion: The Classical Genre and Children and the Process of Civilization.* New York: Wildman, 1983.

Zipes, J., "Semantic shifts of power in folk and fairy tales," *The Advocate*, 1985, 4(3), 181–188.

Zipes, J., *Don't Bet on the Prince: Contemporary Feminist Fairy Tales in North America and England.* New York: Routledge, 1986.

Part 13

PUBLISHING AND TELEVISION

74

Extracts from NOTES ON THE CHILDREN'S BOOK TRADE: ALL IS NOT WELL IN TINSEL TOWN

John Goldthwaite

Source: *Harper's Magazine* (1977): 389–402.

When I was a little girl, I was satisfied with about six books. . . . I think that children now have too many.

—BEATRIX POTTER

No children's book publisher would dream of suggesting that he was in business for reasons other than to bring children what Walter de la Mare, the librarians' darling, called 'only the rarest kind of best'. With 80 per cent of the sales of the more than 2,000 titles published each year going to institutions staffed by the secular legions of the muse, allowing any motive less noble would be folly. A children's publisher, to succeed, must assume the guise of doing good deeds, and to do that he must keep the muse, old and toothless though she be, out front in a rocker, gumming platitudes. Some publishers and editors are not insincere about this. Excellent children's books do get published. On the other hand, the department must profit the house; each editor must earn his keep. That means marketing a whole heap of books that are less than good, and warehouses of books that are downright awful. Every trifle must be decked out as handsomely as possible, every author and illustrator made out to be God's gift to children. This requires a certain suspension of disbelief on the part of publisher and editor, and inevitably some insensibility will set in, until the publisher and the editor, and soon the librarians as well, can themselves no longer tell the difference between a work of art and a commodity.

Sales now assume their spurious legitimacy; the search for excellence is lost to the art of the hype. Librarians, be it noted, do not buy books in hand but promises out of catalogues and trade reviews that read like a cross between a card-catalogue entry and a publicity release. The publishers' easy optimism and librarians' frequent lapses of literary discretion, riding high on public moneys and the lack of resistance from most quarters, enable endless crates of stuff to be bought sight unseen. It is a nice piece of work for the many writers and illustrators who have come to this lucrative field from the only incidentally literate worlds of the kitchen and the commercial arts. Really, it is a nice piece of work for everyone, for there is much at stake beyond literature—careers, prizes, income, fame; and often, as one Caldecott Medal winner pointed out, paying the bills may call for the production of two and preferably four titles a year, every year, forever.

So the proliferation of pretty little books must continue unabated, and not only unabated but celebrated. A multi-billion-dollar industry knows no law but the momentum of its own survival. The prizes must come thick and fast, the muse be rocked more and more quickly. Sooner or later some enthusiast will conjure up an aesthetic that makes it all ring good and true. College courses will spring up coast to coast. The people at the paper mills will be happy, the printers, the binders, and jobbers will be happy. The entrepreneur who manufactures the little chairs kids sit in during story hours can add another snowmobile to the family fleet.

People with a vested interest in children's books suffer from feelings of cultural inferiority. They are also hungry for the prestige of yesteryear, when children's books were the Cinderella of literature. Accordingly, they are eager to promote the illusion that the present day is a second Golden Age, all aglitter with the glories of the picture book, and loud with the brave clatter of its mounted authors. To anyone not dazzled by the shine and show, the place may look suspiciously like tinsel town; but saying so can be a risky business. To point a finger is to get it lopped off. The replies awaiting those who would seek to rescue Cinderella from the ashes are prompt and humorless. If you don't like the books you see, snaps one voice, you haven't seen the right books. It is the illusion of people in the snug world of children's books that no one can read the 'right' books and not love them. They have been turning up in tinsel town since the mid-Twenties at the rate of a dozen or so to half a hundred each year. Only the laziest malcontent could fail to see it.

The child psychologist Bruno Bettelheim, an unlikely prince but one with his wits still intact, stuck up a finger recently in behalf of Cinderella, and, as was to be expected, they took a good whack at it. Dr Bettelheim's serious critical study of fairy tales, *The Uses of Enchantment*, is exactly the kind of book that you would expect children's authors, critics, and librarians to have written many times over. The truth is, what good essays we have on children's stories are the work of such gifted amateurs as J. R. R. Tolkien and C. S. Lewis, or of folklorists such as Iona and Peter Opie. They have come, in other words, from everywhere but inside the field of children's books itself, where the most popular form of disquisition seems to be the after-dinner speech. They ought to be a little embarrassed about this in tinsel town, but they are not. They are miffed. Not only has Dr Bettelheim bested them at their own game, he has had the temerity to suggest that in contrast to the fairy tales modern children's books are shallow and at cross-purposes with their didactic aims: 'Strictly realistic stories run counter to the child's inner experience . . . [and] inform without enriching.' Illustrated storybooks 'direct the child's imagination away from how he, on his own, would experience the story.' 'The trouble with some of what is considered "good children's literature" is that many of these stories peg the child's imagination to the level he has already reached on his own. Children like such a story, but benefit little from it beyond momentary pleasure.' And so on. A frightful man, this Freudian. *The Horn Book*, the most prestigious of all children's book journals, whose opinion of a book can make or break its library sales, gathers up her skirts and sniffs haughtily. Dr Bettelheim is a carper. Shame!

Dr Bettelheim might be dismayed to think that this is what his good work could come to, but he does not make his living writing for children and so can be excused for not caring less what *The Horn Book* thinks. A children's book author, on the other hand, has a much riskier time of it. Should he agree that modern children's books are shallow—and even dishonest—the people with the vested interests have his fortune and his personal honour squeezed tight in the notion that a children's author is by definition sweet and reasonable. Reasons for his lighting the fuse of disgust, reasons perhaps desperate and aesthetic and good enough for an incident or two of auto-catharsis on the adult circuit, will at the great seminar on children's literature only soil his reputation as a good person, worthy to write for children. In the second Golden Age of Children's Books Hans Christian Andersen, to survive, must come whistling down the lane a certified Danny Kaye.

Children's authors generally write in one of two ways, either to please children or to please themselves. The more numerous of them, those who write to please children, have traditionally been the purveyors of ephemera and dreck; those who write to please themselves have given us most of the best children's books we have, though they, too, have produced many sad and silly books of the sort penned by the old lady down the lane. The quality of literature is not threatened by the latter, the child is not deprived by them, but by the book consciously directed at the child and written presumably to his or her liking. This book, the 'Chopsticks' of children's literature and virtually the only tune we hear being played today, has been deplored by nearly every writer on the subject who is not in thrall to the industry; yet it is what most people have been led to assume a good children's book to be, and so it is precisely the sort of book—short of another

Babar or *Charlotte's Web*—that every editor is most eager to publish. Each new season brings an avalanche of such kiddie confetti, and the air right now is thick with it. In addition to the usual superfluity of ABCs, counting books, folk tales 'retold', holiday and Bicentennial specials, and other commercial artifacts, we have—many from notable authors out of the most reputable houses—such three-minute epics as *Oh, What a Busy Day! The Most Delicious Camping Trip Ever; A Special Birthday; A Wet Monday; Around Fred's Bed; Betsy and the Chicken Pox; Much Bigger Than Martin; Everett Anderson's Friend; My Teddy Bear; It's Not Fair! Two Is Company; A Little at a Time; I Love You, Mouse; I Like You; Like Me; I'll Tell on You; I'm Going to Run Away; I Wish I Was Sick, Too; and You Can't Catch Me.*

No less numerous than your local author's home movies are Casper the Friendly Ghost cartoons—*Monster Mary, Mischief Maker* and *Clyde Monster*, for example—and cat tales. Writers and illustrators with only a few cute tricks to turn on paper can always be counted on for funny monsters and cats; indeed, some respectable careers have been built on the low but universal appeal of funny monsters and cats and precious little else. Sifting through the latest batch of kitty litter, we find *Count the Cats, More Cats, Oh, No, Cat!, The Christmas Cat, The Convent Cat, The Post Office Cat, Kittens for Nothing, The Surprise Kitten, A Cat Called Amnesia*, and *Great Grandmother's Cat Tales.* Granny does rattle on these days. Who else but some venerable goodbody could be responsible for such geriatric titles as *Rupert Piper and the Dear, Dear Birds; Coo-My-Dove, My Dear*; or *Grandparents Around the World, Loving and Sharing?*

No more serious corruption of literature can be imagined than one which cheats children of their language even before they can read, and trivializes life before they have lived. Yet we are enjoying such an affluence of cultural frivolity that in the next few months librarians will, without blinking twice, spend tens of millions of tax dollars on these trifles. Call them educational toys, which many of them are, or pet rocks, which are more rewarding, or funny T-shirts with too much starch; but do not call them literature. *Pinocchio* is literature and so is *Babar. Peter Rabbit, The Wind in the Willows*, the *Jungle Books*, and the tales of the Brothers Grimm are literature. Take a good look at the next picture book your child brings home. Is it really any different in kind from the Saturday cartoons and Sunday funnies which children's-book people profess to despise? Or is it just an episode, when you come right down to it, from a TV family sit-com; a dramatization from a mother's field notes on the neighborhood kids; a case study from a child-training manual; a bit of toothless Aesop; or one more imitation of any children's book that ever showed a profit or won a prize? It is called 'children's literature', this bit of merchandise. It will probably win a prize. The author will move to Connecticut because 10,000 librarians said what the hell, and bought the thing. Children, because they cannot choose wisely for themselves, ought to be better served.

We have come to accept less and less and somehow the familiarity of it all comforts us. In a recently published fantasy the reward for saving the kingdom is not the kingdom but a roller skating party. Sad, paltry fare, but fully in accord with our lowered expectations. Like most of the rest of us, editors hope to reduce life to a series of small, manageable moments, and so they encourage authors to find their stories close to home, in the everyday, and publish whatever comes of it: timid little thoughts about snowflakes and shoes, lunch pails, snails, and sidewalks; inane fables about losing friends, making friends, being fat, hating war, holding hands. The clichés are old and tired and suspicious even to children: there's no place like home, a boy's best friend is his mother, one step at a time, arms are for hugging. These are not good thoughts for children to grow on; they are the sentiments of adults writing to pacify the next generation, not excite it; to make the world a safer place for people without curiosity, dreams, or bravery. Such books as *The Happy Day, The Snowy Day, So What If It's Raining!, I Love My Mother, I Like Old Clothes, A Tree Is Nice, Hold My Hand, That Makes Me Mad!, The Unfriendly Book, The Quarreling Book, Just Me*, and thousands of homey primers as like them as clothespins on the line do little but suggest to the child, if only subliminally, that he is so small, so afraid, and so blind that he cannot, as children have always done, discover the horrors and wonders of his backyard for himself, without some well-meaning, tedious grown-up playing tour guide. Apparently no one believes any more that tales told by the fireside ought to be about the big, dangerous, rewarding world outside the door. Anatole France once wrote that children 'find the writer who binds them in the contemplation of their own childhood a terrible bore,' but senior editors throughout the industry have for some forty years been operating on a contrary assumption. They have made this the age of the domestic children's book—until now our best writers, housebroken, suffer from daring too little.

Our best writers have been in thrall to the domestic sensibility too long, and they have had to bow to the primacy of illustration too long. In so doing they have all but forgotten how to do what writers are supposed to do, which is use language to animate the world. Our worst writers, trying to please children by writing about childish things, think they have been able to do this in their stead. Whether or not they actually do please children is of little concern. You can please a child by slipping on a banana peel; it proves nothing. What is of concern is that even in pleasing children they will have failed them utterly. Their books are bad because the world has been left out of them. So has an intuition about life that once informed all our greatest children's books and most of the lesser ones as well, an intuition unknown to children's writers content to busy themselves with the details and worries of childhood itself. It is indefinable but there is no mistaking it, once heard. It is as detectable in the slightest picture book as in the longest epic—a naive longing in the author's voice, an acceptance that one cannot embrace the world without fearing its kick, and at the same time a celebration of curiosity and bravery. This is behind every great children's book from the tales of the Brothers Grimm to *Pinocchio*, from the verses of Mother Goose and Edward Lear to Wanda Gag's *Millions of Cats* and Carl Sandburg's *Rootabaga Stories.* G. K. Chesterton caught its spirit when in praising fairy tales he wrote, 'Life is not only a pleasure but a kind of eccentric privilege.' That is the voice of the comic spirit talking, and it is a voice both missing and sorely missed.

How has so much that is bad for literature and children been allowed to eat away at what ought to be—whether high, humble, or vulgar in origin—at the very least honest work honestly arrived at? Failures of nerve and the imperatives of profit aside, much of the hanky-panky (tinkering with classics, the attendance on special-interest groups) can be attributed to ordinary lapses in taste and good sense. Much more can be laid to the work of nepotism, cronyism, and the energies of not a few people without modesty or shame, despite their public resemblance to your favorite aunt. Here, for example, can be lumped the published efforts of those ethically suspect pains in every honest writer's billfold, the editors themselves. Gone are the days when a senior editor, feeling the need for a particular book, commissioned an author to write it. Now, assuming neither her daughter nor best pal needs a shot of glory at the moment, she will write it herself, appropriating a top illustrator and a goodly slice of the ad budget to do herself justice. One senior editor did recently do the honorable thing, submitting her manuscript elsewhere under a pseudonym; but here is an ethical standard a world apart from the realities of the children's-book industry.

Naturally, no one who lives in such a cozy niche of literature would for a moment entertain the following modest proposals:

1. *The pink slip for every other children's editor who is a woman.* There are too many women in children's books, and far too many holding down editorial positions. This imbalance of male and female sensibilities might have been accepted in 1919, when Macmillan put together the world's first juvenile department, and, under the delusion that children's books belonged to the ladies, gave it over to one; but there is no excuse for it today. There is no evidence that women understand more than men what children need and want; and, even if there were, it would hardly affect the verdict on books given us by several generations of women editors who have proven that, whatever their good intentions, their standards are timid and commercial.

2. *The termination of the picture book.* Even with superior examples offered at prices that would allow for home use, one cannot avoid suspicions that what is told in a picture book is not worth a book for the telling, and that too many pictures, however good, may only divert the child away from any lasting encounter with his imagination. Worse, it is guilty of

absolving parents of having to read—really *read*—to their children. The idea that children can learn to read words by first learning to read pictures is so bizarre one wonders if the educators responsible for it have got their heads screwed on straight. No one, children least of all, can get the feel of a language from nothing, nor from a few sentences. They must hear the sounds of whole books. Language is more than pretty captions; it is the rhythms of action and ideas, of expectation and consequence. It is the ultimate music. To abandon the verbal at an early age is to abandon the child.

3. *The promotion of the storybook.* Not to be confused with the picture book, the storybook is longer, livelier, and usually more complex. Books in the tradition of *The Tale of Peter Rabbit, Millions of Cats, The Story of Babar*, and Maurice Sendak's *Higglety Pigglety Pop!* are, together with the children's novel (see below), the best hope for reaffirming Chesterton's eccentric privilege of life and for redeeming children's books from commercialism and banality.

4. *The termination of teen-age fiction.* No one has ever satisfactorily explained why there is or ought to be such a thing as teen-age fiction at all. In the case of science fiction and fantasy, for example, there is little being written for adults that could not be understood by any literate twelve-year-old. Conversely, some prizewinning fantasies for teen-agers have a turgidity of style the worst SF hack would be hard put to achieve. As for all that novelized stuff about alienation, drugs, and pregnancy, the great bulk of it might be more enjoyable presented in comic books. There are any number of very good underground cartoonists on the West Coast who need the money and might be willing to make something halfway real of such material.

5. *The rediscovery of the children's novel.* This is a form not much practiced by American writers, perhaps because of all books for children it is the hardest to do well, and perhaps too because by the time a writer has acquired the necessary skills he may be too corrupted or too dispirited either to make the attempt or to keep from botching the job. In this henpecked world, no one speaks the unspeakable: that, with the exception of Beatrix Potter, every great children's novel was written by a man, and nearly all of them by a man with little or no professional interest in children or their literature: Perrault, the Grimms, Andersen, Lear, Carroll, MacDonald, Stevenson, Twain, Collodi, Kipling, Grahame, Milne. (Carl Sandburg's *Rootabaga Stories* and more recent books by E. B. White, Tolkien, C. S. Lewis, and I. B. Singer seem to make it axiomatic that any remarkable children's book of this category will be the work of a gifted male 'amateur'.) It is instructive to note that while the Grimms, Andersen, Lear, and Carroll were doing their work, the ladies, self-appointed pros every one, were busy as bees edifying children with religious tracts and moral instructions. They have been at it ever since.

6. *The termination of the Newbery/Caldecott awards.* Each year for fifty-three and thirty-seven years respectively, the Newbery and Caldecott

Medals have been awarded by the American Library Association to 'the most distinguished contribution to American literature for children' and to 'the most distinguished American picture book.' That's ninety distinguished books in all, and a taste of dust in the mouth. The average N/C book is just another average book—often decently done, always terribly earnest, always ordinary. The best Newbery books, such as *The Slave Dancer*, by Paula Fox, glide along on good ideas that never wake up even the sympathetic reader. Most are haunted by the genteel ghost of that winner who announced she had never done anything to make her mother ashamed. Even less can be said for the prints and posters which have dominated the Caldecott awards for the past thirty years.

Everyone has a right to his style and his prize, of course. Were it not for the pernicious effects of the N/C awards, they would hardly matter. But mediocrity tends to gather glory these days, and everywhere the N/C books are set up as little idols of sensibility and style by teachers and librarians dedicated to the cultural uplift of kids who just might be on their way to some larger literacy than is encouraged by such books.

7. *The removal of writers, poets, and illustrators from the schools and libraries.* They mean to spur the imagination of the child, but all they do, I suspect, is make the world a little more banal. Artists cannot enter the classroom without the emphasis shifting, however subtly, from art to celebrity. I do not care, as a reader, and I do not think most children, unaided, care how or why or by whom a book is made. That they are asked to know as much as they are can only debase the mystery of what is in a particular book, and the mystery of all books as magical things.

8. *The termination of undergraduate college courses in children's literature.* These courses are doing literature and generations of children more harm than good by following the texts now standard in the field—chronologies, most of them, and appreciations of librarians, editors, booksellers, and other good souls who were legends in their time—the sort of uncritical histories in which nosegays are thrown Howard Pyle's mother for raising such a nice boy, and Margaret Wise Brown, author of *The Runaway Bunny*, is elevated to the rank of genius. Children's-book scholars can't help but write these clubhouse surveys, of course, because there is not a lot you can say about most children's books (they resist explication in a way adult literature does not), and because the usual scholar does not often have the perception to cut through the wisdoms that pass for critical thought in the enchanted world of children's literature. Elaborating for more than two minutes on, say, *The Wind in the Willows*, she will likely tell you that what she reveres about the book—what sets it apart for her as a work of literature and raises it to the level of the sublime—is the chapter 'The Piper at the Gates of Dawn', that intrusive prelude to Kahlil Gibran in which Rat and Mole hear the unearthly pipes of Pan and fall to their knees in teary reverence. C. S. Lewis was quite right that the child who has met the creatures of *The Wind*

in the Willows 'has ever afterwards, in its bones, a knowledge of humanity . . . which it could not get in any other way'; but the child encouraged to swallow the pseudo-classical pantheism of Grahame's piper runs the risk of growing up soft at the core and of wearing fads for a soul. Such rambles with the muse are nice for American college students, however, who seem at last to have found, in children's literature, the universal gut course.

9. *The hiring of a few fast guns; or, a good critic is hard to find.* Despite the high regard in which our several trade journals are held, professional reviewing of children's books in America is depressingly second rate. Only a handful of outsiders—Jean Stafford in *The New Yorker* for example, or the collectively disgruntled voice of the *New York Times*—have anything worthwhile to say on the subject, and they, because they operate sporadically and from without the field, can be discounted as having much effect on sales, let alone on the way we think about our children's books.

How we do, and at the same time, do not, think about our children's books, is best reflected by that infuriating form of benign neglect, the roundup review. In varying degrees the roundup rules the shape of each of the journals on whose brief opinions the fortunes of every new book must ride: *School Library Journal*, the American Library Association's *Booklist, Publishers Weekly, Kirkus Reviews*, and, to a lesser extent, *The Horn Book.* With a nice feel for democracy in action, a list of books for review is gotten up, a paragraph of a certain length is allotted to each book, and pretty near equal space is shown to all. Week after week, year after year, mountains of these paragraphs heap up, and few are willing to sort them out. The industry which knows no law but the momentum of its own survival rolls on like a great conveyor belt, and the journals have their pages full just maintaining a spot check on the titles.

In this way children's journals and reviewers inadvertently become what Eliot Fremont-Smith has called shills for the industry because, accepting not the performance but the *occasion* of each book as equal to that of all others, they allow themselves to be made into list-makers. No idea of quality is put forward; none is recalled and none demanded.

The visible results of such a leveling of literature will be evident to anyone who has ever come up against the fact of what retailers and librarians do and do not carry on their shelves as a consequence of the reviews they read. Among bookstores only a Scribner's or an Eeyore's in New York or a small-town gem like the Andover Bookstore in Massachusetts is likely to salt its stock with anything worthwhile. For the rest, relying heavily on *PW*'s roundups of winsome and commercial choices, it's the same old story: bad but noticeable books by name authors, didactic tracts, domestic candy, calendars, and the like. What is depressing is not that the stores carry such books, but that they carry them to the exclusion of too much else that is as good and better. A parent in an above-average store with a selection of perhaps 300 children's titles—say, one in a college town supplying a course in children's literature, to go to upstate New York for an example—ought reasonably to expect to find among the current crop of titles at least a few of the highest quality. What he will find, typically, is a fat sampling of the domestic dross mentioned earlier in this article. He will not find *Lizard Music* (Manus Pinkwater), *Moon Whales* (Ted Hughes/Leonard Baskin), *Nightmares* (Jack Prelutsky/Arnold Lobel), *The Red Swan* (John Bierhorst), or any number of other promising new books. He will find no books at all, from this or any other season, by Tove Jansson, William Steig, Natalie Babbitt, Nancy Elkholm Burkert, M. B. Goffstein, William Kurelek, Margot Zemach, Edward Gorey, or Uri Shulevitz. He will find one entire shelf devoted to the once-amusing and now repetitive books of James Marshall, and another to wordless picture books and miniature boxed sets. Wordless books—most of them idiot cartoons about sneezing, running, falling down—are a bastard genre, but they sell like bubble gum. Boxed sets derive from no compelling cause beyond the desire to be cute and make money. Having borrowed every one of Maurice Sendak's turns of style, the hacks must now rip off his *Nutshell Library* as well—in two instances without even doing him the courtesy of calling their junk by another name. But that's business.

Given half a chance, children will often choose to read, or be read, much humbler fare than the best we can offer them, and they will be moved in strange, unknowable ways by it. They will always want comic books, for example, which they love because comic books are theirs, not ours. Unless we can claim to know what we are doing—and I suspect when it comes to children none of us can—they may be better off with their own choices, insofar as their freedom to choose anything may kindle a love of reading. [. . .]

75

RAISING THE ISSUES

Michael Rosen

Source: *Signal* 76 (1995): 26–44.

I would like to begin with a story. About three years ago I was approached by an editor at one of the big publishing houses, I'll call them – let's say Berlusconi and let's call her Caroline. She had just been promoted to the job of what seemed like chief commissioning editor, a post that had been occupied for I think about a year by – let's call her Anne, who had replaced Josephine who had been there for some time. So Caroline said, what we would like, Mike, is for you to have a go at writing a book for our series (I'll give it a pseudonym) Sonics. They're really innovative. Each page has a flap that when you open reveals the secret thoughts of the people in the story. What do you think? I said yes, I did like the idea and I had seen some books in the series that I thought were very inventive and my step-daughter had actually turned from being a hesitant reluctant reader into an avid confident one using Sonics. She loved the flaps.

So I went away and had a go at writing a Sonic. I thought I had done quite a good job. Let's say it was a story about a cucumber that terrorized a supermarket. I sent it in but got the thumbs down, but this didn't matter too much because another publisher took it and now it's doing quite well even though the reviewer in the *Independent* said that it was 'crass' because children couldn't cope with the idea that the cucumber killed off some rather jolly carrots. A few months later I got another call from Caroline, who said that there was going to be a change with Sonics. They were going to start up Giant Sonics. These would be books that you could buy big or small so that teachers could buy them as shared-reading big books but children could buy small, and teachers would probably buy both, which would double the sales. Would I please, please, please have another go at writing one? I said yes, and came up this time with, let's say, a story about a child who is blind and becomes a rock star. Caroline came straight back to me with a yes. I had got it just right. She would be back to me soon with one or two changes and my book would be on the first list of Giant Sonics that were going to be launched in about a year's time. Before she did get back to me, I changed the ending that was kind of too predictable – number one hit, that sort of thing – so I put in a twist where the girl would have got a number one hit but she was let down by her band. Great, said Caroline, she was thinking it needed something like that.

Then there was silence for two or three months, then I heard that Caroline had left Berlusconi and was now chief editor at Rockefeller's – though actually the new company wasn't called Rockefeller's, it was called Bentley. Bentley was an old English nineteenth-century family firm that had been taken over first by Robert Maxwell, who sold it to the German company Axel Springer, who then sold it on to Rockefeller.

I then didn't hear about my Giant Sonic – it was called *Chart Attack* by the way – for three years. I wasn't that bothered because I had received half of my advance and anyway I was doing a lot of radio work and was heading for a big legal bust-up with another of my publishers, Ronson's. Ronson's had taken over Grodzinsky's who, in the two years before the take-over, had published four of my books. Since the take-over, Ronson's had dragged their feet on the four titles, neither selling them to a big paperback house like Puffin or Collins, nor publishing them themselves under the Ronson paperback imprint Acorn. The four books were dying. I was fed up, I felt undervalued. I started to think that maybe the four books weren't up to much anyway. Every time I wrote to the chief editor at Ronson's – Amanda – I either got no reply or some strange letter about how they really valued my work, but they were thinking of a strategy and maybe that book I wrote about Galileo's dog would fit into their new series called Format Fantasy. The other book, the one about Moses, was, she thought, absolutely brilliant and they were working on a way of repackaging it along with some other titles they had on great journeys. They were doing brilliantly with Format Nightmare and Format Dateline, but though, yes, the book I had done for teachers about children's storytelling had sold out in three years, it wasn't really for them and the picture book about a girl who wakes up each morning and finds that a bit more of her has disappeared actually needed reillustrating. Come in sometime, let's do lunch and we'll talk about it.

Then there was a mysterious little postscript that alluded to a problem that I thought had blown over. This was over the question of my book: *Tomorrow is a new banana.* This had sold for ten years and was still selling very well in paperback in the Daffodil imprint, a subsidiary of the massive Archer combine. When Ronson's bought up Grodzinsky's they said they wanted to get back the paperback rights of *Tomorrow is a new banana* from Daffodils and print it themselves under their paperback imprint: Jollywelly. I had said no, because I might as well stick with Daffodils because they had great distribution, did lots of publicity, had a high profile, did posters and paid my expenses on trips and I liked the people there. Amanda's mysterious little postscript said that there had been a little question mark over my loyalty to Ronson's ever since I had said they couldn't put out *Tomorrow is a new banana* as a Jollywelly.

Three years from the time I wrote the Giant Sonic I got a phone call from Lucy, the new editor at Berlusconi, who said that the page proofs were ready for *Chart Attack.* Would I like to see them? I didn't call back because I thought she would send them anyway, but for several days Lucy rang leaving a message so in the end I called back and said, sure send them, I would love to see them and Lucy said, great but they were really pressed for time on this one, we had to do a turnaround on it of one weekend because a whole week had gone by when I hadn't got back to her. Fine, I said, so the page proofs arrived and actually it was a kind of mock-up of the finished Giant Sonic and at first I thought this was brilliant, I loved the pictures, I had completely forgotten the story, so it was like reading someone else's book. I showed it to my step-daughter, who said that this wasn't the story she remembered. She remembered that the blind girl didn't get to number one with her song but in this version she did. And then weren't there a whole set of gags about the blind girl 'seeing' (geddit?) what was going on in the pop business while people all around her were talking about how marvellous it was that she was doing so well given that she couldn't see what was going on. All these gags had gone. Then it suddenly came back to me that this was the old version of the story, not the corrected version. I thought where in heaven's name *is* the corrected version? I know, on the old computer disk of the Amstrad which we don't use anymore since we became plutocrats and bought an Apple.

So we unearthed the Amstrad, wound it up, got out the story and on the Monday arranged to see Lucy a.s.a.p. to discuss *Chart Attack.* She said she had never seen a version of the story where the girl doesn't get to number one with her song, she just picked up the manuscript that was on file when Caroline left and worked with that. So I rushed over to Berlusconi and managed to shunt a few things round, put in some of the changes I had made three years before, get back in one of the fourteen gags I had written and hopefully the artist wouldn't get too pee-ed off about this, do some more work and just as planned *Chart Attack* would be in the launch of Giant Sonics next year.

Meanwhile the row with Ronson's rumbled on. I didn't do lunch because there didn't actually seem to be anything to talk about but I had rung to get some copies of an old title of mine: *Up Your Nose, Mr Prune.* Four weeks went by and I didn't receive them, so I rang again and waited two months and still didn't receive them. Melissa in publicity at Ronson's rang to see if I would do a signing in Waterstone's in Orpington. I said rather churlishly that there was no point in my spending a couple of hours getting to Orpington, sitting in a bookshop with four people coming to see me, two of whom thought I was Roger McGough and two of whom told me that they had rather hoped that I would be with Quentin Blake. I much preferred doing visits to schools who wanted me to come where I would talk to four hundred children, meet teachers, do a parents-and-teachers' session in the evening for another two hundred, sell two hundred books and come home with two hundred quid or more fees. Melissa sounded rather cheesed off about this, because Waterstone's were very keen. I said Waterstone's were keen because it made the manager look good when he or she reported back to central office but it was busywork and it didn't benefit me, Waterstone's, or sales of the books but of course it also looked good to Melissa's boss at Ronson's because at the publicity meeting she could say she had arranged for Michael Rosen to visit Waterstone's in Orpington and this would look like things were moving. When in fact they weren't. I said if she had money in a publicity budget to spend on authors or me in particular then she could subsidize my visits to Canada, Australia and the States that neither Ronson's nor Grodzinsky's before them had ever come up with any dough for. This didn't go down too well, and then I said, oh yes, and where are the copies of *Up Your Nose, Mr Prune*? Ah, yes, Mike, she said, I'm awfully sorry about this, Mike, I meant to get in touch with you about this but what with summer and things it must have slipped my mind but it's out of print.

So I banged out a fax to Amanda, chief editor at Ronson's, saying that this was news to me that *Up Your Nose, Mr Prune* was out of print, couldn't I have been told? Doesn't it say on the contract that I should have been told? If it is out of print, doesn't this mean that it must have sold quite well, so shouldn't it be reprinted? Amanda sent me a curt little fax back saying it was news to her that it was out of print but just because it sold out in three years in hardback and trade paperback didn't mean that it had sold well and was worth reprinting. That was six months ago and I haven't heard from Ronson's since then. The Giant Sonic is in production and should, repeat should, be in my mitts in about six to nine months' time. There my story ends.

This talk is called 'Raising the Issues' and my first intention in preparing for it was to do what I often do which is to try and take some kind of overview of what's going on. Where are we as a community of writers, editors, readers, publishers, teachers and children? What are the problems? What are we getting right? What are we getting wrong? But the more I thought about the overview, the more my specific situation kept popping up and hitting me on the head. Go away, I kept saying, I'm thinking about my IBBY talk, the politics of children's literature – stop bothering me with all your moaning about Berlusconi and Ronson. Then, of course, it dawned on me: it was trying to tell me something. My specific situation was the place to start in talking about the politics of children's literature.

When talking about children's literature it's useful to see it not as one simple kind of cultural practice but rather as a human activity that plays a part in a range of different institutions. So, rather than seeing children's literature as a discipline unto itself, we should see it within other disciplines, other practices. Other institutions? Which ones?

Clearly, children's literature is part of the book trade and the book trade is part of the media and communications business, which is in turn part of world capitalism. Children's literature is perhaps also part of what the French Marxist, manic depressive and homicide Louis Althusser called the Ideological State Apparatuses. That is to say, we live in a society which not only makes sure we do as we are told with police, secret police and the army but also tries to ensure our behaviour follows certain lines through the institutions of the law, education, the mental health provision, and the media and information industry. So in some respects children's literature is part of what everyone now calls popular culture. Or at least some of children's literature is.

But children's literature is also part of what anthropologists would call nurturing practices, which involves firstly the home unit and, in an advanced society, education. On closer examination this means that children's literature not only plays a part in how we bring up children but also in how we view children, how we try to construct notions of them.

If children's literature is a player in these practices, what philosophers call the subject, it is also in other spheres the object, that which is looked at and dealt with. This way children's literature can be seen to be part of the institution of Literature (with a big L), a community of academics, informed readers, journals, broadcasts, reviews, university courses that ascribe status and value to certain kinds of books and not to others. But then it can also be the object in the institution of child psychology, a human activity that sometimes tries to understand children. An argument can be pursued here that if somebody like D. W. Winnicott understood children and we understand Winnicott then maybe using our knowledge we can understand better what children's literature is about and/or what children make of it.

Seeing children's literature in each of these different ways – sometimes as subject, sometimes as object – might shed some light on what actually is going on at the moment. Now let's return to my story. I told it partly because I am in a highly niggled state but partly because it is very easy when talking about literature to treat it as some kind of spiritual intercourse, a circulation of pure ideas, detached from the circulation of things, detached from considerations of how we organize ourselves to make sure we can eat, stay warm and enjoy and use all the goods and services in our lives. The discussion of literature often goes on in such a way that we can talk about such things as imagery, structure, identity, character and the like in ways that don't have to relate to such things as, say, the latest technological advances or the funding of the welfare state. My story is a crude and vulgar example of one of the ways in which writing literature in 1994 is to inevitably take part in capitalism.

That is to say, anyone who works in the publishing industry, no matter what their beliefs and aspirations, has to obey the conditions that prevail. As you can imagine, I'm not someone who thinks that these are conditions that must and will always prevail but simply that each material concrete act within publishing, whether it be signing a contract, turning over a printing press, or selling a book, is a part of a world economic system. Every book we read, every line I or any other author writes, or picture that an artist makes, is affected by the prevailing conditions within that system. Let's tease some of this out of my story.

Why in the story am I writing a Sonic and then a Giant Sonic? Not simply because someone has had a good idea but because it is possible to cut down on production costs if you can produce series and if – I left this bit out of the story – if you can co-produce your series with another publishing house. Whole chunks of the story I had wanted to write wouldn't fit the format of the Giant Sonic so even though I thought they worked and my step-daughter thought they worked, it didn't fit the commercial reality.

Then there was the whole business of the lost manuscript, which could easily have meant, given the quick turnaround, that completely the wrong story would have been published. How did that come about? Well, that was because publishing houses are no different from any other capitalist enterprise: they hire, they fire, they take over, they are taken over. Editors are what industrialists used to call in less mystificatory days 'hands'. This means that one day they might be there and the next they might be gone, either because the editor thought that she could get a better deal somewhere else or because she was sacked. Meanwhile, quite curiously people in these companies talked the language of feudalism and talked about loyalty.

So where does new, quirky, unorthodox writing fit in here? Quite clearly, if you are within the big combines it is becoming more and more difficult to produce one-off books that may start out life intended for what might be called 'a local market'. Notice I said, 'within the big combines'. Obviously, the big combines are not the sole players in the publishing game. With new technology it is now possible for very small units to produce children's books. This means that in theory community groups, minority-language groups, pressure groups of any complexion and persuasion could get together enough money to produce a children's book and break even on a sale of anything over five hundred copies.

So I think there are two processes going on here: in jargon terms: globalization and localization. Globalization is hot and strong, it's Disney, it's the international company, it's the we-must-sell twenty thou or forget it. It means return on investment must show within a year or clear the book off the warehouse shelf, it's taking up space and space costs money. It means more and more titles because any book stands a better chance of selling more in its first year than in any other year of its life, so ideally a publishing house should be a place that is selling hundreds of titles for one year. It is no strange artistic or economic mystery why seven thousand children's books a year are being produced in the U.K. That's not something creative, critical people can alter by being pious and analytic about. It is the inexorable anarchy of capitalism that is insisting: more titles, more authors, quick quick, write write, no time to edit, no time to rewrite, get it out, sell it, drop it, pulp it. Publishing children's books is moving more and more towards the structure of publishing magazines.

The impulse to localize is cool and weak. Very clever idealistic people are trying to set up outfits that are attempting commitment to a principle – bilingual books, for example, or multicultural books. They can't always pay authors and illustrators enough money to live off, they can't compete with the big geezers in distribution and publicity, so the buyers and readers find it difficult to get hold of the books or, to put it another way, they don't actually hear of them.

Judging by today's programme, I would guess that this room is full of people who want to see books that represent minority views, dissenting views, that challenge the obvious, status-quo type ideas, that pose all kinds of questions about the way human beings treat the environment, the way they abuse each other, exploit and oppress each other, the way they ignore and exclude each other, the way some human beings can gain immense power and dominate others. If I am right that you are that kind of audience – and I count myself as one of you – then what I have said so far represents a challenge to us. When we enter the institution of the big combine we go into a place with an agenda that is not immediately apparent. People talk as if they are dealing purely and simply with ideas, plots, characters, jokes. But there is also an agenda of will this co-produce with America? Germany? Spain? Will it fit into a low-budget series? Will it sell out in a year? Or have you got a name like Duchess of Rutland or Frank Sinatra which would mean that any story, literally any story at all would be marketable? If we enter the institution of the small independent, a whole set of ideological requirements might be met but the outcome could well be that the book doesn't always, or even often, reach the very children that you most wanted it to reach. Of course, this is not to say that the effort isn't worth it. Precisely the opposite. It is something we all have to fight for.

Now what I have said so far may strike you as very crude, very unsubtle. Cultural production under capitalism isn't simply the production of uniform ideas: it is only partly a matter of producing mainstream conformist ideas, but what also takes place is that people contest these ideas whether they are writers, illustrators or maverick editors. And, with just as much power, readers find themselves in contexts that contest what is given them and demand change. How does this happen?

I spoke earlier of Althusser's notion of Ideological State Apparatuses and anthropology's nurturing practices. Children's literature finds itself in families and schools. It enters relationships that are already there where it is expected to do all kinds of jobs. This is a very complex area. In families, children's books are sometimes part of how adults and children physically make contact with each other: on laps. They are sometimes part of how adults and children talk to each other about how they talk to each other: you're like Goggle-eyes, a child might say to a step-father. They might be part of how a child carves out a world for herself slightly removed from the hurly-burly of downstairs or the kitchen, in the quieter places of bed-rooms and toilets. But families, we might say, are themselves part of where identities are forged, and in economic terms, where the new generation of workers, supervisors, managers, salespeople and owners is produced.

Children's books enter this process too, which means that when they appear to question dearly held notions of order they go to the very heart of what many parents think it is their duty to be doing: reproducing the next generation of people like themselves. Or to put it another way, it is very much easier and profitable if we produce books that affirm the ideas that conform to the ideal family, where families are shown in the end to be comforting, reassuring places, where when wolves eat small red-cloaked girls, big strong men come along and cut open wolves, release small helpless girls and get rid of big bad wolves. It is easier and more profitable if we produce books that suggest that the world is an unchangeable sort of place, that attempts by ordinary, nonruling human beings to change their conditions are futile, pointless or inevitably unsuccessful, che sera sera, inshallah, Allah, Fate or God wills it.

Once again, this is simplistic. The family, like every other institution, is contested. Why else would the government have spent so much time and effort telling us how necessary it is to have a nuclear family, when everywhere around them and amongst them, people are busting it apart? So children's books do not enter a monolithic, uniform family. They enter a contested, fought-over place. Children find themselves within many kinds of ways of being at home. Some, perhaps many of these children face the fact that their way of life is not legitimized, not given status. They are invisibilized within the media machine. In spite of what the anti-PC chorus says, it is not the case that most children's books are about so-called split and dysfunctional families. In fact most of the main, powerful, mass-selling images for children affirm, normalize or yearn for resolutions in nuclear reunions. *The Lion King* manages not only to do this but to do it within a plot that suggests that a whole civilization rests on the survival of one key patriarch. In situations like that it's hard to see that mothers, daughters (or if you prefer lionesses who know how to hunt and kill and provide) have any use at all.

But I have cause for optimism here. You may remember in *King Lear* Gloucester sees that he is living in a time of enormous change: '. . . nature finds itself scourged by the sequent effects. Love cools, friendship falls off, brothers divide. In cities, mutinies; in countries, discord; in palaces, treason;

and the bond cracked 'twixt son and father.' He goes on, '. . . there's father against child. We have seen the best of our time: machinations, hollowness, treachery, and all ruinous disorders, follow us disquietly to our graves.'

Gloucester blames it all on the late eclipses of the sun and moon but Edmund, who is both rational and evil, despises this fatalistic view and mocks it. Whatever else is going on here, it is clear that there is some kind of contest in which two or more views are being aired about the way in which society is rocked from top to bottom with upsets in the way people relate to each other. The Elizabethan period was indeed the beginning of an acceleration of social change that would lead to the rise of the merchant and then manufacturing class. The old certainties of how people related to each other were being rent asunder by the relationships required when people treat each other as buyers and sellers of goods and skills and not only or simply as friends, lovers, parents and the like.

I would argue that we are living in a similar time of crisis. We are taking part in a long process in which the ability of the capitalist system to provide for all our wants and needs is day by day becoming less certain, less possible. In these circumstances, the ways in which we relate to each other are rent asunder. This causes many people, including children of course, great pain, but you will also remember that Edmund says 'Stand up for bastards'. At the very moment in which these old relationships fall apart, new ones emerge. If most women want a paid job outside the home and men don't leap into the home to fill the space, then we shall collectively have to come up with other ways to nurture children. When I said children's literature enters the family, this is the situation it enters.

Raymond Williams ascribed three movements to culture: dominant, emergent and residual. At any given moment we are confronted with combinations of these three forces: dominant culture telling us to conform to the norms of society, residual culture reflecting and expressing nostalgias and past structures, and emergent culture expressing new ideas, new hopes, new feelings that may or may not become the dominant culture of the future. One of the things that an active, lively children's literature can do is show these three forces at work; another thing it can do is avoid sentimentality by harking back to the residual, or it can avoid doing our masters' job for them by expressing the dominant, or again it can help voice the emergent, and show us glimpses of what is possible for human beings to do when they are not dominated by ideas of fate and the unchangeability or the incomprehensibility of society, technology, machines or the human condition in general.

This also applies in the other key area where children's literature finds itself: education. Now here is a delightful paradox that further complicates my simplistic picture of children's literature within capitalism. The circulation of children's books does not purely and simply depend on the free actions of the market. What we call the market – the place where books are bought – is affected by certain massive forces that are not directly controlled by the individual's whims, needs and tastes. Education in this country is a complex institution of central ideological control, relatively autonomous academic expertise, hired managers in the form of inspectors, and the mass of teachers who still have quite a large degree of workplace control. We have seen ten years of bitter struggle over this very situation: just how much autonomy – or, if you prefer, ideological autonomy – can be left to the low-paid, highly unionized, nonconforming mass of classroom teachers? Children come into schools in large collective portions and are divided up on an age-ranked basis where they learn many things apart from what is known as the curriculum: they learn what they imagine are their limitations and their due roles in life. But their lives in schools are beset with contradictions: the most striking of which is that at the very moment schooling teaches that each child must act as a striving individual who must do better than his or her friend, outpoint someone else, children are brought *together* in all kinds of collective enterprises, one of which is to face what often seems like a totally arbitrary discipline system that is outside of their control.

I think children's literature is affected in all kinds of ways by this picture of education. There is on the one hand a great pull for it to do the job the controllers of education want it to do: like produce simplified, dull texts that will teach the process of reading as a function not as an interactive, imaginative act. Like follow a canon of repute that will help cement ideas of taste to ideas of class: the good book just happens to coincide with the book that reflects and celebrates middle-class life and aspirations and Raymond Williams's residual culture of heritage, nation, and phony unreal ideas of a past rural peace. On the other hand, as it becomes necessary to educate more children for longer in more complex processes in order that the wheels of industry, commerce and service can function, so there is a need to make a wider range of children interested, literate and biddable within schools. Where in the 1930s and 1950s millions of children could effectively be by-passed after the age of eleven, now it can't be done. So teachers find themselves face to face with the children and grandchildren of people who didn't receive much education. Relevant texts have to be found.

For the last thirty years, teachers have been demanding books that will hold the attention of all their children, not just the white middle-class ones. They have cried out for images, themes, language and ideas that originate outside of southern English leafy suburbs, or the world of shopkeepers, managers, and artists. And because teachers tend more and more towards a nonconforming section of society – if only now because they have been on the receiving end of some of the most fanatical, unpleasant and irrational government activity – they have provided a huge upswell of desire for nonconforming, nonstable texts. And here's the rub: teachers affect that hallowed site of capitalism: the market. They talk to each other, they go on courses, they attend conferences, they circulate journals, they do MAs and diplomas, they question the nature of language. They do not simply buy the most conformist texts. They hunt out the local, the regional, the minority, the dissenting, the unorthodox. So that enemy of the market, the state, through its institution of education – which by rights should be doing the job of turning out unquestioning round pegs for round holes and square pegs for square holes – defies the rules and in so doing affects the market.

Whatever else happens, we must support each other in the process of making knowledge ourselves: having conferences, producing magazines, circulating ideas. Many kinds of authors, not least non-white ones, but also ones that are difficult, or awkward, or puzzling have been sustained by the fact that teachers have asked for and used such texts.

It is possible to paint a much more pessimistic picture. The ten-year assault on teachers' autonomy has had its effects: not least in the form of financial cuts. But also in the ludicrous attempts to overload the curriculum with useful knowledge and to stipulate what should be read and when. I will pause here to congratulate myself and anyone else in the room who fought to remove the lists of prescribed authors from the national curriculum: something won this week for key stages 1 and 2 at any rate. Teachers, parents and children can be trusted after all. Amazing. People remember Mr Gradgrind from Dickens's *Hard Times* as someone who kept demanding that children learn and only learn facts. But he had another tenet as well. 'Never wonder.' Dickens shows this to be an idiotic and self-defeating axiom, and so it has come to many of us watching the government's antics in education that they appeared to be following the same line of thought: as the overloaded primary curriculum forced literature into humanities as a tool of history, science, geography or whatever, I could hear Gradgrind nodding in support: never wonder. But of course it is just as self-defeating for those in power because though ideologically they yearn for ordered, conforming children chanting times tables (and as I saw in a school recently: a noun is a naming word, a noun is a naming word, a noun is a naming word – that's what I learnt in school today). They also know that their allies, the captains of industry and commerce, are crying out at them saying: give us flexible workers, give us people who one day can work a VDU and tomorrow can work in a planning team. We need creative, technologically literate people by the million or we won't be able to compete.

This poses one of the major problems both for education and for the future of the book. The key battle for the next twenty years in education is not where Ron Dearing says it is, over whether children can do mental arithmetic or know what these linguistically ignorant people keep calling 'grammar'. It turns on: who has access to state-of-the-art information technology? Or, in children's terms, who gets the time to play with the latest, most advanced computers? Who gets the chance to use computers to solve problems, create new possibilities and entertain us in the most interesting and exciting ways? Well, it ain't the not very well-off kids in local authority-controlled state schools. It's children who come from well-off homes and/or kids who go to city technology colleges and private schools. Coming as we do from the world of children's literature, this puts us into a difficult position.

Firstly, to be anti-computer is just another kind of philistinism but if it is differentially available, when and as we provide and work with CD-ROMs and whatever else the future holds, we enter once again a world of haves and have-nots or at least have-lesses. If tomorrow I were to devise a poetry CD-ROM I will have to face the contradiction that, egalitarian and socialist that I am, it will be used and consumed for the most part only by those with the money to get it. Books at this moment, under present conditions, are more democratically available. What will this mean for the immediate and long-term future? In the immediate (and it's already happening) working-class children are only getting hold of the most basic, least sophisticated of computerized entertainment: Nintendo and the like. This means they are getting little or no chance to use the new technology to make or receive the most inventive, creative and useful products available. I foresee that we will have to be shouting about this from the rooftops and exposing all the talk about mental arithmetic and grammar as a smokescreen for what is the real carve-up. In the long term I can see that there might be a time when the book is a kind of poor child's substitute for what is the really exciting medium of the day. On the other hand it might work like the automatic camera and the camcorder before it, that a massive democratization of media will take place in which the old distinctions of producer and consumer go on being broken down.

Once again, thinking of Gloucester in *King Lear*, these are strange and disruptive times. The kind of person who today calls herself a children's author might well be doing something very different in twenty years' time. It is probably well within the abilities of everyone in the room here to devise some kind of interactive narrative game incorporating old texts, coming up with new ones, which if you had the means here in this room now, to amalgamate video, cartoon and sound, you could knock up fairly quickly.

The point is we don't. The point is that such a high level of technology is capital intensive. Just as it takes a team as powerful as the one that sat in the desert in 1943 making the atom bomb to make *Bambi* or *The Lion King*, so it takes one helluva whack to turn out CD-ROMs. Just as it seemed as though children, teachers and parents could produce books, tapes and films and so demystify the grandness and awesomeness of such media, along comes another one that is just beyond the ordinary person's grasp. Or will it be?

In my sketch earlier, I mentioned that children's literature is not only the subject – that is, the participator in processes of trade, family and school – but also the object of Literature and psychology. I also mentioned that as a subject it participates in the process of the construction of the child.

Society as a whole through the media and politicians' utterances frequently uses children and childhood in order to say something about all of us. So children are largely seen in the media by both right wing and liberal as victims. The right use the image of child victim as evidence for the innate beastliness of criminals who need to be disposed of in sanitary ways. The left use the image of child victim as evidence of the innate beastliness of our rulers, who have allowed children to be poor, illiterate, or abused. It's a dangerous game to play because the people singled out for passivity and feebleness – quite apart from whether it is true or not – seem to become vulnerable to those people who need to express their own fear of feebleness by beating up someone else.

Children's literature is a marvellous institution if for no other reason than that, in general, by taking children's desires and abilities seriously, it tends to defy dominant notions of children's supposedly innate feebleness and vulnerability. Nearly everyone I ever meet in the world of children's literature holds firm to one idea above all others: children are active, creative, imaginative people who can, if they want, do almost anything. In some ways this is an idealized utopian notion but a crucial and central one to the spirit of literature – that is, to hold the mirage of other possibilities, beyond the mundane, beyond the limitations of what powerful people say and imply are inevitable. From Gretel to Alice, yes even Blyton's Famous Five, to children in the books of Anne Fine, Robert Westall, Gillian Cross, Nina Bawden, including Dennis the Menace, children's literature's children again and again defy society's stereotypes of them. Then again, the complexities of many children's books, the use of in-group knowledge as with somebody like Jon Sczieska, can imply a notion of the child as someone who can do things, imagine things, who has resources, who has knowledge and culture and is not in the image of the victim of the national curriculum, someone who will simply start out schooling as an empty cultureless shell, waiting to be filled up with useful, canonical knowledge, as stipulated by clever people behind closed doors.

Of course some books imply a more active and more creative child than others, some books show images of more active and more creative children than others. Sometimes such children become so active and capable they become Superchild and such a fantasy that we might wonder whether it merely confirms the feelings of ordinariness in the reading child. Perhaps so, perhaps not: we don't know what fantasy does for people. Or to put it another way, we don't know what fantasy does for people in new situations. Those of us in the room who are anxious for children's literature to be alive and creative are, by implication at the very least, keen that we can support notions of children as active, creative, capable people, as able as Gretel to overcome problems, or as able as the reader of *Rosie's Walk* to figure that that fox is in big trouble, Rosie is darned lucky and some kind of joke is going on here and whoever reads this thing out loud to you never tells you the whole story – a story you yourself can tell even if no one else manages it. Such pictures, such processes we must cherish and build on. No matter what

I say, we will, and I find myself often thinking that no matter what images of ideological conservatism I might find in many children's books, no matter how much I might be irritated by, say, the beginning of *The Iron Man* where we are told that the origins of this technological titan are unknown, no matter how much I lament that this turns the technological into the mythic dominator of humankind when in reality it is the servant of dominating humans, I can still comfort myself that Ted Hughes knew he had to find a capable child to solve the problem of the story and he knew he wanted to keep his audience gripped and fascinated not only with what would happen next but also by extraordinary pictures of things in the heavens and unusual, bizarre language. Hooray.

So finally to children's literature as object. Briefly, children's literature within Literature is a pathetic shadow of its real self. Literature within academe, the *T.L.S.*, the *London Review of Books*, the Booker Prize, *et al.*, can scarcely bear to recognize that everything rests on the edifice of initiated and charged child readers. Even when literary theorists discovered intertextuality, that process of writing that draws on all literature before it and around it, our theorist friends nearly always manage to leave out the primary source of writers' and readers' intertextual repertoires, their childhood reading. As adults our notions of narrative, of openings, denouements, goodies, baddies, red herrings, first-person narrators, third-person narrators, third-person narrators who get inside people's brains and then come out again, identification, projection – the list is, in all seriousness, endless – all these ways of reading and writing are laid down when reading *children's* literature. Yet, incredibly, when people talk about adult books, this period in reader-formation is kept out of the picture. This is an integral part of the politics of children's literature. It serves to help serious literature define what it isn't. It isn't childish. And children aren't grown up.

Literatures and literacies that defy this age-ranking are particularly interesting. At the moment, most frequently the way they are defied is within the context of something called family viewing: *The Cosby Show* and the like. But this doesn't have to be the case. Intergenerational reading and viewing doesn't have to have nuclear family situations as its images. To give Disney his due, his massive family viewing enterprise nearly always produces epics that begin with some dysfunctional, disrupted family unit: *Snow White*, *Bambi*, *Pinocchio*, *Beauty and the Beast*, *The Lion King*. You might counter by saying that these are resolved mostly in entirely conventional ways. Indeed. But part of their power is in the panic and anxiety created early on with the disruptions. I often wonder why, if Disney seems to be able to pull it off, can't more of us create nonconforming intergenerational literature? Not *instead* of what we call children's literature but *as well as.* There's nothing wrong with adults and children enjoying things together, is there? What is interesting is the way the industry and discourse of literature manage mostly to keep us apart. Why? For whose benefit? Mostly to confirm the notion that adults are people who have achieved a higher order of civilization than children. This is doubtful. Adults have achieved a higher order of power than children, which is a very different matter.

Finally, children's literature enters the discourse of child psychology; or, rather, quietly waits outside the door. How the child becomes the adult, what kind of child becomes what kind of adult remains a central problem for the human mind. We all know that there is some kind of continuity between childhood and adulthood, but we also know that there is also some kind of discontinuity. We hunt for analogies and metaphors like 'the child within' or we say 'the best years of your life' and the like. We constantly run to and fro in our minds between what we were and what we are, what we did and what we do. As adults we wonder if what we do to children and with children produces them, makes them. A fully fledged determinist picture says yes. Children are just products, sums of the total amount of environmental influence. But the picture is faulty because it denies human agency, an immeasurable force, the key force which explains all change and flux – that is, that humans from the start act on whatever they receive, actively construct meanings and interpretations of what they receive, make efforts to affect the environment that is affecting them, they interact with it and interact with each other.

Children's literature gets mixed up with all this because it provides a forum in which children's agency is recognized. For the realist children's novel to be successful it has to show children figuring, making meanings, trying to interpret actions. The supreme example of this, it seems to me, is Nina Bawden's work. It's not that her children are overly wise or overly clever because quite often they make mistakes, it's much more their attempt to figure in the first place that is important. This too strikes me as something terribly important, for we will only solve the massive problems facing us as a society and as a world if we recognize that we can all figure and interpret and we can't afford to count ourselves out of the process. Of course, as presently constituted, outside is precisely what we are, *hors de combat*, outside of the process of governing our own lives, but the figuring children of the realist novel show glimpses of what we are all entitled to do. So children's literature inevitably draws on whatever is the contemporary level of understanding of children's abilities, and ways of developing and changing. Or to put it another way, it is actually part of the discourse about children's thinking and child psychology. If our conception of child psychology does not simply mean an immutable sequence of structures and hurdles that the textbooks call child development, but is widened to include notions of the changing culture – or if you like social psychology of children – then it can be seen that children's literature plays some kind of part in the changing psychology of children. This is partly why at various key moments it becomes such a highly charged matter. Judy Blume broke a taboo with *Forever . . .* because she appeared to be allowing children to imagine that they could treat each other's bodies in the way her protagonists do. It represented a psychological shift that some people weren't ready for or were sure was a threat to order. Perhaps it was.

To turn the matter round, it is possible that psychological knowledge and speculation can illuminate something for us practitioners: namely, how children receive the literature we give them. Literary theory is now full of words once only used by psychologists: projection, transference, condensation, identification, splitting, the gaze, the transitional object, return of the repressed and constructs and many others. As ever, critics and writers are trying to come to terms with what it means to write and read. Some psychologists have specialized in children and some, like Nicholas Tucker and the Rustins, are very much part of the discourse about children's literature. Whatever we say about what children's literature does to people who read it, or what people are doing when they write, it will inevitably be in part a statement about child psychology. In an ideal world those of us involved in this enterprise of making and distributing children's books would find the time to do quite a lot of figuring in this area, rather like Nina Bawden's children. Not that we should all dash off and do courses in reductive psychometric psychology that regale us with human limitations, determined pathways of consciousness, and crude staged patterns of development, but somehow we need to escape from the uninformed chat that begins: 'What kids really want is . . .'

I'm not finishing here as if I am offering a final key that will unlock a magic answer. I am merely throwing into the pot of how we improve our practice – how we try to make what we do more thoughtful, more fun, more useful, more exciting, more dissenting and nonconformist – the notion that here lies a massive body of ideas that impinge directly on what we do. One of the consequences of taking it seriously was Catherine Storr's *Clever Polly and the Stupid Wolf* books. I wonder if they would have seen the light of day if she had started out writing with publishers standing over her saying: could you shorten that for our new series called Whizzers we're launching in the autumn. And could you change biscuits to cookies, we're off to the Bologna Book Fair next week, and we're hoping to interest Gulf Oil Children's Books in it.

In conclusion, I intended in this paper to view children's literature from different angles and in so doing see ways in which it is caught up in prevailing conditions and ways in which we can intervene to keep it an alive, hopeful, nonconforming, questioning place to work.

76

IN THE WORST POSSIBLE TASTE

Children, television and cultural value

Hannah Davies, David Buckingham and Peter Kelley

Source: *European Journal of Cultural Studies* 3(1) (2000): 5–24.

STEVE: (aged 6):	I love *Animal Hospital.* It's my best programme.
CHARLIE:	Did you watch the monkey one?
STEVE:	Yeah, that was so funny. It started itching other monkey's bums and they started spitting down on people's heads.

Debates about children and television have largely been preoccupied with the potential impact of 'harmful' material. Such debates implicitly define children as a special audience, with distinctive characteristics and needs. Children, it is argued, are in need of protection, not just from commercial exploitation or ideological manipulation, but also from the consequences of their own vulnerability and ignorance.

One of the implicit concerns in these debates is with the question of children's *taste.* It seems to be assumed that, left to their own devices, children will choose to watch material that is not only morally damaging but also inherently lacking in cultural value. Dietary metaphors are common here: children, it is often asserted, will opt for chips and chocolate bars in preference to the nourishing cultural food that adults consistently tell them is good for them. Children's 'natural' taste, it is argued, is for vulgarity and sensationalism, rather than restraint and subtlety; for simplistic stereotypes rather than complex, rounded characters; and it is led by the baser physical instincts rather than the higher sensibilities of the intellect. Children and 'good taste' are, it would seem, fundamentally incompatible.

In this article, we investigate some of these assumptions using data arising from a broader research project about children's television culture. The project used a multi-disciplinary approach to consider changing assumptions about children's characteristics and needs as an audience. Thus, we looked at the implications for children of broader economic and institutional changes in the media environment; at the ways in which broadcasters, regulators and policy-makers define the child audience; and at how children are directly and indirectly addressed and constructed as an audience by the television schedules, and by the formal strategies of specific programmes. Against this background, we were also interested in how children defined *themselves* as an audience – in the kinds of programmes they identified as being uniquely or primarily 'for children', and their reasons for these judgements. As we shall indicate, these different definitions of children's characteristics as an audience necessarily invoke broader assumptions about the meaning of childhood itself.

Children's television/adults' television

Historically, the main focus of public concern in this area has been on the effects of material that is aimed at *adults*, rather than on programmes aimed specifically at children. In 1996, for example, a British market research report revealing that children's preferences are for 'adult' sitcoms and soap operas resulted in outraged headlines about 'the scandal of the "view as you like" generation'.[1] In fact, this story is far from news. Right from the beginnings of television, children have always preferred to watch programmes that were not specifically made for them (Abrams, 1956).

A closer look at the ratings, however, reveals a more interesting story than simply that of children watching 'unsuitable' material or 'growing up too fast'. To be sure, children's programmes are rarely among the top rating shows for children; and there is a good deal of overlap, with the same popular sitcoms and soap operas featuring on both adults' and children's charts. Nevertheless, many of the most popular programmes with children are not especially popular with adults, and vice versa. Our analysis of the ratings for 1995, for example, found that some entertainment-based 'adult' programmes, which were peripheral in the general chart, were consistently in the top 20 for children; while some more serious home-produced dramas, which featured in the general top 20, were absent from the children's chart (Buckingham *et al.*, 1999). To some degree, of course, these differences can be explained through scheduling and availability to view: some of the most popular programmes with adults run after the 9 p.m. watershed, while the most popular 'adult' programmes among children are often screened in the early evenings, especially at weekends. Nevertheless, this kind of comparison should lead us to question any easy opposition between 'children's' and 'adults'' programmes.

Clearly, these categories are much more relative – and indeed, more valueladen – than straightforward institutional definitions would seem to imply. Just as sociologists of childhood have increasingly questioned the unitary category 'children', we should acknowledge that what it means to be 'adult' is also heterogeneous and negotiated. Obviously, there are different kinds of grown-ups – in traditional socioeconomic terms such as class and education, but also in terms of lifestyle and culture. Similarly, 'adult' television – that is, television not made specifically for children – offers different kinds of grown-up subject positions, from that of the serious, intelligent citizen who watches a news magazine like *Newsnight* to the ironic, playful viewer of the salacious *Eurotrash* (who might, as often as not, be the same person).

Nevertheless, when we look at the kinds of 'adult' programmes that children watch in their millions, there seem to be particular features and conventions that they have in common, such as action, humour and narrative simplicity. So to what extent can we talk about an *aesthetic* dimension to children's preferences – or indeed a distinctive 'children's taste culture'?

Falling standards

If much of this debate continues to focus on 'adult' programmes, the impact of deregulation and commercialization has given rise to new concerns about the nature and content of *children's* television. Here again, the issue of children's taste is often an underlying – and frequently unacknowledged – concern.

For example, Stephen Kline's (1993) critique of the commercialization of children's culture repeatedly invokes what it assumes are shared assumptions about cultural value. Kline looks back wistfully to the golden age of classic children's literature. These stories, he argues, 'took on the ability to enthrall and delight the child' as 'writers joyfully undertook experiments that charted new courses for the literate imagination' (1993: 81). Through the development of popular literature and comic books and thence to television, Kline traces a steady cultural decline, resulting from the 'homogenising' and 'levelling' influence of the mass market. While the Victorians are unstintingly praised for their 'rich emotional texture' and their 'unfettered imagination', contemporary television is condemned for lacking their 'psychological depth', 'exuberance' and 'innocence'. Cartoons in particular are condemned as universally 'formulaic', 'predictable', 'inane' and 'banal': by virtue of their 'truncated characterisation', their 'stylised narratives' and their 'stultified animation', they are judged to be unable 'to deal adequately with feelings and experience' (1993: 313–14).

The problem with these kinds of judgements is not just that the key terms themselves remain undefined, but that the *evidence* that might exemplify and support them is simply taken for granted. It is easy to condemn *The Care Bears* and *My Little Pony*, as Kline (1993: 261) does, for lacking 'the wit, individuality and subtle humour of A. A. Milne's eternal characters', not least when very few of one's readers will ever have seen such programmes. If there is any doubt, a few silly quotations taken out of context will easily do the trick. Such assertions are seen as self-evidently true, and as somehow neutral. In the process, the *social* basis for such judgements of taste is simply evacuated.

As Ellen Seiter (1993) suggests, social class is certainly one dimension here. As in a great deal of Marxist cultural critique, Kline paradoxically takes the position of the 'old' bourgeoisie in his attack on the new ruling ethos. He implicitly judges *The Care Bears* by the criteria one might use to evaluate the relative claims of *Middlemarch* and *The Mill on the Floss*: depth of character, complexity and moral seriousness are seen as 'eternal' qualities whose value is self-evident. As Seiter suggests, such distinctions between 'quality' children's television and 'trash', or between 'educational' and 'non-educational' toys, could well be seen as a reflection of what she calls the 'smug self-satisfaction of educated middle-class people'.[2]

Yet this debate also raises questions about what it might mean for *adults* to pass judgements on *children's* media culture (see Buckingham, 1995a). The problem here is partly to do with the implicit assumptions about the audience that are at stake – and in particular, the notion that adults should be in a position to define what children *need*, irrespective of what they appear to *want*. Why is it that children positively prefer the 'crude' to the 'complex'? Why do they actively seek out 'one-dimensional' characters and 'predictable' narratives, rather than those which possess 'rich emotional texture'? Might there not in fact be very good reasons for these choices? Yet the problem here is not only to do with audiences: it is also to do with the criteria that are being applied in making such aesthetic judgements. Could it be that the value of such apparently 'inane' and 'stultified' productions might need to be judged according to *different* aesthetic criteria, *irrespective* of whether or not they are popular with audiences? And if so, how (and by whom) are those criteria to be identified?

Interpreting taste

To raise the question of taste in this context is inevitably to invoke the work of Pierre Bourdieu (1979). As Bourdieu amply demonstrates, aesthetic judgements cannot be divorced from social relations: distinctions of taste are a means of displaying and sustaining distinctions of class and social power. The preferences and judgements of those who have the power to ascribe cultural value become the apotheosis of 'good taste'; and in this way, the maintenance of aesthetic hierarchies becomes a means of perpetuating social inequalities.

While his argument about the social basis of taste has been widely accepted, Bourdieu's analysis has also been criticized for its deterministic analysis of social class, and for its neglect of other factors such as gender. Furthermore, it has been argued, Bourdieu implicitly sees the hierarchy of taste from the perspective of the dominant classes, failing to take account of the subordinated classes who may not recognize it, or indeed actively refuse to accept it (Frow, 1995; Mander, 1987; Robbins, 1991; Schiach, 1993).

Despite Bourdieu's (1998) denunciation of the medium, discussion of taste in relation to television also rather complicates neat distinctions between 'high' and 'low' culture. Television can obviously offer traditional high culture (opera) as well as low culture (game shows) and many points in between. Indeed, some have argued that it is precisely because of this blending that it has helped to break down traditional distinctions between elite and popular culture (Hartley, 1992).

In this respect, the relationship between taste, aesthetics and social power in the case of television is more complex than such essentialist distinctions allow. There is more heterogeneity both in the cultural objects that are consumed and within the audiences that consume them. Furthermore, for certain groups within the dominant class – particularly those characterized by Gouldner (1979) as the 'new class of intellectuals' or the 'knowledge professionals' – preferences for the low or the popular can themselves be a form of cultural capital. And of course it is precisely these kinds of people who are making popular television programmes.

The white, urban 'knowledge class' seeking to appropriate certain versions of ethnic culture; the gentrification of football as a kind of working-class tourism; or the application of 'camp' as a way of flirting with definitions of sexual difference (Simpson, 1994) – these and many similar phenomena reflect the evolution of new taste cultures that both reflect and serve to construct new social positionings that are not simply tied to fixed class distinctions.

Before cool

To what extent can *generational* differences be interpreted in these terms? Thus far, much of the debate on this issue in cultural studies has centred on the category of 'youth'. As Simon Frith (1998) has noted, the idea of 'hip' or 'cool' is both symbolically and empirically tied up with youth and change. For the 'knowledge professionals', to be youthful, or (more importantly) to *know* about what is youthful, provides a key source of cultural capital which can be traded on the employment market (Peretti, 1998). In this analysis, 'youth' becomes a symbolic construct that is to some extent divorced from biological age. Youth is a pattern of consumption rather than a demographic category: you don't have to be young to go to rave clubs, wear Nike trainers or listen to drum and bass (although undeniably it helps). When Tony Blair talks about Britain as a 'young country', or when media advertisers, schedulers and producers chase the elusive 16–25-year-olds, 'youth' is being defined as the ultimate desirable quality, far removed from the actual experiences of unemployed young Britons on government training schemes.

Where do children, and children's tastes, fit into this matrix? For some market researchers and media producers, children seem to be perceived as a kind of 'pre-youth', a taste avant-garde, symbolically at the cutting edge of cultural innovation. What children like today will be what is cool and hip tomorrow. Youth, it could be argued, is getting younger every day. Within the discourse of the children's cable channel Nickelodeon, for example, children are constructed as 'sovereign consumers': sophisticated and difficult to reach, they know their own minds and they are not afraid to speak them (Buckingham *et al.*, 1999). However, as with youth, this new symbolic construction of children – as innovative, smart, street-wise and hip – can obscure the actual experiences of children themselves.

Here again, if we examine the kinds of 'adult' programmes that children watch and like, and the reasons they give for liking them, the picture is more complicated. Their tastes are quite distinctive, but not necessarily 'cool' or 'fashionable': they prefer *Gladiators* to *Inspector Morse*, but they also like the mass market music of *Top of the Pops* rather than the more youth-oriented *TFI Friday*. Children are choosing to identify with and to occupy *some* 'adult' subject positions rather than others, while at the same time avowedly retaining aspects of 'childishness'.

In the remainder of this article, we intend to explore these questions about children's taste via an analysis of extracts from discussions with children themselves. As we shall indicate, the socially performative nature of the kind of focus group discussions we undertook highlights quite acutely the social uses of judgements of taste (Buckingham, 1993). Like those of adults, children's expressions of their tastes and preferences are self-evidently social acts: they are one of the means whereby children lay claim to – and attribute meaning to – their preferred social identities. This is not, of course, to imply that they are free to select from an infinite variety of subject positions as and when they choose. We need to recognize children's agency in constructing and defining their own tastes and identities; but we need to avoid the sentimental view of children as necessarily 'media-literate active viewers'.

As we shall indicate, children's judgements about the cultural value of television articulate power relations, both within the peer group and in terms of the wider social groupings to which these children belong. Proclaiming one's own tastes, and thereby defining oneself as more or less 'mature', represents a form of 'identity work', in a context in which being a 'child' is effectively to be seen as vulnerable and powerless. Such statements clearly cannot be taken at face value, as evidence of what children 'really' think or believe. On the contrary, it is through such negotiations and performances that the *meanings* of 'childhood' are constructed and defined.

Talking taste

The data presented in this article are drawn from a larger study of changing views of the child audience for television.[3] In addition to looking at how the television industry defines and constructs the child audience – through practices such as programme production, scheduling and research – we wanted to understand how children perceived *themselves* as an audience (cf. Buckingham, 1994). We decided to focus this aspect of our research around one key question: how do children define what makes a programme either 'for children' or 'for adults'?

We took this question to two classes of children in a socially and ethnically mixed inner-London primary school. Year 6 – the top year of primary school – was selected because of its transitional position. At the age of 10 or 11, these were the most senior or 'grown-up' children in the institution, looking towards secondary school, where they would be the least grown-up (cf. de Block, 1998). We chose to compare this with a Year 2 class of 6–7-year-olds, whose position as 'children' we expected to be more secure and less problematic. In total, we had contact with each class for two mornings a week over the length of the term; and we were therefore present in the school for four days out of five every week. Though our research was not intended to be ethnographic, we did become a regular feature of the classroom routine.

We began with a series of relatively open-ended discussions about the children's likes and dislikes in television.[4] These were followed by two more focused activities. The first was a sorting exercise, in which the children were invited to categorize a broad assortment of programme titles (provided on cards) in terms of whether they were 'for children' or 'for adults' – although in practice, of course, many groups chose to have more than these two categories. The second exercise was a more complicated scheduling simulation, in which the children were given a similarly broad selection of programme cards and asked to fit them into five programme slots on a weekday afternoon and on a Saturday evening. These activities thus attempted to tap into the children's understanding of how childhood and adulthood are constructed within television schedules, and how far they challenged these definitions of space and time.

Throughout each of these activities, the children were invited to comment and reflect on their choices and decisions. They were also permitted to make changes as the discussion progressed. The activities were thus intended to facilitate discussion, rather than to accurately reflect children's viewing tastes or habits; and it is these discussions, rather than the 'results' (that is, the choices themselves) that we primarily focus on here.[5]

What makes a children's programme?

In effect, our research activities deliberately set up the opposition child–adult and asked the children to negotiate it. For various reasons, they found this very difficult. New categories emerged such as 'in between' or 'for everyone'. The older children in particular were uneasy about defining their favourite programmes as 'children's'; while some of the younger ones constructed the category 'babies' to differentiate their tastes from those of their younger siblings. In this respect, the process of classifying programmes explicitly served as a means of social self-definition. For example, when a group of 6-year-old boys collapsed into laughter at the mention of *Teletubbies*, they were clearly distancing themselves from the younger audience for whom the programme is designed – and from the girls in their class who had appropriated its 'cuter' aspects. Similarly, when a group of girls covered their ears every time football was mentioned, they were self-consciously constructing their own girlishness by rejecting the male world of football. In this respect, our activity effectively dramatized Bourdieu's (1979) famous statement: 'classification classifies the classifier'.

In the children's explorations of what makes a programme 'for children', a number of quite predictable factors emerged. Perhaps unsurprisingly, the strongest arguments were negative ones. Programmes featuring sex, violence and 'swearing' were singled out by both age groups as being particularly 'grown-up'. Likewise, children's programmes were predominantly defined in terms of absences – that is, in terms of what they do *not* include. By contrast, the most persuasive and insistent reason given for a programme being 'for children' was simply that they watched and enjoyed it. This definition had an unarguable logic; and it also allowed for more flexibility than a purely institutional definition based on the schedule or on what actually appears on children's channels. Yet in these terms, many of the programmes that they liked and wanted to talk about were actually 'adults' programmes.

In the process of these activities and discussions, a set of loose oppositions emerged that were used by the sample to explain the differences between children's and adults' programmes. We have interpreted these oppositions as follows:

parents	children
grannies	teenagers
old-fashioned	cool
boring	funny
talk	action

These categories are broadly related to each other, with those on the right being associated with each other in opposition to those on the left. While we acknowledge that this kind of schema ignores the fluidity and the contradictions that this kind of discussion inevitably produces, it does provide a useful way of identifying how our sample defined the distinctiveness of children's taste.

Broadly speaking, the children argued for their preferences by emphasizing the criteria on the right of our schema and disavowing those on the left. Of course there were disagreements within groups about *which* programmes they preferred, but the *reasons* put forward for liking or disliking a programme were generally within this broad paradigm. For example, one group of girls disagreed about the long-running soap opera *Coronation Street*: two rejected it on the grounds that it was 'boring' and 'for grannies', while one defended it on the grounds that it had 'good stories' and that it was 'funny'. Despite the differences between them, there was considerable agreement about the basic *grounds* for judgement.

As we have noted, the most obvious criterion for selecting a programme as being 'for children' was that of personal preference (I like it, so it must be for children). Such expressions of preference often involved contrasting their own personal taste with that of parents, most noticeably in relation to news or current affairs programmes. However, this opposition between parents and children was often expressed in quite complex ways. In some cases, the children made a clear distinction between 'parents' in the abstract and their *own* parent(s). While parents in general were seen to like 'boring stuff' such as *The News*, talk about their own family lives often involved anecdotes about their parents watching and enjoying the same kinds of programmes that they liked. Two 6-year-old boys, for example, referred to the comedy *Mr Bean* in this way:

DANIEL: My mum likes watching it and she's nearly 29.
PAUL: My dad loves it, my dad laughs at it!

In the everyday reality of these children's lives, then, the viewing preferences of the 'grown-ups' (parents) are not independent of the tastes of their children, nor do they necessarily correspond to what are seen as adult norms.

To a large extent, this could be regarded as simply a consequence of the routines and structures of family life: people (parents included) do not always choose what they watch, and they may decide to watch programmes together for the experience of companionship rather than because they actually prefer them. In this sense, the opposition between parent and child is not necessarily fixed and stable.

Aspirational tastes

This parent/child distinction had greater currency among the younger children, who were generally more inclined to accept their dependence on parental and adult authority. The 10-year-olds, looking forward to adolescence and secondary school, tended to make more nuanced distinctions *within* the category of 'childhood'. On the brink of becoming teenagers themselves, they associated particular programmes or types of programmes with this age group. These choices were clearly informed by a broader sense of a 'teen' lifestyle, to which many of them aspired, even though they didn't see themselves as teenagers quite yet. Being a teenager was seen to offer a degree of autonomy and control over their lives which was just around the corner. Thus, they recognized that programmes like the sitcoms *Sister Sister* or *Sabrina the Teenage Witch* might feature teenage characters, but they were quite clearly claimed as programmes for people like them. Unlike older people, however, it was felt that teenagers – the actual bearers of this projected future identity – might also share some of their own tastes:

INTERVIEWER: Do you think it [*Sister Sister*] is a programme for teenagers?
ALL: No.
INTERVIEWER: Why is that? Aren't the characters sixteen?
SHARON: Yes, but they're the sort of age where, you know, we can understand . . .
ANNIE: I think teenagers can like it as well.

Certain lifestyle options were consistently associated with this slightly older age group. Teenagers, it would seem, have social and emotional lives, characterized by boyfriends, girlfriends, fashion and music. During our group interviews, conversations around these subjects were frequent and unsolicited. These conversations clearly had a social, performative role and were used partly as a way of articulating their own (heterosexual) gender positions (for a fuller discussion, see Kelley *et al.*, 1999). However, the identity of the teenager was not only differentiated through sexual and romantic knowledge; it was also about having greater access to the public world. In our scheduling exercise, when groups of older children were asked about what they would watch on a mid-week afternoon, discussion would frequently move on to other things that they did or would like to do at that time – playing football in the park, or 'hanging about' with friends. Spending more time out of the house was also something that they looked forward to and associated with being a teenager.

However, looking forward to being teenage was not at all the same thing as wanting to be grown-up. Certain programmes that were seen as the kinds of things that teenagers would like were enjoyed because of their almost 'childish' silliness and rebellion against adult authority. For example, one boy singled out the character George Dawes in the quiz show *Shooting Stars* as a particular reason for liking this programme, because he was a grown man dressed as a baby:

INTERVIEWER: What's so funny about him?
SIMON: He's a baby and he plays the drums with his hand up and he says 'silly git' and everyone laughs on the show.

The juxtaposition between babyishness and adult humour and swearing is clearly a source of enjoyment to this boy. In cases like this, enthusiasm for the 'childish' and silly aspects of comedy were also combined with a sense of exclusivity. In discussion, it was important for certain children to show that they could 'get' the joke, in order to demonstrate that they were grown-up and sophisticated.

In a sense, then, these were clearly *aspirational* preferences. As Liesbeth de Block (1998) notes, comedies like *Friends* and *Men Behaving Badly* seem to be particularly popular with children in this age group, partly because they allow them to rehearse a kind of adulthood that is independent, autonomous and self-sufficient (living in your own flat with your friends, having control over your own space and time) while at the same time allowing irresponsibility, irreverence and immaturity (watching lots of television, getting into trouble with more 'responsible' grown-ups). Yet, unlike characters in more serious adult soaps or dramas, the male characters in these comedies are not portrayed (or indeed perceived by children) as particularly mature. As de Block suggests, their appeal rests largely on the fact that they are men behaving like boys. Such programmes thus offer children a version of 'adulthood' that combines elements of autonomy and freedom with irreverence and irresponsibility.

It was these qualities, as much as the music or the clothes the characters wore, that defined such programmes as inherently 'cool', as opposed to 'old-fashioned'. As one 10-year-old boy – Luke – with a particular self-esteem problem explained: 'I have to admit this, but I'm quite – I'm not a cool guy. I don't watch *Friends*.' In this aspirational world of 'cool', there seems to be an almost narcissistic relationship between reader and text. It is partly that the qualities of the programme are seen to transfer across to the individuals who watch it; but also that one's existing qualities are somehow necessarily reflected in what one chooses to watch in the first place. In Luke's account, classification very definitely classifies the classifier.

How uncool can you get?

If the cultural identity labelled 'teenage' is characterized by fun, rebellion and sex, it was necessary for a contrasting identity to be constructed – as something that was none of these things, and indeed was actively opposed to them. This category was identified by several groups of girls in particular as that of 'grannies'. Given the highly gendered nature of this classification, it is interesting that it was more clearly formulated by the girls. The identity of the granny was defined as boring, old-fashioned and censorious:

INTERVIEWER: Why do you think it [the quiz show *Countdown*] is so boring?
ANNIE: Because it's full of all these words that you have to make.
INTERVIEWER: Who do you think would like those kinds of programmes?
JULIA: Grannies.
ANNIE: Yeah, grannies!

Likewise, 'grannies' or (more charitably) 'people in their sixties' were also seen as the least appropriate audience for the children's own favourite shows. This renouncement of old age was also used as a strategy in arguments about programmes. In a mixed group, one girl expressed a preference for the sitcom *Frasier*, only to be put down by one of the boys with the withering comment: 'What, old people living in a flat? That's not funny.'

In this way, certain types of adults and adult viewing are very explicitly rejected. Being old and female, it would seem, is the ultimate cultural stigma. Of course, this expression of cultural taste is not unrelated to questions of social power and status, not least as defined by the media themselves: when younger women are valued for their physical desirability, older women are frequently invisible – and, when they are represented at all, often serve as the butt of young people's humour. This might go some way to explaining why it was the girls rather than the boys who were so hostile to 'grannies' and all that they were seen to represent.

You've got to laugh

In response to our somewhat earnest questions about why a programme was chosen or preferred, the most common answer across both age groups was simply that it was 'funny'. Like most audiences, our sample enjoy television that makes them laugh, as one 6-year-old girl related when talking about *Mr Bean*:

INTERVIEWER: What makes it a children's programme?
TONI: Because I like it, because it's funny and I like funny things.

On one level, this kind of explanation is so obvious as to be banal. However, it is important to understand its significance a little more fully. In fact, comedy is one of the areas in which children's tastes are frequently seen to differ fundamentally from those of adults. Children's humour is often (revealingly) dismissed as 'puerile' or 'infantile'. Indeed, in our experience, the children's programmes that are the hardest for adults to watch are the highly stereotyped, slapstick comedies like the BBC's *Chucklevision* and *To Me, To You* – programmes that make *Mr Bean* look like Jane Austen. Such programmes are often highly successful in the ratings.

As we have noted, contemporary critics of children's television tend to adopt a conservative notion of cultural value. Such critics do not deny that children's television can and should be entertaining; but what gives children's television value is not the fun stuff (the cartoons and comedies) but the factual programmes, the literary adaptations and the 'socially relevant' contemporary drama. In this rather sanctimonious context, very few critics seem prepared to stand up for children's right to just 'have a laugh' – although, it should be noted, programme-makers certainly have.

While children's expressions of enthusiasm for comedy are, on one level, simply an assertion of 'personal' pleasure, there are also social functions in talking about what makes them laugh. Different kinds of comedy had different kinds of value in this respect. Programmes like *Mr Bean* or the camcorder show *You've Been Framed* are primarily physical, slapstick humour, although the children's accounts of them focused particularly on the subversive or 'carnivalesque' element of adults behaving like children and making fools of themselves. On the other hand, programmes such as *Shooting Stars* were valued for different reasons. Central to their appeal for the older children was the idea that in 'getting the joke' they were gaining access to an exclusive world of irony and media-references inaccessible to younger children:

ANDREW: *Friends* is – it's not a little kids thing. Like *Shooting Stars* is a show for older people.
JAMES: Little kids don't have the patience to watch them.
ANDREW: Yeah, someone younger won't find *Friends* or *Shooting Stars* funny.

For James and Andrew, the 'older people' identified here are implicitly people like them.

Talking about these kinds of programmes seemed to be more important for the boys in the group – which may reflect an aspirational identification with the men who tend to dominate these shows. In several of these programmes, the humour often involves a characteristically male form of banter and one-upmanship. To some extent, being seen to be 'in on the joke' was more important than actually finding it funny. As one 10-year-old boy explained in relation to *Shooting Stars* and other such shows: 'You see them maybe once and sometimes you don't get the jokes, but you still laugh because you know it's meant to be funny. . . . But you don't really know why' (David).

Laughing with the big boys, as it were, has the most social and cultural currency: this is what you *should* find funny. For one particular 10-year-old boy – who saw himself as a taste leader in the class – this became apparent when he discussed the US sitcom *Sabrina the Teenage Witch*. As a less sophisticated, more girl-oriented show, he almost apologized for liking it:

INTERVIEWER: So what's good about *Sabrina*?
JAMES: It's just good.

ALAN: I have to admit, it's not the kind of thing you'd think is good. But it's good, it's funny.

Particular kinds of comedy, then, clearly have a social function, which is again associated with being more sophisticated and 'teenage'. To this extent, talking about comedy is a serious business: it can be used to mark out social status and knowledge as well as simply expressing pleasure.

If what is 'funny' was seen to be particularly appropriate for children, then what is 'boring' (and hence lacking in pleasure) was consistently equated with adults – and particularly with 'grannies'. For this group of 6-year-old girls, being boring is a defining characteristic of adult programmes:

INTERVIEWER: So what makes it [*The News*] a grown-ups programme?
TONI: It's boring.
INTERVIEWER: So does that mean that grown-ups are boring?
RUTH: Yes, because they like the news.
TONI: I hate the news.
INTERVIEWER: Why do you think grown-ups like the news?
TONI: Because they want to know what's happening?
INTERVIEWER: And aren't you interested?
TONI: No!

News as a genre is inherently and essentially defined as adult. A group of 6-year-old boys, for example, saw no clear difference between *The Six o'clock News* and *Newsround*, despite *Newsround*'s very clear institutional status as children's television:

INTERVIEWER: What about *The Six o'clock News*, is that for grown-ups?
FRED: Yeah, sort of.
JACK: That's like *Newsround*, isn't it?
INTERVIEWER: Do you think there's any difference between them?
JACK: No, they're the same.
MICHAEL: Yes, it's just that one's on later.

Here again, the criteria that were used to define a particular programme as 'boring' – and hence to proclaim one's dislike of it – were quite diverse; but the association between what was 'boring' and what was identified with 'adults' was very consistent. Thus, for a group of 10-year-old girls, *Shooting Stars* – which was a preferred programme among their male peers – is defined as boring, in part because it is associated with one of their parents:

SHARON: My dad would laugh at *Shooting Stars* . . . sometimes I think it's really boring.

INTERVIEWER: Is there anything in particular about the programme that makes it for grown-ups?
SHARON: It's boring. And it's –
JULIA: They laugh about stupid, dumb things.

Being boring – while it means different things for different children – is thus a cardinal signifier of a lack of cultural value. In contrast, being funny (and 'getting the joke') is seen to convey value on these children as individuals as well as on the programmes that they consume. In the process, the cultural hierarchy that elevates seriousness and civic responsibility is effectively inverted.

Cut to the action

For the younger children in particular, one of the characteristics that was seen to make television boring was *talking*. Needless to say, perhaps, this resistance to talk extended to our research activities: sorting out programme titles on cards could be perceived as an acceptable game, but having to rationalize their choices in response to our questions was something that many of the children resisted. Talk is seen as the antithesis of action. As one of the younger boys explained:

INTERVIEWER: Why aren't soaps for children, then?
ANDREW: Well, it's just that there are lots of conversations in them. Nothing happens, no funny things.

This opposition between talk and action was also a key dimension of responses to news, as these 6-year-olds indicated:

GEOFF: And I watched this really, really boring one [*Newsround*]. All it was really – you didn't see any pictures at all – all you heard was talking, talking, talking.
LAURA: [*News*] is boring for children because it's got no acting in it.

As in this instance, television talk is generally *adult* talk. Even children's news programmes like *Newsround* rarely feature children talking in their own right, whether as presenters or as participants in news events (Buckingham, 1997).

In contrast, programmes claimed as children's programmes would often be talked about in terms of their physicality and visceral appeal. The game show *Gladiators* was described in these terms by children in both age groups:

INTERVIEWER: What do you like about *Gladiators*?
TONI: Well they do activities and stuff.

RUTH: And they wear –
ROBYN: – bright clothes and stuff.
TONI: I'm going to be a Gladiator when I grow up.

(6-year-olds)

MARK: I like to see how they, I just like the activities they have. I don't really care about the people, I just want to see how they do in the activities.

(10-year-old)

Typically, talking was associated with fact, while action was associated with stories or performing. However, this distinction was not necessarily the same as that between fiction and non-fiction. Programmes such as *Gladiators* or *Wildlife on One* are non-fiction, but because of their visceral and dramatic content, they were associated by these children with fictional action programmes like *Hercules* or *Xena Warrior Princess*. This preference for action, event and spectacle also underlines the popularity in ratings terms of programmes featuring sport – particularly football – and the National Lottery draw. Whether human, animal or environmental, action – often expressed through 'violence' – is a key criterion in determining these children's television tastes, for both boys and girls. Children, it would seem, like to see things happen.

Conclusion

On one level, children clearly do have distinctive tastes in television. Allowing for other social differences, they seem to enjoy things that adults don't, and vice versa. And even where they watch the same programmes as adults, they often appear to be enjoying them for different reasons.

Psychologists would seek to explain these differences by recourse to notions of development. Thus, children's apparent liking for what we as adults judge to be simplistic narratives, stereotyped characters and crude humour would be seen as evidence of their cognitive and emotional limitations. More charitably perhaps, such tastes could be seen as a developmental *necessity* at a given stage: children, it might be argued, need to see the world in simple binary terms before they can learn to understand its full complexity. While outwardly quite different, psychoanalytic explanations would be inclined to take a similar form. Scatological and sexual humour, for example, would be seen as a necessary stage in the sublimation of the id and the development of the mature ego.

Such analyses have some truth, but they are unavoidably normative – both in terms of *texts* and in terms of *audiences*. Truly 'mature' viewers simply would not get excited by *Gladiators* or *Xena Warrior Princess*; they would not be amused by *Mr Bean* or the silly behaviour on *Shooting Stars*; and they would simply refuse to watch *You've Been Framed* or game shows like *Blind Date*. On the contrary, their television diet would consist solely of *Newsnight*, serious dramas like *Inspector Morse* and perhaps the occasional glimpse of *Coronation Street*. Such normative judgements are, to be sure, partly about social class and gender; but they are also frequently defined and expressed in terms of *age*.

The reality, as we have suggested, is rather different. As 'adults' – albeit of different generations – the authors of this article will confess to enjoying *Shooting Stars*, *The Simpsons*, *Blind Date* and *Top of the Pops* – although we would also confess to drawing the line at *Mr Bean*, not to mention *Chucklevision*. Viewing such programmes is partly a professional necessity, but it is also something that we consciously choose to do in our 'real lives', insofar as we have any. This is not to say that we do not also watch 'adult' programmes like *Newsnight* or *Inspector Morse* – although again we would probably draw the line at *Countdown*. The point is that, as adults, we have multiple tastes – and multiple subjectivities.

More to the point, these tastes are also socially defined. As we have attempted to show in this article, children's assertions of their own tastes necessarily entail a form of 'identity work' – a positioning of the self in terms of publicly available discourses and categories. The labels 'child' and 'adult' are categories of this kind: they are defined relative to each other (and to other age-defined categories such as 'teenagers' and 'grannies'), and as such they are necessarily flexible and open to dispute. Definitions of what is 'childish' or 'adult' – 'mature' or 'immature' – are therefore subject to a constant process of negotiation.

Like the practice of film classification, which publicly defines maturity in terms of age categories, social hierarchies of taste thus provide a scale against which children can calibrate their own maturity and hence make claims about their identity. This is, as we have shown, partly a form of *aspiration* – although for the children we have studied, this is a matter of aspiration towards a 'teenage' identity rather than a fully 'adult' one. Yet it can also be a matter of *subversion* – a celebration of 'childish things' that self-consciously challenge or mock adult norms of respectability, restraint and 'good taste'.

This subversive option has also become increasingly popular for many adults (or at least young adults) in recent years. Just as some older children appear to want to 'buy in' to adulthood, so some adults want to do the reverse. The cult status of the BBC's pre-school series *Teletubbies* among twenty-something clubbers; the camp nostalgia associated with 'retro' children's TV of the 1970s, currently being revived on cable channels; the child-like anarchy and game-playing of Chris Evans's *Big Breakfast* and *TFI Friday*; and the crossover success with adults of children's hosts like Zoe Ball – all these phenomena point to the growing appeal (and indeed the commodification) of 'childishness' as a kind of style accessory. Childhood, it would seem, isn't just for children anymore.

Some academics and media commentators appear to be particularly disturbed by what they perceive as this infantilization – or 'paedocratisation' – of the television audience (Hartley, 1987; Preston, 1996). Television, they argue, increasingly addresses the adult audience as emotional, excitable and wanting to be pleasured – characteristics more usually attributed to children. Yet there is a kind of puritanism about this argument. One could interpret this phenomenon more positively, as a necessary process of recovering 'child-like' pleasures – in silly noises and games, in anarchy and absurdity – for which irony provides a convenient alibi. This kind of nostalgia for past pleasures could be seen to reflect the ambivalent status of television as a kind of 'transitional object', which plays a significant role in young people's growth towards adulthood.[6]

Yet to pose this argument in such terms – as a matter of 'infantilization' or alternatively of 'getting in touch with one's inner child' – is to resort to psychologistic interpretations. By contrast, we would argue that this elevation of an apparently 'child-like' anarchy and irresponsibility as the ultimate in cool is a *social* and *political* act on the part of adults. The 'immaturity' of some of these programmes is also a front for a kind of machismo; their self-regarding enthusiasm for celebrity sanctions a barely concealed contempt for the apparent inadequacies of their audience. Without being merely nostalgic, one could see such programmes as a kind of retreat from the public spaces which were partly colonized by more threatening forms of youth culture in previous decades.

Above all, it should be emphasized that this exchange is far from equal. When adults – or at least particular kinds of adults – seek to appropriate children's culture, they inevitably select the aspects that have resonance for their own lives. In the process, there may be a risk of forgetting the material inequalities between children and adults, and the way in which children's autonomy is currently being undermined in the era of educational testing, curfews and enforced homework quotas. When children laugh at the incompetent child-like adult in *Mr Bean* or the spectacle of adults humiliating themselves in *You've Been Framed*, it is partly because these programmes speak to their sense of their own powerlessness. In contrast, when adults revel in the *faux* children's television of shows like *TFI Friday*, the irresponsibility invoked there is a conscious choice. Adults, it would seem, can *choose* to be childish. Children cannot.

Notes

1 *Daily Mail* (20 June 1996).
2 For a fuller discussion, see Buckingham (1995b).
3 'Children's Media Culture: Education, Entertainment and the Public Sphere', based at the Institute of Education, University of London, and funded by the Economic and Social Research Council UK (award no. L126251026). Further material from this research is presented in Buckingham *et al.* (1999).

4 Space precludes a more detailed discussion of the research methodology. For accounts of similar studies, see Buckingham (1993) and Robinson (1997). These discussions and activities took place outside the classroom, in the library or a teacher's office. The groups were taped and the tapes were transcribed. Groups were selected on the basis of existing friendship groups and seating arrangements in the classroom. Each child in both classes was interviewed at least twice.
5 Further interpretations of this data, focusing on different issues, can be found in Kelley *et al.* (1999) and Davies *et al.* (1999).
6 We owe this argument to Mica Nava, in a presentation at the Institute of Education in February 1998. The notion of television as a transitional object is drawn in turn from the work of Roger Silverstone (1994).

References

Abrams, M. (1956) 'Child Audiences for Television in Great Britain', *Journalism Quarterly* 33(1): 35–41.

Bourdieu, P. (1979) *Distinction: A Social Critique of the Judgment of Taste.* London: Routledge & Kegan Paul.

Bourdieu, P. (1998) *On Television and Journalism.* London: Pluto Press.

Buckingham, D. (1993) *Children Talking Television: The Making of Television Literacy.* London: Falmer.

Buckingham, D. (1994) 'Television and the Definition of Childhood', in B. Mayall (ed.) *Children's Childhoods: Observed and Experienced.* London: Falmer.

Buckingham, D. (1995a) 'On the Impossibility of Children's Television: The Case of Timmy Mallet', in C. Bazalgette and D. Buckingham (eds) *In Front of the Children: Screen Entertainment and Young Audiences*, pp. 47–61. London: British Film Institute.

Buckingham, D. (1995b) 'The Commercialisation of Childhood? The Place of the Market in Children's Media Culture', *Changing English* 2(2): 17–41.

Buckingham, D. (1997) 'The Making of Citizens: Pedagogy and Address in Children's Television News', *Journal of Educational Media* 23(2–3): 119–39.

Buckingham, D., H. Davies, K. Jones and P. Kelley (1999) *Children's Television in Britain: History, Discourse and Policy*. London: British Film Institute.

Davies, H., D. Buckingham and P. Kelley (1999) 'Kids' Time: Childhood, Television and the Regulation of Time', *Journal of Educational Media* 24(1): 25–42.

De Block, L. (1998) 'From Childhood Pleasures To Adult Identities', *English and Media Magazine* 38: 24–9.

Frith, S. (1998) 'Is Youth the Future?', paper delivered at Institute of Education, London University, March.

Frow, J. (1995) *Cultural Studies and Cultural Value*. Oxford: Oxford University Press.

Gouldner, A. (1979) *The Future of Intellectuals and the Rise of the New Class*. New York: Seabury Press.

Hartley, J. (1987) 'Impossible Fictions: Television Audiences, Paedocracy, Pleasure', *Textual Practice* 1(2): 121–38.

Hartley, J. (1992) *Teleology*. London: Routledge.

Kelley, P., D. Buckingham and H. Davies (1999) 'Talking Dirty: Children, Sexual Knowledge and Television', *Childhood*. 6(2): 241–2.

Kline, S. (1993) *Out of the Garden: Toys and Children's Culture in the Age of TV Marketing*. London: Verso.

Mander, M. (1987) 'Bourdieu, the Sociology of Culture and Cultural Studies: A Critique', *European Journal of Communication* 2(4): 427–53.

Peretti, J. (1998) 'Middle Youth Ate My Culture', *Modern Review* 5 (March): 14–19.

Preston, P. (1996) 'Watch Out, Sex and Violence Are About', *The Guardian* (13 Dec.): 19.

Robbins, D. (1991) *The Work of Pierre Bourdieu*. Milton Keynes: Open University Press.

Robinson, M. (1997) *Children Reading Print and Television*. London: Falmer.

Schiach, M. (1993) '"Cultural Studies" and the Work of Pierre Bourdieu', *French Cultural Studies* 4(3/12): 213–23.

Seiter, E. (1993) *Sold Separately: Parents and Children in Consumer Culture*. New Brunswick, NJ: Rutgers University Press.

Silverstone, R. (1994) *Television and Everyday Life*. London: Routledge.

Simpson, M. (1994) *Male Impersonators: Men Performing Masculinity*. London: Routledge.

Part 14

PSYCHOLOGY

77

GOOD FRIENDS, OR JUST ACQUAINTANCES?

The relationship between child psychology and children's literature

Nicholas Tucker

Source: Peter Hunt (ed.), *Literature for Children: Contemporary Criticism*, London: Routledge, 1992, pp. 156–173.

The time lag between psychological theory and any popular take-up outside the profession varies from the almost immediate to the still pending, watch this space. Some psychoanalytic ideas, for example, made themselves felt fairly soon in terms either of passionate endorsement or else indignant denial. Cognitive psychology, dealing with the less emotionally charged issue of how we learn, has had to wait longer before making any general impact. Much depends therefore on how dramatic the psychological findings are and on the salience of their chief advocates. There is also the matter of how close the psychological theory is to the general mood of the time. Psychoanalysis, with its perpetual looking back into every past aspect of the individual, was particularly suited to a culture where fascination with the self had often come to replace more typical nineteenth-century interests in social, religious or community issues. Behaviourism, by contrast, always found fewer resonances in this same self-absorbed culture, and what literary references there are to its particular techniques are generally hostile.

Turning specifically to children's literature, the number of nods within it aimed in the direction of any specific school of psychology have always been sparse. This is not surprising. Authors with ready access to childhood themselves in terms of either personal memory or private fantasy generally have no need for any psychological key before feelings and memories about the past can begin to flow. Indeed, the ability to write about childhood can itself act as a process of therapy and understanding where past experience is concerned. Children's authors can therefore become their own psychologists when reconstructing their own childhoods and that of the imaginary characters they invent. Any child psychologists writing with similar authority about childhood matters can in this sense seem rivals to children's authors rather than colleagues. So what psychologists actually have to say about childhood often stands a good chance of either being ignored or else mocked by authors happy with the maps of childhood that they create in their books. Any child psychology they need can be made up as they go along in accordance with the demands of the plot and the personalities of the characters they have created.

Yet to the extent that children's authors are inevitably influenced by the culture within which they live, some of those psychological theories of childhood which have become widely taken up will eventually begin to work their way into their writing. This is particularly likely to happen in those stories where questions of motivation and personality figure most prominently. How should unpleasant or badly behaved child characters be portrayed, for example; as born nasty or as the result of poor parenting? What are the really important influences upon children when young? In both framing and attempting to answer such questions, individual authors usually prove laws only to themselves. But while some will have nothing to do with psychological explanation at all, others may indeed follow up some current psychological theory concerning childhood every now and again.

The exact contribution made by psychology to the writing of children's fiction can therefore never be described as a consistent, across-the-board phenomenon. Even so, the broad psychological movements I shall now briefly outline have all had some important effects on children's literature both past and present. Discussing these movements in rough chronological order does not imply that succeeding psychological theories necessarily always replaced those that went before. More commonly, various aspects of all these theories may be used at times by children's writers when it comes to trying to explain different types of human behaviour in their novels. The end results often amount to something of a psychological mishmash, with many children's writers following a tradition of partial psychological explanation and partial moral assessment so common in the fictional treatment of child characters past and present.

In the novels of Charles Dickens, for example, the explanations put forward to account for the different way various child characters behave change from child to child at the whim of the novelist himself. In *Oliver Twist* (1837–8), the Artful Dodger is shown clearly as a creature of his environment while Oliver is portrayed as driven by purely inner forces of goodness and nobility consistent with the exalted social origins whose existence he only discovers at the end of the book. In *David Copperfield* (1849–50) Steerforth's poor character is shown as the result of unwise parenting; David himself is always guided by a good inner spirit, while Uriah Heep seems born evil. But while psychologists must try to be consistent when searching for a developmental theory to explain human behaviour, novelists are perfectly free to pick and choose between theories of behaviour ranging from the environmental to the demonic, often in the same novel. So if various important psychological theories have been sampled by different novelists at times, few have ever been followed to the letter except perhaps for the theories of Jean-Jacques Rousseau (1712–78), the first quasi-psychologist to have a major effect on the fictional treatment of children in literature.

Rousseau actually condemned book-reading in his famous study of a perfect childhood, *Emile* (1762). As he puts it himself, 'Men may be taught by fables; children require the naked truth' (Rousseau 1969: 1). So apart from *Robinson Crusoe* (1719), which Rousseau did approve of, children were expected to turn to nature rather than to books for knowledge both about life and about themselves. A rather similar message was later suggested by Wordsworth, particularly in *The Prelude* (1850), once again with childhood in mind. The results of such influences have been endemic in much children's literature ever since, with the great bulk of stories written for them set in the countryside rather than in the town and often featuring children shown learning the hard way how to sail a boat, build a fire or catch a fish.

Just as characters in today's television soap operas are never seen watching or talking about other soap operas, children in such literature are rarely shown doing any reading. They are too occupied instead learning at first hand from Mother Nature, with real mothers usually as well out of the way as they were in *Emile* itself. The paradox of trying to advocate such do-it-yourself adventures through the agency of private reading, an activity involving little more physical effort from a child than merely sitting in a chair, can be a hard one for an author to outface. In the novels of Richard Jefferies and Arthur Ransome, for example, the determination of the author to get across the physical skills they write about with such enthusiasm shows itself in periodic, densely written descriptions of this or that activity. But as technical details multiply and paragraphs get longer, the final result is often obscure. What begins as a description of physical skill may finish as a highly abstract discussion well beyond the reach of all but the best-informed young readers, who – should they already possess and therefore understand such skills themselves – might anyhow be just as likely to be exercising them at that moment as to be reading a story about them.

A possible element of compensatory fantasy must also be borne in mind here, both on the part of the reader and the writer. Authors, often from quite bookish childhoods themselves, may get an extra kick from writing about real or imagined unbookish childhood activities. Writing in a reasonably lively way about the influence of reading, on the other hand, is a much harder task, even though it may well be that books themselves have often proved the most important influence in many an author's early years. Child readers, meanwhile, indulging in solitary reading may also get an agreeable thrill from imagining themselves coping heroically within an active environment. But for whatever reasons, the image of the child always learning best from or in the presence of nature remains an important literary ideal right up to our own times, despite evidence from contemporary surveys revealing the loneliness and privation of many children living in the British countryside now. Dissident stories hinting that all may not always be well for modern country children written by keen-eyed authors like Jan Mark (*Handles*, 1983) or Jill Paton Walsh (*Gaffer Sampson's Luck*, 1987) continue to chip away at this image in their own fashion.

Some parents after reading *Emile* actually tried to raise their own children on such principles, almost invariably with little success (Darton 1982: 146–7). A number of children's writers also accepted Rousseau's message in its entirety, as in Mrs Inchbald's witty fable *Nature and Art* (1796). But in general, Rousseau's ideals were part of a general cult of sensibility holding that it was more important for children to follow their instincts at their own pace than for them to become acquainted through books and teaching with the culture in which they were born. Almost the opposite was true of the earlier and never quite so influential theories of another great quasi-psychologist, John Locke. In his ideal education, children were to be allowed plenty of books so long as these were reasonably informative rather than full of 'useless trumpery' (Darton 1982: 18). For Locke believed that the child, born with no knowledge, could only learn from appropriate experience, with well-designed children's books a particularly good way of providing such learning.

This idea, shared of course by many who had never heard of Locke himself, has also remained as a pervasive influence in children's literature. Children's books today may not slip in the odd educational lesson as obtrusively as did nineteenth-century writers like R. M. Ballantyne, who rarely missed an opportunity to dwell on the flora and fauna found in the foreign parts he chose as settings for his adventure stories. Yet there is still a strong tendency to instruct both morally and about diverse matters of random knowledge in much modern children's literature. By the same token, children's books now that deal with matters thought undesirable, whether sexually, morally or politically, are still often attacked for the 'bad' message they convey to readers. Those making this type of criticism are consciously or unconsciously holding to the theory of learning by association outlined by Locke. This stated that children are affected by all experience, positively in the case of good experiences and negatively when the reverse is true. Each child, therefore, is the sum of all such experiences, and where literature is concerned, Locke believed that it behoves us to see that children's stories always aim at being wholesome, educational and generally useful. Such a message can still be heard on many an educational platform today.

The last quasi-psychologist I would pick out as particularly influential on children's literature is the German educationalist Friedrich Froebel. His insistence on the importance of storytelling, folk songs and traditional games in the education of young children gave the cause of literature a large boost both within schools and without. Locke might well have suspected more 'useless trumpery' at work as Froebel's kindergarten children sang their nursery songs or listened to fairy tales. But the concept of play as the best type of early learning helped put an end to the idea that books should always act as a form of instruction for young readers. Henceforth nonsense often stood as good a chance as solemn commonsense in the nursery, with importance now given to the intrinsic appeal of language itself as well as to its particular content.

Championing myth and legend as a form of wisdom rather than as undesirable relics of peasant superstition also allowed more children access to that special type of magical thinking that has always been so meaningful to them, either in literature or in oral tale-telling. Taking up the cause of very small children meant too that their particular needs were treated more seriously, including their literary needs. This belief would eventually lead to increased nursery education, more children's libraries and of course to many more books. With picture books in particular getting both cheaper and brighter with the advance of new printing techniques towards the end of the nineteenth century, the stage was set for the massive growth in children's literature for all.

The biggest upset facing conventional ideas about children and their favourite literature was still to come, in the shape of Freud. In a sense his essential message remains as subversive today as it was when psychoanalytic concepts began to become better known. Something of a literary man himself, Freud often used ideas from fiction and myth to illustrate his theories. Thus, 'It begins to dawn on us that the many fairy tales which begin "Once upon a time there was a king and queen" only mean to say that there was once a father and mother' (Freud 1973: 192). Or: 'The poet enables us to enjoy our own daydreams without shame or guilt' (Freud 1925: 5). In dreams, and no doubt in children's stories too, Freud believed that large animals were often symbolic representations of parents while small animals either stood for siblings or for child-readers themselves (Peller 1959).

It was the reasoning behind these bold pronouncements which was to have such an effect. For while traditional associationist psychology believed that children were the sum of their external experience, Freud reversed this equation. For him, it was a child's inner life that really mattered. Particularly important here were the fantasies and feelings that were either inherited as part of the human condition or else were the inevitable outcome of the tensions inseparable from all family life, happy or unhappy. Such fantasies could often be extremely aggressive not to say sadistic, frequently revolving around strong sexual interest.

Many myths and fairy tales contain vivid reflections of those fantasies mentioned by Freud as illustrating a child's pent-up aggressive feelings towards its parents at moments when tempers are lost and imaginary revenge is sought. *Snow White*, for example, explores the idea of the murderous mother-figure who must be killed to safeguard the life of her own child. *Jack and the Beanstalk* describes how a boy kills off a father-figure with the compliance of his mother. Many authors have incorporated elements of these themes in their own stories. A version of *Cinderella* can be found in Jane Austen's *Mansfield Park* (1814), for example, and aspects of *Beauty and the Beast* are suggested in Dickens's *Great Expectations* (1860–1). The continuing popularity of such fairy-tale themes suggests that Freud was right in believing that the inner tensions these fantasies reveal have always been present throughout history and have always found some reflection in favourite stories.

Most prevalent of all in fairy stories is the Oedipal myth, central to all Freudian psychology and reflecting a child's principal need to kill off in fantasy their main parental rival of the same sex, so allowing them unlimited access to the desired parent of the opposite sex (Freud 1973: 118). While any direct wish to kill a parent even in fantasy would generally arouse too much guilt, Freud argued that it was a different matter to enjoy reading stories about the extermination of parental symbols suitably disguised as traditional-style villains. As it is, giants, ogres, dragons and other monsters can stand very well for the resented, powerful father in the child's imagination. Witches meanwhile symbolize the resented side of motherhood, together with those wicked stepmothers, coiled, silky-voiced serpents and tempting mermaids who get their evil way by sexual allure rather than through traditional spells. And who other to outwit or slay these monsters than the young fairy-tale hero or heroine, setting out from home little more than a child, yet a couple of pages later often ready to take on marriage and a respected adult place in society? Although such fairy tales were once enjoyed by all ages, Freudian critics constantly stressed how much there is in them for those younger members of an audience, always particularly appreciative of any story in which they can at last walk tall and act big.

Hunting the symbol in this way quickly became something of a literary-psychoanalytic game, helping make children's literature more interesting to some adults who might otherwise have cared little for it. But any implications here for new ways of critically assessing contemporary children's literature remained vague. Books once considered good for children mainly because they were about good child characters setting good examples now indeed sometimes looked more questionable. Just as Freud defined the 'good' as merely dreaming about what the 'bad' actually get up to, so too could extra-pious literature be seen as another form of repression through which child-readers are denied any insight into the less respectable side of their own fantasy lives.

On the other hand, neither Freud nor his followers, almost all of whom led conventional middle-class existences, would ever have countenanced a modern children's literature giving direct expression to the unsocialized, aggressive and acquisitive forces existing within every individual which Freud believed always had to be kept at bay if civilization is to continue. As it was, American-style horror comics in the 1950s were quite as condemned by psychoanalytic spokesmen as they were by representatives from education and the church (Barker 1984). Yet their pseudo-Gothic, sadistic imaginings did in fact often resemble the descriptions of unconscious aggressive fantasies found for example in the work of Melanie Klein, another influential psychoanalyst.

One answer psychoanalytically inclined commentators found to the critical dilemma of what exactly should be included in modern children's books was to ignore such literature altogether. Instead, they concentrated on those traditional fairy stories and myths that most clearly lend themselves to Freudian interpretation. Various stories in the Grimm collection were especially relevant here, dealing as they do with taboo matters such as cannibalism, incest, torture, murder and bestiality. Because these stories were traditional they could get away with using such strong material in a way that would not be true of modern writing for children. A psychoanalyst like Bruno Bettelheim in his study *The Uses of Enchantment* (1976) not only totally endorsed the genius of fairy tales for the way they discuss those feelings that mean most to children, but also dismissed all modern children's literature as vapid by comparison. Indeed, his opinion of it was so low that he did not even attempt to sample it properly, citing only two examples of such modern decadence in the whole of his book (Tucker 1984: 33–41).

This ignorance of modern children's literature among most psychologists is typical, although some psychoanalytic critics did eventually get round to discussing classics from the more immediate past. *Alice's Adventures in Wonderland* (1865), *Peter Pan* (1904), *Treasure Island* (1883) and various other books have in time received psychoanalytic scrutiny, with more modern writers now also beginning to be considered in studies like Margaret and Michael Rustin's *Narratives of Love and Loss* (1987). In fact, modern children's literature by authors like Robert Westall, Anne Fine, Katherine Paterson and many others now offer all readers, including interested psychologists, a particularly rich mixture of human emotions for attention and analysis. But while it could once be assumed that almost every educated adult would be acquainted with children's classic novels read during their own childhood, common knowledge today about any modern classic for children can no longer be taken for granted. In our televisual age, every plot of every modern children's book must first be painfully spelled out in detail before any further type of analysis can begin. This helps make any reasonable discussion of contemporary children's fiction, psychological or otherwise, very difficult for a general audience.

The upshot of this is that while children's books themselves have changed enormously in the last fifty years, many adults remain ignorant or unconvinced of the reality of such changes. Those adults answering to this description would be genuinely surprised, for example, to know that there is now much more emphasis upon sexual feeling in children's books. The greater frankness following on from the psychoanalytic revolution has also played an important role in helping lead to this change. Sibling rivalry too – something particularly stressed by Adler, one of Freud's psychoanalytic contemporaries – can also now be mentioned as a normal family phenomenon. Family rivalry in former children's books was only alluded to in order to condemn it for its possibly appalling consequences, as in Mrs Sherwood's *The Fairchild Family* (1818) or Annie Keary's remarkable novel *The Rival Kings* (1857). Late twentieth-century children's writers by contrast have so absorbed the idea of the inevitability and occasional ferocity of sibling rivalry that if anything it is now over-stressed in many stories, leaving those families that get on fairly well somewhat unrepresented in contemporary fiction.

Other crumbs from the psychoanalytic table seized on by literary critics include the endorsement of fantasy not simply as a context for winning imaginary victories in the unconscious but as a valid metaphor for the passage of human life itself. For Carl Jung, fairy tales are often symbolic of the individual's struggle from the primitive, animal level to the world of higher consciousness and personal fulfilment. Forests, monsters, castles, valued helpers and all the various trials encountered on the way are aspects of the positive and negative side to the reader's own self. Although J. R. R. Tolkien and C. S. Lewis wrote their own literary fantasies from a Christian rather than a psychoanalytic background, the seriousness with which Tolkien himself has since been treated owes something to the way that Jung and others have helped turn the idea of myth into a psychological treasure-house for those setting out on their own quest for personal understanding.

Melanie Klein's particular psychoanalytic vision of children's capacity for sadistic reverie has not so far had much effect on children's literature. For her, infancy was a time for intense aggression aimed at the mother, arising from an infant's overriding wish to keep this parent all to themselves. When balked of this fierce desire, Klein believed that the infant took revenge by indulging in fantasies of destroying the mother in various painful ways. But at the same time, such violent fantasies can also come back to haunt the child, terrified (once their bad mood has passed) that all their aggression might actually have killed off the mother. Klein also believed that infants projected their own aggression on to persecutory parental figures in their imagination, who would then come back in nightmares or fantasies to threaten the infant with the same violence that the infant had originally wished upon them.

Klein's one essay about children's literature, where she writes about Colette's fable *L'enfant et les sortilèges*, is neither well known nor easy to read (Mitchell 1986). Yet some of her main ideas have to an extent been absorbed, often by those who have never heard of her. There is, for example, greater tolerance today of depictions of violence and death in books for smaller children. Those rougher, tougher nursery rhymes once shunned by inter-war anthologists now grace the pages of Raymond Briggs's influential collection *The Mother Goose Treasury*, first put together in 1966. Picture books since, like the *Frances* series by Russell and Lillian Hoban (1960–), Maurice Sendak's *Where the Wild Things Are* (1963), and John Burningham's *Come Away from the Water, Shirley* (1978) and many others have all explored childish fantasies revolving around resentment of parents, jealousy towards siblings or the occasional wish for murderous revenge.

Psychoanalytic influences apart, much else in psychology this century has had its own effect upon children's literature. Jean Piaget, for example, did a great deal to change attitudes towards small children. Like his fellow-countryman Rousseau, Piaget was not a great advocate of books for the young. Instead he always believed that children learn best when confronted by experience itself rather than by pre-digested, bookish instruction. Because of his teaching, backed up by educationists like Susan Isaacs and Maria Montessori, a new child-centred theory of teaching was established, based on advocating a better understanding of how small children think during their early years. Such thinking, Piaget argued, was not simply the result of arbitrary misunderstandings of adult thought. Instead, it had its own rules and structures. Those wishing to communicate with children effectively had better learn such rules for themselves first.

One result of this change of emphasis was the decline of the bad old textbook written in a style well above most children's heads. These were gradually replaced by books placing more emphasis on illustration and less on verbal explanation. Such illustrations were now often drawn without too much fussy detail, making it easier for pupils to understand and learn from them. Piaget's constant stress here was on the active nature of learning, with pupils in his estimation always eager to make their own sense of the material that most interested them. Books that still tried to anticipate this process by telling young readers exactly how they should be thinking about any topic would now more often be seen as merely counterproductive.

Instead, children were increasingly presented with clearly illustrated books written in plain language at an intellectual level they could be expected to follow. Whether the topic was sexual instruction, religious knowledge, history or geography, the main aim was always to get information across at a child-centred level. The effect of this approach was always clearer in non-fiction than in fiction, with *Comment la souris reçoit une pierre sur la tête et découvre le monde* (1971) – the one children's picture book Piaget ever worked on as a special adviser – little more than a lifeless compendium of childlike guesses about the general workings of the daily weather. But Piaget's particular genius was always more concerned with the development of children's logical thought than with the development of their imagination.

Once presented with interesting stories written at their own level, many children often proved to be more advanced than Piaget ever estimated in terms of their understanding of ordinary human thoughts, feelings and behaviour. Ideas of empathy, individual psychology or comparative justice, for example, could all make sense even to a very young audience once described in the context of a lively story involving characters around the same age and stage as their readers. As various post-Piagetian psychologists were to discover, even children under six were capable of making intelligent comments on their favourite stories, at times showing evidence of quite complex reasoning ability (see Donaldson 1978). The same children, faced by Piaget's more abstract questions, might indeed have seemed bewildered simply because they could not understand or identify with the way things were being put to them.

One serious limitation of Piaget's theories was their neglect of children's feeling for narrative as opposed to logic. He himself always saw children principally as lone explorers of the inanimate world. Post-Piagetian psychologists, by contrast, believe that children in fact often find social situations a good deal easier to comprehend, and indeed at times can manifest a certain social sophistication in their understanding much in advance of their comprehension of the non-social world. This school of thought was enormously enhanced by the rediscovery during the 1960s of the work of the great Russian psychologist Vygotsky, whose principal argument was that the true significance of language as the essential tool for learning had hitherto been overlooked.

For Vygotsky, play and language represented the most fundamental of human attempts to transcend the here and now in order to construct symbolic models for the better understanding of the nature of the world we live in. Because of a child's highly developed social sense, the different cultural associations surrounding the use of language will often mean as much to him or her as will the actual meaning of individual words. One child, for example, will quickly learn that language in all its variety is something to be relished and encouraged; another will, equally quickly, soon understand the reverse if this happens to be true. It is parents then later on schools that principally hand down linguistic tools to children. Those that provide them with plenty of positive verbal stimulation are also providing them with the abundant mental scaffolding necessary to help them in time to construct their own rich models of the world.

For children brought up in this type of linguistic atmosphere, language will be seen as a vital and empowering process, invaluable for asking questions or conversing about mutual interests. Such children can also borrow potentially useful 'scripts' from their parents, for example in learning how to imitate the way a parent answers the phone or constructs a shopping list. But parents and schools who are niggardly in their attitudes towards play and language will be passing on a much more limited set of tools for children trying to make sense of the present and also plan in the imagination for the future.

The implications here for children's literature are considerable. Fiction has always been a medium wherein the child's here and now can be transcended, enabling the child to move into foreign worlds and different social roles. The ability to indulge in this type of imaginative play constitutes what Vygotsky saw as the ultimate difference between humans and animals, since only humans can use their brains to envisage a different way of doing things at another period of time. Such ideas can be tested out first in language, play or through the imagination. For Jerome Bruner, an American psychologist working along the same lines, part of the appeal of myth is that it offers readers a range of metaphysical identities against which the individual can compare his or her own spread of multiple identities (Bruner 1979). By reducing the complexities of everyday life to a series of symbolic forms and choices, myth can also help readers find a pattern in their own concepts of themselves and the reality within which they live.

Myth, and mythopoeic literature in general, first frames then offers some answers to many of the immemorial problems of existence. At other levels, fiction provides a more mundane commentary on human affairs. It describes, for example, what people say or do in which situations, so suggesting a link between a reader's own sense of self and their understanding of how others may operate in the same social situation. It also describes feelings that readers recognize from their own experience, or emotions foreign to particular readers but still important when it comes to trying to understand the thoughts and behaviour of others.

In this way fiction maintains a continuous form of dialogue with those readers who find themselves comparing their own personalities, reactions, emotions, thoughts and modes of speech with those of the author and the characters in his or her book. Such comparisons can suggest new possibilities to readers in the conduct of their own lives. Whether readers then take up any of these possibilities is another matter. But giving them a type of choice that is both wide and informed is something else that literature at its best has to offer.

Vygotsky's emphasis on the important cultural overtones of language also helped focus more attention on the meaning behind words in fiction. The issue of racist or sexist uses of language in children's books was once dismissed as a comparatively unimportant matter. But when it was argued that particular words or phrases carried a whole network of implications for young readers, some of which might prove to be extremely negative, then such matters came to be seen as more significant. Vygotsky's belief that children usually learn more from each other also had important implications for the treatment of fiction in the classroom. Much of the recent work on reader response now focuses on the interaction between individual readings of a story and the way such readings once expressed in public so often grow, modify and deepen (Hayhoe and Parker 1990).

This realization that others' opinion on anything may be different from one's own is an essential step in Vygotsky's outline of how young brains best develop. As he saw it, the more different hypotheses an individual is aware of, the more able that individual then becomes at understanding complex situations that demand to be looked at from a number of points of view. The fact that children often learn this type of developmental step better from each other relates to their ability to follow childlike reasoning, their own and other's, more easily than they usually follow most adult reasoning. To the extent that children's fiction provides a highly appropriate forum for discussion and speculation about motivation, character, or even simply what comes next at a stage half-way through a story, successful classroom discussion of different reader responses lends itself well to Vygotsky's main purposes.

So it is no accident that arguments for the importance of providing fiction in schools now often stress not simply the literary merits of books but also the opportunity they give pupils for the better understanding both of themselves and of others through discussion, comparison and introspection. At the same time, modern children's authors like Alan Garner, William Mayne, Jan Mark and Margaret Mahy no longer write fiction that can always be understood easily at first glance. Instead, they often leave gaps in their stories for interested readers to fill in for themselves, either privately in the imagination or out loud in classroom discussion.

The most recent psychological developments have tended to concentrate more on the nature of fiction, and the covert as well as overt nature of its message, and also on the personal nature of each individual reader's response to it. Modern linguistic critics such as Saussure insist that meaning in a text is something necessarily imposed on readers by the arbitrary nature of language itself. Other critics like Norman Holland (1974) go along with Barthes and others in the various structuralist schools of criticism. The main belief here is that each individual can make sense of a text only by creating their own version of it in their imagination in accordance with their own particular needs and experiences.

Such arguments have yet to have any serious impact on the writing of children's fiction, and later developments in psychoanalytic thinking, particularly in the work of Lacan, may well remain too obscure for all but a tiny coterie. However, the effect of all these recent critical theories upon the current discussion of children's literature has been marked. On the question of the personal nature of all literary responses, some have argued that no critic can ever attempt to justify their own reaction to a text as in any way valid for everyone else. If that critic is also trying to answer for child-readers, there is more doubt now whether he or she can be sure that their own reconstruction of what a child wants can ever have any meaning for all children, or even for one. This particular point of view has alarmingly nihilist implications for all critics of children's literature. It is not an argument that will simply go away, and must eventually be met one way or another.

The general obscurity of much recent critical discussion of literature has led to a chasm opening up between the academic treatment of children's literature and criticism of it at a more popular level. Many children's authors must now be puzzled by the latest, more recondite developments in critical theorizing about their books; so too will most teachers, parents and of course child-readers as well. This is not a healthy situation, and the days when authors like C. S. Lewis and J. R. R. Tolkien could address their audience equally clearly both as writers and as critics already seem remote. Yet the present gulf between literary practice and literary theory could widen even further as more ingenious academic critics give it their full attention.

But while discussion of reader response often exists at present at a dauntingly jargon-infested level, other psychological approaches continue to have a more accessible type of influence on public opinion. The patient observations of child behaviour earlier on this century made by psychologists like Arnold Gesell have provided a much clearer picture of the different stages of child development. More is known now about how children play, what they believe and what they like doing best. Baby-care books have taken up many of these findings, and picture books increasingly reflect a closer knowledge of developmental stages in the early years. If and when small children go through a phase of mild anxiety or disturbance, for example, it is now less easy to put the blame on the influence of undesirable books. On the contrary, research almost always concludes that such specific influence to the bad is highly unlikely to come from one source alone, given everything else going on in a child's life at the time. The modern author or illustrator therefore has much greater freedom now, with the public pillorying of fiction as a prime suspect for leading a child astray now a thing of the past.

On the other hand, most leading children's authors and illustrators are also much less well known now than would once have been the case, and must consequently fight harder for any sort of public recognition. The fact that television and video are blamed more than books for sometimes having a bad influence upon the young simply reflects the greater importance today of visual over literary stimulation in the lives of most children. Whether this occasional scapegoating of television is as unfair and unfounded as was so much criticism of former children's literature remains a controversial area, in need of more research.

Social scientists have an obvious future role to play here, just as they have already done this century when it comes to adding to the public grasp of important social issues. The complex nature of deviancy, handicap or poverty, for example, is much better understood today, and this increased understanding has manifested itself in some children's literature tackling such issues. Villains in children's books were once regularly drawn from various social minorities, the physically odd or the mentally unstable. Today, we have been taught that the mere fact of coming from a different race, class or physique to the majority is no longer enough to label any fictional character as suspect even before anything else becomes clear about them.

Greater knowledge and awareness of gender issues has also helped the slow process of seeing off those out-of-date sexual sterotypes once such a feature of children's publishing. More too is known about the actual readership of children's books. What few nineteenth-century surveys of reading there were existed at a very amateur level, producing unlikely candidates such as *Alice's Adventures in Wonderland* or the novels of Charles Dickens as children's favourite reading. But better-organized research using social science techniques has helped force publishers and writers into realizing that the standard audience for children's books is not simply a middle-class two-child family living quietly with mother in the suburbs while father goes out to work. Today's greater awareness of changing family patterns, new ethnic minorities and the needs of previously marginalized readers such as the handicapped has helped lead to more adventurous writing and publishing for all types of children.

At an individual level, the old moral-medical model for explaining individual deviancy has also wilted in the face of psychological research. Maladjusted children are less often seen now as diseased or merely missing out on some essential moral fibre. The new stress on individual disturbance as something that is often compounded by severe social problems has led to stories that show far more understanding of those bullies, tell-tales or juvenile thieves whom it was once so satisfying to dislike and then condemn out of hand in the former, morally polarized world of so much children's fiction. This more complex view of the causes of individual behaviour has resulted in a number of stories that may appear fairly static on the surface but where the main adventures are more taken up with inner journeys of psychological understanding where some of the chief characters are concerned. Those adventures where physical danger and ultimate survival are the chief concern are still with us in the world of children's books. But even they more commonly discuss the psychological dimension to heroism as well, in contrast to the former stress on courage and endurance alone.

As to the future, there is no guarantee that today's commonly accepted psychological theories at either a popular or an academic level will last with the years. Psychology is a far more normative study than those who argue for its purely scientific status are prepared to admit. Both it and children's literature will go on evolving, setting new norms in time and continuing to have a two-way influence upon each other. For while psychologists are now quite good at painting the wider picture of different developmental processes, individual psychological portraits have always been best created by novelists. What possible effects such literature may in turn have had upon psychological thinking over the years remains an even more mysterious and still relatively unexplored topic.

References

Barker, M. (1984) *A Haunt of Fears*, London: Pluto Press.

Bettelheim, B. (1976) *The Uses of Enchantment: The Meaning and Importance of Fairy Tales*, New York: Knopf.

Bruner, J. (1979) *On Knowing*, New York: Belknap.

Darton, F. J. H. (1982) *Children's Books in England*, 3rd edn. Cambridge: Cambridge University Press.

Donaldson, M. C. (1978) *Children's Minds*, London: Collins.

Freud, S. (1925) 'The relation of the poet to the daydreamer' (1908), in *Collected Papers IV*, London: Hogarth Press.

—— (1973) *Introductory Lectures on Psychoanalysis*, Harmondsworth: Penguin.

Hayhoe, M. and Parker, S. (1990) *Reading and Response*, Milton Keynes: Open University Press.

Holland, N. (1974) *Five Readers Reading*, New Haven: Yale University Press.

Mitchell, J. (1986) *The Selected Melanie Klein*, Harmondsworth: Penguin.

Peller, L. E. (1959) 'Daydreams and children's favourite books: psychoanalytic comments', *The Psychoanalytic Study of the Child*, 14: 414–33.

Rousseau, J. J. (1762/1969) *Emile*, Harmondsworth: Penguin.

Rustin, M. and M. (1987) *Narratives of Love and Loss*, London: Verso.

Tucker, N. (1984) 'Dr Bettelheim and Enchantment', *Signal* 43: 33–41.

78

PSYCHOANALYSIS AND CHILDREN'S LITERATURE

The case for complementarity

Kenneth Kidd

Source: *The Lion and the Unicorn* 28(1) (2004): 109–130.

What can psychoanalysis tell us about children's literature? And what, we should also ask, can children's literature tell us about psychoanalysis? What work connecting these two fields has already appeared, and how might we productively imagine their relation in the future? Although psychoanalysis and children's literature have much in common, psychoanalytic criticism of children's literature is a fairly recent undertaking. Generally speaking, there are three kinds of psychoanalytic work on children's literature so far: close readings of individual texts, analyses of particular genres, and broader meditations on the enterprise of children's literature and/or children's literature criticism.

The 1980s and 1990s saw an upsurge of psychoanalytic work on children's literature. Hamida Bosmajian's engaging treatments of *Charlie and the Chocolate Factory* (1964) and *Johnny Tremain* (1943) set a high standard, offering nuanced psychoanalytic consideration alongside attention to the sociohistorical dimensions of the texts under scrutiny. In their co-edited volume *Psychoanalytic Responses to Children's Literature*, Lucy Rollin and Mark I. West furnish not only lively analyses but also a bibliography of the burgeoning scholarship. Two special issues of the *Children's Literature Quarterly*, edited by Roberta Seelinger Trites, have been devoted to psychoanalysis and children's literature; the second issue specifically explores Freud's *unheimlich* or the uncanny.

Scholars are now looking at genre as well as specific texts, using psychoanalysis to take up broader issues of literary and cultural formation. Exemplary writings include Lucy Rollin's book-length analysis of nursery rhymes, and Karen Coats's essays on alphabet books and young adult fiction.

Coats's treatment of young adult fiction draws from Julia Kristeva's theory of abjection to argue that "the exploration of abjection has come to dominate the [young adult] genre" ("Abjection" 291). Like Coats, Martha Westwater turns to Kristeva to suggest a strong affinity between adolescence and abjection in her book *Giant Despair Meets Hopeful: Kristevan Readings in Adolescent Literature*. Westwater reads Kristeva as a theorist of hope as well as abjection, as does Coats, and while I disagree with Westwater's sense of the current cultural moment, I find intriguing her idea that adolescence and abjection go hand in hand.[1] Critics often see the so-called "problem novel" as emblematic of the young adult's problem interior (along these lines, see Crew).

Identifying the workings of genre does help foster a more dynamic practice of criticism. In such discussions, scholars are starting to underscore the interdependence, or mutuality, of psychoanalysis and writing for young people. This emphasis is promising, as it moves criticism away from a one-way and applied mode, in which psychoanalysis discovers its own truths in the literary text. Psychoanalysis, after all, is not merely a method, but a rich intellectual and narrative tradition. It's time to leave behind the "psychoanalytic approaches" or "responses to" model of scholarship. It seems more productive to treat psychoanalysis and children's literature as discourses that revolve around similar concerns and themes, and which may be mutually constitutive.[2]

As I show in the first section of this essay, however, disciplinary assessments of children's literature as an enterprise (as opposed to more local readings of text or genre) too often assume an oppositional rather than a complementary relation between psychoanalysis and children's forms. Whatever their orientation, such oppositional readings stage a showdown between psychoanalysis and literature, usually centering around a canonical case of the literary "child" (or child figure): Peter Pan, Pinocchio, Winnie-the-Pooh. These readings treat the very scene of canonicity as symptomatic of analytical and cultural malaise, usually recuperating the text from its sorry social context.

Against this assumption of irreconcilable differences, I then trace some of the relays between psychoanalysis and children's culture. I sketch a provisional genealogy of the psychoanalytic investment in child analysis and children's forms, which I think helped set the stage for the psychoanalytic interpretation of literature more broadly. First, I outline some general thematic and disciplinary parallels between child analysis and children's literature, looking at both as "mother-centered" fields. Next, I consider the psychoanalytic interest in children's play. The study of children's play, as advocated by Melanie Klein especially, helped shift attention to processes of human symbolization more broadly, even as children—actual and/or figurative—remained the grounding subjects of psychoanalysis. Klein's work with actual children made it possible to produce knowledge about children's symbolic activity, including drawing and writing. In a sense, psychoanalysis "textualized" childhood, through case history writing as well as clinical theory, such that the children's story or work became just as legitimate an object of inquiry as the child herself.

In the last section, I address the centrality of folklore to the field of children's literature. Folklore is often taken as the most primal form of children's literature, since young children listen to stories before they read (or write) them. Folklore has also long inspired psychoanalysis, even as psychoanalysis has been applied to folklore. I suspect that the interest in folklore across the twentieth century owes something to the extraordinary success that psychoanalysis has enjoyed in the United States, as a profession and a discourse that emphasizes the importance of childhood experience and fantasy. Put another way, we reproduce folklore, keep it in circulation, in part because we think it's psychologically useful and/or appropriate for children—something we learned from Freud, Klein, and other theorists (who themselves drew from oral narrative). Thus folklore, like children's play, makes possible both psychoanalytic theory and children's literature, two seemingly different projects that actually have a lot in common.

Oppositional case writing

The most notorious oppositional reading of children's literature and psychoanalysis is Jacqueline Rose's now-canonical *The Case of Peter Pan, or The Impossibility of Children's Fiction* (1984), designed to disabuse us of childhood innocence, textual simplicity, and other wishful notions. If we believe Rose, children's literature hinges upon the "impossible" relation of child to adult (1). Psychoanalysis, on the other hand, is the discourse through which we understand that impossible relation as such, through which we interrogate the innocence of both childhood and children's literature. For Rose, it is Sigmund Freud who tells more truthfully the story of childhood, exposing it as a myth (if not quite an "impossibility") that gives coherence to otherwise alarming experiences of self and otherness. If we learn to read the "real" Freud, she says, and not the revisionist Freud of ego psychology and object relations theory, we'll realize that Freud sought to dismantle the very ideologies allegedly underwriting children's literature. "In most discussions of children's fiction which make their appeal to Freud," Rose complains (and justifiably so), "childhood is part of a strict developmental sequence at the end of which stands the cohered and rational consciousness of the adult mind" (13).

Rose builds her case around Freud and J. M. Barrie's *Peter Pan* (1904), with shorter discussions of Rousseau, Alan Garner, and Robert Louis Stevenson's *Treasure Island* (1883). *Peter Pan* functions for Rose as a quasi-folkloric foil to that duplicitous enterprise known as children's literature. She seems to think that *Peter Pan* is the closest thing we have to good psychoanalysis in the imaginative register. Although Rose introduces a useful hermeneutics of suspicion into children's literature studies, she also dismisses children's literature in keeping with a familiar bias. While she makes brilliant use of *Peter Pan*, her celebration of psychoanalysis hinges upon her caricature of this vibrant, diverse field.

A more local and recent example of this oppositional line of thinking is Jennifer Stone's spirited discussion of "Pinocchiology." Noting that virtually every major writer and cultural critic in Italy has written about Carlo Lorenzini's *The Adventures of Pinocchio: Story of a Puppet* (1881), Stone criticizes the discourse of "Pinocchiology" for its obsession with native Italian culture and its evasion of Freud's central insights into the psyche, an evasion that she playfully christens the "Pinocchio Complex." Here the fetish of a child-text serves as a form of resistance to Freud. The *true* story of Pinocchio, she holds, much like the true story of Peter Pan as retold by Rose, confirms Freud's wisdom and exposes the mechanisms of cultural denial. Both Rose and Stone urge respect for the Freudian canon as a safeguard against the cult of childhood/nativism.

Also in this tradition is Karín Lesnik-Oberstein's *Children's Literature: Criticism and the Fictional Child* (1994), which declares the impossibility of children's literary criticism. The first five chapters are devoted to the familiar argument that children's literature criticism relies upon various constructions of the child that are finally impossible to maintain. Specifically, she holds, children's literature criticism doesn't own up to its own investment in the "emotional education" of children—a persuasive point in and of itself, even if it doesn't necessarily follow that attempts to theorize childhood are disingenuous. The final chapter ushers in the hero of the story, psychoanalysis, or more particularly, D. W. Winnicott. Lesnik-Oberstein feels that because he especially attends to issues of transference, interpersonal relation, and the analytic space, Winnicott avoids essentializing "the child" and works to accommodate particular children. While children's literature criticism is "inextricably tied to a *prescriptive* role," in her view, psychoanalysis and psychotherapy allegedly function "*non-prescriptively*" (176).

In her compelling study *Hide and Seek* (1995), Virginia Blum comes to different conclusions. Psychoanalytic theories that claim to illuminate childhood, she argues, really mythologize it. The psychoanalytic child is not the actual child; the latter is an "unknowable subject" and indeed the "ultimate blind spot" of psychoanalysis (23). Blum's analyses of the writings of Freud, Anna Freud, Melanie Klein, D. W. Winnicott, and other prominent child analysts make compelling her own deconstructive case. She usefully identifies key truth claims of psychoanalysis—among them, for instance, that the child has direct access to the Real, and that there is later a fall into sexuality and discourse alike. "Any concept of estrangement, Otherness, alienation, mediation," Blum holds, "depends for its signification on a fantasy of undisrupted wholeness" (53). According to Blum, psychoanalysis obsessively posits a difference between child and adult that it can neither tolerate nor sustain.[3]

Both Rose and Blum insist that the adult-child relationship is "impossible," but they disagree over how that impossibility is best represented or handled. While Rose prefers the real Freud as a counterdiscourse to children's literature, Blum puts her faith in literature rather than psychoanalysis. Blum's book begins with three chapters on psychoanalysis, then moves into a discussion of canonical literature about (if not for) children: texts by Charles Dickens, Henry James, and Vladimir Nabokov. While Peter Pan is Rose's poster boy, Blum concentrates on a different child-figure, the "go-between" child of literature, who serves as a mediator and messenger. As with Peter Pan, the go-between is a liminal or hybrid child, whose function reveals the difficulties of language and love. Blum understands literature as usefully ambivalent. Literature does not promise us the same kind of truth as psychoanalysis, she maintains, and so we should trust it more.

Rose examines three discourses—children's fiction, *Peter Pan*, and psychoanalysis (or four, if we distinguish the real Freud from bad psychoanalysis)—using the latter two to expose the falsehood of the first. In Blum's work, two discourses receive scrutiny—psychoanalysis and go-between narrative—neither quite children's nor adult literature. Blum doesn't disparage children's literature, but she has little to say about it (aren't there plenty of go-between figures in children's books?). It seems that for these critics, children's literature is either misleading or inadequate. Other scholars, of course, rightly emphasize that children's literature is sometimes *quite* self-conscious about its own "duplicity" and (in any case) that it shouldn't be so quickly dismissed.

The oppositional spirit is not limited to the academic field of criticism, but indeed crosses over into mainstream book culture. I'm thinking of what we might call (after Stone) Poohology, the popular and critical discourse of Winnie-the-Pooh. Over the years, some very creative books for adults have drawn from A. A. Milne's classic *Winnie-the-Pooh* (1926), such as Benjamin Huff's *Tao of Pooh* (1982) and *The Te of Piglet* (1992), and Frederick Crews's spoof of criticism, *The Pooh Perplex* (1963). In 2001, Crews gave us a sequel to the *Pooh Perplex* entitled (predictably enough) *Postmodern Pooh*. As in the earlier book, Crews makes fun of the excesses of literary criticism, this time parodying queer theory, postcolonial studies, and so forth. In his review of *Postmodern Pooh*, Jan Susina observes that "[w]hat Crews is trying to suggest in both of his Pooh books is that the best way to show the limitations or flaws of a critical approach is to apply it to a children's text" (276). As Susina notes, Crews mocks the likes of Homi Bhabba, Judith Butler, and Gayatri Spivak but is respectful toward the work of children's literature scholars, as if the wisdom of Pooh extends to that critical field (and that field alone). Here, even more than in the case of Peter Pan, literature wins. Unlike Rose, Crews is not interested in affirming psychoanalysis. He is, in fact, one of its most impassioned critics, having renounced his earlier psychoanalytic study of Hawthorne. Like Rose, however, he invokes a canonical children's book to make his case against culture, in this instance the culture of criticism.

Operating in the same vein is John Tyerman Williams, whose *Pooh and the Psychologists* (2000)—subtitled "In Which It is Proven that Pooh Bear is a Brilliant Psychotherapist"—completes his trilogy of Poohology primers (the others are *Pooh and the Philosophers* and *Pooh at the Millennium*). Pitched to a wider audience than Crews's Pooh books, *Pooh and the Psychologists* offers a tongue-in-cheek look at twentieth-century psychology and psychotherapy. The way Williams explains it, Pooh is a clinician whose seeming ineptitude is actually proof of his therapeutic genius. Pooh helps Piglet to mature, Rabbit to confront his xenophobia, Owl to communicate with the masses, and Eeyore to overcome his clinical depression. Like all good therapists, Pooh is eclectic in approach, borrowing from Freud, Jung, Winnicott, Piaget, and Lacan, among others. Despite the parody, or maybe because of it, Williams's book is weirdly informative. Williams mocks not only psychoanalytic concepts, but also psychoanalytic writing practices, among them character studies and close readings. Williams, of course, isn't seriously arguing for the profundity of Pooh, but he is certainly poking fun at our collective faith in mind science.

There are responsible academic models of children's culture "case" writing, privileging neither literature nor analysis, which do not assume children's literature to be deceptive or innocent. I have in mind Jonathan Arac's "*Huckleberry Finn*" *as Idol and Target* (1997) and Carolyn Steedman's *Strange Dislocations* (1995), both of which invoke an iconic child figure (Mark Twain's Huck Finn and Goethe's Mignon, respectively) to underscore the complementary, if often contested, relation of literature to other discourses of culture. In both books, the very liminality of these representative child figures suggests the absurdity of championing literature over psychoanalysis or vice versa. Steedman, an historian, shows how childhood became a mode of interiority through and across literature and psychoanalysis alike; Arac addresses the literary and pop-psychological operations of what he calls "hypercanonization." Arac and Steedman manage to move beyond a polemical practice of oppositional case writing, even as they appropriate to their own critical ends the rhetorical power of the liminal child.

Child analysis and children's literature

Psychoanalysis and children's literature should not be seen as oppositional. A more informed understanding of both disciplines will not only help to challenge oppositional posturing, but also to situate more local readings of text and genre within the wider scene. Even more, an understanding of child analysis will illuminate psychoanalysis's affinities with children's literature. Actually, we could invert the usual practice of seeing child analysis as a subset of psychoanalysis, and argue that psychoanalysis is really a mode of child analysis that recognizes explicitly the adult's early memories and fantasies.

From the start, psychoanalysis was part and parcel of a new interest in childhood that drew from evolutionary metaphor and the emergent social sciences. That interest in turn transformed the scene of children's literature. "When the late nineteenth century found that its researches into origin and development focused attention on the child," writes Juliet Dusinberre, "it simultaneously produced for those children a literature which revealed as clearly as possible adult hopes for the new generation" (32). Dusinberre's *Alice to the Lighthouse: Children's Books and Radical Experiments in Art* (1987) chronicles that simultaneous interest in children's development and children's books through the modernist period, pointing to the influence not only of Freud but also of Charles Darwin, Friedrich Froebel, James Sully, and others. While there may be no direct or simple correspondence between psychoanalysis and children's literature, it's safe to say that the whole project of writing for children was profoundly altered by the insights of psychoanalysis, and child analysis especially. This period also marks the beginning of professional writing about children's literature; one of the earliest treatments was E. M. Field's *The Child and His Book* (1891), and others soon followed.

In America, the successful popularization of psychoanalysis coincided with the early-twentieth-century heyday of children's book culture. The 1910s and 1920s saw the anxious solicitation of "quality" children's books, often defined against syndicate-produced series fiction. Even as they decried the evils of mass production, more and more people, most of them women, got involved in book publishing and reviewing. They worked to contain and channel the forces of commercialism, and thus became a vital part of the children's book industry. In 1916, Bertha Mahoney opened the first small American bookshop for children in Boston. She also distributed book lists which, by 1924, evolved into *The Horn Book Magazine*, still going strong today. In 1918, Anne Carroll Moore, of the New York Public Library, began reviewing children's books in *The Bookman*. The year before, Children's Book Week was launched, and the Macmillan Publishing Company created the first department of children's books within a major house, headed by Louise Seaman Bechtel. Doubleday Page soon followed suit. In 1921, publisher Frederic Melcher (of *Publishers' Weekly* fame) launched the Newbery Medal, the first award for excellence in children's literature and still one of the nation's most prestigious literary prizes.

Melcher's place in this larger movement is often overemphasized at the expense of the women librarians, booksellers, and reviewers who are largely responsible for inaugurating this new, largely middle-class public sphere.

Like the movement to introduce "quality" children's television programming that began in the 1960s (and that produced *Sesame Street*, itself vital to the success of the Public Broadcasting System), this earlier public sphere was conceived and realized largely by women. I mention this because there's a rough parallel between this American culture of children's literature and the contemporaneous scene of child analysis in Europe. Sigmund Freud and his Hungarian colleague Sándor Ferenczi felt that the analysis of children would make significant contributions to the discipline, and they encouraged women to pursue work along these lines. As Freud was inspiring his daughter Anna to expand upon her work as a teacher by becoming an analyst of children, Ferenczi was helping his assistant Melanie Klein to pursue her own studies in this area. Hermine Hug-Hellmuth, a former Viennese schoolteacher, had paved the way, and Freud and Klein were quick to follow her lead. That child analysis long remained the calling of women is clear from the histories of psychoanalysis. Ferenczi, one of the most sympathetic parties and the author of several essays about child abuse, nonetheless pitched child analysis as "a suitable endeavour for a woman" (Grosskurth 74).

Despite their many and acrimonious differences, Anna Freud and Melanie Klein invoke the maternal in their advocacy of child analysis. Anna Freud's work is directed largely at teachers, and she appropriates pedagogical authority, presenting herself as the mother of teachers. Analysis for Klein was clearly a form of mothering: not the kinder, gentler form of education that Anna Freud advocated, but rather a rough-and-tumble sort of mothering, a practice of tough love. Klein even analyzed her own children—standard analytical practice in the early years of psychoanalysis—but gave them pseudonyms in her case studies. Janet Sayers argues that the influence of woman pioneers, such as Anna Freud and Melanie Klein, effectively transformed psychoanalysis from a patriarchal to a matriarchal system. This conclusion seems premature and a bit simplistic. While psychoanalysis may be "mother-centered," thanks to the legacy of Klein especially, men still dominate the profession, especially in terms of the theoretical canon.

We might instead conclude that as child analysis underwent professionalization, it was masculinized; in the object relations school, for example, it was W. R. D. Fairbarn and D. W. Winnicott who rose to prominence after Klein. The current psychoanalytic experts on childhood development are men, foremost among them John Bowlby. The teaching and study of children's literature—like teaching, social work, and other professions devoted to children and families—has likewise been denigrated as a feminine project and then recuperated as a proper vocation for men. My fear is that children's literature has become a more legitimate field in English studies as more men have adopted it. Never mind that Francelia Butler of the University of Connecticut was the major mover and shaker for decades, founding the MLA Division and the journal *Children's Literature*. Or that most children's literature scholars are women, as are most authors of children's literature. To this day there exists a divide in children's literature studies between scholars working in English and scholars based in the disciplines of education, library science, and social work. This divide is not so dramatically gendered as to suggest conspiracy, but I do think that the respectability of children's literature as a specialty has come at the professional expense of women across the disciplines.

Women analysts and women specialists in children's literature are routinely figured as mothers, not only because they often *are* mothers, but also because mothering furnishes a lingua franca for professional practice. In the 1920s and '30s, mothering became nearly analogous with both children's book reviewing and with the analytic situation in clinical work. With respect to the latter, in her recent assessment of Klein, Kristeva observes that "Klein's strong tendency to 'mother' the unconscious endured and even insinuated itself into her most coherent and objective practices later in her career" (*Melanie Klein* 45). After Klein, Winnicott imagined analysis as clinical reclamation of "good enough" mothering and the enabling of regression: "I have found that the patient has needed phases of regression to dependence in the transference," he writes, "these giving experiences of the full effect of adaptation to need that is in fact based on the analyst's (mother's) ability to identify with the patient (her baby)" (137). Whether socially progressive or reactionary, this mother-speak permeates both child analysis and children's literature (and later advocacy for children's television). Kristeva even suggests that Klein's work and thought flourished in England precisely *because* that nation had long been preoccupied with the interiority of childhood and had produced an impressive tradition of children's books (*Melanie Klein* 37).

What I'm trying to outline are some transatlantic institutional and disciplinary parallels between children's literature and psychoanalysis worth further investigation. The relation of psychoanalysis to child analysis itself is, of course, also complex, and I don't mean to oversimplify that scene either. But even there we can see resemblances to the equally vexed scene of children's literature, in the sense that both psychoanalysis and "adult" literature at once affirm and disavow their investments in childhood.

Consider briefly the case of Jacques Lacan, who in his famous Rome discourse of 1953 ("The Function and Field of Speech and Language in Psychoanalysis") made quite clear his reservations about child analysis. Lacan attributes the decline of interest in speech and language—Freud's real concern, he holds—to work on the imaginary, to object relations theory, and to discussions of countertransference. These three new emphases are "pioneer activities" that have nonetheless led psychoanalysis astray, in his view. The first he attributes directly to "the analysis of children, and . . . the fertile and tempting field offered to the attempts of researchers by access to the formation of structures at the preverbal level" (35). Freud, he says, knew not to venture too far into this field; Lacan praises Freud for discovering infantile sexuality indirectly, through the analysis of adults and through parental mediation in the case of Little Hans.

Lacan's critique of child analysis is interesting for many reasons, not the least of which is that his own essay on the mirror stage returns us to Freud's foundational speculations on infantile helplessness (not just infantile sexuality) and depends upon the existential primal scene of the baby in front of the mirror. Even if he's working to counteract the assumptions of ego psychology and object relations theory, Lacan still reinvents psychoanalysis through childhood; it's no coincidence that he arranged the mirror stage essay first in *Écrits* (1977). We could even argue that Lacan develops his discourse of the imaginary, the symbolic, and the real largely through the case studies of childhood conducted by other theorists and his students (Klein's case of Little Dick, for instance, as well as the research of Rosine Lefort). Lacan clearly owes much to Klein, especially her ideas about symbolization. Presumably what differentiates Lacan from child analysis is his attention to language and/as the unconscious, and his remove from the compromised world of mother-analysis. "We would truly like to know more about the effects of symbolization in the child," he remarks, "and psychoanalysts who are also mothers, even those who give our loftiest deliberations a matriarchal air, are not exempt from that confusion of tongues by which Ferenczi designated the law of the relationship between the child and the adult" (36).

Lacan refers to "The Confusion of Tongues between Adults and the Child: The Language of Tenderness and of Passion" (1933), Sándor Ferenczi's final professional paper. Ferenczi notes the tendency of patients to embrace the secret desires of their analysts, much as children unconsciously bind themselves to the secret wishes and emotions of their caregivers. The child/patient thus abandons her native, or "mother," tongue to accommodate the parent/analyst. Lacan holds that mother-analysts do not really listen to the unconscious, and his accusation is part of a larger conversation about transference and countertransference.

The confusion of tongues is likewise central to children's literature and to assessments of it, in that critics routinely accuse one another of forgetting the child's mother tongue or, from the opposite point of view, of subscribing to such a silly notion to begin with. Put reductively, the big debate in children's literature studies is whether or not children's literature is really children's literature, since, after all, it is nearly always written by adults. Is the very idea of children's literature sheer fantasy? What does it mean to write "for" or in the name of children? Do we need their consent to be legitimate? Clearly critics such as Rose and Lesnik-Oberstein find the enterprise problematic at best, while others reply that the "impossibility" of childhood (and of clear child-adult boundaries) is neither news nor something to fret about. In any event, much like child analysis within the larger field of psychoanalysis, children's literature is at once embraced and disavowed in the academy, sometimes treated as a separate (even abject) field, sometimes seen as coterminous with or indistinguishable from adult writing.

But we don't even need to reconstruct these scenes of professionalization to see psychoanalysis and children's literature as complementary. There are canonical texts of children's literature that coincide historically with formative texts and/or moments in psychoanalysis. The case of *Peter Pan*, for instance, is worth consideration beyond Rose's fine treatment, as it dramatizes as early as 1905 many central themes of psychoanalysis, among them the dreamwork. Rose hints that Barrie was working through the same issues taken up by Papa Freud, but stops short of suggesting that psychoanalysis and children's literature could be intersecting explorations of identity, desire, and subjectivity. Kevin Shortsleeve points to a similar and fascinating "coincidence" of the publication of Edward Gorey's melancholic "picture book" *The Object Lesson* (1958) and the intellectual ascendance of object relations theory in the late 1950s. As Shortsleeve's essay suggests, it would be a mistake to read Gorey's book simply as confirmation of the wisdom of object relations theory; something messier is happening.[4] As such examples show, children's literature has been contemporaneous with and even germane to intellectual and artistic work.

Fort-da: play and symbolization

Psychoanalytic attention to the material culture of childhood preceded and made possible psychoanalytic readings of children's literature. The earliest readings of children's forms were concerned with folklore and with children's play. As an activity and an idea, play furnished a bridge from the study of children to the analysis of literature, from the simple drawings and stories of children to literature by and for adults. Even if psychoanalytic criticism is a relatively recent arrival on the scene of children's literature criticism, the project of analyzing children's texts owes much to child analysis and its emphasis on play. As Rollin and West acknowledge, Sigmund Freud's *fort-da* game "has become the most famous children's game in psychoanalysis," having inspired *Beyond the Pleasure Principle* (1920) (5). Rollin and West hint at the significance of play in psychoanalysis, but don't connect play to children's literature.

Although Hug-Hellmuth and Anna Freud were also interested in children's play, it was Melanie Klein whose research on play and "symbolisation" led to dramatic innovations in child analysis. Klein gave her first paper on child analysis in 1921 at the Berlin Psychoanalytic Society. Her interest in play began with her observations of her son Fritz (dubbed "Erich"), but it was with another patient, Rita, that Klein discovered the usefulness of toys. Later, looking back at her long career, she would identify the play technique as the defining element of her practice. Critics of Klein often miss the significance of her insights into play and symbolization, distracted by her dramatic claims about inner objects, unconscious phantasy, and the depressive position.

Klein increasingly turned to toys and other objects in her sessions with children. Nearly any object could be a toy, and in one of her early essays, "The Role of the School in the Libidinal Development of the Child" (1923), Klein shows how the pedestrian objects of the classroom—desk, slate, penholder, and chalk—bespeak internal objects and imagoes. Klein, in fact, links the child's mastery of the alphabet with his libidinal and symbolic maturation. Young Fritz/Erich recreates the erotics of the schoolroom within the confines of Klein's consulting room, playing with the cushions on her divan, drawing various characters, even doing math homework. "It can be repeatedly demonstrated," Klein writes in that essay, "that behind drawing, painting and photography there lies a much deeper unconscious activity: it is the procreation and production in the unconscious of the object represented" ("Role" 72). By describing even the letters of the alphabet as objects, and by likening child's play to the free association of adults, Klein alters our very understanding of language and narrative. Hence the importance of objects, such as toys and books, to the study of childhood; studying children's forms isn't that far removed from the direct observation of children, the logic runs. At the same time, critics of children's literature tend to disavow the psychoanalytic dimensions of literary criticism, as if forms of close reading or case writing have no history.

In "The Importance of Symbol-Formation in the Development of the Ego" (1930), otherwise known as the case of Little Dick, Klein emphasizes how destructive desires, in tandem with the dread to which they give rise, enable the child's ability to symbolize. For Klein, symbolization offers relief from the intense anxieties and hostilities of early childhood. In this essay, she acknowledges the influence of Ferenczi and Ernest Jones, both of whom also speculated on the origin of symbolization (and by way of folklore). Revising an earlier formulation of the problem, Klein writes:

> Since the child desires to destroy the organs (penis, vagina, breasts) which stand for the objects [the adults to whom those organs belong], he conceives a dread of the latter. This anxiety contributes to make him equate the organs in question with other things; owing to this equation these in their turn become objects of anxiety, and so he is impelled constantly to make other and new equations, which form the basis of his interest in the new objects and of symbolism. ("Importance" 220)

For Klein, fear and anxiety motivate symbolization, not, say, the child's innate curiosity or the structure or culture of language. "Thus," she continues, "not only does symbolism come to be the foundation of all phantasy and sublimation but, more than that, it is the basis of the subject's relation to the outside world and to reality in general" ("Importance" 221). Little Dick suffers from an arrest of symbolization. Because his ego's defenses against sadistic wishes are "excessive and premature" (232), he is no longer able to bring into phantasy the sadism he feels toward his mother.

As Kristeva emphasizes, Klein's play technique was not merely a means to an end, but indeed was constitutive of her work, inseparable from the work of observation, interpretation, and healing. Klein's appreciation of play wasn't limited to the child's physical manipulation of objects, but eventually included the play of words, linguistic and semantic play alongside more nonverbal forms of interaction and fantasy. "By relying on the interplay of the child's diverse semiotic codes, the creativity of psychodrama, and the interplay among the signifiers of free association," holds Kristeva, "Melanie unwittingly foresaw the path that analytic treatment would take in the wake of Freud" (*Melanie Klein* 56). Klein's attention to language, which anticipates Lacan's "return" to Freud, also anticipates the semiotic interest in literature. Whereas Freud recognized man as a symbol user, suggests Kristeva, Klein described the child as a symbol maker.

Kristeva underscores Klein's growing interest in the reparative work of art and literature; certainly Kristeva is the direct inheritor of Klein's vision of art as comprising a "way of caring for other people" as well as raw material for analysis. Klein did try her hand at literary criticism, writing not about children's books but about Colette as well as Julien Green's 1947 novel *If I Were You* (*Melanie Klein* 187–88). But her legacy is more diffuse. Would it be far-fetched to think of children's literature as a mode of reparation, as a way of making up for the adult abuses of childhood? If adults write children's books, as is routinely pointed out by more suspicious critics of the field, couldn't adult intentions be more generous (less manipulative) than we often assume? In any case, play is the vital link for Klein between child analysis and the study of children's literature and culture.

For mother-analyst Winnicott, play is *the* fundamental human experience; in his system, childhood play expands into adult creativity and "creative living." He repeatedly talks about "the cultural field," thus reenacting the disciplinary trajectory of play's emergence into that broader frame of reference, such that playing and reality become synonymous. For Winnicott, even more than for Klein, interpretation is a form of (child's) play. Psychoanalysis, he writes, "has been developed as a highly specialized form of playing in the service of communication with oneself and others" (41).

I may overemphasize the relevance of child analysis to the field of children's literature, but certainly in the twentieth century, play became the central focus not only of writing for children but of children's literature studies. Histories of children's literature routinely note that, beginning in the late eighteenth century, didactic and rationalistic children's literature was challenged by a literature of play and amusement; this advance ostensibly represents the dawn of a new sensibility. It's important to realize that, like Klein and Winnicott, the authors of children's literature and children's literature criticism take "play" to mean not merely recreation, but also "creative living," even moral and emotional maturation. Play and symbolization—the learning and making of meaning—have replaced, as much as displaced, reason as our *modus operandi*; their ascendance marks less a dramatic shift in sensibility than a modernization of terms. Lesnik-Oberstein finds that "'amusement' starts its career as a form of claimed love and commitment to learning" and remains "the cry of educators up to the present day" (68).

In their study of postwar children's literature, Margaret and Michael Rustin hold that children's literature is always already child's play, even when play is not thematized. The authors they examine create emotional depth through "symbolic equivalents or containers for states of feeling," which amounts to "a kind of poetic communication, analogous to the symbolizations of children's imaginative play" (3). Literature, they confirm, is a form of play, and critics of children's literature arguably have as much knowledge about childhood as do those who work directly with children and write up case studies, statistical analyses, and other documents.

The classical genre and beyond

Klein shows at least a passing interest in folklore, especially the fairy tales assembled by the Brothers Grimm. In her earliest essay on child analysis, "The Development of a Child" (1921), Klein reviews Fritz/Erich's interest in such material. Like Freud's Wolf-Man, Fritz is both afraid of and obsessed with wolves in fairy tales and picture books, and like the Wolf Man, dreams about wolves. "Here is another dream," continues Klein, "that was not, however, associated with feelings of fear. Everywhere, behind mirrors, doors, etc., were wolves with long tongues hanging out. He shot them all down so that they died. He was not afraid because he was stronger than them" ("Development" 40–41). At the essay's end, Klein remarks: "I have particularly selected listening to Grimm's tales without anxiety-manifestations as an indication of the mental health of children, because of all the various children known to me there are only very few who do so" (52). These tales suggest for Klein a litmus test for mental health.

In "The Early Development of Conscience in the Child" (1933), Klein again refers to fairy-tale characters as screens for terrifying parent figures (249). Unlike Sigmund Freud, however, Klein does not use the fairy tale to reconstruct the primal scene, because for Klein, aggression and anxiety are already primal enough and don't depend on a traumatic episode. As Klein has it, the child's fascination with fairy-tale figures—sometimes confident, sometimes anxious—represents both an expression of, and defense against, infantile aggression and ambivalence. Like Bruno Bettelheim, she implies that fairy tales are therapeutic, even as she censures the ego for interfering with the child's mental health. Klein didn't speculate further about fairy tales or children's literature, but other psychoanalysts, psychologists, and cultural critics have taken up that task.

I've argued elsewhere that what I call the "feral tale," the folkloric-turned-literary story of a child raised by animals and/or living in isolation from humanity, is central to the psychoanalytic imaginary as well as to children's literature. The Rat Man and Wolf Man histories are (among other things) psychoanalytic variants of the feral tale, variants that Freud uses to dramatize his theories about psychosexual drama and development. In that sense, they are comparable to Kipling's *Jungle Books* (1894, 1895), which Freud knew well, and Edgar Rice Burroughs's many Tarzan tales. Of course, throughout his writing, Freud explicitly and deliberately draws from psychoanalysis to explain folklore, and vice versa. But he also invokes the folkloric to advance his own ideas, in ways that are more implicit and perhaps unconscious. Sarah Boxer's recent *In the Floyd Archives: A Psycho-Bestiary* (2001) pays clever homage to the psychoanalytic feral tale (as well as to Janet Malcolm), casting Freud as a birdish Dr. Floyd and his famous animal-identified patients as Mr. Wolf-man, Lambskin (Mr. Wolf-man's alter ego), and Ratma'am. Boxer's cartoon book, surely also inspired by Art Spiegelman's *Maus* books (1986) and other graphic novels, could be likened to the dreamwork, at once representing and distorting Freudian thought, very much in the tradition of Freud's own lively and creative feral refashionings.

Freud's writing inaugurates the mutual entanglement of psychoanalysis and folklore as documented by Alan Dundes. Dundes acknowledges the early psychoanalytic work on folklore and mythology conducted by Freud's contemporaries Karl Abraham, Ernest Jones, Carl Jung, and Otto Rank, among many others. "Actually," notes Dundes, "almost every single major psychoanalyst wrote at least one paper applying psychoanalytic theory to folklore" (21). Such "application" was a foundational practice, even as psychoanalysis has been folkloric in less conscious ways. Case histories, for example, are written transcripts of oral narrative. Dundes writes partly to challenge the success of Bettelheim's best-selling *The Uses of Enchantment* (1976), filling in the historical gaps and all but proving that Bettelheim plagiarized this book (a claim subsequently substantiated). Arguably it was Bettelheim's book that made psychoanalytic interpretations of children's literature more palatable within as well as outside of the academy. Like Klein, and unlike A. A. Brill, who warned against their use, Bettelheim thought that fairy tales were useful in monitoring mental health.

For better or for worse, the European fairy tale canon—especially the work of Charles Perrault, the Brothers Grimm, and Hans Christian Andersen—is generally understood as the baseline of children's literature.

Most survey classes and introductory texts begin with folklore and other oral genres, then move on to picture books, and finally more sophisticated genres. It's not surprising that children's literature critics interested in psychoanalysis at first turned to literary fairy tales and other folkloric literary and cultural forms (among them Disney's early films). In his first of many books on the subject, for example, Jack Zipes describes the literary fairy tale as the "classical genre for children" (from his book's subtitle), and sets the stage for a Marxist and New Historicist understanding of children's literature. His reading is residually psychoanalytic—in his words, "an historical psychological point of view" (33)—in suggesting a correspondence between "psychogenetic" and "sociogenetic" factors in the socialization of children through fairy tales. Like Freud himself, who returned again and again to what I call the problem of ontogenetic-phylogenetic correspondence, Zipes tries to account for both cultural inheritance and individual experience. Few people have done more than Zipes to establish the cultural and critical significance of children's literature. Like Bettelheim before him, Zipes capitalizes on the popularity of fairy tales, but this time to the benefit of leftist literary criticism. It's hard to imagine children's literature without folklore, and children's literature criticism without Zipes, Marina Warner, Maria Tatar, and other scholars who have written about the fairy tale, with or without endorsing a psychoanalytic perspective. Children's literature is a very heterogeneous field, but folklore is arguably where it all began.

The debate about the use-value of psychoanalytic interpretation has been staged largely around folklore, with historically oriented critics rightly objecting to static Freudian interpretations of individual tale variants. Zipes, Tatar, and other scholars have taken Bettelheim to task for his essentializing and ahistorical readings of select tales. Their criticism is just. For too long, critics have invoked psychoanalytic concepts—oedipality, for instance, or abjection, or the mirror stage—as if they don't have a history, and as if that history isn't indebted to folklore, literature, and art. Even the kind of complementary readings that I'm envisioning in this essay run the risk of being reductive and tyrannical if either children's literature or psychoanalysis is understood ahistorically.

It's not surprising that the "classical genre" has received the lion's share of psychoanalytic interpretation so far, since folklore and psychoanalysis have a symbiotic relationship. That relationship is often implicitly acknowledged even by scholars who repudiate psychoanalysis as a method. But what of other genres? Picture books, like fairy tales, are fundamentally about the child and her experiences and anxieties and fantasies; like psychoanalysis, they are preoccupied with language and desire. Despite their provocative mix of word and image, however, picture books have not yet received much psychoanalytic attention. In *Inside Picture Books* (1999), Ellen Handler Spitz implies a correspondence between the "inner possibilities" of younger children (10) and the visual and verbal work of picture books, but she doesn't really offer sustained readings of texts. Still to emerge is a full-length study of picture books that emphasizes the dynamic relation of psychoanalysis and children's literature. I suspect that some scholars resist psychoanalytic readings of picture books because of the pervasive myth of innocence. Young children are innocent, runs the myth; so too must be their favorite objects.

Presumably, psychoanalytic criticism is more suitable for young adult literature since that literature (like the adolescents it serves) is less innocent. But our assumption that adolescence is a time of stress and growth is itself psychoanalytic; that's why psychoanalytic criticism seems a viable approach to young adult literature. Kristeva writes in her essay "The Adolescent Novel" (1995) that adolescence, psychic turmoil, and writing are linked in complicated ways. Arguing that the novel itself is a perpetually "adolescent" genre, Kristeva affirms the association of psychoanalysis with adolescence as well as proto-adult writing.

It would seem that our assumptions about the richness and/or maturity of particular genres have been psychoanalytically inflected from the start. Folklore is ostensibly about primal wishes and fears, the product of a primitive/child-like folk mind even when filtered through the adult consciousness of Charles Perrault or the Brothers Grimm. Picture books, on the other hand, as well as other genres for preadolescents, are assumed to be empty of sexual meaning, or at least, such meaning is deemed latent rather than blatant. With young adult literature allegedly comes the return of the repressed, the flowering of sexual agency and autonomy.

Even if I exaggerate the degree to which we read childhood psychoanalytically, it's clear that play and folklore helped make possible children's literature as well as child analysis. We're just starting to move past an oppositional practice of criticism, to see how psychoanalytic discourse has shaped our understanding of childhood and children's literature, and vice versa. As Freud recognized, psychoanalysis doesn't know anything that literature doesn't also know, which is why he fashioned psychoanalysis not only as a science, but also as a form of literature with children as its principal characters.

Notes

1 Like Kristeva, Westwater believes "that we are in a state of cultural decay and that writing—whether for children or adults—may preserve for us values that are on the verge of decline" (xvii). But Westwater's sense of crisis is much more dramatic than Kristeva's; she writes, for instance, that "[w]e seem unable to discern between good and evil. We've lost our passion for absolutes and cannot find replacements . . . Apparently, violence and ugliness have replaced idealism and beauty as youthful realities" (2). Predictably, she bemoans the breakdown of the family, never acknowledging the dramatic social gains of the 1960s and 1970s She is also much too eager to see literature as redemptive.

2 To keep this essay manageable, I pay no attention to children's film (both about and for children), which also has intimate connections with psychoanalysis.
3 Blum goes so far as to rewrite Freud and Lacan as invested not so much in the oedipal triangle as in the dyadic relation of mother and child, describing the latter as a metaconceit of psychoanalysis that assures the child's alternating sense of presence and absence, selfhood and otherness.
4 I'm indebted to Kevin Shortsleeve's essay "The Object (Relations) Lesson: A Psychoanalytic Reading of Edward Gorey and the Characters in His Books," written for my graduate seminar on children's literature and psychoanalysis at the University of Florida.

Works cited

Arac, Jonathan. "*Huckleberry Finn*" *as Idol and Target: The Functions of Criticism in Our Time*. Madison: U of Wisconsin P, 1997.

Bettelheim, Bruno. *The Uses of Enchantment*. New York: Alfred A. Knopf, 1976.

Blum, Virginia. *Hide and Seek: The Child between Psychoanalysis and Fiction*. Urbana: U of Illinois P, 1995.

Bosmajian, Hamida. "*Charlie and the Chocolate Factory* and Other Excremental Visions." *The Lion and the Unicorn* 9 (1985): 36–49.

——. "The Cracked Crucible of *Johnny Tremain*." *The Lion and the Unicorn* 13.1 (June 1989): 53–66.

Boxer, Sarah. *In the Floyd Archives: A Psycho-Bestiary*. New York: Pantheon Books, 2001.

Coats, Karen. "Abjection and Adolescent Fiction." *Journal for the Psychoanalysis of Culture & Society* 5.2 (Fall 1999): 290–300.

——. "P is for Patriarchy: Re-Imaging the Alphabet. *Children's Literature Association Quarterly* 25.2 (Summer 2000): 88–97.

Crew, Hilary S. *Is it Really "Mommie Dearest"? Daughter-Mother Narratives in Young Adult Fiction*. Lanham, MD: Scarecrow P, 2000.

Crews, Frederick. *The Pooh Perplex*. New York: E. P. Dutton, 1963.

——. *Postmodern Pooh*. New York: North Point P, 2001.

Dundes, Alan. "The Psychoanalytic Study of Folklore." *Parsing through Customs: Essays by a Freudian Folklorist*. Madison: U of Wisconsin P, 1987.

Dusinberre, Juliet. *Alice to the Lighthouse: Children's Books and Radical Experiments in Art*. New York: St. Martin's, 1987.

Ferenczi, Sándor. "Confusion of Tongues between Adults and the Child: The Language of Tenderness and Passion." 1933. Rpt. in *Ferenczi, Final Contributions to the Problems and Methods of Psycho-Analysis*. Ed. M. Bálint. Trans. E. Mosbacher, *et al.* New York: Brunner/Mazel, 1980. 156–67.

Gorey, Edward. *The Object Lesson*. New York: Harcourt, 1958.

Grosskurth, Phyllis. *Melanie Klein: Her World and Her Work*. New York: Aronson, 1986.

Klein, Melanie. "The Development of a Child." 1921. Rpt. in *Melanie Klein: "Love, Guilt and Reparation" and Other Works, 1921–1945*. Ed. R. E. Money-Kyrle, *et al.* London: Vintage 1988. 1–53.

——. "The Early Development of Conscience in the Child." 1933. Rpt. in *Melanie Klein: "Love, Guilt and Reparation" and Other Works, 1921–1945*. Ed. R. E. Money-Kyrle, *et al.* London: Vintage, 1988. 248–57.

——. "The Importance of Symbol-Formation in the Development of the Ego." 1930. Rpt. in *Melanie Klein: "Love, Guilt and Reparation" and Other Works, 1921–1945*. Ed. R. E. Money-Kyrle, *et al.* London: Vintage, 1988. 219–32.

——. "The Role of the School in the Libidinal Development of the Child." 1923. Rpt. in *Melanie Klein: "Love, Guilt and Reparation" and Other Works, 1921–1945*. Ed. R. E. Money-Kyrle, *et al.* London: Vintage, 1988. 59–76.

Kristeva, Julia. "The Adolescent Novel." *New Maladies of the Soul*. Trans. Ross Guberman. New York: Columbia UP, 1995. 135–53.

——. *Melanie Klein*. Trans. Ross Guberman. New York: Columbia UP, 2001.

Lacan, Jacques. *Écrits*. Trans. Alan Sheridan. New York: W. W. Norton, 1977.

Lesnik-Oberstein, Karín. *Children's Literature: Criticism and the Fictional Child.* Oxford: Clarendon P, 1994.

Rollin, Lucy. *Cradle and All: A Cultural and Psychoanalytic Study of Nursery Rhymes.* Jackson: UP of Mississippi, 1992.

Rollin, Lucy, and Mark I. West, eds. *Psychoanalytic Responses to Children's Literature*. Jefferson, NC: McFarland & Co, 1999.

Rose, Jacqueline. *The Case of Peter Pan, or The Impossibility of Children's Fiction.* Philadelphia: U of Pennsylvania P, 1984.

Rustin, Margaret, and Michael Rustin. *Narratives of Love and Loss: Studies in Modern Children's Fiction*. London: Verso, 1987.

Sayers, Janet. *Mothers of Analysis*. New York: W. W. Norton, 1991.

Shortsleeve, Kevin. "The Object (Relations) Lesson: A Psychoanalytic Reading of Edward Gorey and the Characters in His Books." Unpublished essay cited with permission.

Spitz, Ellen Handler. *Inside Picture Books*. New Haven: Yale UP, 1999.

Steedman, Carolyn. *Strange Dislocations: Childhood and the Idea of Human Interiority, 1780–1930*. Cambridge: Harvard UP, 1995.

Stone, Jennifer. "Pinocchio and Pinocchiology." *American Imago* 51.3 (Fall 1994): 329–42.

Susina, Jan. Rev. of *Postmodern Pooh*, by Frederick Crews. *The Lion and the Unicorn* 26.2 (Apr. 2002): 274–78.

Trites, Roberta Seelinger, ed. Special issue: "Psychoanalytic Approaches to Children's Literature." *Children's Literature Association Quarterly* 25.2 (Summer 2000).

——, ed. Special issue: "The Uncanny in Children's Literature." *Children's Literature Association Quarterly* 26.4 (Winter 2001–2002).

Westwater, Martha. *Giant Despair Meets Hopeful: Kristevan Readings in Adolescent Fiction*. Edmonton: U of Alberta P, 2000.

Williams, John Tyerman. *Pooh and the Psychologists: In Which It is Proven that Pooh Bear is a Brilliant Psychotherapist*. New York: Dutton, 2000.

Winnicott, D. W. *Playing and Reality*. New York: Routledge, 1989.

Zipes, Jack. *Fairy Tales and the Art of Subversion: The Classical Genre for Children and the Process of Civilization*. London: Heinemann, 1983.

Part 15

SPECIAL TOPICS

79

METAFICTIONAL PLAY IN CHILDREN'S FICTION

Ann Grieve

Source: *Papers: Explorations into Children's Literature* 8(3) (1998): 5–15.

> *What we need is not great works, but playful ones. . . . A Story is a game someone has played so you can play it too.*
>
> (Sukenick 1960, pp. 56–57)

Notions of play in metafictional texts apply both to the role-playing activity of writing and the different roles created for the reader. Toys, cartoons, comic books, TV shows, video games, movies and role-playing games such as 'Dungeons and Dragons' are the most obvious models of imaginative play and storytelling with which children will be familiar, but many metafictional children's texts also draw on several kinds of playful textual strategies: the game as a text or fiction, utilising the game structure or rules of an actual game; characters represented as players in a game; the physical book as a game; and the text as a game – that is, books or texts which cannot be fully recuperated without reader participation or interaction.

Before discussing these categories of textual play, I'll first expand two crucial terms: 'metafiction' and 'play'. Metafiction is generally associated with terms such as 'reflexive' or 'self-reflexive', 'self-conscious', 'auto referential', 'narcissistic', 'introverted' or 'postmodern fiction'. The term 'metafiction' itself dates back about a quarter of a century and as Wenche Ommundsen argues, *if* it is a genre, (and even that is debated, many taking the position that metafiction is a tendency *within* a novel) it is a genre in the making (Ommundsen 1989, p. 264). The point of consensus among theorists is that 'metafiction' is a fiction about fiction – that is, fiction that includes within itself a commentary on its own narrative and/or linguistic identity. It is also a fiction preoccupied with problematising the mimetic illusion and laying bare the construction of fictional reality.

Ommundsen identifies 'three different ways of accounting for the phenomenon of fictional reflexivity' (Ommundsen 1990, p. 171). One is to declare metafiction a genre apart, an anti-mimetic form concerned with the process of fiction writing and seeking to destroy the fictional illusion. The second approach declares that all fiction, including nineteenth century realism, is fundamentally self-reflexive. This argument can be extended to incorporate the position that all fiction carries within itself the potential for a metafictional reading. The third position locates metafiction firmly in the eyes of the beholder; a metafictional reader will find textual signals 'functioning as statements about the artefact in which they figure' (Ommundsen 1990, p. 172), so that metafiction is seen as the product of a certain practice of reading, a particular kind of attention brought to bear on the fiction text. This position argues against the concept of metafiction as a separate genre of writing.

Some texts, such as Italo Calvino's *If On a Winter's Night a Traveller*, are so overtly metafictional that they set themselves apart from realistic fiction; but apart from examples such as these, the borderline between metafiction and non-metafiction is difficult to identify. If establishing boundaries of covert or overt metafictional territory is problematic for theorists, the question is: How does the reader 'recognise a metafiction when she sees one'? The answer to this question would require a discussion of its own, but it is particularly relevant when the discussion of metafiction is extended to children's fiction. A question that frequently arises is whether metafiction is an appropriate literary from for children's books; for example, Geoff Moss asks, 'Do metafictional texts have any place in children's literature . . . [or] are metafictional texts for adults only?' (Moss 1990, p. 50).

Derived from a long humanist tradition which has been challenged only recently, the dominant model of children's stories has produced stable, knowable, readable texts which set out comfortably to seduce the child reader. They generally deploy features such as chronological sequence; well-made plot; authoritative omniscient author/narrator; and the primary narrative modes of first person narration by the main character, which includes the commonly used diary format; and third person narration of a series of events focalised by the central character. Children's books also have a strong ideological function and, historically, exert social control, functioning as part of an educational apparatus – a means of teaching and influencing children.

Children are inexperienced readers. That is not to say that they cannot read the words or understand them, but that they are inexperienced in decoding texts. Accordingly, the forms and language of metafiction in children's books are not normally so far removed from realism as to be entirely beyond young readers' knowledge of narrative or modes of communication. So children's metafictional works incline towards texts which, on Waugh's 'sliding scale of metafictional practices', implicitly invoke some 'context of the everyday world' rather than emulating those radically indeterminate texts in which the only 'frame of which the reader is certain is the front and back covers of the book he or she is holding' (Waugh 1984, p. 115). Metafiction for children functions by preserving a balance between the innovatory and the familiar, so that the reader can make predictions and construct coherence.

An author who wishes to challenge or even abandon mimesis in books for children, who wishes to foreground the fictional illusion as illusion, must ask how fiction can be created which will still engage and satisfy the reader. Brian Stonehill argues that the answer to this is to be found in the *ludic* theory of art – the conception of art as a game or form of play (Stonehill 1988, p. 12).[1] Many self-conscious novels are concerned with, or have been compared with, game playing, some well known examples being Robert Coover's *The Universal Baseball Association Inc. J. Henry Waugh Prop*, based on a tabletop baseball game; Fiona Moorhead's *Still Murder*, shaped by the form of a jigsaw puzzle; and Vladimir Nabokov's novel *The Defence*, which is centred around the game of chess. Add to such adult works, those most playful of stories for children, *Alice's Adventures in Wonderland* and *Through the Looking Glass*, which foreground chess and card games.

Playful fiction can be extended beyond the use of the 'actualised game model' or fiction built around the idea or rules of an actual game, to include metafictional devices such as puzzle-solving (including the detective novel); multiple narrative endings; playful, 'lying' or unreliable characters and narrators; linguistic play; playing with the book as an object, and playing with or 'reworking' genre conventions and established literary codes by means of parody and intertextuality to discover the new possibilities of the literary game.

The broadest conception of 'play' and 'game' is that seen as synonymous with the concept of reader involvement, the textual means by which the metafictional reader is provoked into an awareness of the role she plays in activating the text: 'By theorising and problematising the reader's function, metafiction produces readers at once aware of their participation in the fictional game . . .' (Ommundsen 1993, p. 77). The reader has increasingly become the focus of much postmodern and metafictional discourse, not just as a receiver of the text but as a producer; Barthes argues that discursive authority has shifted from the originating author to the reader or textual Scriptor who exists only in the time of the text and its reading (Barthes 1977, p. 145).

It is important to emphasise that this paper is concerned with interrogative or metafictional play rather than works which may be simply playful or which have children's play as a central theme. The books selected for this study are works which self-reflexively make the reader aware of the interplay between reality and illusion.

The game as a text

Power and Glory, by Emily Rodda and Geoff Kelly, is a picture book which foregrounds the computer game and interrogates the boundaries of fantasy and reality. In another time and space is the solipsistic world of the computer game – a world of hyper-reality; an independent, free standing world of its own, providing a semi-permanent or even permanent escape from consensus reality: 'The player loses him or herself in a fantasy world and actually becomes the role being played (a favourite metafictional theme)' (Waugh 1980, p. 41). In *Power and Glory*, the game is depicted as a miniature escape fantasy, a world-within-a-world in competition with the primary world of the text.

Because of the high level of participation and interaction required by the player, the computer game, like a 'Choose your own adventure' narrative, is constantly being 'written'; *Power and Glory* depicts the 'I' of the story as lost in his role as a player and a co-creator. He has completely given himself over to the illusion of the game and, by his participation in the game, to the act of writing in a non-literary context – he has become a maker of fiction. The characters of the game do not exist as independent characters; they are generated by the narrator, produced by his interaction with the game which becomes an activity enclave into which he can escape. This projection of himself into the imaginary world of the game begins to shape his perception of his frame world to the extent that any return to 'reality' is encumbered by the signifiers of the game, such as 'THE WITCH' and 'THE GOBLIN', so that the signifiers begin to apply to signifieds beyond the game, and the familiar realm of his family becomes replaced and dislocated – 'a mirror image, a paraxial realm, on the edge of reality' (Jackson 1981, p. 109). Representation begins to turn to reality, and defamiliarises the 'real' world. In other words, reality begins to copy art; because the game breaks the boundaries of the frame, the 'real' becomes a notion which is under constant interrogation. And the capacity of the world of the game to take over the 'real' world implies, as Waugh comments, that 'human beings can only ever achieve a metaphor for reality, another layer of 'interpretation' (Waugh 1984, p. 15).

The use of rebus within the text is in itself reflexive. Rebus demands a special type of attention: it breaks up the page, undercutting its transparency and ease, and it requires the reader to make sense out of apparent nonsense. A rebus is a mixed form of coding which changes from the verbal to the visual, often mid-sentence, and has all the playful elements of a puzzle: 'The fracture lines between letters and images offer the child the pleasure of juggling back and forth from one code to another. . . . [It] is especially telling because it underscores the puzzling aspect of the reader's encounter with a gap between one code and another' (Higonnet 1997, p. 40). In *Power and Glory*, the visual rebus does not replace the verbal; the two are juxtaposed as competing semiotic systems, so that the reader can 'read' either or both and must constantly cross-check two forms of signification.

The computer screen is a metaphorical mirror, a frequently used motif or self-reflexive image in metafiction. The computer/mirror in *Power and Glory* which allows the narrator through the looking glass into another time and space does not allow the reader through. The reader is positioned as an observer who witnesses both the construction and the deconstruction of a pseudo-reality, since as Bersani explains,

> *By presenting images of the self in another space (both familiar and unfamiliar), the mirror provides versions of self transformed into another . . . It employs distance and difference to suggest the instability of the 'real' on this side of the looking glass.*
>
> (in Jackson 1981, p. 87)

In *Beyond the Labyrinth*, Gillian Rubinstein appropriates a game motif, the 'Dungeons and Dragons' role play. She has also deliberately used a metafictional technique that ironically parodies 'Choose your own adventure' stories, and self-reflexively comments on the fatalistic outlook which sees Brenton randomly resolving life decisions through the throw of a dice. Rubinstein is well aware that children understand the shared terminology of fantasy and the rules or codes of these popular game and fiction conventions. This understanding gives them greater access to the rich diversity of an ambivalent text which can be read at many levels.

Rubinstein points out that the labyrinth of the title echoes the structure of a book.[2] The text does not contain a spatial labyrinth but a metaphysical labyrinth in which the basic story ramifies into many other stories offering a range of choices and directions for the reader to take. Rubinstein uses the labyrinth with irony by setting it against the enigmatic message of the anonymous graffiti artist, 'DEAD END', 'DEADEN', 'DEADN'. When Brenton asks what the graffiti means, the creator answers 'Mean? I don't know if I can explain what they mean. I just stand there, facing an empty space, and the words come to me. They feel right, so I put them into space. They can mean whatever you want them to mean' (p. 166). The game book that Brenton is reading is called *Labyrinth of Dead Ends*; while Borges sees the labyrinth as a model for infinite possibilities, Brenton paradoxically sees it as a dead end, as though 'he is playing out a fantasy game in which all the rules have been written and the moves preordained – a game which is now approaching its climax and its end' (p. 152).

One of the most powerful conventions of story is narrative closure. The sense of ending, however, can easily be disturbed; we expect some sort of resolution in a story but if that resolution is deferred or made inaccessible to the reader, this can result in dislocation and disorientation. Gillian Rubinstein exploits this expectation through the double ending of *Beyond the Labyrinth.* How does a reader respond to narrative rupture in which closure is denied or subverted? Many readers will assume they have misread and reread the text for verbal clues they may have missed. Or they may feel that they have not misread and attempt to give meaning to the apparently incomplete narrative. They will extrapolate, try to fill gaps; in fact, they will become co-creators in their desire to make meaning. Rubinstein maintains the game play theme by giving the reader the power to change the story by the role of a dice: 'The one who speaks into the poised silence is Cal. "*Throw the dice*!" Her eyes are bright and feverish, her voice harsh and urgent. She is not speaking to Brenton and Victoria. She is speaking to *you*, the Reader. You who have been the observer so far. You who have been watching the whole story. Throw the dice!' (p. 143). And the reader, having to choose an ending, becomes a player in the game.

The Westing Game, by Ellen Raskin, is an example of a plot which has parodically appropriated the framework or construct of a popular fiction genre, the detective novel. It rewrites the detective genre reflexively, explicitly relating the acts of reading and investigation, with the detective often functioning 'as the model for the reader's activity' (Ommundsen 1993, p. 10). Waugh comments that, 'In metafiction, . . . writers experiment more commonly with the formulaic motifs of popular fiction . . . science fiction, ghost stories, westerns, detective stories, popular romance' (Waugh 1984, p. 81), partly because genre fiction foregrounds its conventions and is therefore itself self-referential. This kind of metafictional reworking of a popular genre must be accompanied by a thorough reworking of its constitutive conventions. Detective fiction operates most commonly as the literature of concealment, but also paradoxically contains mechanical certainty and hyper-logic represented by the detective who is the agent of order and meaning. It is a construct in which the readers are often left to fill gaps and to sort through both over-determined and under-determined 'clues' which are part of the puzzle or intellectual game played within the fictional construct of the genre. The character of the detective echoes the task of interpretation undertaken by the real reader.

The Westing Game has not one detective, but sixteen. Sixteen named beneficiaries have been called together under the terms of the last will and testament of Samuel W Westing, described in his obituary as a person who believed in fair play, 'never drank, smoked or gambled. Yet he was a dedicated gamesman and a master at chess' (p. 19). The beneficiaries are instructed to work in pairs to solve a puzzle, with the winning pair to inherit the Westing fortune. The puzzle itself is obscure and the words of the will ambiguous: 'my life was taken from me – by one of you!' (p. 29). Each pair is given one set of clues, consisting of four single words on a piece of paper. In some cases even the word is obscure: for example, 'ON' could be 'ON' or 'NO', depending which way the paper is turned, and MT could stand for 'Mount' or 'Empty'. The reader must participate in this linguistic play, the kind of play which 'functions to disengage words from syntax, thus hindering the reconstruction of the projected world, and foregrounding the ontological difference between the stratum of worlds' (McHale 1987, p. 162). By removing the word from any known context, the author has broken down the idea of a natural affinity between the signifier and signified.

This disengagement of words from syntax also forces the reader to reflect on the assemblage of the words. Is this a word list, and if so, what governed the selection of the words, and their arrangement in this particular order? The reader is confronted with a verbal collage in which the play of meanings is infinitely plural, and to try and bring meaning to the words, is tempted to make lists, to write down each 'clue' and, like the main players in the story, to rearrange, reconstruct, manipulate, order and apply learned codes and rules to try and make mimetic order out of linguistic chaos. Readers, more often than not, willingly participate in Coleridge's 'willing suspension of disbelief' in the act of reading; but '*self-depicting* fictions, by acknowledging the limitations of imitations, invite us to suspend our disbelief not only willingly, but wittingly' (Stonehill 1988, p. 15).

The reader is also reflexively aware that she has been given information not available to the characters in the story. The narrator, whilst impersonal, is distinctly in control, having an authoritative voice with an implied knowledge of completed events. But the alert reader will find the narrator's storytelling practices odd; at some point the reader ceases to be lulled into a false sense of security and begins to wonder what sources the narrator draws on for the story, uncomfortably aware that this omniscient and implied presence appears to, but cannot, share the same ontological world as the reader. On the first page, the reader is told that the letters delivered to the new tenants of Sunset Towers are signed 'Barney Northrup', and that, on the other hand, 'there was no such person as Barney Northrup' (p. 1). In what Brian Stonehill calls a 'conspiratorial mystique' (Stonehill 1998, p. 8), the reader is told that she has all the clues, whereas the characters have only selected clues. But, whilst the reader might hold all the clues, the narrator cannot be counted on to supply the answers, but only to prod the reader into making further efforts to make meaning of the clues.

Throughout *The Westing Gam*e the game of chess is used as an image of the text. It sustains the artifice of the game and mirrors the manipulation of the sixteen heirs/players, comparing them to chess pieces, and the carefully constructed Westing Game to the chess board on which they must play. Chess, like language, is infinitely plural but some aspects are given – sixteen pieces, eight black, eight white, and strict game rules as to how these pieces may behave or move. The heirs are temptingly aligned as black or white through references to their appearance or clothing, but these clues ramain tantalisingly incomplete. Throughout the mystery, references to chess occur: 'The judge says she is a pawn and Otis Amber says he's a king, Crow's the queen' (p. 51). But the work never fully resolves the possible combinations and permutations of chess pieces and characters. The reader will be compelled to try and make meaning of this game within a game, filling in the spaces on the board as she proceeds, interpreting and ordering, but the very structured, traditional rules of chess are undermined by textual indeterminacy in much the same way that metafictional devices undermine the realism of a text. Thus the reader must construct his or her own game to fill the void, to activate the work.

Characters as players in the game

Readers have traditionally been drawn to the liberal humanist treatment of characters as full-blooded and three dimensional, and can, like Annie in Stephen King's *Misery*, become so involved with the character that they lose sight of the fact that the character on the page is a literary construct. Metafictional authors will systematically flaunt this artifice and foreground a fictional character as an artistic creation: 'Within their fictions characters become dehumanised counters, abstractions that are manipulated with the same freedom as non-human elements of the novel like the plot, setting or symbol . . . to be a character is to be an assortment of words on a page' (Boyd 1983, p. 29).

Gary Crew's *Inventing Anthony West* reminds us that Anthony West exists only because he is created. The term 'invented' is used, but he is really 'reinvented', being a pastiche of 'real-life' images of young men published in magazines. The illustrations and photographs imitate the real thing, but they are not the real thing; they are merely representations, symbolising something which is absent.

The creation of Anthony West begins as a game between two teenage girls who, like Frankenstein creating his monster, decide to invent the perfect boy from various parts of other boys depicted in magazines. When the 'perfect' physical image is created, the girls realise they must give him an *identity*, and in order to create such an identity they select the symbols of a pen and an axe, and name their character Anthony West. Metafictional works such as this foreground the arbitrary control of the author in naming a character and highlight the paradox of referentiality in fiction where the naming and description of an object brings it into being. This fictional arbitrariness is continually brought to the reader's attention by the girls' disagreement over whether their creation is named Anthony – intellectual owner of the pen, or Tony – macho owner of the axe.[3]

The figure of Anthony West demonstrates that 'a fictional character both exists and does not exist' (Waugh 1984, p. 91). In the case of a character in a mimetic or realistic novel, a reader may 'know' the literary/fictional character and discuss him/her like a real person. The figure of Anthony West denies the reader that intimacy, since as a metafictional character he is clearly meant to lack substance, and his presence is at best nebulous and changeable. He wavers in and out of parodic popular culture stereotypes; he is dehumanised, and finally, disappears back to the paper construct where he began:

> *held high above them, they waved a poster – an old, faded movie poster. Libby recognised it at once. It was Tony – or all that was left of him. Tony 'The Axeman' West, Tony the Star, still flashing his million dollar smile, still rippling his million dollar muscles . . . but all on paper, on faded yellowing paper . . . which was what he had become.*
>
> (p. 89)

In his discussion of Robbe-Grillet, Brooks describes his works as 'impressive examples of what can be done with the leftovers of the traditional novels as with the 'ready-mades' of consumer society: the mannequins, the glossy photos, the clichés of desire:

> *Narrative becomes a combinatoire; a game of putting together, a kind of metonymy in which the given elements – as the given products and paradigms of culture and society – provide, as it were, the metaphoric glue . . . The reader never is vouchsafed anything we would want to call a plot, in the traditional sense, but he himself is left to engage in plotting, if not towards the creation of meaning, at least in exploration of the conditions of narrative meaning.*
>
> (Brooks 1984, p. 316)

Such a description could well apply to *Inventing Anthony West* and could be expanded to argue that Anthony West – collage, pastiche, invention – serves as a metonym for the pastiche-like 'invention' or construct of this fiction, with its overt and playful embracing of pop-culture, popular fiction and film (especially cult films) where codes are made and learned, and sophisticated and complex narrative techniques are experienced.

A fascinating use of metafictional character is to be found in the picture book *Bad Day at Riverbend* by Chris Van Allsburg. In this work, Van Allsburg blurs the world of the reader with that of the book. This play of ambiguities culminates on the last page, when it is discovered that the reader of the book is also a protagonist. Although inscribed, she is silent and temporally and spatially removed from what appears to be the natural main plot, which takes as its generic model the traditional Western. This reader is also, paradoxically, a playful encoder without whom the story cannot exist. The fictional world has acquired an invisible maker and along with that, the status of an artefact.

Bad Day at Riverbend problematises the layers of 'worlds' that can be embedded in a work of fiction and explicitly lays bare the framing devices which are part of the formal, conventional organisation of novels. To begin with, there is the 'paramount world' or what is thought of as the real world, and there are the invented worlds of fiction. In some fiction, invented worlds can be found within invented worlds; Eco calls these worlds-within-worlds 'subworlds' (1979, p. 234) and Pavel calls them 'narrative domains'

(1980, p. 108). In these doubly fictional worlds, one possible world is said to be accessible to another by manipulating the first world's entities . . . a second world is accessible if it can be conceived by the inhabitants of the first world (McHale 1987, p. 35). In the case of *Bad Day at Riverbend*, the first world entities (those who 'inhabit' Riverbend) are manipulated by the character, whose playful act of creating 'textual' changes to that world with crayon causes disruption to a narrative world which has already been 'written'.

The text calls into question the gap between characters who occupy different universes. It is impossible in this work to determine which world is hierarchically superior and which is subordinate. In *Power and Glory* the characters of the fantastic universe of the game belong to a secondary world and cannot conceive the character of the fictively 'realistic' primary world, but in *Bad Day at Riverbend* the fictively 'real' world is fully conceived by the characters of the fantastic world even though they do not understand that their fictional border is being manipulated and trespassed upon by an unseen character from another possible world. Ontological boundaries are seen to be permeable and unstable when a character can migrate from one world to another and the space of the fictional world is exposed for what is – a construct – just as the characters and objects within it are, or the actions that unfold within it. Borges asks,

> *Why does it disturb us that Don Quixote be a reader of the Quixote and Hamlet a spectator in Hamlet? I believe I have found the reason: these inversions suggest that if the characters in a fictional work can be readers or spectators, we, its readers or spectators, can be fictitious.*
>
> (Borges 1970, p. 230)

It is also interesting to see the authority of the visual image in *Bad Day at Riverbend* so ambiguously subverted. For the book's visual images, rather than inviting a suspension of disbelief, in the end disrupt any possibility of a mimetic reading; the fictional worlds are so annexed to the physical space and physical elements of the book that a realistic reading becomes literally and paradoxically impossible. Further, the auto-referential image of the book on the last page as it sits closed upon the desk signals not only the virtual nature of the story which precedes it, but highlights the nature of the book-as-an-object.

The physical book as a game

Reflexive books for very young readers often require active involvement in the material substance of the book, for example through the devices of split pages, pop-ups, fold-outs, holes, lift-up flaps, and so on. One example is that of strip or 'mix and match' books, in which 'The break between strips offer points of entry for the child, who can play with the creation of her own absurdity . . . [and] permits the child to act as the blind hand of chance, creating her own aleatory structures' (Higonnet 1990, p. 40). In such cases, the very fabric of the book is part of the game.

Another work which requires visual, if not physical manipulation of the split page device is Macauley's *Black and White.* It is layered and multi-diegetic in such a physical way that to recoup the narrative the reader must decide first of all how to read the book. Every page is divided into four narratives which are enigmatic and apparently unrelated to each other. The reader is forced to decide on some arbitrary order of reading since simultaneous reading is nearly impossible. This may require each page to be opened and read four times. There is no unifying narrative and the reader must interpret the shifting perspectives of various narratives, all of which offer their own constructions of reality.

Similarly, in Martin Waddell and Philippe Dupasquier's *The Great Green Mouse Disaster*, the reader must choose from 'reading' several narratives on one page as a horde of green mice create havoc in a hotel. Each page shows every room of the hotel simultaneously so that the reader has the choice of reading several narratives on one page or following the strand of one narrative from beginning to end and recommencing at the beginning with another narrative. McHale describes this procedure of improvising an order of reading as 'glossing a text'. He points out that we are forced to 'manipulate the book as a physical object, thus never losing sight of the "ontological" cut between the projected world and the material world. Such manipulations certainly serve to keep the materiality of the book in the forefront of the reader's consciousness' (McHale 1987, pp. 192–3).

The Stinky Cheese Man and Other Fairly Stupid Tales shows just how far the form of the book-as-object can be subverted. This overt parody of traditional nursery tales is reflexive literally from cover to cover. It declares its reflexivity from the blurb on the dust jacket, which in the tradition of advertising announces, 'only $16.00! 56 action-packed pages. 75% more than those old 32 page 'Brand X' books. New! Improved! Funny! Good! Buy Now!' On opening the book, the reader is confronted by a diatribe by the Little Red Hen, interrupted by the narrator Jack (of the beanstalk), who points out that she must not tell her story at this point, because this is only the book's endpaper. The book continues to self-consciously comment on itself as an object; its every physical aspect is interrogated, including publishing and copyright details, author and illustrator biographies, and the 'ugly' ISBN number. *The Stinky Cheese Man* plays with its readers; it upsets their expectations not only of how the story should be told but how the book should proceed in a cohesive, linear format from beginning to end. In this way, readers' expectations of an ordered creation are completely frustrated, resolution is denied, chaos rules, and as page numbers rain down on unsuspecting characters, the reader is constantly reminded that narrative is constructed and that the book is an artefact.

The text as a game

Linda Hutcheon comments that 'the most extreme example' of the contemporary 'aesthetic and theoretical interest in the interactive powers involved in the production and reception of texts' is that of 'interactive fiction' or computerized, participatory 'compunovels'. Here, she says, 'process is all; there is no fixed product or text, just the reader's activity as producer as well as receiver' (Hutcheon 1988, p. 77). 'Choose your own adventure' books could well fit within the parameters of Hutcheon's 'interactive fiction' in that they successfully question linear, traditional narrative strategies, problematising the whole process of the reception of texts and the role of the reader as a producer of text by inviting the reader to re-run and replay a text.

In these books, the reader is typically 'the star of the story'; the narrative is written in second person, 'the most immediate of all narrative voices, a strategy which makes the choice of action seem like the reader's own . . .' (Higonnet 1987, pp. 42–43). In these texts, bifurcating, mutually exclusive possibilities are juxtaposed. It has been argued that fictions such as these still set themselves against a conventional framework, since readers will try hard to shape a narrative result which is meaningful compared to traditional works with which they are familiar, and because they are free to make choices only within terms of the options presented: 'The traditional reading is preserved as a foil for the act of transgression, a constraint without which the various liberties would not so much be free as meaningless' (Ommundsen 1990, p. 178). On the other hand, children reading these texts are made aware of the notion that they are 'eternally written here and now' (Barthes 1997, p. 145), in a way which contests the notion of the original and originating author.

Containing the same textuality disruptive elements as 'Choose your own adventure' books are those personalised books which Sharon Clarke discusses as metafiction:

> *The action of these texts work in the same way as Calvino's description of 'you' . . . the child is conscious of not having met such figures/people, visited such places or performed such feats as those described within a personalised book, and so therefore would realise that s/he is being moved about like a character. . . . The text thereby becomes the site of a 'game' signalling this to the child/reader/listener through every encounter with personalised detail. Thus the text sheds its realistic cover and openly and continually declares itself a fiction which is relying on reader-participation.*
>
> (Clarke 1991, p. 85)

These two forms of interactive books are the forerunners of the electronic 'texts' – computer story-games such as 'Power and Glory' – which contain the elements of a story in which the player must make decisions about characters, the action, the moral structure – or what Aidan Chambers calls the 'why' of the story (Chambers 1985, p. 75). These are strikingly similar to the process-driven 'compunovels' which Hutcheon describes.

A number of children's books which could not be described as adhering to the 'Choose your own adventure' form nevertheless reflect a collaboration with the reader and a high level of reader participation. Strip books, as previously mentioned, are just one example, allowing readers to create absurd characters by manipulating the top half of the page with any combination on the bottom half. Books such as *Black and White* and *The Great Green Mouse Disaster* could also be described as reader participation books which require a high degree of play and interaction.

Other texts in this style are multi-choice books. Perhaps one of the best known examples for young reader is John Burningham's *Would you Rather . . .* (1978). Although this work presents as one narrative, it is in fact a series of fragmented narratives, each with a multiple ending – sometimes as many as five – and there is no 'right' ending. The reader is left with a choice that relies on his or her own personal preference or on their socialisation rather than on any preconceived knowledge of the conventions of traditional texts which may lead the reader towards an ending which appears to be 'right' in literary terms. This work cannot be recuperated into a narrative structure which is controlled by preceding conventional narrative structures.

A large part of the game strategy repertoire comprises narrative gaps and ambiguities which force the reader into active rather than passive reception, and within this repertoire the most common action is re-reading to search for 'clues' to make meaning. For example, I defy anyone to read Crew and Woolman's *The Watertower* just once. One reader describes her experience with this work as following: 'With courage and optimism I read [*The Watertower*] through once, twice, thrice . . . then backtracked yet again' (Lamond 1994, p. 15). Even more interesting is her next response: 'I recorded phenomena. I counted prongs on pitchforks, I noted odd reflections and chilling thoughts in the natives' eyes. I examined rippling water and the slant of shadows' (p. 15). Despite being disturbed and unsettled by the work, this reader has been provoked into engaging herself intellectually in its co-creation; she has become a participant in a world she is forced to acknowledge as fictional.

The Watertower appears, superficially, to be a conventionally crafted picture book but the page design and layout are active tools for creating layers of information or misinformation. The physical properties of the illustrations have been so manipulated that in the course of reading, the book moves through 360 degrees, echoing the uncanny circular leitmotiv and, more broadly, suggesting cinematic influences. Readers' imaginative responses will depend on their literary and filmic points of reference, which may include American Gothic, 1950s B-grade science fiction, and *cinema noir*.

The illustrator has reflexively provided far too much visual information. By divorcing seeing from knowing, he has engaged the reader in a type of metaphysical game in which no amount of obsessive and exasperated revisiting can discover the significance of the excessive clues in this work. Recurring symbols, visual subplots, red herrings and the disconcerting juxtapositions of buildings, cars and fashion of the 1950s with modern objects such as satellite dishes and the advanced technology of the tower itself, all add to the reader's task of deciphering the story from over-determined illustrations and an under-determined text in which the resolution is endlessly deferred. *The Watertower* is 'a text of absolute epistemological uncertainty: we know that something is happening here but we don't know what it is . . . Inevitably, epistemological doubt as total as this has ontological consequences as well; in particular [the work] flickers in and out of existence, depending on which hypothesis we choose to entertain' (McHale 1987, p. 18).

Metafiction poses ontological questions about the nature and existence of reality, the creation of literary universes and the nature of human artefacts. It reminds the reader of the book's identity as an artefact and of the reader's own role in realising the text. Reading and writing are considered vital functions in most modern societies and metafiction involves the reader in both – metafiction is both a process and a product which denies the reader a passive role. Barthes points out that:

> *reading, in the sense of consuming, is far from playing with the text. 'Playing' must be understood here in all its polysemy. The reduction of reading to a consumption is clearly responsible for 'boredom . . . to be bored means that one cannot produce the text, open it out, set it going.*
>
> (Barthes 1977, p. 163)

In conclusion, when theorising metafiction for children, it is important to remember that 'children are remarkably competent at handling all sorts of technical devices of story telling provided that the story is clearly of their culture, for them' (Sarland 1983, pp. 169–70) and can quickly recognise when a code has been violated and the fictional illusion destabilised. As Brian Caswell observes,

> *Far from being turned into mindless sponges, the video generation is far more sophisticated in the demands it makes of its story tellers . . . The post-Spielberg generation demands a style of narrative which allows for interactive reading – Not the patronising narrator who sets*

> *the moral agenda [but] multiple narrators, mixed genre, fragmented narrative, shifts in person, episodic and cinematic plot sequencing – bold experiments . . . to address the sophistication and needs of young readers.*
>
> (Caswell 1992, pp. 7–8)

Secondly, it is important to consider what 'pre-knowledge' children bring to a text that will affect the way they make meaning. The context in which children read or listen to stories includes their dealings with adults, their world knowledge, and their participation in the shared underground oral culture of the playground in which the child as transmitter is also the author. Any significant theory of children's literature cannot ignore the texts children hold in common, or their encounters with popular culture or their games, with their complex rules and elaborate role-play.

Notes

1 The term 'ludic' derives from Huizinga's 1938 study *Homo Ludens: A Study of the Play Element in Culture*, but the idea that play should be taken seriously, as a way of representing the experiences of writing and of reading, was proposed much earlier by Immanuel Kant and extended in Frederick von Schiller's *Letters on the Aesthetic Education of Man* (1795).

2 The theme of the labyrinth or maze is commonly used in metafiction. The paradigmatic text is Jorge Borges' *Garden of the Forking Paths*, in which the narrative agent is faced with a bifurcation at each point in the story. Choosing one, he is faced with another branching; choosing again, he is faced with yet another – the labyrinth (see McHale 1997, p. 106).

3 Naming is, of course, a primary act or invention. Henry, in Coover's *The Universal Baseball Inc . . .*, creates a dice game of baseball, inventing the dialogue, looks, and mannerisms of his players. But names are crucial: 'Strange. But name a man and you make him what he is. Of course he can develop . . . but the basic stuff is already there. In the name. Or rather: in the naming' (Coover 1968, p. 46–47).

References

Atwood, Margaret (1987) *The Handmaid's Tale*. London, Virago Press.

Barthes, Roland (1977) *Mythologies.* London, Granada.

Borges, Jorge (1970) 'Garden of the forking paths' in *Labyrinths: Selected Stories and Other Writings*. Harmondsworth, Penguin, pp. 44–54.

Boyd, Michael (1983) *The Reflexive Novel: Fiction as Critique*. London, Bucknell University Press.

Brooks, Peter (1984) *Reading for the Plot: Design and Intention in Narrative*. Oxford, Clarendon Press.

Burningham, John (1994; 1978) *Would You Rather . . .* London, Random House (Red Fox).

Caswell, Brian (1992) 'Literature and the changing society', *Reading Time* 36, 1, 4–8.

Chambers, Aidan (1978) *Breaktime.* London, Bodley Head.

Chambers, Aidan (1985) *Booktalk: Occasional Writing on Literature for Children.* London, Bodley Head.

Clarke, Sharon, 'There are no new stories only new ways of telling: A discussion of personalized children's books as postmodern texts', in Michael Stone (ed) *Children's Literature and Contemporary Theory.* Wollongong, New Literatures Research Centre, 76–90.

Crew, Gary (1994) *Inventing Anthony West.* St. Lucia, University of Queensland Press.

Crew, Gary and Steven Woolman (1994) *The Watertower.* Adelaide, Era.

Eco, Umberto (1979) 'Lector in Fabula: pragmatic strategy in metanarrative text' in *The Role of the Reader: Explorations in the Semiotics of Texts.* London, Indiana University Press.

Higonnet, Margaret (1990) 'Narrative fractures and fragments', *Children's Literature* 15, 37–54.

Jackson, Rosemary (1981) *Fantasy: The Literature of Subversion.* London, Methuen.

Lamond, Magrete (1995) 'Enigmatus Interruptus or The frustration of being lured, snared and thrilled, only to be ultimately disillusioned: the saga of an interaction with *The Watertower*', *Reading Time*, 39, 3, 15–16.

Macauley, David (1990) *Black and White.* Boston, Houghton Mifflin.

Marsden, John (1996) *Creep Street: You Make it Happen.* Sydney, Pan Macmillan.

McHale, Brian (1987) *Postmodernist Fiction.* New York, Methuen.

Moss, Geoff (1990) 'Metafiction and the poetics of children's literature', in *Children's Literature Association Quarterly*, 15, 50–52.

Ommundsen, Wenche (1990) 'The reader in contemporary metafiction: freedom or constraint?', in John Hay and Marie McLean (eds) *Narrative Issues*, AUMLA 74, 169–184.

Ommundsen, Wenche (1989) 'Narrative navel gazing, or how to recognise a metafiction when you see one', *Southern Review* 22, 265–274.

Ommundsen, Wenche (1993) *Metafictions? Reflexivity in Contemporary Texts.* Melbourne, Melbourne University Press.

Pavel, Thomas (1980) 'Narrative domains', in *Poetics Today* 1:4, Summer.

Raskin, Ellen (1978) *The Westing Game.* New York, Penguin (Puffin).

Rodda, Emily and Geoff Kelly (1994) *Power and Glory.* Melbourne, Allen & Unwin/ Little Ark.

Rubinstein, Gillian (1988) *Beyond the Labyrinth.* Melbourne, Hyland House.

Stonehill, Brian (1988) *The Self-Conscious Novel: Artifice in Fiction from Joyce to Pynchon.* Philadelphia, University of Pennsylvania Press.

Sukenick, Ronald (1984) 'The new, tradition' in *In Form: Digressions on the Act of Fiction.* London, Methuen.

Van Allsburg, Chris (1995) *Bad Day at Riverbend.* Boston, Houghton Mifflin.

Waddell, Martin, and Phillipe Dupasquier (1981) *The Great Green Mouse Disaster.* London, Anderson Press.

Waugh, Patricia (1984) *Metafiction: The Theory and Practice of Self-Conscious Fiction.* London, Methuen.

80

THE CHANGING AESTHETICS OF CHARACTER IN CHILDREN'S FICTION

Maria Nikolajeva

Source: *Style* 35(3) (Fall 2001): 430–454.

Character and characterization are such an obvious part of fiction that they are very seldom discussed in critical works. Despite the postmodern and poststructural denigration of characters, however, they are still central in fiction; basically, we read fiction because we are interested in human nature and human relationships as revealed through fictive characters. In this essay, I will deal with two aspects of the vast field that may be called a theory of character: (1) the changes in characters themselves as they are presented in children's literature of the past two centuries and (2) the changes in the devices of characterization, that is, the artistic means authors employ to reveal characters to readers.

1

In his treatment of literature as the displacement of myth, Northrop Frye discerns five consecutive stages: myth, which presents characters as gods, superior to both humans and the laws of nature; romance which presents characters as idealized humans who are superior to other humans, but inferior to gods; high mimetic narrative, which presents humans who are superior to other humans, but not the laws of nature; low mimetic narrative, which presents humans who are neither superior nor inferior to other humans; and, finally, ironic narrative, which presents characters who are inferior to other characters, such as children, the mentally handicapped, animals, and so on (Frye 33–34). By this definition, all characters in children's fiction would appear at the ironic stage, since they naturally lack experience and knowledge and are therefore inferior to adults. But even a brief glance at a number of classical and contemporary children's novels demonstrates that this is not the case. Characters in children's novels are empowered in a variety of ways and operate on all the displacement levels.

According to Frye, contemporary Western literature has reached the ironic stage, at which most of the characters we meet in novels are weak, disillusioned men and women. But this is true only of quality literature, since formulaic fiction operates within the romantic mode (romance, adventure, fantasy). Further, at least some contemporary adult fiction still uses mimetic modes. Children's literature is historically a recent form of fiction. Its emergence coincides with the establishment of realism (mimetic modes) in the mainstream; therefore, Frye's five stages seem to coexist more frequently in children's literature than in the mainstream of any given period. In contemporary Western children's fiction, we meet characters from all Frye's modes.

The mythic hero is, however, not a common figure in children's fiction, for myth as such is absent in the history of Western children's literature. Since children's literature emerged long after Western civilization had lost its traditional mythical belief, this stage is not represented in children's fiction. The most important mythic figure is the cultural hero, whose story teaches his people to use fire, to hunt, and to cultivate land. Such stories were not relevant—as living narratives, essential for survival—for young readers at the time children's literature became a separate artistic form. Of course, if we treat Judeo-Christian belief as myth, we can naturally say that Bible stories retold for children are mythical children's narratives. This view would have them correspond to the mythical stories of archaic people, told indiscriminately to children and adults alike. In certain cultures, mythical stories are still prominent as instructional narratives for young people. Classic myths, such as the Greek, Celtic, native American, or African, however, are in the Western world retold for children who have no direct belief in them—myth has been displaced and instead functions as romance.

In his study *The Hero with a Thousand Faces*. Joseph Campbell presents an analysis of the monomyth, the universal mythical pattern we find in the vast majority of narratives. The movement of the monomyth, separation, initiation, and return (Campbell 30), corresponds exactly to the "basic plot" of children's fiction, identified as home, away, and homecoming (see, e.g., Nodelman). The hero in Campbell's model is a young person going through a rite of passage. In this respect, the pattern of all children's literature is similar to the monomyth, and all characters in children's fiction are a further development of the mythic hero. Like the mythic hero, the child character must depart from the ordinary situation in order for there to be a plot. In children's novels, popular devices for achieving physical dislocation are sending characters away either simply for summer vacations (*Five Children and It*, by Edith Nesbit), or else because of illness in the family (*Tom's Midnight Garden*, by Philippa Pearce) or some danger (air raids in *The Lion, the Witch and the Wardrobe*, by C. S. Lewis). The characters then receive a message about their special task and acquire help that, depending on the genre, is either natural or supernatural. At the next step, in a plot element present in all forms of narratives, the character must cross a threshold. In fantasy novels, the threshold is tangible, as the character is transported into a different world. Rarely, if ever, does children's fiction present the painful and sometimes rather graphic dismembering or annihilation of the mythical hero this threshold crossing sometimes involves. Rather, in children's fiction this element it either omitted or transferred to a secondary character, presumably to spare young readers the horrors of empathic identification with the hero's suffering.

The mythical hero is subjected to a series of trials, as is the character of children's fiction. The trials and tasks are more tangible in romantic modes (fantasy, adventure). In mimetic modes, they assume symbolic forms, for instance the quest for identity. One might argue that the central episode of Campbell's schema—the hero's meeting the Goddess—is not present in children's fiction, mainly since the purpose of such an encounter is marriage, involving initiation into sexuality. But the original myth is displaced in fiction, and in children's fiction, censorial filters may be imposed. Many child characters do indeed meet either a friend or an opponent of the opposite sex who initiates a turning point in the protagonist's life (Leslie in *Bridge to Terabithia*, by Katherine Paterson). Campbell mentions the figure of the goddess-temptress, an evil figure seducing the hero; we encounter this figure for instance as the Snow Queen in Andersen's fairy tale or the White Witch in *The Lion, the Witch and the Wardrobe*. According to Campbell, the Goddess in myth represents the hero's mother, and by marrying—mastering, conquering—her, the hero replaces his father in the universal hierarchy. While such an interpretation may seem repulsive in connection with children's fiction, the transformation of the pattern can be traced in many novels. The next stage in Campbell's schema, atonement with the father, is also frequently found in children's novels (Jess's reconciliation with his father in *Bridge to Terabithia*). The hero's triumph is almost indispensable, as is the following reward. Further, like the mythical hero and unlike most characters of adult fiction, the child character returns to the point of departure, sometimes through flight and rescue, crossing the return threshold to ordinary life. There is a promise of further adventure: that is, as long as children remain children, they can cross the boundaries between the ordinary and the magical world (Wendy in J. M. Barrie's *Peter Pan* can go to the Neverland until she grows up; Lucy in the Narnia Chronicles can return to Narnia until she becomes too old for it). This very brief comparison between Campbell's description of myth and some basic patterns of children's fiction demonstrates that although myth as such may not be part of children's fiction, the mythical hero is a major source of inspiration for children's writers (see Stephens and McCallum).

The romantic hero, superior to ordinary human beings, is one of the most common character types in children's fiction. We encounter it primarily in fairy tales and fantasy, where the child is empowered by being able to travel through space and time, by possessing magical objects, or by being assisted by magical helpers. In fairy tales retold for children, characters are usually empowered in a way that makes them superior to other human beings. They are endowed with magical agents enabling them to be transported in space, or to metamorphose into animals or other, presumably better, human beings (Cinderella's transformation from ashes to diamonds). Fairy-tale heroes, however, normally have helpers possessing stronger powers than themselves, without whom they would be unable to achieve their goals. If fairy-tale protagonists are demi-gods, their helpers are gods. Ultimately, this difference reflects the power relationship between children and adults in society.

With few exceptions, fairy tales have always been regarded as suitable for children, apparently because fairy-tale protagonists, like children, grow from being the underdog to being strong and independent. Another essential trait of fairy-tale heroes is their lack of complexity, a feature considered appropriate for young readers from a didactic viewpoint. Fairy-tale heroes know no nuances: they are one hundred percent heroic, they never doubt, fear, or despair. In fact, they are seldom individualized. If described at all, they possess a standard set of traits: brave, clever, kind, or beautiful. The exact content of these traits may change with time and culture; the behavior of fairy-tale tricksters, involving cheating, stealing, and killing, would be considered highly immoral in contemporary Western societies. Nevertheless, the fairy-tale hero or heroine, the oppressed youngest brother or sister, empowered by magical means, is decidedly the origin of contemporary character of children's novels, not only in fantasy stories, but everyday stories as well.

The romantic hero of children's fiction has, like the fairy-tale hero, a standard set of traits, such as strength, courage, loyalty, and devotion. Although the origin of this type is unmistakably the classic epic hero, the premise for the romantic child hero is the idealization of childhood begun during the Romantic era. It is based on the belief in the child as innocent and therefore capable of conquering evil. Although this ideal child is now being interrogated by some critics (see essays in McGavran), it affects the ways in which child heroes are still constructed in certain text types, especially formulaic fiction.

I have already shown how mythic patterns are displaced on the romantic level. The most important difference, that allows reiteration, is the return to the initial order, the disempowerment of the hero, and the reestablishment of adult authority. That the mythic hero kills his father and usurps his place would be highly improper in a children's book. From magical journeys to alternative worlds or histories, the child hero is brought back to the ordinary, sometimes being explicitly stripped of the attributes of previous power (most tangibly seen in the transformation of the Kings and Queens of Narnia back to children at the end of *The Lion, the Witch and the Wardrobe*). The magical object is irretrievably lost or loses its magical power (*The*

Story of the Amulet, by Edith Nesbit), the magical helper is removed (*Mary Poppins*, by Pamela Travers), and the character once again stands alone without assistance, no longer a hero. Thus in many children's fantasy novels, the characters become displaced yet further away from myth, onto low mimetic and ironic levels. This displacement would appear not to be the case in high fantasy, such as Lloyd Alexander's *Prydain Chronicles*, that at first glance follow meticulously Campbell's myth model. At the end of the five-novel cycle, however, Taran is left without magical assistance as all magic forces leave Prydain and thus suddenly transform it from a mythic realm into ordinary Britain.

Even though contemporary authors may lean heavily on myth, they will inevitably deconstruct it in some way (see Hourihan). Only in formulaic fiction can purely romantic characters still exist today. Interestingly enough, while the romantic hero has been a prominent source of influence for children's fiction, the romantic heroine, the object of the hero's desires (see Rabine), is a conspicuously absent figure. Presumably the nature of relationships between hero and heroine in a romance is irrelevant for the young characters of children's fiction. While some children's novels certainly depict romantic friendships, portraying characters such as Becky Thatcher in Mark Twain's *The Adventures of Tom Sawyer*, there is no correspondence in children's literature to the great romantic heroines of the mainstream.

High mimetic characters are humans superior to other humans, for instance, in terms of bravery, wisdom, or patriotism. High mimetic narratives for children emerged almost simultaneously with the early retold fairy tales. Two types are hagiographies (lives of saints) and plutarches (lives of important historical and political figures). Being superior to other humans, including the reader, high mimetic characters are supposed to serve as models not only for the other character in the story, but for the readers as well. In children's fiction, such characters are used for didactic purposes.

One of the possible modes for employing high mimetic characters is allegory. *Pilgrim's Progress*, by John Bunyan, has been widely utilized as children's reading. Very few contemporary children's novels are intentionally written as allegories, and allegorical characters seem to belong in the past (there are exceptions, such as *Terrible Things: An Allegory of the Holocaust*, by Eve Bunting). Since allegory is by definition a didactic literary form, contemporary children's authors, who tend to avoid didacticism, seldom choose purely allegorical characters for their work. Further, it is likely that most young readers will ignore the potential allegorical interpretations of some children's novels, such as *The Lion, the Witch and the Wardrobe*, unless these are brought to their attention. Partly such an attitude depends on the fact that contemporary readers in general are not trained in allegorical reading.

In the vast majority of pre-twentieth-century children's literature, child characters are used as models for young readers. They are virtuous beyond measure, good and kind, pious, obedient and humble. In many cases, as we read these texts today, the characters seem either ridiculous or hopelessly sentimental (for instance in *Jessica's First Prayer*, by Hesba Stretton). There are naturally exceptions, such as Diamond in *At the Back of the North Wind*, by George MacDonald. Because the purpose of all such characters is to set a good example for the reader, the positive traits of the characters are amplified beyond natural proportions. *Struwwelpeter* (*Slovenly Peter*), by Heinrich Hoffmann, has exactly the same function, only in reverse.

Modern examples of the use of characters as models can be easily found in children's literature of the former Soviet Union: young war heroes and revolutionaries, vigilant scouts who reveal spies and saboteurs, boys who save other children or adults from drowning or fire, or children who assist the country by collecting recyclable materials. These heroes have few other traits than being heroic. Similarly, in China today, stories of revolutionaries and war heroes still constitute the majority of children's fiction. In the USA, biographies of presidents published for children are popular, and in France there are dozens of books about Joan of Arc.

Another clearly didactic use of characters is their serving as mouthpieces for the authors' ideas and opinions. Here, however, an interesting difference can be noted between children's fiction and that of the mainstream. Young readers are supposed to identify with young protagonists and thus learn lessons together with them. This assumption implies that the protagonists themselves cannot be used as mouthpieces, but rather wisdom must necessarily come from a secondary character, whether adult or a child. Indeed, we see a variety of such mouthpiece figures who explain, preach, and warn, seldom leaving readers room for further contemplation. Although one would assume that such novels for children belong to the past, one recent international bestseller, mysteriously crossing over from children's fiction to mainstream, *Sophie's World*, by the Norwegian Jostein Gaarder, employs such an adult as didactic mouthpiece character.

Low mimetic narratives such as domestic stories, school stories, and so on, present ordinary children in ordinary situations. Although "realistic" characters seemingly have existed in children's fiction from the beginning, I would argue that characters appearing on a low mimetic level—neither superior nor inferior to other character—are a relatively recent development. Considering the protagonists of some classic novels for children, we discover that they are portrayed as anything but ordinary. The four March sisters in *Little Women* are exceedingly virtuous and become still more so as they go through their self-imposed "pilgrimage." Tom Sawyer finds a treasure ensuring him a pleasurable future in the adult world. Anne of Green Gables becomes a brilliant student and is eventually described as quite good-looking. Besides inheriting great wealth, Cedric Errol in Burnett's *Little Lord Fauntleroy* is nauseatingly blameless.

We can probably regard Laura in the *Little House* series as an early low-mimetic character, ordinary in every respect. Modern low-mimetic characters appear on a larger seale in Western children's literature after the Second World War as a result of major changes in society, rapid urbanization, and changes in family structure, as well as the influence of child psychology. Low-mimetic characters offer the most natural subject position for contemporary young readers: they are not freed from the obligation to attend school by eternal summer holidays; they are not extremely lucky so as to be in the right place at the right time to have exciting adventures; they are not exceedingly bright, nor brave, nor handsome; they do not marry princes or millionaires; and they do not find treasures that will allow them to live happily ever after.

It has taken children's fiction a long time to venture into the ironic mode and depict characters who, in addition to being inferior to their parents and other adults, are weaker, physically and spiritually, than their peers. Unlike fairy-tale heroes, these characters are not empowered at the end of the story. At best, they remain the same (for instance in *The Planet of Junior Brown*, by Virginia Hamilton, or *Slake's Limbo*, by Felice Holman), at worst they perish, incapable of coping with surrounding reality, as do many characters in Robert Cormier's novels.

We have recently witnessed a radical change in the narrative perspective of children's novels whereby the didactic, authoritative narrator is supplanted by character focalization. This change enables some contemporary authors to portray the world through the eyes of a naïve and inexperienced child. Children's fiction authors have a wider scope of expressive means than their colleagues in the mainstream, who have to employ, for instance, mentally disturbed characters to achieve the same effect. While most narratologists are limited in exemplification of the totally naïve perspective to Benjy from *The Sound and the Fury*, children's literature scholars can easily enumerate several dozen children's novels using the same device. An excellent example is Ramona in Beverly Cleary's series. On her first day of school, she has to learn "a puzzling song about 'the dawnzer lee light,' that Ramona did not understand because she did not know what a dawnzer was. 'Oh, say, can you see by the dawnzer lee light,' sang Miss Binney, and Ramona decided that a dawnzer was another word for a lamp" (Cleary 21). Apparently, the character's confusion is based on her ignorance and naivete. That readers are supposed to recognize the words gives them superiority over the character. But if for some reason they do not, the situation leaves them as helpless and puzzled as Ramona.

Low mimetic and ironic characters are the first ones historically and the only ones typologically who presuppose and allow a portrayal of internal life. Therefore we are most likely to find such characters in contemporary psychological novels for children. If, as the title of Harold Bloom's study *Shakespeare: The Invention of the Human* suggests, a psychological human being was invented by Shakespeare, in children's literature it was invented collaboratively by such authors as Katherine Paterson, Patricia MacLachlan, Beverly Cleary, Maria Gripe, Nina Bawden, and Michelle Magorian.

It is not always possible and still less fruitful to draw a definite boundary between low mimetic and ironic characters in children's fiction. As pointed out above, all child characters are by definition ironic, that is, inferior to their surroundings and, it would seem, to readers. In children's fiction, however, readers may be just as inexperienced and disempowered as the ironic character. In other words, young readers may find themselves at the same level as the character, as in the case of Ramona, above. Although as adult coreaders we may see the young protagonist's faults and mistakes, a young reader may fail to do so. Contemporary writers have developed means of drawing the readers' attention to the ironic status of their characters, for instance through detachment and alienation.

In traditional fiction, for children as well as for adults, readers are expected to identify and empathize with at least one character, to adopt a subject position coinciding with a character's. One of the main premises of postmodern aesthetics is the subversion of subjectivity, often achieved by making the protagonist repulsive in some way. Physically unattractive, obnoxious, morally depraved, a criminal, or even an inhuman monster, some characters in contemporary children's fiction efficiently alienate the reader by being unpleasant and thus offering no clear-cut subject position. While in Burnett's *The Secret Garden*, Mary Lennox, repeatedly described as "disagreeable," quickly gains the reader's sympathy, because she is an orphan and exposed to the adults' indifference, a character staying unpleasant throughout a story may leave readers concerned and even frustrated. In Katherine Paterson's *Flip-flop Girl*, Vinnie's father is dead, and since her little brother has taken the worst damage of his death, Vinnie feels neglected. Although the situation may seem similar to that of Mary Lennox, Mary makes the most of it and improves, morally, physically and mentally, while Vinnie is consistently presented as exceedingly nasty, not to say destructive. Here, the narrative device of the filter—shifting the reader's point of view away from the character's—enables the reader to dissociate from the focalizing character.

The use of alienating characters in children's fiction is problematic, and some authors do not manage to be consistent in their creation. Stanley in *Holes*, by Louis Sachar, starts as a typical ironic character: he is obese, not particularly likable, and even though we are told that he is innocent of the crime for which he is punished, the way he is described provokes alienation rather than empathy. He is also presented in an oppressed position: in a labor camp, literally deprived of his freedom, humiliated, and abused. Half-way through the novel, Stanley develops more heroic, high mimetic traits as he risks his own life to save a friend: and in the end he finds a treasure ensuring him and his family a carefree life ever after. This sudden elevation of the character to the romantic mode is not only implausible, but incompatible with the ironic outset of the novel. Presumably it is the author's capitulation to the conventions of children's fiction that demand a happy ending.

Yet another possible detaching strategy is metafiction. The prefix "meta-" in the postmodern terminology refers to framing, that is, the deliberate construction of the narrative on more than one diegetic level. Patricia Waugh includes fantasy among metafictive devices (Waugh 108–14). With such a view, all characters traveling between the real and the fantastic world, or, in time-shift plots, between two real worlds by fantastic means, must be counted as metafictive. Fantasy is a considerably more conspicuous frame-breaking element in mainstream fiction than in children's fiction. Therefore I do not see any point in discussing one of the most common narrative devices in children's fiction, the magical journey, as metafiction. Instead, I will reserve the notion of a metafictive character for those who in some way transgress the frame boundaries of the narrative, for instance, by appearing on different diegetic levels or even by being aware of the existence of other levels. True, fantasy with its explicit heterotopia allows for endless metafictional options. Bastian, in Michael Ende's *The Neverending Story*, enters the fictional world he is reading about, and one of the characters in Geraldine McCaughrean's *A Pack of Lies* wanders in and out of his own fiction. Too-ticki of the Moomin novels, by Tove Jansson, sometimes seems to be watching the events from another narrative level, and Snufkin is aware of being inside an adventure story. Christopher Robin is a metafictive character in the sense that he appears on two different diegetic levels. Yet we do not actually see him pass from one level to another; the passage is implicit, the metafiction covert. None of these characters really leave the reader puzzled, since the character's ability to break the diegetic frames is perceived as part of the fantasy convention.

In a novel written in a mimetic mode, metafictive characters create a sense of uneasiness, since the reader is left uncertain as to their ontological status. Hal in Aidan Chamber's *Dance on My Grave* comments: "I have become my own character" (221). Ditto in *Breaktime*, by the same author, exists on two diegetic levels: the frame story and his own first-person narrative. Moreover, at the end of the novel, not merely the credibility of Ditto's narrative, but the very existence of the character himself is questioned. Ditto is perhaps the closest juvenile fiction has so far come to the concept of a canceled character, that is, a character totally lacking any psychological features whatsoever, existing exclusively as a textual construction, one consisting only of words. Canceled characters are no longer possible to discuss in terms of personal integrity. Some critics have pointed out that Sarah in John Fowles's *The French Lieutenant's Woman* has no mimetic function in the story, that she does not "represent" anything. By introducing a character like that, the author breaks the illusion of mimetic reality. We can perhaps say something similar about Johnny in the Swedish Peter Pohl's *Johnny My Friend*. The enigmatic Johnny is a catalyst initiating a change in the protagonist without herself being affected. Yet such characters are unusual in children's fiction, since children's writers most often wish, probably for didactic purposes, to offer their readers a psychologically acceptable objects of identification.

The various types of irony in character construction are especially tangible in female characters. Not surprisingly, male myths and male narrative patterns have been most influential for traditional children's fiction. We can easily discern figures such as Odysseus, Hercules, or King Arthur behind a large number of protagonists in children's fiction. Trying to recall great Western myths that have inspired female characters, we might perhaps count Joan of Arc as the model for contemporary juvenile novels about girls in disguise; otherwise our sources are extremely limited. Personally I am not convinced by attempts to squeeze female characters into Campbellian male mythical patterns (Pearson and Pope). It is hypothetically possible to put a female character in a mythical or romantic narrative, but this will be simple gender permutation, creating a "hero in drag" (see Paul: see also Nikolajeva, *From Mythic* 147–49).

Annis Pratt's *Archetypal Patterns in Women's Fiction* can be regarded as a feminist reply to Campbell's overtly masculine analysis of a hero. Although Pratt's patterns are clearly connected with sexuality and eroticism, some parallels with children's fiction can still be made. For instance, the green-world archetype, a girl who lives close to nature, is one of the most common female protagonists in children's fiction. Wendy in Barrie's *Peter Pan* is one of these heroines, escaping into her green world away from both urban civilization and her parents' oppression, and returning to it in her recuperating memories as adult. The protagonists of Johanna Spyri's *Heidi*, Burnett's *The Secret Garden*, and Astrid Lindgren's *Ronia the Robber's Daughter* are further examples of the green-world heroines.

The growing-up-grotesque archetype implies meeting the incompatibility of personal freedom and societal demands by going into depression or seclusion. As Pratt observes, in literature boys grow, but girls shrink (30). This shrinking has also been described in terms of abjection, a girl's feeling of aversion towards her own body as it develops into a young woman's. The tomboy archetype in children's fiction is an excellent example of abjection. Rather than accept their own femininity, heroines such as Jo March and Anne Shirley suppress it by manifesting nonfeminine behavior. Both characters have to subdue hot tempers incompatible with feminine norms. Anne is literally silenced as she abandons her imaginative, poetic language. Cross-dressing and androgyny are two more ways of denying one's body and gender. In contemporary novels, the archetype of the grotesque can be stretched quite far, since today's young women's unwomanly manners are slightly more tolerated than in Jo March's days. Louise in Katherine Paterson's *Jacob Have I Loved* suppresses her femininity to distance herself from her pretty and talented twin sister. She is also trying to fulfil her father's secret desire for a son. Louise dresses carelessly, has a male occupation, fishing, and seemingly makes no attempts to grow up as a "normal" woman. Portraying this survival strategy, the author explicitly describes her as unattractive (among other things, with an ugly scar from chicken pox), the way she perceives herself. A much younger Paterson heroine, Gilly Hopkins, employs a similar survival strategy by being deliberately nasty.

In children's fiction, girls are doubly oppressed: as women and as children. Such oppression implies that in a children's novel, a female character's development is more universal than that in mainstream fiction, where femininity is overt and explicit. Not least, because girls' fiction is historically a relatively recent genre, masculine patterns, as in many other fields, are "default value" in children's fiction. Paradoxically enough, the contemporary ironic character of children's fiction has inherited significantly more traits from the female archetypes as drafted by Pratt than from those of Campbell's hero with a thousand faces.

2

Viewing the characters' ontological status from a historical perspective, we can clearly see that contemporary characters tend to become more like "real people," since they appear on low mimetic and ironic levels. Our shifting criteria for "plausible" characters depend on several factors, for instance on our growing knowledge of human nature (a knowledge young children normally lack), on our changing values regarding human virtues and vices, and finally on the variety of human behavior. Examples of real heroes are today found only in formulaic fiction. Even when child characters are temporarily elevated to high mimetic and romantic levels, they are subsequently brought back to ordinary life, and romantic heroes are deconstructed in a variety of ways. Contemporary characters are not meant as examples for young readers to admire, but as subjectivities recognizably equal to one's own. The opposite trend, prominent in contemporary mainstream postmodern fiction, that increasingly makes characters resemble empty verbal constructions, is as yet extremely rare in children's fiction.

The tremendous popularity of the Harry Potter novels may be partly ascribed to J. K. Rowling's successful attempt to reintroduce the romantic character into children's fiction. The character of Harry Potter has all the necessary components of the romantic hero. There are mystical circumstances around his birth and infant years, he is displaced and oppressed until suddenly, on his eleventh birthday—a common age of initiation—he is given unlimited power. He has a whole group of gurus and supporters and an infinitely evil and powerful opponent. His innocence and his intrinsic benevolence, however, make him superior to the evil—adult—powers.

Yet, Harry Potter is a child of his time, of the twenty-first century. He appears as a reaction to a long chain of ironic characters who show ambiguity in their concepts of good and evil, transgress gender, and exhibit other tokens of the postmodern aesthetics. By contrast, Harry Potter is a very straightforward hero. We know what to expect from him. After decades of parody, metafiction, frame-breaking and other postmodern games, it may feel liberating for readers to know where to place their sympathies and antipathies. Of course it is conceivable that Harry will eventually go over to the dark side. But such a development would feel almost trivial today, especially in the wake of *Star Wars—the First Episode*. After so many anti-heroes in children's as well as adult literature, a hero is welcome. Still, the appeal of Harry is exactly that he is not a hero of the Superman caliber, but an ordinary clumsy and bespectacled boy. A boy who turns out to have magical powers, yet receives most praise for his sporting achievements. A boy who is disobedient and curious, who is not at all brilliant in school, but quite average. A boy who has friends and enemies, who needs to eat and sleep, and who, in book four, is at long last awakening to the charms and mysteries of the opposite gender. Harry Potter is at once human and non-human, with the same emotions we all know: longing for mom and dad, loneliness, insecurity, curiosity about his identity and origin. In this respect, he differs from traditional romantic heroes, devoid of any such sentiments. Thus Harry is repeatedly taken down to mimetic and ironic levels, only to be elevated to hero status again at moments of decisive struggle. As critics, we might find Harry Potter conventional: for readers, he presents a welcome alternative to characters they may find too sophisticated.

A crucial question in connection with the development in children's fiction from "hero" to "character" is the adult authors' capacity to adopt a child's subject position. It would be reasonable to assume that adult writers would feel most comfortable writing from their own superior position, presenting child characters as inferior physically, morally, spiritually, in terms of knowledge, experience, economy, and societal power. Yet even a very brief glance at a number of children's novels reveals that the ironic mode is the most complex and demanding, for the writer as well as the reader. By contrast, the romantic mode allows adults to empower the child, thus creating an illusion for the character and the reader that such empowerment is indeed possible. On the high mimetic level, adult writers can use characters to provide young readers with examples and ideals. Which endeavor is to be regarded the most successful depends exclusively on the purpose authors have in writing for children. The development from hero to character in children's fiction is thus not a simple linear process. It reveals the attitude toward childhood and toward children's reading at any given moment, in any given society.

Further, subjectivity as such is an essential issue in children literature. In mythic, romantic, and high mimetic modes, subjectivity is outside the text and, moreover, frequently connected with an adult narrative agency. Subjectivity in low mimetic and ironic modes is inside the text and therefore usually connected with a child character. Thus we may regard the development from outside to inside subjectivity as a process parallel to the development from hero to character.

Another very prominent change in the aesthetics of character in children's fiction, one closely interconnected with the movement from hero to character, is the shift from authorial to figural discourse; from predominantly external characterization, such as that found in description, narrative statements, and presentation of actions, toward representation of inner life. Considering this shift poses about characterization a number of epistemological questions, ones such as the ways we can get to know and understand them and the strategies authors have to reveal characters for the reader. Several critics argue that while literature allows us an intrinsic knowledge of other people, in real life we have only intrinsic knowledge of ourselves and extrinsic knowledge of other people. While real people are always opaque to us, literary characters may be presented in a vast continuum from opacity to full transparency. For many critics, the appeal of literature is exactly the fact that we can more easily understand literary figures than we can ever learn to understand real people. Although children's literature has been for a long time utilized mainly for didactic purposes, the young reader's aesthetic appreciation of characters cannot be neglected. Literary characters are indeed transparent in a way real people can never be. Far from all means of characterization, however, allow this transparency. In children's literature, characters are usually less transparent than those in the mainstream, because children's writers for a number of reasons have a tendency to use external rather than internal characterization devices. This is an interesting paradox. On the one hand, children's literature is supposed to be simple and easy to understand. We might then expect writers to employ narrative devices that would enable readers to come closer to characters and understand them better. But on the other hand, such devices are the most complex and ambiguous and are therefore used only sparsely in children's literature. In fact, children's literature has substantially lagged behind in the development of psychological characterization, that has to do with the aesthetic of children's literature as such. The majority of children's books are plot-oriented, that is, they focus more on actions and events than on character and characterization. Until recently, few children's books portrayed characters with personality traits other than ones suggesting good or evil. Certain scholars of children's literature, for instance, Perry Nodelman, go so far as to maintain plot-orientation as one of the foremost aesthetic features of children's literature (192); I must hasten to add that I do not share this opinion.

The fact that children's stories often are indeed plot-oriented implies that children's writers have closely followed the conventions of Aristotelian poetics long after their colleagues in the mainstream have abandoned them in favor of psychological characterization. Aristotle claimed that characters should possess only one of the two traits: nobility or baseness. In many cases this "rule" is also true about characters in children's fiction: they can be easily divided into "good guys" and "bad guys," for instance, in fairy tales (hero versus dragon), fantasy novels (Aslan versus the White Witch), adventure (Tom Sawyer versus Injun Joe), mystery (Nancy Drew versus the numerous villains), and so on. That characters are noble or base, good or bad is revealed to us primarily through their actions, and those traits are used to propel the plot. This type of characterization through actions is predominantly used for romantic and high mimetic characters, who are thus, in one of the common dichotomies of character analysis, static and flat.

In dealing with characterization, we should therefore ask what is sufficient in order to understand a character in a particular text type. In fantasy or adventure, it may be enough to know on which side to place our sympathy. We do not necessarily require romantic heroes to have ethical choices or in general to possess any ambivalent qualities. In psychological novels, ones, that is, portraying characters on low mimetic and ironic level, we normally expect them to have traits other than merely goodness or badness; moreover, we expect the traits to add up to a consistent whole. In other words, we postulate that low mimetic and ironic characters should be round and dynamic. In children's literature, the issue is especially relevant, since young readers may misjudge characters or fail to assemble a number of traits into a whole. Until recently, it was believed that young readers lack the ability to understand psychologically complex characters or the skills necessary to construct a coherent portrait from the information provided by the text, for instance, if a character's self-evaluation contradicts the other people's opinion or the narrator's overt comments. These presumptions about the cognitive capacity and aesthetic needs of the young audience have considerably impeded the development of more sophisticated characterization in children's fiction. Not unexpectedly, this belated development, coinciding with the emergence of low mimetic and ironic characters, is one that in its turn is connected with the shift toward figural discourse, toward character-oriented children's fiction.

Since conventional children's literature is plot-oriented, it is natural to expect the dominance of external representation in children's novels. Indeed, up to recently, the vast majority of characters in children's fiction were portrayed only externally: by their appearance, by narrator's explicit judgements, by their actions and reactions, and by direct speech. External representation is essentially authorial and therefore considered suitable for the didactic purpose inherent in conventional children's fiction. External representation is also the least complex way of revealing characters and therefore regarded suitable for the young audience. Although external representation is seldom the only means of characterization in a novel, we can speak about external orientation in characterization, meaning that *most* facts we learn about a particular character are conveyed through such external means as, for instance, description, narrator's comments, actions, and events.

The predominance of external orientation in children fiction is closely connected to several literary factors. First, it occurs in older rather than in modern texts. Comparing, for instance, Louisa M. Alcott's *Little Women* with Katherine Paterson's *Jacob Have I Loved*, that have some superficial similarities in plot and theme, we will immediately notice that the former employs external description, authorial comments, actions, and dialogue for characterization, while the latter is wholly concentrated on the character's inner life. The first-person introspective narration in Paterson's novel is the natural result of the author's focus on character.

Second, for obvious reasons external orientation is typical for plot-oriented narratives where it is more important what characters do than how they feel about it. Comparing an adventure story such as *The Adventures of Tom Sawyer* with a domestic story, such as *Anne of Green Gables*, we can see that the former presents characters primarily through their actions and reactions, while the latter delves deep into the protagonist's mind. Domestic stories, not least *Little Women* and *Anne of Green Gables*, sometimes have been condemned for their "lack of action," while critics have obviously missed that the novels depict internal rather than internal events.

Third, external orientation is more likely to be used in formulaic fiction than in psychological narratives. Adventure, mystery, and horror devote little attention to the psychological life of their characters, and young readers choosing to read formulaic stories are not in the first place interested in the characters' inner life.

Fourth, external orientation is more likely to be used in texts addressed to younger children. This statement does not exclude the existence of highly sophisticated picture books that allegedly are supposed to be understood by very young readers. Maurice Sendak's *Where the Wild Things Are*, Anthony Browne's *The Tunnel* and *Gorilla*, or John Burningham's *Granpa* show psychological dimensions well above the average middle-level children's novel. Yet it is true that books geared toward younger readers, for instance Laura Ingalls Wilder's *Little House* series or Beverly Cleary's *Ramona* series, reveal the characters through actions and dialogue rather than through the depiction of their mental states.

Last but not least, external orientation more or less presupposes an omniscient perspective. Description of both the characters' looks and their actions requires an external narrative voice, whether it is overt or covert. Narrator's comments are by definition authorial. As soon as the narrative perspective shifts onto a character, either through first-person narration or character focalization, an internal, subjective dimension is imposed on the story. The traditional extradiegetic-heterodiegetic narrator in children's fiction allows an authoritative, didactic manipulation of the readers in their understanding of characters.

All these factors are highly relevant for the discussion of the changing aesthetics of character since they provide at least some insight into why and how these changes occur in contemporary children's fiction. Of them, description is the most elementary way of presenting a character, especially block description in the beginning of the book providing us immediately with a full and direct portrait. Its abundance in classic literature, including classic children's novels, presumably has something to do with the late eighteenth-century theory of physiognomy, directly connecting people's physical appearance with their psychological traits. Although this theory has been completely discredited in the twentieth century, its influence is manifest in children's fiction. For instance, the initial description of the protagonist in *Anne of Green Gables* includes a "very pointed and prominent" chin, "big eyes [. . .] full of spirit and vivacity, " "sweet-lipped and expressive" mouth and "broad and full forehead," with the immediate conclusion that "no commonplace soul inhabited the body of this stray woman-child" (12).

Although we assume that descriptions have an aesthetic purpose in a children's novel, that they have implications, they may be employed merely because the author wants to have a fuller portrait of the character, or even simpler, because it has always been done in children's books. Quite often, indeed, descriptions seem to be an end in themselves, something included because "young readers like to know 'how people look'" (*Little Women* 5). The description is not motivated otherwise than by the presumed expectations of the implied readers. Being an authorial narrative form, external description is tangibly didactic.

Further, descriptions have different functions for different kinds of characters. In a formulaic novel, blond hair is likely to indicate innocence, while dark hair will indicate evil. In a realistic novel, the color of hair does not necessarily imply moral qualities. Yet, even in realistic modes, certain external traits, such as moles, crooked teeth, or extreme facial hair are often ascribed to evil characters. If this tendency is manifest in formulaic fiction for adults, it is all the more tangible in such mystery and adventure stories for children as the Nancy Drew or the Hardy Boys books. By contrast, in contemporary children's novels, descriptions are used sparsely and mostly in figural discourse: a character is described through another character's eyes. For instance, in *Bridge to Terabithia*. Leslie as well as Miss Edmunds, the schoolteacher, are described through Jess's perception, one that is subjective as compared to the objective description by an omniscient narrator. Although such figural descriptions have been widely employed in the mainstream novel since the nineteenth century, for children's fiction they remain an unusual device.

Yet, when used for overtly didactic purposes, even an authorial description may be a powerful characterization device in a children's novel. In *The*

Secret Garden, Mary is first presented as a girl with "a little thin face and a little thin body, thin light hair and a sour expression. Her hair was yellow, and her face was yellow because she has been born in India and had always been ill in one way or other" (7). As the story evolves, the narrator frequently returns to Mary's looks, noting successive changes in them: she is gaining weight, getting a rosy shade on her cheeks, her hair is turning thick and shiny, and so on. This physical change, as she develops from a spoiled, lazy, selfish brat into a strong-willed, active, and alert young lady, is used to emphasize the mental and moral improvement of the protagonist.

The narrator of *The Secret Garden* not only describes the change in Mary's looks, but also the change of her disposition. Narrative statements are frequently used in children's fiction to comment on a variety of characteristics, such as the character's external appearance (pretty, ugly, tall, fat), social position (rich, poor), intelligence (clever, stupid), actions (brave), attitudes (greedy), manners (well-behaved, kind), and finally on the character's temporary feelings (cold, hungry, tried) or state of mind (agitated, frightened, glad). They can refer to a permanent, inherent quality (brave or clever by nature) or to a concrete action or reaction (brave or clever in a particular situation). Like descriptions, narrative statements are of course also didactic; they manipulate readers toward a certain interpretation of character and are therefore often associated with traditional, didactic children's fiction: "Flopsy, Mopsy, and Cottontail, *who were good little bunnies*, went down the lane to gather blackberries/But Peter, *who was very naughty* [. . .] (Potter n.p.; emphasis added). At the time the story was written it was habitual to have such comments in children's books, as if the author did not trust her readers to recognize the three bunny girls as well-behaved and Peter as naughty. Similarly, in *The Secret Garden*, although the narrator frequently condemns the protagonist as lazy, inactive, and disagreeable, her actions occasionally contradict the statements. Yet because of the strong authoritative narrative voice, there is not much left for young readers to do than accept such statements as, for instance "she was a self-absorbed child" (13). As with *The Tale of Peter Rabbit*, it seems that the author does not trust readers themselves to make the necessary inferences from the character's actions and reactions.

Actions present characters in a more indirect way and involve at least some engagement from the reader. For instance, Pippi Longstocking repeatedly treats her friends to nice food and gives them presents. Readers are encouraged to understand that she is generous. Reactions to events can also reveal character properties: Pippi reacts strongly when she encounters injustice and violence. She does not hesitate to save two small children from a fire. But the narrator of *Pippi Longstocking* does not explicitly say that Pippi is generous, righteous, and brave. Although characterization by actions is external and hence authorial, readers are to a certain extent free to interpret the actions and reactions according to their own understanding.

Is Tom Sawyer clever or naughty when he cheats other boys into whitewashing the fence for him? How does coming to his own funeral characterize him: is he clever, cynical, silly, thoughtless? Is Anne Shirley stupid when she gives Diana wine to drink or does she simply not know better? In these cases, the authors seem to trust their young readers to draw their own conclusions, a trust that is otherwise far from common in children's fiction.

Let us agree that external orientation does not imply deficient characterization. While we today, especially in the field of adult fiction, attribute higher aesthetic quality to psychological portrayals that penetrate the innermost parts of human mind, it is wrong to assume that external characterization is artistically inferior, that it is merely a different device. Moreover, external characterization is part of the overall didactic adaptation of children's fiction to the cognitive level of its implied readers. Presumably, young readers may more easily understand and judge characters' actions, external description, or the narrator's direct statements than subtle psychological changes and motivations. Since literature is dependent on language to describe emotional life, it demands a rich and multi-faceted vocabulary to convey the nuances of meaning that young readers may not have mastered yet. Although some contemporary children's writers, such as Katherine Paterson, Patricia MacLachlan, or Virginia Hamilton, do not hesitate to use advanced vocabulary to portray their characters' internal lives, the bulk of contemporary children's fiction still resorts primarily to external means. Further, as already mentioned, in fiction for younger children, there is a clear tendency toward external characterization, while young adult fiction, frequently employing internal means, thus comes closer to the mainstream. Whether this tendency reflects the actual limitation in the young audience's cognitive capacity or, instead, the conventions of, not to say prejudices about, children's fiction, is another question.

One of the common characterization devices that I find highly problematic in children's fiction is direct speech. One would assume that is it simple and explicit, since characters' direct speech presents them immediately, through what they say as well as through how they say it. Yet, paradoxically, in children's fiction, direct speech is used far more often to carry the plot than to develop character. Further, we must once again pay attention to the didactic issues manifest in the relationship between direct speech and narration. Narrator's comments and reported speech manipulate the reader to interpret the characters' utterances in a certain way. Assuming that the narrative authority is an adult, we may notice that even when a child character is given a voice through direct speech, there is normally an adult voice accompanying it and adjusting it to guide the reader toward "correct" understanding. Although direct speech may seem a characterization device that presents characters in the most immediate manner, we should not forget that there is usually a narrative agency nearby to amend whatever impression we as readers might get. Even a specific verb, adverb, or additional comment may immediately manipulate our understanding of the character, for instance: "'Who is going to dress me?' *demanded* Mary" (*The Secret Garden* 29; emphasis added); "'I'm sorry I was late,' he said *shyly*" (*Anne of Green Gables* 12; emphasis added); "'I suppose you are Mr. Matthew Cuthbert of Green Gables?' she said *in a peculiarly clear and sweet voice*" (*Anne of Green Gables* 12; emphasis added).

It is often argued that young readers prefer direct speech to narration (some metapoetic comments from writers confirm this assumption: for instance, Lewis Carroll's Alice thinks her sister's book boring because it has "no conversations"). Several pedagogical studies of children's literature, applying as one of the criteria for "readability" the ratio between narration and direct speech, claims that the abundance of dialogue makes texts more reader-friendly. This claim may be true in terms of pure reading skills. Direct speech utterances, especially coming from child characters and imitating their syntax and vocabulary, are usually shorter and simpler than authorial discourse, and a more everyday, colloquial idiom is used. A swift interchange of lines in a dialogue makes a fast progression of the plot. Besides, dialogue in conventional children's literature is most often used in combination with narrator's comments and reported speech that manipulate the reader's understanding of the characters' conversations. So if dialogue is used exclusively or primarily for plot advancement, it is indeed a simple, reader-friendly device.

In terms of characterization, however, direct speech may be an extremely demanding and confusing form, for the absence of narrative agency leaves readers without guidance. Are the characters honest and frank in their utterances? How can we know whether they are? Empirical studies of young readers show that until a certain age children do not understand irony; they tend to interpret the characters' statements at their face value. Why would readers trust some characters, but perceive others as liars and hypocrites, unless there were narrator's comments to assist them? For instance, without the narrator's comments, would we know that the White Witch was evil if we only had the dialogue between her and Edmund to judge?

In extreme cases, when most of the text is comprised of dialogue, readers must work hard to comprehend what is going on. For some reason, Hemingway's short story "Hills Like White Elephants" is frequently included in high school anthologies, but, in my experience, students find it totally incomprehensible. The dialogue in the story hides more than it reveals. The man and the woman do not mean what they are saying, and their real thoughts and feelings remain beyond the text. Their speech only characterizes them implicitly, by omission. One would assume that such a narrative form would be unlikely in a children's novel, and indeed it occurs very seldom. *Red Shift*, by Alan Garner, is an example of a young adult novel where the story is narrated almost wholly in direct speech, without tags. Such a "dialogue novel" is a postmodern narrative form; in Garner's case, his novel is a deliberate intellectual puzzle. Its purpose is to confuse rather than clarify, and most of its characterization lies beyond the text itself. There are few similar novels, and *Red Shift* naturally implies mature readers, as does Robert Cormier's *I Am the Cheese*, partly written in dialogue representing tape-recorded conversations. Thus if we regard direct speech as a characterization device rather than a plot engine, it is rarely used to its full capacity in children's fiction. Besides, contemporary children's writers have discovered a more efficient characterization device, one their colleagues in the mainstream have employed for many decades: internal representation.

The incentive to reflect characters' internal life is a relatively recent development also in adult Western literature, one often connected with Henry James, on the one hand, and Virginia Woolf, on the other. In Western children's literature, this tendency has become prominent only during the last twenty or thirty years; indeed, in some countries, it has not emerged yet. The development toward predominantly internal representation can be clearly described in a terminology taken from Mikhail Bakhtin as a shift from epic toward polyphone discourse, from depicting primarily an external flow of events toward attempts to convey the complex nature of human consciousness (see The *Dialogic Imagination, Problems of Dostoyevsky's Poetics*, and "Author and Hero on Aesthetic Activity"). The premise for this mode of writing—the blending of the narrator's and the character's discourse—results in a variety of narrative techniques classified as stream of consciousness, interior monologue, free indirect speech, narrated monologue, or dual-voice discourse. All these techniques presuppose that authors through their narrators penetrate the minds of their characters and are able to convey their state of mind to readers by means of language. This statement in itself presents a problem, for language does not always have adequate means to express vague, inarticulate thoughts and emotions. Yet in children's fiction, the prerequisites for successful internal representation are, if possible, still more disputable.

A general consensus about children's literature seems to be that adult writers can easily penetrate a child character's mind, while logically it should be infinitely more difficult to enter than the mind of another adult. By analogy, it is often questioned, especially by feminist, postcolonial and queer theories, whether male writers can successfully depict female characters, white writers—black characters, or heterosexual writers—homosexual characters. This skepticism is based on the unequal power positions, in which the "oppressors" presumably have limited possibility to understand the mentality of the "oppressed." Even though *all* adult writers have been children once, profound differences in life experiences as well as linguistic skills create an inevitable discrepancy between the (adult) narrative voice and the levels of comprehension of both the focalized child characters and young readers. Critics of children's literature refer to this dilemma as the "double address" (Wall 9 and passim), a term meaning that an adult writer inevitably addresses the adult co-reader together with the child reader. Indeed, because in some cases this adult co-reader will be addressed at the expense of the child, some critics go so far as to declare, as Rose suggests in the subtitle of *The Case of Peter Pan*, "the impossibility of children's fiction."

The many successful attempts to breach the discrepancy—for instance, by using strong internal focalization of a child character or first-person (autodiegetic) child perspective—do not eliminate the dilemma as such. That mental representation is uncommon in children's literature naturally depends on its implied readers. We need certain life experience to be able to interpret characters' thoughts, and still more their unarticulated emotions, such as fear, anxiety, longing, or joy. Of course, a writer can simply say "He was anxious" or "She was scared." But the words "anxious" or "scared" are very simple labels for complex and contradictory mental states. Not even a long description can necessarily convey all the shades of a person's feelings. Still, the most profound consequence of the different modes of mental representation in children's fiction is the discrepancy between the (adult) narrator and the child character. Naturally, this discrepancy can also be the case in the mainstream first-person novels depicting the protagonist's childhood, such as *David Copperfield* and *Great Expectations*, as well as third-person narration focalizing a naïve child, as in *What Maisie Knew*. The latter example, featured in many narratological studies as a unique and innovative device of James's, corresponds to the widely used technique of internal focalization of the child protagonist in modern children's fiction. Even though children's fiction has not as yet produced a counterpart to Molly Bloom's interior monologue, we can find examples as the following:

> Well, I'm eleven now, folks, and, in case you haven't heard. I don't wet my bed anymore. But I am not nice. I am brilliant. I am famous across this entire county. Nobody wants to tangle with the great Galadriel Hopkins. I am too clever and too hard to manage. Gruesome Gilly, they call me. She leaned back comfortably. Here I come. Maime baby, ready or not.
>
> (*The Great Gilly Hopkins* 3)

The various modes of depicting internal life also clearly show a shift from authorial toward figural discourse. Quoted monologue, corresponding to direct speech, is the most primitive way of conveying characters' state of mind, because the narrator's and the character's discourse are kept clearly apart, and the authoritative narrator can always correct whatever erroneous views the young characters may express in their own thoughts. Narrator's comments create either ironic or didactic discrepancy between the narrator's discourse and the character's discourse, emphasizing the cognitive difference between the two. Since quoted monologue is the easiest device to understand, it is used most frequently in children's literature, for instance: "'Thank goodness,' *said Edmund*, 'the door must have swung open of its own accord.' [. . .] 'She's angry about all the things I've been saying lately,' *thought Edmund*. [. . .] 'Just like a girl,' *said Edmund to himself*, 'sulking somewhere, and won't accept an apology'" (*The Lion, the Witch and the Wardrobe* 31; emphasis added). The tags "said," "thought," and "said to himself" are in this case full synonyms and do not of course imply that the character is talking aloud to himself. The novel is clearly plot-oriented, and quoted monologue has the same function as dialogue in conventional children's literature, namely, to carry plot rather than contribute to characterization.

Blended narratives, such as free indirect discourse or psychonarration, are often used in children's literature to manipulate readers, to create an illusion that the text directly reflects a character's mind, while it is in fact a narrator's discourse about a character's mind. In order not to sound false, writers must keep a delicate balance between the narrator's and the character's discourse. The best contemporary children's writers have managed to keep this balance. Katherine Paterson is one of several writers who excel in consonant psychonarration used to convey young characters' disturbed states of mind, "subverbal states." Here, a passage from *Bridge to Terabithia* describes Jess's attempt to come to terms with his friend Leslie's death:

> It came into his mind that someone had told him that Leslie was dead. But he knew now that that had been part of the dreadful dream. Leslie could not die any more than he himself could die. But the words turned over uneasily in his mind like leaves stirred up by a cold wind. If he got up now and went down to the old Perkins place, Leslie would come to open it, P. T. jumping at her heels like a star around the moon. It was a beautiful night. Perhaps they could run over the hill and across the fields to the stream and swing themselves into Terabithia.
>
> (106)

To separate authorial and figural discourse here is virtually impossible. Such phrases as "[l]ike leaves stirred up by a cold wind" or "like a star around the moon" are similes, poetical language Jess, a non-reading and non-verbal eleven-year-old boy, would not have as a part of his idiom. Yet the passage is a poignant rendering of the boy's thoughts and feelings. The narrator is articulating them for him because Jess lacks the language to do so himself, but that does not mean he lacks the emotions. Needless to say, this technique is one more advanced than quoted monologue, and brings us closer to the character's mind. It is exactly this technique that allows the creating of ironic characters.

In blended narration, readers may be confronted with the difficulty of adopting a subject position, since at any given moment, the source of internal discourse and the textual point of view are ambiguous, as the example above shows. Whether intentionally or not, when authors lose control over the readers' subjectivity, they give them greater freedom of interpretation and demand more of them in text decoding. While internal representation in itself is the most complex characterization device, the development in children's fiction toward psychonarration has contributed to the overall complexity of contemporary novels for young readers.

Through visual illustrations, children's literature has access to a device to convey complex mental states superior even to verbal ones. When words are no longer sufficient, visual images may take over. In Anthony Browne's *The Tunnel*, the words merely say: "The girl was frightened." But a pictorial image accompanying the text may convey a much wider spectrum of her unspoken thoughts—memories and fantasies—and such emotions as fear and anxiety, and so on. The visual picture affects our senses in a stronger and more immediate way than words. Despite the essay by Graeme Harper in this issue of *Style*, little attention has so far been paid to this specific aspect of the aesthetic of children's literature; indeed, as Harper suggests, use of the device itself is a relatively recent achievement.

3

As my discussion has surely suggested, the different narrative modes for conveying consciousness are seldom employed consistently throughout a text, but are mixed and combined, the transition often being very vague, almost indiscernible. Further, contemporary children's and juvenile fiction has also given us examples of experimental multiple techniques, for instance, a combination of personal and impersonal narration (*Breaktime*), of self-narration and witness-narration (*Dance on My Grave*), of dialogue and self-narration (*I Am the Cheese*), and so on. In these novels, authorial presence is almost eliminated, while subjectivity is obscure and ambivalent. Such experiments aim at still more elaborate ways of expressing the complex inner world of a young protagonist. As we return to our initial discussion of the shift from "hero" to "character" in children's fiction, it becomes clear that the transition, successively, from authorial to figural discourse is closely interconnected with those historical changes in narrative mode that Northrop Frye outlines in *Anatomy of Criticism*. For romantic and high mimetic heroes, devices of external characterization seem quite sufficient, since story is plot-oriented, and characters possess only a limited number of stock traits. Characters appearing in low mimetic and ironic modes demand complex techniques of internal representation that enable readers to partake of their psyches. Yet while this development seems to be trivial in the mainstream fiction, it is far from universally acknowledged in children's literature.

In several previous studies, I have demonstrated the manifest evolution of contemporary children's fiction toward the complexity and ambiguity inherent to postmodern thinking (see, for instance, *Children's Literature Comes of Age*, "Exit Children's Literature," and *From Mythic to Linear*). In the present essay, I have shown not only the changes in the aesthetics of character but also how the changes overall contribute to the trend toward a general postmodernist aesthetics.

Works cited

Alcott, Louisa May. *Little Women*. 1868. Harmondsworth: Penguin, 1994.

Bakhtin, Mikhail. *The Dialogic Imagination*. Austin: U of Texas P, 1981.

——. *Problems of Dostoyevsky's Poetics*. Minneapolis: U of Minnesota P, 1984.

——. "Author and Hero on Aesthetic Activity." *Art and Answerability: Early Philosophical Essays*. Austin: U of Texas P, 1990. 4–256.

Bloom, Harold. *Shakespeare: The Invention of the Human*. New York: Riverhead Books, 1998.

Burnett, Frances Hodgson. *The Secret Garden*. 1911. London: Penguin, 1995.

Campbell, Joseph. *The Hero with a Thousand Faces*. 2nd edition. Princeton: Princeton UP, 1968.

Chambers, Aidan. *Dance on My Grave*. 1982. London: Random House, 1995.

Cleary, Beverly. *Ramona the Pest*. 1968. New York: Avon, 1992.

Frye, Northrop. *Anatomy of Criticism. Four Essays*. Princeton: Princeton UP, 1957.

Hourihan, Margery. *Deconstructing the Hero: Literary Theory and Children's Literature*. London: Routledge, 1997.

Lewis, C. S. *The Lion, the Witch and the Wardrobe*. 1950. Harmondsworth: Penguin, 1959.

McGavran, James Holt, ed. *Literature and the Child: Romantic Continuations. Postmodern Contestations*. Iowa City: U of Iowa P. 1999.

Montgomery, L. M. *Anne of Green Gables*. 1908. New York: Bantam, 1992.

Nikolajeva, Maria. *Children's Literature Comes of Age: Towards a New Aesthetic*. New York: Garland, 1996.

——. "Exit Children's Literature?" *The Lion and the Unicorn* 22.2 (1998): 221–36.

——. *From Mythic to Linear: Time in Children's Literature*. Lanham, MD: Scarecrow, 2000.

Nodelman, Perry. *The Pleasures of Children's Literature*. New York: Longman. 1992.

Paterson. Katherine. *Bridge to Terabithia*. 1977. New York: Harper Collins, 1987.

——. *The Great Gilly Hopkins*. 1978. New York: Harper Collins, 1987.

Paul, Lissa. "Enigma Variations. What Feminist Criticism Knows about Children's Literature." *Signal* 54 (1987): 186–201.

Pearson, Carol, and Katherine Pope. *The Female Hero in American and British Literature*. New York: Bowker, 1981.

Potter, Beatrix. *The Tale of Peter Rabbit*. London: Warne, 1902.

Pratt, Annis, with Barbara White, Andrea Loewenstein, and Mary Wyer. *Archetypal Patterns in Women's Fiction*. Bloomington: Indiana UP. 1981.

Rabine, Leslie W. *Reading the Romantic Heroine: Text, History, Ideology*. Ann Arbor, MI: U of Michigan P. 1985.

Rose, Jacqueline. *The Case of Peter Pan, or The Impossibility of Children's Fiction.* London: Macmillan, 1984.

Stephens, John, and Robyn McCallum. *Retelling Stories, Framing Culture: Traditional Story and Metanarratives in Children's Literature*. New York: Garland, 1998.

Wall, Barbara. *The Narrator's Voice: The Dilemma of Children's Fiction.* London: Macmillan, 1991.

Waugh, Patricia. *Metafiction: The Theory and Practice of Self-Conscious Fiction.* London: Methuen, 1984.

81

THE VALUE OF SINGULARITY IN FIRST- AND RESTRICTED THIRD-PERSON ENGAGING NARRATION

Andrea Schwenke Wyile

Source: *Children's Literature* 31 (2003): 116–141.

An examination of the conventions of restricted third-person narration in relation to the concept of immediate- and distant-engaging first-person narration can teach us a lot about the constructedness of texts and reader response; it raises the obvious question of how the narrator's telling of the story is related to the character's perceptions as well as readers' understanding, a question that underlies many discussions of children's literature. The specific forms of retrospective narration I am calling "engaging narration" share the desire to bring readers back to the feelings of the character-focalizer at that moment in time, rather than to provide them with an analysis of the narrator's current views on the situation. Here the word "engaging" is key. The narrator seeks to reconstruct the events being related in a way that engages readers, a way that invites them to consider themselves in, or close to, the position of the protagonist.

In restricted third-person as in first-person narration, readers' engagement in the narration is determined by the singularity of perspective and the intensely personal relationship that they develop with the central character as a result of the limitations of narrative perspective. Restricted third-person engaging narration, like first-person engaging narration, fosters a trusting and personal relationship between narrator and narratee, a relationship that is ultimately deflected onto the character due to the anonymity of the narrator. That is to say, because the narrator's sole purpose is to convey the character's story, readers' attention is drawn to the subject of the telling, the character, rather than by the teller, whereas in first-person engaging narration the teller and subject are the same being although they are always separated temporally, as Chatman reminds us:

> [The narrator] resides in an order of time and place different from that occupied by the characters; his is a different "here and now." And that's true for every narrator, no matter how minimal his/her/its distance from the "here-and-now" of the story (as, for example, in the epistolary novel).
>
> (*Coming to Terms* 142)

Thus, because the focus is entirely on the character who limits the narration in restricted third-person engaging narration, readers' awareness of the narrator is routinely overshadowed. Obviously, the narrator does not actually disappear, but because the focus on the character is so intense, it creates a kind of spell that has the effect of enhancing our identification with what is being related rather than directing our attention to the incongruity or gap between the character's understanding and the narrator's explication of it. The effect of restricted third-person engaging narration is to present a fuller and more sophisticated explanation of events and feelings than the character would be capable of, without explaining more than the character knows. If one believes in reading as a form of experience, one could claim that such singular emphasis on character within a narrative can build character in readers as well.

In "Expanding the View of First-Person Narration," I identify two forms of "engaging narration" that narrative theory has not previously accounted for, immediate- and distant-engaging narration. Of these two, the first appears to be common to children's and young adult literature and to only be sustained in specialized forms of first-person genres, like the epistolary novel, in writing for adults. "[I]mmediate-engaging-first-person narration [. . .] precludes both an adult narrator and the use of dramatic, romantic, and structural irony in the representation of the narrator-protagonist" (186), and "the subject of the narrator-protagonists' narratives is themselves at a particular point in time in their immediate past. The characterization of the narrators is substantial because everything they say about themselves and others reflects on them in some way" (187). The difference in the second type, "distant-engaging" narration, "is the narrator's overt acknowledgment of the time that has passed between the events being narrated and their telling" (189). These types of first-person narration seek "to draw the reader in and establish confidence between the narrator and the narratee" such that the narratee feels like "the listener in the story rather than a reader outside the story," rather like what Aidan Chambers calls an implicated reader (192).

Given the similarities in reading experience between first-person narration wherein the narrator is also the protagonist (autodiegetic) and restricted (or limited) third-person narration (heterodiegetic), I would like to explore whether one can apply the idea of engaging narration to restricted third-person narration and to consider what, if anything, is desirable and distinguishable about this form. Admittedly, first- and restricted third-person narrators engage readers somewhat differently due to their differing relations to the main characters. Yet, because both these forms of narration are based on limitations, they invite a particular set of relations between narrator and narratee and between writer, text, and reader, a set of intimate interactive narrative relations that bring character to life in significant ways.

The relation between readers and the texts they bring to life in the process of reading will naturally depend a great deal on their experience as readers and as people. The work of cataloguing these different relations will serve to inform and refine the theoretical distinctions I will outline in this article; however, at this point the ideas I am presenting are the groundwork for future practical applications. I am drawn by the idea of an engaging narrator because I think it helps to explain the power of certain types of narratives that invite or foster an earnest and personal, if fictional, relationship between characters or narrator-protagonists and readers. I lean toward the cluster of readers who "lose" themselves in books, though the more I try to explain how such absorption comes about, the less fully I myself can achieve it—the very pattern J. A. Appleyard describes in *Becoming a Reader: The Experience of Fiction from Childhood to Adulthood*—an occupational hazard. Mollie Hunter's Bridie McShane's mother describes her as "deaf as a post when she has her nose in a book" (17) in *A Sound of Chariots*; this type (or idea) of complete immersion in fictional worlds, which is of course never really complete, makes Robyn Warhol's idea of an engaging narrator compelling, though I am persuaded that such a narrator can go well beyond narrative interventions and can compel such engagement throughout an entire narrative. By working through the terminology on offer for discussions of first- and third-person narration in conjunction with the idea of an engaging narrator, I will argue that there are certain forms of narration that are sustained throughout children's and young adult texts that serve to inform and expand narrative theory and our understanding of narration, reading, and the creation of character that binds the two.

Engaging narrators and personal voice

The concept of engaging narration is premised on an earnest telling of events in which the narrator is entirely devoted to relating one character's experiences. The result is that the "text provides a single voice that is so highly confident that it is ultimately unassailable within the text" (Cadden 148). In first-person narration, the engaging narrator is also the main character. Susan Sniader Lanser's discussion of personal voice in *Jane Eyre* pinpoints the particular relationship set up by engaging narration:

> In public narration, in contrast [. . .] the narrator appears primarily as an "I" and speaks to an unidentified and readerly "you," thus mirroring the narrative situation of nonfictional autobiography and encouraging readers to conflate writer and character in ways that anonymous publication, and fluid boundaries between fact and fiction, could only reinforce. (142)

In first-person engaging narration, the narrator uses what Sniader Lanser calls a "public personal voice" (178), where the distinction between private and public is based on whom the narration is directed toward. The private voice directs the narration "toward a narratee who is a fictional character" (what Genette calls the intradiegetic narratee ([*Narrative Discourse Revisited* 131]) and the public voice directs the narration "toward a narratee 'outside' the fiction who is analogous to the historical reader" (15) (Genette's extradiegetic narratee). Some narrators, like Jane Eyre, use direct address to signal their "self-conscious relationship with [their] narratee[s]" (185), thereby also involving readers in their narration more actively, while other narrators do not (for example, the first-person narrators of Jean Fritz's *Homesick* or Bernice Thurman Hunter's *Booky* or *Margaret* trilogies).

Thus, as I claim in "Expanding First-Person Narration," engaging narration can be either *active* or *passive* depending on whether or not the reader is directly called upon, as in "dear reader" or "you." This distinction affects the reading experience: generally speaking, passive engaging narration allows readers to remain more fully immersed in their reading, whereas active engaging narration provides a number of reminders to immersion prone readers that they are reading, while also serving as an invitation to actively consider the relationship between their reading and their experience of the world (Schwenke Wyile 198). Readers may feel more compelled to question narrators that engage them actively because of the direct address prompts. However, there are other strategies besides direct address that narrators can use to draw attention to the constructedness of their texts even within the confines of first-person immediate-engaging narration. Diana Wynne Jones's first-person *Black Maria* provides an interesting example. Mig, the narrator-protagonist, relates a strange tale of her stay of a few weeks at her Aunt Maria's in the tucked-away town of Cranbury-on-Sea. The tale itself is not the issue for this example; what matters is that at the end of Mig's odd and engaging story she adds a postscript that calls into question the immediacy in which it appears to be told and the validity of its construction. She notes: "That was all six months ago now. I have spent the time rewriting this autobiography and doing the end. Sometimes I have added bits and sometimes I have cheated a bit so that it looks as if I wrote more than I did. Chris says if I really wrote that screed at Aunt Maria's I wouldn't have had time to do anything else. But I want it to be good when I finish it" (239–40). Mig's admission could be construed as unreliability; yet, given Mike Cadden's points considering the ethical risks in single-voiced first-person narration, in "The Irony of Narration in the Young Adult Novel," we can also view her remark as a valuable reminder regarding the constructedness of all narratives. In this passage, Mig's comment indirectly urges us to consider the relation between experiencing and writing, between the events being related themselves and the way they are told, a relation that relies on a very personal tone and the establishment of trust in engaging narration.

Both Warhol's and Sniader Lanser's formulations of an engaging narrator are based on an active relationship between narrator and narratee and also suggest a blurring between the narratee and the reader in the act of reading. That is to say, when Genette's "possible reader," a term he feels is better than "implied reader" (*Narrative Discourse Revisited* 148), becomes actualized by a real reader, the question of who is theoretical and who is real (first the possible reader/narratee, then the implied author/narrator) is turned around—a simple fact of writing and reading that engaging narration wants us to question. The interaction between engaging narrators and their engaged readers results in a focus on the main characters of single-voiced narration. In first-person immediate-engaging narration, narrator and character blend into one another in many readers' minds despite the fact that one can make a technical distinction between the "I" who narrates and the "I" who experienced the events—that is, between the narrator and the character—because the narration is subsequent to the action nevertheless. The closeness of these two positions is amplified due to the immediacy of the narration and due to great temptation to conflate the two, as suggested by Sniader Lanser above (though she says "writer" and "character" because she is speaking about narrative interventions).

In the case of Jane Gardam's *A Long Way From Verona*, it is taxing to separate the telling done by Jessica Vye the narrator from the actions of Jessica the protagonist. The temptation is to discuss these separate positions as one, as the term "narrator-protagonist" encourages us to. This closeness and tempting conflation is similar to the blending of the narratee and the reader; when readers are fully engaged in a narrative they may feel that they, personally, are being addressed, a feeling that Sniader Lanser explains as the result of a personal public voice. Genette states, "It is completely legitimate to distinguish in principle the narratee from the reader, but one must also take into account cases of syncrisis," and he notes that Gerald Prince "implicitely gives up the idea of distinguishing the reader from the narratee (extradiegetic of course)" (*Narrative Discourse Revisited* 132).

While the intimacy in restricted third-person engaging narration also results from the triadic relation between the narrator, the character, and the narratee, here the temptation to conflate positions is lessened, although the narration can be decidedly engaging and the identification between the reader and the character just as highly charged as in first-person narration. In *A Sound of Chariots*, for example, when the limiting character, Bridie, performs at the community children's Christmas party a few months after her father's death, she intends to recite a poem but is moved, within the split second of opening her mouth, to sing one of her father's songs instead. The separation between her actions and what is going on in her mind—a recurring separation that marks her as an unnatural child in the minds of many of the adults in her community—is recounted by the narrator as follows:

> The sadness poured out of her in the song, a sadness that was somehow not only for herself now, but for them all. She saw the hall as she sang and it was no longer a big place to her, a gay and exciting party place. It was small suddenly and shabby, the floor greasy with spillings and squalid with littered ice-cream cups. But it was only with the background of her vision that she saw it for she was watching the women's faces as she sang and seeing on each one of them the shadow of the cripple that stood behind it. And she was aware too, as she sang, of the darkness outside the hall, aware of it not only as the ordinary dark of night but as a great and terrible something surrounding them all; and her mind cried out through the song to the women that here inside the hall they were safe together in a little oasis of light in the big darkness. (117–18)

This description is both very detailed and very compact as it draws our attention to the things Bridie notices in the divided state in which she so often finds herself, between performing actions and watching herself perform them and noting the reactions of others. While the terminology Dorrit Cohn provides in *Transparent Minds* allows us to discuss the different ways in which consciousness is presented in the context of third-person narration, it does not characterize entire narratives. The use of psycho-narration (the narrator's discourse about a character's consciousness [15]) in the above passage draws the narratee and the reader into Bridie's personal darkness as she stands in front of all the women, who are judging her with a mixture of compassion and disdain, as well as into the significance of the bigger darkness of the world, and the emotions that this description elicits in readers are the result of their involvement in the story as well as of the projections and recognitions they contribute from their own lives. The combination of the narrator's telling and the readers' reactions is what brings Bridie's character "to life" in the act of reading, and that life is as fleeting as the insight Bridie gains above.

Three paragraphs later, as Bridie and her siblings are on their way home, we are told, "It was difficult enough to explain what had happened to herself, never mind being forced to do so to the Others over a barrage of jeers; for now that the moment's insight the song had given her was gone, she had no conception of why she had felt that rush of compassion for the women in the hall or of why she had reached out from it to identify herself with them" (118–19). Could the narrator be telling this to just anyone? The intensity and personal nature of the insights given provide readers with the illusion that they are witness to something very private; in engaging narration this feeling and the resultant trust we have in the anonymous covert narrator is never broken, even while we may think our entire attention is absorbed by the character. The particulars of different types of narrative relations need to be identified so that we can distinguish between them. Because restricted third-person narration is not necessarily engaging, the current terminology on offer for discussions of restricted third-person narration needs to be expanded.

Forms of retrospection

The idea of engaging narration is very suggestive and could lead in a variety of directions; however, I propose a very specific use in relation to first-person and restricted third-person narration. In first-person narration the engagement between the narrator and the narratee is affected by both the temporal relationship between events and their telling and by the absence of some forms of irony. When narration is retrospective, the narrator can choose whether or not to highlight the fact or degree of retrospection, a decision that also affects the reading experience. Dorrit Cohn posits two forms of retrospective self-narration, dissonant and consonant. Engaging narration shares features with consonant narration but distinguishes the type of consonance based on the temporal relation between events and their telling, as well as on the lack of structural, dramatic, or romantic irony used by the narrator. In the case of *Jane Eyre*, Sniader Lanser says that "the novel's suppression of retrospectivity re-creates the immediacy of epistolary fiction" (186), yet readers know, or come to realize, that retrospectivity has been suppressed because the novel follows the typical pattern of the adult autobiography, *Bildungsroman*, and *Künstlerroman* in which narrators look back over their own lives, or the lives of the characters whose tales are being related, and arrive at the present of the telling by the end of the narrative, thereby alerting readers to the size of the temporal gap that may not have been clear at the beginning of the narrative. Genette states, "These effects of final convergence [. . .] play on the fact that the very length of the story gradually lessens the interval separating it from the moment of narrating" (*Discourse* 221). This temporal span is important by virtue of the fact that it exists and is highlighted, on occasion, by the narrator.

The narrator's periodic recognition of the temporal span between the events and their telling, as well as the greater span of time covered by the story are what distinguish distant-engaging from immediate-engaging narration; the immediate-engaging narrator tells the story shortly after the events have happened, usually within one year, whereas the distant-engaging narrator tells the story ages hence. The recognition of the time-span between the events can either be suggested or stated explicitly. At the opening of chapter 2 in *Jane Eyre*, the narrator recounts her resistance to the punishment that is about to be imposed upon her for angering her aunt and guardian in terms that vividly describe her emotional state as a nine-year-old girl, but in language that uses analogies and explanations that would not have been available to her as a nine-year-old. Here the distance is implied:

> I resisted all the way: a new thing for me, and a circumstance which greatly strengthened the bad opinion Bessie and Miss Abbot were disposed to entertain of me. The fact is, I was a trifle beside myself; or rather *out* of myself, as the French would say: I was conscious that a moment's mutiny had already rendered me liable to strange penalties, and like any other rebel slave, I felt resolved, in my desperation, to go to all lengths. (12)

Jane only learns French some time after this incident—the narrator's description of her character-self's actions here can be usefully compared to the relation between restricted third-person narrators and the characters whose tales they relate, with the significant difference that restricted third-person engaging narrators must remain more stringently within the confines of what the characters know. Restricted third-person engaging narrators further differ from distant-engaging first-person narrators in that they cannot look ahead to the outcome of the characters' stories in order to make sense of an event being related. An example of the explicit acknowledgement that the narrator is at a significant temporal remove from the events being related occurs three pages later in the same chapter of *Jane Eyre*. The narrator elaborates on the agonies she suffered while she was locked in the infamous red room:

> What consternation of soul was mine that dreary afternoon! How all my brain was in tumult, and all my heart in insurrection! Yet in what darkness, what dense ignorance, was the mental battle fought! I could not answer the ceaseless inward question—*why* I thus suffered: now, at the distance of—I will not say how many years, I see it clearly. (15)

Although the number of years is not specified, the distance is both indisputable and clearly significant to the telling to the story.

Gardam's *A Long Way From Verona* provides a useful point of comparison to *Jane Eyre* as both stories are *Künstlerromane*, both narrators use direct address, and both stories begin when the character-narrator is nine. *Verona*, however, is immediate-engaging first-person narration. The first chapter of the novel details the key events that took place four years previously, events which are key to the rest of Jessica Vye's narration and mark the threshold of her career as a writer. At the end of the first chapter, her family is not only in the process of moving, she also receives a package from a writer, who had visited her school some months previously, including a note stating that she is a writer beyond all possible doubt. Her response to this information concludes the analepsis (flashback) and provides the necessary context for the narrative proper, which begins in chapter two:

> This experience changed me utterly, like Heaven, "in the twinkling of an eye," and I believe is the reason for the next point I have to make clear before getting on with the story. Which is that I am not really very popular. Some people in fact do not really like me at all. In fact if you really want to know quite a lot of people absolutely can't stand me. (14)

The contrast with the excerpt from *Jane Eyre* above is telling: here we are dealing with the voice of the thirteen-year-old narrator as well as with an immediate telling of events that provides an intense look at the transitional period of adolescence—there is little distance of any kind to be found within this narrative, and it decidedly captures the confusion and exuberance of adolescence. Jessica's admissions to uncertainty, as well as the lack of explanations of setting or of cultural and literary allusions in her narration, all support the category of immediate-engaging first-person narration. Thus, both immediate- and distant-engaging narration demand some level of personal involvement, eschew intended irony, and also serve to distinguish between two kinds of consonant narration rather than to replace it as a term.

Distancing factors

The terms "dissonant" and "consonant" narration allow us to describe the first-person narrator's relationship to his or her earlier self, whereas in restricted third-person engaging narration the relationship between the narrator and the character to whom the narration is restricted is determined by the narrator's covertness and the proportion of direct to indirect reporting. In dissonant first-person narration, the narrator is clearly older and wiser than the younger self whose exploits are being related, and this fact is made evident by critical and judgmental comments; the effect of the narration is based upon the sharp distinctions "between the protagonist and the mature detached narrator who can look back critically upon her former self" (Sniader Lanser 179). Narration that privileges the conceptions of the older narrator looking back often makes liberal use of dramatic irony and/or provides explanations for things that the character doesn't know and might therefore be called *distancing* narration rather than *engaging* narration (Schwenke Wyile 185). While the term "distancing narration" serves to help clarify the relation between readers and their involvement in first-person narration, it doesn't contribute new understanding to the concept of dissonant narration; however, it does provide a useful general contrast to the concept of engaging narration, particularly for third-person narration wherein narrative distance is not the result of a dissonance so much as the degree of the narrator's overtness. While readers can be just as interested in what a dissonant narrator has to say, there is much less of a chance that they will feel personally involved in the events being related because they are being kept at a distance. Similarly, in third-person narration one can distinguish between narrators who build in distance and narrators who beguile us by closing the distance between themselves and their narratees by maintaining their focus on the central characters.

In restricted third-person narration, an overt narrator, or an audible narrator, effects a similar feeling of distance (Chatman, *Story and Discourse* 196). While the narrator is always overt in first-person narration, we only perceive the narrator to intervene in distant-engaging narration, where the older narrator comments on the behavior or judgement of his or her younger self. The narration of overt narrators is marked by "descriptions of what characters did not say or think" and their commentary includes interpretation, judgment, and generalization (Chatman, *Story and Discourse* 197), or by providing additional information to assist readers in a variety of ways. James Berry, for example, uses an overt narrator in many of his stories in *A Thief in the Village and Other Stories*. The overt narrator in "Elias and the Mongoose" inserts a brief history of the mongoose's introduction to Jamaica for the benefit of the reader; it is of no concern to the characters in the story.

Karen Cushman's *The Midwife's Apprentice* draws a fine line between engaging and distancing narration, but the line is clear nonetheless due to the overt narrator. While the narration is largely restricted to the perspective of the girl apprentice, the narration ultimately does not qualify as engaging because the narrator occasionally tells us what the girl doesn't know or provides an insight into another character that qualifies it as unrestricted narration, despite the fact that most of the narration is restricted to the focal character's views and understanding. The first indication of this comes toward the end of the first chapter, where the homeless girl meets the village midwife. Here one sentence gives us a glimpse into the midwife's motives, "The woman's sharp nose smelled hunger, which she could use to her own greedy purpose" (4). While the narrator mostly focuses on the girl and we become drawn into her story, the accumulation of little details and narrator intrusions that are beyond the girl's experience soon add up to disqualify this story from being considered engaging narration and restricted third-person, though the lines of separation are not very strong. When the girl (known as Beetle) has rescued the cat from the burlap bag after its near drowning by the village boys, she puts it in a safe and warm place in the hope that it will live. The narrator says:

> If Beetle had known any prayers, she might have prayed for the cat. If she had known about soft sweet songs, she might have sung to him. If she had known gentle words and cooing, she would have spoken gently to him. But all she knew was cursing: "Damn you, cat, breathe and live, you flea-bitten sod, or I'll kill you myself." (9)

While the character is still the point of limitation, the fact that the narrator explains her actions based on what she doesn't know disrupts the immediacy of the narrative engagement. Similarly, the description of her first experience of a fair and of receiving a gift is also presented to readers in terms of what she doesn't know:

> The comb was hers. Beetle stood breathless for fear someone would snatch it back. Never had she owned anything except for her raggedy clothes and occasional turnips, and now the comb with the cat was hers. The wink and the comment about her curls, *though Beetle didn't know it*, were also gifts from the generous merchant, and they nestled into Beetle's heart and stayed there.
>
> (30, emphasis added)

Finally, ten pages later at the beginning of chapter 7, after Beetle has taken on the new name Alyce and saved a boy named Will from drowning, the narrator intrudes, "If the world were sweet and fair, Alyce (for she must be called Alyce now) and Will would become friends and the village applaud her for her bravery and the midwife be more generous with her cheese and onions. Since this is not so, and the world is just as it is and no more, nothing changed" (40). This intrusion clearly demarcates the triadic relationship between narrator, character, and narratee and therefore breaks readers' sustained engagement with the character. While such an intrusion is similar to the use of direct address in first-person engaging narration, the effect is different because the narrator is not the character and therefore readers are engaged by two separate forces: the whole idea of restricted third-person engaging narration is to foster the illusion that the reader is wholly involved with the character; an engaging narrator directs this involvement unobtrusively.

Engaging factors

The covert narrators of engaging narration find all kinds of ways to remain hidden in the discursive shadows. In restricted third-person engaging narration, the statements made by the narrator are so close to our understanding of the character, there is clearly such sympathy between them, "that it does not matter to whom we assign the statement" (Chatman, *Story and Discourse* 207). This affinity is evident in Louise Fitzhugh's *Harriet the Spy*, wherein the affinity is emphasized by the similarity in tone between the covert narrator's telling of the story and the excerpts of Harriet's diary that are interspersed throughout the narrative. While Peter Hunt rightly states that Fitzhugh's novel is focalized entirely through Harriet, the fact remains that a narrator relates her story. This means that we are still dealing with a voice that is not Harriet's. While the seeing may direct the telling, it is nevertheless still subordinated by the telling. Therefore, restricted third-person engaging narration, like distant-engaging first-person narration, is less limiting than immediate-engaging first-person narration because the narrator makes sense of the character's perceptions, and this greater freedom is what determines a writer's choice of narrators. However, for writers wishing to present a singular story shaped by the views and understanding of just one character, this greater freedom can be as risky as it is welcome. The trick is to stick to the limited awareness being presented, no mean feat for the adult writer who "knows [it] to be incomplete and insufficient" (Cadden 147); it is this very challenge that I believe we need to recognize as a valuable contribution to the array of characters and positions to be found in children's and young adult literature, because the experience of negotiating singular views is as important as that of negotiating a plurality of views. It is these very limitations that draw readers into the narration and into an intimate or personal relationship with the character at the point in time being described, a relationship that fosters the sense of having been there or of having had the experience first hand.

Restricted third-person engaging narration uses all of the modes for representing consciousness that Cohn describes in *Transparent Minds*;[1] it does not replace any of Cohn's terms, but rather serves to describe a type of sustained narration. Its key features are—as in immediate- and distant-engaging first-person narration—first, the absence of dramatic, romantic, and structural irony; and second, an anonymous and covert narrator who addresses an extradiegetic narratee in a public personal voice, as described by Sniader Lanser above. In terms of our reading experience, engaging narration, be it first- or restricted third-person, causes readers to feel personally involved in the ideas and events being related, often because they identify with the character. Appleyard says, "One may wonder whether a reader who talks about identifying with a character may be implying a mixture of 'the me I am' and 'the me I'd like to be' and whether involvement does not operate on the promise of straightening this uncertainty out" (105). He also suggests that this process of identification changes over one's lifetime "from undiscriminating identification in childhood to a sense in adolescence of both the power of the ideal and the pathos of the gap, then to a more realistic appreciation of what the disparities mean in adulthood, or even to an ironic rejection of idealism altogether" (105). This progression in one's reading experience and needs is important to keep in mind with regard to the absence of irony in engaging narration; although the narrator endeavors to present the character's experiences and understanding in a limited and unassailable fashion, experienced readers may see the inevitable irony of a situation that a character cannot, despite the fact that the narrator is not trying to undermine the character—a fact which is proven by the lack of any explanation.

An example from *A Sound of Chariots* serves to illustrate this distinction very clearly. As I've already indicated, this novel's subject matter is extremely complex; the story details Bridie McShane's relationship with her father, her reaction to his death when she is nine, and her early development as a writer (until the age of fourteen). While the heart of the narrative is to convey Bridie's immediate experiences, this could not be achieved to the same degree of complexity and intensity if Hunter had written it within the confines of a child narrator through the ages of nine to fourteen. *A Sound of Chariots* is unquestionably a remarkable example of restricted third-person engaging narration. In the long analepsis that makes up the first part of the story, Bridie's mother at one point cautions her father about his behavior at his political meetings, and in seeking to address Bridie's concern about this grown-up discussion, he tells her that Christ was also a revolutionary, to which she responds that she will follow in her father's footsteps and be a revolutionary, too:

> "That's the stuff, my girl! Up the revolution, and we'll both ride to Heaven on Marx's coat tails."
>
> He was still laughing when her mother seized her and hustled her out of the kitchen so that she had no chance to ask who Marx was. But thinking it over in bed that night she decided that, whoever he was, it would be much more exciting to ride to Heaven on his coat-tails than to get there by crossing over from the Sinners to the Saints. (32)

An engaging narrator cannot explain who Marx was; all the narrator can tell us is what happened or was said and how the character to whom the narration is restricted made sense of it; no comment can be made to disabuse readers of Bridie's new notions concerning her salvation. Here she is clearly pitted between the call to follow her mother by changing sides in Church and her father's call to bypass the Church in favor of political activism. A distancing narrator, on the other hand, would leave no doubt that the character (and perhaps the less experienced reader) had missed or misunderstood something.

Michael Bedard's *Redwork* provides a similar example insofar as it can be interpreted on different levels, depending on the experience of the reader;

yet, in this case, these levels are not contingent on irony. In *Redwork* the limiting character is fifteen-year-old Cass, whose mother is in the midst of writing her M.A. thesis on William Blake. As the pressure is on for her to finish, Cass takes on most of the home responsibilities. About two thirds of the way into the book when they are having supper, his mother delivers a short speech on the significance of "The Book of Thel" in the development of Blake's thought. The speech is reported directly. Cass's reaction to it is significant because, as with the case of Bridie's lack of information about Marx, he does not understand the significance of this information, significance the implied author clearly intends. Immediately following his mother's speech we are told:

> It was the most she had said in more than a week. It was a shame he didn't have a clue to what she was talking about. Reciting her name over a few dozen times would have been more enlightening. There was no point in telling her that though. It would just start her off explaining it all for the next half hour, and he wouldn't be any the wiser at the end of it anyway. He nodded and smiled. (174)

This paragraph provides an out not only for Cass, but for any reader who also has no clue. Readers who do have a clue can relate what his mother says about Blake's work to Cass himself as well as to the novel overall. This example demonstrates one of the ways in which restricted narration can broaden the reading horizons without compromising the rules of engaging narration—the additional information is there for those who know what to do with it, but it is not explained for those who do not. This is the reverse strategy from James Berry's previously mentioned short story, "Elias and the Mongoose," where the characters are not even aware of the information the narrator provides for the benefit of readers who are presumed not to know it. In restricted third-person engaging narration, the descriptions of the character's awareness or understanding can be articulated in a way that is more sophisticated than what the character would be capable of, but only if it represents what the character knows or feels, and additional information that may guide readers' interpretation of the novel can be included if it is reported directly, but the narrator cannot make sense of it for the character or reader. Thus, singular narratives could be said to require even more sophisticated reading strategies than plural ones; however, such sophistication requires experience, and therefore such stories often risk frustrating younger readers by not making sense of such reported information. I see this as a worthwhile and necessary risk, although such risks can be argued to walk a fine line between danger and value.

Narrative theory makes claims that need refining if we are to discuss categories such as immediate- and distant-engaging narration. While consonant narration generally aims to suppress any advantage provided by hindsight, there often is no such advantage to be suppressed in children's and young adult first-person fiction. For example, Cohn claims that "The experiencing self in first-person narration . . . is always viewed by a narrator who knows what happened to him next, and who is free to slide up and down the time axis that connects his two selves" (145). Nevertheless, this knowing plays a different role in immediate-engaging narration, because there has not really been enough time to process the significance or ramifications of the events. Therefore, although the narrator may know the immediate outcome of events, she or he only knows the short-range effects; that is, the narrator does not yet feel the full effects of "two selves" as the events being described are recent enough not to draw the kind of attention we typically associate with the telling self with regard to the experiencing self. An example of a story that does not open with a kind of prologue or with a different temporal frame, as *Verona* does, is Kevin Major's *Hold Fast*, which covers the last six months of the narrator-protagonist's life since his parents' death in a car accident. When Michael begins his narration, he does, presumably, know that he will continue to live in his small hometown, Marten, with his aunt and brother. However, the story he relates takes us chronologically from his parents' funeral, through his critical time of separation when he lives with his uncle in the considerably larger town of St. Albert, and to his return to his home. He never once looks forward throughout his narration, though he does admit to keeping back a few details at one point. As we read the story, we are (re) living the events as Michael describes them. He cannot make any great claims about his experiences because the anguish and anger are still too fresh—looking back over half a year hardly gives one the same sense of perspective as looking back five, ten, or twenty years. Thus there is considerably less freedom to be found in sliding up and down the time axis, and it seems very useful, therefore, to have some means of distinguishing between stories that have such freedom and those that do not.

While this kind of sustained immediacy can be found in adult short stories, in diaries, and in epistolary novels, it is not easily found in longer first-person narratives. Dorrit Cohn cites Knut Hamsun's *Hunger* as exemplary of consonant narration, but also remarks, "*Hunger* is a rare specimen, and I know of no other novel that duplicates its purity" (158). Further, according to her description of consonant narration, "though the retrospective narrative stance is maintained, the narrator never draws attention to his hindsight: neither analyzing nor generalizing, he simply records the inner happenings, juxtaposing them in incongruous succession, without searching for causal links" (156). There is a complete "absence of self-exegesis and of all references to the narrating self" (158). Engaging narration, whether immediate or distant, is not limited to a "depiction of the inner life" (154) of the narrator-protagonist, though inner life can certainly be part of the narration. Hindsight does not usually come into play in immediate-engaging narration, but it does make intermittent appearances in distant-engaging narration. Restricted third-person engaging narratives like Louise Fitzhugh's *Harriet the Spy* and Janet Lunn's *Shadow in Hawthorn Bay* can also follow this pattern of relative temporal immediacy, but this does not set the engaging quality of their narration apart from works that cover a longer span of time, such as Mollie Hunter's *A Sound of Chariots*.

Engaging narration, then, is consonant, and, in children's and young adult literature, where it occurs frequently, it is often sustained for the duration of a novel, despite what Patrick O'Neill says in his discussion of three levels of focalization in *Fictions of Discourse: Reading Narrative Theory*. O'Neill distinguishes between "*simple* focalization when there is only a single focalizer involved"; "*compound* focalization when there is more than one focalizer involved, as when a character-focalizer's vision is embedded in an external focalizer's enveloping perspective"; and "*complex* focalization in cases where the focalization is essentially ambiguous or indeterminate" (89). His remark concerning simple focalization clearly indicates the need for narrative theory to take children's and young adult literature into account:

> Simple focalization, involving a single focalizer, can be said (provisionally) to occur when, for example, a single narrator also functions as focalizer for the entire duration of the text under consideration. *In practice, however, this is rarely encountered in texts of more than a few sentences in length.*
>
> (90, emphasis added)

Simple focalization, albeit a provisional category limited to narrator-focalizers in O'Neill's discussion, in conjunction with single-voicedness, is a distinguishing feature of immediate-engaging first-person narration and can be found in many children's and young adult novels. O'Neill's warning,

> We especially need to remember in this context that the narrator is always a focalizer, having no choice whether to focalize or not (just as he/she/it has no choice whether to verbalize or not), only how to do so. The narrator, in other words, necessarily has a particular 'vision' of the narrative world he/she/it projects. As we have seen, the narrator may focalize objects directly or may choose to focalize them indirectly through one or more interposed character-focalizers." (90)

is of importance to restricted third-person engaging narration because while one can speak of simple focalization in immediate-engaging first-person narration, both distant-engaging first-person and restricted third-person engaging narration necessarily employ compound focalization. However, as Cadden argues, the unassailable first-person narrators of YA fiction are never truly simple focalizers because they all have invisible adults behind them, a point O'Neill explains as the result of the fact that readers are only "fully aware of the most recent focalization . . . [they are] consequently almost entirely unaware throughout of the most important focalizer, the implied author" (97). While this fact does ultimately mean that all focalization is therefore complex, it should not, I think, eliminate the pertinence of the three categories of focalization O'Neill sets out, nor should it mean that we dispense with all notions of singularity in narration, particularly when so many YA novels explore the very parameters that a singular vision and/or voice make possible.

Character building

One of the key distinctions between immediate-engaging and distant-engaging first-person narration and restricted third-person engaging narration is the difference in relations between the relay points along the theoretical narrative line of communications. Which of these points are relevant in the transaction of story from real live authors to real live readers has been explained in a number of ways by different narratologists. In Seymour Chatman's version as explicated by Barbara Wall (4), the chain has real players (author and reader) on either end, implied players in the next layer, and the narrator and narratee in the center. This model leaves out the entity that interests me the most in narrative fiction—the character. There has been considerable debate about the relevance and/or necessity of some of these positions, particularly that of the implied author. In immediate- and distant-engaging first-person narration, the implied author is extremely difficult to discern. An engaging narrator also makes the positions between narratee and reader very hard to distinguish; as I explained above, these positions become easily conflated. The result is that the character takes precedence in engaging narration: in first-person because the narrator is also the character, and in restricted third-person because the narrator is effaced due to the absolute focus on a single character.

In *Fictions of Discourse*, Patrick O'Neill offers productive theoretical grounds to further explore how we engage in narrative relations. Most notable for my purposes is his suggestion that both the narrator and the narratee create the character. This joint creation is the very process that underpins engaging-narration because the character is the product of the narrative relationship, the engagement, between the narrator and the narratee. This relationship is clarified by the contrast in the way in which Chatman and O'Neill schematize it. In Chatman's model, all of the arrows between the points on the chain of narrative communications point in one direction, from left to right, from author to reader, despite the fact that his discussion of the relationship between these points is bidirectional. In one of his diagrams (78; figure 1 below), O'Neill, on the other hand, has arrows pointing inward from both edges to suggest the mutual relationship between author (A), implied author (A′), and narrator (N) as well as between reader (R), implied reader (R′), and narratee (N′) on the creation of the central focus, the

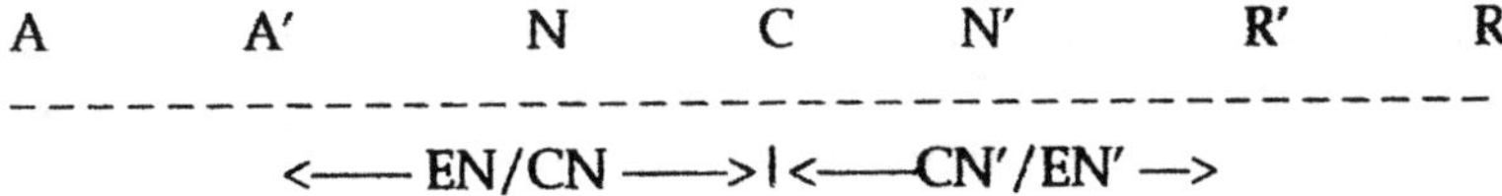

Figure 1 Narrative shifters, from Patrick O'Neill, *Fictions of Discourse: Reading Narrative Theory* (Toronto: U of Toronto P, 1994) 78.

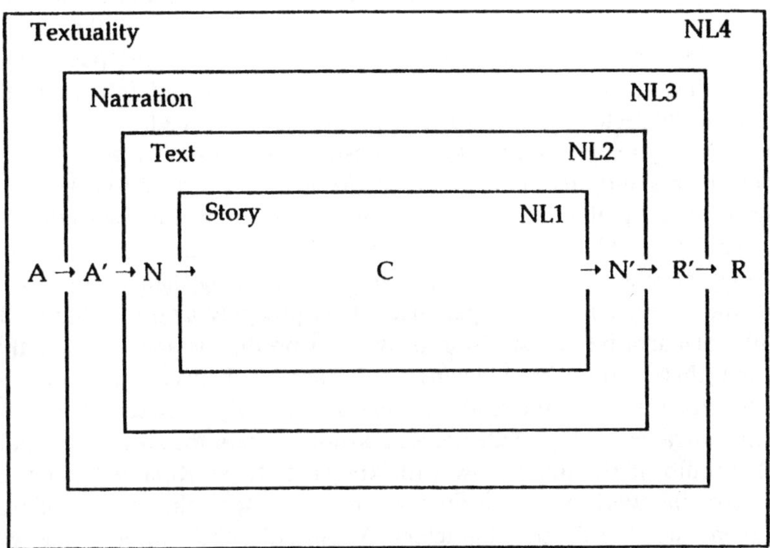

Figure 2 Narrative levels, narrative worlds, from Patrick O'Neill, *Fictions of Discourse: Reading Narrative Theory* (Toronto: U of Toronto P, 1994) 111.

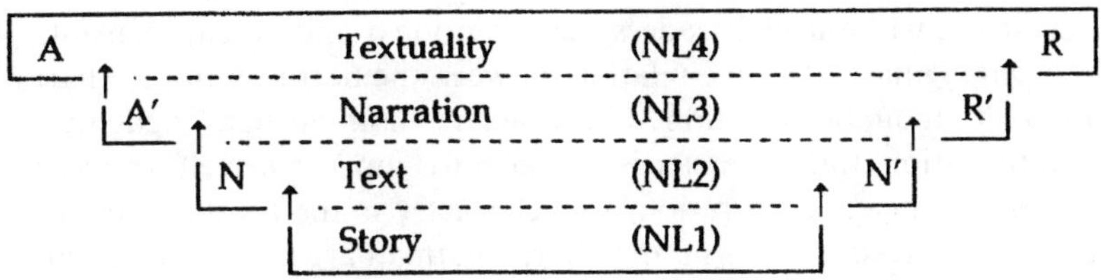

Figure 3 Nested narrative worlds, from Patrick O'Neill, *Fictions of Discourse: Reading Narrative Theory* (Toronto: U of Toronto P, 1994) 114.

character (C), and in another variation (see figure 2) has the character in the center of a series of nested frames that represent a series of narrative levels and narrative worlds (111, 114).

O'Neill also identifies four distinct terms to delineate a narratological framework: story, text, narration, and textuality (24–25; see figure 3). Of these four, textuality has "not been one of the concerns of classical narratology in the French tradition" (25). O'Neill argues that the "major advantage of its inclusion [is] to focus more attention on the essentially interactive nature of the narrative transaction as a whole, neglected to date by classical narratology. Put another way, textuality [allows] us to consider within the general conceptual framework of narratological concerns the nature and significance not only of authorial but also of readerly (including critical) *intentionality*" (25). That is to say, both authors and readers have their own designs on the *text*, which in O'Neill's scheme is the same as Roland Barthes's term *work*—the unchanging words on the page, and it is the collision and/or negotiation of these designs and intentions that realize the character the narrator presents to us as we read.

While many readers are unlikely to desire explanations of such narrative entanglements and are content to read closer to the surface to satisfy their primary interest in the characters and their actions, this doesn't mean that they are completely oblivious to other forces directing their reading, although they may have a difficult time expressing or analyzing their narrative relations and/or their reading experiences. It is precisely at this juncture that the line of narrative transmission provides a productive means of thinking through this relationship. Placing the character between the two most closely related poles in the reading equation—namely, between the narrator and the narratee—can provide the long-awaited flip of the switch that makes the lightbulb of the mind glow with knowing. If, as Roland Barthes has proposed, the work comes to life (becomes a text) in the process of reading, then surely so do the characters. Admittedly, the author of the work has provided all of the ingredients, but without adding water, there can be no life; no matter how luscious the ingredients were when the author prepared the literary repast, they become dehydrated by theoretical force once they are out in public and the book sits, awaiting readers, on the shelf. Implied reader or no, without real readers there is no text and no engagement.

In engaging narration, the relation between the narrator and the narratee is all built upon the creation of character. In immediate-engaging first-person narration, this character is the narrator him- or herself. In restricted third-person engaging narration, this character is the focalizer, or, to use Chatman's more specific term, the filter. Chatman argues that as the mental experiences of the narrator and character are different kinds of experiences (*Coming to Terms* 142), we need to have separate terms for each one, and he proposes *filter* for the character and *slant* for the narrator:

> What I like about the term "filter" is that it catches the nuance of the *choice* made by the implied author about which among the character's imaginable experiences would best enhance the narration—which areas of the story would the implied author want to illuminate and which to keep obscure. This is a nuance missed by "point of view," "focalization," and other metaphors. (144)

The reason we care about the narrator in first-person narration is because the narrator *is* the character; thus, any choices the narrator makes in the telling also directly illuminate the character. In restricted third-person engaging narration, we tend to overlook the narrator because the narrator *is not* the character. Here the notion of character as filter may also work in two ways: whereas narrators filter the story through the characters, the narratees' responses to the story are also filtered by their personal contributions to the understanding of those characters. Although narrators are obviously crucial players in the relation of story, readers who become lost in the fiction, while they may appreciate the tellers on some level, give their hearts and souls over to the characters. As Aristotle insisted on the vitality of plot to a story, I insist on the vitality of character. My insistence stems directly from the form of engaging narration wherein character, not plot, is what makes or breaks the story. Indeed, many engaging narratives have been accused of having no plot (Bernice Thurman Hunter's *Booky* trilogy, for example).[2]

The very lack of contestable information and views in these, by definition, limited forms of narration leave readers with a considerable responsibility to sort out what they have read without the assistance of alternate views from within the text; the tendency is to view this fact as a failure on the part of the author for not providing "immature" readers with some guidance. John Stephens cautions against the practice of encouraging reader identification with such limited narratives, arguing that because "Readers remain unaware that their perceptions and attitudes are being conditioned by this process" (69), the combination of these texts and the readings they invite are effectively "dangerous ideological tool[s]" (68). While I do not dispute these very real dangers, my aim here has not been to delve into the ideological implications of such texts, but rather to define their parameters so that we can identify them by name. Stephens identifies a broad textual distinction "between narratives which encourage readers to adopt a stance which is identical with that of either the narrator or of the principal focalizer, and narratives which incorporate strategies which distance the reader" (68). Similarly, Mike Cadden distinguishes between assailable and unassailable narrators, wherein the former provide clues to the very construction of the narrative and the latter efface such clues under the guise of authenticity, which Cadden argues can't really exist. Immediate-engaging first-person narration, which is typically unassailable, encourages one to adopt a stance identical to the narrator's, and restricted third-person engaging narration with that of the principal focalizer.

Given that there are many such narrators and focalizers in young adult fiction and that writers have consciously decided to use single-voicedness over double-voicedness (to follow Cadden's use of terms), we need to consider whether there aren't, in fact, advantages to such variety despite the potential danger. Like a fine wine, the pleasures of engaging narration are both delicious and intoxicating, if you like that sort of thing. If you drink too deeply and too often, you put yourself at risk; both Stephens and Cadden rightly suggest that young readers are unlikely to recognize this risk without some assistance. Although I am a pluralist at heart, I am advocating singularity here with the understanding that readers of all ages benefit most from a balanced diet; because stories restricted to singular views and voices do not exist in a vacuum, they are beneficial when savored in moderation and/or within a wider spectrum of reading. Furthermore, engaging with singular characters builds readers' characters as well precisely because there is no guidance—we all learn through experience and we are often duped along the way.

Ultimately, what the term "engaging narration" conveys is quite specific: such writing, filtered through one character, is a form in itself, a form that encourages us to focus on the singularity of experience and of voice, and a form that requires readers to make their own judgements without much help. When asked, in an interview with Dannette Dooley, to what degree her writing is related to her own adolescent experiences, Janet McNaughton responds, ". . . But I don't think much of fiction that's just hauled out of real life. I think there has to be a creative background and I really am more interested in a creative interpretation of life than a not-very-well-digested reality" (Dooley 5). Immediate-engaging narration presents itself as "not-very-well-digested reality" because the narrator-focalizer has not had sufficient time to digest the experiences being related; what makes the narration engaging, however, is the tension and balance between that very rawness of experience and the "creative interpretation" of both the real and implied authors whose roles are critical in shaping the ultimate narrative relations and thus our reading experience. In distant-engaging first-person, as in restricted third-person engaging narration, reality is presented in decidedly more advanced stages of digestion, but the narrators' creative interpretation of the characters' experiences is driven by a similar tension and balance of the intensely personal relationship and the singularity of views that is fostered between the narrator, character, and narratee in immediate-engaging narration. O'Neill issues an important reminder about how such a creative interpretation is narrated: "no matter how simple and straightforward a narrative may initially appear to be, it *can* never be a single, undivided discourse" (81); and yet, having a means of identifying the discourses that present themselves as singular in voice and/or filter provides a key step in distinguishing between the aims and results of the broader spectrum of both first- and restricted third-person narration. Perhaps I've come around to agreeing with Wayne Booth more than I ever thought I would on this particular point: it is not the question of "person" alone that needs to be belabored after all, but rather the distinctions between the types of narrators to whose company I now hope we'll admit the engaging narrators of first- and restricted third-person narration.

Notes

1 "1. psycho-narration: the narrator's discourse about a character's consciousness; 2. quoted monologue: a character's mental discourse; 3. narrated monologue: a character's mental discourse in the guise of the narrator's discourse" (Cohn 14).

2 Judith Saltman states, "Because there is no real plot other than the chronicling of Booky's growth from ten-year old child to teenager, there is plenty of room, against the backdrop of colourful incident and family drama, for character development" (58).

Works cited

Appleyard, J. A. *Becoming a Reader: The Experience of Fiction from Childhood to Adulthood.* Cambridge: Cambridge UP, 1990.

Bedard, Michael. *Redwork.* Toronto: Lester, 1992.

Berry, James. *A Thief in the Village and Other Stories.* Penguin, 1988.

Booth, Wayne. *The Rhetoric of Fiction.* 2nd ed. Chicago: U of Chicago P, 1983.

Brontë, Charlotte. *Jane Eyre.* 1847. London: Oxford UP, 1980.

Cadden, Mike. "The Irony of Narration in the Young Adult Novel." *Children's Literature Association Quarterly* 25 (2000): 146–54.

Chatman, Seymour. *Story and Discourse: Narrative Structure in Fiction and Film.* 1978. Ithaca: Cornell UP, 1986.

——. *Coming to Terms: The Rhetoric of Narrative in Fiction and Film.* Ithaca: Cornell UP, 1990.

Cohn, Dorrit. *Transparent Minds: Narrative Modes for Presenting Consciousness in Fiction.* Princeton: Princeton UP, 1978.

Cushman, Karen. *The Midwife's Apprentice.* 1995. New York: Harper Trophy, 1996.

Dooley, Danette. "Under the skin: An interview with Janet McNaughton." *Atlantic Books Today* 35 (Fall 2001): 5.

Fitzhugh, Louise. *Harriet the Spy.* 1964. New York: Harper Trophy, 1990.

Fritz, Jean. *Homesick: My Own Story.* New York: Dell, 1982.

Gardam, Jane. *A Long Way From Verona.* 1971. London: Abacus, 1989.

Genette, Gerard. *Narrative Discourse: An Essay in Method.* Trans. Jane Lewin. Ithaca: Cornell UP, 1985.

——. *Narrative Discourse Revisited.* Trans. Jane Lewin. Ithaca: Cornell UP, 1994.

Hunt, Peter. *Children's Literature.* Oxford: Basil Blackwell, 2000.

Hunter, Bernice Thurman. *As Ever, Booky.* Richmond Hill, ON: Scholastic, 1985.

——. *That Scatterbrain Booky.* Richmond Hill, ON: Scholastic, 1981.

——. *The Margaret Trilogy.* Richmond Hill, ON: Scholastic, 1988.

——. *With Love from Booky.* Richmond Hill, ON: Scholastic, 1983.

Hunter, Mollie. *A Sound of Chariots.* 1973. London: Fontana Lions, 1975.

Lunn, Janet. *Shadow in Hawthorn Bay.* 1986. Toronto: Puffin, 1988.

Major, Kevin. *Hold Fast.* 1978. New York: Stoddart, 1997.

O'Neill, Patrick. *Fictions of Discourse: Reading Narrative Theory.* Toronto: U of Toronto P, 1994.

Saltman, Judith. *Modern Canadian Children's Books.* Toronto: Oxford UP, 1987.

Schwenke Wyile, Andrea. "Expanding the View of First-Person Narration." *Children's Literature in Education* 30 (1999): 185–202.

Sniader Lanser, Susan. *Fictions of Authority: Women Writers and Narrative Voice*. Ithaca: Cornell UP, 1992.

Stephens, John. *Language and Ideology in Children's Fiction*. London: Longman, 1992.

Wall, Barbara. *The Narrator's Voice: the Dilemma of Children's Fiction*. London: Macmillan, 1991.

Warhol, Robyn R. "Toward a theory of the engaging narrator: Earnest interventions in Gaskell, Stowe and Eliot." *PMLA* 101 (1986): 811–18.

Wynne Jones, Diana. *Black Maria*. New York: HarperCollins, 2001.